RIVERS OF THE WORLD

A SOCIAL, GEOGRAPHICAL, AND ENVIRONMENTAL SOURCEBOOK

RIVERS OF THE WORLD

A SOCIAL, GEOGRAPHICAL, AND ENVIRONMENTAL SOURCEBOOK

James R. Penn

A B C CLIO

Santa Barbara, California Denver, Colorado Oxford, England

Library of Congress Cataloging-in-Publication Data

Penn, James R.
Rivers of the world : a social, geographical, and environmental sourcebook / James R. Penn.
p. cm.
Includes bibliographical references and index (p.).
ISBN 1-57607-042-5 (hardcover : alk. paper) — 1-57607-579-6 (ebook)

1. Rivers—Encyclopedias. I. Title.
GB1201.4 .P46 2001
910'.91693—dc21

2001004556

06 05 04 03 02 01 10 9 8 7 6 5 4 3 2 1

This book is also available on the World Wide Web as an ebook. Visit abc-clio.com for details.
ABC-CLIO, Inc.
130 Cremona Drive, P.O. Box 1911
Santa Barbara, California 93116–1911

This book is printed on acid-free paper.
Manufactured in the United States of America

For Laura

You cannot step into the same river twice.
Heraclitus

Rivers are more than hydrology; they have lives and souls...
Louise Wagenknecht

CONTENTS

RIVERS OF THE WORLD: A SOCIAL, GEOGRAPHICAL, AND ENVIRONMENTAL SOURCEBOOK

PREFACE

Reference works arranged in alphabetical order have been a staple of the book business for some two and a half centuries, ever since a group of French *philosophes* had the audacity to try to encompass all of human understanding within the bindings of volumes they chose to call encyclopedias. The name stuck, and more importantly the idea, including the Enlightenment belief that the widely disseminated printed word had a progressive power and shaping influence in the world. Although many would consider the idea to treat *all* of human knowledge in a single set of reference works to have reached its physical limitations with the publication of the 11th edition of the *Encyclopedia Britannica* (1911), the usefulness and commercial viability of the treatment of specific topics, of which this book is an example, have been demonstrated over and over again.

No one can read the future, of course, but the use of the Internet for research and the reading of books made available as digital files or printed on demand at individually controlled sites are significant trends that will inevitably affect the course of book publishing. As I was writing this book, I happened to read a provocative review of a new reference book on the American West that acknowledged the excellence of the volume but at the same time questioned its need in a digital age, comparing the editor and authors to absurd Wile E. Coyotes in the *Roadrunner* cartoon series, forever missing the electronically fast desert bird who was zipping by on the fast-track Internet and eluding the print-bound coyote. The publisher of this book, ABC-CLIO, has been at the forefront of innovations in reference books with its *Historical Abstracts* series and interesting thematic reference volumes, and this book is being offered as either a hardcover book or an ebook.

This volume is a comprehensive treatment of the major rivers of the world in their physical, cultural, and environmental settings. All of the great rivers of the world—the Nile, Niger, Amazon, Mississippi, Yangtze, and many others—are included here, as well as many lesser rivers, including some comparatively small waterways that illustrate important themes or represent significant trends. This raises the question: What were my criteria for selecting rivers to include in this volume? I must confess to a certain amount of arbitrariness, but I tried to consider the size of the river and its drainage basin, the frequency with which the river was referred to in historical accounts, and the role it plays in the increasingly decisive relationship to human activities in the present. For practical reasons I operated within the constraint that I didn't want the number of entries to exceed about 200. To write as complete an account as I wanted to, and to give each river an individual description with a personal style rather than writing in the monochromatic style of, say, a dictionary, I needed to keep my entry list within bounds. Without such limits it would have taken even a team of writers and editors at a large press many years to complete this project in a reasonable period of time. As it is, the research, writing, and editing of this work required about three years of my time and proved every bit as daunting as my first book. In short, I included all of the great rivers of the world and then added rivers that were of particular significance for cultural, historical, or environmental reasons, all within the constraints of not exceeding 200 entries.

The famous nineteenth-century French writer Jules Verne once read an account of his life and work that was written late in his career. He noted that the Italian critic Mario Turiello had failed to comprehend Verne's purpose, which the Frenchman felt had been "the teaching of geography, the description of the earth. For each new country I had to invent a new story. The characters are only secondary, whatever you may think." At the risk of being overly subtle and exposing myself to the charge of comparing my abilities to those of Verne, I am tempted to say that my purpose isn't so much the recounting of a large quantity of geographical information as the telling of a story or at least opening up numerous anecdotal lines. If the author of such popular novels as *Journey to the Center of the Earth* and *Around the World in Eighty Days* wanted to teach themes about the earth's regions through his spellbinding tales, I am trying here to make use of the materials of substantive research and expository prose (no one would call this a work of anything but nonfiction) to offer glimpses of historical drama, poetic significance, and cultural relationship. Though at times wearing the trappings of a scientist, I had too many good courses in literature and history as a student at the University of Wisconsin to be able to dissociate myself from an essentially humanist core. Each day I live, read, and think, I hope to add integuments to the thought and work of Erasmus, Montaigne, and Shakespeare.

This book is no substitute for a good atlas, that most essential reference work, which I recommend each reader have at hand while perusing this volume. An atlas will indicate the location of the myriad streams, towns, and other places referred to in the text beyond the ones shown on my few maps, and show other relevant locational and situational material that the text doesn't treat.

It is always a pleasure to acknowledge the numerous debts incurred in the writing of a book. I would first like to thank Alicia Merritt at ABC-CLIO, who was much more than my acquisition editor; she was the one who originally suggested the idea for this book and frequently offered encouragement along the way. Dr. H. Jesse Walker, Boyd Professor of Geography at Louisiana State University, generously contributed a number of excellent photos to illustrate this book, as he did my first. Jesse influenced the text of the book as well, especially in matters concerning coastal processes in deltas. I am grateful to Jesse for showing me articles and reprints based on his long and productive career as a coastal geomorphologist with a special interest in the Arctic. I am glad to acknowledge two colleagues of mine going back to graduate school days, Pascal Girot and Kent Mathewson, who contributed information that was useful in writing the entries respectively on the San Juan on the border between Costa Rica and Nicaragua and the Casiquiare in northern South America. I would like to thank Martin Hanft for his deft editing of the manuscript to tease out my sometimes obscure meanings. By researching the image archives, Chava Boylan added some excellent photos and prints to illustrate the text. At ABC-CLIO, Carol Smith handled production, and Liz Kincaid coordinated the artwork and secured permissions. Finally, I owe a debt of gratitude to my wife, Laura, who not only provided the kinds of emotional and personal support required of a spouse during such a long undertaking but also drew the figures and contributed some of her own photos.

INTRODUCTION

Rivers don't really begin or end. Hydrographers can't identify a single source in the highly fissured Alpine glacier where the Rhine begins any more than they can pinpoint the precise location where western Europe's greatest river slows and separates into a number of branches as it crosses the Low Countries en route to the North Sea. Which particular rivulet, seep, or puddle in the environs of Lake Itasca in north-central Minnesota is the source of the Mississippi? If you travel south from New Orleans, no one can tell which of the many branches of the Birdfoot delta, the current outlet of the river, is the real mouth of the Mississippi.

It's not just a question of "Who cares?" (a lot of people do), but a question of the continuity of a hydraulic system. A river is but one segment of the water cycle—from the evaporation of water over a broad ocean, to the drifting of a cloud over a continent, to precipitation being gathered in countless rivulets to form a regular channel (some goes to recharge groundwater). By a devious course the channelized flow of a river eventually reaches the sea, where the cycle begins anew. There is yet another sense in which a river doesn't begin or end. We don't need the Victorian poet laureate to tell us that though we die and pass away, Philip's Brook, in Tennyson's words, goes on forever.

I considered providing a short course in this introduction to certain themes and concepts in geomorphology—the science of river forms and processes—but found it too cumbersome and so decided to make this material available in a glossary. Where appropriate, I have integrated these concepts into the text, and the reader can refer to the glossary if he or she wants additional elaboration. For example, if an entry on a river with a major falls or rapids (for example, Niagara) refers to such a technical concept as *knickpoint,* which I will usually briefly define in the text as an aid to comprehension, the reader can consult the glossary for a fuller discussion of the term, perhaps also looking at a related term such as *longitudinal profile.* I would recommend that the reader peruse the glossary at least in a cursory way before reading the book, as this would give the fullest understanding of individual rivers in relationship to geomorphic processes. Some of the key terms and concepts that I had planned to elucidate here, but put instead into the glossary, include *floodplain, meander, delta, estuary, river network,* and *drainage pattern.*

For North American rivers I can happily refer the reader to an excellent series of books written by some of America's most gifted writers during the last generation or two. The Rivers of America Series published by Farrar and Rinehart (under various corporate names) between 1937 and 1974 represented a major effort to get popular and authoritative authors to write vivid, readable, and comprehensive accounts of America's primary waterways. A total of sixty-four books on individual rivers (and one songbook) eventually appeared in this award-winning series. Noted authors included Carl Carmer (the Hudson), Edgar Lee Masters (the Sangamon), Hodding Carter (the lower Mississippi), August Derleth (the Wisconsin) among others, and original illustrations were contributed by the likes of Andrew Wyeth and Lynd Ward. For the rivers covered here that were included in the series I have listed references in the Further Reading sections and in the bibliography. I am not aware of any authoritative listing of these popular books, although clean copies with dust jackets intact are much in demand by book collectors.

This encyclopedia consists of 192 alphabetically arranged entries ranging from 250 words to 2,100 words. It has been my aim to make the contents of the entries as thoroughly researched, vividly written, and clearly organized as possible. I attempted to provide a comprehensive treatment of the rivers of the world—large and small—from the River Aare in Switzerland to Africa's Ziz, with an eye toward revealing the physical, economical, political, and environmental character of the world's alluvial landscapes and regions.

Each entry begins with key information on the source of the river, its length, major tributaries, and outlet for quick reference. Within this key information readers will find boldface cross-references for rivers that have their own entries. Most entries contain references at the end for further reading. A complete bibliography of works consulted can be found at the back of the book. *See also* references at the end of entries are used to refer the reader to other relevant portions of the book. For the nagging problem of multiple and changing names, cross-references will help guide the reader to the appropriate entry (for example, Yellow River—*See* Huang He). I have included a selection of quotations to open another window on the world of rivers. Though rivers in North America and Europe do not receive short shrift in this work, I think that my more-or-less complete treatment of rivers in other parts of the world is one of this volume's primary contributions. Also, environmental and land use problems of flooding, pollution, and river regulation have not received such broad coverage before.

Let me send the reader off with an original riddle. Can you detect the four rivers referred to, however indirectly, in the following lines (all four are covered in this book)? *By the waters of the somber river I babble on and muse.* Bon voyage!

(Answer: somber = Sambre; babble on = Babylon, thus the Tigris and Euphrates; muse = Meuse)

MAPS

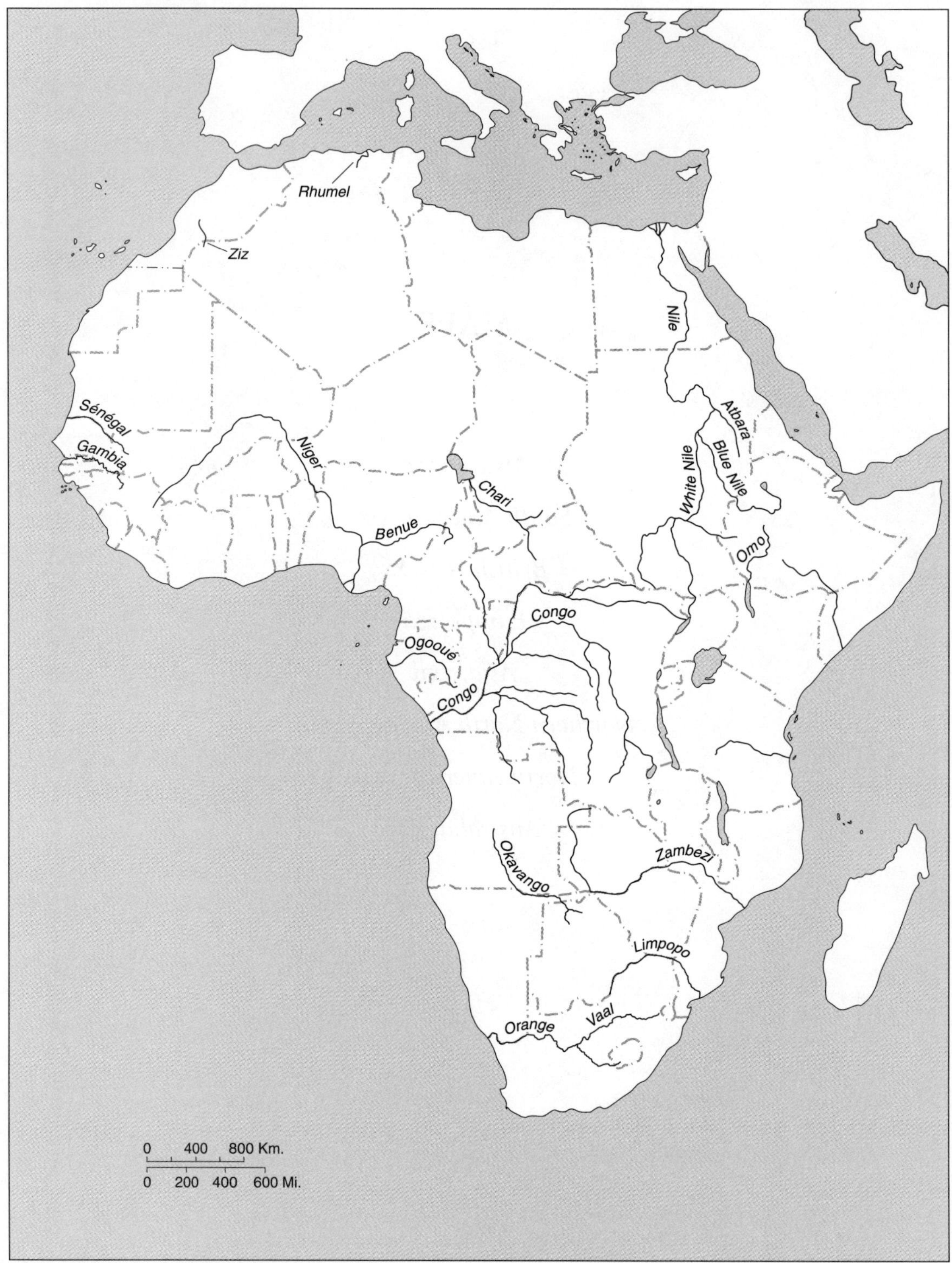
Rhumel
Ziz
Nile
Sénégal
Gambia
Niger
Atbara
Blue Nile
White Nile
Chari
Benue
Omo
Congo
Ogooue
Congo
Zambezi
Okavango
Limpopo
Vaal
Orange
0 400 800 Km.
0 200 400 600 Mi.

Map 1 Africa

Map 2 South America

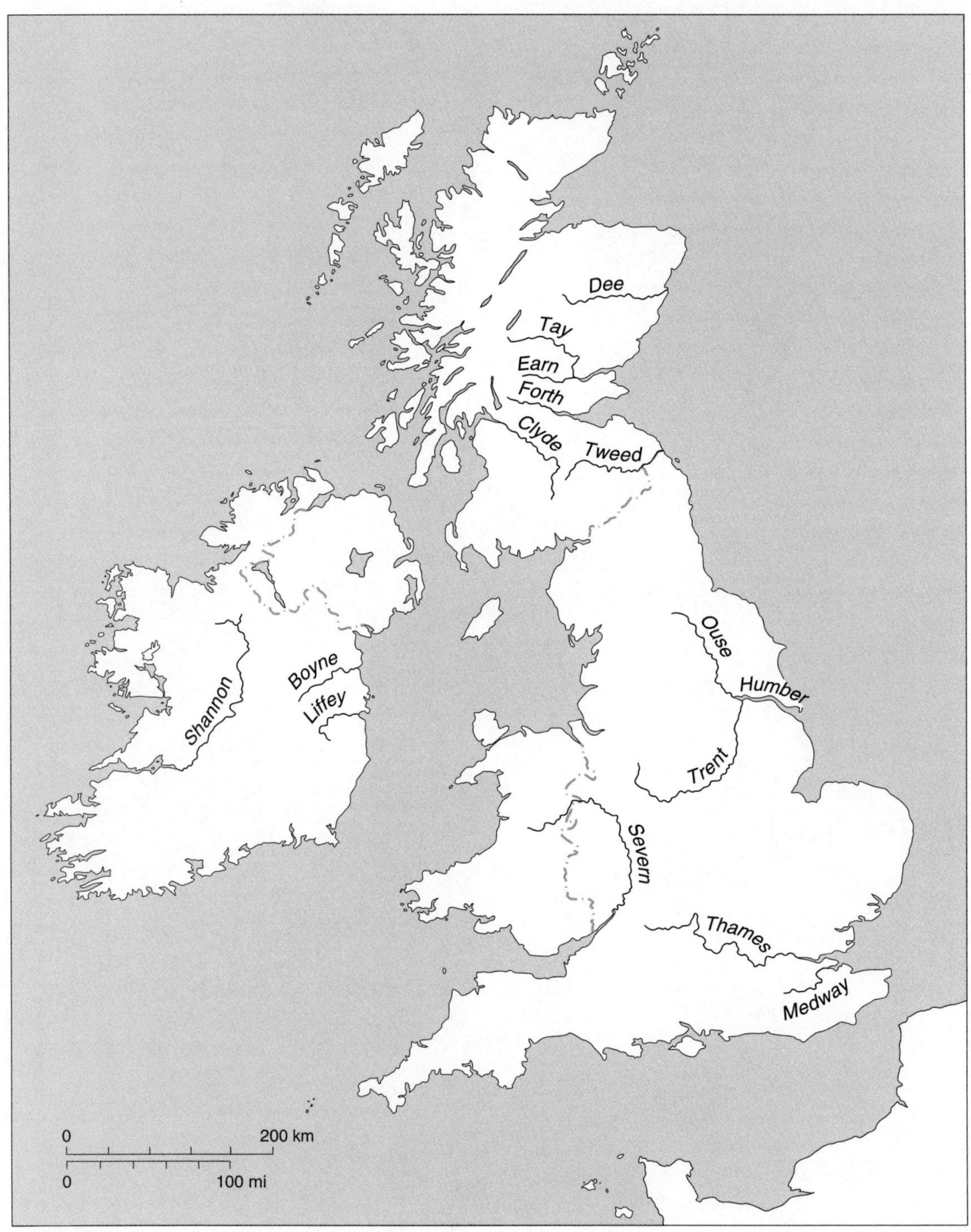

Map 3 British Isles

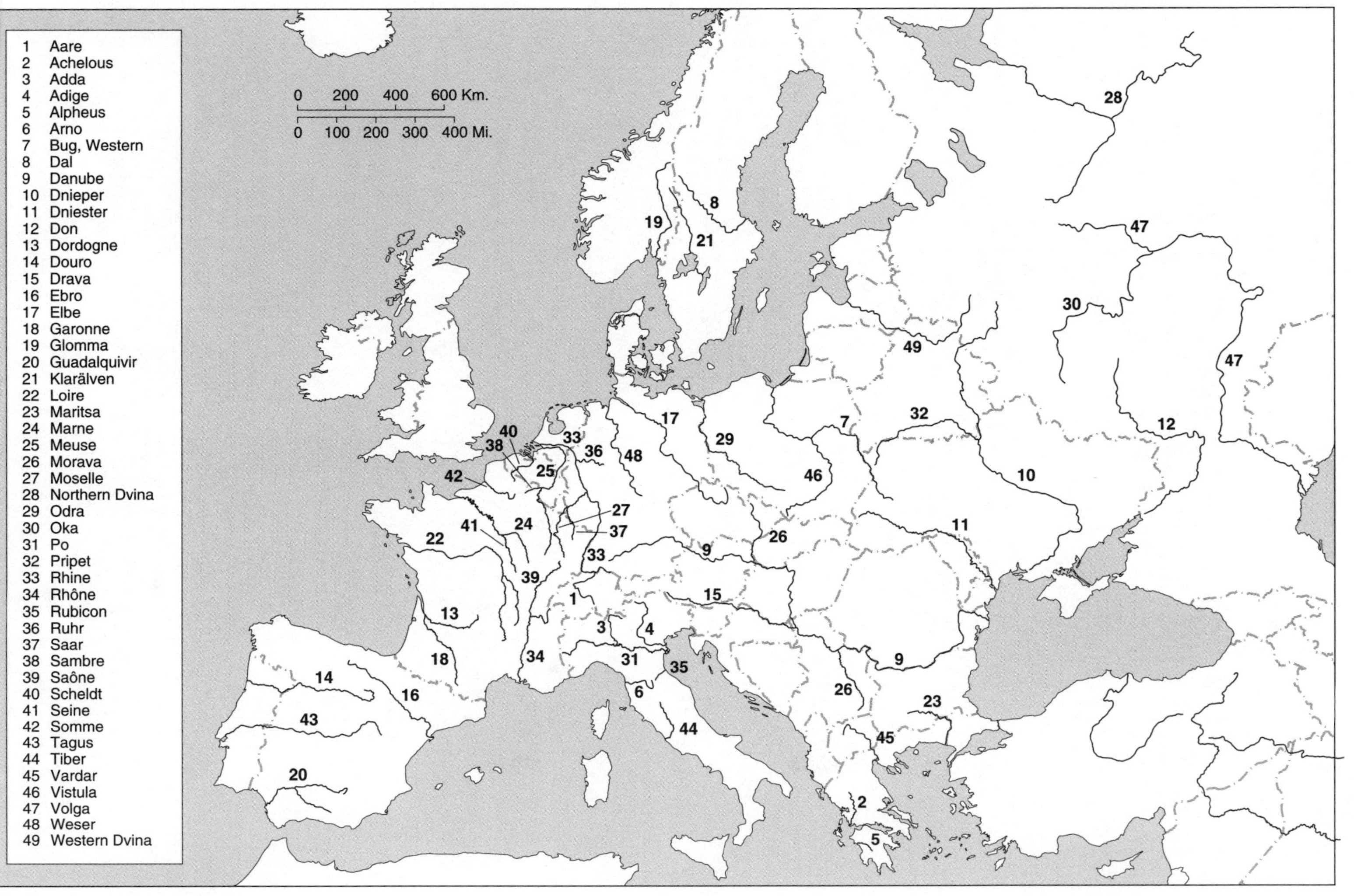
1 Aare
2 Achelous
3 Adda
4 Adige
5 Alpheus
6 Arno
7 Bug, Western
8 Dal
9 Danube
10 Dnieper
11 Dniester
12 Don
13 Dordogne
14 Douro
15 Drava
16 Ebro
17 Elbe
18 Garonne
19 Glomma
20 Guadalquivir
21 Klarälven
22 Loire
23 Maritsa
24 Marne
25 Meuse
26 Morava
27 Moselle
28 Northern Dvina
29 Odra
30 Oka
31 Po
32 Pripet
33 Rhine
34 Rhône
35 Rubicon
36 Ruhr
37 Saar
38 Sambre
39 Saône
40 Scheldt
41 Seine
42 Somme
43 Tagus
44 Tiber
45 Vardar
46 Vistula
47 Volga
48 Weser
49 Western Dvina
0 200 400 600 Km.
0 100 200 300 400 Mi.

Map 4 Europe

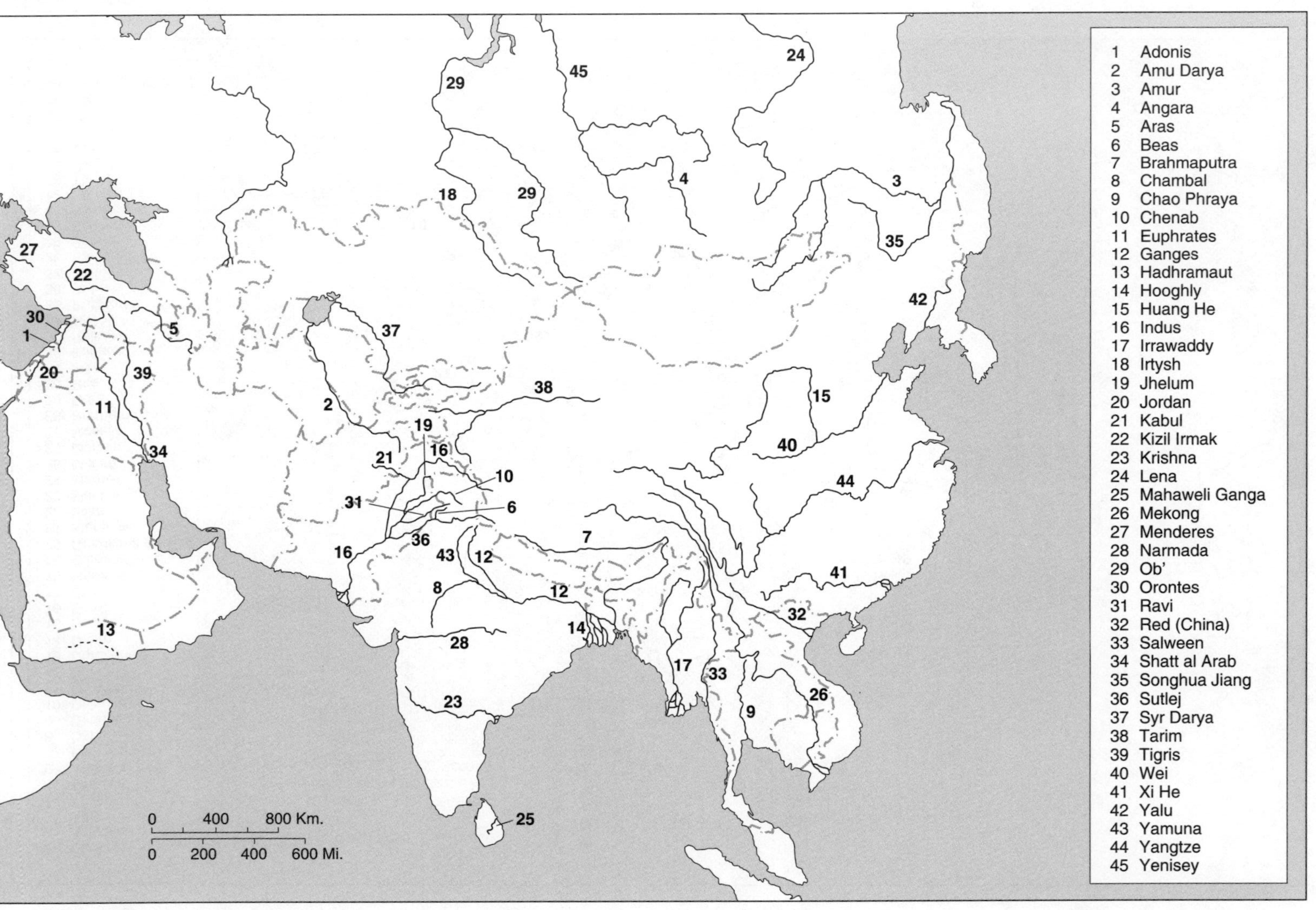
1 Adonis
2 Amu Darya
3 Amur
4 Angara
5 Aras
6 Beas
7 Brahmaputra
8 Chambal
9 Chao Phraya
10 Chenab
11 Euphrates
12 Ganges
13 Hadhramaut
14 Hooghly
15 Huang He
16 Indus
17 Irrawaddy
18 Irtysh
19 Jhelum
20 Jordan
21 Kabul
22 Kizil Irmak
23 Krishna
24 Lena
25 Mahaweli Ganga
26 Mekong
27 Menderes
28 Narmada
29 Ob'
30 Orontes
31 Ravi
32 Red (China)
33 Salween
34 Shatt al Arab
35 Songhua Jiang
36 Sutlej
37 Syr Darya
38 Tarim
39 Tigris
40 Wei
41 Xi He
42 Yalu
43 Yamuna
44 Yangtze
45 Yenisey
0 400 800 Km.
0 200 400 600 Mi.

Map 5 Asia

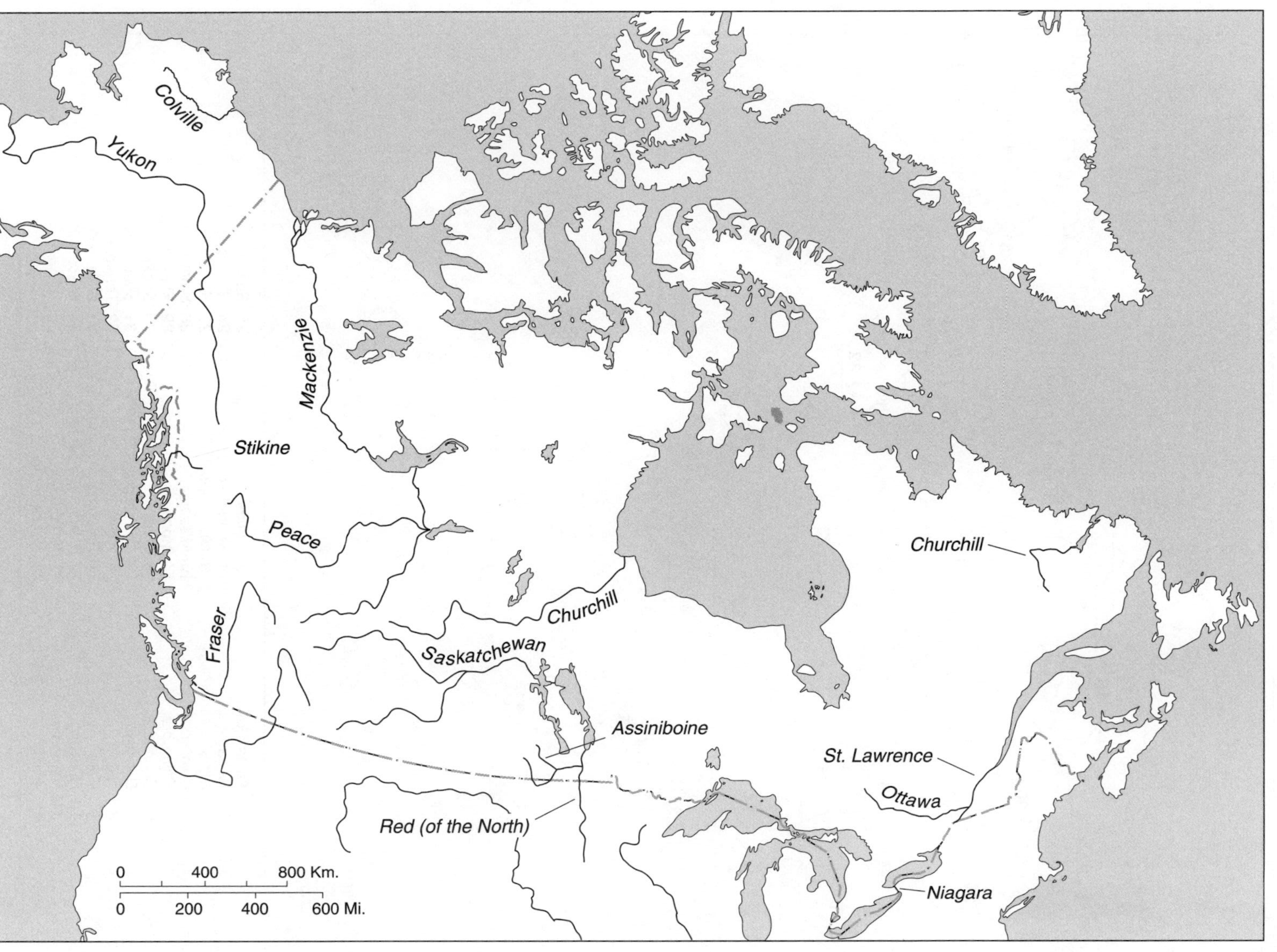

Map 6 Northern North America

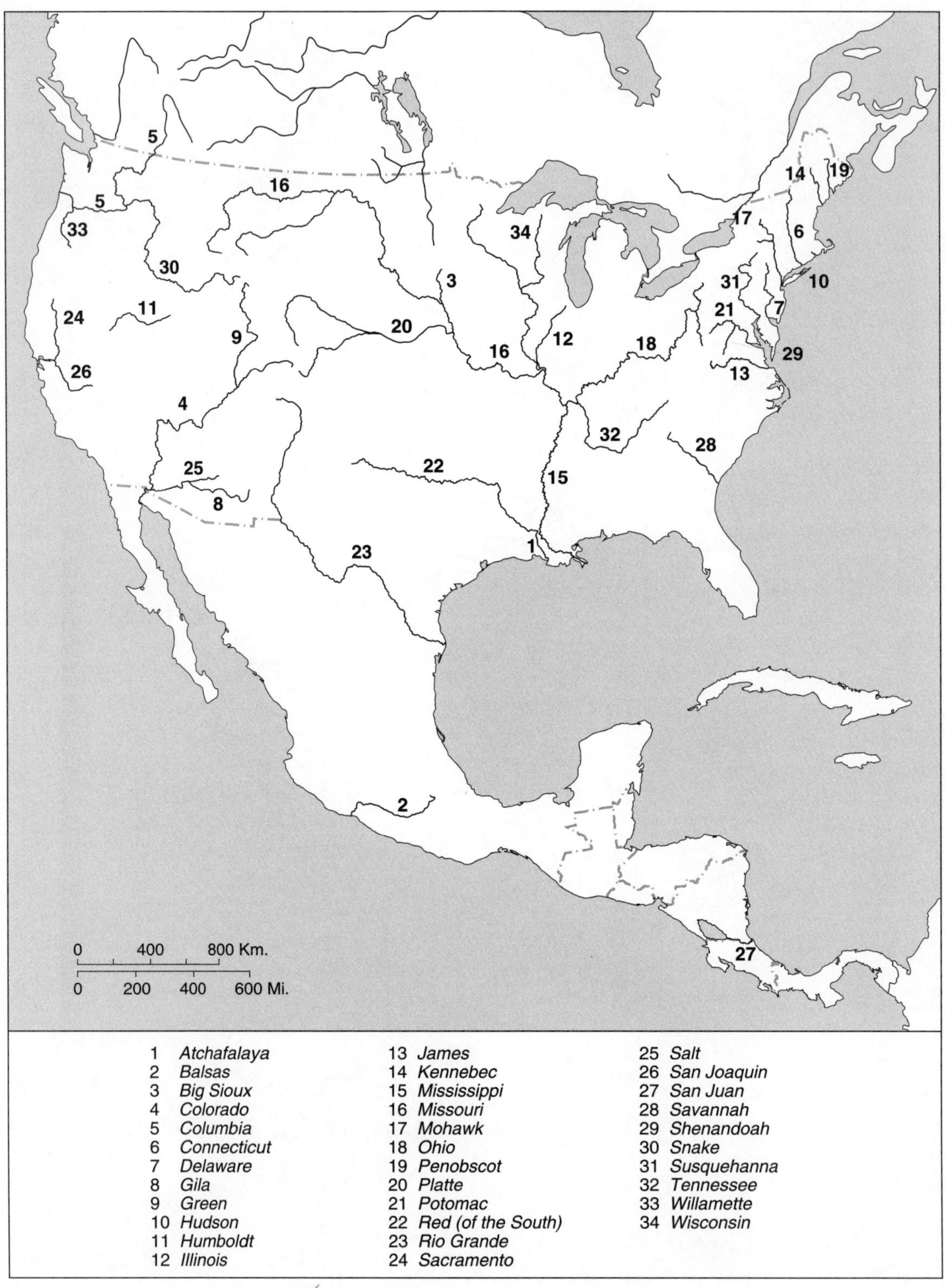

Map 7 North America

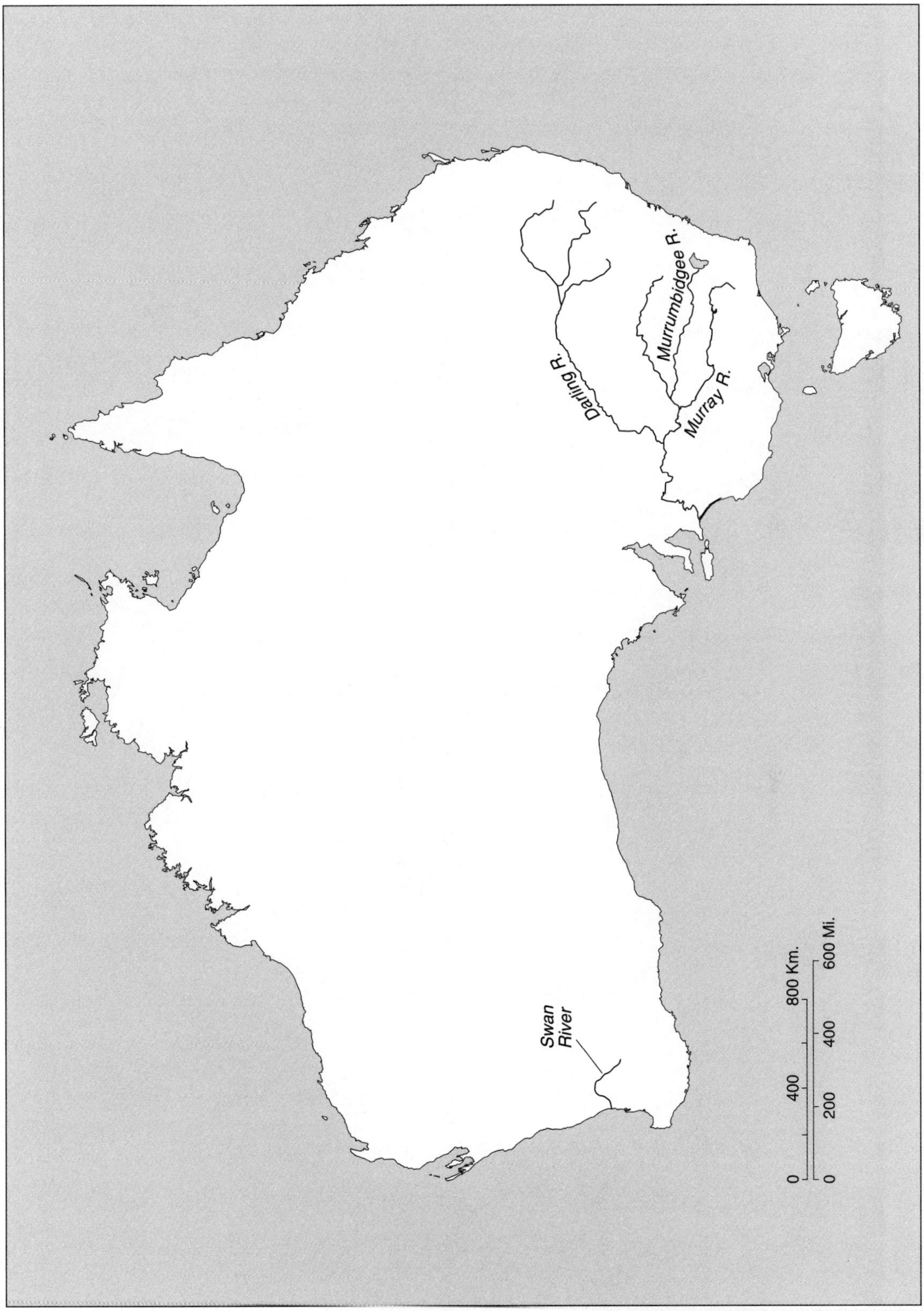

Darling R.
Murrumbidgee R.
Murray R.
Swan River
0 400 800 Km.
0 200 400 600 Mi.

Map 8 Australia

AARE

Source: Grimsel Lake, in the Bernese Alps
Length: 183 miles (294 kilometers)
Tributaries: Reuss, Limmat
Outlet: **Rhine**

The Aare (pronounced AH-re) is the longest river flowing entirely in Switzerland. Its name has a linguistic root that is derived from the Indo-European syllable *Aa,* meaning "water." The same root is found in the Latin *aqua,* as well as in the names of hundreds of small streams in northern Europe, especially in France and Switzerland. One of the Aare's tiny tributaries is even named the Aa, emptying into the lower river via a series of lakes.

The Aare River rises in the Bernese Alps (German Berner Oberland), in the north-central portion of Europe's highest mountain range. Draining much of Switzerland, the Aare flows across a lake plateau whose terrain is continuous with German Bavaria. Pleistocene glaciation has interrupted the natural flow of the stream and dispersed lakes along its course.

The glacially fed headwaters of the Aare pass through the scenic gorge of the Aareschlucht near Meiringen. The river runs generally westward through Lake Brienz in the direction of the resort town of Interlaken, where it is canalized. From there it passes through Lake Thun, the head of navigation. Continuing northwest the river loops around the picture-book city of Bern, the Swiss capital, whose medieval core with its splendid town hall and elaborate clock tower is contained in a wide meander of the river. Next the river turns northeast past Solothurn and Aarau before joining the upper Rhine River opposite Waldshut, Germany.

The lower river has been much altered by human activity, with dams, canals, channelization, and reservoirs much in evidence. There are more than forty hydroelectric plants on the river, and two canals join the river to Lake Biel. For many the Aare is the entranceway to the Bernese Oberland. On the way north from the national capital to Thun—on the lake of the same name—there are delightful river scenes of meadows, forests, reed grasses, sedges, and backwaters, much of which has been preserved today. Upon reaching the interconnected lakes of Thun and Brienz, the traveler is presented with dazzling views of lofty Alpine peaks, including the Jungfrau. Although the hourly animated diversion of Berne's celebrated Zytgloggetum (Clock Tower) is not without interest, for those with a love of raw nature the highlights of this portion of Switzerland are sure to be the high Aare, its cataracts, the passes to the south (toward Italy), and the surrounding peaks.

Further Reading: Banks, Francis Richard, *Your Guide to the Bernese Oberland*, London: A. Redman, 1965.

ACHELOUS

Source: Pindus Mountains
Length: 137 miles (220 kilometers)
Tributary: Meghdova
Outlet: Ionian Sea

This comparatively short Greek river, without a major concentration of population, nevertheless has a rich and fruitful association with mythology.

The south-flowing Achelous (Greek: Akhelóos, the name of a river god who wrestled with Hercules) rises in western Thessaly in the Pindus Mountains. Like most Mediterranean rivers, it receives most of its precipitation in the winter months. Eighty inches (203 centimeters) of rain fall on the area each year, and the river carries two hundred times more water in winter than in summer. Dams and weirs have been installed along the lower course of the river to control flooding and to direct the river's water to where it is most needed. One of the stream's tributaries, the Meghdova, has been diverted to cross the mountain divide to the east, to provide irrigation waters for the well-settled Thessalian Plain. In ancient times ships could sail quite a distance up the Achelous, which was one of the largest rivers in Greece, and dock at Oiniadai. Because of siltation, this city today lies well away from the coast. Tectonic activity has depopulated the lower valley, and the river's upper course has traditionally been home to pastoralists and bandits rather than the cultivators that are the basis of large cities.

Although the Achelous valley has never been a major focus of Greek settlement, the ancient Greeks held the river in special esteem and accorded it divine powers. Achelous was a Greek river god, born of Oceanus and Tethys. He had the ability to take on the guise of a bull, a speckled serpent, or a bull-headed man. Streams of water continually flowed from Achelous's shaggy beard. Achelous once fought the most popular of all Greek heroes, Hercules (Greek: Heracles). Fresh from accomplishing his twelve labors, Hercules, renowned for his extraordinary strength and courage, sought the hand of the beautiful Deianeira, who drove a chariot and practiced the arts of war. Achelous, in the form of a bull-headed man, taunted Hercules, saying that he, Achelous, was a famous personage, the father of all Greek waters, whereas Hercules was a footloose stranger. Announcing that he was a better fighter than debater, Hercules began to wrestle with Achelous. When the river god was thrown onto his back, he turned into a serpent and slithered away. Hercules had strangled twin serpents while still in his cradle, so he advanced unafraid, but Achelous shifted his shape into that of a charging bull. Hercules deftly stepped aside, grabbing the bull's right horn as it passed and breaking it off. In one version of the story, this is the origin of the cornucopia, the ever-full horn of plenty associated with fertility. It is appropriate that fertility should result from breaking off a horn from a livestock animal, as the Greeks revered bulls and goats as embodiments of natural vitality. In the myth of Achelous, the ancient Greeks thus showed their awe of the natural force of rivers.

The Hellenes were also aware of how rivers create new land by the accumulation of silt at the river's mouth, and they created a characteristically clever tale. Alcmaeon, the conqueror of Thebes, misinterpreted the Delphic Oracle's instructions and murdered his wife, who upon dying uttered a curse: "Lands of Greece and Asia, and of all the world: deny shelter to my murderers." Pursued by the avenging Erinyes, or Furies, Alcmaeon could not settle on any land in Greece, or anywhere else. Upon further advice from the Delphic Oracle, however, he found a solution: he married Achelous's daughter, Callirrhoë, and settled on land formed by the silt of the river, land that had not been included in the original curse.

Hercules was believed to have drained some of the marshes in the lower course of the Achelous, whether as part of a wrestling match with the river god or as a further feat of strength we don't know. The home of wandering Odysseus was Ithaca, one of the Ionian Islands, lying offshore from the mouth of the Achelous River. Toward the end of Odysseus's epic voyage, he escapes the lure of the Sirens, strange birdlike creatures with enchanting voices, by plugging his men's ears with wax and having himself strapped to the mast. Since the Sirens were sometimes called the children of Achelous, it could be concluded that their island may have been one of the Echinades, located at the mouth of the Achelous River.

See also Alpheus
Further Reading: Graves, Robert, *The Greek Myths,* 2 vols., Baltimore: Penguin Books, 1955.

ADDA

Source: Rhaetian Alps, in northern Italy
Length: 194 miles (312 kilometers)
Tributaries: Mera, Brembo, Serio
Outlet: **Po**

A comparatively short left-bank tributary of the Po River, the Adda rises in several small lakes in the south-central section of the Alps. This portion of Europe's highest mountains—the Rhaetian Alps—exhibits spectacular scenery along the river's upper course. The Adda follows the southern part of Stelvio Pass between Italy and Switzerland. Farther downstream, the valley broadens and forms the Valtellina, extending from the Ortles group of the Alps to Lake Como. The river valley is fertile and prosperous, and several hydroelectric power plants have been installed to harness the river's tumbling energy. Exiting Lake Como at Lecco, a manufacturing and resort town, the river flows across the Lombard Plain, one of the largest agricultural districts in Mediterranean Europe and the prize of would-be conquerors since Roman times.

The only important town on the lower Adda is Lodi, 20 miles (32 kilometers) southeast of Milan. In early May 1796 the commander of the French army, Napoleon Bonaparte, advanced with lightning swiftness down the Po valley along its southern bank and came between the Austrian army and its main stronghold at Mantua. After capturing Piacenza, just upstream from where the Adda empties into the Po, Napoleon directed his army across the Po in an advance on the bewildered Austrians under the command of Beaulieu, who, despite his Gallic surname, was no friend of the French Revolutionary forces. The Austrian army was caught in the region north of the Po drained by a series of parallel streams coursing out of the Alps, from the Sesia River on the west to the Adige River on the east. The Adda was one of those streams in a broad zone of glacial materials skirting the foothills of the Alps.

The Austrians' first surprise was Napoleon's decision to mount an essentially rearguard battle, rather than facing the enemy directly in conventional, squared formation. The second was the decision of the "little corporal" to fight at the unprepossessing town of Lodi, not in itself valuable as a diplomatic counter in any possible future negotiations. Even today this small town set in the midst of rice fields and lush meadows is better known for cheese-making than as the site where Napoleon's military genius was first demonstrated.

Lodi was situated at the intersection of the Adda River and several major routes that linked it to Milan, Pavia, and Piacenza. Striking rapidly northward from the Po, Napoleon's army came upon the escaping Austrian army, which was passing through Lodi en route to Cremona, a Gallic site built upon by the Romans located just downstream from where the Adda empties into the Po. The city was a river-crossing site, with a 300-foot wooden bridge extending out from the city walls across the river, resting at midpoint on a sandy island. This bridge was wide enough only for a single cart, and the Austrians did not have enough time to burn or destroy it as they retreated across, but they did the next best thing: they swung fourteen cannons into place to cover the narrow passageway.

The Corsican-born commander surprised the Austrians yet again by his decision to assault the heavily defended bridge at Lodi. At 7:00 P.M. on May 10, 1796 (21 Floréal, An IV, of the French Revolutionary calendar), under a westering sun, French grenadiers, the elite of the French forces, rushed six abreast onto the bridge over the Adda, shouting "Vive la République!" This initial wave sustained massive casualties, but the French continued to charge, officers joining privates and Napoleon pulling his horse up alongside the river to view the battle. Some carabineers reached the island by climbing along bridge timbers, and they opened a murderous sniper fire just as French columns again surged forward. French soldiers crossed a wall of fire and advanced all the way to the cannoneers at their pieces, bayoneting them.

Bonaparte knew he needed a daring victory in Italy: "I needed some bold stroke to set a special stamp on my deeds; I resolved to astonish the enemy by so daring an operation." The bridge at Lodi and Napoleon's destiny would henceforth be linked in historical memory. Although the Italian campaign was only in its early phases, the victory at the Adda was decisive in Napoleon's conquest of northern Italy. Many battles have been fought along the lower course of the Adda, inasmuch as it formed the border between the territories of Venice and Milan, but Napoleon's was certainly the most important. When the commander of the French forces returned home, he found a disorganized, late-revolutionary state looking for a strong man and finding one in the future emperor.

See also Adige

Further Reading: Asprey, Robert B., *The Rise of Napoleon Bonaparte,* New York: Basic Books, 2000; Connelly, Owen, *Blundering to Glory: Napoleon's Military Campaigns,* Wilmington, Del.: Scholarly Resources, 1987; Ferrero, Guglielmo, *The Gamble: Bonaparte in Italy, 1796–1797,* London: G. Bell, 1961.

ADIGE

Source: Rhaetian Alps, northern Italy
Length: 255 miles (410 kilometers)
Tributaries: Isarco, Noce, Aviso
Outlet: Adriatic Sea

A series of streams in northern Italy drain the Alps southward in the direction of the Po Plain. These rivers—from the Sesia on the west to the Brenta on the east—generally parallel one another and flow into the Po River itself, or, in the case of the Adige and the Brenta, enter the alluvial plain of the Po and then drain eastward to the Adriatic south of Venice. The Adige, the second longest river in Italy, rises in three small lakes in the Rhaetian Alps (south-central Alps), where Italy, Switzerland, and Austria meet. Flowing southeast through spectacular mountain scenery, the river passes the resort town of Merano, which was Austrian until 1918. This region, known as the South Tyrol, was annexed to Italy after World War I, and despite repeated attempts to impose an Italian character on the area, many of its people still speak German. The cathedral city of Trent farther downstream, where the Catholic powers in the sixteenth century met to map their Counter-Reformation strategy, marks the linguistic frontier and is a completely Italian town. Farther south yet, the river flows parallel to the eastern shore of Lake Garda before turning southeast and entering the broad plain of the Po.

In the first Italian campaign of 1796 to 1797, Napoleon Bonaparte made the control of the exits from the Alpine passes, notably the Brenner Pass in the eastern Alps, the key to his military strategy. This hinged on an attempt to assault the so-called quadrilateral fortresses that guarded the pass routes along the valleys of the Chiese, Adige, and Brenta Rivers. The western pair of key forts were Mantua and Peschiera, both located on the River Mincio, linking Lake Garda to the Po. The eastern pair, Legnano and Verona, were both on the Adige River. Mantua was the ultimate prize captured by Bonaparte in 1797, since it was the military and administrative center of Austrian rule in northern Italy. Numerous battles along the lower Adige and the other paralleling rivers were fought pitting the French Revolutionary forces against their Austrian opponents. Bridges were often key control points in these battles. To avoid such constrictions, armies relied on their engineers to erect temporary pontoon bridges to span streams. Marshy ground along rivers created strategic dry-point sites, as at the famous battle of Arcole, where mighty armies contended along the narrow causeways crossing the region between the Adige and Alpone Rivers.

Verona is the only important settlement on the lower Adige. In the late medieval period many north-Italian communes attained independence, but that did not keep the Italians from fighting among themselves. The most notable of the struggling families were the Guelphs and the Ghibellines, who feuded in Verona as elsewhere in

Italy. Shakespeare used this historical background and the "fair city" of Verona in his tale of the star-crossed lovers, *Romeo and Juliet.*

This Alpine valley had been the subject of contention before Napoleon. The Romans, the Goths, Charlemagne—all had passed this way. The Austrian-Italian campaign of 1916 during World War I resulted in many battles being fought here. The valley today is the site of numerous hydroelectric power plants and irrigation works. The threat of flooding has been reduced by the construction of flood-control works. The Adige empties into the Adriatic Sea southeast of Chioggia, a port at the southern end of the Venetian Lagoon.

See also Adda

Further Reading: Asprey, Robert B., *The Rise of Napoleon Bonaparte,* New York: Basic Books, 2000; Taylor, Griffith, "Trento to the Reschen Pass: A Cultural Traverse of the Adige Corridor," *Geographical Review* 30 (1940): 215–237.

ADONIS

Source: Central Lebanon
Length: 14 miles (22 kilometers)
Tributaries: None
Outlet: Mediterranean Sea

This short stream in central Lebanon was associated in ancient mythology with death and seasonal renewal.

The source of the Adonis River (or Nahr Ibrahim) is a large cavern contained in a rocky precipice 5,000 feet (1,524 meters) above sea level. A rough track climbs to this spot from the valley below. Each spring, heavy rains wash so much red soil into the river that it seems to flow with blood. In ancient times a large throng of worshipers would climb to the river's source to view the rosy river associated with sacrifice and fertility. A chaotic mass of hewn stones in the valley indicates the location of former shrines and sacred places. It has been suggested that human sacrifice may have been practiced here to ensure agricultural fertility.

The ancient Greeks appropriated the river's legends for their mythologies. They named the river after the beautiful youth who was gored to death by a boar. Both Aphrodite and Persephone loved the boy and claimed him as their own, so Zeus stepped in and settled the dispute between the goddess of love and the queen of the underworld. Adonis was allowed to spend half the year, the summer months, above the ground with Aphrodite, and the other half in the underworld with Persephone. Adonis's death and resurrection thus ensured the yearly cycle of the vegetation.

Where drops of Adonis's blood were spilled, flowers sprang up, traditionally called anemones. The most common red flower in the Adonis valley, however, is the scarlet buttercup (*Ranunculus asiaticus*). The river drops in a series of falls from its source. Farther downstream it cuts its way through the mountains via an impassable gorge, and it is only a short distance from the sea where the river is bridged.

The river's outlet is almost as storied as its source. Near the mouth of the river lies the city of Byblos (Jubayl), one of the oldest cities in the world, going back four thousand years before Christ. Situated 20 miles (32 kilometers) north of Beirut, Byblos was an important commercial and religious center on the eastern Mediterranean coast. It was a meeting-place of Asiatic, Egyptian, and Mycenaean cultures. The Phoenician city exported papyrus to Egypt, hence the Greek word *byblos,* meaning "book" and the English "Bible." It was here that the goddess Astarte was first worshiped and associated with the dying god Adonis. The Greek worship of Aphrodite and later the Roman Venus arose from these origins. One of Shakespeare's few nondramatic works, *Venus and Adonis,* celebrated the relationship between the amatory Venus and the reluctant, rose-cheeked boy; it is a work written during a period of enforced leisure for the bard, as playhouses were closed on account of the plague.

Further Reading: Thubron, Colin, *The Hills of Adonis: A Quest in Lebanon,* Boston: Little, Brown, 1968.

ALPHEUS

Source: Taiyetos Mountains, southern Greece
Length: 70 miles (121 kilometers)
Tributaries: None
Outlet: Ionian Sea

The Peloponnesus (former Morea) is a mountainous peninsula at the southern end of Greece joined to the mainland by the narrow isthmus of Corinth. The most powerful ancient city-state in southern Greece was Sparta, best known for its military discipline and rivalry with Athens. It was located in the valley of the Eurotas. West of the Spartan province of Laconia lies the old district of Elis, through which the sacred Alpheus River flows.

The longest river in southern Greece, the Alpheus rises in the Taiyetos Mountains, a range of highlands extending from the interior of the peninsula as far south as the jutting coastal fingers. The headwaters of the stream pass through the uplands of Arcadia, a verdant oak woodland interrupted by fertile valleys, which in ancient times had a reputation for harmony and rustic happiness (cf. W. B. Yeats: "The woods of Arcady are dead / And over is their antique joy"). The Alpheus flows northwest through gorges before reaching Olympia in the province of Elis. The prestige of this ancient town was enhanced by the enactment every fourth year of the Olympic Games in honor of Zeus on the north bank of the Alpheus. A giant statue of Zeus made by Phidias in the shrine at Olympia was one of the Seven Wonders of the Ancient World (better described as the Seven Wonders of the Ancient Western World). The Alpheus flows northwest across the Olympia plains before emptying into the Ionian Sea near Pyrgos.

The ancient Greeks were not averse to mingling the divine and natural worlds. Although the Alpheus River is only about 70 miles (110 kilometers) in length—not long compared with the great rivers of the world—it was considered a god, an immortal spirit partaking of physical qualities. A river that continues to flow because of the hydrologic cycle would seem to be a good choice for an immortal. The river god Alpheus, son of Thetis, dared to fall in love with Artemis (the Roman Diana), the virgin goddess of the hunt and protector of women. Alpheus chased her all across Greece, but she reached Letrina in Elis. She daubed her own face and the faces of her accompanying nymphs with white mud, and when Alpheus could not distinguish the object of his desire among the company, he left humiliated. In Athens, worshipers of Artemis focused on her famous statue, called "the White-Browed." Artistic depictions of chastity and the symbolic use of white relied on this association between the fleeing goddess and the river god Alpheus.

This story of hopeless pursuit may have been modeled on that of Alpheus chasing Arethusa, which turned her into a spring at Syracuse, while changing him into a river. The ancient Greeks believed that the Alpheus River flowed from Greece under the sea and emerged in the fountain of Arethusa in Syracuse harbor. One of the twelve labors of Hercules was the cleaning of the stables of Augeas at Elis, which the Greek hero accomplished by turning the Alpheus through them.

In Samuel Taylor Coleridge's short poem "Kubla Khan" (1816), the river Alph is a key feature in the romantic poet's evocation of an exotic, mystical landscape:

> In Xanadu did Kubla Khan
> A stately pleasure-dome decree:
> Where Alph, the sacred river, ran
> Through caverns measureless to man
> Down to a sunless sea.

But this paradise turns out to be a troubled place. Disturbing signs appear. Shaking rocks issue forth in a fountain, the sacred river, which meanders for 5 miles (8 kilometers) before reaching the "caverns measureless to man." Generations of critics and students alike have tried to puzzle out the meaning of Coleridge's mystifying but strangely alluring lyric, which the poet himself dismissed as being the result of a drug-induced dream. (One is reminded of Archibald MacLeish's dictum that a poem should not mean but be.) The source of the poem—as opposed to its stimulus—lies in the story of the river god Alpheus and the fountain Arethusa. Coleridge was able to fuse in his creative imagination Greek mythology with exotic travel literature to produce one of the most memorable poems in the English language.

See also Achelous

AMAZON

Source: Andes Mountains, Peru
Length: 3,900 miles (6,276 kilometers)
Tributaries: Ucayali, Javari, Juruá, **Negro, Madeira,** Tapajós, Xingu, Tocantins
Outlet: Atlantic Ocean, near Belém, Brazil

We were within the southern boundary of this great equatorial forest, on a river which was not merely unknown but unguessed at, no geographer having ever suspected its existence. The river flowed northward toward the equator, but whither it would go, whether it would turn one way or another, the length of its course, where it would come out, the character of the stream itself, and the character of the dwellers along its banks—all these things were yet to be discovered.
Theodore Roosevelt, *Down an Unknown River*

The Amazon is truly a river of superlatives. Gathering water from both hemispheres, the second longest river in the world (the Nile is the longest) generally flows eastward from its sources in the Andes Mountains. The Amazon drains much of northern Brazil and parts of the adjoining countries of South America. Since the river parallels the Equator along most of its course, flowing slightly to the south of this global division, the main channel and its numerous tributaries cross a wide zone in which tropical air masses converge. Although precipitation is abundant throughout the year, temperatures are not as extreme as many think and not as high as in the cloudless subtropics. The enormous drainage area of approximately 2,500,000 square miles (6,475,000 square kilometers) covers 35 percent of South America and is the largest in the world. The river ranks number one in discharge, its annual outflow representing one-fifth of all the fresh water draining into the world's oceans. It has an uncounted number of tributaries,

Dense rain forest covers the banks of the Amazon River in Brazil. (Wolfgang Kaehler/CORBIS)

with more than two hundred in Brazil alone. Seventeen of the largest tributaries are more than 1,000 miles (1,600 kilometers) in length. Three million tons of sediment are washed into the sea each day. This discharge alters the Atlantic Ocean's salinity and color as far as 200 miles (322 kilometers) out to sea. The vast alluvial plain of the Amazon and its tributaries encompass the largest remaining extent of species-diverse tropical rain forest in the world.

The main-stem Amazon is formed in northern Peru by the junction of two north-flowing streams that drain the snow-covered Andes: the Ucayali, the longer tributary, and the shorter Marañon. Turning eastward, the river passes the major commercial outlet of the upper Amazon: Iquitos, a river port that is reached from the east by 3000-ton ships even though the town is 2,300 miles (3,700 kilometers) from the river's mouth. As the river exits Peru and enters Brazil its name changes, at least on atlas maps, to the Solimões, a name that refers to the upriver part of the Amazon in western Brazil. The name changes to the Rio Amazonas at Manaus, which is actually located on the Rio Negro, a major northern tributary, near its junction with the Amazon. The Rio Negro derives its name from the heavy load of silt it carries, noticeably darkening the lighter-colored waters of the Amazon at their meeting. Below Manaus the river is normally a broad highway several miles in width, but it stretches across the horizon whenever seasonal floods overflow its banks. The early Portuguese explorers gave the name O Rio Mar, or Ocean River, to this alluvial immensity.

The Amazon enters the Atlantic through a broad estuary estimated to be 150 miles (240 kilometers) in width. Since the Atlantic has sufficient wave and tidal energy to carry most of the river's sediments out to sea—it is a high-energy coastal environment—the Amazon does not form a true delta, a large, fan-shaped tract of land at the mouth of a major river. The great deltas of the world are all located in relatively protected bodies of water that allow the buildup of silt into new land, whereas the Amazon flows into the turbulent Atlantic. The river braids into two branches, or distributaries, at its mouth. The northern arm, a maze of islands and channels, is separated from the southern channel, called the Pará River, by the Switzerland-sized Marajó Island. The southern channel is the site of Belém (Portuguese: "Bethlehem"), the major city of the river mouth and the primary entrepôt and gateway to the Amazon region.

The immense alluvial plain, broadening as one proceeds upriver, is covered with an evergreen forest (*selva*) of inconceivable biotic diversity. Along a small drainageway in southern Peru encompassing only a few acres, one researcher identified 1,209 butterfly species (Wilson, 1992). Tropical rain forests like the Amazon Basin occupy only 6 percent of the world's land surface but are believed to contain more than half of the earth's plant and animal species. A distinguished group of nineteenth-century naturalists, including Darwin, Wallace, and Agassiz, were attracted to the region in the pursuit of what Darwin called "the mystery of mysteries," the origin of species.

Unlike the Anglo-Saxons elsewhere in the Americas, the Catholic Portuguese, under the influence of the Jesuits, did not so uniformly extirpate their indigenous peoples. Practicing a type of agriculture known as shifting cultivation, in which fields rather than crops are rotated to ensure soil fertility, the native tribes of the Amazon were well adapted to the local environment and its drainageways. Their technology, though primitive, was sustainable (and still is). The low levels of nutrients and humus in the tropical oxisols (highly oxidized soils low in fertility) do not allow for long-term use of the land for commercial grazing or cash crop cultivation, and the effects of mining on the local cultures and environment are even more deleterious. Native tribes such as the peaceful Yanomamö; the Waiwais, a tribe of fishermen; and the headhunting Jívaro sustained population densities in the lush rain forest that were lower than those in the Sahara Desert, although the low populations may have been partly a result of post-Columbian contact with European diseases and disturbances.

The mouth of the river was probably first discovered in 1500 by Vicente Yáñez Pinzón, the commander of the *Niña* on Columbus's 1492 voyage. Exploration did not really begin until 1540 or 1541, however, when Francisco de Orellana followed the Napo River downstream in what is now Ecuador and reached the Atlantic Ocean. Orellana's fanciful stories of female warriors may have given the river its name, though an alternate etymology is that the river is named after the awesome tidal bore or wave front from the ocean that sweeps hundreds of miles upstream at speeds in excess of 40 miles per hour (65 kilometers per hour). The native term *amassona* ("boat destroyer") may be the origin of the name. Pedro Teixeira undertook the first upstream voyage (1637–1638) when he ascended to the source of the Napo River and crossed the Andes to Quito, Ecuador.

This began the Portuguese legal, if not always effective, occupation of the region. The valley continued to be sparsely populated by indigenous people of Tupi-Guaraní linguistic stock. (The Brazilian language, though essentially Portuguese, has been more influenced by the Indian languages than, say, American English, whose primary influence from native peoples is seen only in colorful place-names and a few loan words.) Brazilians were well aware that they had for long only "scratched along the sea like crabs," a vivid but accurate description of Portuguese peripheral settlement made by one of Brazil's first historians, the seventeenth-century Franciscan Vicente do Salvador. This pattern would begin to be drastically altered in the mid-twentieth century by the Brazilian strongman President Getúlio Vargas, who ruled from 1930 to 1945 and again from 1951 to 1954. Vargas inaugurated a campaign to occupy the interior in his "march to the west," and by the relocation of the capital from coastal Rio de Janeiro to Brasília (1960), a forward location on the interior plateau. The construction of access roads to the north, including the notorious Highway BR-364, brought thousands of land-hungry settlers into the territory (now state) of Rondônia. Migration peaked in 1986, but the Belém-Brasília Highway and the Trans-Amazon Highway continue to open up new parts of the Amazon valley to settlement and exploitation. Although the Brazilian government requires protection of the intervening corridors, many believe that the last large block of tropical rain forest is now being reduced to shreds and tatters.

See also Madeira, Negro

Further Reading: Davis, Wade, *One River: Explorations and Discoveries in the Amazon Rain Forest,* New York: Simon and Schuster, 1996; Margolis, Mac, *The Last New World: The Conquest of the Amazon Frontier,* New York: Norton, 1992.

AMU DARYA

Source: The Pamirs
Length: c. 1,600 miles (2,580 kilometers)
Tributaries: Kokcha, Kunduz, Balkh
Outlet: Southern end of Aral Sea

Crossed by the ancient Silk Route connecting the Orient to Europe, this great river plain of Central Asia has attracted settlement, conquest, and imperial control throughout history.

The source of the Amu Darya, known to the ancient world as the River Oxus, lies in the confluence of two large headstreams, the Pyandzh and Vaksh, which drain glaciers of the Pamirs on the flank of the world's highest mountains. The upper course of the river for about 170 miles (274 kilometers) downstream is the boundary between Afghanistan and independent Tajikistan. The lower course of the river also forms a boundary: it is the border between Uzbekistan and Turkmenistan. With the exception of Afghanistan, all these countries were formerly part of the Soviet Union.

The river flows generally northwest across the sandy deserts of interior Asia to its outlet on the Aral Sea, which it reaches via a large delta. The river corridor contains a long string of oasis cities. The lower course divides the Kyzyl Kum Desert (or Red Desert) to the north from the Kara Kum Desert (or Black Desert) to the south, the latter lying between the Elburz ranges of northern Iran and the Amu Darya.

The town of Balkh, legendary birthplace of the prophet Zoroaster and Islamic center of learning, is situated south of the Oxus on the Balkhab River. It gave the name to the ancient Persian province of

Bactria. In 329 B.C. Alexander the Great crossed the massive ramparts of the Hindu Kush mountains from Kabul in the south. Alexander used the Khawak Pass, at an elevation of 11,500 feet (3,505 meters), on the eastern shoulder of the mountains representing the major topographic division between India and Central Asia. That would be the route—in reverse—of Tamerlane, Genghis Khan, and other invaders of India. The long column of Alexander's army stretched out for miles across the pass and found it hard going in such precipitous terrain, so far from their sources of supply. They finally reached Balkh, the Persian capital, located strategically between the Afghan highlands and the plateau lands stretching north to the Oxus. The Persian leader Bessus, the murderer of, and self-proclaimed successor to, the great Persian ruler Darius, had fled his capital. Balkh is today a ruined city, with only vestiges of its mud walls remaining, though the city was once a crossroads on the Silk Route and conquering Arabs in the eighth century referred to it as the "Mother of Cities."

In pursuit of Bessus the Macedonian leader traveled north to the Oxus, which was about 50 miles (80 kilometers) away. Short of water and burned by the wind-whipped sands, the army finally reached the river, where it gladly quenched its thirst. It took five days to cross the river, because Bessus had commandeered and burned all the riverboats; Alexander's army had to cross in improvised boats made from skins stuffed with chaff. Alexander moved out ahead of his army, advancing across the region known as Sogdiana—the region between the Oxus and the Jaxartes (Syr Darya).

The region that Alexander crossed in the northernmost reaches of his conquest was the place where in the nineteenth century the Great Game was played out between the British and Russian powers. The Amu Darya River was then important strategically, as it was a line of control of the Russians, who were sweeping out of the steppe lands of Central Asia in their conquest of the native Muslim *khanates* (kingdoms). The British, from their base in India, were concerned that the Russians would not stop there and might advance on their northwestern frontier in Afghanistan or move in the direction of the British-protected Persian Gulf. The balancing of the two empires involved two separate but related requirements: Afghanistan was established as a buffer between the nations, and the Amu Darya became the dividing line between the hegemony of the two powers. After midcentury there was much jockeying back and forth, with the backing of one or another local potentate, before this settlement was reached, but in 1873 Russia accepted the ancient Oxus as the northern boundary of Afghanistan. That fact was not officially affirmed until 1887. In 1920, after the Russian Revolution, the Soviet Union accepted the Amu Darya as its southern border.

This region has not only been the meeting-place of diverse cultures and civilizations along the Silk Route but also the site of the legendary cities of Samarkand and Bukhara, both located on the Zeravshan, a northern tributary of the Oxus. Alexander's army suffered severe privations living away from home for so long in a desert, but the conqueror eventually secured the Bactrian plain and the farther reaches of Sogdiana (Trans-Oxiana). Only after two years of fighting in Central Asia would Alexander be able to recross the Hindu Kush and enter India.

The river has provided water for irrigation since prehistoric times. Archaeological evidence shows that irrigation systems were established there as early as 1200 B.C. It is along the last 200 miles (322 kilometers) that irrigation is most developed today, especially along the left bank, where the oasis widens to 40 miles (64 kilometers). During modern times canals supplied by the Amu Darya have enlarged the area under cultivation. The largest of these, the Kara Kun Canal, leaves the Amu Darya near the Afghan frontier and crosses the desert westward to the oases of Mary and Ashkhabad in present-day Turkmenistan. The delta has not attracted so much irrigation, as it mostly comprises a swamp forest of poplar and tamarisk. Much of the irrigated land is given over to cotton, which is barged along the river to Chardzhov. From there it moves via the Tashkent-Caspian Railway to its eventual destination.

Under the economic pressure of the Soviet

Union, the region drew so much water from the Amu Darya that the river no longer replenishes the Aral Sea. That inland body of water—more accurately described as a lake, as it is completely enclosed—presently occupies only about 30 percent of its pre-1960 area. Evidence of the changing shoreline can be seen in the boats left stranded miles from the water's edge. The Trans-Caspian Railroad has lessened the importance of the river as a transport route, but the string of oases that attracted conquerors from Alexander the Great to the Russian czars continue to exert a pull of influence, not least as an exotic focus of the geographical imagination.

The Amu Darya border lasted from the nineteenth century well into the twentieth. The British withdrawal from India in 1947 created a political vacuum in south Asia. The United States did not want to provide the counterforce needed to balance the Russians. Even before the 1978 Afghan Revolution brought to power a socialist government in Kabul, the Russians had been working behind the scenes to establish their preeminence in the country. In December 1979 the Russians moved approximately 80,000 troops across the Amu Darya in their attempt to bring the whole of Afghanistan under their control. The failure of their efforts to hold a mountainous country whose terrain offered untold number of hideouts for opponents of the regime became evident in February 1989, when Russia withdrew from Afghanistan. With the collapse of the Soviet Union in the early 1990s, the Amu Darya is no longer a frontier between the U.S.S.R. and Afghanistan but is now a border between the newly independent countries of Uzbekistan and Turkmenistan, as well as between Afghanistan and Tajikistan.

See also Syr Darya

Further Reading: Hopkirk, Peter, *The Great Game: The Struggle for Empire in Central Asia,* New York: Kodansha International, 1994; Meyer, Karl E., and Shareen Blair Brysac, *Tournament of Shadows: The Great Game and the Race for Empire in Central Asia,* Washington, DC: Counterpoint, 1999; Wood, Michael, *In the Footsteps of Alexander the Great: A Journey from Greece to Asia,* Berkeley: University of California Press, 1997 (companion volume to BBC television series).

AMUR

Source: Confluence of Argun and Shilka Rivers in northeast Asia
Length: c. 1,800 miles (2,897 kilometers)
Tributaries: Ussuri, Sungari, Zeya, Bureya
Outlet: Tatar Strait

The Amur has long been an important accessway between interior Asia and the Pacific Ocean, as well as forming the border along much of its length between China and Siberian Russia. The Amur River (Chinese: Black Dragon River) is formed by the confluence of the Shilka and Argun Rivers in the region where southern Siberia meets Inner Mongolia. Counting the Shilka and the Shilka's main tributary, the Onon, the river system consisting of the Amur-Shilka-Onon Rivers is 2,800 miles (4,500 kilometers) long, making it the eighth longest in the world.

In its upper course the Amur crosses the high, rolling plateaus of Mongolia and southern Siberia. The river here is a mountain stream with steep valley slopes covered with coniferous forest. Gradually the mountains fade away and cedars and deciduous trees appear on the river's banks. Trending southeast, the river passes the twin cities of Blagoveshchensk (Russian) and Heihe (Chinese). The two banks of the stream are a study in contrast: Blagoveshchensk is a bleak industrial city, an eastern outpost of a Russian regime mired in corruption and ideological rigidity; Heihe is a gleaming modern city that has sprung up in the recent period of economic modernization in China. A brisk border traffic crosses the river by ferry, carrying mostly Chinese-made goods because the Russians aren't producing anything of use. There are plans to build a bridge linking these two cities in an effort to regularize trade and political relations between the two countries.

Southeast of Blagoveshchensk the river enters a narrow gorge cutting across the Lesser Khingan Mountains. Emerging from this constriction, which runs for 95 miles (150 kilometers), the river opens onto the vast open plain of its lower course. Where the Ussuri empties into the Amur from the south, the river turns northeast away from the

Manchurian border at Khabarovsk. Then the river winds across a swampy plain choked with numerous islets and shifting sandbars. Navigation of the lower Amur is treacherous. The channel is wide and subject to shifting, and it is difficult for the barges that ply this stretch of the river to maintain their course in the deepest parts of the channel, even with the help of guide buoys. Crossing coastal flatlands, the Amur finally reaches an outlet 10 miles (16 kilometers) wide on the Tatar Strait, opposite Sakhalin Island.

The comparatively fertile and temperate valley of the lower Amur has been the principal attraction in this isolated region of the Far East. Cossack explorers in the seventeenth century pushed forward the limits of the czar's domain, searching for the valuable resources of the vast taiga: furs, minerals, and timber. The political frontier was contested until the treaty of Nerchinsk (1687) granted the Amur region to the Chinese. Facing the declining Ching dynasty in the nineteenth century, a confident and growing Russia was able to obtain the left bank of the Amur in the Treaty of Aigun (1858). So was created the 1,100-mile (1,770-kilometer) border between China and Russia in the Far East that has persisted for almost 150 years.

In the late nineteenth century a revival of conflict occurred in the border area of the lower Amur. The construction of the Trans-Siberian Railroad (1891–1905) opened up Russia's vast Siberian frontier as far as the Pacific. The original route across the Far East passed through parts of Manchuria en route to the Vladivostok terminus, even though the Chinese objected to this incursion into their territory. (Today the route follows the left bank of the Amur and is entirely in Russian territory.) However it was not to be the Chinese but the Japanese who would successfully resist Russian expansion. The secret Japanese military organization known as the *Kokuryukai,* or Black Dragon Society, was founded in 1901 to agitate for a war with Russia and an advance to the Amur River. Taking its title from the Chinese name for the river, the Heilung Kiang, or Black Dragon River, this highly trained and effective military society with Samurai roots would be important in later Japanese aggressions (the annexation of Korea, 1910; the seizure of Manchuria, 1931). On February 8, 1904, the Japanese struck without warning—as they would at Pearl Harbor, thirty-seven years later—at the major Russian naval base of Port Arthur, thus initiating the Russo-Japanese War (1904–1905). The settlement of the war, brokered by the rising economic and military power of the United States, gave the southern half of oil-rich Sakhalin Island to Japan. Although the czar didn't lose any territory in the key Amur valley, for the first time a Western power had been defeated by an oriental nation. Russia's forward movement in Asia was effectively checked, and the loss contributed to the fall of the Russian monarchy twelve years later.

With the emergence of differences between Chinese- and Soviet-style communism in the 1960s, the Amur again became contested terrain. Russia began construction of a new railroad parallel to the Trans-Siberian but passing several hundred miles farther north. The Baykal-Amur Mainline (BAM) Railroad, completed in the 1980s, extends 2,200 miles (3,540 kilometers) eastward from Taishet directly to Komsomolsk on the lower Amur, crossing the northern end of Lake Baykal. Russia gained thereby a strategic route for military deployment if the Trans-Siberian, lying so close to Chinese territory, were seized. Numerous border conflicts along the Amur in the 1960s occurred: strategic islands in the river were taken and retaken.

The Amur-Ussuri river corridor has become the most important axis of urban and industrial development in Russia's Far East. Vladivostok, Russia's largest city on the Pacific, lies to the south. It has large military installations as well as shipbuilding and fish-processing plants. Khabarovsk, near the confluence of the Amur and Ussuri, has centrality: its manufacturing specialization has been in the machine and metal-working industries. To the north, the city of Komsomolsk was founded in 1932 by members of the Komsomol, the Communist youth organization. The city expanded greatly after World War II as a steelmaker, on the basis of nearby iron ore, and it has benefited from its location at a crossing point on the BAM. The river is navigable during the summer and fall months and continues to be an important transportation artery. It transports bulk commodities such as timber, foodstuffs, and oil (from Sakhalin Island) as well as finished and processed goods, making connections with the great railroads that tie the region to European markets. The proximity of this temperate corner of Russia's Far East to Japan makes it likely to be the focus of future investment and growth linked to the resource needs of the world's second largest economy.

See also Songhua Jiang
Further Reading: Bobrick, Benson, *East of the Sun: The Epic Conquest and Tragic History of Siberia,* New York: Poseidon Press, 1992; Winchester, Simon, "Black Dragon River: On the Edge of Empires," *National Geographic,* February 2000, pp. 2–33.

ANGARA

Source: Lake Baykal
Length: c. 1,150 miles (1,851 kilometers)
Tributary: Ilim
Outlet: **Yenisey**

The vast region of Siberia is conveniently divided into three major physiographic units: the West Siberian Plain, crossed by the Ob' and Irtysh Rivers; the Central Siberian Plateau, lying between the Yenisey and Lena Rivers; and the Eastern Highlands east of the Lena. The Central Siberian Plateau, whose western portion is drained by the Yenisey and its tributaries, including the Angara, is a heavily dissected plateau of complex rock structure that rises occasionally to subdued mountains. This stable and ancient rock platform is also known as the Angara Shield (or Angaraland). Much of the area consists geologically of pre-Cambrian crystalline rocks that have resisted tectonic activity as younger mountains have risen to the south and east. Extensive areas of younger sedimentary strata overlie the crystallines, and large lava flows emitted from recent fault lines attain a thickness of 1,000 feet (305 meters).

The Angara is the outlet for the mile-deep gash known as Lake Baykal, the lake with the largest volume of water in the world. This lake was

Bratsk Dam on the Angara River (Jesse Walker)

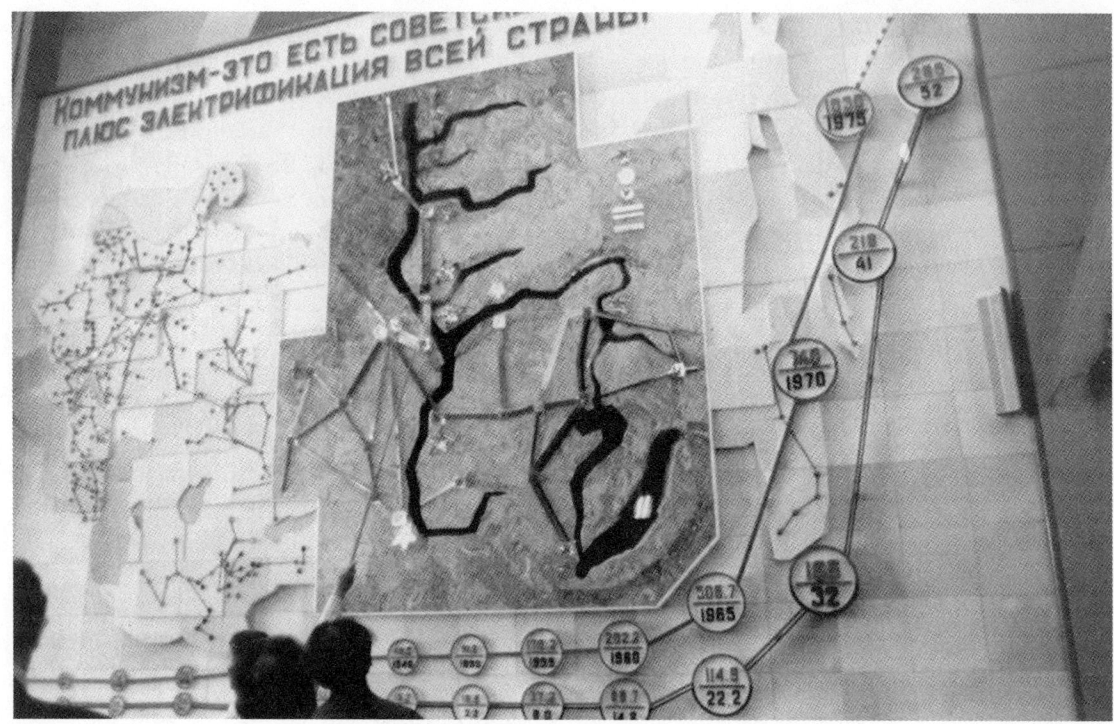

Model of the electrical grid around Bratsk Dam on the Angara River (Jesse Walker)

formed as a result of the foundering of the earth's crust along parallel fault lines, in a process similar to that which produced the lake with the world's largest surface area, Lake Superior, one of the Great Lakes on the U.S.-Canada border. Lake Baykal has hundreds of species of plants and animals found nowhere else in the world as a result of its isolation and the depth of its waters. The Angara rushes steadily out of the southwestern end of Lake Baykal past Irkutsk, the major city of southern Siberia. The lake freezes over in the winter, but because the water flowing down the Angara has such a steep gradient and high speed, the river itself does not freeze.

This region of southern Siberia did not really open up until the construction of the Trans-Siberian Railroad. The building of the railroad, the longest single track in the world, was delayed for more than a decade by the difficulty of crossing the precipitous cliffs of mountain spurs at the southern end of Lake Baykal. As a result, for a time trains were ferried across the lake in summer and tracks were laid across the ice in winter. The Trans-Siberian crosses the Angara at Irkutsk, 45 miles (72 kilometers) from the lake, promoting the city's growth as a transportation and industrial center.

In the 1950s the Soviet Union began to construct a series of high dams along the Angara. The hydroelectric dam at Irkutsk backs the water all the way to Lake Baykal. Despite the enormous capacity of this lake—it has been estimated to contain 10 percent of all the fresh water in the world—its level has been raised 20 feet (6 meters) by the Irkutsk Dam. The even larger dam farther downstream at Bratsk has created its own sea, the Bratsk Sea, which stretches all the way to Irkutsk, some 300 miles (483 kilometers) away. The Bratsk Dam is one of the largest hydroelectric plants in the world, generating roughly 4.5 million kilowatts of power. Other dams have been constructed or are planned below Bratsk, making the region an even larger producer of hydropower than the Povolzhye (the Volga valley) in western Russia. Since south Siberia, with its small population, lacked a significant demand for residential or consumer electricity, the massive amounts of power generated were devoted to energy-intensive industries such as aluminum manufacturing and pulp processing, or for electrifying the Trans-Siberian, which in the past had to carry large quantities of coal for its steam engines.

The Angara flows north out of Lake Baykal past Irkutsk and Bratsk. After receiving the Ilim River, the Angara turns west to the Yenisey near Strelka. The lower course of the river below its junction with the Ilim is known as the Upper Tunguska (Russian: Verkhnyaya Tunguska). Though often overlooked, the Upper Angara River (Russian: Verkhnyaya Angara) is a stretch of the river roughly 200 miles (322 kilometers) long rising northeast of Lake Baykal and flowing southwest into the lake.

ARAS

Source: Bingol Dag (in Turkish Armenia)
Length: 568 miles (914 kilometers)
Tributaries: Hrazdan, Qareh
Outlet: Caspian Sea

The Aras (Russian: Araks) is the chief river of Armenia, and its valley contains the largest concentration of population in the country. It forms a long stretch of the border between Iran and two of the Trans-Caucasus republics—Armenia and Azerbaijan—and a shorter section of the boundary between Armenia and Turkey. A political dividing line along much of its length, the river is also a traditional entryway for those invading Iran from the northwest.

The Aras (in ancient times, the Araxes) rises in the mountains of Turkish Armenia. In its upper course the river flows in an entrenched valley through an undulating lava plateau. It forms a long east-west corridor of which the ancient garrison of Erzurum is the center. To the east the river forms the political frontier with Armenia, approaching the fertile Yerevan Plain, the center of the ancient Armenian kingdom, which included, besides present-day Armenia, parts of Turkey, Azerbaijan, and Iran. The biblical Mount Ararat (16,854 feet, or 5,137 meters) is a prominent feature at this meeting-place between the former Soviet Union, Turkey, and Iran. Farther downstream the Aras enters a gorge at the road and railway crossing-point of Julfa before opening onto a broad plain. The river leaves the Iranian border and crosses into Azerbaijan territory, joining the major waterway of the Kura close to the Caspian Sea. Since 1897 part of the river's flow has entered the Caspian by its own mouth.

The fruitful Aras valley has been associated with the legend of the Garden of Eden, just as Noah's ark is believed to have come to rest on Mount Ararat. An ancient civilization flourished in the Aras valley in the first millennium B.C., which appears to have been an offshoot of Mesopotamian cultures to the south. An ally of Rome, Armenia later developed as an independent Christian state. In the nineteenth century the rising Russian power increasingly encroached into the Trans-Caucasus. In 1827, Russia wrested control of Erivan (today's Yerevan) from the Persian shah, who was disappointed that British forces did not come to his assistance. Subsequently Russian Armenia passed to the Soviet Union during the period of Communist rule. In modern times many Armenians, known for their business ability, have immigrated to the United States.

ARNO

Source: Northern Apennine Mountains, central Italy
Length: c. 150 miles (240 kilometers)
Tributaries: Chiani, Sieve, Bisenzio, Elsa, Era
Outlet: Ligurian Sea

A densely populated river valley of north-central Italy is the heart of historic Tuscany. The Arno River valley, with its remarkable cluster of Renaissance geniuses and its repositories of some of the most celebrated artworks of the Western world, is truly a stream of treasure. Glorious paintings, breathtaking statues, and magnificent architecture grace the museum towns along its banks. Rising in the northern Apennine Mountains, the Arno flows generally south to Arezzo, the birthplace of Petrarch, the fourteenth-century poet and humanist who anticipated the Italian Renaissance. From Arezzo the river turns northwest, flowing past Florence and Pisa on a mostly westward course as it crosses a fertile plain dotted with hill towns. From its source on Mount Falterona in the Apennines to its outlet on the Ligurian Sea, an arm of the Mediterranean, the Arno travels about 150 miles (240 kilometers)—not long as great rivers go.

Tuscany embraces a wider region than the river valley. Known in ancient times as Etruria, this land of hilly plateaus, low mountains, alluvial plains, and coastlands was the home of the Etruscan population before being conquered by the Romans. The Tuscan Hills south of the Arno form an undulating plain interrupted by the tall, quadrangular towers of its defensively situated hill villages, which resemble the background of a medieval fresco. Most notable among these hill towns is Siena, known for its Gothic architecture, school of early Renaissance painting, and boisterous summer horse races run on a fan-shaped main square. Siena and Florence were home to the two main political factions of late medieval history: the Florentine-supported Guelphs and the Siena-sponsored Ghibellines. Proud to be free of larger political entities like the Holy Roman Empire or the Papal States, the Italian communes did not hesitate to fight among themselves.

The Val d'Arno drains the northern third of Tuscany. The alluvial plain is intensively cultivated with typical Mediterranean crops—olives, grapes, and cereals. Terraced hill slopes give the impression of a carefully tended and much-loved landscape. The Tuscan cities of Pisa, Lucca, Siena, Arezzo, and Florence became independent city-states and strong republics in the eleventh and twelfth centuries. Florence had attained supremacy in the region by about 1450 but failed to conquer one of its traditional enemies, Pisa, a port city near the mouth of the Arno. Florence's bankers and merchants grew prosperous with cloth production (the wool came from sheep grazing the hilly pasturelands nearby) and artisanal manufacture, especially of fine jewelry, metalwork, glass, and marble, for which the primary requirements seemed to be skill and taste. Today the City of Towers is the outstanding center of art and culture in Italy.

Florence was originally a river crossing when Rome founded the city as Florentia in 59 B.C. The shop-lined fourteenth-century Ponte Vecchio, or Old Bridge, stands at the approximate position of this ancient ford. Florence derived its early growth from its position astride the interior routes from Rome to Bologna and Milan along a waterway that initially was an obstacle for the northward-moving Romans. The major Roman roads forked around Tuscany, passing east of the Apennines along the Via Flaminia and west along the coastal plain on the route of the Via Aurelia, the latter avoiding the great swamps of the Maremma in southwestern Tuscany. This relative isolation permitted ancient Etruria to develop its own distinctive language and culture independent of the cosmopolitan influence of Rome—including the mongrelizing effects of the large barbarian population of the Eternal City on the Latin tongue. Today's Italian language resembles the sweet Tuscan speech standardized in the poetry of Dante, Petrarch, and Boccaccio.

It was near the small hill town of Vinci, located on a northern tributary of the Arno, that in 1452 was born the person whom many consider the greatest intellect of the Renaissance—Leonardo da Vinci. After moving to Milan in the 1480s, Leonardo began an inquiry into both the practical and scientific aspects of flooding, irrigation, and river transportation. His *Notebooks* contain frequent comments on the destructive capabilities of rivers, and they demonstrate a knowledge of the highly variable flow of Mediterranean streams. Leonardo's earliest known drawing, dated August 5, 1473, is a sketch of the Arno River winding among the Tuscan Hills. The Arno had flooded a number of times in the fourteenth and fifteenth centuries: in 1333, 1466, and 1478 the river had overtopped its banks, destroying crops and damaging buildings. Leonardo is of course best known for his masterful paintings (few in number) and daring flights of scientific advance that seem to anticipate so much twentieth-century science and technology. He was more likely to earn his keep, however, in the pay of Italian cities working as an

Churches, towers, gates, and bridges are evident in this print of historic Florence (Firenze) on the north bank of the Arno River. (Bridgeman Art Gallery)

engineer and military architect, applying the knowledge he had gained from first-person, empirical investigations. Among the most outstanding of these practical projects were his ideas relating to the Arno River itself.

As a result of new documents that have surfaced in Madrid in the last 30 years, we now know that between 1503 and 1506 Leonardo collaborated with Niccolo Machiavelli, the second chancellor of the government of Florence, on a grand scheme of river basin development that was partly intended as a military strategy. The project was first of all a plan to make Florence a seaport by improving the navigability of the Arno between Florence and the sea. Second, the scheme was meant to deprive Pisa, with which Florence was at war, of water by cutting off its riverine position through a diversion of the outlet. Pisans would not only lack for drinking water; in addition, they would not be able to receive aid from their Genoan allies, who relied on river transportation up the Arno.

Leonardo's design included a plan to dig two large canals along the lower course of the Arno near Pisa. The waters of the Arno would thereby be drawn away from Pisa into the marshes of the Stagno di Livorno, a large wetland near Leghorn (Livorno). The project failed because of a lack of leadership on the part of the superintending engineer—Leonardo only designed the plan, he didn't dig the ditches. Leonardo estimated that about one million tons of earth would need to be removed, requiring some fifty thousand worker days. Leonardo even devised a mechanical canal digger for the project, which he sketched in his *Notebooks*, but it was never built. Another Florentine, Dante Alighieri, in the *Divine Comedy* had imagined a dam on the lower Arno to flood Pisa into submission. And the architect Brunelleschi, whose most famous work is the elegant cupola of Florence cathedral, attempted a similar strategy against Lucca; its failure was considered an object lesson in how overly grandiose schemes can go awry. That was to be the case with Leonardo's and Machiavelli's collaboration; hence its being hushed up in the official record. During a storm Florence lost a number of ships at sea, and the Pisans filled up the diversionary canals. The war dragged on for another five years before Florence finally triumphed. While Leonardo was employed by Florence as an advisor on military strategy and fortification, he painted the most famous picture in the world, a portrait of the third wife of the Florentine merchant Francesco del Giocondo; it now hangs in the Louvre.

The detailed maps that Leonardo drew of the Arno headwaters, the Val di Chiana, show his awareness of the need for sufficient water in the dry summer months. The watershed between the Arno and Tiber Rivers was a sensitive geopolitical boundary between Florentine power and the widely ranging papal influence to the east and south of Florence. Nor could the political point have been missed by Leonardo's partner in this affair, Machiavelli, the father of political science and inventor of *realpolitik:* the government that controlled Tuscany would also have to control the Val di Chiana.

Few people look past the mysterious smile in the *Mona Lisa* (also known as *La Giocanda*) to observe the conventionally painted background. A sinuous river winds across a hilly landscape. The valley is almost certainly that of the Arno, or a composite image of a river valley influenced by the Arno. The peak in the background resembles the sketch of Monte Verucca made in preparation for its fortification. The ethereal quality of the picture derives partly from the way in which Leonardo has chosen to paint the wife of Giocondo: she seems to rise above the river. This technique of aerial perspective known as bird's-eye view, popular in the Renaissance, was invented by Leonardo.

Politicians since Leonardo's time have often promised to control the Arno's floods and to prevent its destructiveness. However, no overall plan has been put into effect, even five hundred years after Leonardo's grand but abortive proposals. In 1966 a major flood of the Arno put the magnificent artworks of Florence again in jeopardy. This capricious river still threatens the treasures along its banks.

See also Po, Tiber

Further Reading: Masters, Roger D., *Fortune Is a River: Leonardo da Vinci and Niccolo Machiavelli's Magnificent Dream to Change the Course of Florentine History,* New York: Free Press, 1998.

ASSINIBOINE

Source: Southern Saskatchewan
Length: 590 miles (950 kilometers)
Tributaries: Qu'Appelle, Souris
Outlet: **Red River of the North**

Rising in eastern Saskatchewan Province, the Assiniboine River flows southeastward into Manitoba, then turns east before joining the Red River of the North at the plains city of Winnipeg. Its most important feeder streams are the Souris River, which drains from the south out of North Dakota, and the Qu'Appelle River, which enters from the west. The latter stream was so named because at a certain bend in the river there is a strong echo: hence the French *Qu' appelle?* or "Who calls?" The river and its primary tributaries have cut broad river valleys into the 1,600-foot (488-meter) prairie surface. Bluffs along the river and low rounded hills with evocative names like Moose Mountain and Riding Mountain—part of the discontinuous Manitoba Scarp—provide the only relief from the gently undulating prairie plain. West of Portage la Prairie the Assiniboine enters the lowlands of glacial Lake Agassiz, which range in elevation from 500 to 1,000 feet (152 to 305 meters), formed by ice blockage of drainageways during the Pleistocene epoch.

Brandon, Manitoba, is the largest city along the Assiniboine River. It is just upstream from the junction with the Souris. Brandon was originally a fur-trading center before the late-nineteenth-century arrival of the Canadian Pacific Railway, which more than anything else reoriented the economy and settlement pattern of this commercial wheat-growing region. The major city of southern Manitoba is Winnipeg, located at the southern end of an immense lake of the same name. Both Red River and Lake Winnipeg drain ultimately via the Nelson River into Hudson Bay.

The river was named after the local Native Americans, the Assiniboine, whose name means "those who cook with stones," referring to their practice of boiling water by placing heated stones in a skin container. The river was explored by the Frenchman La Vérendrye in 1736, and forts for conducting the fur trade were soon built at the two key strategic sites in the region: at the mouth of the Assiniboine (present-day Winnipeg) and near the site of Portage la Prairie, where the lake plain is first encountered by the eastward-flowing Assiniboine.

In the early nineteenth century, agricultural settlement spread upriver from the colony founded on the lower river by Lord Selkirk (5th Earl of, 1771–1820, Scottish philanthropist). Though lacking in the petroleum resources boasted by Alberta, Manitoba has prospered on the basis of a diverse, hardworking population and its key location astride the gateway to western Canada. Still an agricultural region focusing on wheat, the Assiniboine valley is no longer dependent exclusively on cereal cultivation.

See also Red (of the North)

ATBARA

Source: Ethiopian Highlands
Length: c. 500 miles (800 kilometers)
Tributaries: Tekeze, Angereb
Outlet: **Nile**

The Atbara is a right-bank tributary of the world's longest river. It joins the Nile just above the fifth cataract in northeastern Sudan about 200 miles (322 kilometers) north of Khartoum and the junction of the Blue and White Nile. The river rises not far from Gondar in Ethiopia and, after flowing through ravines, enters Sudan, where it receives its two major tributaries, the Angareb and the Satit (in Ethiopia, the Tekeze), both of which have large catchment basins but low annual discharge. The Tekeze forms part of the boundary between Ethiopia and the newly independent country of Eritrea (est. 1993).

The population of the region is small and includes some nomads. Parts of the valley are severely eroded, forming "badland" topography. Recent irrigation projects, as at Khashm el Gerba, have resulted in the relocation of an increasingly sedentary population. The Atbara has a highly variable flow. It rises at the end of May, reaches a maximum in August, and falls off abruptly in the fall; during the winter and early spring, only rock pools remain. At its peak the river contributes 22 percent of the Nile's flow, but this diminishes to nil during the dry season. The only sizable town along the river has the same name as the river. Atbara is a rail junction and rail headquarters located near the place where the river empties into the Nile.

After the humiliating slaughter at Khartoum of the British governor, General Charles Gordon, in 1885, an Anglo-Egyptian army was sent out to squash the forces of the charismatic Muhammad Ahmad (the Mahdi). The defeat of the Mahdists in 1898 at Atbara ushered in a period of British paramountcy in the region, though the Sudan was never a British colony but instead was administered as an Anglo-Egyptian condominium until independence was attained in 1956.

ATCHAFALAYA

Source: Near where the **Red** (of the South) and **Mississippi** almost meet
Length: c. 170 miles (270 kilometers)
Tributaries: None (maze of interconnected waterways in Atchafalaya Swamp)
Outlet: Atchafalaya Bay, Gulf of Mexico

The only active distributary of the Mississippi River in Louisiana is one of the nation's largest river swamps and a critical floodway protecting the major cities of southern Louisiana. Where the 31 degrees north latitude line intersects the Mississippi River is the convergence of three major rivers, though they are not all connected to each other. The rivers of the three-river floodplain roughly form the letter *H,* with the left side the Red-Atchafalaya, the right the Mississippi, and the cross-bar the Old River.

As background for understanding this key region in the hydrology of the lower Mississippi valley, it is necessary to look at some basic principles. There are no major natural tributaries of the Mississippi in Louisiana. South of the central part

Buttressed cypress trees in the Atchafalaya Swamp in southwestern Louisiana (John Elk)

of the state—where the narrowing of the political boundaries has given rise to the description "waistline of the state"—several distributaries take water away from the main-stem Mississippi. Three of these distributaries, or effluents, are below Baton Rouge: Bayou Manchac on the east bank is just below the capital city, while Bayou Plaquemine and Bayou Lafourche (pronounced la-FOOSH) lie on the opposite bank, farther down the river. Beginning in the nineteenth century these outlets were sealed off by the Army Corps of Engineers, the federal agency primarily responsible for flood control and navigation on the nation's waterways.

Only the Atchafalaya remains open to the overflow of Mississippi water. This river, whose name in Choctaw was Hacha Falaya, or "long river," is the linchpin of the Corps's flood control program, almost in a literal sense since the Corps's efforts are embedded in the massive concrete structure known as the Old River Control Structure (ORCS), built into the mainline levee where the Mississippi and Atchafalaya come together.

The Atchafalaya is a shorter route to the sea than the current path past Baton Rouge and New Orleans—155 miles (249 kilometers) versus 325 miles (523 kilometers). Rivers prefer a shorter route because the gradient or slope of the river (the vertical drop per mile) increases with a shorter path. The Mississippi River would naturally jump its banks during high water and take the shorter Atchafalaya route to the Gulf of Mexico. In the wake of the disastrous 1927 flood and the Corps's studies in the 1940s, which showed that the Atchafalaya was developing an insatiable appetite for the Mississippi, the federal government launched a massive construction project in the 1950s. Completed in 1962 at a cost of $67 million, the project had a number of components. A lock and dam were installed to allow boats to move back and forth between the Mississippi and the Atchafalaya via the connecting Old River. Today the water of the Mississippi is about twelve feet above the level of the Atchafalaya. Just upstream from the lock is what locals call the "second locks," actually not a lock at all but a flood control structure, the ORCS. A spring flood in 1973, ten years after the completion of the control structure, washed out flanking wing walls, scoured deep holes that threatened to join under the structure thereby preventing control, and undermined part of the foundation. An auxiliary structure, built at a cost of $206 million, was ready to back up the ORCS by 1986.

By law no more than 30 percent of the Mississippi's water can flow down the Atchafalaya—approximately the percentage taking the shorter Atchafalaya route when the Corps's control was first established. Land along the upper Atchafalaya is farmed by corn, soybean, and livestock farmers behind protective levees. The Atchafalaya Swamp begins farther downstream, below where the floodplain is joined by the Morganza Spillway—an opening in the west bank of the Mississippi River just below Old River that provides additional flood protection. This inundated forest or swamp is filled with numerous lakes, bayous, marshes, and cypress swamps. Original homeland of the Cajuns, this maze of interconnected waterways challenges the navigational abilities of the people who migrated here from Acadia or French Nova Scotia. The Cajuns—the name "Acadian" was inevitably shortened—actually prefer some dry land for their characteristic farmer-fisherman means of subsistence, just as the cypresses require some temporarily dry patches of ground for sprouting. When this exiled group of French Canadians began to arrive after 1753 (they refused to sign a loyalty oath to the conquering English), there was little dry land available in south Louisiana. Though the Cajuns are more thickly settled along Bayou Lafourche and in the city of Lafayette, which received large numbers of Cajuns during the oil boom that followed World War II, swamp dwellers made a life for themselves amid the moss-draped cypresses, combining fishing, moss collection (moss was gathered and used to stuff furniture), and other such traditional livelihoods in a semisubsistence economy. Few settlements dot the floodplain of the lower Atchafalaya today—in fact, building is prohibited in the section of the river that is to be used as a floodway in the event of a century flood (a flood that has a statistical probability of occurring once every one hundred years, although that might not necessarily keep them from occurring in consecutive years—it merely means that the chances each year are one in a hundred).

The only major city along the river is Morgan City, established 150 years ago by the shipper Charles Morgan, who, tired of dockage fees and waterfront hassles along the New Orleans waterfront, built a competing port near the mouth of the Atchafalaya. The original Tarzan movies were filmed nearby, with the jungly growth of the cypress swamp and the Black extras who were hired locally suggesting darkest Africa. Morgan City has benefited from a succession of booms, but it has also been vulnerable to the inevitable busts. Cypress logging gave way to the shrimp business, which in turn receded, without completely losing its importance, before the powerful offshore oil industry. Guide levees in the swamp above Morgan City narrow and demarcate the largest river swamp in North America. The Atchafalaya Basin functions as a protective floodway to ensure that New Orleans and Baton Rouge stay high and dry in case of a once-in-a-century flood. The levees around Morgan City, known locally as the seawall, do not, however, guarantee that Morgan City will stay dry. To the ever-present danger that the seawall will be topped is added the threat of backwater flooding. During the 1973 flood water was shunted around the city but then came back and assaulted the city from the south, after it had reached the end of the levees some 6 miles (10 kilometers) below town. If the Atchafalaya Swamp is a funnel with its narrow end at the Gulf of Mexico, Morgan City represents the tip. Or even more vividly, as the travel writer John McPhee has put it, Morgan City is like a large tumbler glued to the bottom of an aquarium.

See also Mississippi

Further Reading: McPhee, John, "Atchafalaya," pp. 3–92 in *The Control of Nature,* New York: Farrar, Straus and Giroux, 1989.

AYEYARWADY

See Irrawaddy

B

BALSAS

Source: Tlaxcala state, south-central Mexico
Length: 426 miles (685 kilometers)
Tributaries: Tepecoacuilco, Cutzamalá, Tácambara, Tepalcatepec
Outlet: Petacalco Bay, Pacific Ocean

Rivers do not feature as prominently in the narrative of Mexican life and history as do threatening volcanoes, temperate mountain basins, and towering sierras. The country described as being so close to the United States but so far from God straddles the subtropical belt of latitudes with their tendency toward aridity. Its rivers have low discharge and often are intermittent. One of the longest rivers in Mexico, the Río Balsas, is an exception. Flowing in a broad curve from north to west, the river passes through the states of Puebla and Guerrero, where it waters a fertile agricultural valley. After passing along the border between the states of Guerrero and Michoacán, the river turns southwest across a hot, dry region before emptying into the Pacific Ocean at Petacalco Bay.

In its upper course in Tlaxcala and Puebla states, the stream is called the Atoyac, while in Guerrero it is known as the Mexcala. Rising in the volcanic highlands east of Mexico City, the river has numerous rapids that make it unnavigable. The Balsas passes through the densely populated basin of Puebla southeast of Mexico City. This region was already densely populated by Indian farmers before the arrival of the Spanish, and it has continued to be one of the major Mexican population clusters. Puebla has been a key link between Vera Cruz and Mexico City, and as varied a company as Cortez, Winfield Scott, and Diaz have gained military fame there.

The river keeps to the mountains in Guerrero but passes through a densely wooded fertile valley. A humid environment and irrigation projects have produced one of the richest agricultural regions in Mexico. Corn, coffee, cotton, sugar cane, and tropical fruits are among its staple crops. The river in its middle course lies beneath the sharply uplifted Morelos region, where many isolated Indian communities nestle in the valley heads of tributary streams or in miniature basins. The river is dammed in its hot, arid lower course where it penetrates the rugged coastal sierra, forming the Presa de Infiernillo, an artificial reservoir backing water far upstream along the Balsas and its tributaries.

Further Reading: Webber, John W., "Down Mexico's Río Balsas," *National Geographic,* August 1946, pp. 253–272.

BEAS

Source: Western Himalayas
Length: 250 miles (402 kilometers)
Tributary: Parvati
Outlet: **Sutlej**

Although better known on the Punjab plains, the Beas begins its journey in the high Himalayan peaks of Himachal Pradesh in western India. The upper course of the river is popular with trekkers and river rafters. The headwaters lie about 200 miles (322 kilometers) northwest of the upper Ganges. The scenic Kulu valley descends from snow-capped peaks at the river's source. The tourist and outfitting center of Manali, described as the "end of the habitable world," is the primary destination for those seeking adventure or picturesque scenery in the headwaters region. Surrounded by mountains on three sides, primitive roads and trails wind their way northward over rugged Rhotang Pass at 4,000 meters (13,100 feet) in elevation.

The Beas is a mountain stream in its upper course. Fed primarily by snowmelt from the upper peaks, the river varies between relatively quiet stretches of smooth, flat water and boiling turbulence in the gorges, which are carefully rated for use by kayak and canoe. About 50 miles (80 kilometers) south of Menali lies the district capital and provisioning point of Kulu. Immediately downstream the valley widens to become a fertile basin of apple orchards and wheat fields.

The Beas empties into the Sutlej—another of the five rivers of the Punjab—south of Amritsar. The lower section of the river, above where it joins the Sutlej (a tributary of the Indus), is more characteristic of the Punjab region. An overlapping of valley plains from five great rivers has produced an enormous alluvial plain with hardly a hill visible anywhere (see Figure 1). This vast plain is suitable for irrigated agriculture on a grand scale, and though irrigation goes back to early times, it was during the British Raj that the landscape of tanks, ditches, canals, and wells was fashioned. Much of this country is now in Pakistan, but the Bari Doab—so called because it is between the **B**eas and the **R**avi—is located farther to the east than other parts of the Punjab. It is more elevated and cool, and, receiving more precipitation, is less dependent on irrigation than the parched western Punjab.

The Beas-Sutlej line approximately delimits the Punjab border to the south and east. The Beas marks the eastern limit of Alexander the Great's invasion of India in 326 B.C., the first firm date in India's history amid the swirlings of her legendary and colorful past.

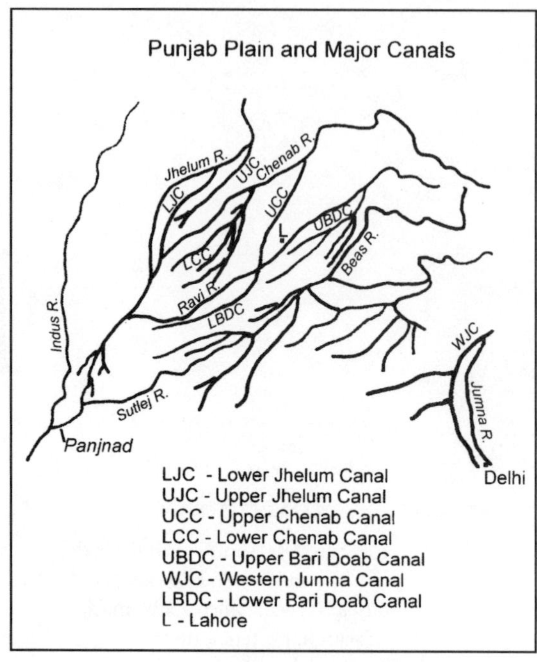

Figure 1

Several hydroelectric dams have been constructed on the Beas. The Indian state of Himachal Pradesh has a dozen hydropower projects. The coincidence of heavy monsoonal precipitation in the late summer and early fall with snowmelt has led to increased problems not only of flooding but also of siltation of generators. Hydro projects have had their economic lifetimes shortened by excessive silt entering the turbines during floods. Linking canals among the Punjab's major arms, such as the Beas-Sutlej Canal, have become shallower as a result of siltation, and their effectiveness has been reduced. Landslides in the tectonically active Himalayas have aggravated these problems. Blockage of rivers increases the potential for flash flooding and silting, and construction of roads for power projects has also worsened the situation. Much of the soil removed from hillsides during blasting and mining finds its way into streams, and landslides on destabilized slopes have increased in the upper reaches of both the Sutlej and Beas Rivers.

See also Chenab, Jhelum, Ravi, Sutlej

BENI

Source: Northern Bolivia, eastern slope of Andes Mountains
Length: 994 miles (1,599 kilometers)
Tributaries: Madidi, Madre de Dios
Outlet: **Madeira**

One of two landlocked countries in South America, Bolivia has a striking diversity of terrain. Most of its population lives in the western part of the country in the Andes Mountains and on the Altiplano. Draining the eastern slopes of the Andes in northern Bolivia, the Beni River and its tributaries cross a highly variegated mosaic of ecological zones, including elevated cloud forests, savannas, and evergreen lowlands, where human activity is scant.

One of the river's major tributaries, near the border with Peru, is the Madidi River. The financially strapped Bolivian government in 1995 agreed to adopt a conservation policy in this species-rich region as part of a Debt-for-Nature Swap (contemporary parlance for the practice of reducing Third World countries' debt in exchange for the promise not to develop rain forests and other natural areas). The Madidi National Park is supposed to be maintained as a corridor with high biological diversity and intact ecosystems. Preservation of plant and animal species as well as protection of indigenous human communities are to be topmost priorities. The mandate is for exploitation of resources, but only in sustainable ways. Unfortunately, as of 1999 plans are afoot to construct a hydroelectric dam, the Bala Dam, on the Beni, which would flood large sections of jungle lowlands in the park.

Farther downstream the Beni receives another important tributary, the Madre de Dios. The town of Riberalta was founded in 1882 in the middle of the jungle at this junction as an outpost for rubber collection. Only a little farther downstream lies the town of Villa Bella at the confluence of the Beni and the Mamoré River, the latter the major drainage of Bolivia's Oriente region and the country's longest navigable stream. The Beni and Mamoré together form the Madeira, one of the great tributaries of the Amazon Basin. The head of navigation on the Amazon system is at Porto Velho on the Madeira. In the early years of the twentieth century, with rubber prices rising (but about to collapse), Brazil began construction of a railroad linking Porto Velho, to which ocean steamers could come, to Riberalta on the Río Beni above the uppermost rapids. The line was completed to the Bolivian border by 1913, but before a bridge could be built across the Madeira and a short length of track extended beyond to Riberalta, the rubber boom collapsed, a result of competition from new producing areas such as British Malaya. A distinctive mode of resource and labor exploitation amounting to a *Raubwirtschaft* (robber economy) had come to an end, but it would not be the last phase of a cyclic, boom-bust commodity economy with associated mistreatment of the indigens in the Amazonian region.

See also Amazon, La Paz
Further Reading: Kemper, Steve, "Madidi: Will Bolivia Drown Its New National Park?" *National Geographic,* March 2000, pp. 2–23; for efforts to protect natural areas in Bolivia, see the website: http://www.ecobolivia.org.

BENUE

Source: Adamawa Mountains, northern Cameroon
Length: c. 880 miles (1,416 kilometers)
Tributaries: Mayo-Kebbi, Faro, Gongola, Katsina Ala, Donga
Outlet: **Niger**

The Benue, the primary eastern tributary of the Niger River, begins in the remote Adamawa Mountains in northern Cameroon. It rises in a broad zone comprising plateaus and occasional mountains, the Adamawa, that lies between the Bight of Biafra and Lake Chad. First explored by the Germans, this 50,000-square-mile (129,500-square-kilometer) area was divided in 1919 between a British and a French mandate. The French mandate became part of Cameroon, while the British mandate split between Nigeria and Cameroon. The Benue crosses this region in its upper course as it flows in a generally northerly direction.

The river drops about 900 feet (274 meters) before it is joined by a right-bank tributary, the Mayo-Kebbi, linking the Benue and Logone at high water through extensive swamps, thus occasionally joining the Niger and Chad drainage systems. The city of Garoua is situated near this confluence on the right bank of the river. An important trade center for a large cotton and peanut growing area, Garoua is a river port located at the head of navigation for shallow-draft boats. The town also functions as a transfer point for commercial transactions with the republic of Chad.

Below Garoua the river turns westward and crosses into Nigeria. From Yola to its outlet, the Benue is navigable throughout the year. Significant seasonal variations in water level do occur, with high water in August and September as much as 75 feet (23 meters) above low water in March and April. This affects navigation and flooding, not only on the Benue but also on the Niger, the great river of West Africa into which the Benue empties opposite the town of Lokoja.

South of the Benue, at Katsina Ala, terra cotta statues from a previously unknown culture were unearthed in the middle decades of the twentieth century. These figures include realistic representations of human heads, some animal figures, and pieces of much larger statues. The creators of these works have been identified as belonging to the Nok culture, after similar but earlier finds from Nok, some 130 miles (209 kilometers) to the north. The beautiful figures have puzzled archaeologists, who believe that the statues belong to a civilization more than 2,000 years old. Artifacts of the lost civilization of the Benue valley predate any other West African archaeological finds by some 1,000 years. Most intriguing of all is that we don't know what the significance of the figures is, or what brought the culture to an end.

See also Niger

BIG SIOUX

Source: In northeastern South Dakota
Length: 420 miles (676 kilometers)
Tributaries: Floyd, Rock
Outlet: **Missouri**

The states of Iowa and South Dakota have an undeserved reputation for flat terrain and bland culture. It used to be said jokingly that Iowa leads the nation in nothing but corn production. The valley of the Big Sioux in northwestern Iowa and eastern South Dakota, however, is a fertile, well-settled region belying that stereotype. Though possessing level land in the alluvial valley bottom and growing large amounts of corn for hog raising, the region departs from the uniformly negative image in its historical importance and in its recent economic advances.

Located on the western margin of the Corn Belt, the Big Sioux rises in the moraine country of northeastern South Dakota. It flows in a generally southerly direction, paralleling the nearby border with Minnesota. Numerous small glacial lakes lie just to the west. The river passes on its east the graceful small town of Brookings, site of one of the state's major universities and its agricultural school, South Dakota State University. After passing the town of Sioux Falls, South Dakota, which functions as a market and service center, the river forms the border with northwestern Iowa. The Big Sioux receives from the east the important tributary of the Rock River (not to be confused with the Rock River in Wisconsin and Illinois), which drains the elevated Coteau des Prairies in southwestern Minnesota and northwestern Iowa. About 75 miles (120 kilometers) farther downstream on the left bank, in Iowa, is another regional entrepôt, Sioux City. It is here, at the extreme southeastern corner of South Dakota, on the western boundary of Sioux City, that the river empties into the Missouri River.

Even before European settlement, native Indian tribes were attracted to the valley for its bountiful resources. The nomadic Sioux were less interested, however, in its fertile agricultural bottomlands than in the famous quarries nearby that furnished a smooth, pinkish-red stone used in making ceremonial pipes. The warlike Sioux showed their displeasure when settlers began arriving in the 1850s. The possession of the land by farmers and stockmen was delayed not only by the need to build railroads and by the interruption of the Civil War but also by Indian resistance. The city of Sioux Falls—today the largest in South Dakota—was founded in 1857, but it had to be abandoned during a Sioux uprising in 1862; not until 1870 did permanent settlement begin. The people who came to this southeastern corner of South Dakota were hardly homogeneous: Scandinavians, Germans, and Russians were almost as common as the Anglo pioneers who were born in the states farther east.

The importance of the river valley lies in its geographical situation. Bordering three states, the Big Sioux straddles a broad transition zone between the densely settled Corn Belt to the east and sparsely populated cattle country to the west. Precipitation and the height of grass decline sharply though smoothly to the west. The Sioux Indians were attracted to the plentiful game and resources along this ecological boundary between sharply contrasting natural environments. In the 1930s, economic depression and drought sent many farmers scurrying back east to more humid climates and less marginal economic and environmental conditions. Indeed, mortgage foreclosures and evictions were so common in 1933 that armed bands of farmers and their neighbors guarded their properties against the agents of creditors. Most of the counties in the valley today have a lower population than they did in the early decades of the twentieth century, though the meat-packing plants in Sioux Falls and Sioux City continue to operate around the clock. The relocation of the credit card operations of a major New York bank to Sioux Falls in the early 1980s suggests the beginning of a shift toward service and finance, at least in the larger towns.

BLUE NILE

Source: Lake Tana, in northwest Ethiopia
Length: c. 1,000 miles (1,600 kilometers)
Tributaries: Bascillo, Dinder, Rahad
Outlet: Merges with the **White Nile** at Khartoum to form the **Nile**

The shorter of the two branches of the world's longest river rises in the Ethiopian Highlands. Known in the rugged headwaters region as the Big Abbai, the Blue Nile begins its thousand-mile course as a quiet stream flowing languidly out of the southern shore of Lake Tana, a small but important body of water that has played an important role in Ethiopian history. The southern outlet of Lake Tana, and the river's source, lies near the village of Bahardar. Only a short distance downstream from Lake Tana the river enters an inhospitable gorge thousands of feet below the level of the plateau. The river can be reached only by following the numerous tributaries down into the gorge, but the Ethiopians, who are accustomed to the bright light and distant horizons of the open plateau, rarely venture down to the damp and malarial heat of the riverbottom. Numerous cataracts made this portion of the Blue Nile unnavigable and virtually unknown until the third decade of the twentieth century. As late as 1925, the British consul and explorer Colonel Cheesman found that maps of Ethiopia indicated the uncharted course of the Blue Nile with a series of dotted lines.

Cheesman followed the lead of the early Scottish explorer James Bruce, who had visited the headwaters in 1769–1771. At the time, the source of this eastward branch of the Nile was believed to be a small swamp south of Lake Tana, Ghish Abbai, which drains into the lake, but there is no evidence of a continuous current across the lake. Southeast from the lake's outlet, rough hills and small rapids are encountered almost immediately, and after only about 20 miles (32 kilometers) the thundering, foaming, rainbow-arched Tisisat Falls, one of the great waterfalls of Africa, second in height only to Victoria Falls on the Zambezi, can be seen and heard at a distance. The winding gorge of the upper river makes a large bend and begins to flow to the west. The precipitous cliffs of the gorge have rebuffed Europeans and Africans alike. Many places along the river had never been seen until the arrival of the airplane, although a curving line of fleecy clouds hanging about a thousand feet above the water marks the river's course.

Signs of human activity do not reappear until the river passes the Sudanese frontier, some 470 miles (756 kilometers) downstream from Lake Tana. As the plain broadens, mud villages begin to sprout along the river's banks. The ancient gold-mining center of Fazughli nearby has attracted as many African as European fortune seekers to a region that could hardly be described as having a great abundance of the alluring yellow metal. The relatively primitive and poor black-skinned Christians of the Highlands have been left behind; in the Sudan one encounters more lightly complected and prosperous Muslims. A short way downstream from Fazughli lies the town of Roseires, where the river passes its last cataract and opens onto the wide spaces of the parched Sudan. The only reminder of the mountains left behind are the isolated outcrops of rock known to the Arabs as jebels. The name of the river here changes: it is known locally as Bahr al-Azraq.

The Blue Nile then enters the ancient kingdom of Sennar, which once extended its domain west across the White Nile to Kordofan, north almost to the present Egyptian border, and east to the Red Sea. Two tributaries join the river from the east, the Dinder and the Rehad, each crossing the desert by a different route from the mountains in the vicinity of Lake Tana. By the time the Blue Nile joins the White Nile at Khartoum, the former river is a formidable current carrying more silt than the longer branch of the Nile, especially during the wet season, from mid-June through September. As in many cases, the colors of the rivers do not accurately reflect their names, but it is true that the White Nile, with its lighter sediment load, usually has a muddy, gray look, while the Blue Nile, eroding the Ethiopian Mountains, carries more grit and soil and has a darker, brown-green color that looks blue at dawn and in the evening. For a few miles below Khartoum the two rivers flow side by side, and a distinct dividing line between them is visible, before they merge in the mighty Nile on its long, northern course to the Mediterranean Sea. The Blue actually provides six-sevenths of the combined flow of the Nile, and it is primarily responsible for the abundant current of the Nile through Egypt. The last tributary of the Nile, the Atbara, joins the river only a short distance above Khartoum. After that, the world's longest river receives neither affluents nor precipitation, crossing the world's largest desert. The Nile is a textbook example of an exotic stream, one that flows in a dry region and receives its water from somewhere else, in this case from the Blue Nile.

The Blue Nile has been a more important thoroughfare in history than the White Nile. Though the shorter of the two branches of the great river, its influence has been greater because of its association with early Christianity. The ancient kingdom of Abyssinia, with its air of exoticism and romance, was centered on the isolated plateau of Ethiopia. The region was always relatively inaccessible because the Blue Nile, with its daunting gorge and numerous cataracts, did not provide a natural route for reaching the Highlands. The upper river and Lake Tana could be reached only by the time-honored caravan tracks, crisscrossing desert and mountains, linking the Nile valley with the Red Sea.

The Scotsman Bruce was not the first European to reach the river's headwaters. Two Portuguese priests, Pedro Paez and Jerome Lobo, traveling separately, visited Lake Tana in the early seventeenth century. Nearly a century later a French doctor, Jacques Charles Poncet, reached Gonder, just north of Lake Tana, the Ethiopian capital for most of the modern period until, in the twentieth century, Addis Ababa became the capital.

The last two centuries have proved to be devastating to African peoples and cultures, here as elsewhere on the continent. Several invasions showed the superiority of European arms to those of the Africans in the Nile region: Napoleon's overthrow of the Mamelukes in his Egyptian campaign of 1798–1799; Muhammad Ali's consolidation of power by murderous raids on Nubian tribes down the Nile; and, most important, the 1868 British invasion of Ethiopia from the Red Sea, which had become vitally important to the British Empire. The British invaded to bring to heel the recalcitrant Ethiopian emperor Theodore II, who had taken some European captives, including the British consul. No less a fighting man than Field Marshall (later Lord) Napier of the Indian Army was given command of an enormous force of men and modern armaments with which to eject the pretentious and unbalanced emperor from his rock at Magdala. The expeditionary force crossed the plateau with thousands of men, building roads and bridges as they went; after defeating the emperor's intimidated army (Theodore finally committed suicide), they promptly left, dragging everything back with them to the Red Sea port from which they had embarked and going home without leaving a trace. The resulting political vacuum in Ethiopia led to an almost predictable series of events: a long period of civil wars among rival tribes; two Italian incursions (the first in 1896, a defeat, the second a revenging victory in the 1930s); increased British and French interest in establishing spheres of influence in the region, especially after the opening of the Suez Canal in 1869; and the eventual achievement of independence for Ethiopia during World War II, when with British approval Hailie Selassie was placed on the throne.

See also Nile, White Nile
Further Reading: Moorehead, Alan, *The Blue Nile*, New York: Harper and Row, 1962.

BOYNE

Source: Bog of Allen (County Kildare, Ireland)
Length: 70 miles (113 kilometers)
Tributaries: Blackwater
Outlet: Irish Sea, near Drogheda

In many parts of the world rivers are referred to as "mothers": Narmadai, "Mother Narmada"; the Volga is Mat' Rodnaya, "Mother of the Land." The Thai word for river, mae nan, translates literally as "mother water." Rivers have often been linked with divinities, especially female ones. In ancient Egypt, the floods of the Nile were considered the tears of the goddess Isis. Ireland's River Boyne, which is overlooked by the island's most impressive prehistoric burial sites, was worshipped as a goddess by Celtic tribes.
Patrick McCully, *Silenced Rivers*

As a rule, Irish rivers are neither long nor straight. Draining from interior depressions rather than elevated peaks, their courses usually follow a circuitous path to the sea. The relatively short Boyne exemplifies this pattern. Rising in the Bog of Allen west of Dublin and west of the looping Liffey, which winds around the Irish capital, the Boyne heads up near Edenderry. The source region is a low-lying, featureless country with elevations of less than 300 feet (91 meters) above sea level. The drainage is confused by canal feeders. For the first half of its course the river flows sluggishly in a northeasterly direction across a glacial plain. At Trim, the capital of County Meath, the river is overlooked by the ruins of the largest Anglo-Norman castle in Ireland, the site of early parliaments and a mint. After passing through the rich pasturelands of County Meath, the Boyne is joined by a large tributary, the Blackwater, at Navan. The Blackwater drains the hilly country of Cavan in the north. Below Navan the valley begins to deepen, cutting a small gorge at Beauparc near Slane, best known for its salmon fishing. The river flows in a broad, well-defined valley from Slane to the sea.

The river is best known for rich cultural and prehistoric associations, combined with a historic battle fought along its banks. Bronze Age burial mounds lie north of the river at Newgrange, Dowth, and Knowth. Nearby are the ruins of monasteries, the Round Tower, and free-standing, sculptured early-Christian crosses. Located on an important drainageway astride the east-west axis between Dublin and the Shannon, the Boyne attracted early colonization and became a focus of Celtic civilization.

The settlement of the English in their midst led to the conquest of the Irish by an antipathetic Protestantism. After the Stuart king James II was deposed in a series of events known as the Glorious Revolution (1688–1689), he retreated from England and gathered a force in eastern Ireland. The Catholic James was, however, pursued by the superior army of the Protestant William III, Dutch prince of Orange, who had been placed on the English throne subject to parliamentary strictures amounting to a bill of rights and the requirement that parliamentary powers be accepted and enshrined in the English constitution. The Battle of the Boyne, fought near Drogheda on July 1, 1690, resulted in the defeat of James II by William's army. James fled to France, the last Stuart king and one who would never return to his kingdom again. The Battle of the Boyne was referred to by the poet W. B. Yeats as the second of the "Four Bells," crucial historical events, all coming at the turn of a century, by which England established its ascendancy over a submissive Ireland.

See also Liffey, Shannon

BRAHMAPUTRA

Source: Near the Kailas range of Himalayas, in southwest Tibet
Length: c. 1,800 miles (2,897 kilometers)
Tributaries: Lhasa, Luhit, Tista
Outlet: Bay of Bengal

A monk was anxious to learn Zen and said: "I have been newly initiated into the Brotherhood. Will you be gracious enough to show me the way to Zen?" The master said: "Do you hear the murmuring sound of the mountain stream?" The monk answered: "Yes, I do." The master said: "Here is the entrance."
from *The Transmission of the Lamp,*
as quoted by D. T. Suzuki

According to traditional belief, a spring at the foot of the west Himalayan peak Mount Kailas is the source of the waters of the four great rivers of south Asia: the Ganges, the Sutlej, the Indus, and the Brahmaputra. After emerging from copper pipes through Lake Manasarowar and circling the mountain seven times, the rivers are believed to take their courses east, south, west, and north. Mount Kailas, elevation 22,028 feet (6,714 meters), is revered as the center of the universe by Hindus, Buddhists, and Jains alike. Pilgrims travel to this remote place and make the 30-mile (48-kilometer) trek around the summit as many times as possible in imitation of the sacred river (the number 108 is particularly auspicious to Tibetan Buddhists). The actual source of the Brahmaputra is not far from legend. Based on recent expeditions, it is now known that the river arises in a small stream gushing out of a glacier about 60 miles (97 kilometers) southeast of Kailas in the Chemayungdung range. Two peaks behind the glacier have the appearance of a pair of ears, hence the name of the headwaters stream: Tamchok Khambab, or "river coming out of the horse's mouth."

The "son of Brahma the Creator"—the meaning of the river's name—begins near the meeting-place of India, Nepal, and Tibet. It flows for almost half its length on the other side of the Himalayas from densely populated India, draining parallel to the grain of the mountains in a generally easterly direction. Crossing the dry, elevated plateau of Tibet in western China, the river goes by the name of Zangbo, or "the purifier," a name applied by Tibetans to any large river. Most Tibetans live along the section of the Yarlung Zangbo and its tributaries between Xigase and Zetang, where Tibetan Buddhism developed from the late eighth century. The culture depends not only on Buddhism but also on the irrigation potential of the great river to nourish the parched lands of the region and bring forth rich harvests of crops, though the economy relies heavily on pastoralism, too, with large herds of sheep and yaks. This part of the river is navigated in yak-skin coracles and crossed by suspension bridges.

Not until the early twentieth century was it known for certain that the Zangbo and the Brahmaputra—the latter name strictly applied to the river in the midcourse section of Assam—were the same. The precipitous gorges below Pei, where the river makes a large bend to the south, are as much as 18,000 feet (5,486 meters) deep and are covered with rain forest. Politics more than inaccessibility has restricted exploration of this border region. China has always rejected the nearby McMahon Line, drawn by the British between China and British India in 1914. The Indian state of Arunachal Pradesh, home of tribal populations, is still on occasion subject to border disputes, with the inevitable massing of Indian and Chinese soldiers on the frontier. The last unexplored part of the gorges was visited by the botanist Kingdon Ward in 1924. Deafened by the roar of plunging water, the intrepid plant hunter described being pulled across the river on a stout cable—just as passengers are ferried across today. The poet W. H. Auden, whose brother worked as a geologist in south Asia, described the mighty range of the Brahmaputra:

Growth cannot add to your song:
    as unchristened brooks
already you whisper to ants what,
    as Brahma's son,

descending his titanic staircase
into Assam, to Himalayan bears you thunder.
"Streams"

Where the Luhit joins the main-stem river in Assam, the river becomes the Brahmaputra proper. It flows across a wide valley in a channel as broad as the lower Rhine. The Assam lowlands occupy a geological depression between the folded sedimentary formations of the Himalayas and arcs of hills to the south and east. Flowing through rather than carving its valley, the Brahmaputra has nonetheless deposited enormous loads of silt and gravel, resulting in a series of well-defined terraces. Fast-flowing tributaries on either flank are slightly incised in the alluvium, crossing densely forested hills or tea gardens on well-drained gravels. The villages of Assam lie on the lower terraces, with permanently embanked fields of rice, sugar cane, jute, and tea around them. Assam has been virtually isolated from the rest of India since partition (1947), linked to the rest of the country only by a narrow corridor in the south. The Brahmaputra provides access deep into the country, with Dibrugarh the traditional head of navigation for steamboats. Hindus consider the river divine and celebrate the farming seasons with festivals called bihus in which participants bathe in the sacred Brahmaputra, the only male river in Hindu cosmology. The highest recorded rainfall in the world occurred on the south slopes of the Khasi Hills at Cherrapunji in south Assam, where monsoonal flow from the Bay of Bengal brings an average 450 inches (1,143 centimeters) per year—and reputedly more than 900 inches (2,286 centimeters) in 1861.

The river changes its name to Jamuna as it crosses into Bangladesh (formerly East Pakistan). It receives a major right-bank tributary, the Tista, which before the eighteenth century flowed farther to the west and emptied into the Ganges. The main stream of the Brahmaputra formerly flowed southeast through Mymensingh, but that course receives significant flow only during the high waters of the monsoon season. The Ganges joins the river near Aricha, and farther down the river a complicated braiding of channels gives evidence of the beginning of the deltaic portion of the river. The apex of the fan of distributaries is near Chandpur. The bulk of the sediment and most of the water in this world's largest delta originates with the Brahmaputra. The water of the mighty river, beginning in Tibetan trickles, roaring down titanic Himalayan stairs into Assam, and ambling across the Bangladesh delta, is finally received by the broad Indian Ocean embayment of Bengal.

Further Reading: Van Dyk, Jere, "Long Journey of the Brahmaputra," *National Geographic,* November 1988, pp. 672–711.

BUG, WESTERN

Source: Western Ukraine, near Zolochiv
Length: c. 500 miles (805 kilometers)
Tributaries: Krzna, Liwiec, Mukhanets, Nurzec
Outlet: **Vistula**, near Warsaw

A major river of eastern Poland forms the political boundary with Ukraine and Belarus for much of its length. The Western Bug (Ukrainian: Buh) rises at the western edge of the Podolian Plateau in Ukraine 9 miles (14.5 kilometers) east of Zolochiv. Draining northwest past Bus'k and Sokal' in the western part of the former socialist republic of Ukraine (part of the former Soviet Union), the river alters its direction to a more northerly course to become the border first between the independent country of Ukraine and Poland, and then between the independent country of Belarus and Poland. Just below Brest (Belarus) at the western end of the Pripyet Marsh, the river begins to pull away from the boundary, passing in a generally westerly direction to its junction with the Vistula (Wisla) near Warsaw. Just before the confluence the Bug is joined by the Narew, another major drainageway of eastern Poland. The Western Bug should not be confused with the Southern Bug, a nearby river that flows in almost the opposite direction, south toward the mouth of the Dnieper and the Black Sea.

The importance of this north-flowing affluent lies in its frontier status, changing though it may have been throughout history. As a natural artery, the Bug was a corridor for the eastern extension of Polish population and cultural influence. On the map it is evident that the Bug acts as an eastern branch of the Vistula, since the latter, Poland's major river, swings away to the southwest in its upper course above Warsaw. The Bug is navigable as far as Brest, where today a canal links the city to the Dnieper system to the east. Caught between a strong Germany and a strong Russia (later the Soviet Union), Poland's fate has been to be swallowed up by its neighbors, even disappearing from the map in the nineteenth century after its partition among Prussia, Russia, and Austria. Much of the present eastern border of Poland follows the central course of the Bug and corresponds to the Curzon Line, proposed by Britain's foreign minister after World War I. The signing of the Treaty of Brest Litovsk (1918) between Russia and Germany, which took Russia out of World War I (immediately after the Bolshevik Revolution), took place on the north bank of the river at Brest. Since 1945 about 200 miles (322 kilometers) of the river's course have been marked as the boundary between Poland and the Soviet Union and, after 1991, between Poland and the former soviet socialist republics of Ukraine and Belarus.

Brest was once a Polish city and the capital of the Polish department of Polesie. Russian and Polish influences overlap in this border region, as in the sparsely populated Pripyet Marsh to the east. No one knows for sure the precise location of the homelands of the ancestral Polish Slavs. German scholars of the twentieth century tended to locate the earliest evidence of Poles far to the east—up the Bug—while Russian researchers displayed an equally biased scholarship by focusing farther west, in Pomerania along the Baltic coast or near the mouth of the Vistula. The rationale behind this murky research is that political boundaries have been drawn and redrawn in the twentieth century on the basis of such cultural historical studies. Since the Treaty of Paris (1918) at the end of World War I enshrined the principle of self-determination, linguistic and cultural delineation of a nation or people has been the primary basis for drawing political boundaries in Europe. The effects have been particularly far-reaching in eastern Europe, large parts of which were subject to evanescent empires. Thus the Bug's course has intersected with geopolitics and territorial aggrandizement, affecting the fortunes and fate of an often subdued but not finally conquered people.

See also Vistula

C

CASIQUIARE

Source: South Venezuela, near Brazil border
Length: 222 miles (357 kilometers)
Tributaries: Pamoni, Siapa, Baria
Outlet: Guainía (tributary of the **Negro**)

The catchment area of a river—the land drained by the river and its tributaries—is usually bounded by a distinct ridge or low plateau known as a drainage divide. This definition is more easily applied to uplands than to level plains or to the lower courses of rivers, where drainage divisions are not so easily distinguished. The presence of numerous lagoons and channels in deltas of course makes the mouths of rivers especially problematical in delineating hydrological boundaries. The blurring of watersheds along the upper courses of streams is less common, though it does sometimes occur, as on the border of Poland in the Pripet Marshes, whose waters are diverted both to the southeast along the Dnieper system and to the north via the Bug and Vistula systems. The Casiquiare (Portuguese: Cassiqiere) Channel in South America represents the fusing of the two major watersheds of northern South America—the Orinoco and the Amazon—across the expanse of lowlands extending eastward from the Andes.

The Venezuelan Orinoco River flows in a great arc northward and eastward across the jungles and grasslands of northern South America from its source near the Brazilian border to its outlet on the Atlantic Ocean. Like most great rivers, it picks up numerous tributaries along the way. Along its upper course, yet some distance from its headwaters, 12 miles (20 kilometers) west of the small settlement of Esmeralda, there is a broad opening in the south bank of the river: it is the beginning of the Brazo Casiquiare, or Casiquiare Channel. This stream doesn't flow into the Orinoco but flows away from it. More than 200 miles (322 kilometers) to the southwest the Casiquiare joins a tributary of the Río Negro, the Guainía, and forms a link to the great Amazon river system to the south. In flood stage after the spring equinox, a large proportion of the Orinoco's flow passes down the Casiquiare, while during the drier fall months less water is so diverted. Rather than reversing its flow, an idea that is sometimes presented to schoolchildren, the Casiquiare has a highly variable discharge subject to the alternation between wet and dry seasons.

The distinguished naturalist and geographer Alexander von Humboldt explored the river during the course of his epochal expeditions to Central and South America (1799–1804). Reaching the Casiquiare in 1800, he surveyed and mapped the unusual intermingling of the two major drainages. Appropriately enough for someone who was imbued with a deep-seated Enlightenment temperament, Humboldt did not so much solve a mystery concerning the Casiquiare as clear up a hydrological problem about which much already was known, but not publicized, in Europe. Humboldt approached the problem rationally: "When immense rivers may be considered as composed of several parallel furrows of unequal depth; when these rivers are not enclosed in valleys; and when the interior of the great continent is as flat as the shores of the sea with us; the ramifications, the bifurcations, and the interlacings in the form of net-work, must be infinitely multiplied." In other words, though the natural canal linking the upper Orinoco to an Amazon tributary lay well into the interior, the land drained was low and level and would be subject to linkages. Humboldt reviewed what was known about the Casiquiare from the missionaries and slave traders who had used the shortcut between the two drainages throughout the eighteenth century. La Condamine, during the course of his navigation of the Amazon in 1743, collected information from native tribes who regularly made the traverse between the upper Orinoco and the Rio Negro. Conclusive proof of the link was made the following year by the Spanish missionary Father Manuel Roman, who traveled from the lower Orinoco to the Rio Negro and back by the shorter route. Half a century later Humboldt collated the evidence and reports and assessed the information in a geographical perspective.

He could not have known the full story of how geological erosion had produced the level depression of the Casiquiare that made possible such a maverick linking. This unusual hydrological phenomenon is a result of the erosional peeling away of sedimentary strata known as the Roraima formation, yielding a nearly level surface of underlying Guiana Shield crystallines. As the divide between the Orinoco and Amazon drainages was lowered, the south-flowing Casiquiare extended its catchment area farther and farther northward by the process of headward erosion. Finally, during a flood, it breached the low divide between the two river systems. Swollen today by one hundred tributaries, the channel is 720 feet (219 meters) wide. Humboldt may have cleared up a small but significant hydrological conundrum, but he was clouded by his Enlightenment belief in progress, and he mistakenly forecast a time when boats would pass back and forth between the Orinoco and Amazon Rivers as commonly and unremarkably as canal boats pass between the Loire and the Seine valleys in France.

See also Negro, Orinoco
Further Reading: von Humboldt, Alexander, *Personal Narrative of Travels to the Equinoctial Regions of America, During the Years 1799–1804 by Alexander von Humboldt and Aimé Bonpland,* vol. II, ch. 23, London: Bohn Scientific Library, 1852, pp. 372–432.

CHAMBAL

Source: Vindhya Range, in central India
Length: c. 550 miles (885 kilometers)
Tributaries: Sipra, Kali, Sind, Parbati, Banas
Outlet: **Yamuna**

The Chambal (pronounced CHUM-buhl) River of central India is a short stream compared with the great rivers of south Asia. Although the river is tributary to the densely populated alluvial districts of the Indo-Gangetic plain to the north, it is not navigable for most of its length and therefore has a measure of enforced isolation. The land around its headwaters is the homeland of a prominent Indo-Aryan people—the Marathas—who fought as militant Hindus against the waning power of the Moslem Moguls and the rising influence of the British in the late eighteenth and early nineteenth centuries.

The river rises in the Vindhya Range, a district of east-west trending hill lands in west-central India. Along with the similarly trending Satpura Range to the south, this region encompasses a zone of transition between Aryan people living in the north who speak Indo-European tongues and Dravidian, or non-Indo-European speakers, in the south. The source of the Chambal lies about 8 miles (13 kilometers) southwest of Mhow, in Madhya Pradesh state. The city of Indore, the capital of one of the most powerful Maratha states of the same name, is located just east of the river in the headwaters region. With a population of more than a million as of 1999, Indore is a major industrial center with cotton mills, engineering works, and chemical plants. The state of Indore lost much of its territory after its defeat by the English general

Lake (1804) and became a British dependency in 1818 (it was not governed by the Crown initially, but rather by the administrators of the British East India Company).

The river flows in a generally northeasterly direction, entering southeastern Rajasthan state before flowing past Kota along the Rajasthan–Madhya Pradesh border. It then turns east-southeast along the Uttar Pradesh–Madhya Pradesh boundary to join the Yamuna River (not to be confused with the Jamuna, the name of the Brahmaputra in Bangladesh). The Yamuna is a Ganges tributary, flowing parallel to the holiest of Indian rivers for some distance before joining it at Allahabad. The Yamuna is part of extensive lowlands in the Indo-Gangetic plain, the most densely populated region of a country with a population in excess of a billion people as of 2001. The junction of the Chambal with the Yamuna occurs just west of the town of Kanpur (English: Cawnpore). Located on the right bank of the Ganges, Kanpur was the scene of the notorious massacre of British soldiers and European families during the Indian, or Sepoy, Mutiny (1857–1858). This rebellion, though confined to certain regions and backed by a relatively small number of native troops under the British Raj, was decisive in changing the relationship between Indians and Europeans on the subcontinent.

The course of the Chambal winds through steep ravines amid dense, jungly vegetation. The natural growth does not resemble the tropical rain forest through which Tarzan swung in his jungle films as much as the bush country of Kipling's *Kim* stories. The summer monsoon brings enough precipitation to ensure that the stream is perennial, yet like most rivers in south Asia it is subject to sudden flooding. For nearly half the length of the river an unusual land tenure arrangement exists by which land rights are subject to conservation policy.

The monsoon forest in the valley is subject to the Wildlife Protection Act of 1972 and is thereby considered a government sanctuary. The long-snouted crocodile known as the gharial (*Gavialis gangeticus*) has as its preferred habitat high-banked rivers with clear, fast-flowing water and deep pools, conditions that prevail along the upper Chambal. This endangered animal has been "gazetted"—that is, listed for protection along with various fish species. The name *gharial* derives from the distinctively shaped growth of tissue near the nostrils of adult males resembling an earthen pot known as a *ghara* in northern India. The Chambal wildlife refuge is unusual in that the project is totally funded by the Indian government, which coordinates the three large Indian states with land in the sanctuary. Several game rangers, research assistants, guards, and boatmen make up the staff of the Chambal preserve.

See also Yamuna

CHANG JIANG

See Yangtze

CHAO PHRAYA

Source: Mountains of northern Thailand
Length: 140 miles (225 kilometers)
Tributaries: Meping, Mewang, Meyom, Menam
Outlet: Gulf of Thailand

The north-south trending hills of northern Thailand are drained by numerous watercourses that flow into four streams that eventually merge at about 16 degrees north latitude to form the Chao Phraya. Formerly known as the Menam, or The River, Thailand's major riverine highway and agricultural valley begins at the confluence of the four branches near Nakhon Sawan. Farther north, narrow forested gorges alternate with broader open tracts along the river. The northern Thai city of Chiang Mai on the westernmost tributary, the Meping, is a commercial center connected to Bangkok by rail.

Thailand (formerly Siam) may be said to have only one great river of its own—the Chao Phraya. Though the Salween and Mekong drain a considerable area of the country in the north and form part of the political borders, respectively, with Myanmar (Burma) and Laos, only the Chao Phraya and its

Buildings elevated on piles above the floodplain of the Chao Phraya (John Elk)

tributaries lie entirely within the kingdom of Thailand. The Chao Phraya is to Thailand what the Irrawaddy is to Burma. As the river crosses a wide alluvial valley, it braids into a number of courses. On an island along one of these waterways is situated the old capital of Ayuthia, many of whose inhabitants live on boats.

The low banks of the river are thickly fringed with bamboos and tall palms that almost manage to hide the straggling villages that dot the waterway. Not the romantic Eden of the lotus that many Westerners are looking for, the small population of the Buddhist kingdom of Thailand has traditionally been bound to the harsh and demanding rhythms of paddy rice cultivation.

The capital and largest city, Bangkok, is located along the river 25 miles (40 kilometers) from its mouth. The city has for its site a loop in the river that has afforded a natural defense. Only an agricultural village and fort before 1767, when it became a stronghold against the Burmese, the original town had the river for protection on the north, west, and south sides, and needed only to extend a *klong,* or canal, on the east with reinforcing walls to form a riverine defense. The old town with its canals and buildings on piles resembles a primitive Venice of the East, but today the more than five million people who inhabit the Bangkok metro area live in a city that has added modern services and industrial economic activities to its traditional role as a river port.

The outlet of the river—not so much a single, discrete channel as several paralleling channels—is at the northwest end of the Gulf of Thailand (formerly the Gulf of Siam). The bar at the entrance to the river prevents the largest ships from reaching Bangkok, but a deep-water anchorage exists on the island of Ko Sichang. Used for transportation by a bewildering variety of vessels and for the irrigation of one of Asia's leading rice-producing areas, the Chao Phraya has a less important role in the economy today than in the past, but it is still the most significant geographic feature of the country.

Further Reading: Van Beek, Steve, *The Chao Phya: River in Transition,* Oxford: Oxford University Press, 1995; Wyatt, David K., *Thailand: A Short History,* New Haven: Yale University Press, 1982.

CHARI

Source: Uplands of Ubangi-Chari Plateau, in north-central Africa
Length: c. 650 miles (1,046 kilometers)
Tributaries: Bahr Aouk, Bahr Sara, Bahr Salamat, Logone
Outlet: Lake Chad

The Chari, or Shari, River of tropical Africa, the longest river of interior drainage on the continent, is an important transportation artery as well as a vital source of food and water for the fishermen, farmers, and herdsmen who live along its banks. Most of the population of the valley occupy the river's lower course in Chad, one of the poorest countries of Africa. Chad has no railroad and only a scant network of paved roads, yet it is served in true Third World style by regular air flights not only to places elsewhere in Africa but to the capitals of Europe as well.

The river begins to the south in the uplands of the Central African Republic 105 miles (169 kilometers) west of Ndélé, where a number of headstreams and tributaries meet. Descending the Bamingui-Bangoran region onto the flat Baguirmi plain, the river begins to flow northwest to Lake Chad, joining with its only significant tributary, the Logone, at N'djamena (Fort-Lamy) at the head of a wide delta. The river soon empties into the large interior lake basin of Lake Chad. In the land between the Chari and the Logone are numerous channels and distributaries that are inundated during the rainy season, producing what is sometimes called the "Mesopotamia of Chad."

The Chari forms part of the political boundary between Cameroon and Chad. A political as well as a resource problem is created by this riverine border. In the rainy season, the river floods so much of the surrounding district that some outflow even reaches the Benue, a Niger tributary, and thereby finds an outlet, at least seasonally, to the sea. Because water is a precious commodity in a semiarid environment, boundary disputes in the water-deficient Chad Basin are perhaps inevitable. An international commission comprising the countries bordering Lake Chad—Chad, Cameroon, Nigeria, and Niger—has been given a mandate to deal with such hydrological and political disputes from its headquarters in N'djamena. The hydrological regime of the Chari and Logone Rivers concerns the surrounding countries, which fear a progressive drying up of the lake—a problem aggravated by increased demands for irrigation and drinking water (cf. the desiccation of the Aral Sea in central Asia. See Amu Darya).

The small river steamers that navigate the river in the rainy season may seem puny by modern standards, yet the Chari continues to be a primary axis of Chad life. The chief division of the country is between nomadic Arabic-speaking people who live on the Sahelian edge of the Sahara to the north and sedentary French-speaking villagers living along the Chari and Logone in the south. The geographic congruity of a comparatively dense population, light network of roads, and river access in the southwestern part of the country is not a mere coincidence. The primary source of foreign exchange for this economically strapped and politically unstable country is the export of cotton, grown on an irrigated basis in the valley. The Chari-Logone confluence is one of the most productive freshwater fisheries of central Africa, and seasonal fishermen from northern Nigeria have visited the region since 1952.

See also Benue

CHENAB

Source: North Indian state of Himachal Pradesh
Length: 675 miles (1,086 kilometers)
Tributaries: **Jhelum, Ravi**
Outlet: **Indus**

The political borderland between central Pakistan and northwest India is drained by five large and important eastern tributaries of the Indus. Converging on the Indus from the northeast, the valleys of these rivers coalesce and overlap to form the Punjab, a Persian word meaning "Land of the Five Rivers" (see Figure 1 on p. 24).

The largest of the five rivers of the Punjab plains, the Chenab rises in the north Indian state of Himachal Pradesh, flowing northwest through the Kashmir Himalayas. Its name, meaning "river of China," suggests erroneously that it crosses the highest mountains of the world. In fact the river drains the southern flank of the Himalayan chain, with its source about 150 miles (241 kilometers) south of the main trans-Himalayan town of Leh. The course of the Chenab roughly parallels the Indus, running first northwest, then southwest. The Chenab in its natural state was prone to destructive flooding, especially along its lower course.

Alexander the Great crossed the river on boats and floats, reporting it to be a little under two miles wide and littered with jagged rocks over which the river violently roiled. The floats got over well enough, but several boats were broken up and their men drowned.

The Chenab is joined in the northern part of the Punjab plains by the Jhelum, the northernmost of the five rivers. These two in turn are joined some 40 miles (64 kilometers) downstream by the Ravi. Yet farther downstream the next rivers come in together, the Beas and the Sutlej. At this point all five of the Punjab streams are known as the Panjnad. The ancient city of Multan, situated astride an old crossing route of the Indus, lies 60 miles (97 kilometers) to the north.

Under British imperial rule, the Chenab, being the largest of the Punjab rivers, received early attention from her majesty's hydraulic engineers. All of the Punjab rivers drain snow-clad peaks of the Himalayas. Spring meltwater is augmented by monsoon gushes in the summer. During the dry season, by contrast, the rivers are shallow and sluggish, and occupy only a small portion of their wide beds. As early as 1892 the Lower Chenab Canal was opened, watering the dry lands on the left bank of the river. The canal irrigated a vast district known as the Rechna Doab (note the nomenclature: **Ra**vi + **Chenab**), with an elaborate system of headworks (at Khanki, Gujranwala district), and branches, subbranches, and distributaries. The Upper Chenab Canal, opened in 1912, runs 120 miles (193 kilometers) south to the Ravi, over which it is carried by an aqueduct, after which it becomes the Lower Bari Doab Canal (Bari = **Beas** + **Ravi**). This scheme, known as "The Triple Project," has been described by one of the preeminent British geographers of Asia in the twentieth century, L. Dudley Stamp, as "one of the cleverest examples of irrigation in the world." When irrigation started, it was discovered that so much water left the upper Chenab to water the Bari Doab that there was not enough water remaining to fill the existing Lower Chenab Canal. So an Upper Jhelum Canal was built to bring water from the Jhelum to the Chenab at Khanki.

Ingenious though the various engineering projects associated with the Chenab are, environmental problems caused by excessive irrigation have emerged. Because of a high water table, the soils of the Punjab plains are prone to waterlogging. Accumulation of salts by evaporation—a perennial problem bedeviling dry subtropical irrigators—has taken place. And deforestation is not a problem just on the steep slopes of the nearby Himalayas. Deeply rooted trees on the Punjab plains promote the permeability of water, whereas overcultivation of wheat, millet, cotton, and other crops has led to the ponding of water. Divided politically between Pakistan and India, the Punjab is being tested both politically and environmentally. As one of the major irrigation districts in the world, the region is a test case for the use of intensive irrigation in a dry environment.

See also Beas, Jhelum, Ravi, Sutlej

CHURCHILL

1. Source: Methy Lake, in northwest Saskatchewan, Canada
Length: c. 1,000 miles (1,609 kilometers)
Tributaries: Beaver, Reindeer
Outlet: Hudson Bay
2. Source: Ashuanipi Lake, in southwest Labrador
Length: c. 600 miles (966 kilometers)
Tributaries: Nonc
Outlet: Atlantic Ocean (Lake Melville and Hamilton Inlet)

Perhaps only in such a vast country as Canada—the second largest in the world—can there be two major rivers of the same name that are named after different, though related, people.

The Churchill River of central Canada drains the northern parts of the provinces of Saskatchewan and Manitoba past the town of Churchill at its mouth. The roughly 1,000-mile (1,609-kilometer) waterway connects a series of glacial lakes as it travels in a generally easterly direction from its headwaters at Methy Lake in northwest Saskatchewan en route to its outlet on the western shore of Hudson Bay. It receives its major tributary, the Beaver, at Lac Ile-à-la-Crosse, Saskatchewan. This aquatic waterway allowed penetration of the remoter parts of the Canadian Shield, the geologically archaic foundation of the continent, by fur traders who once dominated this isolated region. The river was first explored in 1619 by Jens Munck, a Scandinavian sent by King Christian IV of Denmark to search for the elusive Northwest Passage. The town of Churchill became the primary entrepôt for the British trading company named after the bay that forms a central, sunken depression on the shield's ancient rocks.

The Hudson's Bay Company distributed food and supplies to its traders and trappers and received beaver pelts in return. The company was responsible for the characteristic seasonal pulse of activity in the northern forests. In 1717 the British established a stronghold at Fort Prince of Wales, which was captured by the French in 1782 under Jean La Pérouse; it was subsequently regained by the British and renamed Fort Churchill. The fort, the town, and the river were not named, as one might think, after Sir Winston Churchill, the twentieth-century prime minister, but after his ancestor, John Churchill, duke of Marlborough, the famous general and statesman of the late seventeenth and early eighteenth centuries whose fame derived from his victories on the battlefield in the War of the Spanish Succession (1701–1714).

The other Churchill River in Canada is shorter and of less historical significance, though the harnessing of its hydroelectric power has made it of increased economic importance. Rising in western Labrador at Ashuanipi Lake, this eastern Canadian river flows north over the rugged Labrador Plateau. It is perhaps best known for a series of rapids and cataracts and, immediately below, McLean Canyon; these are found some 200 miles (320 kilometers) upstream from the river's mouth at saltwater Lake Melville. Once a spectacular sight, the water of the falls has been diverted to drive the massive turbines of the Churchill Falls underground hydroelectric plant, one of the largest hydro plants in the world. The river's tumbling water has generated not only power but conflict: the provincial governments of Quebec and Newfoundland (Labrador is the mainland portion of Newfoundland) both claim a share of the electrical power produced by the river. Formerly known as the Hamilton River, the waterway was renamed after Marlborough's descendant, Sir Winston Churchill, following his death in 1965. The waterfalls, known previously as Grand Falls, adopted the name of the person who is arguably the most important statesman of the twentieth century.

CLYDE

Source: Southern Uplands of Scotland
Length: 106 miles (171 kilometers)
Tributaries: Daer Water, Potrail Water
Outlet: Firth of Clyde

The Clyde is not a long river as great rivers go, but it is the major river of Scotland. Along its lower course, and particularly at its mouth, can be found the primary concentration of Scottish population, shipbuilding, and industry.

The Clyde is the principal river of the Strathclyde region of west-central Scotland (*strath* is Gaelic for "valley"). The river really has no important tributaries, but the name is given to the stream formed by the confluence of the Daer Water and the Potrail Water. A small right-bank tributary, called the Clydes Burn, dribbles from the west side of the low hill of Clyde Law. These picturesque headstreams drain the rounded green hills of the Borders, long contested by the English and the Scots but today peacefully grazed by Cheviot sheep. The upper Clyde flows northwest, then northeast,

Crowds gather to watch the new liner the Queen Mary *leave her fitting-out berth at Clydebank and make her way down the river to the sea. (Topical Press Agency)*

through a broad, open valley that presents excellent opportunities for trout fishermen. It reaches the railway junction of Symington, where it again turns northwest, although the northeastern path of the valley is continued by a broad throughway used by road and rail. This valley, no longer traversed by stream, indicates the capture by the present lower Clyde of its headwaters from a formerly larger Tweed basin by a process of headward erosion.

After Douglas Water comes in from the left, the course of the river straightens out and heads generally northwest until it reaches the upper part of the estuary, the Firth of Clyde. The river falls several hundred feet after its junction with Douglas Water, forming a series of waterfalls: Bonnington Linn, Cora Linn, Dundaff Linn, and Stonebyres Linn. The potential for water power was early exploited with small mills, but with the Industrial Revolution came larger water-driven textile mills. The burgh of Lanark, capital of the former county of the same name, is located near the falls. In 1785 English industrialist David Dale and manufacturer Richard Arkwright founded New Lanark just southwest of the city, which became the scene of the early-nineteenth-century social and industrial experiments of the Welsh socialist Robert Owen.

The river flattens out below the falls, its broad valley prone to flooding. The banks are quite steep though not precipitous, gradually becoming gentler as the river approaches Glasgow. The river flows in its middle course through a noted farming region—Clydesdale—with orchards, market gardening, and, of course, the famous Clydesdale draft horses.

The Clyde passes through the coal field of Lanarkshire before reaching Glasgow. The river has been deepened and widened and is navigable for ocean-going vessels as far as the lowest road and rail bridge in the heart of the city. The lower valley, known as Clydeside, contains the primary concentration of Scotland's population and industrial activity, and the river functions as the main route of commercial waterborne traffic. No longer the world's leading shipbuilding center, this much-dredged estuary still sees the launching of some of the world's finest ships and boasts of having constructed the world's biggest passenger liners, including the *Queen Mary* and the *Queen Elizabeth.* The waterway is such a narrow place that large ships have to be launched at an angle. Clydeport comprises the docks of Glasgow; Clydebank on the north bank of the Clyde, 6 miles (9.7 kilometers) downstream; and Greenock, an important general cargo, oil, and container port. The river is connected to the Firth of Forth by the Forth and Clyde Canal. A ten-lane bridge, opened in 1970, crosses the Clyde at Glasgow. From the center of Glasgow the river runs past several concentrations of shipyards and engineering works before it reaches Dumbarton. A twin-peaked hill rises abruptly from the river's bank here, the defensible fortress site for the medieval Celtic capital of the kingdom of Strathclyde.

Scottish firths and Norwegian fjords share more than a linguistic root. Both are funnel-shaped indentations of the coastline caused by the drowning of the lower ends of glacial valleys. The inundation of former valley mouths is a result of the melting of Pleistocene icesheets and the consequent rise in sea level. The Firth of Clyde, on the west side of central Scotland, is in a protected location behind sheltering islands. The large island of Aran as well as the nearly enclosing peninsula of Kintyre protect this arm of the sea from the roughest winds and weather. The hills and mountains that border the Firth, along with the long tributary fjords receding into the distance, have a beauty enjoyed by proud Clydesiders. Rimmed by summer resorts, yacht basins, and links golf courses, the Firth of Clyde entices tourists as well as Glaswegians (the peculiar name for Glasgow's residents) to take a holiday "doon the water" on a pleasure steamer.

See also Forth

COLORADO

Source: On the Continental Divide in northern Colorado, in southwestern Rocky Mountain National Park
Length: 1,450 miles (2,333 kilometers)
Tributaries: Gunnison, **Green**, San Juan, Virgin, **Gila**
Outlet: Gulf of California

The most fought-over water in the United States is a life-giving artery of the arid Southwest. Although one of the most visited national parks includes as its main attraction the spectacular canyon carved by the river in northern Arizona, most visitors do not see the reddish-colored waters that give the river its name, for the view of the river from the rim of the Grand Canyon is blocked by the precipitous cliffs of the inner canyon.

The mighty Colorado begins in the Rocky Mountains of northern Colorado some 65 miles (105 kilometers) northwest of Denver. The source lies in the southwestern corner of Rocky Mountain National Park, surrounded on three sides by the Continental Divide. The river flows through Grand Lake (Shadow Mountain Reservoir) and Lake Granby. Crossing the state of Colorado in a generally southwesterly direction, it passes Glenwood Springs, Rifle, and Grand Junction, where it receives the Gunnison River from the southeast.

The Colorado then enters Utah, where the erosive force of the river and its tributaries has carved the nearly level sedimentaries of the Colorado Plateau into scenic wonders that must be included among the most visually stunning of America's natural places. The river forms the southern boundary of Arches National Park at Moab, Utah. Farther downstream, in Canyonlands National Park, the river receives the Green River, its longest tributary draining from the north. The Green is longer than the upper Colorado, as it drains territory as far away as central Wyoming. Some authorities therefore consider the Green to be the real Colorado, and support for this position can be seen in the original name of the upper Colorado from Grand Lake to the Green confluence: the Grand.

The river then enters Lake Powell, the second largest reservoir in the United States, formed by the

Hoover Dam (formerly Boulder Dam), a giant arch-type dam on the Colorado River completed in 1936 (Jesse Walker)

Glen Canyon Dam at Page, Arizona. A short distance downstream from the dam, Lee's Ferry is one of the few places along this stretch of the river where the sheer walls of the canyons open to permit a crossing to be made, as the Mormons discovered. Lee's Ferry is considered the hydrologic division between the upper and lower basin for purposes of allocation of the scarce water of the river among competing uses.

The river flows generally on a westerly course across northern Arizona, entering via Marble Canyon the 271-mile (436-kilometer) stretch of the majestic Grand Canyon. After leaving the park the river flows through the second of its artificial impoundments, Lake Mead, which has been designated a recreational area. Backed up behind Hoover Dam (originally Boulder Dam), Lake Mead is the largest reservoir in the United States, and its construction in the 1930s, guaranteeing employment and income during the Great Depression, was a monument to man's age-old attempt to control nature.

The river generally flows south from this point, forming the Arizona-Nevada state line, then the Arizona-California line. Next in a series of dams below Hoover is Davis Dam, forming Lake Mojave, built to control releases from the giant dam above it. Farther south, Parker Dam and its associated Lake Havasu were meant to provide for the water needs of Los Angeles. These multipurpose dams not only are a source of drinking water and irrigation storage for the parched Southwest but also generate hydroelectric power, regulate the flow of water and prevent flooding, and provide recreational opportunities. All the way from Lake Powell on the Utah-Arizona border to the series of irrigation dams around Yuma, Arizona, near the Mexican border (Imperial, Laguna, and Morelos), the river has been harnessed in an effort to reclaim this parched land. Phoenix's end-of-the-millennium claim to be the fastest growing city in the United States would have been unimaginable without the relentless efforts of the Bureau of Reclamation during the preceding century.

The Colorado River, looking downstream from Hoover Dam (Jesse Walker)

By the time the Colorado—paradoxically the wildest and yet the most shackled of Western rivers—is diverted through Morelos Dam in the northwestern corner of Mexico to irrigate the fertile Mexicali valley, the river has been reduced to a braided trickle. Its final 95 miles (153 kilometers) form the border between the Mexican states of Baja California Norte and Sonora. The river—such as it is—enters the northern end of the Gulf of California (the Sea of Cortez) opposite Montague Island.

The Colorado delta is not shaped like a triangle, but rather like an overturned *Y* with its arms pointing to the northwest and the south, the silt-laden river flowing in a southwesterly direction and entering the base of the *Y* near Yuma. For the last 60 miles (97 kilometers), the river is known as the Hardy. Before the approximately thirty dams were installed on the river, naturalist Aldo Leopold visited the lower river and described the delta as a "milk-and-honey wilderness." Once a bountiful land for hunter and conservationist (in the 1920s Leopold was both), the delta today receives but a fraction of the sediment, fresh water, and nutrients it once did. As a result, the ecology of the delta has been compromised and the area of wetlands reduced; the region hardly qualifies any longer as a paradise, either for hunter or naturalist.

A key thread that binds the tangle of controversy and dispute over the river's use is the Colorado River Compact of 1922. Signed by six of the seven basin states in 1923 (and by Arizona in 1944, the same year as the Mexican Water Treaty), the compact in essence allocates the river's water between upper and lower parts of the basin (in approximately equal amounts) and between different uses, with agriculture getting the lion's share. The problem is that there is not enough water to go around. The river's average annual flow of about 15 million acre-feet (1.8 hectare-meters) has been divided up for multiple uses that total more than 16 million acre-feet. Moreover, exotic streams (with headwaters in humid regions) have highly variable flow. The Colorado's annual discharge can be as low as 5 million acre-feet (0.6 hectare-meter) in dry years and as high as 25 million acre-feet (3.1 hectare-meters) in wet years. With millions of people all the way from Denver to Los Angeles depending on the river for drinking water, and thousands of farmers relying on it for irrigation, the Colorado's average flow falls short of demand. The average is only a statistical calculation, but based upon it developers have proceeded with multiple and often conflicting plans.

Unintended consequences and negative environmental impacts have been numerous. The porous Navajo Sandstone of the reservoir of Glen Canyon absorbs an estimated 4 percent of the river's annual discharge as bank storage, which cannot be used for irrigation or hydropower. As the river's name implies, the Colorado is rich in silt, and the lakes formed behind the behemoth dams are slowly filling with sediment, reducing their potential. The clear, fast-moving water below the dams scours the valley, removing sandbars and reorganizing downstream ecology. Exotic plants like the spiny camel thorn, a plague to campers; peppergrass, in the mustard family; and ornamental Ravenna grass have colonized disturbed beaches since dam closure. As if overdrawn water resources and the environmental impacts of dams weren't enough, pollution has emerged as a problem on the Colorado Plateau. In an ironic twist, the curbs put on the building of a dam that would have flooded part of the Grand Canyon in the 1960s led to the need for a coal-fired generating plant, the smoke from which reduces visibility in these much-visited canyon lands. A huge pile of uranium mill tailings near the river at Moab, Utah, threatens the drinking water of Nevada, Arizona, and southern California, and has been termed a "radioactive time bomb."

The one-armed veteran of the Battle of Shiloh and former Illinois schoolteacher John Wesley Powell was the first to successfully descend the Colorado River through the Grand Canyon (1869); he later became director of the U.S. Geological Survey (1881–1892). Powell was as prescient about the Colorado River as he was about so many other matters in the West. The noted historian and Western writer Wallace Stegner recalled in his biography of Powell, *Beyond the Hundredth Meridian,* the events of the 1893 international irrigation conference held in Los Angeles, when Powell responded to delegates bragging that the entire arid West could be conquered and reclaimed: "I tell you, gentlemen, you are piling up a heritage of conflict and litigation over water rights, for there is not sufficient water to supply the land." The pioneering explorer, geologist, and ethnologist was booed from the hall—not the first or the last time that a prophet has been so unappreciated.

Not only have Powell's predictions about the quantity of Western water resources proven to be accurate, but his qualitative concerns about people and community, including a respect for the native Americans, are increasingly at the forefront of public awareness. People look to a great river like the Colorado for more than just kilowatt-hours of electricity and acre-feet of reserve storage. There is today an appreciation of the aesthetic and scientific value of untamed rivers. People now value the integrity of a wild river ecosystem and appreciate the fine micropatterns of islands, dune deposits, and vegetation along its course. There are those who want to experience an exhilarating boat or raft trip down such a river and to listen (really listen) to the music of running water.

See also Gila, Green

Further Reading: Fradkin, Philip L., *A River No More: The Colorado River and the West,* rev. ed., Berkeley: University of California Press, 1996; Lopez, Barry, *Crossing Open Ground,* New York: Vintage, 1989; Powell, John Wesley, *Exploration of the Colorado River and Its Canyons,* New York: Dover, 1961 (orig. pub. 1874); Waters, Frank, *The Colorado,* New York: Rinehart and Company, 1946 (Rivers of America Series); Zwinger, Ann H., *Downcanyon: A Naturalist Explores the Colorado River through Grand Canyon,* Tucson: University of Arizona Press, 1995.

COLUMBIA

Source: Columbia Lake, in southeastern British Columbia
Length: c. 1,210 miles (1,947 kilometers)
Tributaries: Kootenai, Pend Oreille, Spokane, Yakima, **Snake**, **Willamette**, Cowlitz
Outlet: Pacific Ocean on Oregon-Washington boundary

Vertical joints in basalt exposed by Columbia River (Jesse Walker)

> *Way back in 1940 or '41, I made a fast walking trip up and down the Columbia River and its tributaries, the Snake, the Hood, Willamette, Yakima, and the Klickitat, making up little songs about what I seen.*
>
> *I made up about 26 songs about the Bonneville dam, Grand Coulee dam, and the thunderous foamy waters of the rapids and cascades, the wild and windward watersprays from the high Sheliloh [sic] falls, and the folks living in the little shack house about a mile from the end of the line.*
>
> *The Department of the Interior folks got ahold of me and took me into a clothes closet there at the Bonneville Power Administration and melted my songs down onto records.*
>
> Woody Guthrie, *People's World*

The great "River of the West" discharges from its mammoth basin more water than any other river in the United States except the Mississippi. Best known for its middle and lower course in the states of Oregon and Washington, more than one-third of the river's path lies in Canada. Its largest tributary, the Snake, drains 49 percent of the basin. The Columbia River system has four distinct provinces: the Rocky Mountains; the basaltic Columbia Plateau and Snake River Plain; the Columbia Gorge, cutting across the Cascade Range; and the Puget Trough, a lowland area between the Cascades and the Coastal Range, drained by Oregon's Willamette and Washington's Cowlitz River.

The river rises west of the sharply faulted and uplifted eastern edge of the Canadian Rockies in southeastern British Columbia. It flows initially northwest through a long, narrow valley called the Rocky Mountain Trench. After hooking sharply around the Selkirk Mountains, the river flows southward, passing through Upper Arrow Lake and Lower Arrow Lake. It next receives the Kootenay (spelled Kootenai in the United States) and Pend Oreille Rivers before entering the state of Washington. Both the Kootenay and Pend Oreille drain sizable parts of the United States (the latter has only a short section in Canada), but each empties into the mainstream Columbia in Canada just north of the international boundary.

Passing into Washington, the river flows south before traversing a great arc known as the Big Bend. Near the mouth of the Spokane River, the Columbia is forced to veer sharply to the west by extensive lava beds, an extension of the Columbia Plateau. The river flows west, then south around the Channeled Scabland, a dry, eroded portion of eastern Washington that turns out to hold the key to the glacial history of the region. The breaking up of Pleistocene glacial Lake Missoula high in the Rockies caused swollen floodwaters of biblical proportions to short-cut the Columbia's wide bend west of Spokane, flowing across, indeed creating, the channels and glacial lakes now distributed on the scabland. The argument that the broken and irregular landscapes contained within the curving arm of the Columbia were the result of a prehistoric flood was first proposed by pioneering geologist Harlen Bretz in the 1920s, but the idea was initially rejected because such catastrophic notions were anathema to the uniformitarian orthodoxy of the day, which favored explanations emphasizing slow, uniform changes. The New Deal's massive hydropower and irrigation project in this part of Washington filled the reservoir of Grand Coulee, whose site is a dry channel where the Columbia once flowed when its course was blocked by ice during the Pleistocene.

The river runs in a narrow, entrenched valley across the Columbia Plateau, a basaltic tableland formed by successive flows of lava emitted nonexplosively from multiple vents in the Cascades. Near the confluence of the river's chief tributary, the Snake (and just below the juncture with the fertile fruitlands of the Yakima valley), the Columbia turns westward, in the direction of the sea. Along this section of the river, it forms the boundary between Washington and Oregon.

The river, however, must cleave the Cascade Range and the lower Coast Range before reaching the Pacific. There are several constrictions here, attesting to the erosive work of the river and the varying resistances of the geological formations. Traveling upriver from the sea, several obstacles to navigation present themselves. The Cascades (now Cascade Locks) are located some 160 miles (257 kilometers) from the mouth. They are a series of rapids so violent that locks had to be installed for navigational purposes in the late nineteenth century. Thirty-five miles (56 kilometers) farther, the Dalles is a narrow basaltic channel whose turbulent waters needed to be portaged in the early years. The constriction of the Dalles ended upriver at the horseshoe falls called by the Indian name Celilo. Here natives using long poles and special nets once stood on long platforms built over the rapids and scooped thousands of spawning salmon from the river.

The earliest travelers tried to run the Dalles; they found it uncomfortable at best, and sometimes fatal. Narcissa Whitman, wife of the missionary Marcus Whitman, described the Dalles as "a terrific sight, and a frightful place to be in." Indian middlemen resided along the narrows on both sides of the river, exacting tolls from travelers and exchanging the goods of upper-river Indians for those of lower-river Indians. Neither Lewis and Clark nor the fur-trading Astorians had pleasant experiences with these Indians.

When the first whites arrived, they found heavy native settlement along the coast, in the estuary, and at the Dalles. More than 125 tribes were counted in the region. Particularly noteworthy were the Chinooks, Clatsops, Willamettes, and Tillamooks. The Chinooks of the lower Columbia couldn't have contrasted more with the warlike tribes of the Plains, such as the Sioux. Their entire culture and religion centered on the life of the river, and the salmon was of key importance both as a food source and a symbol of fertility and prosperity. The natives practiced the celebrated potlatch ceremony, by which affluent tribesmen expressed generosity and social standing by feasting their neighbors—a cultural practice with remarkable similarity to the conspicuous consumption by wealthy Americans, as noted most famously by the anthropologically trained economist Thorstein Veblen. Fish are still taken out of the river, but the construction of dams and the heavy settlement along the river and its tributaries have reduced the salmon runs.

The American captain Robert Gray is credited with being the first European to reach the

Columbia, anchoring his ship *Columbia* (after which the river is named) off the mouth in 1792. A few months later, in the same year, British lieutenant William Robert Broughton crossed the sandbar in a small boat and rowed about 100 miles (161 kilometers) upstream. In 1805, Lewis and Clark, at the end of the first leg of their epochal journey, floated down the Columbia to the sea. Lewis's *Journal* records: "The fog suddenly clearing away, we were at last presented with the glorious sight of the ocean—that ocean, the object of all our labors, the reward of all our anxieties." The explorers erected Fort Clatsop near the south bank of the river and wintered there in 1805–1806.

The first to travel the river from source to mouth was a scientifically minded employee of the British North West Company, David Thompson, who crossed the Canadian Rockies at the Athabasca Pass and traveled the entire length of the river to its mouth. He reached it in July of 1811, only to discover that the representatives of John Jacob Astor, an American, had already established Astoria to draw off the fur trade of the lower Columbia. The stage was set for that traditional staple of early American history: the diplomatic and geopolitical struggle between Great Britain and the United States for control of the Oregon Country (the British called it Columbia). Once the Spanish agreed to the northern limits of California at the 42nd parallel (the present boundary of California and Oregon) and Russia accepted the southern limit of Russian Alaska at 54 degrees 40 minutes, England and the United States began in the 1820s to contest the intervening terrain. Numerous books have recounted this struggle for the primary access route and settlement corridor of the Pacific Northwest. A key factor in the eventual incorporation of the region into the United States was that the Oregon Trail crossed the Rockies over the low divide of South Pass and reached the Columbia River in the Walla Walla area, near where the river turns west after rounding the inhospitable Columbia Plateau. Until 1846 the Oregon Trail

Log handling on the Columbia River (Jesse Walker)

ended at the Dalles, and weary pioneers had to raft down the river to finish the final stages of their arduous journey. Subsequently, a wagon road, the Barlow Road, led around the southern edge of Mount Hood and took immigrants to the Sandy River, a tributary of the Columbia.

In the twentieth century the major thrust of human activity in the region was a push for modern economic development. That led to the building of numerous multiple-purpose dams along the middle and lower course of the river. The Columbia River Project received its impetus in the economically depressed 1930s, when authorization was obtained to impound the waters of the middle Columbia at Grand Coulee. Completed in 1942, this flood control and irrigation dam is the key dam in the project that today counts several dams along the middle Columbia, as well as a number of lower-river dams that provide a slackwater-navigation channel as far as the Snake. The immense scale of the Grand Coulee Dam can perhaps best be appreciated by citing a single fact: during spring surges, water running over the spillway creates a waterfall half as wide and twice as tall as Niagara Falls. With the aid of the folk singer and Dust Bowl balladeer Woody Guthrie, who celebrated the project with a number of songs in the spirit of hydro-socialism (jobs and income for poor migrants), the Grand Coulee was completed in January 1942, a month after America went to war. The enormous success of the project stemmed from the fact that aluminum skins for bombers could be turned out rapidly from Columbia River plants. Jobs were available, now that the economy was humming with Columbia-generated electricity.

There are today six federal and five nonfederal dams on the Columbia River, and the only section with some resemblance to the river observed by Lewis and Clark lies between the mouth and Bonneville Dam. As a result, mortality of small salmon trying to reach their spawning beds is high despite the use of fish ladders. The cumulative effect of all the dams has been to raise the average water temperature five degrees Fahrenheit. The Hanfort atomic plant, located along the river in central Washington, raises the water temperature yet another degree.

Further Reading: Clark, Robert, *River of the West: Stories from the Columbia,* New York: HarperCollins, 1995; Gayton, Don, "The Cartography of Catastrophe: Harlan Bretz and the Great Spokane Flood," *Mercator's World* 4, no. 3 (May-June 1999): 54–61; Holbrook, Stewart, *The Columbia,* New York: Rinehart and Company, 1956 (Rivers of America Series); Harden, Blaine, *A River Lost: The Life and Death of the Columbia,* New York: W. W. Norton and Company, 1996; Meinig, D. W., *The Great Columbia Plain: A Historical Geography, 1805–1910,* Seattle: University of Washington Press, 1968.

COLVILLE

Source: De Long Mountains, western Brooks Range, northern Alaska
Length: 375 miles (600 kilometers)
Tributaries: Awuna, Killik, Chandler, Anakktuvuk
Outlet: Beaufort Sea, Arctic Ocean

The Colville drains a strip of land that slopes seaward from the range of mountains lying at the northwestern end of the Rockies chain. The river flows east and then north, emptying into the Arctic Ocean about halfway between Barrow and Barter Island. Encompassing about one-third of the catchment area of Alaska's North Slope, the river lies entirely within the zone of continuous permafrost, unlike other, larger Arctic rivers that rise in temperate climates farther south. The drainage basin includes both a coastal plain and a piedmont section. The major town along the river, Umiat, lies near the junction of the low foothills and the level Arctic plain, west of the big bend in the river. The dominant vegetation of the region is tundra, and woody growth is lacking except for low shrubs and some dwarf trees. Although the river's delta is only 5 percent the size of the Mackenzie's (the Mackenzie River of northwest Canada, the nearest great river, has the second largest Arctic delta), it exhibits most of the processes and landforms characteristic of Arctic deltas.

Most of the river's tributaries rise on the northern flanks of the Brooks Range, a folded mountain

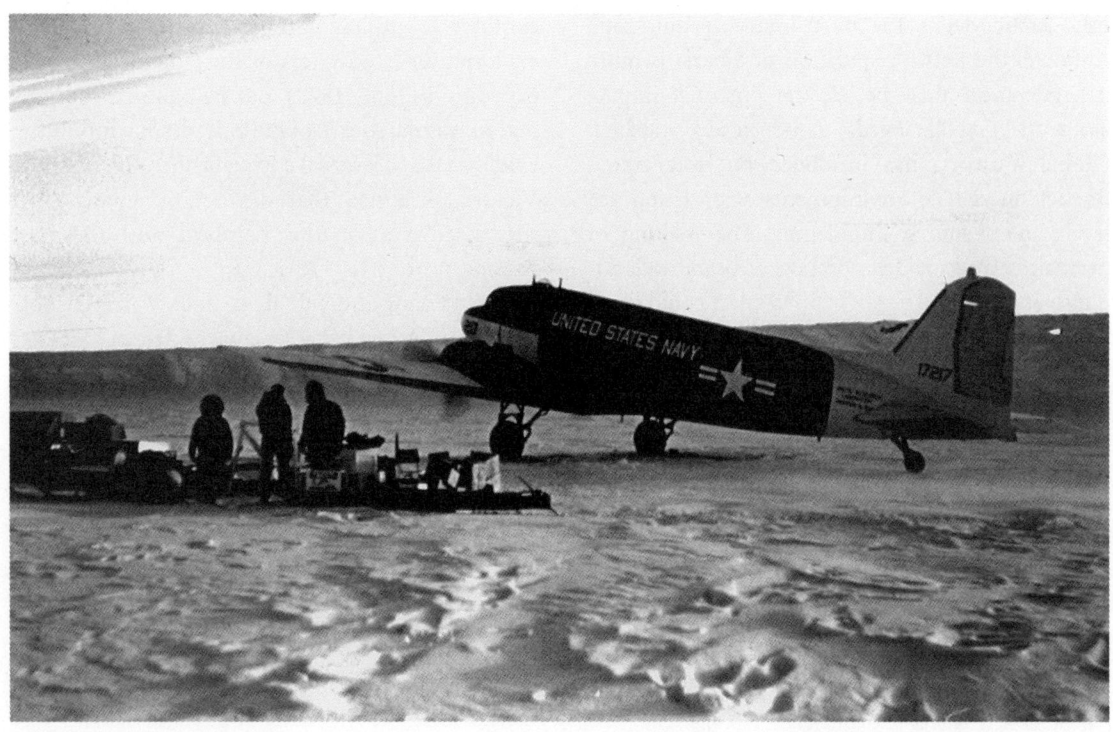

Supply shipment by DC-3 from Barrow, Alaska, on the frozen Colville River (Jesse Walker)

system extending east-west across northern Alaska. The upper courses of these tributaries were glaciated during Pleistocene times. Once the main stream collects these numerous affluents it flows across a stark, nearly level terrain that was never glaciated. That may seem somewhat puzzling, until one recalls that contemporary glaciers are to be found in southern, not northern, Alaska, dependent as they are on the moist maritime breezes of the Gulf of Alaska.

Ice-free in the past, the landscapes of the North Slope and its major river basin are shaped by the present-day action of frost, ice, and snow. Not until May or June does the temperature rise above 32 degrees Fahrenheit long enough to melt winter's accumulated snow and ice. River breakup occurs at the moment when ice begins to flow. The largest amount of riverbank erosion and geomorphic activity generally occurs when the river is carrying large blocks of ice, at or near flood stage.

The apex of the approximately triangular delta is located about 25 miles (40 kilometers) from the sea. The main distributary channel lies to the east, while a secondary outlet, the Nechelik Channel, flows past the delta's only town, Nuiqsut, along the western boundary. The fan of constantly shifting distributaries is impressive for such a relatively small delta. It has been calculated that from the head of the delta there are more than 5,200 routes that can be taken by water flowing to the sea. Common Arctic landforms and processes evident in the Colville delta include ice-wedging, polygonal ground, and pingos (conical hills cored by ice). Features that are common to deltas worldwide are also seen here: sandbars, mudflats, dunes, lakes, and shifting channels.

Although the northern terminus of the pipeline transporting oil from Prudhoe Bay lies off to the east, increased economic activities along the Arctic coast have led to greater potential for negative environmental impact. In 1998 the first major oil activity began in the Colville River delta. Whitefish is an important part of the Arctic fishery, with both subsistence and commercial uses. The whitefish uses Arctic deltas for its primary feeding site. Although the native population of Siberia is more dependent on this species, the potential impact along the Colville needs to be closely watched. Global warming has produced an exaggerated impact on deltaic environments with rising sea levels and resulting inundation. The melting of permafrost and the deterioration of peaty wetlands is also of concern. The last-named effect could cause a positive feedback in the environmental system with runaway consequences on warming, since large reserves of peat are locked up in Arctic permafrost, which acts as a global storehouse of carbon.

Further Reading: Walker, H. Jesse, "Arctic Deltas," *Journal of Coastal Research* 14 (1998): 718–738.

CONGO

Source: Chambesi, near the border with Tanzania
Length: c. 2,720 miles (4,380 kilometers)
Tributaries: Lualaba, Lomani, Kasai, Lulonga, Ubangi, Aruwimi, Itimbiri
Outlet: Atlantic Ocean

Sometimes we came upon a station close by the bank, clinging to the skirts of the unknown, and the white men rushing out of a tumbledown hovel, with great gestures of joy and surprise and welcome, seemed very strange—had the appearance of being held there captive by a spell. The word "ivory" would ring in the air for a while—and on we went again into the silence, along empty reaches, round the still bends, between the high walls of our winding way, reverberating in hollow claps the ponderous beat of the stern-wheel. Trees, trees, millions of trees, massive, immense running up high; and at their foot, hugging the bank against the stream, crept the little begrimed steamboat, like a sluggish beetle crawling on the floor of a lofty portico. It made you feel very small, very lost, and yet it was not altogether depressing, that feeling. . . . The reaches opened before us and closed behind, as if the forest had stepped leisurely across the water to bar the way of our return. We penetrated deeper and deeper into the heart of darkness.
Joseph Conrad, *Heart of Darkness,* 1902

The major river of equatorial Africa rises on a savanna plateau just south of Lake Tanganyika. The nineteenth-century medical missionary and explorer David Livingstone first discovered and explored the headwaters of the Congo on his last expedition (1866–1873), but he believed that this region was the source of the Nile, despite mounting evidence that a large lake lying farther north—Lake Victoria—claimed that distinction. Livingstone, the discoverer of the Zambezi and the first European to cross Africa from coast to coast, inspired many individuals to follow in his footsteps, not least the ace reporter Henry Morton Stanley, whose "discovery" of the good doctor attracted international attention in the late nineteenth century. The headwaters of the Zaire, as the Congo is also known, lie in a short, meandering stream—the Chambesi—which drains southwest from near the border with Tanzania into Lake Bangwelo (Livingstone died on the southern shore of this lake on May 1, 1873). A drainage from the marshy southern end of this lake is known as the Luapula. This river in turn flows into Lake Mweru, whose outlet has the name of Luvua. Thus the river at its farthest eastern reach and highest topographic point has three names and drains two lakes as it cuts across its savanna rim.

Then the major stream of the upper course is encountered, the Lualaba, which flows through dark, forbidding rain forest. Because of its length, many consider the Lualaba itself to be the main stem of the Congo. Livingstone had once struck out west from Lake Tanganyika in the direction of the Lualaba, but, upon reaching the river, he was unable to obtain canoes from the unfriendly tribes there, who had a reputation for cannibalism (they feared further incursion of Arab slavers). As a result, he could not follow the Lualaba downstream to what he hoped would lead to a tributary of Lake Albert and an outlet on the Nile.

At the confluence of the Lualaba and the Luvua, the headwaters of the Congo end, and the upper Congo, under the name of the Lualaba, begins its long descent from the savanna into the immense rain forest river basin. The Lualaba flows relentlessly north for more than one thousand miles before crossing the equator and then making a broad counterclockwise arc to the west and then the southwest, crossing the equator again as it flows

A partial clearing along the banks of the Congo River in equatorial Africa (Paul Almasy/CORBIS)

toward its mouth on the Atlantic. No other major river in the world crosses the equator even once, let alone twice. The circuitous course of the river caused explorers to mistake the river's direction and to consider its unexplored parts to be segments of other African rivers. The early British explorer and discoverer of the Niger, Mungo Park, believed the mouth of the Niger to be the lower Congo, while, as we have seen, the Scottish missionary-explorer Livingstone thought the upper waters of the Congo were the fountains of the Nile, described in Herodotus and believed by the devout Livingstone to be prefigured in biblical scripture.

Since the Congo's course lies in both hemispheres, the river is unlike other tropical rivers that have notable periods of high and low flows in response to alternating wet and dry seasons. The rainy season is always occurring on one side of the equator, and as a result, the Zaire's flow is amazingly constant, especially considering its volume, which is second only to that of the Amazon. The lower end of the Upper Congo is reached at Stanley Falls, a series of seven cataracts and rapids, which, over a course of some 60 miles (96 km), drop the river to an elevation of 1,500 feet (457 meters). The falls were named after the discoverer of Livingstone, who, after the death of his mentor (and father figure as well, since Stanley was an orphan), followed the Congo to the sea and later worked in the employ of the king of the Belgians, Leopold II, to open up the region for commercial exploitation. Just below Stanley Falls is the city of Kisangani (formerly Stanleyville), which was the main river port for shipping out rubber and ivory harvested in the surrounding forest; the brutal conditions of that trade are described in Joseph Conrad's *Heart of Darkness* (1902). Downstream stretches a thousand miles of navigable river along the Middle Congo, terminating at Kinshasa (formerly Leopoldville) just above the tremendous falls that for so long kept Europeans and Congo natives of the lower river (for example, the Bkongo) from penetrating the interior. Livingstone Falls is not a stupendous plunge like Niagara Falls or Victoria Falls, but instead, like its upriver counterpart, it comprises a long stretch of treacherous waters. In this case the falls has at least thirty-two cataracts covering 220 miles (354 km). A number of major tributaries join the Zaire along its middle course: the Lomami and Kasai from the south, draining the mineral-rich Katanga; and the Ubangi from the north.

Located just above Livingstone Falls, the broad waters of Stanley Pool (now Malebo Pool) form the lower limit of the middle Congo. Here occurred an intense European rivalry in the late nineteenth century. The focus of the dispute was the rush to establish a settlement above the falls to serve as a point of attachment for the commercial exploitation of the interior. The French explorer Pierre Savorgnan de Brazza reached the pool first, in 1880, traveling from French Gabon via the Ogooué River. The handsome and socially well-placed Frenchman made a treaty with one of the tribes on the pool guaranteeing French rights in the region and permitting the construction of a settlement (present-day Brazzaville). Henry Morton Stanley, representing the Belgian king Leopold II, had achieved fame as the discoverer of Livingstone, but because of his lowly origins as a workhouse orphan, his efforts were sometimes mired in difficulties (he was initially dismissed when he claimed to have found Livingstone). Stanley busied himself constructing roads and stations along the route from the lower river around the falls, and when he reached the pool he too negotiated a makeshift agreement with one of the many tribes in the area. The Belgian point of entry so established became present-day Kinshasa.

This French-Belgian rivalry precipitated a crisis in Europe. Although no great power was very interested in the malaria-plagued river whose indigenous people had a reputation for cannibalism (the reports were often exaggerated), no one wanted to see a potentially rich region attached to a competitor. Leopold II, king of a minor country, had since childhood pondered over maps and atlases looking for an overseas territory where he might extend the influence of his tiny kingdom. Fabulously wealthy, Leopold created a number of sham benevolent societies whose ostensible purpose was to civilize the peoples of the river basin; under this smoke screen, the European powers, by means of the Berlin Act of 1885, granted the Congo to Leopold II—not as a Belgian colony but as Leopold's personal kingdom. The Belgian Free State so created became a proper colony in 1908 under the name of the Belgian Congo, the name it retained until 1960, when independence was attained.

The lower course of the Congo below Livingstone Falls crosses a nearly level coastal plain for about 200 miles (322 km) before emptying into the Atlantic. The river is navigable for 83 miles (134 km) to Matadi. The estuary is about 7 miles (11 km) wide as the river enters the sea between Banana Point on the north and Sharks Point on the south.

The Portuguese naval captain Diogo Cão first discovered the mouth of the Zaire in 1482, as part of the Portuguese exploration of the west coast of Africa in search of a water route to India. Cão erected stone pillars inscribed with the name of his monarch, King John II, on the southern bank of the river near its mouth. The Portuguese made contact with the large Kibongo settlement of Mbanza Congo (previously São Salvador) south of the river, but, unable to cross the Crystal Mountains into the interior, they later transferred their primary interest farther south and established the coastal colony of Angola.

With independence in 1960 came the need to foster African identity. Since 1971 *authenticité* campaigns have resulted in erasing the traces of European colonialism on the map and substituting African names: Stanleyville became Kisangani; Leopoldville, Kinshasa; and the name of the river and the country encompassing the largest extent of this great equatorial basin changed from Congo to Zaire (and then, more recently, changed back again). "Zaire" is an ancient African name for certain tribes along the lower river, actually a Portuguese mispronunciation of the Kibongo word *nzadi* or *nzere*, meaning "the river that swallows all rivers." By whatever name, the river follows its meandering course for 2,920 miles (4,700 km) on its way to the sea, resembling a giant snake suggestive of both the river's power and its terror.

Further Reading: Forbath, Peter, *The River Congo: The Discovery, Exploration and Exploitation of the World's Most Dramatic River*, New York: Harper and Row, 1977; Hyland, Paul, *The Black Heart: A Voyage into Central Africa*, New York: Henry Holt and Company, 1988.

CONNECTICUT

Source: Connecticut Lakes, in northern New Hampshire
Length: 407 miles (655 kilometers)
Tributaries: White, Ashuelot, Deerfield, Millers, Westfield, Chicopee, Farmington
Outlet: Long Island Sound

The largest alluvial lowland in New England has not played as important a role in history as one might think, but its significance for agriculture, town development, and the rise of manufacturing cannot be doubted.

The longest river in New England, the Connecticut drains four of the six New England states (only Rhode Island and Maine do not lie in its path). It rises in lakes of the same name in far northern New Hampshire. The three linked lakes of the headwaters are named—appropriately for the region, whose people pride themselves on their plain, direct speech—First, Second, and Third Connecticut Lakes. Third Connecticut Lake, or just Third Lake, lies close to the Canadian (Quebec) border and is the source of the river.

The Connecticut River flows generally southward along the border between Vermont and New Hampshire. Then it cuts across Massachusetts and Connecticut to enter Long Island Sound at Old Saybrook, a small town that was the original site of Yale University (now at New Haven).

The Connecticut is the only major river in the United States without an important city at or near its mouth. This curiosity can be explained by two geographic facts. An obstructive sandbar off the river's mouth has allowed the development only of the towns of Old Saybrook and Old Lyme, on opposite banks of the river. Old Saybrook, or just Saybrook for short (remember the New Englanders' laconicism), was established as an independent colony of English residents in 1635 by Viscount Saye and Baron Brooke, but its founders sold the town in 1644 to Connecticut colony. The other geographical circumstance working against the rise of a city near the river's outlet relates to the divergence between the broad lowlands of the valley and the actual path of the river in its lower course. In the state of Connecticut the river flows through only the northern half of the valley. Then it veers off to the southeast at Middletown, crossing resistant rocks; as a result, the present river carves only a narrow valley there. The hinterland of any emerging city in the lower valley is thereby diminished. The growth of cities was promoted farther upstream, however, at falls (Hadley, Holyoke) and crossing points (Springfield, Hartford). Other cities in the valley grew in response to agricultural and industrial specializations among the hardworking Yankee settlers.

The first European to view the river was the Dutch fur trader and explorer Adrian Block, best known for the resort island bearing his name at the eastern entrance to Long Island Sound. Block explored the sound and sailed upriver as far as Enfield Falls. He named the river "De Versche Riviere," or Freshwater River. The natives had previously called this northward-stretching river Quoneklacut (or Quonehtacet), meaning "long river" or "the river without end." The Pequot Indians inhabited the shore of Long Island Sound, while other tribes including the Podunk, Poqunock, Mohegan, and the Massacoe lived nearby. Though the Dutch responded to Block's enthusiastic report by creating a palisaded trading post and a fort near present Hartford, the river and its fertile valley passed to the English at the same time that New Amsterdam became New York. Pilgrims from Plymouth Colony were the first to realize the potential of the rich agricultural lands of the Connecticut

Covered bridge across the Connecticut River connecting Cornish, New Hampshire, and Windsor, Vermont, built in 1866. This is the longest covered bridge in the northeastern United States. (Jesse Walker)

valley; they established a trading post near present-day Windsor, Connecticut, in 1633. Three years later, small English settlements existed at Windsor, Wethersfield, and Hartford, Connecticut. The native peoples did not pass peacefully from the scene. The short Pequot War of 1637 was followed, after a long period of peace, by the bloody and destructive King Philip's War in 1675–1676. The prolonged conflict of this latter war marked the turning-point in the relationship between the Indians and the colonists. Subsequently, peaceful coexistence was not an option.

By the early nineteenth century a distinctive pattern of agricultural specialization and protoindustrial development was apparent in the valley. Wethersfield was becoming known for its onions. Other areas concentrated on beef cattle, dairy cows, but not yet sheep. Places in the upper valley specialized in one of the first intensively tilled crops: broomcorn. Introduced from India at the end of the previous century, broomcorn, a crop with a distinctive, tall profile, became the basis of the manufacture of whisk brooms from its dried panicles in such Connecticut River towns as Hadley and East Hampton. As would occur later in the Midwest, commercial agriculture and manufacturing were yoked together like a team of horses and a wagon. Grist- and sawmills serving local farmers at falls along the river could be adapted as fulling and carding mills—the latter initially serving home producers of textiles. Most early manufacturing, at least until midcentury, either involved processing of agricultural products or relied on farm families in a putting-out system whereby merchants advanced raw materials to domestic producers and collected the finished goods. Only slowly did factory-based textile making emerge, and the distinctive Connecticut valley industry of machine tools was a later development yet. The palm-leaf industry of Amherst was typical of early-nineteenth-century manufacturing, with its small-scale organization and dependence on family labor. In the mid-1840s there were no fewer than ten hat merchants in Amherst, and hundreds of families split, braided, and shaped the leaf, which had been sent out and would be gathered by town merchants. By such modest means manufacturing arose in the Connecticut River lowlands. The opening of a factory in Hartford in 1848 for the production of what would soon be famously known as the Colt revolver would not have occurred without these simpler beginnings, when manufacturing was essentially a sideline activity.

Entrepreneurial zeal was manifested in the building of canals to circumvent the falls at South Hadley and Turner's Falls. Although by the 1840s and 1850s the canals were obsolete because of the construction of the first railroads, both canals and railroads revealed the same underlying motivation: the search for a larger market.

Since the river was long and relatively straight, the network of towns in the valley exhibited a linear arrangement absent in other parts of New England. The Connecticut River has a regular series of terrace surfaces rising from the floodplain. In most cases there are three or four levels formed by the cutting down of the river into young sediments in response to the changing sea level. The terraced steps of the Connecticut valley were important in the laying out of settlements by town fathers. The main north-south streets paralleling the river were laid out on the dry terrace surface. The second terrace above the river was preferred for the village core, as it was believed to be beyond the level of flooding and likely to promote greater healthfulness—or "salubrity," to use a term of the time. The rise to the next or third terrace was described as the "meadow hill." A closely knit community fronting a boulevard-like main street characterized many early Connecticut valley towns. The streets of nearby villages were eventually joined to form a long and narrow "street village"—a transitional settlement form between the compact villages of earlier communities and the scattered, isolated farmsteads of later periods.

Further Reading: Clark, Christopher, "Household Economy, Market Exchange and the Rise of Capitalism in the Connecticut Valley, 1800–1860," *Journal of Social History* 13 (1979): 169–189; Hard, Walter, *The Connecticut River,* New York: Rinehart and Company, 1947 (Rivers of America Series); Wilson, Roy R., "An Integrated River Management Model: The Connecticut River Management Program," *Journal of Environmental Management* 41, no. 4 (1994): pp. 337–348.

D

DAL

Source: West-central Sweden, near the mountainous border with Norway
Length: 325 miles (523 kilometers)
Tributaries: Österdal, Västerdal
Outlet: Gulf of Bothnia

The Dal, or Dalälven, River is regarded by Swedes with particular affection, even more so than the great lakes in the south or Lapland in the north. Flowing out of the Norwegian mountains, the river has two main branches: Västerdal, or West Dal; and Österdal, or East Dal. The former rises on the slopes of Fulufjället at an elevation of 3,425 feet (1,044 meters), while the latter begins on Storvatteshägna at 3,950 feet (1,204 meters).

Like many Swedish rivers, the Dal drains to the southeast. Both branches of the river begin high up in the mountains, in deep glacial valleys with characteristic *U*-profiles. Above the headwalls of the upper valley can be found barren fells (fjelds), while slopes below are tree-covered. About 100 miles (161 kilometers) from its source, Österdal broadens to form Lake Siljan, a densely settled agricultural region from whose shores many Swedish emigrants came to the American upper Midwest (especially Minnesota) in the late nineteenth century. In this part of the upper Dalarna, or valley of the Dal, excellent soils have formed around the geologically distinctive Siljan Ring, a basin of relatively young sedimentary rocks with recent moraine deposits. As a result, there is a denser pattern of rural settlement here than in most other regions of Sweden. The principal market towns in this wide, hilly basin are Rättvik and Mora.

About 15 miles (24 kilometers) downstream from Lake Siljan, the Västerdal joins the Österdal, and the characteristic shape of the valley narrows until the river reaches the industrial town of Borlänge. This region possesses abundant iron resources that have long provided the raw materials for the Swedish steel and engineering industry, which has been at the forefront of European manufacturing. In the Bergslagen—the most important Swedish mining region—resource extraction dates back to the dawn of prehistory. This historic region extends from the lower Klar to the bend of the Dal. Not only iron ore but also copper, silver, lead, zinc, and gold have been quarried from these shapeless hills. The largest steel and paper mills in Sweden are concentrated at Börlange, not far from rapids that have been harnessed for hydroelectric power.

Just off the main stream of the river, on the tributary Faluän, lies elongated Lake Runn, at whose northern end is the copper town of Falun. The mining of copper at this site goes back at least twelve centuries. Farther downstream, the town of Säter, at the lower end of Säterdal, was founded in 1626 by Gustavus Adolphus, the Swedish ruler (reigned 1611–1632) who made his country a great European power (his establishment of Göteborg as Sweden's major westward-looking port in 1619 was decisive in this).

The oldest town on the river is Hedemora, located about 12 miles (19 kilometers) above where the river makes its turn at Avesta, another important steel manufacturing center. One of the numerous faults of the Swedish coastline diverts the Dal toward the northeast into Gävle Bay. Along the lower course of the Dal, the uniformity of the coniferous forest is dispersed by deciduous trees such as oak, ash, and lime, and a touch of color appears in the fall that early frosts do not end so abruptly here as elsewhere in Sweden. Before emptying into the Gulf of Bothnia, the Dal forms a chain of lakes, with a series of intervening waterfalls. Although one thinks of deeply trenched fjords on the west coast of Norway, there are river widenings in eastern Sweden along the lower Dal, as at Bysfjärd, Färnebofjärd, and Lanfjärd, that possess some of the same characteristics and the same linguistic root as their more spectacular cousins. Low waterfalls between some of these lakes make the lower course unnavigable and not suitable for timber floating. The nearest part of the river is only 100 miles (161 kilometers) from Stockholm, and about half that distance from Uppsala, so the Dal River and its valley, the Dalarna, are accessible to a large number of people.

See also Klarälven

DANUBE

Source: Black Forest, in southwestern Germany
Length: c. 1,770 miles (2,850 kilometers)
Tributaries: Inn, **Drava**, Tisza, Sava, Prut
Outlet: Black Sea

The second longest river in Europe is the major commercial artery and accessway linking central and eastern parts of the continent. The river of many names and many nations is the only major European river that flows from west to east.

The polyglot Danube rises in two short headstreams in the hilly plateau of the Black Forest in southwestern Germany, only a short distance from a segment of the upper Rhine. Known to the Germans as the Donau, the river flows initially northeast through Württemberg and Bavaria past Ulm, the head of navigation, and Regensburg, where it makes a large bend at its northernmost point before turning to the southeast and entering Austria below Passau. Following a generally easterly course across upper and lower Austria, the Danube cuts across wooded hills in the scenic Wachau region just above Vienna, which many consider the most beautiful part of the valley and the likely inspiration for the lilting waltz of Johann Strauss the Younger, the "Blue Danube." Splendid castles, isolated abbeys, and opulent palaces along the German and Austrian Danube evoke the bygone times of the high Middle Ages in Germany and the Hapsburg prosperity that followed. Although the river is rarely blue—it is more often gray or green—Strauss's haunting tune captures a romantic nostalgia for the past: it is said that in lovers' eyes the waters of the river appear blue.

Below the Austrian capital the river passes Bratislava, the major river port in former Czechoslovakia (now in Slovakia). Bratislava, or German Pressburg, is today a major industrial city that discharges a large amount of pollution into the river. The Danube makes a large bend to the south, flowing across the land of the Magyars—Hungary. The Duna (Hungarian: Danube) bisects the historic city of Budapest, which consists of the garrison heights of Buda to the west and the level lands of Pest to the east, stretching away to the horizon to form the Great Hungarian Plain (Alföld). The Danube broadens and slows below Budapest, resembling a flatland river like the Mississippi with its large freight of silt, carried down from the mountains, settling out in the channel and forming numerous bars and islands. The marshy and shallow middle section of the river receives the largest of the approximately 300 tributaries of the Danube—the Drava, the Tisza, and the Sava. The Roman province of Pannonia lay on the right bank of the Danube in the key region drained by the Sava. The low-lying and accessible Pear Tree Pass was located here and provided the primary line of communication between Italy and the Balkans. Rome's first emperor, Augustus, annexed the Balkan territory in 29–28 B.C. and later selected the middle course of the Danube as the boundary

Danube Delta, shelters used for harvesting grass (Jesse Walker)

between the empire and the rest of Europe. Thus began the process whereby an artery of navigation and access became a political boundary and zone of conflict. In a geopolitical sense, little has changed from the time of Augustus to the unraveling of Yugoslavia in the 1990s at the end of the Cold War.

The confluence of the Sava and the Danube occurs at Belgrade, the capital of Yugoslavia (both the larger political entity, consisting of six autonomous republics that came into existence in 1918, and the smaller Yugoslav Federal Republic comprising Serbia and Montenegro, created in the 1990s). Like Budapest, this historic city was originally a Roman frontier position and a bridge crossing. Below Belgrade the river enters the boiling rapids of the Iron Gate constriction, one of the key strategic sites of eastern Europe. The roughly two-mile-long gorge has been cut between the western Transylvanian Alps and the rugged Balkan ranges. Sheer rock walls as much as 1,000 feet (305 meters) high once struck fear into the hearts of navigators, but today the Sip Canal bypasses the treacherous rapids; a large hydroelectric dam was built in the 1970s. As evidence of the river's turbulent power in this narrows, large potholes have been excavated to a depth of 246 feet (75 meters), some reaching below sea level. The Danube changes once again below the cataracts, becoming a broad, sluggish river forming the boundary between Romania and Bulgaria. On the north side of the river in Romania the river goes by the name Dunarea, while to the south, in Bulgaria, the river is known as the Dunav. Near Silistra the river leaves the Bulgarian border and turns north to Galati. About 50 miles (80 kilometers) from the Black Sea, the Danube branches into numerous distributaries to form an enormous delta, a mosaic of land and water—marshes, lakes, sandbars, and floating reedbeds. The second-largest delta in Europe is home to large numbers of wading and water birds that inhabit a delicate ecological zone increasingly endangered by industrial development. The northernmost of the three main channels of the delta is the Kiliya, which is also the main arm for shipping. The Bessarabian towns of Izmail and Kiliya lie just north of this distributary channel and are part of Ukraine (formerly part of the Soviet Union).

The significance of the Danube is that it is the key accessway between central and southeastern Europe. Ever since the Romans built forts at crossing points along the river, the Danube has been a boundary zone and region of conflict: between Romans and barbarians, Ottoman Turks and Austrian Hapsburgs, Russian-dominated communist regimes and West European democracies. Despite the bucolic fields and quaint villages of the valley, the armies of Augustus, Charlemagne, Napoleon, and Hitler have all passed this way. After the collapse of the Roman imperium in the fifth century A.D., a diverse group of tribes invaded the region: Goths, Huns, Avars, Magyars, Pechenegs, Cumans, Mongols, and others. The river served as a transportation corridor for eastward-moving crusaders beginning in the eleventh century, while Ottoman Turks advanced in the other direction in the fifteenth century, reaching as far as the gates of Vienna before they were turned back for the last time in 1683.

In the nineteenth century the Danube was a key link between the industrializing centers of Germany and the agrarian Balkans. At that time most of the river's middle and lower course lay within the territory of the Austro-Hungarian Empire, whereas the lower part belonged to the decaying domain of the Ottoman Turks. As Turkish political control waned, Russian influence was on the rise, and a strategic nightmare appeared on the horizon: the possibility that Russia might acquire or control the Danube delta.

The treaty that concluded the Crimean War (1853–1856) placed control of the Danube delta in the hands of a European commission. In 1890 the Austrian government initiated a series of projects meant to improve navigation at the Iron Gates. Following World War I another commission was established to ensure free navigation of the Danube above the delta. During World War II, Nazi Germany abolished these commissions and controlled all of the river from 1940 to 1944.

Today the Danube is the object of renewed international concern and negotiation. Since the end of the Cold War, issues related to economic development and the environment have come to the fore. To the traditional issue of navigation have been added those of hydroelectric dam building and pollution. The Danube not only serves as a

Dredging the channel on the upper Danube (Jesse Walker)

transportation artery; it also provides drinking water, irrigation, and industrial water to ninety million people in seventeen countries. The river acts as a disposal site for municipal, agricultural, and industrial wastes. Pollution of two of its main tributaries—the Sava and the Drava—has led to increased loads of phosphates and pesticides, which threaten Black Sea fisheries and the ecology of the Danube delta. The eleven riparian countries under the Danube Convention of 1948 have agreed to international regulation of the river. In 1986 eight countries agreed to a nonbinding Danube Declaration regulating water quality in the face of increasing pollution. A political problem arises since different countries have organized their regulatory apparatus at different levels of the government. In Austria, governmental authority over the river is spread over six government ministries; in Hungary, almost all control is vested in one body, the National Water Authority; in Germany, state governments have primary responsibility for rivers.

Perhaps the best example of a controversy related to these concerns is the construction of the Gabcíkovo Dam in southern Slovakia in the 1980s. The diversion of the Danube southeast of Bratislava by Slovakia aroused the ire of the Czech, Hungarian, and Austrian governments. Hungary and Austria withdrew from the project because of pressure from environmental and other groups (the dam seals off the river from its former course and doesn't allow the natural inundation of the vast Pannonian Plain of the middle Danube). With the dissolution in 1993 of Czechoslovakia into its component political units, the Czech Republic and Slovakia, the more economically prosperous Czechs withdrew from the project. Slovakia unilaterally went ahead with the construction of the giant hydroelectric plant and dam, despite vociferous protests by the Hungarian government, which demanded the redrawing of the international boundary to reflect the Danube's northward shift. With a large Hungarian minority, Slovakia found itself with cultural opposition, an all-too-common problem in this ethnically diverse part of Europe. The control of the Danube today—both as a resource and an environment—is an excellent test of the relative strengths of cooperation and conflict among the people living along the banks of this important river.

See also Drava, Morava
Further Reading: Edwards, Mike, "The Danube: River of Many Nations, Many Names," *National Geographic,* October 1977, pp. 454–485; Magris, Claudio, *Danube: A Sentimental Journey from the Source to the Black Sea,* London: Harvill Press, 1999 (orig. pub. 1986).

DARLING

Source: Western slope of Great Dividing Range, southeastern Australia
Length: 1,702 miles (2,739 kilometers)
Tributaries: Barwon, Culgoa, Bogan, Warrego
Outlet: **Murray**

The Darling-Murray river system is the largest drainageway in the predominantly dry island-continent of Australia. The Darling, which is a tributary of the Murray, is the longer, though the Murray figures as being more important in the settlement history of the Land Down Under.

The Darling begins near the eastern edge of the continent at about the latitude of Brisbane. The river rises on the far or western side of the Great Dividing Range, a generally north-south-trending chain of mountains whose elevation, geological character, and position on the landmass resemble those of the American Appalachians. The upper tributaries drain the flanks of the Dividing Range and the agriculturally productive tableland known as Darling Downs, which extends west from the range in southeastern Queensland. Gathering headstreams and intermittent channels, the river flows southwesterly across northern New South Wales, the earliest settled and still largest Australian state. But most of the population of New South Wales lives along the coast and in Sydney, and the upper course of the Darling is only sparsely populated. Isolated sheep farms known as "stations" spread across an open and largely untenanted landscape. Along the banks of the river redgums and leopard wood provide some shade, but the interminable red plains stretch out to the horizon, dotted with occasional gray-green mulga trees. The region occupies a semiarid belt between the continent's wet eastern rim and its dry interior. With the semiarid climate goes a grassland or steppe environment. When the infrequent rains do fall, the land comes alive with waving grasses and bright flowers, rather like a red-tinged American Great Plains.

The Darling proper begins just north of Bourke in northern New South Wales, formed by the confluence of the Barwon draining from the east and the Culgoa from the north. These two streams are fed in turn by numerous subtributaries, including the Condamyne, McIntyre, Gwydir, Castlereagh, Macquarie, and Bogan Rivers. As these place-names suggest, the early settlers and explorers often came from Scotland or were of Scotch-Irish descent. Below Bourke the river flows across an increasingly dry plain, and only the Warrego empties into the river.

Even generalized atlas maps show many dashed watercourses, indicating intermittent flow in these channels. The Darling itself sometimes dries up entirely, its waters swallowed by the dust of the world's driest continent (excepting Antarctica, which is a cold desert). Weirs have been constructed along the dry Darling to pond water for storage and future use. At Menindee a series of lakes with aboriginal names have been filled to supply water to the nearby mining center of Broken Hill and to irrigate market gardens in the vicinity.

The mines around the city of Broken Hill, the only city in the Darling region, have been worked since 1883. The district got its start when a German immigrant, Charles Rasp, who was employed as a boundary rider on a nearby sheep station, chipped a sample of rock from a long, jagged ridge that ran across the property. Although this sample assayed low in silver, later finds were more promising. The Broken Hill district has since produced enormous quantities of silver, lead, zinc, and tin. At the end of the nineteenth century, one-third of the world's silver was mined here. As the mineral resources have been depleted, Broken Hill has become an important tourist destination and artist colony. Many of the original artists were miners who painted in the primitive style during their time off. This was true as late as 1965 when the writer Elspeth Huxley toured and studied in Australia. The largest Australian business concern, the Broken Hill Proprietary Company, began at this mining center but left the city in 1939.

The Darling flows east of the city of Broken Hill near Menindee. After separating into two channels and subsequently recombining, the river merges with the Murray at Wentworth near the border with South Australia.

In search of grazing lands, the English explorer Charles Sturt reconnoitered the river's headwaters in 1815. Thirteen years later, diverted westward by the Macquaire Swamps, Sturt reached the Darling but was disappointed to discover that its waters were salty. He named the river after the governor of New South Wales at the time, Sir Ralph Darling. In 1830, Sturt made an incredible journey down the Murray River and identified its major northern tributary as the Darling. Settlers found the country dry, but they were able to tap into subterranean, artesian supplies of water.

River traffic never flourished on the Darling as it did on the Murray, since its flow is sporadic and navigation is treacherous during dry seasons. Before the arrival of the railroad, small steamers plied its waters, carrying wool tinted red with dust. By a curious historical twist, the first boat to reach Bourke in 1861 carried liquor to thirsty, waiting men, and the last boat on the Darling, in 1943, also carried liquor—for troops in Queensland. Irrigation has improved conditions in this Aussie outland, but the general impression remains one of aridity and isolation.

See also Murray

Further Reading: Huxley, Elspeth, *Their Shining Eldorado: A Journey through Australia,* New York: William Morrow, 1967.

DAUGAVA

See Western Dvina

DEE

Source: Pools of Dee, in Aberdeenshire, Scotland
Length: c. 90 miles (145 kilometers)
Tributaries: Clunie Water, Girnock Burn, Water of Feugh, Burn of Sheeoch, Gormack Burn
Outlet: North Sea

Although not a major river measured by length or volume of discharge, the Dee commonly surpasses expectations in its scenic beauty. The river rises on the slopes of the high Cairngorms in some of the most spectacular hill country in Britain. It originates in three clear pools along a rough track about a mile (1.6 kilometers) below the summit of the Lairig, a high pass joining Speyside to Deeside. Subterranean wells connecting the Pools of Dee are fed by rainfall from the slopes of Braeriach to the west and Ben Macdhui to the east.

Draining the Grampian region of eastern Scotland, the river initially flows south before veering to the east as it reaches the Linn of Dee, a narrow cleft where opposing rock walls approach one another. The river plunges down a long chasm before broadening for its 6-mile (9.7-kilometer) journey to Braemar, the site of the world's most famous Highland Games.

The next 17 miles (27.4 kilometers), between Braemar and Ballater, form Deeside, where the valley exhibits its classic form: a sparkling river rushing over small falls through pine woods against a background of blue hills. Just below Braemar stands a castle of the same name, an imposing edifice used as barracks by red-coated British soldiers stationed here in the early eighteenth century to keep the Highlanders in check.

Eight miles (12.9 kilometers) farther downstream is the royal residence of Balmoral. Designed and planned by Prince Albert, Queen Victoria's husband and consort, the residence stands on extensive grounds. It was built in 1854 of white Crathie granite quarried nearby. This stretch of the river is reputed to be one of the best salmon fishing streams in Britain.

The tourist town of Ballater is situated near where the Dee exits from the Highlands. The river broadens into a less picturesque valley on its way to the North Sea. Though receiving many minor burns, the river has no major tributaries. The Dee finally reaches the sea near Aberdeen, an important port on the northeast coast of Scotland. Nearly a mile (1.6 kilometers) of the river's course was diverted in the nineteenth century to improve the harbor. Aberdeen has benefited recently from its connection by pipeline to the crude oil fields of the North Sea.

DELAWARE

Source: Catskill Mountains, in southeastern New York
Length: c. 280 miles (451 kilometers)
Tributaries: Neversink, Lehigh, Schuylkill
Outlet: Delaware Bay

Although one of the most important rivers of the midsection of America's East Coast, the Delaware is relatively unknown. No literary genius is associated with the river in the way that the Hudson is identified with Washington Irving. No one has penned songs or ditties about its rivermen. Serving parts of the heavily populated states of New York, New Jersey, Pennsylvania, and Delaware, the river in its lower course is a hardworking river: a place of freeways, canals, warehouses, factories, and airports. Americans may not know its geography, but in their daily lives they use many of the industrial and consumer products made along its banks.

The Delaware is formed by the junction of East and West Branch, which meet at Hancock, New York. The headwaters region lies in the Catskills, a portion of the Appalachian Highlands extending west from the middle Hudson valley in the vicinity of Kingston. The river flows to the southeast along the New York–Pennsylvania border to Port Jervis, then follows the Pennsylvania–New Jersey boundary in a generally southward route. The upper river's proximity to the Hudson has long been noted by those attending to the water needs of New York City. Diversions of the upper Delaware provide about a third of the city's water supply. A now-abandoned canal connecting the Hudson and the Delaware was built in 1834 to link Pennsylvania anthracite coal supplies to the Hudson valley and New York City.

The best known feature of the upper river is the picturesque Delaware Water Gap located near Stroudsburg, Pennsylvania. Long a destination for tourists and travelers, this site is now a National Recreational Area. The river retained its channel even as the Kittatinny Mountains rose across its path, resulting in a precipitous gorge 1,600 feet (484 meters) deep. Hiking trails, lookouts, river activities, and the inevitable Lovers Leap early attracted visitors from New York City and Philadelphia, especially once cheap rail connections were established. The Delaware, Lackawanna & Western Railroad ran round-trip excursions from New York City in 1895 for $3.40, extolling in its advertisements the virtues of clean-burning Pennsylvania coal in the person of the fair Phoebe Snow, whose immaculate dress accented with a corsage of violets remained unsoiled by coal soot. Mark Twain, after making a trip on the DL & W in 1899, sent a telegram to the company: "Left New York on Lackawanna Railroad this A.M. in white duck suit and it's white yet." Baedeker, the early travel-guide series, counted the Delaware Water Gap among the fifteen scenic marvels of the United States.

The lower course of the river encompasses a broad, fertile alluvial plain. This land was originally well timbered, but the forest has long since been cut down. Low ridges separate the valleys of tributary streams. The Neversink joins the main valley at Port Jervis; the Lehigh comes in from the west at Easton, Pennsylvania; and the Schuylkill merges with the Delaware at Philadelphia. The rich soils of the valley benefited not only from the decomposition of the broad leaves of its native deciduous trees but also from the mix of glacial deposits that extended southward to within 60 miles (96 kilometers) of the current location of Trenton.

The head of navigation is at Trenton, a contributing factor in promoting manufacturing in this New Jersey city known for its blue-collar industry. (The steel town of Allentown in the tributary Lehigh valley has a similar hardworking reputation.) Philadelphia is near, but not located precisely on, the Fall Line, the boundary between the crystalline rocks of the Piedmont and the lower sedimentaries of the Coastal Plain. Artisanship and small-scale industry developed in the City of Brotherly Love before the advent of Industrial Revolution methods and machinery. Manufacturing in Philadelphia was actually fostered by the lack of a significant water power potential, as workers and employers had to find alternatives to traditional manufacturing industries focused on milling. The need to break bulk at a transshipment point combined with the proximity of the rich agricultural hinterlands of the Pennsylvania Piedmont fostered Philadelphia's rise to industrial prominence, which was well under way even before the city established itself as an important railroad center in the mid-to-late nineteenth century.

The industrial products and materials issuing from the lower Delaware were the stuff of early American industrial dominance: Robert Fulton's shipyards, John Roebling's wire works, and Baldwin's locomotives. Du Pont established gunpowder mills along the Brandywine in the vicinity of Wilmington, Delaware, near the head of Delaware Bay. Common consumer products made in the lower valley include Campbell's soup, Fels Naphtha soap, Tastykake, Jack Frost sugar, and Stetson hats. Industrial canals lace the region, linking population centers and nearby valleys. In addition to the already-mentioned Hudson Canal, there is the Raritan Canal, now abandoned, linking the Delaware and Raritan Rivers, joining Bordentown, Trenton, and New Brunswick, New Jersey; and the still-used Chesapeake and Delaware Canal joining the river to the north end of Chesapeake Bay.

The region was originally inhabited by the Lenni-Lenapes, an Iroquoian tribe that became known as the Delaware. They were hardly a match for the encroaching Dutch, Swedish, and English settlers, who began arriving soon after the Dutch navigator Henry Hudson explored the mouth of the river in 1609. The river, bay, and state were named after Lord Delaware, or De la Warr, the governor of the Virginia colony in 1609. The granting of land to the Quaker William Penn in 1681 by Charles II (to pay off a debt to Penn's father) led to the establishment of Philadelphia and the founding of the colony of Pennsylvania, meaning "Penn's Woods." This mid-Atlantic colony was pivotal among the thirteen original colonies, serving as a bridge between theocratic New England and the plantation South. George Washington seemed to make a career out of crossing the Delaware during the course of the Revolutionary War, and most Americans, if they have an image of him at all, think of a tall man standing in the bow of an open boat crossing the Delaware, after the German artist Emanuel Leutze's famous, much-reproduced painting. Washington actually crossed the Delaware three times during the American Revolution, but the most famous crossing occurred on Christmas 1776 during the night, when the young, unproven American army ferried 2,400 soldiers, 200 horses, and 18 cannons east across the ice-filled river some 8 miles (13 kilometers) above Trenton, New Jersey, where Hessian mercenaries were celebrating the holiday. The surprise attack was effective: no Americans were killed, and Hessian soldiers, guns, and supplies were captured. Confidence in Washington and the revolutionary army was restored. The Delaware was the scene of the most intensive fighting in the early years of the Revolutionary War. Battles were fought at Trenton, Princeton, Brandywine, Germantown, and Monmouth, while Washington's winter camp at Valley Forge became a patriotic symbol of American tenacity and survival.

The Delaware Basin Commission today includes representatives from four states plus the federal government. Established in 1961, this regional association attempts to regulate and allocate the use of water among the states of the basin. The Delaware Basin Compact did not come about a moment too soon, as a severe drought began in August of 1961, lasting until June of 1965. New York City withdrew so much water at this time from the upper Delaware that the water supplies of downriver towns like Trenton and Philadelphia were threatened.

The salinity of Delaware Bay has on occasion increased to harmful levels, threatening the safety of the estuarine habitat. (Similar problems occur on the Chesapeake Bay when freshwater supplies from its major feeder, the Susquehanna, decline because of drought or overuse.) Although the Delaware Basin Compact forbids open dumping of untreated sewage, pollution problems emerged as early as the late nineteenth century. These problems continue to plague the river, whose indigenous fish population, including shad, perch, herring, and sturgeon, has been severely depleted.

Further Reading: Stutz, Bruce, *Natural Lives, Modern Times: People and Places of the Delaware River,* New York: Crown, 1992; Wildes, Henry E., *The Delaware,* New York: Farrar and Rinehart, 1940 (Rivers of America Series).

DNIEPER

Source: Valdai Hills, in western Russia
Length: 1,420 miles (2,285 kilometers)
Tributaries: Byarezina, Desna, **Pripet**
Outlet: Black Sea

The Dnieper River is the third longest European river, after the Volga and the Danube. Draining the western portions of European Russia, Belarus, and Ukraine, the Dnieper (Russian: Dnepr; Ukrainian: Dnipro) flows in a generally southerly direction to empty into the Black Sea near Kherson, in Ukraine.

The headwaters of this important north-south route across eastern Europe lie west of Moscow near Sychevka in the Smolensk oblast. The river flows at the southern end of the Valdai Hills within a short distance of rivers flowing into the Volga and the Western Dvina. The source region is low and swampy and not especially suitable for intensive cultivation. At the crux of an intricate system of riverine transportation and associated portage routes, the upper river benefited from its access to rivers flowing into the Baltic Sea (for example, the Western Dvina). The river early became the key link in the trade route joining the Baltic and Black Seas.

The river winds south to Dorogoburgh, the head of navigation, before turning west in the direction of the old city of Smolensk, which is an important route junction. Passing into Belarus, the Dnieper flows by Orsha and Mahilev in the eastern part of "White Russia," once part of the enormous

Soviet Union but today a sovereign country. Below Mahilev the high glacial banks of the river drop away, and a broad, flat lowland covered by swamp begins. There the river drains the eastern end of the Pripet Marshes, a forbidding land that has always been an important divide for Slavic populations. The Pripet River enters the Dnieper from the west just inside Ukraine. The confluence is near the site of the largest nuclear disaster in history, the 1986 meltdown of nuclear reactors at Chernobyl. The Pripet drains into a large reservoir upstream from Kiev near where the disaster occurred.

The Dnieper is the major waterway of Ukraine. Just north of Kiev the river is deflected in its course by the scarp of the Volyno-Podolsk Upland (also known as the Dnieper Upland). Running along the foot of this dissected plateau of west-central Ukraine, the Dnieper leaves the vegetation zone of mixed forest—oak, birch, spruce, and pine—and enters the zone of the steppe, a grassland with deep black-earth chernozem soils that have made Ukraine a traditional breadbasket for European Russia. The historic city of Kiev was the first capital of the Slavic Rus, dating back to the ninth century. The city derived its wealth from the control of trade routes along the Dnieper. Kiev was the most important entrepôt city on the route linking the Viking lands of the Baltic to the Byzantine Black Sea ports, including the fabled city of Constantinople located on a key strait joining the Black Sea to the Mediterranean. Kiev stands on the high right bank of the Dnieper, from which it overlooks the level floodplain on the opposite side.

The giant Dniprohes Dam and hydroelectric station at Zaporizhzhya, Ukraine. When first built in 1932, the power plant was the largest in Europe. The dam had to be replaced after it was destroyed by the Germans during World War II. (Novosti)

Below Kiev the river enters a series of rapids. Giant dam projects initiated by the Soviet Union beginning in the 1930s have resulted in the creation of several reservoirs that have inundated the low rapids that previously hindered navigation. Especially noteworthy is the Dniprohes Dam (1932) at Zaporizhzhya, which flooded the rapids stretching from that town upstream to Dnipropetrovs'k. The river's natural cascades have been transformed into a comprehensive suite of dams, locks, and reservoirs. Although the drop in elevation is not great, hydroelectric stations have been installed at the dams. The power provided by the hydroelectric plant at the huge Dniprohes Dam is used in the large steel-making and engineering concentrations in the cities of Dnipropetrovs'k, Zaporizhzhya, and Dniprodzerzhyns'k, and in the manganese-mining towns of Nikopol' and Marhanets'. The Kakhovka Dam is the last dam on the river, lying at the lower end of this chain of hydraulic monuments to the Soviet regime along the lower Dnieper. These dams and impoundments do not have just utilitarian value. They have been a reflection of the patriotic and ideological fervor of the Soviet people and its system. During World War II the government dismantled the power plant before the advancing German army. The dam was rebuilt after the war, not just to provide hydroelectricity but also to allow barges carrying grain, timber, and steel to pass along the stretch of river just above the dam. The level of the water backed up by the dam just covered the outcrop of crystalline rocks that had resulted in the falls, which were a restriction to navigation. Although the river and many of its tributaries are navigable today along most of their length, ice impedes traffic for three or four months in the winter.

The river swings to the southwest below the large industrial cities associated with the dam at Zaporizhzhya. At Kherson the Dnieper begins to break up into distributary channels. The delta is complicated and does not appear as a classic triangular shape. The swampy lower course of the river debouches into a long, narrow estuary known as the Dnieper Liman, an arm of the Black Sea that also receives the waters of the Southern Bug River.

Known in ancient times as the Borysthenes, the Dnieper has long been a boundary, not only between natural regions but also between cultural groups and political formations. In the seventeenth century part of the Dnieper became a frontier between Russia and Poland—in fact, *ukraine* means frontier. With the help of giant reservoirs to improve navigation, and with the aid of canals joining the river and many of its tributaries to other major waterways, the age-old dream of forming a commercial artery linking the Baltic and Black Seas across eastern Europe has become a reality. The irony is that after the demise of the Soviet Union the major commercial and industrial towns of the lower Dnieper lie outside Russia. An admittedly broad frontier zone is now an independent state.

See also Dniester, Don
Further Reading: Reid, Anna, *Borderland: A Journey through the History of Ukraine,* Boulder, Colo.: Westview Press, 1997.

DNIESTER

Source: Carpathian Mountains, western Ukraine
Length: c. 850 miles (1,362 kilometers)
Tributaries: Stryy, Bystrytsya, Seret
Outlet: Black Sea

In the culturally and politically fragmented Shatter Belt of southeast Europe, rivers often are used to define borders. This holds true for the Dniester (Russian: Dnestr; Ukrainian: Dnister; Romanian: Nistrul), a part of which forms the boundary between Moldova and Ukraine.

The river rises on the northern flanks of the central Carpathians near where Poland, Slovakia, and Ukraine meet. It flows generally southeasterly through western Ukraine past Halych, Khotyn, and Mohyliv-Podilskyy. The head of navigation is at Halych. The river flows in a broad trough at the foot of the mountains between rolling foothills to the south and the historic province of Volhynia to the north, a borderland between Russia and Poland. The river meanders frequently in this densely settled rural district known for its flourishing agriculture focused on wheat, sugar beets, maize, and tobacco. The large number of incised meanders are a conspicuous feature of the valley here.

Entering Moldova, the river initially forms the political border between Moldova and Ukraine. Then the river pulls away from the border as it veers off to the south. The easternmost section of Moldova between the Dniester and its border with Ukraine, consisting of so-called Trans-Dniestria, was the scene of conflict between ethnically Russian separatists and the Romance-speaking Moldovans in 1992.

The only city of any size located on the river is Tiraspol, at the southern end of Moldova. Other towns are found on tributary streams. The hills of Moldova overlooking the river are the site of prosperous orchards and vineyards, the dry uplands furnishing excellent soils. Only a sliver of limestone between Ukraine and Romania, Moldova was a prized farming region of the agriculturally deficient Soviet Union. The river carries a large amount of bulk cargo, including grain, vegetables, cattle, and timber. It is navigable most of the year, with ice blocking traffic for about two months each winter.

The lowest reaches of the river have a slow current, with numerous shoals and sandbars. It enters the northwest corner of the Black Sea via a broad estuary known as the Dniester Liman. This estuarine lagoon has a complicated pattern of channels with numerous marshy arms. Its outlet southwest of Odessa is almost sealed off from the Black Sea by a sandy spit.

From 1918 to 1940 the Dniester formed the boundary between the Soviet Union and Romania. During World War II battles were fought along its banks between German and Romanian invaders and Soviet defenders. Subsequently, the Soviet Union recovered Bessarabia, the historical province between the Prut and Dniester Rivers, and incorporated the region as the Moldavian Socialist Republic. Renamed Moldova, the country attained its independence in 1991.

See also Dnieper, Don
Further Reading: Reid, Anna, *Borderland: A Journey through the History of Ukraine,* Boulder, Colo.: Westview Press, 1997.

DON

Source: Southwestern European Russia
Length: c. 1,200 miles (1,931 kilometers)
Tributaries: Voronezh, Khoper, Medveditsa, Donets, Manych
Outlet: Sea of Azov

The fifth-longest river in Europe is also one of the best known in Russian history. The headwaters of the river lie in the northern part of the central Russian upland, near the industrial town of Novomoskovsk. The river flows along the eastern edge of the upland in a generally southeasterly course. It forms a narrow valley in its upper reaches, with a steep right bank rising nearly 300 feet (91 meters) above the river.

The Don drops only slightly in elevation in its upper course. Considered as a whole, the river loses an average of only 1 foot (0.3048 meter) every 2 miles (3.2 kilometers). The resulting slow flow has earned the river the nickname "Quiet Don," as in Sholokhov's famous novel *And Quiet Flows the Don.*

South of Dankov the river valley broadens after it receives the first major left-bank tributary, the Voronezh. An important industrial town of the same name stands on the bank of this tributary just upstream from the confluence. The Don now leaves the transitional forest steppe, a vegetation mosaic of grassland and oak woods, and enters the true steppe. The deep, rich, organic soils of the natural grassland have long since been put under the plow to produce the bounteous cereal harvests for which Ukraine is famous. Bulk cargoes of grain, coal, and timber move freely on the navigable portions of the Don, which is open for most of the year except during the depth of winter. Plowing of the steeper slopes of the Don's right bank has led to widespread gully erosion. Eroded materials have washed into the river, as is evidenced by numerous sandbars and shallows, impeding navigation. Seagoing vessels reach only as far as Rostov-na-Donu (or Rostov on the Don), though shallow-draft boats can go farther upstream. Below Liski, the Don's valley follows the trough between the low hills of Belogorye and the Kalach uplands, outliers of the central uplands. The Don maintains its high right bank in this section of the river. An extensive floodplain on the left bank stretches for miles, with a regular series of alluvial terraces rising from the valley bottom like steps.

This part of the river is the home of the famous Don Cossacks, who lived in elongated "street villages" along the river in the manner of French Canadians along the Saint Lawrence River. Driven from Muscovite Russia during medieval times, the ancestors of the fiercely independent Cossacks settled the Don basin in the early seventeenth century as semi-independent warriors defending the frontier (*ukraine* means "frontier") against Tatars and Turks. Even after coming under the nominal sovereignty of the czar, the Cossacks retained a quasi-independence that permitted them their own administration until 1917. Superb horsemen, they were the elite of the Russian cavalry and had a well-deserved reputation as explorers and defenders of the eastern Siberian lands.

Below the left-bank confluence of the Medveditsa, the Don makes a large bend and flows to the southwest. The "Don Elbow" was the scene, in August 1942, of bitterly fought battles. The German invaders approached the key lower Volga city of Stalingrad (now Volgograd) where the Don and the Volga approach one another to within 40 miles (64 kilometers). A ship canal built in

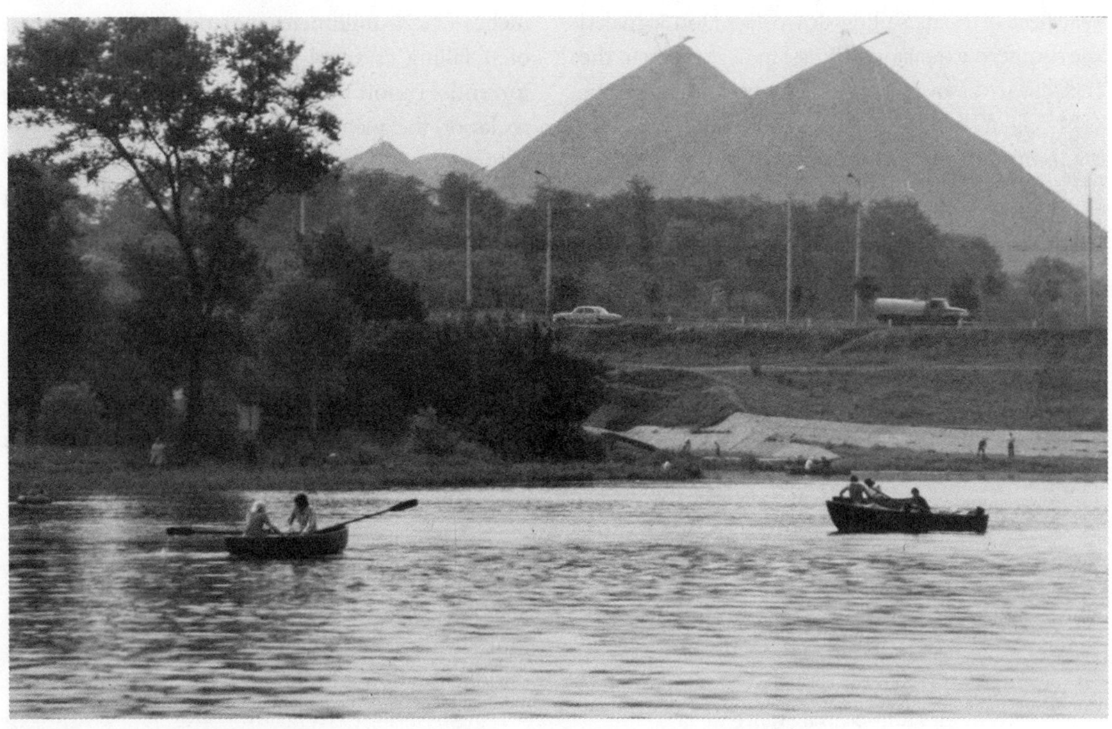

Pleasure boating on the quiet Don River (Novosti)

1950–1952 links the two rivers. The canal scheme, with thirteen locks, a hydroelectric plant, and the enormous Tsimlyansk Reservoir, is a monument to the Soviet system's attempt to control nature for economic purposes and to provide ideological showpieces. Below the dam the broadening river is joined by its longest tributary, the Donets, on the right, and by the Manych on the left. The Donets taps the Donets Basin, or Donbas, a reserve of high-quality coal that has been mined continuously for more than a hundred years. Less than 200 miles (322 kilometers) to the west, on the far side of the Dnieper River, lie the rich iron ore deposits of Kryvyy Rih (Krivoy Rog). Wherever high-quality coal and iron ore are brought together—at the northern end of the Appalachians in Pittsburgh, or in the Donets-Kryvyy Rih region—the result is a concentration of steel-making and heavy industry. The greatest concentration of factories and heavy industry in the former Soviet Union was located in this south Ukrainian region, where manufacturing had its origins in late-nineteenth-century czarist Russia. The chief city and port of Rostov-na-Donu stands on the right bank of the river, 30 miles (48 kilometers) from its mouth. The major port for the river as well as for the Donbas industrial region, Rostov also has important engineering works and other factories. At Rostov a dredged canal takes ships through the Don delta. Although the waters of the Don eventually make their way to the Black Sea, the two are not directly connected but are instead joined by a ramifying series of bays and seas. The Don flows first into the Gulf of Taganrog, at the northeastern corner of the Sea of Azov. The delta is gradually extending itself out into this shallow gulf. The Sea of Azov in turn is connected to the Black Sea by the 25-mile-long (40-kilometer-long) Kerch Strait.

At the southern end of the delta stands the ancient fortress city of Azov, established as a Greek colony in the sixth century B.C. and known as Tanais (the Greek name for the Don). Later this town was taken by the Genoese and then the Turks. Peter the Great's capture of the town in 1696 by a vast fleet of boats sailing down the Don signaled the southern extension of Russian hegemony to the Black Sea. Rostov has now taken over the functions of the old town, whose site has silted up.

In the ancient and medieval world, the Tanais, or Don, was often portrayed on maps as the boundary between Europe and Asia. Today, the Ural Mountains are considered to form the boundary between the only two broadly conjoined continents in the world (North and South America are joined by a narrow land bridge), yet it is not hard to see why the Don, long an important border region, was once accorded this geographical significance.

See also Dnieper, Dniester

DORDOGNE

Source: Le Mont-Dore, in the Massif Central, in south-central France
Length: c. 300 miles (483 kilometers)
Tributaries: Cère, Vézère, Isle
Outlet: **Garonne**, to form Gironde estuary of Bay of Biscay

The Dordogne region of southwestern France encompasses diverse landscapes and traditional regions (*pays*) yet retains a distinctiveness and unity that have persisted since ancient times. Its four principal rivers impart a coherence to this land of great castles, fortified abbeys, and prehistoric caves. Draining the western slopes of the Massif Central, the Dronne, Isle, Vézère, and Dordogne form a branching network of rivers oriented from northeast to southwest. Although the Isle is the most centrally located and accessible of the four, and contains the administrative center Périgueux, the Dordogne is the largest and most important river. All the others are either tributaries or subtributaries of the Dordogne.

The river rises at an elevation of 5,600 feet (1,707 meters) on the northwestern flank of Le Mont-Dore, an ancient volcano in the Auvergne Mountains, the highest part of the Massif Central. With high elevations and a windward location, this part of south-central France receives more than 50 inches (1,270 millimeters) of precipitation, much of it falling as snow during the winter. There is torrential runoff from the impermeable crystalline rocks of the plateau. River levels are low in the summer. At Bort-les-Orgues the ratio between maximum and minimum flow is 780 to 1. As a result, the gorgelike valleys of the upper Dordogne and its tributaries have been modified by a series of dams to regulate flow and to generate hydroelectric power. The power plant near Bort-les-Orgues is the largest project in the Dordogne valley.

Farther downstream, the Dordogne leaves the crystalline rocks of the Massif and flows across the porous and soft limestone first of the Petits Causses, then of Périgord. The latter is the name of the ancient territory and diocese that is roughly coextensive with the Dordogne region. The name goes back to the Roman occupation of Gaul, when four Celtic tribes—the Petrocorii—occupied the middle portion of the Isle River as well as the Dordogne valley. These four tribes were conquered and incorporated into the Roman Empire as one of the three divisions of Aquitania (Land of Many Waters), with Vesunna (Périgueux) as the capital.

Paleolithic cave art is a principal attraction of the valley of Vézère. Paintings and designs in rock shelters (*abris*) and subterranean caverns provide some of the textbook examples of early human creativity and artistic impulse. The natural shelters and caves were hollowed out of the porous limestone by percolation of slightly acid rainwater, which dissolves the calcium carbonate in limestone. So many archaeological sites are found near the village of Les Eyzies that it has been described as the "Capital of Prehistory." Farther up the Vézère, the comparatively recently discovered cave at Lascaux reveals particularly striking colored paintings of bulls and horses, but this site is not open to the public.

The valleys of the middle Dordogne and its tributaries are quite wide, and the rivers meander from side to side between limestone bluffs. In the larger valleys, there is an alternation between narrow, gorgelike valleys and open alluvial basins. The basins are well cultivated and have attracted farmers and villagers since the time when the cave dwellers left their rock shelters. The broad zone

Prehistoric cave painting of a horse in Lascaux Cave in Dordogne Valley, in southwestern France (Art Resource)

between the rivers—the interfluve—possesses scrubby vegetation and was forested and feared by the earliest inhabitants. Tributary valleys provided access between the major rivers, so that the territory developed a coherent and unified culture and economy. Truffle-gathering in stunted oak woods may have given way to commercial strawberry cultivation, but a distinctive polycultural agriculture of a Mediterranean type persists. Viniculture is especially important in the lower valley, where modern commercial fruit and market gardening also concentrate.

The broad floodplain of the lower Dordogne crosses gently undulating sandstone formations as it forms a broad floodplain. In winter, surging waters often inundate a large area, especially near Libourne, where the river receives the waters of the Dronne and Isle from its north bank. Finally, the river joins the Garonne at Bec d'Ambes, 14 miles (23 kilometers) north of Bordeaux, to form the Gironde estuary, an arm of the Bay of Biscay.

Four barons ruled the four rivers of Périgord during the troubled but religiously unified Middle Ages. Peasants retreated to forest clearings during times of tension, returning to the open alluvial basins when peace was restored. The large number of surviving *bastides*—planned, fortified towns—dating from the late thirteenth and early fourteenth centuries testify to the need for security during those difficult times. The hilltop site of Domme, built on a crag overlooking the Dordogne, is a classic example of such a defensive new town.

The Dordogne River was a linguistic boundary in the Middle Ages, representing the northern limit of the Provençal language, known as langue d'oc, spoken in southern France. During the Hundred Years War (1337–1453) the river was the boundary between English control to the south (in Aquitaine) and the French north. When people crossed from the south to the north bank of the river, they were said to "go to France." The hostilities of the Hundred Years War ended in 1453 with the defeat of the English on the banks of the Dordogne at Castillon and their expulsion from southwestern France.

After the French Revolution put an end to the ancien régime, the Constituent Assembly of 1789 created the Dordogne as one of eighty-three *départe-*

ments; its boundaries closely corresponded to those of historic Périgord. The traditional region went into eclipse in the last decades of the nineteenth century, with a declining population and the emigration of the younger, more enterprising population. As elsewhere, the arrival of the railroad spelled doom for once-vigorous river traffic. The catastrophic destruction of its vines by the phylloxera insect pest forced a major adjustment in the region's agricultural economy. World War I left an older and less vigorous population on the land and in the villages. Though still displaying the feisty, independent spirit that is a hallmark of the region, its people had to reconcile themselves to the closure of charcoal ironworks, the destruction of the vine, and the death of so many young in the war. Conditions had declined so far by the 1920s that migration from heavily populated Brittany was subsidized. In the Sarladais region of the Vézère valley a population density of 374 per thousand hectares (97 per square mile) had fallen to 106 per thousand hectares (27 per square mile) by 1926. The backward-looking and nostalgic may not approve, but the future of the economy lies in adjustments in agriculture such as the commercial growing of strawberries, which began after World War II; the growth of tourist industries focused on the scenery of the valley and prehistoric cave paintings; and the attractiveness of quaint villages to vacation home seekers.

See also Loire
Further Reading: Scargill, Ian, *The Dordogne Region of France*, London: David and Charles, 1974; Web site showing the famous Lascaux cave paintings, closed to the public since 1963: http://www.culture.gouv.fr/culture/arcnat/lascaux/en

DOURO

Source: Picos de Urbión, in north-central Spain
Length: 475 miles (765 kilometers)
Tributaries: Tormes, Esla, Pisuerga, Tua
Outlet: Atlantic Ocean

Spain and Portugal share a watercourse that is the third longest on Iberia and forms the largest drainage basin in the peninsula. The river rises on the semiarid plateau of the Spanish Meseta northeast of Madrid in the province of Old Castile. On the basis of Douro (Spanish: Duero) irrigation water, the dry, red lands of Soria, where the headwaters are located, have been converted into a rich farming district.

The river begins as a trickle on the flank of Picos de Urbión at an elevation above 5,000 feet (1,524 meters). Here in the Iberic Mountains, one of many sierras that cut diagonally across and interrupt the tableland, mountain torrents and cascades are gathered into a small, shallow stream that flows past Duruelo de la Sierra and Covaleda at the base of the mountains. The gently rolling red lands of Soria are largely unpeopled today, yet the region is redolent of history, with medieval castles and earlier Roman ruins much in evidence. The upper river is the core of Castilla-León, a prosperous, grain-producing region that is the heart of old Spain. This land was a border between Christian and Moorish forces during much of the Middle Ages. Spain's oldest epic poem, *Cantar de Mío Cid* (*El Cid*), colorfully portrays the fortunes of the chivalrous knight who seemed to fight for both sides for the cause of himself. The real-life champion on whom the account was based, Rodrigo de Vivar, lived from around 1043 to 1099.

The river flows generally westward past the historic towns of Gormaz and Sardón de Duero. The valley broadens by the time it receives the right-bank tributary of the Pisuerga, on whose banks not far from the confluence lies the historic town of Valladolid. Here was the seat of the Castilian court until about 1600, and here were married Isabella of Castile and Ferdinand of Aragon in 1469, an event considered crucial in the formation of the modern Spanish nation; here, too, died in 1506 Cristóbal Colón, better known as Christopher Columbus. Today, Valladolid is the only major industrial city along the Spanish Duero.

Just downstream on the Duero is Tordesillas, where in 1493 Spanish and Portuguese authorities drew up the famous treaty concerning the division of the newly discovered lands opened up by Columbus's voyage the year before. The Tordesillas Line, running north-south through eastern South America, specified that Spain receive all lands west of the line, Portugal all lands to the east. The Protestant powers of northern Europe naturally did not look with sympathy on such an amicable agreement among the major Catholic powers of Europe.

From Miranda the river marks the boundary between Spain and Portugal for about 75 miles (125 kilometers), cutting precipitous gorges in crystalline rocks. This forbidding border, constituting one-seventh of the river's length, is part of the desolate land of Trás-os-Montes, or "Beyond the Mountains," where there are few hamlets and poor communications. Both Spain and Portugal have installed hydroelectric plants in the Douro gorges, and reservoirs and canals are now used for irrigation and flood control. Almost the entire course of the river in Portugal lies within a narrow, gorgelike valley.

Intensively cultivated terraces along the river yield the prized grape used to make port, a fortified dessert wine that has been a carefully guarded and regulated export of Portugal since the late seventeenth century. The name derives from the port city near the river's mouth, Oporto, the second largest city in Portugal after Lisbon. It also is the basis of the country's name. Though Britain receives less port today than France and Belgium, the beginning of port grape cultivation goes back to the time when exports of claret from Bordeaux were restricted and England sought an alternative supply. The Methuen Treaty of 1703 gave Portuguese wines preferential treatment. The historical amity between Portugal and Britain in part stemmed from this trade connection. Originally, port was a heavy table wine, but the practice of adding brandy to arrest fermentation and retain unfermented grape sugar led to its adopting a dessert character. The wine was once transported down the Douro to Oporto in special sailing craft known as *barcos rabelos* ("boats with tails"), designed to withstand the rough waters of the gorges, but trucks and rail carry most of the wine today. The heart of the wine district, the Paiz do Vinho, lies along the middle Douro between Peso da Régua and the Spanish border.

Cavernous warehouses store the prized wine on the south bank of the Douro, opposite Oporto at Vila Nova de Gaia. The outlet of the Douro is so silted that an outport at Leixoes has been constructed to accommodate seagoing vessels unable to reach Oporto. Another commercial outlet is available at the mouth of a small parallel river, the Leca, just north of Oporto. Although fish and other wines are shipped from northern Portugal, port wine produced on the middle Douro and exported from the estuary has an unrivaled economic and historical importance for this Atlantic-facing country.

See also Tagus

Further Reading: Kaplan, Marion, "Iberia's Vintage River," *National Geographic,* October 1984, pp. 460–489.

DRAVA

Source: Eastern Alps, on border between southern Austria and Italy
Length: c. 450 miles (724 kilometers)
Tributaries: Isel, Mura
Outlet: **Danube**

The elongated valleys of the south Austrian Alps parallel the main east-west trend of the mountains. These so-called longitudinal valleys combine with low, easily traversible ridges to facilitate Alpine communications. The Drava (German: Drau) occupies one of these long valleys in the midst of towering mountains. A traditional routeway across the eastern Alps, the Drau, as it is known in Austria, links the Italian South Tyrol with Austria.

The Drava rises on the southern flanks of the Hohe Tauern Alps. It flows as a mountain torrent between the Carnic Alps to the south and the Hohe Tauern to the north, the latter mountains separating the river from another important longitudinal valley to the north, the Salzach. Draining the longest longitudinal valley of the Alps, the Drau flows through the scenic Pustertal toward Lienz, where it is joined by the Isel. It then traverses the northeastern tip of Slovenia. Near Csurgó, Hungary, it is joined by its principal tributary, the Mura.

From there, the river flows southeast for about 90 miles (145 kilometers), forming for most of its length the boundary between Hungary and Croatia. Along the lower reaches of the river, the only part navigable by boats of any size, the Drava runs along the boundary between the rolling hill lands of Trans-Danubia (west of the Danube) to the north and the Croatian hill land to the south, the latter being limestone and crystalline hills interspersed with fertile, loess-covered lowlands. Thus the river forms at once a natural, a cultural, and a political divide. It finally empties into the Danube on the Croatian-Serbian border east of Osijek, Croatia.

See also Danube

DVINA

See Northern Dvina and Western Dvina

E

EARN

Source: Loch Earn, in central Scotland
Length: 46 miles (74 kilometers)
Tributaries: Glen Lednock, Rochill Water
Outlet: **Tay**

Several small streams tumble down from the glacially eroded mountains in western Perthshire to form the source of this scenic Scottish river. Elongated Loch Earn—7 miles (11 kilometers) long and 1 mile (1.6 kilometer) wide—is typical of glacial basins. Though the ribbon lake is near the source of the river, the elevation here is only 317 feet (97 meters) above sea level.

The river flows east and then south in a geologically controlled, faulted landscape. Steep mountain slopes lie in wood and pasture on either side, with only occasional patches of alluvial plains. After passing Comrie and Crieff, small market centers, the river crosses the broad agricultural valley lying between the Highlands and its outlier, the Ochil Hills. For its last 20 miles (32 kilometers), the Earn meanders widely, leaving behind former loops of its path as oxbow lakes. Toward its confluence with the Tay, the river has cut so deeply into its plain that the meanders are entrenched. As a result, the river is bordered by steep bluffs. Where the main Edinburgh-Perth road crosses the river is the functionally named village of Bridge of Earn.

The Earn is celebrated in Scottish ballads as well as in the fiction of Sir Walter Scott. The banks of Loch Earn and its small tributary streams were the scene of the bloody fighting between the Highland clans of the Campbells and the MacGregors, who contended for supremacy in the lawless days of yore. Above the loch in the Braes of Balquhidder, Scott's famous bandit Rob Roy was surprised and imprisoned by the duke of Montrose, before making good his escape.

See also Tay

EBRO

Source: Cantabrian Mountains, in northern Spain
Length: 575 miles (908 kilometers)
Tributaries: Ega, Aragón, Huerva, Gállego, Guadalope, Segre
Outlet: Mediterranean Sea

The Ebro is the only major river in Spain that flows into the Mediterranean. It is the second-longest Spanish river after the Tagus, and the longest river flowing entirely in Spain. In the landmass constituting Spain and Portugal, the Ebro forms the second largest drainage unit. Known in ancient times as the *Iberus,* or the *Hiberus,* the river gave its name to the peninsula.

The Ebro rises on the southern flanks of the Cantabrian Mountains, a western extension of the Pyrenees. The headwaters lie in the province of Santander only 40 miles (64 kilometers) from the Bay of Biscay. The upper course is situated in a geologically trenched basin underlain by sedimentary rocks. The upper river flows at the southern end of the historic province of Navarre. Forming a corridor between the Pyrenees to the north and the Iberian Mountains to the south, the river follows a generally southeasterly course all the way to the Mediterranean. The valley is bordered by extensive alluvial flats and terraces, while tributaries dissect the nearby uplands into a series of flat-topped plateaus and rolling hills. Much of the basin is covered with poor pasture and evergreen scrub, as the region is one of the driest in Spain, cut off from maritime breezes by the rugged coastal mountains of Catalonia to the east.

Because of the scarcity of water and paucity of streams, Aragon's aridity is legendary, at least apart from irrigation oases. A proverb holds that its people could more easily mix their mortar with wine than with water. Like all Mediterranean streams, the Ebro has numerous shoals and is subject to wide variations in discharge. Between the dry month of August and the wet month of January, there is a ratio of 1:45 in the volume of water in the channel. Flooding in the late winter and spring brings large amounts of sand and gravel down the steep tributary streams. Such alluvium spreads out near the junction of tributaries and the main river, clogging the channels and reducing navigation. Though not important for navigation, the Ebro system provides about half of Spain's hydroelectric power and is a valuable source of irrigation.

At the source of the river the Ebro's valley is narrow and steep-sided. From Haro to Tudela the valley broadens to form the basin of the Rioja Alta, where vines are widely grown. Between Tudela and Zaragoza the valley widens again to form an intensively cultivated *huerta* (garden), where two or more crops are grown each year. Since Roman times—*Zaragoza* is a corruption of "Caesar Augustus"—aqueducts have carried irrigation water from the Ebro to wheat fields and orchards along its banks. Zaragoza is the capital of Aragon, the historic kingdom whose union with Castile in the fifteenth century led to the formation of the Spanish nation-state. A Roman town was built on a Celtic site because of its strategic location. Zaragoza commanded this crossing site as well as the junction of the Gállego tributary from the north and the Huerva from the south. Once the Moors were driven out in the early twelfth century, Zaragoza became the prosperous capital of Aragon. After the marriage of Ferdinand of Aragon to Isabella and the removal of the capital to Castile, the queen's domain, the importance of this ancient city began to decline.

The green areas of cultivation produce grapes, wheat, fruit, olives, and vegetables, standing in sharp contrast to the brown lands farther downstream beyond the reach of the major canal. This so-called Imperial Canal had originally been built for navigation, but that function was superseded by the railroad, and the Ebro's waters became used increasingly for irrigation. Farther downstream at the junction of the major left-bank tributary, the Segre, stands the town of Lerida and another fertile irrigated basin.

Not far below Lerida the Ebro cuts through the coastal ranges of the Catalan Mountains. This stretch of the river winds through scenic gorges and romantic defiles that have been carved from the native limestone. The river breaks out abruptly onto the coastal plain near Tortosa (Roman: Dertosa). Like many other places along the Ebro, Tortosa was long fought over between the Moors and Christians during the Middle Ages. The grim old castle overlooking the river reminds us of the long sieges and ding-dong battles fought to control this key position where the hill lands open out onto the plains. This stretch of the Ebro was the site of important battles between Loyalists and General Francisco Franco during the Spanish Civil War (1936–1939). In an offensive in late 1938, Franco's forces defeated the Loyalists, splitting Catalonia from the rest of the Republican territory and thus deciding the outcome of the war.

Below Tortosa the river branches into a wide delta about 80 miles (129 kilometers) south of Barcelona. The river has built up an extensive lowland of salt marshes and sandbars, since the body of water into which the river flows is relatively free of currents and tides that would sweep the sediments out to sea. The delta is covered with many canals and ponds, by which navigation is effected. Though reputed to have once been navigated as far upstream as Logroño, seagoing vessels today proceed only to Tortosa, about 20 miles (32 kilometers) inland. The extensive canals of the delta have been tapped for rice growing. Two major mouths flow out to sea, enclosing the sandy island of Buda. At the northern mouth stands the lighthouse of Cape Tortosa, seen from afar at sea and from the lowland.

Further Reading: Sanchez-Arcilla, Agustin, Jose A. Jimenez, and Herminia I. Valdemoro, "The Ebro Delta: Morphodynamics and Vulnerability," *Journal of Coastal Research* 14, no. 3 (1998): 754–772.

ELBE

Source: Krkonose (Riesengebirge), in northwest Czech Republic
Length: 725 miles (1,170 kilometers)
Tributaries: Vltava, Mulde, Saale, Havel
Outlet: North Sea

Although the Rhine is often considered Germany's river of destiny (*Schickalsstrom*), a case could be made that the slow-moving, gray Elbe (pronounced EL-buh) has been a more significant shaper of German settlement and history. The Elbe is not a heroic river, however, but a river of tears. Unsung by poets, the river has been accorded respect by statesmen, kings, dictators, and warriors, who have treated it as a flowing fortress and a key strategic position ever since it marked the farthest advance of the Romans—who named it Albis—in 9 B.C.

Germany's second longest river doesn't actually begin in Germany. It rises in the Riesengebirge, or Krkonos Mountains, in the northwest Czech Republic. Traversing the Bohemian headwaters, the river goes by the name of Labe. The source lies on a rock-strewn meadow at an elevation of 4,000 feet (1,219 meters) below windswept Hohes Rad. The river is soon joined by a minor tributary, the Weisswasser, at the resort of Spindleruv Mlýn (Spindlermühle). As it approaches the plains, the river passes baroque castles that remind us of the time when rulers of this kingdom dreamed of making the river a trade artery uniting Prague and Hamburg. Karlštejn Castle in Bohemia, and Tangermünde on the lower Elbe halfway between Magdeburg and Hamburg, were the work of Charles IV, king of Bohemia, who planned to regulate the river, make dams, establish river ports, all as part of a scheme to link the Hanseatic cities of the north with the southern hinterlands. This grand scheme was forgotten with Charles's death in 1378. The strategic importance of the Bohemian lands drained by the upper Elbe has never been overlooked, however. Bohemia was once a key region in the delicate geopolitical balance of central Europe. It was like a hinge that swings both ways, and its possession by a major power opened the way for imperial aggrandizement and expansion. The river plains of the upper Elbe were fought over in the Seven Years War (1756–1763) between Austria and Prussia. Frederick the Great of Prussia was defeated decisively during this war at the old town of Kolin, located on the river. A century later the Prussians had their revenge when in 1866 they defeated the Austrians at Königgrätz, also near the river.

At Melník the river is joined by its most famous tributary, the Vltava (Moldau), which is the national river of Bohemia. The Vltava is immortalized by the tone poem of the same name, which functions as a movement in the Czech classic "Má Vlast" ("My Country"). Twenty miles (32 kilometers) below Melník the river is joined by another tributary, the Ohre (Eger). The golden landscape of orchards and vineyards is soon interrupted. The river crosses the Porta Bohemica at Velky Cernosek, passing into the Mittelgebirge, a series of uplands in central Germany and its borderlands. The section of the river between Leitmeritz and Dresden, with its fantastically sculpted sandstone bluffs, has been compared to the Rhine between Bingen and Bonn. A group of romantic painters and writers visited its scenic vistas in the nineteenth century, in much the same way as a similar group toured the gorges along the middle course of its more famous western cousin.

The river passes the ancient town of Dresden, the capital of Saxony. Though located in central Germany, this major city was part of the German Democratic Republic (East Germany) during the Cold War. Most of the Altstadt (or Old City), with its baroque churches and palaces, was destroyed in February 1945 by a sustained fire-bombing raid in

U.S. Soldier carrying a child over a bombed bridge on the Elbe River, Tangemune, May 1, 1945 (Keystone/Archive Photos)

which hundreds of tons of phosphorus bombs were dropped by Allied forces. With clues provided by Renaissance and Baroque portraits of the city, however, landmarks could be reconstructed accurately. Described by the German humanist Johann Gottfried Herder as the German Florence (Dresdeners refer to their city as Elbflorenz), the town has recovered its traditional vitality as the dark cloak of Nazism and communism has been lifted.

The river passes Wittenberg, the cradle of the Reformation, where Luther received the crucial inspiration of justification by faith; nailed his ninety-five theses to the castle door; and burned the papal bull of excommunication. Halfway between Dresden and Hamburg is Magdeburg, an old fortress town and once the eastern limit of Germanic colonization. Here on the northern plains an intricate system of canals and lakes links towns and rivers. The canal network along the lower Elbe includes links eastward to Berlin; westward to Hanover via the Mittelland Canal; and to the Ruhr and Rhine via the Dortmund-Ems Canal. With Prague to the south and Hamburg to the north, this is a large and impressive trade area long coveted by businessmen. The Cold War disrupted the east-west system. The Elbe was connected through the Saale and Havel Rivers and a network of lakes and canals to the Baltic and the Oder. As late as 1938 most of the traffic that reached Hamburg was waterborne.

From Magdeburg to Hamburg the river crosses extensive plains and is bordered by marshes, most of which have been drained. This contributes to flood problems, since overflow lands are no longer able to absorb surplus water. The two banks of the river here are a study in contrast. The left bank, facing the Rhine, is flat and monotonous, while the right bank, facing east, comprises depressions bordered by dry wooded ridges (*Prussia* means "land of spruce"). This is a land of eternal strife, where the river has been crossed and recrossed, battled over, and besieged by conquerors and defenders alike throughout history. In the Middle Ages, Germans pushed Slavic peoples eastward across the river, but the Slavs resisted. The long swing of Germanic expansion to the east might be considered to have reached its limit and to have receded with the decisive defeat of Germany in the two world wars of the twentieth century.

The Cold War in the latter half of the century disrupted the Elbe as a trade artery, reducing the amount of waterborne goods received by its cities but increasing the geopolitical importance of the river. South of Lübeck and east of Hamburg, a section of the river was bordered by electrified barbed-wire fence, constituting a portion of the notorious Iron Curtain. Earlier, on the afternoon of April 26, 1945, World War II in Europe had come to an end when advance elements of the 69th Division of the U.S. First Army met a spearhead of the 58th Guards Division of the Ukrainian First Army on the partially destroyed Elbe bridge near Torgau.

Some 60 miles (97 kilometers) from the mouth of the river lies the large seaport and former Hanseatic League town of Hamburg. Referred to as a German Venice, the city is located where a tributary, the Alster, joins the Elbe in the midst of the lovely lakes of Binnen-Alster and Aussen-Alster. The lowest part of the Elbe below Hamburg is divided by some islands into several branches that reunite 5 miles (8 kilometers) before reaching the river's outlet. This stretch of the river constitutes a wide estuary where fresh and salt water meet, at whose head is the outport of Cuxhaven.

ESSEQUIBO

Source: Guiana Highlands
Length: c. 600 miles (970 kilometers)
Tributaries: Rupununi, Potaro, Mazaruni, Cuyuni
Outlet: Atlantic Ocean

The term "Three Guianas" once referred to the three small European colonies in northern South America whose population composition was decidedly non-Latin. Two of these attained independence during the phase of nation-making that followed World War II. British Guiana became Guyana; Dutch Guiana transformed itself into Suriname. The easternmost territory, French Guiana, remains to this day (2001) an overseas department of France. The inhospitable environment of the Guianas—at least for Europeans—comprises a narrow, swampy coastal strip backed by the rugged and isolated mountains of the Guiana Highlands.

More than half of the area of the westernmost country, Guyana, is drained by the Essequibo, its longest river. The river rises on the northern flanks of the Serra Acqraí, on the border with Brazil. From its headwaters to its outlet on the Atlantic the river follows a generally northerly course. The delta is of an estuarine type, with the river emptying into an inlet of the sea 20 miles (32 kilometers) wide that contains many islands. The opening of the estuary to the sea is about 13 miles (21 kilometers) west-northwest of the capital, Georgetown.

The upper course of the Essequibo is broken by many falls and rapids. Like other rivers of the Guianas, the Essequibo tumbles off the steeply pitched crystalline uplands of the Guiana Highlands onto the level Coastal Plain. Far up a left-bank tributary of the middle river, the Potaro, is one of the largest waterfalls in the world, Kaieteur Falls. Located near the place where Brazil, Guyana, and Venezuela come together, the spectacular falls has been produced by the differential erosion of bedrock resulting in a particularly steep gradient. The tabular sandstone formation of Mt. Roraima at an elevation of 8,635 feet (2,632 meters)—the highest point in the Guiana Highlands—looms above the lower crystalline uplands. The Potaro River plunges 741 feet (226 meters) over the Kaieteur Falls; compare Niagara's 167-foot (51-meter) drop at the American Falls.

The chief town of the Essequibo is Bartica, at the head of navigation for anything larger than a small boat or canoe. The major tributaries of the lower river, the Mazaruni and Cuyuni, both join the river here. A parallel watercourse, just to the east, is the Demerara, a shorter but commercially more important river, since Georgetown is located at its mouth. For purposes of bulk transport, a railroad has been constructed from Rockstone on the Essequibo to Wismar on the Demerara, in order to circumvent the rapids. Large quantities of stone, timber, gold, and diamonds are transported on the river and its tributaries. Guyana's economy epitomizes the dependence of Third World countries on the production of primary commodities. The plantation coast yields rice and sugar, while the species-rich rain forest of the uplands (there are occasional patches of dry savanna) is exploited for tropical hardwoods.

EUPHRATES

Source: East-central Turkey
Length: c. 1,700 miles (2,470 kilometers)
Tributaries: Belikh, Khabur
Outlet: **Shatt al Arab**

The two great rivers of southwest Asia, the Tigris and the Euphrates, rise in close proximity on the rugged Anatolian Plateau in present-day Turkey. The Euphrates (Turkish: Firat; Arabic: Al Furat) is formed by the junction of the Kara (Sarasu) and the Murat Rivers in east-central Turkey. Flowing generally southward through Turkey, the river turns to the southeast across Syria and Iraq. The river joins the Tigris in southeast Iraq, the two together forming the Shatt al Arab before flowing into the Persian (Arabian) Gulf.

The upper river flows rapidly through precipitous gorges along deep, narrow valleys. With the completion of the Ataturk Dam in 1990, Turkey began a series of hydraulic installations along the Tigris and Euphrates that, if finished according to plan, will result in twenty-two dams in southeast Turkey along the upper course of the two rivers and their tributaries. The downstream countries of Syria and Iraq were predictably concerned that Turkish withdrawal of water would reduce the potential for irrigation in their countries—not that Syria hadn't already dammed the Euphrates for its own uses. In Syria the middle Euphrates traverses the low Jazira plateau, and the river is used extensively for irrigating cultivated land along its banks. With Soviet aid the giant Euphrates Dam was constructed at Tabqa, in north Syria, 90 miles (145 kilometers) east-southeast of Aleppo as the main unit in a general barrage scheme. These dams are not meant just to provide irrigation water, as large amounts of hydroelectric power contribute to the development of both agriculture and industry in the region. Below the Euphrates Dam the river receives its only major tributaries, the Belikh and Khabur Rivers, and begins to flow across the forbidding Syrian Desert and the plains of Iraq. Along its lower course the river loses velocity and becomes a sluggish stream, characterized by shifting channels and extensive marshlands. Its waters have been applied to wheat and barley fields in the broad alluvial plains of southern Iraq since time immemorial. Above the confluence with the Tigris at Qurnah, Iraq, the river divides into many channels, forming a marshland and Lake Hammar. The conjoined rivers of the Shatt al Arab divide into two main arms: the western arm flows into a narrow inlet of the Persian Gulf, while the other effluent passes the port of Khorramshahr, Iran, where it receives the canalized waters of the Karun River; it then passes the major oil center of Abadan, Iran, before reaching the gulf.

The Shatt al Arab forms the border between Iran and Iraq. It is not a line, but a broad and changing deltaic region. It is also young, in a geomorphic sense. The Tigris and Euphrates once flowed separately into the gulf, and the Shatt al Arab has been built up as a result of the accumulation of sediment over the last 10,000 years. The protracted military conflict of the Iran-Iraq War (1980–1988) centered on this border area and its associated petroleum resources. The war ended in a stalemate with no important territorial gains, despite a large loss of life on both sides caused by the bombing of the nations' capitals. Within two years of the conclusion of the war, Iraq's leader, Saddam Hussein, had invaded and annexed oil-rich Kuwait at the head of the gulf, which led to the Persian Gulf War (January–February 1991).

The Tigris and the Euphrates Rivers run paral-

Fifteenth-century map of the Middle East, with south shown at the top of the map. The Euphrates and the Tigris Rivers can be seen at the lower left, flowing toward the Persian Gulf. On the right side of the map are the Red Sea and the Nile River (top) and the Mediterranean Sea (bottom). (Archivo Icono graphico S.A./CORBIS)

lel to one another over their long lower courses in Iraq and are never more than about 100 miles (161 kilometers) apart. The lowlands between the rivers receive periodic renewal of their soils from the layers of silt laid down during flooding. The Land Between the Rivers, or Mesopotamia, was the focus of ancient civilizations as early as 5000 B.C., and the rise and fall of legendary kingdoms such as Sumeria, Babylonia, and Assyria depended on the relationship between these civilizations and the rivers that surrounded them. The destructive powers of flooding rivers had to be kept to a minimum, while useful waterworks for irrigation and drainage needed to be kept in good working order.

The Euphrates was an important boundary in ancient times. For centuries it delimited the eastern extent of Roman rule. There are four references to the river in the Hebrew Bible (the Christian's Old Testament): Genesis 15:18; Deuteronomy 1:7 and 11:24; and Joshua 1:4. Abraham's ancestors settled in the southern Mesopotamian land of Sumer between about 5300 and 3500 B.C. A non-Semitic people, the Sumerians invented the system of inscribing moist clay tablets with a wooden stylus. The resulting cuneiform, or wedge-shaped, script was passed on to later cultures inhabiting Mesopotamia, including the Babylonians and Assyrians.

Historical and archaeological sites abound in

this cultural hearth. It might be said that archaeology as an excavational art began with the attempt to unlock the mystery of the numerous flat-topped but steeply sloped mounds of Mesopotamia. The rediscovery of old civilizations that were already ancient to the ancients—some were older than Egypt—and the deciphering of the peculiar cuneiform script came suddenly in the middle decades of the nineteenth century. Initial excavations at Kuyunjik (Ninevah) and Kahlu (Nimrud) in the 1840s focused on the buried towns along the Tigris River north of Baghdad. The meaning of the cuneiform script, which had at first been considered merely decorative, was revealed independently at this time, but the discovery of a library of tablets at one of the sites furthered the translation of the lost language. The excavation of Babylonia on the Euphrates, 55 miles (88 kilometers) south of Baghdad, revealed the temple-tower of the Ziggurat (from the Assyrio-Babylonian word *ziqquratu,* meaning "pinnacle" or "mountaintop"), believed to be the biblical Tower of Babel. This staged pyramid with its terraces and processional steps was at the center of the sacred district of the city and served to connect the people to the heavenly deity via the intercession of the priests of the tower. Ancient Babylonia also was home to the Hanging Gardens, one of the Seven Wonders of the Ancient (Western) World, a series of terraces supported by arches and served by ever-flowing aqueducts. An intricate system of canals and drainageways laced the surrounding district. The present-day state of cultivation of the lower Euphrates lags far behind that of ancient times, as a result of the silting of the canals and the increased salinity of the soils.

In the 1920s the pioneering archaeologist Leonard Wooley unearthed an even earlier cultural stratum than Babylonia in his work in southern Mesopotamia; this was at Ur of Chaldea, as it is called in Genesis. Located along the lower reaches of the Euphrates near its junction with the Tigris, Ur was near the head of the gulf at a time when the two great rivers flowed separately into the sea. The excavations revealed that cuneiform writing, ziggurat towers, metal-working, and inlaying were all cultural innovations of the Sumerians, who lived along the lower Euphrates in the cities of Ur, Erech, Lagash, and Nippur. A town like Ur, which lay near the mouth of the river, must have served as a port, just as Basra on the Shatt al Arab does today. It is believed that the predecessors of the Sumerians may have come from the east over the sea. Ancient Dilmum has been suggested as one possible place of origin, tentatively identified as the sweet water island of Bahrain. On the other hand, the Sumerian language bears similarity to ancient Turkish or Turanian, so it is possible that the original ancestors came from the north, displacing earlier cultures of the region much as the Aryans did in India. The theory that the Sumerians arrived from the forested Iranian Plateau, or from Asiatic mountains farther east, is supported by the discovery that Sumerian buildings were constructed according to principles of a wood architecture that would not be appropriate in the lightly wooded lowlands of Mesopotamia.

See also Shatt al Arab, Tigris

Further Reading: Roux, Georges, *Ancient Iraq,* London: Allen and Unwin, 1964 (Penguin, 3d ed., 1992).

F

FORTH

Source: South-central Scotland
Length: 116 miles (187 kilometers)
Tributaries: Teith, Allan
Outlet: North Sea

Near Aberfoyle in the central region of Scotland two headstreams join to form the River Forth. These two branches, Ducray Water and the Avondhu, drain the northern slope of Ben Lomond at an elevation of 3,192 feet (973 meters), the dominating peak on the east side of Loch Lomond. After running for a dozen miles or so, the headstreams, which have dropped to an elevation of 80 feet (24 meters), converge. The resulting river meanders past the historic city of Stirling—scene of important medieval battles between the English and the Scots—on its way to Alloa. Stirling Castle stands high on a hill above the Forth, overlooking the famous battlefields of Stirling Bridge (1297) and Bannockburn (1314), where the English were routed by the likes of William Wallace and Robert Bruce and the Scots had their moment in the sun. The looping course of the lower river between Aberfoyle and Alloa is rich carse land (see Glossary), giving rise to the saying that "a crook o' the Forth is worth an earldom o' the north."

At Alloa the river reaches the estuarine Firth of Forth, a broad indentation of the east coast. Scottish firths are similar to Norwegian fjords, since both are caused by the drowning of river mouths subsequent to the melting of Pleistocene icesheets and rising sea levels. The Firth of Forth extends about 55 miles (89 kilometers) from Alloa to its eastern outlet on the North Sea. The entrance to the firth is covered by the Isle of May, while just inside the firth are the colorfully named islands of Inchkeith and Inchcolm. The port of Grangemouth is at the eastern end of the Forth and Clyde Canal, linking the Firth of Forth with the River Clyde. On the southern shore of the firth is Leith, which functions as Edinburgh's port, to which it is joined as a result of recent urban growth.

The firth reaches widths of up to 19 miles (31 kilometers), but a peninsula on the northern shore reduces the distance to little more than a mile (1.6 kilometers) at Queensferry, the traditional crossing-point. The Scots are brilliant at nothing if not engineering and bridge-building. The Forth Railway Bridge, the world's first cantilever bridge, was completed in 1889. The Scottish phrase equivalent to the Americans' "washing the windows on the Empire State Building"—meaning a never-ending task—is "painting the Forth Bridge." Carrying road traffic, the modern Forth Road Bridge (completed in 1964) is one of the longest suspension bridges in Europe.

Not far from Edinburgh—the capital and long-time royal residence—the river and the firth have played an important role in Scottish history. Hostile fleets have converged on the firth since the dawn of history, and it is no mere geographical coincidence that the firth has long been used as an anchorage by the Royal Navy. Bridging points and fortified sites along the river were fought over during the Middle Ages between the puissant English and the recalcitrant Scots. The Firth of Forth was the scene of the first air engagement over Britain in World War II.

See also Clyde
Further Reading: Hendrie, William F., *Discovering the River Forth,* Edinburgh: J. Donald Publishers, 1996.

FRASER

Source: Northern Rocky Mountains, in south-central British Columbia
Length: c. 850 miles (1,368 kilometers)
Tributaries: Nechako, Quesnel, Chilcotin, Thompson, Lillooet
Outlet: Strait of Georgia

Canada's northern cordillera presents a striking example of a fault block mountain. Towering, slab-like peaks rise imposingly above the western edge of the plains along the Alberta–British Columbia border. The major river of Canada's Rocky Mountains rises at Yellowhead Pass, at an elevation of 3,717 feet (1,133 meters), in the sharply uplifted Front Range. Its source is not too far from that of the other major drainage of the region, the Columbia, to which it was once perhaps connected. On the west side of the uplifted mountains lies the Rocky Mountain Trench, almost as impressive a geographic feature as the mountains themselves. The trench is a fault line stretching about 1,000 miles (1,600 kilometers) from Flathead Lake in Montana to the Liard River in Canada. This broad structural basin follows the general north-south trend of the mountains and is occupied in turn by Flathead Lake and the Kootenay, Columbia, Fraser, Parsnip, and Finlay Rivers.

The Fraser's upper course veers to the northwest within the Trench, following a path that is at right angles to the direction it eventually takes to reach the sea. The river makes a sharp turn near Prince George around the northern end of the Cariboo Mountains. Now the river flows south for most of its remaining course, turning west in its lower reaches before emptying into the Strait of Georgia opposite Vancouver Island.

The lower river possesses shoals and bars, and as a result the major entrepôt is located away from the river mouth, not an atypical pattern in the siting of port cities in deltaic areas. Burrard Inlet, the harbor of the present city of Vancouver, is only a few miles north of the mouth of the Fraser River. Under British imperial control (which lasted until 1871), the chief city of British Columbia was Victoria, at the southern end of Vancouver Island. With the beginning of a logging boom in the late nineteenth century, Vancouver benefited from its railhead position to become the main city of the province and the only large city on Canada's west coast. The port of New Westminster along the lower Fraser near its mouth was a transshipment point between ocean and river steamers in the early period, but Vancouver soon eclipsed this settlement when the railroad replaced the steamer. Vancouver is today the third largest city of Canada. Much of its growth has occured since the end of World War II. Recently, Vancouver has taken advantage of the growth of the Pacific Rim economy, with Japan replacing Britain as Canada's second trading partner, behind the United States.

The river was first visited by Sir Alexander Mackenzie, the Canadian explorer, who followed its upper course on his 1793 transcontinental expedition to the Pacific Ocean. The river received its name from the Canadian fur trader and explorer Simon Fraser, who was the first to follow the river all the way to its mouth (1808). It was Fraser who first encountered the major problem of the river: the lack of navigability at its lower end. As he descended the river, he must have been dismayed when it plunged into a long, winding steep-sided gorge. Stretching downstream 55 miles (89 kilometers) from the river's confluence with the Thompson at Lytton as far as Yale, the Fraser River Canyon makes for good scenery but is hardly suitable for the passage of a fur brigade. It must have puzzled Fraser, since the upper river flowing in the Rocky Mountain Trench is a placid, smooth stream, the difficult stretches being farther downstream; that reverses the usual pattern of downstream smoothing of the longitudinal profile (see Glossary). The explanation of this anomaly is that the canyon is a result of the river's breaching the Coast Mountains—just as, farther south in the United States, the Columbia cuts across the Cascades at the Dalles. The turbulent river roars through the canyon, tearing at its sides and plunging over bedrock steps. At Hell's Gate, landslides narrowed the river to a width of only 120 feet (37 meters), and the water's velocity and erosive power are consequently increased.

The discovery of gold in 1857 along the lower Fraser just below Yale, and later its discovery along the upper Fraser (the Cariboo), led to a series of gold rushes not dissimilar from those at midcentury in California, though with fewer migrants and with a less feverish intensity. American individualism was muted, though not entirely eliminated, within a framework of British imperial rule. A peripheral fur-trading area and a British colony was transformed, in the process, into a new province of a new country. The rugged Cariboo Road through the Fraser Canyon clung precipitously to the side of the gorge or tunneled through the rock. Crude wagon roads eventually gave way to roads and rail lines. The valley today is followed by two railroads and the Trans-Canada Highway. The influence of the early mining period in British Columbia is echoed by a historical geographer of the region, who noted: "Even today in British Columbia there is both a retrospective Britishness and something of the heady exuberance of a gold rush."

Once it was discovered that the Fraser had the unfortunate characteristic of not flowing into the Columbia or crossing into U.S. territory, the region was launched on its long-term dependence upon producing primary commodities for distant markets. Just as fur trading led to gold-mining, so mining gave rise to a "sawdust empire" based on the harvesting of fast-growing softwoods, particularly cedars and Douglas fir. To Burrard Inlet's natural advantage of deep water was added the steady grade of its site at the waterfront. Until short logging roads were built late in the nineteenth century, logging stayed close to tidewater. Larger logs were skidded on smaller logs down a continuous slope to the beach (the origin of skid row). Vancouver prospered on the basis of railroads, logging, and processing of primary products until, in more recent times, it could take advantage of newer service and technological industries.

The river contains the chief spawning grounds in North America for the Pacific salmon. The salmon fishery along with logging took up some of the slack that came with the waning of the rushes. An indication of the importance that British Columbia attaches to the salmon's spawning grounds is that hydroelectric plants have not been built along the Fraser.

The Fraser delta is the most important agricultural district in British Columbia. Dairying, along with subsidiary poultry, fruit, and vegetable production, concentrates on the lower Fraser. This agricultural region can be considered a northern extension of the Willamette valley and Puget Sound farming areas of the American Northwest. Temperate fruits such as apples are grown in the protected lee of the Coast Mountains on the terraced slopes of the middle Fraser. Since the delta also contains the largest concentration of people in western Canada, a demand for agricultural products is near at hand.

See also Columbia

Further Reading: Harris, R. Cole, *The Resettlement of British Columbia: Essays on Colonialism and Geographical Change,* Vancouver: University of British Columbia Press, 1997 (the quotation is, however, from an earlier work, *Canada before Confederation,* New York: Oxford University Press, 1974); Hutchinson, Bruce, *The Fraser,* Toronto: Clarke Irwin, 1950 (Rivers of America Series).

G

GAMBIA

Source: Fouta Djallon Mountains, in Guinea
Length: c. 700 miles (1,127 kilometers)
Tributaries: Koulountbu, Nieri Ko
Outlet: Atlantic Ocean

At the peak of British influence during Queen Victoria's reign, when one-fourth of the land area on the world map was colored imperial pink, one of the most curious splotches of color must have been the tiny west African colony of The Gambia. Today the smallest country in Africa, it comprises a narrow strip of alluvial land on both sides of the Gambia River extending 200 miles (320 kilometers) above its mouth. The narrow enclave is surrounded by French-speaking Senegal. At no point is this territorial strip more than 30 miles (48 kilometers) wide. The Gambia (the name of the country is always preceded by the capitalized definite article) includes Saint Mary's Island near the mouth of the river, the site of Banjul, the capital.

The Gambia River rises in northwest Guinea on the northern slope of the Fouta Djallon. It flows northwest past Mount Tangé, elevation 5,043 feet (1,537 meters), through Senegal near Kedougou, before turning west, bisecting The Gambia and emptying into the Atlantic Ocean at Banjul. The river is navigable its entire length in The Gambia and is the major transport artery of the country. A sandbar at the mouth of the river is not a major obstacle to navigation, even at low tide. Along the coast are sand beaches, which have recently attracted increasing number of tourists. The upper stretches of the river provide access to interior sections of Senegal and Guinea as well as, via connecting routes, the upper Niger.

The river was first discovered by Portuguese navigators crawling down the west coast of Africa in the mid-fifteenth century. In 1588 the English gained trading rights to the small Malinke and Wolof ethnic states, tributary to the empire of Mali. In 1664 English slavers established the first settlement, Fort James, on a small island upstream from the mouth. The British explorer Mungo Park traveled up the river in 1795 as far as the trading station of Pisania (now Karantaba), before venturing east into unexplored territory, reaching the Niger River at the town of Ségou. He returned a decade later with a second expedition, which traveled down the Niger from Ségou to its mouth. In 1816 Britain purchased Saint Mary's Island from a local chief and founded Banjul (called Bathurst until 1973) as a base against the slave trade.

The colony was alternately governed independently or as part of Sierra Leone until late in the nineteenth century. Soon after its boundaries were defined in 1889, under the pressure of French incursion, the interior of the colony was declared a British protectorate (1894). Independence came in the wave of nation-making that followed World War II. The country attained self-government in 1963 and full independence in 1965.

The fertile alluvial soils of the Gambia River are cultivated with a variety of food crops for subsistence, including rice, cassava, millet, sorghum, and maize. Cattle are raised, and fishing is an important occupation, providing a vital part of the diet. The chief export crop is peanuts. Dependence on a single cash crop subject to price fluctuation is risky here, as elsewhere in Africa. Tourist dollars have augmented exchange earnings, but economic diversification of the alluvial lowlands of The Gambia needs to be advanced.

See also Niger, Sénégal

GANGA

See Ganges

GANGES

Source: Kumaun Highlands, in the Himalayan Mountains
Length: c. 1,560 miles (2,511 kilometers)
Tributaries: Ramganga, Gumti, Jumna, Ghaghara, Son, Gandak, Kosi, Mahananda
Outlet: Bay of Bengal

The most sacred river of Hindu India offers at once a source of refreshment, irrigation, and blessing for the dense population concentrated in its valley. Rising in the mountainous northern part of Uttar Pradesh, the Ganges, or Ganga, drains a broad alluvial lowland in northern and eastern India occupying a historically strategic passageway and settlement zone between the Himalayas to the north and the Thar Desert to the south and west. After passing into Bangladesh, the river joins the Brahmaputra (known in Bangladesh after its junction with the Tista as the Jamuna), the combined waters of two of the world's great rivers making their way to the sea through the world's largest delta.

The Ganges proper forms at the junction of two headstreams at the sacred town of Devaprayag. River sources and confluences are revered by Hindus, so this town, marking the beginning of *Ganga Ma* ("Mother Ganges"), is the first of many pilgrimage destinations found along the river. The lesser headstream, the Bhagirathi, is identified as the true source of the river, as it issues from an ice cave in the Gangotri glacier at 10,300 feet (3,139 meters). The larger headstream, the Alaknanda, lies off to the east near the lofty peak of Nanda Devi, not far from the Tibetan border.

The Ganges cuts through Himalayan foothills before emerging from the mountains at the gorge-mouth city of Hardwar, another pilgrimage site. Hardwar is also the location of the headworks of the Upper Ganges Canal, which links the great river to the Yamuna to the south, providing irrigation water for the tongue of land lying between these two rivers. This interfluvial tract of land is known as the Doab. Elsewhere in India, especially in the Punjab, a doab (Hindi: "two waters") refers to an alluvial strip between two rivers, but the two rivers have to be specified. If one speaks of *the* Doab, it is understood that the reference is to the Ganges-Yamuna interfluve.

Once the river leaves the gorges it passes across an extensive alluvial fan built up over the centuries by sediments sluiced out of the mountains and deposited in predictable fashion, from coarse to fine, away from the gorge mouth, and away from the levees of present or former channels. In cross-section this surface is conical, giving only slight slopes—but important ones in such an extensive plain. The present river's flood plain is narrow and only slightly incised into the fan surface.

At first larger towns stand back from the river. As the river passes the capitals of former princely states, Farrukhabad and Kanauj, major settlements appear on its banks. The large industrial city of Kanpur, scene of a massacre during the Indian Mutiny of 1857, lies farther downstream yet within the upper section of the river. At Allahabad the Ganges merges with its major right-bank tributary, the Yamuna. Despite Allahabad's name, the place was sacred long before Mohammad. Each year a multitude of pilgrims gathers on the river flats between the converging streams for the *Magh Mela,* or religious fair, and every twelfth year pilgrims numbering in the millions converge here to celebrate the much greater *Kumbh Mela.*

Below Allahabad the river follows a generally eastward direction. It makes many meanders and winds around the northeastern shoulder of the

Hindu woman bathing in the Ganges River in Allahabad on January 9, 2001, the first day of the Kumbh Mela, a religious festival held every twelve years (Associated Press)

peninsular block, skirting the Rajmahal Hills before swinging southeastwards across the delta. The valley contains all the features associated with an extensive floodplain: meanders, oxbow lakes, levees (which are lined with villages), and soil textures grading from sandy at the elevated spillbanks to clayey bottoms. Between Allahabad and the great southerly bend lies one of the most densely populated and intensively cultivated rural districts in the world. Wheat gives way to rice as the agricultural staple in this heartland of the Gangetic plain. The overwhelmingly Hindu population remains close to the mother river, not just as a source of drinking water and the revivifying silts resulting from its floods but also because of its spiritual potential. To die along the Ganges, especially at one of its sacred cities, is to ensure that the soul trapped in the coarse shell of the body will be released from the unending cycle of birth, death, and rebirth, and that *mukti,* or union with God, will be attained.

A colorful sacred literature embracing the ancient Vedas, the epic poem *Ramayana,* and the work known as the *Bhagavad Gita* endow the Hindu world with a pantheon of gods and goddesses, including Ganga, who is incorporated as the holiest river. The story of the goddess Ganga is not just a myth to the Hindu people, for it is part of a sacred tradition that dictates their attitude to the revered river. According to the story, the god Brahma sent Ganga down from heaven to wash away the sins of the sons of King Sagar, all of whose souls had been cursed and sent wandering because of their arrogance. Ganga was caught in the snowy Himalayan peaks of Shiva's hair, and only managed to escape many years later through the ice cavern near Gangotri. She then rushed to the sea and in passing redeemed the souls of the 60,000 sons of Sagar.

We need to understand the holy city of Varanasi (Benaras), washed by the Ganges, in such a context. Like Mecca for the Muslim, a visit to Benaras is a devoutly wished for consummation for a devout Hindu. Moreover, Gautama Buddha preached his famous Deer Park sermon on the path to enlightenment at nearby Sarnath. The focus of those who gather here in large numbers is the waterfront, along the ghats, or steps, where both bathing and burning rituals take place. The burning of corpses and the scattering of the ashes of loved ones may be viewed by some Westerners with repugnance, but as part of Hindu traditional belief and practice it is no more crude or cruel than subterranean burial. The red-draped corpse is given a final dip in the river, anointed with ghee (clarified butter), and placed on a pyre scented with sandalwood and camphor. The eldest son of the deceased lights the pyre, cudgeling the skull to release the soul. Later the family returns to scatter the ashes in the Ganges. Bodies are not sent out Viking-style on flaming boats, but the remains of small children are cast into the middle of the river rather than being burned. Hundreds of temples and hostels cluster on the north bank of the Ganges where the winding river has cut a steep bank.

The river flows on past market and administrative centers that were once important river ports. The capital of Bihar, Patna, soon appears. This city was the capital of the ancient kingdom of Magadha, which exploited its strategic position on the Ganges. The powerful Mauryan dynasty in the third century B.C. and the later Gupta dynasty in the fourth century A.D. used Magadha as a base.

The delta of the Ganges begins approximately 200 miles (322 kilometers) from the sea. The lower course of the river passes into Bangladesh (formerly East Bengal) and joins the Brahmaputra to form the Padma, the main channel to the sea. The Ganges-Brahmaputra delta is unlike most other deltas in that it has separate names for many of its distributary channels. The delta is large, complex, and heavily populated.

The two main rivers of the delta flowing together as the Padma are joined just south of Dakha by the smaller Meghna, which drains from the northeast. These three combined rivers, now called the Meghna, constitute the primary distributary of the delta. In fact, the Meghna forms the eastern limit of the 200-mile-wide (322-kilometer-wide) deltaic plain. The most active section of the delta, it debouches into the Bay of Bengal through the traditionally described "Four Mouths of the Ganges." The western limit of the delta is the Hooghly River, a continuation of the Bhagirathi River (also the name of one of the Ganges's headstreams). Though the Hooghly has a broad mouth, it drains the so-called moribund delta, meaning the section receiving only a small share of water and sediment compared with the active, eastern section. The capital of the British Raj, Calcutta, was located at the head of navigation for oceangoing vessels at one time, but low flows and silting have reduced the city's importance as a port. The 1947 Partition of Bengal separated the city from its market and its sources of supply and further emphasized its eccentric location with respect to India. Behind the mud banks and tidal channels of the seaward edge of the delta lies the extensive Sunderbans forest, the largest mangrove forest on earth, half of whose area has been lost since the eighteenth century. Because a large part of the Sunderbans consists of tidal channels, saltwater intrusion and the retreat of shoreline threaten this natural area.

At the mouth of the Hooghly River, some 80 miles (129 kilometers) south of Calcutta, lies one last island, a last pilgrimage site, and a bathing ghat. Hindus view Sagar Island as the meeting-place of the Ganges and the sea. It was here that King Sagar sought advice from the sage Kapila about how to redeem the souls of his sons. The pilgrim rests here and contemplates the work of Mother Ganga.

See also Hooghly, Yamuna
Further Reading: Newby, Eric, *Slowly down the Ganges: An Enthralling and Hilarious Voyage down India's Sacred River,* New York: Viking Penguin, 1966; Putnam, John J., "The Ganges, River of Faith," *National Geographic,* October 1971, pp. 445–483.

GARONNE

Source: Central Pyrenees
Length: 402 miles (647 kilometers)
Tributaries: Neste, Salat, Ariège, Tarn, Lot
Outlet: Gironde estuary, Bay of Biscay

Mountain crests are often chosen to delineate political boundaries. A problem with the use of such a natural frontier is that mountains never provide a continuous, unbroken line over a long distance. Rivers cut across the main ridge line. The result is that drainages may begin on the other side of the frontier, which is the case with the Garonne, cutting across the Pyrenees Mountains along the border between France and Spain. The major waterway of French Aquitaine, the Garonne begins in the Spanish Val d'Aran, an east-west valley in the central Pyrenees. The Val d'Aran might be considered recompense for the Spanish Segre, which begins in French territory.

The scenic source region has long been a focus of transhumance, with flocks of sheep from both France and Spain being led each summer to high mountain pastures. The small district resembles the nearby Pyrenean principality of Andorra, except that it has not attained its political independence. The Garonne exits Spain and the Val d'Aran through the Pont du Roi gorge, a result of the scouring out of a moraine dam by the river's erosive force.

Before passing into the limestone country below and to the north, the river veers off to the northeast. It crosses marble and slate basins and forms a valley whose narrow terraces and shoulders—the work of glaciers—permit cultivators and town sites to be squeezed along its edges. Sun aspect (that is, north-south alignment) often determines land use patterns. At Montrejeau the river is joined by its most westerly affluent, the Neste d'Aure, whose upper course lies in a series of glacially carved cirques separated from the headwaters of the theatrically situated Gave de Pau (which includes the tourist destination of Lourdes). After passing a series of small towns, the Garonne leaves the limestone hill country and becomes a river of the plains. Trenching a wide floodplain into ancient alluvium, it soon reaches Toulouse, where it swings around to the southwest.

Toulouse is the natural collection point for this part of France, for both water and people. Once the capital of the traditional region, or *pays,* of Languedoc, it is still the *chef-lieu* of the department of the Haute Garonne. The town straddles the strategic gateway between the Massif Central and the Pyrenees, permitting passageway between Bordeaux and the Mediterranean. Road and rail routes converge here from the Carcassonne gate, Bordeaux, and the Pyrenean valleys and passes.

Below Toulouse is the middle river. The valley occupies a broad but shallow trench bounded by low limestone bluffs. Many of the classic features of floodplains are evident: the meandering river, extensive marshlands known as *palus,* and terraces standing above the level of the riverbottoms. The well-drained terraces are the most obvious land suitable for cultivation, and they are typically covered with vineyards. The marshlands have often been drained for market gardening or as rich meadows. Several small towns border the river but stand well back from its banks because of the threat of flooding. These towns command the long bridges required to span the channel.

The vine becomes increasingly important as one passes downriver. Viticulture is practiced everywhere: on hill slopes, terraces, and valley bottoms. The French have long recovered from the devastation of the phylloxera (1875–1885) in this famous wine-producing region, whose vintage wines take the name of the principal trading center. The city of Bordeaux stands on the left or west bank of the river, 12 miles (19 kilometers) above its confluence with the Dordogne. The town is at the head of navigation for oceangoing vessels and is at the lowest bridging-point. Though limited today by the river's shifting and shallow channel, and the long passageway of the Gironde, Bordeaux is the fourth largest city of France. Its early growth stemmed from its trade connections with England, dating from the 300-year period when the duchy of Aquitaine and the kingdom of England were under the same ruler. Here French wine is traded for British iron and machinery, Spanish cork and olive oil, Caribbean sugar, and African groundnuts (peanuts). Twelve miles (19 kilometers) below Bordeaux the Garonne is joined by the Dordogne, the major drainage of the western Massif Central. The combined rivers from the point of confluence are known as the Gironde, a broad estuary extending in a northwest direction for 45 miles (72 kilometers). The two rivers join at a beaky tip of land, Bec d'Ambès. The tongue of land between the two rivers, known as Entre-deux-Mers, is all under the vine, as is the Médoc peninsula, lying between the Gironde and the sea. Because of Bordeaux's distance from the sea, a number of outports lie along the left bank of the river where the channel swings to this side. These are about halfway between the city and the estuary's outlet. A lateral canal was built in the nineteenth century (1838–1856) paralleling the Garonne; it is linked at Toulouse to the Canal du Midi, thus allowing passage from Bordeaux to Narbonne and the Mediterranean ports. The amount of time it takes for a boat to traverse this route makes it more likely to be contemplated today by holiday makers than by businessmen.

The Garonne is a poor navigational river, with frequent flooding and shifting channels. There are so many tributaries from both the Pyrenees and the Massif contributing their loads of sand and sediment that it is constantly adjusting its banks and bottom. Only the lower course of the river is navigable—hence the need for the lateral canal. Heavy winter precipitation and early summer snowmelt rush rapidly downstream and cause extensive flooding. Despite attempts to regularize the river's flow, destructive floods recur. Particularly severe flooding occurred in 1770, 1856, and 1930. The Romans were clever to name the region Aquitaine, meaning "Land of Many Waters."

See also Loire

GILA

Source: Southwestern New Mexico
Length: 630 miles (1,014 kilometers)
Tributaries: San Francisco, San Pedro, Santa Cruz, **Salt**, Agua Fria
Outlet: **Colorado**

From its source in the lofty Mogollon Mountains in western New Mexico to its outlet on the Colorado at Yuma, Arizona, the Gila (a Spanish version of the Yuman word *hah-quah-sa-eel*, meaning "running water which is salty") drains some of the most arid land in the United States. Numerous small streams running off the 10,000-foot (3,048-meter) eminences of the Mogollon are gathered to form the main course of the Gila. In its upper reaches the river rushes down steep slopes covered with ponderosa pine and Douglas fir, species more characteristic of northern climates. A part of this headwaters forest has been designated a wilderness area within the Gila National Forest. Practically speaking, this means that the area is not served by roads and is not subject to resource exploitation. The Gila reserve was the first protected wilderness area in the nation, set aside in 1924, four decades before the Wilderness Act mandated a wild land policy. It was the recommendation of a young Forest Service employee then working in the Southwest, Aldo Leopold, that the undeveloped portions of the Gila National Forest remain in their natural state. Leopold went on to a successful career in game management and ecology, and, along with Henry David Thoreau and John Muir, he is today considered to be one of the founders of American environmental thought. Four well-preserved cliff-dwellings are situated in a canyon on the upper Gila in New Mexico, and these, along with the ruins farther downstream at Casa Grande, south of Phoenix, are administered as national monuments.

Leaving the mountains of New Mexico, the Gila drops rapidly in altitude and gives way to grasslands. Where once pronghorn antelope and mule deer browsed, cattle are today corralled and fed with fodder from irrigated tracts. The river crosses southern Arizona, draining one of the most specialized biomes in North America. As a northern extension of the Mexican Sonoran and Chihuahua Deserts, this region displays a rare assemblage of flora and fauna. Cacti predominate among the plants, there being several hundred species—everything from small, ground-hugging forms conspicuous only when they flower to giant saguaro cacti that loom against the sky. Unusual animal life includes giant centipedes, deadly scorpions and tarantulas, and the slow-moving but poisonous lizard named after the river: the Gila monster.

Just inside Arizona, the Gila's major tributary, the San Francisco, joins the river from the northeast. The Gila alternates between several southwesterly and northwesterly stretches as it crosses southeastern Arizona. About midway along this route between the New Mexico border and Phoenix, the Coolidge Dam impounds the waters of San Carlos Lake. Completed in 1928, the reservoir provides irrigation water for the Casa Grande valley along the lower Salt River, 15 miles (24 kilometers) above its confluence with the Gila. The city of Phoenix, one of the fastest-growing areas in the United States (as of 1999), is located on the lower Salt River just above its junction with the Gila. A Hohokam village dating from A.D. 1150–1400 existed here whose irrigation and settlement network was one of the most extensive in the prehistoric New World.

Farther up the Salt, the Roosevelt reservoir primarily provides irrigation water. Another large dam and reservoir, Painted Rock, southwest of Phoenix, lies below the confluence of the Gila and the Salt. The various schemes and projects that exploit the river—for irrigation, hydroelectric generation, and flood control—have so depleted it that below the dams the river's bed is virtually dry all the way to the river's confluence with the Colorado at Yuma.

The Gila basin once lay on the northern periphery of the Spanish New World empire. Apaches and Navajos, linguistic relatives, pushed into the region sometime after 1200, encountering other tribes such as the Pueblos, Zunis, and Pimas, who were related to the lost cultures of what the Navajos called the "Ancient Ones"—the Anasazi. The Spanish were slow to make a mark on the area, on account of distance, isolation, and the fierceness of the fighting Apaches. These retarding factors continued to slow progress and European inroads even as American settlement swept across the semiarid Great Plains in the decades after the Civil War. The Treaty of Guadaloupe Hidalgo at the end of the Mexican War (1846–1848) ceded to the United States all of the Southwest north of the Gila River. When it was discovered that all major trails and a possible railroad route lay farther south, Congress in 1853 approved the Gadsden Purchase, the acquisition of an elongated, east-west strip of land south of the Gila. The addition of this piece of real estate along the Mexican border completed the continental boundaries of the United States.

See also Colorado
Further Reading: Corle, Edwin, *The Gila,* New York: Rinehart and Company, 1951 (Rivers of America Series); McNamee, Gregory, *The Life and Death of an American River,* Albuquerque: University of New Mexico Press, 1998.

GLOMMA

Source: Eastern Norway
Length: 365 miles (590 kilometers)
Tributaries: Atna, Rena, Vorma
Outlet: Skagerrak

The Glomma, or Glåma, River is not only the longest in Norway; it is also one of the longest rivers in Scandinavia. It occupies the easternmost valley of a fan of nearly parallel valleys that debouch into the Skagerrak, the body of water between southern Norway and Denmark's Jutland Peninsula (Jylland).

The course of the south-flowing river is mostly determined by the scouring effects of the Pleistocene icesheet acting in combination with geological structure. The Glomma rises on the elevated plateau, or fjell (related to the English *fell*), near the Swedish border. Over its entire length the river never strays far from the political frontier. The slow-moving glacier gouged out small lakes that dot the headwaters region. Gathering its waters from numerous small lakes and streams, the river flows through the old copper-mining center of Røros. It flows to the southwest for a short stretch then turns southeast, becoming the Österdal (Eastern valley) proper. Though the Glomma is a long and important north-south valley, it lies east of the major population centers and rural districts including the Gudbrandsdal, the adjacent valley to the west. Much of the long southerly course of the upper river is uneventful. Although most of the river is not navigable, it is used to float timber. Logs are traditionally marked with the owners' signs and then removed from the river at various places where they are efficiently sorted like letters in a post office. The river is joined on its right by the Atna River, draining the high mountains to the west, famous for the adventures of Henrik Ibsen's legendary Peer Gynt. Farther downstream the sawmill town of Elverum is best known as the site of the last meeting of the Norwegian parliament after it fled Oslo when the Germans invaded the country in April 1940.

The river turns sharply west at Kongsvinger and begins to cross the well-settled districts of south Norway. It soon meets the Vorma, its major tributary, draining the adjacent parallel valley of the Gudbrandsdal and Lake Mjøsa. When the river enters Lake Oyeren, it is only 15 miles (24 kilometers) east of Oslo. The great pulp-mill center of Sarpsborg is 40 miles (64 kilometers) farther south. The town is located at the head of navigation on Sarp Falls. The tumbling energy of the river has been tapped here by a hydroelectric plant that furnishes power for the district. Only eight miles (13 kilometers) farther along, the river enters the sea at Frederikstad, an important port and shipbuilding center that lies only a short distance east of the mouth of the Oslo Fjord.

Further Reading: Millward, Roy, *Scandinavian Lands,* London: Macmillan, 1964.

GREEN

Source: West-central Wyoming
Length: 730 miles (1,175 kilometers)
Tributaries: Yampa, Uinta, White, San Rafael
Outlet: **Colorado**

The source of the Green is Fremont Peak, elevation 13,730 feet (4,185 meters), in the Wind River Range of Wyoming. From this glacially carved eminence three rivers flow in three directions: the Wind River eastward into the Mississippi; the Gros Ventre River to the northwest into the Columbia; and the Green River to the south into the Colorado. The waters of numerous glacial lakes, creeks, and cataracts gather to form the Green.

The largest tributary of the Colorado initially flows southward across the Wyoming Basin before being interrupted by the transverse Uinta Mountains, the only major mountains in the lower forty-eight states that trend east-west. This stretch of the river from Green River City to the Uinta canyons runs past low bluffs and narrow floodplains and is vegetated on either side by sagebrush (*Artemisia*). Along the base of the mountains, the river veers to the east and crosses the northwestern corner of Colorado before turning south and west into the gorges cut into the Uinta range in northeastern Utah.

John Wesley Powell commenced his pioneering descent of the Grand Canyon in May 1869 from Green River City, north of the Uinta Mountains and the canyons. The takeoff point was chosen because the Union Pacific Railroad crossed the Green River here. Powell's expedition employed four boats that had been built in Chicago and transported via rail to Green River City. Powell named the first canyon he entered as the Green began to cut cross the Uintas Flaming Gorge, after the bright vermilion color of the primary rock mass. Next, the roughly 20-mile (32-kilometer) Canyon of Lodore had to be navigated, with its numerous rapids and falls, horseshoe meanders, and sheer cliffs. Powell climbed up the steep slopes of the valley sides whenever he could to get a good prospect of the surrounding terrain and to note the Indian ruins. Just below where the Yampa joins the river from the east, the Green cuts sharply to the north around a long peninsular rock precipice formed by the winding river. A small opening on the east side of the Green, which was, according to Powell, about the size of a farm, was named Echo Park—because the noise of the men, who were exhilarated from being out of the treacherous canyons, was repeated dozens of times.

A classic geological problem concerning rivers in mountainous areas has focused on the Green in its passage across the Uinta Mountains. An influential geologist who went on to become the director of the U.S. Geological Survey, Powell favored the idea of *antecedence:* that is, that the Green's course was maintained even as the Uinta Mountains were uplifted. More recent geological opinion has relied on the idea of *superposition:* that the Green may have cut through layers of fill onto older rocks and become superimposed on them. Based on the age of the rocks and the age and amount of available fill, contemporary geologists believe that the canyon cannot be explained either by uplift alone or by cutting into superimposed fill, so that an explanation that combines antecedence and superposition is now favored. All of this fascinating scenery and evidence is on display at Dinosaur National Monument, set aside as a federally protected area as early as 1915 for its rich quarries of fossils.

South of the Uinta Mountains the river crosses the Uinta Basin, the northernmost section of the Colorado Plateau. The Uinta Basin forms an embayment between the middle and southern Rocky Mountains. The formations—thick layers of sedimentary rocks—rise gently to the south in the direction of the canyonlands of southern Utah, at whose northern end lie several south-facing escarpments. The river crosses Canyonlands National Park (est. 1964) before emptying into the Colorado, upstream from Glen Canyon.

The natural formations of Canyonlands National Park, including entrenched meanders, vertical cliffs, arched alcoves, spires, needles, mesas, and buttes, are shared with other parts of the canyonlands section of the Colorado Plateau, as well as with the Grand Canyon itself. Since many of these formations are the result of the erosive work of water, which is in short supply in such an arid region outside of the main channels of rivers, it is logical to ask how the landscape could be so intricately and beautifully sculpted. The answer appears to lie in a combination of sparse vegetation and soft rock. Water rushes rapidly down bare slopes during storms, funneling into small gullies and washes. This magnifies the erosive power of the sediment-laden water. Flash floods—not rare events in the desert—scour and deepen canyons.

The Colorado River storage project of the U.S. Bureau of Reclamation has extensively developed the Green River basin for purposes of irrigation, mining, and hydroelectric power. The Flaming Gorge Dam on the upper Green north of the Uinta Range backs up water almost all the way to Powell's starting point at Green River City. Environmentalists gained one of their signal victories in 1956 when they stopped the construction of a dam on the Green River in Dinosaur National Monument that would have flooded Echo Park. Not only were the wild canyons of the Green protected, but in addition the new Colorado River storage bill stated that "no dam or reservoir constructed under the authorization of the Act shall be within any National Park or Monument." A coalition of individuals and groups supporting the protection of the environment had been fostered in this battle: the Sierra Club, the Wilderness Society, the western writer Wallace Stegner, the columnist and historian Bernard DeVoto. Fresh from their success in the Echo Park controversy, they went on to another, even bigger victory with the passage of the Wilderness Act in 1964.

See also Colorado

Further Reading: Abbey, Edward, *Desert Solitaire,* New York: McGraw-Hill, 1968; Powell, John Wesley, *The Exploration of the Colorado River and Its Canyons,* New York: Dover, 1961 (orig. pub. 1874).

GUADALQUIVIR

Source: Sierra de Cazorla, southeastern Spain
Length: c. 350 miles (560 kilometers)
Tributaries: Guadiana, Menor, Guadalimar, Jándula, Guardiata, Bembézar, Genil, Viar
Outlet: Gulf of Cádiz, Atlantic Ocean

Sun-baked blue skies, splashing fountains, and olive-skinned women come to mind when one reflects on the historic south-Spanish province of Andalusia (Spanish: Andalucía). The broad, southwest-flowing Guadalquivir, whose name to the Arabs who long occupied the region was *Wadi al-kebir,* or "large river," is, however, also an important part of the picture of Andalusia. In its lower course the river passes the historic town of Córdoba, which was formerly the head of navigation. On account of heavy silting of the lower river, ships can no longer reach this point. Another historic town, Seville, has as a site the lowest bridg-

Ghost town in the Guadalquivir marshlands (Jesse Walker)

ing point on the river, some 50 miles (80 kilometers) from the outlet.

The major river of Andalusia begins far to the east. It drains the flanks of several sierra that seem to surround the tapering eastern end of the Guadalquivir lowlands. Although the major upstream tributaries flow throughout the year, their discharge is far greater in the wet winter months than during the bone-dry summer, at which time the proximity of Africa's dry air masses is felt. In this eastern portion of the watershed, the courses of subtributaries are shown on maps with dashed lines, indicating an intermittent flow. Supplied by rainwater in the winter and the melting snows of the Sierra Nevada in summer, the Guadalquivir maintains a fairly level flow throughout the year, which is important considering the demands made on the river for irrigation and hydroelectric power.

In its middle course the river travels along the southern flank of the elongated, east-west range of the Sierra Morena. The valley in this section is fertile and densely populated, and the river is used extensively for irrigation. Rich alluvial soils yield excellent harvests of olives, grapes, and sugar cane, as well as providing pasture for horses and livestock (bulls for Spain's famous corrida are bred in this region). The upland margins provide mast in the oak woods for the grazing of pigs, and the thick, corky bark of the native cork oak is harvested for bottle stoppers.

The lower course of the river in southwest Spain traverses extensive marshlands (*Las Marismas*). This tidal wetland extends downriver from Coria del Rio (just below Seville) to the river's mouth at Sanlúcar de Barrameda. As in most cases in southern Europe, there is no large town at the river's mouth because of the problems of silting and low flow; however the ancient port of Cádiz, dating from Phoenician times, lies to one side of the Guadalquivir outlet, much as Marseilles is sited with respect to the Rhône in southeastern France. Although some land has been reclaimed for rice cultivation, an intricate mosaic of land and water exists near the mouth of the river: low-lying islands, ponds, oak savannas, pine forests, sand dunes, and seasonally flooded marshes crisscrossed by river channels. The dunes are best represented by the wind-swept Arenas Gordas, or "fat sands," a sort of cork stopper blocking the river's outlet. A few thousand years ago the river emptied into the Atlantic through an open gulf. During the period of the Roman Empire the outlet had begun to back up and was referred to as Lacus Lagustinus. The transformation was completed when this lagoon was filled in with sediments and became a wetland. Today the barrier of Arenas Gordas extends about 45 miles (70 kilometers) along the coast. Portions of all these habitats—dunes, savannas, pine forest, and marsh—have been set aside as Coto Doñana National Park. Comparatively unscathed by civilization, the Marismas is home to deer, lynx, and wild boar. The reserve is especially noted for its bird populations: flamingos, herons, and spoonbills wade in the wetlands, while rare imperial eagles soar overhead. In the winter months, myriad ducks and geese converge on these flooded plains. Not far from where ships were once launched on voyages of exploration and conquest lies one of the largest and best preserved wilderness areas in southern Europe.

Further Reading: Vincent, Mary, and R. A. Stradling, *Cultural Atlas of Spain and Portugal,* New York: Facts on File, 1994.

H

HADHRAMAUT

Source: Southern end of Arabian Peninsula
Length: c. 400 miles (645 kilometers)
Tributaries: Numerous small wadis
Outlet: Gulf of Aden, Arabian Sea

A coastal region of anciently settled hill lands at the southern end of the Arabian Peninsula also gives its name to a fertile valley containing one of the most important wadis in Arabia. Formerly attached to the British protectorate of Aden, the Hadhramaut (also Hadramawt) today forms the eastern part of unified Yemen and refers to both the range of hills paralleling the Gulf of Aden and the Arabian Sea and the most densely settled wadi of the interior.

Yemen as a whole represents the fractured and dislocated southern edge of the Arabian plateau, a landmass that was at one time connected to eastern Africa. Although the entire tableland tilts toward the east, with higher elevations in the west on the Red Sea, the altitude in the Hadhramaut on the southeastern margin averages about 3,500 feet (1,067 meters), with the highest peak at about 8,000 feet (2,438 meters). The Wadi Hadhramaut is an especially conspicuous topographic feature in the southern coastlands. It represents a broad, well-defined valley, running parallel to the coast some 120 miles (193 kilometers) inland and extending for about 200 miles (322 kilometers) before turning sharply toward the southeast, cutting through the coastal ranges before reaching the Indian Ocean near Saihut. The upper and middle courses of the wadi are broad and have excellent soils that have been cultivated since ancient times for dates and grain. Important ancient centers containing extensive ruins are still for the most part occupied at Shibam, Seiyun, and Tarim. The narrow lower course of the wadi is largely uninhabited. Since streams normally broaden downstream as they pick up tributaries (the major tributary of the Wadi Hadhramaut is the Wadi Duan), it has been suggested that the origin of the valley may have been the result of river capture: a small stream worked its way back through the coastal uplands and eventually captured a large stream that ran parallel to the coast across the southern end of the Arabian plateau.

Yemen was the most advanced center of civilization in the Arabian Peninsula in the millennium before Christ. Unlike other cultural hearths in the Mideast, it did not depend on great rivers, since Arabia has no large permanent drainage features. Yemen's ancient inhabitants were able to make skillful use of small dams across the intermittent streams of the wadis to store winter floods in cisterns and to intensively cultivate the floors and walls of the distinctive small valleys. In addition to a flourishing agriculture, Yemen also controlled the incense trade. Its ports traded with Africa, India, China, the Persian Gulf, and the Mediterranean. Biblical and classical references reveal a social structure little changed even today: a literate hereditary elite; trades divided into noble and ignoble; settled agriculturalists; and wandering tribesmen. In the Bible the region is referred to as *Hazarmaveth.* The Arabic and related Hebrew forms of the name seem to derive from the Arabic word *diram,* meaning "burning heat."

Evidence for the early history of the area is scanty, partly because the main centers of the region, Shibam and Tarim, have been continuously occupied and have not changed their locations, leaving behind extensive desert ruins, as in other places in the Mideast. In addition, the southern Arab tribes (*Qahtan*) are considered to have descended from different ancestors than the northern tribes (*Adnan*), and they have always demonstrated an independence at the margins of political control: at first from their Persian overlords who first introduced Islam to the area; later from the Ottoman Turks, who were even further removed from them geographically and culturally; and finally from the British suzerains, who never exerted direct control over Quaiti and Kathiri tribes in the Wadi Hadhramaut as they did over the Arab population of Aden and its immediate hinterland.

Isolated from the remainder of the Mideast by deserts, south Arabia has looked more to the east and to the west than to the north. Its agricultural crops bear a resemblance to the cultigens of tropical and monsoon lands in Africa and India. Drought-adapted millet is the chief cereal, and tree crops such as date palm, sago palm, mango, pawpaw, and banana are also husbanded. Cotton, indigo, and tobacco are additional cash crops. Frankincense obtained from the sap of trees that grow on the damper hill slopes above 3,000 feet (914 meters) comes from the wadi, as well as from the hill lands around Dhofar. In former times caravans laden with frankincense and myrrh plied the old "Incense Route" between production centers in the wadi and the eastern Mediterranean.

Fishing is more important in the eastern part of the Hadhramaut and along the coast, where economic activities focus on the sea. The traditional, small Arab trading vessel, the dhow, is as common in these waters as it is in the Persian Gulf. The Arabs of the south are the Greeks of the Indian Ocean, and many prominent Hadhramaut families earned their fortunes in sea trade, living abroad for a number of years before returning to establish themselves and their families, building multistoried houses with elaborate woodwork and carving that is reminiscent of East Indian models.

Archaeological research and architectural preservation efforts have lagged behind other parts of the Mideast. Shibam has been termed the "New York" of the Hadhramaut, as a dense cluster of mud-built, multistoried houses with contiguous walls forming a defensive barrier has been built out of a rocky spur that projects from the wadi floor. These five- or six-story skyscrapers were built by prosperous traders who returned from amassing fortunes in places like Singapore, Batavia, and East Africa. Today, Shibam presents a labyrinth of twisting streets, some almost tunnels; livestock running loose amid what amount to hidden passageways; white mosques squeezed between the high walls of nearly contiguous houses; and, in the western parts of town, the odd juxtaposition of shops selling modern gadgets such as stereo equipment and VCRs alongside magnificently carved doors and windows. The proximity of such traditional and modern worlds is something one sees all across the Mideast today. Huge cracks are beginning to appear in the old mud-built houses of Shibam, and even the more prosperous middle-class families cannot afford the high rates workers charge to repair the traditional buildings.

Further Reading: Breton, Jean-Francois, "Manhattan in the Hadramaut," *Aramco World Magazine* 37, no. 3 (May–June 1986): 24–27.

HOOGHLY

Source: Confluence of Bhagirathi and Jalangi in northeastern India
Length: c. 160 miles (260 kilometers)
Tributaries: Damodar, Rupnarayan, Kasai
Outlet: Bay of Bengal

The Hooghly (also Hugli) is the western arm of the Ganges. It extends from the confluence of the Bhagirathi branch of India's greatest river with the Jalangi River at Navadwip to the Bay of Bengal. The city of Calcutta is situated at the head of navigation

Steamboats and barges on the busy river Hooghly at Calcutta, in West Bengal, India, 1929 (E. O. Hoope/CORBIS)

for small oceangoing vessels, some 80 miles (130 kilometers) upstream on the east bank of the river. An active port today, Calcutta was the headquarters of the East India Company and the capital of British India from 1773 to 1912. It is the most important commercial center in the heavily industrialized Hoolyside, a quayside concentration of factories and towns extending from Hoogly town (Hooghly-Chinsura), some 18 miles (30 kilometers) north of Calcutta, as far as the sea. Half of the people in the densely populated Indian state of West Bengal live in the numerous cities lining the Hooghly in this district.

The Portuguese were the first Europeans to settle here. A trading post established by the Portuguese in 1537 was of commercial significance in the sixteenth and seventeenth centuries. Later Dutch, Danish, Austrian, and French traders prospered at settlements established along the Hooghly. The British were attracted to the head of navigation as a site for their settlement. Calcutta grew up out of a factory built in 1692, the term then referring to an establishment for merchants and factors to carry on their business in foreign lands. The English influence grew to dominate the region and to eclipse the trade of the other European powers.

The river is still used extensively for shipping, even though it presents a number of problems: shifting sandbars, a large tidal bore, and as much as a 20-foot (6-meter) difference in level between the dry and wet seasons. The fundamental problem of the Hooghly is that it drains an inactive part of the delta. Most of the water and sediment of the Ganges today pass far to the east, down the Padma channel, discharging into the sea in Bangladesh. A project to divert some Ganges water down the

Bhagirathi-Hooghly arm to flush the lower channel and so to keep the port of Calcutta open is an attempt to counter a century-old tendency for the river to shift eastward, leaving behind stagnant rivers and soils deprived of nutrient-enriching silts.

The port of Calcutta would be in trouble even without these changes, however, because of the eccentric location of the city within India. The old seat of government lies at the eastern extremity of India; it is hardly a central place. The 1947 partition that led to the formation of West and East Pakistan (the latter now Bangladesh) removed a large market area from its orbit.

Even India's old Grand Trunk Road (National Highway No. 1) linking the Punjab in the northwest to the Gangetic plain, passing the historic cities of Delhi, Agra, and Varanasi (Benaras), does not quite reach Calcutta. The eastern terminus of the road that Kipling called "the road of Hundustan" is at Haora on the west bank of the Hooghly, just opposite Calcutta.

See also Ganges
Further Reading: Beattie, Malcolm Hamilton, *On the Hooghly,* London: P. Allan, 1935.

HUANG HE (YELLOW)

Source: Kunlun Mountains, in northwest Qinghai Province, China
Length: c. 3,000 miles (4,828 kilometers)
Tributaries: **Wei**, Fen, Wuting
Outlet: Bohai Bay

When the time of the autumn floods arrived, the hundred tributaries poured into the Yellow River. Its onrushing current was so huge that one could not discern an ox or a horse on the opposite side or on the banks of its islets. Thereupon the Earl of the River [the god of the Yellow River] delightedly congratulated himself at having complete and sole possession of all excellences under heaven. Following along with the current, he went east until he reached the North Sea [North China Sea]. There he looked eastward but could not see the water's end, whereupon he crestfallenly gazed across the surface of the sea and said with a sigh towards its Overlord, "There is a proverb which says, 'He who has heard the Way a hundred times believes no one may be compared with himself!' This applied to me. Furthermore, when I first heard those who belittle the learning of Confucius and disparage the righteousness of Po-yi, I did not believe them. But now that I behold your boundlessness, I realize that, had I not come to your gate, I would have been in danger and ridiculed forever by the practitioners of the great method [The Way (Tao)]."

Chuang Chou—355?–275 B.C.—translated by Victor H Mair

The second-longest river in China frequently inundates the vast alluvial plain at its lower or eastern end. The densely populated North China Plain has been built up over the millennia by a periodically shifting channel—some estimate as many as 1,500 changes, with 9 major ones. The region is extremely vulnerable to flooding, especially during the summer high-water period, when "China's Sorrow" (alternatively, the "river of tears") breaks through retaining walls to cause devastating floods. The failure of the southern levee in 1887, for example, led to more than two million deaths from drowning, starvation, and the ensuing epidemics. Yet China has depended for more than three thousand years on the grain surpluses of the Yellow River and its tributaries. The military and political expansion beginning with the Qin Dynasty (221–206 B.C.) required such a rich agricultural region, and the term *zhongyuan,* or "Central Plain," referring to the broad alluvial plain of the lower river, has always carried as much a political as a geographical meaning.

The Huang He (pronounced HUANG-huh) rises far away from its populated lower course. The headwaters lie at approximately 14,000 feet (4,267 meters) elevation on the eastern flanks of the Kunlun Shan. The source has been identified at two lakes: Kyaring Nor and Ngoring Nor. The river makes a hairpin turn around the Anne Machin Mountains, passes nearby Lake Koko Nor, and enters Gansu Province. Flowing in a generally easterly course, the river meanders through gorges and crosses a fertile valley that includes the site of Lanzhou, because of flooding one of only two cities located on the river, the other being Kaifeng. Receiving the Sining from the left and the Tao from

Guardhouse protecting a levee along the Yellow River (Jesse Walker)

the right, the river enters its characteristic bend—the "Great Northern Bend"—around the Ordos Desert. It is now a wide, slow-moving stream separating the northern uplands from the desert and loess lands of the south (the word *loess* is derived from a German word meaning "to loosen"; it was originally applied to a similar soil in the Rhine valley). At the northern end of the great bend lies the heavily populated Ningxia agricultural region, an extended oasis where cereals and fruits are raised. At the northwest corner of the bend the Huang He divides into numerous branches, watering an ancient cultivated area whose irrigation channels have been repaired and are once again in use today.

Turning south, the river passes through the Great Wall and enters the loessial region from which it receives the yellow silt that gives the river its name. After being joined by the Wei and Fen Rivers, its chief tributaries, the Yellow turns east and passes through San-men gorge, the site of a huge dam completed in 1962 that is used for flood control, power generation, and navigation. During the Han Dynasty (206 B.C.–A.D. 220), grain, lumber, and livestock produced on the Loess Plateau supplied the needs of an expanding empire that rivaled in influence contemporaneous Rome. The gently sloping plateau had previously been covered with dense forests and grasslands that held the loosely packed, fertile yellow soil known as loess. Although extensive areas of wind-blown silt are found elsewhere—northern Germany, the Mississippi valley, and elsewhere in north China—the loess deposits of the middle Yellow River located between the Qinling Mountains to the south and the Great Wall to the north are considered the largest continuous such deposit in the world. Lacking stabilizing vegetation, the yellow hills of Shanxi Province are prominent. The highly fertile soil is easily erodible. Steep faces of hills line the watercourses that feed into the Yellow River. Slopes slump into streams, as more and more yellow silt finds its way into the great river. The highly degraded landscape today presents to travelers an endless panorama of gullies, ravines, and barren hills, with only an occasional scattering of trees or clump of grass. During the Ming Dynasty (1368–1644), grass fires were set to prevent the already defeated Mongols from grazing their ponies. In effect, a barren border zone was created without trees or grass, to keep China's enemies at bay and to accomplish what the Great Wall had failed to do. This was not the last time China would use the environment as a weapon of war.

Farther downstream the Yellow meanders over a fertile plain to reach the Gulf of Bohai (formerly the Gulf of Chihli), an arm of the Yellow Sea. Though the river is the source of the fertility of the soil, it also has been an obstacle. The Communists' mandate to conquer nature has been severely challenged by the Yellow. Dikes and retaining walls restrain the river even as continuous siltation in the channel raises the river's bed, in some places as high as 70 feet (21 meters) above the surrounding plains. During the dry winter months the river is slow moving and choked with silt. It occupies only part of its huge bed. In summer, when flow is high, the river is a raging torrent, always at risk of shifting its channel. The Yellow is distinguished from other large rivers of the world by its extremely large sediment load compared with its discharge. At Ligin, located at the apex of the delta, approximately 62 miles (100 kilometers) from the sea, the river's annual discharge is only about 8 percent of that of the Mississippi. Yet its suspended load—silt and clay—is about five times that of the Mississippi. It is estimated that 90 percent of the sediment load is derived from the Loess Plateau of the river's middle course, even though this region encompasses only 40 percent of the basin's area. The largest Holocene delta in the world embraces parts of the provinces of Henan, Hebei, and Shandong, interrupted only by the hill lands of Shandong Peninsula. The mouth of the river has moved over the course of the centuries as much as 500 miles (805 kilometers) to points north and south of the Shandong Peninsula. Major coastal rivers to the north, the Hai and Huai, are actually distributaries of the Yellow.

Yellow River Delta, 1996, satellite imagery (Jesse Walker)

The three most distinct parts of the Yellow River delta are: (1) the modern delta at the southern end of Bohai Bay (1855–present); (2) an abandoned delta south of the Shandong Peninsula (1128–1855); and (3) an ancient delta, in the vicinity of Tianjin, at the northwest end of Bohai Bay (3400 B.C.–A.D. 1128). The Chinese have not been averse to using the power of the river during periods of warfare. The war of 1128 triggered the shifting of the channel south of Shandong Peninsula. During the Chinese-Japanese War beginning in 1938, dikes were breached so that water and sediment could be diverted southward to block the Japanese invasion. More than 20,000 square miles (51,800 square kilometers) were flooded, killing some 900,000 people, and the Yellow River was not returned to its present course until 1947.

Several tendencies in the modern river valley and its delta can be related to human activity and interference. The hydrology of the lower Yellow has changed drastically since 1972, with the result that the river is often so dry that vehicles can cross it without difficulty. In 1997 no flow was recorded at Ligin for 226 days. Low flow concentrates pollution in the channel and salts and alkalis in the estuarine zone. The once mighty river has been converted to an intermittent stream, rather like the lower Colorado in Mexico, but with greater socioeconomic impact. Because of the heavy sediment load, the Yellow has changed its outlet to the sea during the last century about once every ten years. Since 1976 a southward shift to Qingshuigou, abetted by engineering measures, has resulted in erosion of the coastline farther northward. The coast near Tianjin is receding, not as a result of global sea-level rise but from sediment starvation: the result of damming and diversion of upstream water sources.

See also Wei

Further Reading: Ren, Mei-e, and H. Jesse Walker, "Environmental Consequences of Human Activity on the Yellow River and Its Delta, China," *Physical Geography* 19 (1998): 421–432.

HUDSON

Source: Lake Tear of the Clouds on Mt. Marcy in the Adirondack Mountains
Length: 315 miles (507 kilometers)
Tributary: **Mohawk**
Outlet: Upper New York Bay at New York City

The much-storied Hudson River rises in the Adirondack Mountains in an isolated corner of northeastern New York. As late as 1872 geographers considered its source to be Lake Avalanche. In that year its true source was discovered: a tiny, two-acre pond on the southwest slope of Mt. Marcy, the highest peak in New York state. Lake Tear of the Clouds empties into the river's headstreams, fast-flowing Feldspar Creek and Opalescent River. The upper course of the Hudson has many waterfalls and rapids. The turbulent river has long been favored by trout fishermen.

Lumbering was the opening wedge of exploitation in the region. Sawmills sprang up on the Hudson and on its tributary streams, or "kills" as the Dutch called them. A sawmill was built at Glens Falls as early as 1763. In the first half of the nineteenth century Glens Falls literally became a boomtown as lumbermen were attracted to the river for floating large rafts of merchantable timber. The legendary Big Boom at midcentury, a heavily timbered, chained raft of logs that backed up for several miles above the town, finally snapped in the spring of 1859, hurtling half a million logs down the Hudson, some strewn on the banks of the river as far south as Troy.

The head of navigation of the Hudson is at Fort Edward, below which the river has a drastically altered character. Locks and dams have converted this stretch of the river—many would say the least interesting—into a forty-mile (sixty-four kilometer) chain of sluggish lakes all the way from Fort Edward to Troy. Pleasure boats and self-propelled barges use this section of the river to reach the Champlain and New York State Barge Canals, the old Erie Canal. Below Troy the river has long been polluted by open sewers. The effluent from Albany and Rensselaer downriver only adds to the pollution, as does the waste water from the barge canal flushed into the Hudson at Cohoes, just above Albany. This stretch has received the unlovely appellation Albany Pool; next to the lower Hudson flowing past Manhattan, it is the most despoiled part of the river. Pollution of the Albany Pool has been lamented since the early 1900s, but clean-up efforts began only about 1975.

Below Troy the river does not so much flow to the sea as wash back and forth under the influence of the tides. The Hudson is a tidal estuary as far as 150 miles (240 kilometers) from its mouth. The first explorer, Henry Hudson, was deceived by the lack of current in the river's lower course into believing he had reached a passageway to China.

Along the middle Hudson the dominant features of the landscape are the wooded slopes of the Catskills, and the most notable attractions are the great estates on the east bank of the river between Hudson and Hyde Park. Many of the homes in "Millionaire's Row" are still occupied or run by religious orders, but others are kept as

Scene on the Hudson River, with Rip van Winkle. Washington Irving's stories of early Dutch life combined with romantic paintings of the Hudson River School to popularize an important American river. (James Hamilton, 1845, Smithsonian American Art Museum, Washington, D.C.)

historic houses, such as the Roosevelt home at Hyde Park and the nearby Frederick Vanderbilt mansion. An early style of American painting—the Hudson River School—took its inspiration from idealized scenes in the Catskills along the Hudson. Painstaking attention to detail and the demotion of human beings to a minor role are characteristic of this romantic tradition, whose major practitioners were Thomas Cole, Frederick E. Church (whose castle-home, Olana, still looms over the river), and Albert Bierstadt.

South of Newburgh the river abruptly constricts as it crosses the ancient, metamorphosed Hudson Highlands. At the north entrance to the Highlands stands Storm King Mountain, site of a pivotal conservation battle of the 1960s between Con-Edison, the powerful electric utility that proposed a pumped-storage facility for the mountain, and conservation critics who claimed such a project would mar the scenic beauty of the river. Although the struggle dragged on into the 1970s, it ended with the defeat of the project; the effort was considered to be of signal importance in fostering environmental consciousness and creating enduring political institutions. The Palisades Interstate Park and West Point Military Academy are on the west shore in this rugged stretch of the Hudson, which many consider the river's most beautiful region.

Just below Tarrytown the river broadens to form the 3.5-mile-wide (5.6-kilometer-wide) Tappan Zee. A resident of Tarrytown, Washington Irving, did more than anyone else to imbue the Hudson valley with feelings and an animate folk tradition by means of his colorful stories of the early Dutch settlers. His tales of the rail-thin schoolmaster Ichabod Crane and the sleepy Rip Van Winkle have become part of American folklore. Less conspicuous in Irving's literary efforts were the semifeudal patroons, large land holdings that discouraged settlement and impeded economic development. Landlordism, civil unrest, and antitax demonstrations persisted in the valley well into the nineteenth century.

The lower course of the Hudson is a land of contrasts. On the west bank are the towering cliffs of the Palisades, exposed columnar faces of cooled magma known as diabase, which the Indians called *weehawken,* or "rows of trees." If the columns of rock were placed on end, the formation would look like stairs, so the rock is often called trap rock, from the Dutch word *trapp,* meaning "step." The hematite-containing sandstone layers below the diabase with distinctive and striking color have furnished building materials for the innumerable fashionable "brownstone" houses of Manhattan. Early conservation efforts led by industrial titans such as J. P. Morgan and John D. Rockefeller Jr. succeeded in preventing the Palisades from being turned into a pile of rubble by quarrymen, but mining for building materials still goes on. Maxwell Anderson's *High Tor,* produced in 1936, concerns the efforts to acquire High Tor Mountain, the highest point in the Palisades.

At the mouth of the river are the ports of New York and New Jersey. The two states are linked across the Hudson by the George Washington Bridge and the Holland and Lincoln Tunnels, as well as by railroad tubes. During the colonial and early national period, the East River was the primary center of shipping. Not until the mid-nineteenth century, with the construction of larger steamships requiring more turning room, would the larger harbor on the west side of Manhattan come into its own. The building of a new terminal at Jersey City, the dredging of the bar off Sandy Hook, and the inauguration of new lines such as the Cunard service propelled New York and its harbor into the front ranks of world trading cities.

See also Mohawk
Further Reading: Boyle, Robert H., *The Hudson River: A Natural and Unnatural History,* New York: W. W. Norton, 1979; Carmer, Carl, *The Hudson,* New York: Farrar and Rinehart, 1939 (Rivers of America Series); Howat, John K., *The Hudson River and Its Painters,* New York: Viking Press, 1972.

HUGLI

See Hooghly

HUMBER

Source: Northeast England, confluence of **Trent** and Ouse
Length: c. 40 miles (64 kilometers)
Tributary: Hull
Outlet: North Sea

The east coast of England has historically lain open to North Sea raiders and settlers alike. A cursory examination of a map reveals three significant breaks in the eastern coastline, where the sea extends far into the interior: the Thames estuary, the Wash (a deep embayment north of East Anglia), and the Humber estuary. Known anciently as the Abus, the Humber is formed by the confluence of the Ouse and Trent Rivers 8 miles (13 kilometers) east of Goole. Not a long river (there is a river with the same name that is nearly twice as long in Newfoundland, Canada), nor even an entire one (it represents the lower course of two conjoined rivers), the Humber attains significance in the concentration of industry along its banks and in its history of attracting conquerors and colonizers from across the seas.

The elongated estuary is shaped like a funnel, but a stretched-out one. At its eastern entrance the estuary has a width of 8 miles (12.9 kilometers), while at its head, where the Trent and the Ouse come together, the river is only about 1 mile (1.6 kilometers) across. On the north side of the mouth, a peninsula called Spurn Head, topped by a lighthouse, encloses a shallow bay. Although navigation of the Humber is impeded in places by shoals, the river is an important shipping route. Hull, Grimsby, and Goole are important industrial cities on the river's banks, with shipbuilding, iron and steel production, and chemical refining the major manufacturing concerns. Former ports such as Ravenspur have disappeared, victims of the encroachment of the sea. The river is navigable for large vessels as far as Hull (full name Kingston upon Hull), where the river of the same name joins the

Humber from the north. Near Hull the river is spanned by the Humber Bridge, completed in 1981, one of the longest suspension bridges in the world, with a main span of 4,626 feet (1,410 meters).

Although it is a short river, the Humber derives its significance from the large drainage of its two headstreams and the important trade area of the river and its affluents. Most of the scenic rivers of the Yorkshire Dales—the Swale, the Ure, the Nidd, the Wharfe—drain southeast and eventually empty into the Ouse near the Humber estuary. The cathedral city of York (anciently Eboracum) is located at the head of navigation on the Ouse. The Trent River rises farther south in Staffordshire and drains an industrial section of the English Midlands.

The Humber and Trent have been important divisions, albeit not strictly speaking political boundaries, between north and south England since ancient times. Connected to their western counterparts, the Mersey and the Severn, respectively, are the two sections of England along the Humber-Mersey line, or, alternatively, along the Trent-Severn line, time-honored divisions that have been considered significant in delineating as varied phenomena as terrain, ancient settlement, and present voting habits. That this attribution of significance to the Humber is not a recent notion is suggested by the role the river played in the struggle of the Anglo-Saxons against the Danes in the early Middle Ages. The greatest figure of Anglo-Saxon history, Alfred (ruled 871–899), sought to push the Danes farther north, perhaps as far as the Humber. Like the German Charlemagne, the West Saxon leader Alfred urged a revival of intellectual pursuits and was concerned about the erosion of literacy among the Angles:

> But so clean fallen away was learning now in the Angle race, that there were very few on this side Humber who would know how to render their service-book into English, or to read off an epistle out of Latin into English, and I ween there would not be many on the other side of the Humber. So few of them were there that I cannot think of so much as a single one south of Thames when I took to the realm.
> (translation of Alfred the Great referred to in W. E. Lunt, *History of England,* 4th ed., New York: Harper and Row, 1957, p. 46)

Humberside today is an administrative county—not an old shire—comprising most of the former East Riding of Yorkshire and north Lincolnshire.

See also Trent

Further Reading: Wilkinson, Henry Robert, George De Boer, and Adrienne Thunder, *A Cartographic Analysis of the Changing Bed of the Humber, A Report to the Humber Estuary Research Committee,* Hull: Department of Geography, University of Hull, 1973.

HUMBOLDT

Source: Northeast Nevada, near Wells
Length: c. 300 miles (483 kilometers)
Tributaries: North Fork, South Fork, Little Humboldt
Outlet: None

The famous explorer and naturalist Alexander von Humboldt (1769–1859) lent his name to many different places around the world: mountain ranges, towns, counties, an ocean current (the Peru, or Humboldt, Current), and a glacier in Greenland, the largest in the Northern Hemisphere. But only one important river is named after him.

The Humboldt River is formed by the confluence of Mary's and Bishop Creeks, some 15 miles (24 kilometers) west of Wells in northeast Nevada. The river is one of the few perennial streams in Nevada and the longest in the state. Rainfall is very low in the arid Great Basin, and that accounts for the decrease in volume of flow as one goes away from the mountain springs into the desert. The Humboldt is unusual in that not only the volume of its water but also its length varies seasonally.

Along with its tributaries the river drains much of the northern part of the state. Generally flowing toward the southwest, it first receives the North Fork before flowing past Elko. Then it is joined by the South Fork before passing the small towns of Carlin and Battle Mountain. The river veers to the northwest for a short stretch, receiving the Little

Humboldt from the north, then resumes its southwesterly course as it passes the early trading center of Winnemucca, unfortunately better known today for its legalized prostitution. The river continues through Rye Patch Reservoir, passes Lovelock, then enters Humboldt Sink. Not an ocean outlet, the Humboldt Sink is an intermittently dry lakebed or playa. It is some 11 miles (17.7 kilometers) long, with a maximum width of 4 miles (6.4 kilometers). Like the Carson Sink nearby, it is a relic of ancient Lake Lahontan, formed during the Pleistocene period as a large inland lake. The bed of the playa is salty, and even the lower part of the Humboldt is brackish. The characteristic plant of the sink is greasewood, as not even sagebrush will grow here. Intermittent Humboldt Lake occupies a portion of the undrained depression. It is the fate of the Humboldt's water not to reach the sea but to evaporate or to percolate into parched desert soils.

This "turgid, green, barren-banked, and sullen" stream, as the early explorer John C. Frémont described it, forms a vital link of the "California Trail" taken by emigrants from Salt Lake City to central California in the nineteenth century. Frémont named the river after the great German scientist and traveler Alexander von Humboldt. The route furnished necessary water and grass for wagon teams making the difficult crossing of the Great Basin. The first major party to take the route was the Stevens party in 1844. They came from Fort Hall and reached the river, which they followed downstream to the sink. Then the difficult part of the journey began. They had to make the arduous crossing of the Forty Mile Desert to reach the Truckee River, and thence to the site that one day would be the city of Reno, Nevada. Still looming to the west were the peaks of the Sierra Nevada, separating them from their destination. Such a difficult trail served to open the way for the California gold rush of 1849.

Most of the towns of northern Nevada are on the river whose valley is used by the major transportation lines. The east-west routes of the Union Pacific and Southern Pacific Railroads and Interstate Highway 80 (which replaced U.S. Highway 40 in the 1970s) follow the Humboldt valley. In 1936 the Bureau of Reclamation completed a dam near Lovelock, impounding the waters of the Rye Patch Reservoir. Irrigation is used primarily for forage crops—alfalfa, barley, oats, wheat—that are fed to cattle and dairy cows.

Further Reading: Morgan, Dale L., *The Humboldt,* New York: Farrar and Rinehart, 1943 (Rivers of America Series).

I

ILLINOIS

Source: Confluence of Des Plaines and Kankakee Rivers
Length: 273 miles (439 kilometers)
Tributaries: Fox, Vermilion, Mackinaw, Spoon, Sangamon
Outlet: **Mississippi**

The major river of north-central Illinois begins in the northeastern corner of the Prairie State. It flows diagonally across the state, past rich farmland, industrial towns, and once bustling river ports before emptying into the Mississippi about 50 miles (80 kilometers) above St. Louis. With its numerous tributaries, the Illinois drains 25,000 square miles (64,750 square kilometers) and is second only to the Ohio River among westward-flowing tributaries of the Mississippi. A major commercial artery in the nineteenth century before the arrival of railroads, the broad valley of the Illinois is an American heartland. Traces of former transportation systems and echoes of Lincoln constantly remind one of the historical importance of the region.

Some 45 miles (72 kilometers) south of Chicago, the Des Plaines and the Kankakee Rivers join to form the Illinois. It initially runs westward in a deep, narrow, glacially carved valley before bending to the south around La Salle, the traditional head of navigation. When the Illinois–Lake Michigan Canal was constructed in the middle of the nineteenth century (completed in 1848), commercial vessels could go only as far as La Salle, but with the deeper channel dredged in the 1920s, small towns lying upstream from La Salle—Morris, Seneca, Marseilles, and Ottawa—could now be considered river towns. Ottawa, built on both sides of the river near the junction of the Fox River (the Illinois Fox should not be confused with the Wisconsin Fox), was the site of the first Lincoln-Douglas debate in 1858. The upper course of the river between Ottawa and La Salle has rugged sandstone bluffs, the best known of which is Starved Rock, where the explorer La Salle built Fort St. Louis in 1683. The name Starved Rock derives from the legend that a band of Indians died of starvation there while under siege.

After making its large bend to the south, the river broadens and slows. Extensive sloughs and woodlands border the stream. Wildlife once teemed in the valley, attracting the earliest frontiersmen, who combined hunting and farming as a subsistence livelihood. Commercial farmers were slow to settle the interfluves because of their off-putting prairie vegetation, though the duration of such avoidance of the prairies in Illinois has often been exaggerated. The Illinois country was incorporated into the United States in 1783, but since the region was settled from the south and east, rather than the more obvious point of attachment on Lake Michigan, Americans did not begin to arrive in large numbers until the second quarter of the nineteenth century.

Although the Illinois is for most of its course one-quarter of a mile (0.4 kilometer) or less wide, in the first part of its southern journey it reaches a broad basin known as Peoria Lake. Actually a river outreach or widening, this broad and deep pool forms the site of the largest city of the valley—Peoria—which, despite its reputation as a middle-of-the-road town whose modest aspirations need to be met by admen and politicians, is actually the third largest city in Illinois behind Chicago and Rockford. The city is built on terraces along the bordering bluffs. The valley opens up considerably below Peoria, reaching a width of as much as 15 miles (24 kilometers) where the Sangamon joins the river from the south. The lower river and its once flourishing towns now carry the flavor of the South and also Lincoln's early life (Lincoln was born in Kentucky). Havana is located near the junction of Spoon River, the real place that was the setting for the folksy poetic treatment of Edgar Lee Masters's famous *Spoon River Anthology.* Farther downstream the river is divided by the large island called Grand Island. Below that the river is joined by the Sangamon, which winds past New Salem, which counts as part of its history the years that Lincoln spent there during his early manhood. Downstream the river slips even further into myth, as one passes old steamboating towns and grain-shipping ports. Their colorful names evoke nostalgia for a bygone era: Florence, Montezuma, Pearl, Kampsville, Hardin, Grafton. The town of Hardin is really the last town on the river, situated on a ridge of land between it and the Mississippi. Grafton is on the eastern shore of the great river where the Illinois and the "Father of Waters" meet.

The intersection in the Illinois valley of successive waves of transport innovation—steamboating, canals, and railroads—and the settlement patterns they spawned give historical significance to the river. Algonquin-speaking Indian tribes known to the French as the Illinois were less numerous and more nomadic than the powerful Sac and Fox tribes farther north. These Indians were moved rather easily out of the valley. When in 1832 the U.S. government placed them on a reservation in Kansas, there were only slightly more than one hundred of them left. The first white men to see the river were Father Jacques Marquette and Louis Jolliet, who in 1673 traveled upstream from the Mississippi where they had been exploring. Seven years later, Robert Cavelier, sieur de La Salle, descended the river as far as Peoria Lake, where he built Fort Crevecoeur. The fur-trading empire of the upper Mississippi had already begun to decline by the time Americans reached the rich corn lands of the middle and lower Illinois in the early decades of the nineteenth century.

Only a short water link needed to be forged to join the Illinois to Lake Michigan. The completion of the canal in 1848—construction had begun in 1836 but the economic depression of the following year delayed work—aided the growth of Chicago at the expense of the older river city of St. Louis, as the agricultural bounty of the fat prairie soils found its way northward. The makeover of Chicago into a railroad center after midcentury only accentuated a process already begun with the establishment of the Illinois–Lake Michigan Canal. A series of transformations of the Great Lakes–to–Gulf aquatic link began in the late nineteenth century. During the 1890s construction of the Chicago Sanitary and Ship Canal led to the widening and deepening of the canal, as well as the reversal of the course of the Chicago River. Waters that had formerly flowed into Lake Michigan now carried Chicago's noxious water away from the lake, which was the source of the city's drinking water. Between 1919 and 1933 a new channel was developed between Lockport on the Des Plaines and Starved Rock on the Illinois, which included a series of locks and dams to facilitate navigation. That new aquatic highway, still in use today, is known as the Illinois Waterway; with the completion of the St. Lawrence Seaway, it allows oceangoing vessels access to an inland Atlantic-to-Gulf route.

See also Mississippi

Further Reading: Gray, James, *The Illinois,* New York: Farrar and Rinehart, 1940 (Rivers of America Series); Robertson, Robert A., and Rabel J. Burdge, "The Interface between Commercial and Industrial Development and Recreational Use in an Urban River Corridor: Illinois & Michigan Canal National Heritage Corridor," *Journal of Leisure Research* 25, no. 1 (1993): 53–69.

INDUS

Source: Northern slopes of Kailas Range, in western Tibet
Length: c. 1,900 miles (3,058 kilometers)
Tributaries: Gartang, Shyok, Shigar, Gilgit, **Kabul**, Kurram, Pangnad
Outlet: Arabian Sea

The legendary source of the longest river of the Himalayas is Lake Manasarowar, a holy lake in western Tibet from which the great rivers of south Asia flow to the four points of the compass through the mouths of sacred animals: the Brahmaputra, traveling eastward through the mouth of the Horse; the Karnali, a tributary of the Ganges, flowing southward through the Peacock's mouth; the Sutlej, running to the west through the Elephant's mouth; and the Indus, to the north through Sangi-Kabab, the Lion's mouth. The actual source of the Indus is not far distant from its legendary one. The river rises in a glacially fed spring on the northern slopes of the Kailas on the high, stony plateau of western Tibet. Not finally discovered and mapped until 1907 by the Swedish explorer Sven Hedin, the source lies north of Lake Manasarowar, only some 30 miles (48 kilometers) away. At an elevation of about 17,000 feet (5,182 meters), the source lies only about 100 miles (161 kilometers) from the head of both the Brahmaputra and the Sutlej.

The Lion River swings around the highest mountains in the world, tracing a broad northwesterly arc between the Himalayas to the south and the Karakoram Range to the north, before turning south and making its breakthrough onto the plains of Pakistan. The river that gives its name to India (from the Sanskrit *Sinhu*) as well as to the south Pakistan province of Sind ironically passes through the modern country of India only along part of its upper course, on the farther side of the Himalayas, in the fertile Ladakh region. The capital of Ladakh, Ley, is the traditional crossroads linking northern India to Central Asia and China by storied pass routes. The headwaters pass through deep gorges and scenic valleys, but turbulence makes the river unnavigable. In dry western Tibet, the river to this day is more likely to turn Buddhist prayer wheels than electrical dynamos, though the Chinese have grandiose plans for the region, which they conquered and incorporated into their communist empire in 1959, driving the Tibetan leader, the Dalai Lama, into exile in India.

Ladakh is one of the few places in the upper valley where the river broadens enough to permit settlement. The valley here is fertile and intensively cultivated, mostly for fruit: apricots, apples, mulberries. The provincial capital has for centuries been the pivotal point of a web of trade stretching north into Central Asia across the Karakoram Pass and south into India via the Zoji La route across the Himalayas. The ruggedness of this parched land has bred a durable people of Mongolian descent, short and stocky, whose hardiness is well matched to the rigors of the climate and the harsh landscape. Europeans have often reacted adversely to a people who do not emphasize well-scrubbed looks and elegant coiffures: An English woman once noted that the ladies' hair looked as if it were rubbed in a coal scuttle after which it was dragged through a furze bush. Amid this land of austere beauty, not least in the brilliant earth colors that change during the day, the river flows generally in a northwesterly direction, turning to the southwest after receiving the beautiful Gilgit valley on its right bank. Before making its breakthrough out of the mountains, the river forms a gutter at the west end of the Himalayas, passing between the Karakoram Mountains to the north, topped by K2, the second highest mountain in the world, and to the south the isolated peak of Nanga Parbat, at 26,600 feet (8,108 meters). Treacherous Nanga Parbat was not climbed until 1953, five weeks after the celebrated first ascent of Everest, the world's highest mountain, by the New Zealander Edmund Hillary and the Nepalese Tenzing Norgay.

The Indus emerges from the mountains at Attock at an elevation of 1,100 feet (335 meters). Narrow at this point, the valley at Attock is an important crossing point. The tolerant Mogul Akbar established a regular ferry and built a secure fort here in the sixteenth century. Throughout history, travelers, soldiers, students, and merchants have made the dangerous crossing here.

The vale of Peshawar, with its access to the key Khyber Pass, lies to the west, while to the east along the strategic northwest frontier can be found the old British hill station of Rawalpindi ("Pindi"). Long before the British struggled against recalcitrant Afghan tribes and fierce Sikhs whose warrior religion made them so powerful in the Punjab border region, numerous invaders from the northwest were attracted by the lootable wealth of the Indian population, crossing and recrossing the great plains of the Indus and Ganges. The precise spot where the Macedonian Alexander the Great crossed the Indus in his famous expedition of conquest of 325 B.C. is not known (the name given was Ohind), but the conqueror crossed on a bridge of boats after making an alliance with the king of Taxila, whose domain lay on the east bank of the river. The inhabitants of the tiny village of Hund, located 20 miles (32 kilometers) below Tarbela—the site of the twentieth-century dam—believe that Alexander (or "Sikander," his local name) crossed there. His name in fact is so much part of a living local tradition that it is a common name, and even young boys know he passed this way. Alexander's army reached as far as the Beas River, the easternmost of the Punjab rivers, before the tired and homesick troops demanded to turn back. Reluctantly agreeing, Alexander launched a navy down the Indus, which returned to Persia via the Arabian Sea, while his army marched west along the inhospitable coastlands of the Sind.

With the river's junction with the Kabul River near Attock, the Indus becomes navigable, some 800 miles (1,280 kilometers) from its mouth. Farther downstream at Kalabagh the river narrows again as it enters a limestone gorge, providing the site of another important crossing point and strategic center. Once the river emerges from the mountains, it generally forms a many channeled, braided river rather than a meandering river and flows in a broad alluvial valley across the frontier province of the Punjab, divided today between India and Pakistan. This braided floodplain cuts a fairly straight course roughly to the south or southwest. At first confined by outliers of the Afghan hills to the west and the Potwar plateau and outer folds of the Himalayas in the Salt Range to the east, the valley eventually broadens, presenting sharply defined contrasts between its floodplain, imposing bluffs, and semidesert landscapes of fixed dunes and hills beyond. The gorge at Kalabagh has been utilized for an irrigation scheme to water a tongue-like shape of land known as the Sind Sagar Doab between the Indus and the Chenab. This tract of land, comprising a high-lying, gravelly, alluvial cone, has recently been transformed from a desert landscape where some herding took place into a populous canal colony of farmers.

The Lion stretches itself out on the Punjab plains. Only a mile south of the cliffs of Kalabagh, the bed of the river is 10 miles (16 kilometers) wide. The muddy middle course of the river receives its most important tributaries from the east: the five rivers that give the Punjab its name. The westernmost of the Punjab rivers is the Jhelum, flowing to the west and south from the fertile valley of Kashmir (another long-disputed border region). Where the Jhelum reaches the plains, it is joined by the Chenab, the largest of the five rivers, which flows from the north, and whose name means "the river of China," though it in fact rises on the southern flank of the Himalayas. About 40 miles (64 kilometers) below the confluence of the Chenab and Jhelum, the two rivers are joined by the Ravi, which reaches the plains more quickly and then meanders across the lowlands in a complexity of loops. The last two rivers, the Beas and the Sutlej, come in together, with the Beas marking the easternmost limit of the Punjab and the boundary of the greatest extent of Alexander's oriental conquest (see Figure 1 on pg. 24).

The lower course of the Indus, corresponding to the province of Sind, consists of a harsh, forbidding landscape of wind-blown sand and shifting river channels. The branching of the distributaries begins at the old trade center and crossing point of Hyderabad. No major city is located at the mouth of the river. Karachi, the former capital of Pakistan, which was superseded by the northern city of Islamabad, is a modern port situated just west of the fan of distributaries and the encumbering silt of the delta. The infertile delta of the Indus, with its stretches of blowing sand and frequent changes in the course of its distributaries, does not have the dense population characteristic of other alluvial districts in the Indian subcontinent. Tamarisk trees asterisk the horizon, wind whips the sand against the lone and level shore, and the river trenches the last sand dune before it finally reaches the sea.

Although not possessing a major city or a high density of population today, the Indus valley once was the home of the earliest known civilization of south Asia. A rival of the nearly contemporaneous ancient Egyptian and Mesopotamian civilizations, the prehistoric Indus culture (2400–1800 B.C.) included a large number of sites along the Indus in Pakistan, extending west along the coast to Iran and east into northwest India. The two most important cities of this lost civilization were uncovered in the early 1920s: Harappa, in the central Punjab on the Ravi River; and Mohenjo-Daro, on the lower Indus in northwest Sind. Harappa was discovered accidentally in 1921 by the builder of the Lahore-to-Karachi railway, who found it a convenient source of bricks, thereby badly disrupting the archaeological value of the site. A short time later the larger and better preserved city of Mohenjo-Daro, the City of the Dead, was discovered to the south near the Indus. This mud-brick city had considerable complexity, including elaborate drains made necessary by the high water table, an imposing citadel, and a well-planned gridiron layout of streets. The distinctive square seals of the Indus valley civilization are in contrast with the cylindrical seals of Mesopotamia. They have a line of script across the top of the face of the seal, together with a relief carving, usually of an animal, below. The script is one of the last undeciphered forms of writing in the world. Some scholars regard the apparent emphasis on ritual ablution and the large municipal bath, along with the epigraphic evidence of the seals, particularly the depiction of the Brahmani bull, as support for the idea that the Indus valley civilization represents the foundation of south Asian society and the precursor of the Hindu religion. The origin, development, and disappearance of the prehistoric Indus valley culture remains a mystery.

See also Kabul, Beas, Chenab, Jhelum, Ravi, Sutlej

Further Reading: Fairley, Jean, *The Lion River: The Indus,* New York: John Day, 1975; Wheeler, Sir Mortimer, *Civilizations of the Indus Valley and Beyond,* London: Thames and Hudson, 1966.

IRRAWADDY

Source: Confluence of Mali and Nmai, northern Myanmar
Length: c. 1,000 miles (1,609 kilometers)
Tributaries: Chindwinn, Mu, Myitnge
Outlet: Andaman Sea

Come you back to Mandalay,
Where the old Flotilla lay:
Can't you 'ear their paddles chunkin' from Ran-Goon to Mandalay?
On the road to Mandalay,
Where the flyin'-fishes play,
An' the dawn comes up like thunder outer China 'Crost the Bay!
Rudyard Kipling, "Mandalay"

The principal river of the southeast Asian country of Myanmar (formerly Burma) is both a primary transportation artery and a major food-producing region. Isolated by mountains from Thailand to the east and India to the west, the Burmese state is centered on the broad Irrawaddy (also Ayeyarwady), which contains its many royal capitals along the dry middle course. The major towns of Burma all lie on the banks of the Irrawaddy, or along its tributaries and distributaries.

The river proper forms at the confluence of two streams that drain the hilly Chinese border: Mali Kha and Nmai Kha (*kha* is Kachin for "river"). The narrower but more navigable Mali goes by the same name as the main river for the local Shans. The headstreams flow amid a wild evergreen forest. Just below the confluence lies the settlement of Myitkyina, navigable by motor launch throughout the year. Not far downstream, at a large bend in the river, is the important river port of Bhamo, the beginning of an ancient trade route to Yunnan. Only 50 miles (80 kilometers) from the Chinese border, Bhamo is today a smuggling center, though the contraband passing along the Irrawaddy here is not likely to be drugs but rather more mundane

Traditional boats along the Irrawaddy (John Elk)

items such as painted enamelware from China, bed linens from India (via the Chindwinn tributary), or jade from Kachin. Regular steamer service operates between Bhamo and the celebrated city of Mandalay farther downstream. Two of the three defiles—narrow stretches that present navigation problems—lie in this section of the river. One is best known for its mines, which produce the world's finest rubies.

The river laps the imperial capital of Mandalay in a dry zone of terraced plains. This is the heartland of Burmese culture and also the center of the British territory of upper Burma. A young city and the youngest royal capital, Mandalay was built in 1857, laid out on a gridiron pattern, and dominated by its famous Golden Pagoda. The city bristles with pagodas and stupas, and a modern British traveler, perhaps fresh from London, noted that temples were scattered as profusely as bus shelters. Kipling's poem conferred a kind of immortality on the city, but the great writer of Anglo-Indian parentage, alas, never visited the place.

South of Mandalay the river swings to the west and receives from the right its major tributary, the Chindwinn. An important route for rafted teak, which descends from the monsoon forests farther north, the Chindwinn is navigable for some 200 miles (322 kilometers). The second most important Burmese river, this tributary was the scene of bitter fighting during the reconquest of Burma from the Japanese in 1945.

The river winds along a generally southerly course in the direction of Prome (Pye), an important railhead and river port. The vast Irrawaddy delta, approximately 200 miles (320 kilometers) wide, embraces one of the major rice-producing regions of Asia. The apex of the delta lies near Henzada, with the capital, Yangon (Rangoon), situated on a distributary along its eastern edge. An artificial channel, the Twante Canal, links the main channel of the Irrawaddy to Yangon. The western edge of the delta lies approximately at the town of

Bassein (thus Henzada, Yangon, and Bassein define the corners of a giant triangle). As in the case of the Ganges, the river empties into the sea through multiple mouths, in what are traditionally described as the "Mouths of the Irrawaddy."

Settlement of the delta is of comparatively recent date. Burmese squatters invaded the swamp forests of the delta as far as the maritime mangrove forests between 1850 and 1900. Rice fields were laid out in old channels and oxbow lakes, avoiding the sandbars, and a linear settlement pattern not unlike that found in the dry belt upriver is the result of farms and villages clinging to the curving levees and spillbanks of present and abandoned channels.

The principal highway of Burma since time immemorial has been the Irrawaddy. The most modern Clydeside-built steamers in the world once navigated the river's waters. Though not treacherous in most places, the river presents problems of shoaling and shifting channels. When the Japanese invaded in December of 1941, the British sank most of the steamers of the Irrawaddy Flotilla Company, and many still lie in the water, marked by navigation buoys. The railroads supplemented rather than replaced the river as the primary means of trade. Road and rail connections with India have traditionally been absent or poor. Independence came in 1948, slightly later than in India, and the Burmese, having fought three wars with the British, chose not to become part of the British Commonwealth, as parts of the former British Empire came to call themselves. A people originally of Mongolian stock, who perhaps once emigrated from Tibet, the Burmese added a socialist stripe to their traditional ways during the 1950s and underwent a military coup in the following decade. Through all of this the Burmese kept to their traditional ways along their ancient routeway and granary, making the country one of the most isolated in the region, and for that matter in the world.

Further Reading: Stamp, L. Dudley, "The Irrawaddy River," *Geographical Journal* 95 (1940): 329–356.

IRTYSH

Source: Mongolian Altai Mountains, in northwest China
Length: c. 2,650 miles (4,265 kilometers)
Tributaries: Om', Ishim, Tobol
Outlet: **Ob'**

It is a reflection of the scale of Siberia that the length of a tributary of the principal river of the region's west is measured in thousands of miles. The major tributary of the Ob', the Irtysh (pronounced yir-TIYSH) drains portions of extreme northwestern China, northeastern Kazakstan, and western Siberia. Like many Asian waterways that traverse lowland plains at a considerable distance from their source, it is known by different names along its course. It rises as the Ertix River in Xinjiang Uygur Autonomous Region in far western China. An alternative name for the upper course of the river is the Kara-Irtysh. Flowing northwest through Lake Zaisan in Kazakstan, the river adopts the name of Irtysh. Draining the northern margin of the dry Kirghiz steppe in Kazakstan, the river is cut off from former tributaries on its left bank that have been separated as a result of desiccation following the pluvial regime of the Pleistocene (see Figure 2). The river enters western Siberia (Omsk Oblast) and receives

Figure 2. River Irtysh, with former tributaries separated because of desiccation. "N" represents Novosibirsk, "O" represents Omsk.

from the left its chief tributaries, the Ishim and the Tobol. Each of these subtributaries of the Ob' is more than 1,000 miles (1,609 kilometers) in length. The Ishim River rises to the south in the interior steppe region around Akmola (formerly Tselinograd), while the Tobol drains the southeastern flank of the Ural Mountains. As the Irtysh winds across the southern portions of the West Siberian Lowland—one of the largest expanses of flat land in the world—it passes the major towns along its banks: Omsk, where the Om' River enters from the right; and Tobolsk, where the Tobol River joins from the left. The confluence of the Irtysh and the Ob' occurs near Khanty-Mansiysk. Large hydroelectric stations located at Ust-Kamenogorsk and Zhana Buktyrma, Kazakstan, were completed in 1959.

An isolated area even by Russian standards, the Irtysh valley was occupied by Chinese, Kalmyks, and Mongols until Russians began to arrive in the late sixteenth century. It was not until the early nineteenth century that Russia completed its conquest of the basin. The construction of giant hydroelectric plants in the 1950s was part of Russia's push to develop remote eastern regions, but the effect has been to concentrate population and economic activity along the corridor of the Trans-Siberian Railroad and its feeder lines. The Trans-Siberian crosses the Irtysh at Omsk, which is, not coincidentally, the largest city in the valley, with more than a million people.

See also Ob'

J

JAMES

Source: Confluence of Jackson and Cowpasture Rivers, in west-central Virginia
Length: 340 miles (547 kilometers)
Tributaries: Maury, Rivanna, Appomattox, Chickahominy
Outlet: Hampton Roads estuary of the Chesapeake Bay

Draining eastward across a varied terrain, the James empties into the Chesapeake Bay at its southern end. Though not the longest river with this name in the United States—a tributary of the Missouri is longer—Virginia's James has been the scene of the earliest history of one of the key colonies of the emerging nation.

The James begins on the far side of the Blue Ridge, west of that imposing obstacle that represents the limit of the Piedmont. The river originates amid corrugated ridges of the Allegheny Mountains, which are strongly oriented northeast-southwest. In such rough country the river heads in two separately named branches, the Jackson and Cowpasture Rivers, which, draining from opposite directions, meet to form the main stream. From this point the James flows to the east past Glasgow, where it receives from the north the Maury (or North) River. Then the river makes a precipitous 1,000-foot (305-meter) drop at Balcony Falls. It continues on past Lynchburg, a river port that emerged in the eighteenth century as an important commercial town on the Piedmont. The James then traverses the falls and islands around Richmond, the river's major interior city, which lies on the Fall Line, the irregular, northeast-southwest trending boundary between the Piedmont and the Coastal Plain. The rivers of the Piedmont literally fall down off the Piedmont's elevated crystalline rocks onto the lower, younger sedimentaries of the Coastal Plain. The location on the Fall Line, with its abundant waterpower, almost guaranteed Richmond's status as an important town site, as it did for other interior locations of the South (Raleigh, North Carolina; Columbia, South Carolina; Augusta, Georgia). In the parlance of locals, "widewater" begins at Richmond. All except the largest vessels can reach the rapids and, since canals have been built, proceed even farther upriver. Between Richmond and Bermuda Hundred, located downstream where the river is joined by one of its major tributaries, the Appomattox, the river meanders widely, adding greatly to the distance traveled from point to point. During the Civil War a Union major general, Benjamin Butler, tried to eliminate one of these curves, digging the Dutch Gap Canal, even on one occasion carrying out detonation work under heavy Confederate fire. The project failed, and it would be another ten years before the canal, cutting off seven miles of travel, was completed.

The tidal river continues past a series of historic plantations before it receives another major tributary, the Chickahominy, approximately 12 miles (19 kilometers) west of Williamsburg. By this time the river has widened into an estuary, as do most of the

Statue of John Smith, first governor of Virginia, overlooking the James River at Jamestown, Virginia, site of the first permanent British settlement in colonial America (Laura Penn)

rivers draining the Western Shore near their mouths. The river continues past Jamestown and Newport News to form Hampton Roads, the harbor for Newport News, Hampton, Portsmouth, and Norfolk, before entering the Chesapeake about 20 miles (32 kilometers) west of the mouth of the bay.

The Indians named the river for their chief, Powhatan, but the British colonists called it King's River after their monarch, eventually changing this to the name of the first Stuart king (James I). The first permanent British settlement was at Jamestown (1607) near the mouth of the river at a protected yet tidal location. The site was a small island nearly attached to the north bank of the river. The difficulties of the early settlers, who died in great numbers, seem to have had less to do with food shortages or Indian problems than with diseases, especially of a gastrointestinal kind, which the colonists contracted in the late summer months when salinity levels rose in the river and pathogens were concentrated in the remaining freshwater supplies.

In the early years of the seventeenth century, the history of Virginia was inseparable from that of its longest river. Settlers quickly moved up the James, fanning out in search of timber, minerals, and prime agricultural land. The more imaginative and speculative of the first colonists believed that the James ran all the way across the continent or provided a path to gold, but mundane farmers began cultivating tobacco as a cash crop on the somewhat sandy soils of the coastal plain, while commercial farmers on the Piedmont found wheat well adapted to the environment. Virginians were not content to be just farmers. By the time of the American Revolution a foundry had been established at Westham above the falls and a navy yard at Warwick below the falls. Square-rigged vessels could reach as far as Bermuda Hundred, and smaller vessels up to 150 tons could ascend the river as far as the falls.

"Canal fever" soon reached the East Coast. George Washington recommended a survey of the Potomac and James Rivers. In 1785 the state chartered the James River Company, which built a canal around the falls and cleared a navigable route for raft traffic as far as Buchanan, which lay west of the Blue Ridge. Organized as a state agency after 1820, the company was responsible for major improvements, including the construction of a 7-mile (11-kilometer) canal through the Blue Ridge at Balcony Falls. In the 1830s an ambitious plan to join the James to the Kanawha River and the Ohio valley was conceived. The James River and Kanawha Company, chartered in 1832, completed the task of building a canal from Richmond to Lynchburg by 1840, reaching Buchanan eleven years later. Efforts to reach the Kanawha River, however, failed, despite herculean efforts at building aqueducts and underground waterways, because of excessive debt and competition from the ubiquitous railroad; the Chesapeake and Ohio Railroad eventually bought the stock of the canal company. The canal builders did some clever work. It was arranged in Richmond, for example, that oceangoing vessels could pull up to the docks and be loaded directly from canal packets. As a result of such enterprise, the capital of Virginia became a major exporter of flour and tobacco.

The river retarded the growth of cities in the early days, because planters on the lower James did not need to bring their tobacco to town for shipment. The settlement of the Piedmont varied the economic base and spurred town development. The river exhibited multiple uses long before federal agencies mandated the formula in the exploitation of public resources. Mills, fishing, timber floating, and hauling coal or agricultural products were among the competing uses on the river. As might be expected, conflicts on the James were less common in the early days, although not unheard of. In recent times problems have become more frequent and intense. During World War I the town of Hopewell sprang up as a chemical manufacturing center near the site of the early settlement of Jamestown colony, known as Bermuda Hundred (1613). The Allied Chemical Corporation produced Kepone, a poison, which found its way into the waters of the James, apparently via a sanitary sewer. In 1975 the state banned fishing on the lower James, and the once

Seawall along the south side of Jamestown Island, Virginia, protecting the Jamestown historical site from erosion. The James River is to the left; the building to the right is used to process archaeological finds. (Laura Penn)

extensive crab industry focused on Hampton Roads suffered reduced production. Oystering—a staple of the lower bay—also suffered losses. The varied terrain of the James basin contributed to a broad-based economy. But regular flooding of the steep, narrow upriver valleys of the James and its tributaries has increased of late. Hurricane Camille (1969) and Hurricane Agnes (1972) produced 1,000-year floods—two of them in a three-year period! Commercial lumbering, which peaked in the first decades of the twentieth century, altered the forest cover and contributed to erosion and sedimentation of the stream bed. It is hard to balance the interests of the many people and groups that want to use the river, for mining, manufacturing, and transportation. These activities all suffer when a major pollution problem like the Kepone crisis emerges.

See also Potomac
Further Reading: Earle, Carville, "Environment, Disease, and Mortality in Early Virginia," *Journal of Historical Geography* 5 (1979): 365–390; Niles, Blair, *The James,* New York: Farrar and Rinehart, 1939 (Rivers of America Series); for archaeological information about the recently discovered Jamestown site, see the Web site http://www.apva.org

JHELUM

Source: Himalayan Mountains
Length: 480 miles (772 kilometers)
Tributaries: None
Outlet: **Chenab**

The word *punjab* is a Persian term meaning "five waters" or "five rivers." The Punjab plains lie on the border between northwest India and Pakistan and represent the coalescence of the floodplains of five rivers: the Jhelum, Chenab, Ravi, Beas, and Sutlej (see Figure 1 on p. 24). Draining a dry region, the rivers have been extensively used as a source of water for canal irrigation.

The westernmost of the five Punjab rivers, the Jhelum (anciently the Hydaspes) rises amid snow-clad Himalayan peaks in Jammu and Kashmir, India. It flows northwest through the fertile Vale of Kashmir, passing Srinagar, before turning to the southwest and passing out of India. In Pakistan the river follows a generally southerly course on the western edge of the dry Punjab. It joins with the Chenab; then the two merge with the Ravi. The joint course of the Jhelum, Chenab, and Ravi is known as the Trimab, or "Three Rivers." All five rivers eventually unite to form the Panjnad, which empties into the Indus. That such a detailed vocabulary exists suggests the importance of the riverine zone for human settlement.

The tonguelike territories between major rivers are termed *doabs*. These fertile interfluves have always been the focus of colonization, as the dry soils are productive only with irrigation. The area between the **Jhe**lum and the **Ch**enab is termed the Jech doab as a kind of acronymic abbreviation. Irrigation by natural inundation and small wells had been carried on before the arrival of the British in the mid-nineteenth century. Hydraulic engineers under imperial edict undertook a series of projects and began to produce an extensive irrigation system, whose major works date from the 1890s.

The Lower Jhelum Canal, opened in 1901, brought water from the Jhelum at Rasul to irrigate parts of the Jech doab. The Upper Jhelum Canal, completed in 1915, was made necessary when another, more ambitious canal, the Upper Chenab Canal, took so much water and not only carried it to adjacent lands but also lifted it by aqueduct across the Bari to another doab, the Bari (Bari doab = **Bea**s + **Ravi**). As a result, the Upper Jhelum Canal had to be constructed to bring water from the Jhelum to the Chenab to help supply the Lower Chenab Canal. The Mangla Dam (1960) and Reservoir have greatly improved irrigation on the Jhelum's lower course, as well as providing hydroelectric power.

JORDAN

Source: Hula basin, north Israel
Length: c. 200 miles (320 kilometers)
Tributaries: Yarmuk, Jabbok
Outlet: Dead Sea

The longest and most important river of Palestine rises at the foot of Mt. Herman in the three springs near Tel Dan, Banias, and Hasbani. It then

Restaurant on the shore of the Sea of Galilee (Jesse Walker)

descends rapidly to the Huleh valley, a shallow lake until recent times. From this point the river, now properly called the Jordan, plunges through a gorge to the Sea of Galilee at an elevation of 696 feet below sea level (212 meters). This rapid drop continues south in the main course of the river on the way to the Dead Sea (anciently the Salt Sea), which lies at the lowest point in the valley, at an elevation of 1,292 feet (394 meters) below sea level. This rapid drop probably explains the river's name (from the Hebrew "to go down").

The middle and lower courses of the Jordan are sluggish, even as it receives its major tributaries from the east: the Yarmuk and the Jabbok. Below the Sea of Galilee the river takes on a character very different from that of the upper river. It meanders widely across the soft alluvium of its lower level, requiring about 200 miles (320 kilometers) to cover the 65 miles (105 kilometers) between the south end of the Sea of Galilee and the north end of the Dead Sea. The distinctive lower level of the Jordan, known as the Zhor, is covered with a dense thicket of tamarisk, willows, papyrus, and thornbushes that in the past harbored an assortment of wild animals, reputedly including lions. This virtually impenetrable jungle of vegetation resembles that of tropical locations farther to the south. The Zhor varies in width between 200 yards (180 meters) and a mile (1.6 kilometers) and is separated from the higher level of the Ghor, a 150-foot (137-meter) step above the riverbottom suitable for cropland and pasturage, by highly eroded marl badlands.

The Jordan valley is part of the Great Rift System extending from the Bekáa (Arabic: Beqa'a) valley in Lebanon southward through the Jordan, the Red Sea, and the East African lake country. It is a conspicuous north-south trending trough lying between the ranges of Galilee and Samaria to the west and Gilead to the east. Although the Jordan receives a considerable volume of water, its low gradient (in the lower course), crumbling river bluffs, extremely high temperatures (especially in the summer), and lack of navigability have made the region less desirable as a focus for settlement than the adjacent highlands. In

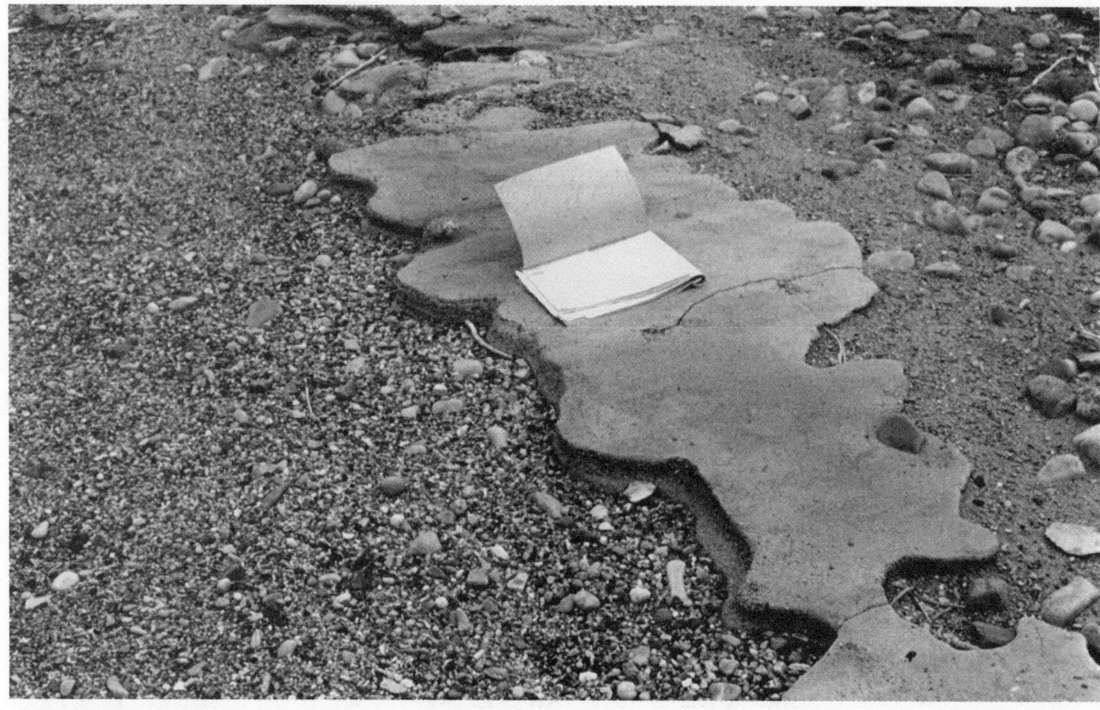

Sediments deposited at the mouth of the Jordan River (head of the Dead Sea) (Jesse Walker)

ancient times the sluggish, mud-colored Jordan was often compared unfavorably to clear, fast-flowing rivers nearby such as the Euphrates.

References in the Bible to the Jordan are not as frequent as one might expect. The river was more important as an obstacle to be overcome than as an attractive place in itself. As the boundary of Moab, the Israelites had to cross over it to reach the "Promised Land." Featured in the miracles of Elijah and Elisha, the river assumes central importance in the Gospel story of the New Testament. Jesus was baptized by John in the Jordan, the traditional site being "Bethany across the Jordan," near Jericho.

Today the waters of the Jordan are as much a source of contention between rival powers of the region as the surrounding land. In the 1960s Israel first began to tap the reservoir of the Sea of Galilee, channeling water as far away as the Negev desert, with the inevitable reduction in water along the lower Jordan River. The Hashemite kingdom of Jordan was late in bringing its water projects on line, and it was not until the 1970s that the East Ghor (King Abdullah) Canal was extended from the Yarmuk River south along the Jordan. This canal provides irrigation water for Jordanian farmers, who returned to the East Bank, which had been left vacant since the shelling of the 1967 war. Joint Jordanian-Syrian efforts to dam the Yarmuk (it defines part of their political border) have been hampered by warfare and a diplomatic impasse. Although groundwater pumping, desalinization plants, and more efficient use of drip irrigation, especially by the Arabs, would go far to extend the resource, the surface waters of the Jordan will continue to be important in the economic and political geography of the Holy Land.

Further Reading: Lowi, Miriam R., *The Politics of Water: The Jordan River and the Riparian States,* Montreal: McGill Studies in International Development no. 35, 1984.

JUMNA

See Yamuna

K

KABUL

Source: Paghman Mountains, west of Kabul, Afghanistan
Length: 320 miles (515 kilometers)
Tributaries: Chitral, Panjshir, Kunar, Swat
Outlet: **Indus**

The alluvial lands of the Kabul, a western tributary of the Indus, are a major focus of agricultural settlement and urban concentration in eastern Afghanistan and Pakistan. Like rivers elsewhere in the northern part of the Indian subcontinent, the Kabul has not been used extensively for transportation. The steep gradient and precipitous gorges along its upper course have made the 30-mile (48-kilometer) Khyber Pass route across the Safed Koh Range just south of the Indus a strategic gateway to the plains of India. Connecting Kabul and Peshawar across the political border, the famous Khyber route linked a series of passes and narrow defiles. On the northwest frontier of British India, the Kabul River joined the frontier garrison of Peshawar with the Afghan capital of Kabul. In the nineteenth century, British imperial strategists attempted to establish buffer states in places like Persia and Afghanistan in order to block the southern expansion of Russia. The Khyber route, along with other potential avenues for invading India, became an obsessive concern of diplomats, military leaders, and adventurers who engaged in high-stakes imperial intrigues that came to be known as the Great Game.

Known in ancient times as the Cophus, the Kabul rises in the Paghman Mountains at the foot of Unai Pass, some 45 miles (72 kilometers) west of Kabul. It flows eastward past Kabul, Jalalabad, and Nowshera to the Indus just north of Attock. The most important cultivated area in Afghanistan is the alluvial plain around Kabul, which is irrigated by the Kabul River to produce a rich harvest of wheat, barley, and diverse fruits including oranges, figs, and date palms. The Vale of Peshawar across the border in Pakistan is also a fertile, irrigated oasis of fruit and cereals amid dry or mountainous surroundings. The large Warwick Dam on the Kabul River where the river enters the Peshawar plain generates power and is the headworks for an extensive system of irrigation distributaries.

The frontier hill lands west of Peshawar are the homeland of fierce, depredatory Afghan tribes collectively known to the British as the Pathans (rhymes with *batons*). They were the scourge of travelers and invaders, as they swept down from their mountain fastnesses on the rough tracks that crossed the narrow defiles in the short but treacherous distance separating Peshawar and Kabul. Many a victim caught in such a circumstance may have wished he had chosen instead to navigate the gorge of the Indus that lies just to the north of the Khyber route.

The series of passes between Kabul and Jalalabad—part of the Khyber route, but not the Khyber Pass itself—were the scene of the most complete and humiliating defeat experienced by the British army in the nineteenth century. At the end of the First Afghan War (1839–1842), an army of 16,000 British and Indian soldiers retreating eastward from Kabul into the mountains were preyed upon by tribesmen, who had previously given their word to protect them, amid the snowy ravines and icy defiles of the pass route. In the end, only a single survivor, a surgeon from the medical corps, reached the mud-walled fort flying the Union Jack at Jalalabad. In retaliation, the British returned the next year and burned Kabul.

The Afghan mountains were a classic ground for playing the Great Game, the struggle between Britain and Russia for supremacy of Central Asia and the Indian perimeter. The British strategy was to secure the northwestern corner of India and to establish and stabilize buffer states like Afghanistan. They would accomplish just such a goal when they put a compliant ruler in charge of Afghanistan at the end of the Second Afghan War (1878–1880). A hundred years later, in 1979, the Russians entered this unruly country, hoping to create a docile satellite; they left ten years later, having learned the lesson of how difficult it is to rule distant, rebellious people occupying mountainous terrain.

See also Indus
Further Reading: Edwards, Mike W., "An Eye for an Eye: Pakistan's Wild Frontier," *National Geographic,* January 1977, pp. 111–139.

KENNEBEC

Source: Moosehead Lake, in northwest Maine
Length: 164 miles (264 kilometers)
Tributary: Androscoggin
Outlet: Confluence with Androscoggin forms Merrymeeting Bay, an arm of the Atlantic

The south-draining Kennebec was an entranceway to the Maine woods for early New Englanders. In the twentieth century, the river has furnished hydroelectric power and attracted industry, but in at least one significant case it has not generated so much power or employed so many people that the possibility of removing a dam on the river could not be considered.

The Kennebec lies in a broad zone of ecological transition. To the south, and along the moderate environment of the coast, lies a mixed forest of broadleaf, deciduous trees (such as maples and birch) combined with pine and hemlock. To the north and farther upstream stretches the great spruce-fir forest extending into Canada. The physical character of coastal Maine is transitional at the mouth of the river. To the south the coast is often open, with sandy beaches, while farther north a steep, rocky coastline presents a stern face to the north Atlantic.

The river begins in the glaciated lake district of western Maine, not far from the New Hampshire border. Flowing from Moosehead Lake, the river follows a southerly course past the small industrial town of Waterville and the state capital, Augusta, before joining its major tributary, the Androscoggin, at the estuary of the Kennebec at Bath, about 28 miles (45 kilometers) northeast of Portland. The head of navigation is at Augusta, where a dam built in 1837 prevented boats and anadromous fish (fish that migrate upstream to spawn) from going any farther up the river—until recently.

Explored by Samuel de Champlain in 1604–1605, the river early attracted attention for its potential for trade and suitability for forts. Augusta on the lower river was founded in 1628 as a trading post by members of the Plymouth Colony of Massachusetts. Fort Western, the first permanent structure in the town, was built in 1754 as a supply base during the French and Indian War (1756–1763). In the American Revolution, General Benedict Arnold gathered 1,100 men at Augusta and traveled up the Kennebec to Quebec during the course of his unsuccessful march on the British.

In July 1837, while visiting a college friend in Maine's new capital, the not-yet-famous writer Nathaniel Hawthorne watched a stone-and-timber dam being constructed on the Kennebec River. First used to divert water to local mills, electric generation was added in 1913. At the end of the twentieth century, the dam was owned by the Edwards Manufacturing Company and the city of Augusta. It generated only 3.5 megawatts of electricity, about one-tenth of 1 percent of Maine's annual energy use.

In the 1990s the venerable Edwards Dam came under a barrage of criticism from anglers, environmentalists, and a host of citizen associations. Residents in the late 1700s and early 1800s had reported catching hundreds of salmon and shad before the dam cut off the natural migration and breeding of these anadromous fish. A powerful coalition of conservation groups, fishermen's lobbies, and aroused environmentalists brought enough pressure on authorities that by the late 1990s it became possible to think the unthinkable: removing the dam. A lengthy series of legal and governmental maneuvers then ensued. In December 1997 the Federal Energy Regulatory Commission denied the dam owners a new license and ordered the removal of the dam. On January 1, 1999, the property of the 160-year-old dam was transferred from its owners to the state of Maine. A shipbuilder, Bath Iron Works, and the Kennebec Hydro Developers, a group of dam operators upstream of the Edwards Dam, created a $7.25 million fund to remove the dam and restore the fishery. Dismantling the dam began in July 1999, with Secretary of the Interior Bruce Babbitt personally supervising the breaching of the dam.

The national press carried the story, whose impact was especially noticeable in the western United States. A note of trepidation could be detected in the reports carried there. Secretary Babbitt reassured the public that the great dams of the West were not threatened, but a significant policy change regarding rivers had clearly been made. The door had been opened for removing other dams across the country. The value of free-flowing rivers in the future would have to be weighed against energy needs, not just in the building of dams but also in their continuing existence.

See also Penobscot

Further Reading: Coffin, Robert P. Tristram, *Kennebec,* New York: Farrar and Rinehart, 1937 (Rivers of America Series); McPhee, John, "Farewell to the Nineteenth Century: The Breaching of Edwards Dam," *New Yorker,* September 27, 1999, pp. 44–53.

KIZIL IRMAK

Source: Kizil Dag, north-central Turkey
Length: 715 miles (1,150 kilometers)
Tributaries: Gök, Delice
Outlet: Black Sea

The greatest rivers in Turkey are undoubtedly the Tigris and Euphrates, whose upper courses drain the southeastern mountains, but their destiny is to flow to the south and east out of the country to form the historic region of Mesopotamia in Iraq. The Kizil Irmak rises in interior Turkey not far from the upper Euphrates and completes its wide, arcing course—west, then north, then northeast—before emptying into the Black Sea. It is thereby the longest river flowing entirely in Turkey, but even at that not so important as some of the streams debouching directly westward into the Aegean Sea.

The topography of Asia Minor, as Turkey was once called, has been compared to a hollow-crowned, narrow-brimmed hat of a kind that is no longer fashionable. Between the rims of the northern Pontic Mountains paralleling the Black Sea and the Taurus Mountains along the Mediterranean lies a central, plateaulike depression in which can be found the dry, shallow Lake Tuz and the great sweep of Kizil Irmak. Known in ancient times as Halys, the river rises on the flank of the peak Kizil Dag east of Sivas. Like most rivers in Turkey, its path to the sea—long, almost circuitous—is dictated by the east-west trend of the mountains. Whereas the rivers that run into the Aegean Sea run out between unfused, mountainous fingers forming broad deltas, the rivers draining into the Black Sea, including the Kizil Irmak, descend the steep slopes of the Pontic Mountains, which descend almost to the shore. Sheltered harbors and cultivable land are at a premium. The Bafra plain along the lower Kizil Irmak is one of the few extensive tracts of arable flatland along the northern coast. The deltaic plain lies approximately halfway between the ports of Sinop to the west and Samsun to the east. The alluvial tracts of the north coast around Sinop, Bafra, and Samsun produce a diversity of crops, the best known of which is Turkish tobacco.

The climate of the interior of Turkey is more

akin to the steppe lands of southern Russia and central Asia than the mild Mediterranean coastlands. The rainfall regime is that of a semiarid grassland, and dust storms can create a foglike dust that hangs in the atmosphere for hours. The flora, fauna, and even the human geography resemble the steppe more than Europe, and it must be remembered that the Turkic language and culture derive from once-nomadic peoples of interior Asia. As a result of the dry climate, the Kizil Irmak has an irregular volume of flow. The river is dammed at a number of points to provide water and hydroelectric power, as at the Hirfanli Dam southeast of Ankara. With the exception of the Bafra district the population density of the river valley is not high, especially compared with western Turkey, but the government is committed to harnessing the power of the river for the multiple purposes of economic development.

Further Reading: Russell, Richard Joel, "Alluvial Morphology of Anatolian Rivers," *Annals of the Association of American Geographers* 32 (1954): 149–154.

KLARÄLVEN

Source: Southwestern Sweden, near border with Norway
Length: 215 miles (345 kilometers)
Tributaries: Varån, Tåsan, Halgån, Uvån
Outlet: Lake Vänern

Scandinavia presents a variety of faces: the Danish islands, Norway's fjord coast, the Finnish Lake Plateau, and Sweden's river plain. Most of Sweden's large rivers parallel one another and flow out of the Norwegian Mountains from northwest to southeast. The Klarälven, the most southerly of the major rivers, has a more nearly southward direction once past the bends of the valley's upper course.

The river rises in the mountains of Härjedalen near the Norwegian border. It flows through Lake Rogen and then crosses the border into Norway. After passing through two more lakes—Faemunden and Isteren—the river recrosses the Norwegian border and passes back into Sweden, for good this time. The Klarälven's course is now toward the southeast or south as it passes through Värmland on its way to its outlet on Lake Vänern, one of the great lakes in south-central Sweden west of Stockholm. The mouth of the river at Karlstad is approximately at the latitude of Oslo and Stockholm, which lie in opposite directions a reasonable distance away.

The valley of the Klarälven has been carved from a thick mantle of Pleistocene glacial deposits. During the last ice age the valley was essentially a fjord, as a narrow inlet of the sea extended higher sea levels northward from the Edebäck region as far as Norra Finnskoga in the upper valley of the river near the Norwegian border. As the land rose with deglaciation and isostatic rebound, the former fjord became a valley. The Klarälven deepened its channel in the loose deposits, leaving along its sides at a slight remove elevated terraces.

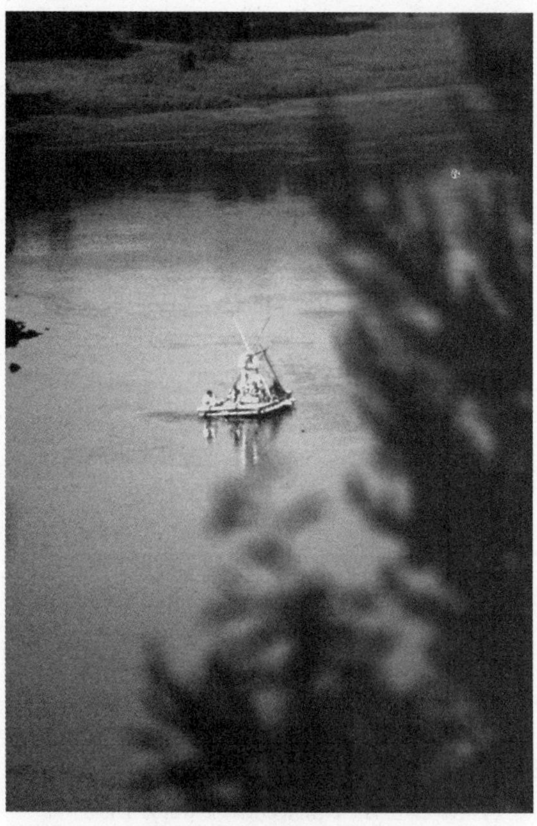

Raft floating downstream on the Klarälven River in southwestern Sweden (Jesse Walker)

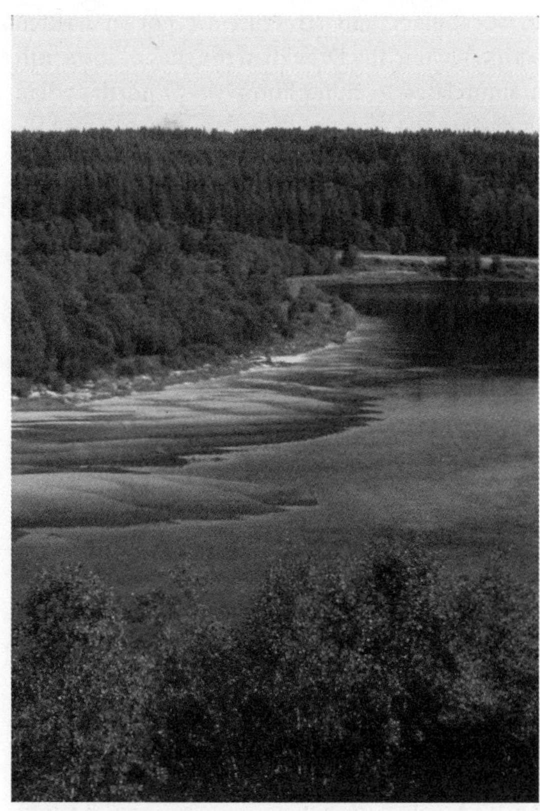

Gravel bars on the Klarälven River in southwestern Sweden (Jesse Walker)

The middle course of the river between Vingängsjön and Edebäck follows an almost straight valley, but one with a well-developed, regular sequence of meanders. Within the narrow valley bottom whose average width is 1 kilometer (0.62 mile), the river turns frequently from side to side. A regular meander pattern is the result, with erodible headlands (Swedish: *näs*) on the outer bends of the curves and inundated shelves or point bars on the inside bends. The focus of agricultural activity has traditionally been the elevated headlands because they lie above the level of most floods, but these lands are also the most subject to erosion by slumping into the river where the energy of the water is most concentrated (the outer bend of a river has the deepest and fastest water). Records from the seventeenth and eighteenth centuries show the claims made to local courts for damages done by the Klarälven. From 1760 to 1827, the *Storskifte,* a land tenure arrangement by which parcels of land were reassigned, resulted in the reallotment of almost all arable and pasture land in the valley in an attempt to consolidate farmland in larger blocks and to avoid piecemeal strips. The most erodible edge of the river along the headland was in many cases converted to common land.

The surveying and mapping beginning in the late eighteenth century not only demonstrates the wisdom of the Swedish people in adapting land use to the environment of valley by means of objective, reliable information; it also established a benchmark against which later alterations in the river and its meanders could be compared.

The Klarälven does not possess any great political or strategic significance, except perhaps in a minor way that its upper course forms the border with Norway. However, this humble river has received the careful attention of numerous scientists in geology, hydrology, and fluvial geomorphology, who have attempted to understand the basic principles of how water flows in channels and the related matter of how sediments are transported and deposited. The nature of the alluvial materials in the erosion scarps of the headlands and the manner by which meander loops migrate downstream have been studied in detail in a landmark study of the valley.

See also Dal

Further Reading: Sundborg, Åke, "The River Klarälven: A Study of Fluvial Processes," *Geografiska Annaler* 38 (1956); pp. 127–316.

KRISHNA

Source: Western Ghats of India
Length: c. 800 miles (1,287 kilometers)
Tributaries: Tungabhadra, Bhima
Outlet: Bay of Bengal

The Krishna River (formerly spelled Kistna) rises about 40 miles (64 kilometers) east of the Arabian Sea in the Western Ghats. These highlands parallel the west coast of the tapering peninsula of south India for some 600 miles (965 kilometers). The descent to the west is steep, down deep gorges and waterfalls; the Krishna drains the longer, gentler slope to the east, emptying into the Bay of Bengal approximately where the coastline bends toward the northeast in the direction of Calcutta.

The 800-mile-long (1,287-kilometer-long) river crosses three Indian states on its passage to the sea: it begins in the Western Ghats in Maharashtra, not far from Bombay; it flows southeasterly through the northern end of Karnataka; then it turns to the east to form the traditional boundary between Madras and Hyderabad. Today this entire lower course lies in the state of Andhra Pradesh. The river enters an extensive delta at Vijayawada (formerly Bezwada). The major tributary of the Krishna is the Tungabhadra, which drains from the southwest. Along the upper reaches of the Tungabhadra in 1336 was founded the city of Vijayanagar ("city of victory"). From here a Hindu culture spread over the entire southern peninsula and served as a bulwark against Islamic expansion from the north, holding out until the sixteenth century when a confederation of Deccan Muslim sultans overcame the city. The Bhima River, rising north of Pune, is the major left-bank tributary of the Krishna. It joins the sacred river near the town of Raichur in the fertile Mesopotamian region lying between the Krishna and Tungabhadra. In contrast to the thin, red lateritic soils of the surrounding areas, the soils in this district are dark and rich because of the regular accumulation of silt from the flooding of its two rivers. This region was a marchland, a frontier, between the Muslim sultanates inching down the peninsula from the north and Hindu Vijayanagar. It is still an area of overlapping political jurisdictions and of cultural and linguistic encounter. The Tungabhadra has been the traditional divide between the Indo-Aryan languages of the north and the Dravidian, non-Aryan tongues of the south. This is important within the broad perspective of cultural history—the mixing and encounter of cultural elements—because the prehistoric Aryan invasion of the north left behind such Indian languages as Hindi and Bengali, which are related to European languages in vocabulary and structure (if not in written scripts), while the Dravidian tongues of the south are unrelated to either European or north-Indian languages.

At the other end of the river lies another historical focus and political alignment. Littoral Andhra Pradesh state extends roughly between the seaports of Vishakhapatnam to the north and Nellore to the south and finds its midpoint along the spreading distributaries of the lower Krishna. Lacking an indented coastline with safe harbors, the region's cities tend to be at interior locations well away from the coast. The cities also lie well away from the ravaging, flood-prone rivers. Just upstream from the head of the delta was located the ancient capital of the Andhra kingdom, Amaravati. Situated on the south bank of the Krishna River about 60 miles (96 kilometers) from its mouth, Amaravati is today in ruins, but its elaborately carved stupa with scenes of Buddha's life is evidence of a once-flourishing south Indian culture that, in the first few centuries of the Common Era (that is, A.D.), managed to reconcile Brahmanical sanctions of kingship with Buddhist worship. The deltaic lowlands of eastern Andhra Pradesh are actually a composite of several rivers' lower courses: in addition to the Krishna, the Penner River (in the south) and the Godavari River (in the north) have contributed their share of silt to the broad depositional surface of the coastal plain.

During high flood the Krishna can be a menacing threat, as evidenced, for example, by the flooding caused by late and heavy monsoon precipitation in the fall of 1998. The headwaters of the Krishna lie in the Western Ghats, which receives its precipitation from the seasonal monsoons that blow up from the Arabian Sea every summer. Unlike the rivers of the Indo-Gangetic plain, which are fed by the melting snows of the Himalayas, the Krishna is subject to highly variable and irregular seasonal flow. The plain is intensively cultivated with rice, sugar cane, cotton, and peanuts, which all do well in a tropical climate, especially when irrigated. The site of Vijayawada some 45 miles (72 kilometers) from the coast is a 3,900-foot (1,189-meter) gap in a gneissic ridge that is utilized as the head of an extensive canal system. Irrigation works also function as hydroelectric dams and reservoirs.

Within the delta the Musi River joins the Krishna from the north, flowing from Hyderabad city with its legendary fort at Golconda, the seat of the diamond industry in the sixteenth and seventeenth centuries. Diamonds cut and sold in Golconda were mined along the Krishna. The principal port today is Vijayawada at the head of the delta, but it was at the seaport of Machilipatnam (or Masulipatnam) on one of the many mouths of the Krishna River that the British East India Company established a "factory" or trading post in 1611, the earliest British settlement on the Coromandel Coast. Contested by the Dutch during the seventeenth and eighteenth centuries, the port was securely held by the British following 1759.

The headwaters of the Krishna River are considered sacred to Hindus. The god Krishna is one of the avatars, or incarnations, of Vishnu, who in turn is one of the most important gods in the Hindu pantheon. Krishna appears in the Sanskrit epic the *Mahabharata* as a friend of native princes when his divinity is revealed, most notably in the celebrated *Bhagavad Gita*, a work almost as well known in the West as in the East (T. S. Eliot and W. Somerset Maugham were both influenced by this classic writing). Foster child of cowherds and lover of milkmaids (*gopis*), Krishna has the lightness of heart and virtue of a living river.

See also Narmada

Further Reading: Sastri, K. A. Nilakanta, *A History of South India, from Prehistoric Times to the Fall of Vijayanagar*, Oxford: Oxford University Press, 1958; Watson, Francis, *India: A Concise History*, London: Thames and Hudson, 1974.

L

LA PAZ

Source: Cordillera Oriental, in western Bolivia
Length: c. 100 miles (161 kilometers)
Tributaries: Palca, Luribay
Outlet: **Beni**

The La Paz River begins high in the Andes Mountains not far from the Bolivian city of the same name. It rises on the flank of the Chacaltaya, a peak in the Cordillera Oriental that overlooks the eastern shore of Lake Titicaca. The upper course of the river runs southward across the Altiplano, the high, wind-swept intermountain plateau. The river parallels the cordillera until, just before reaching the towering mountains, it plunges into a canyon where La Paz is situated. The site of Bolivia's chief commercial city and political center is an unlikely one. Located at an average elevation of 12,000 feet (3,658 meters) above sea level, the world's highest big city is squeezed into a chasm excavated by headward erosion of the loose lakebed deposits near the eastern edge of the Altiplano. Bolivia's largest city does not so much lie *on* the Altiplano as *in* it: the chasm that contains the town lies 1,400 feet (427 meters) below the rim of the plateau, and it is possible for residents to rise or descend some 3,000 feet (914 meters) without ever leaving town. To give an idea of the elevation to a North American audience, Denver, the mile-high city, is at less than half the elevation. Founded in 1548 by Alonso de Mendoza, La Paz offered protection from the harsh winds of the Altiplano and was near the place where the colonial road from Lima to the silver mines of Potosí crossed Lake Titicaca.

The river curves gently past La Paz, flowing northeasterly and descending the eastern slopes of the Andes. Not far downstream the river traverses some exotic landscapes made even more impressive by snow-capped Andean peaks such as Illimani and Illampu looming in the distance. The Valley of the Moon, a popular tourist destination for sightseers from La Paz, consists of desertlike badlands with eroded spires and columns of rock deeply dissected by narrow ravines. The soft sedimentary rocks capped in places by harder volcanics have been eroded into a variety of eerie forms by water rushing down from the surrounding highlands. Elsewhere valley walls have been steepened to produce characteristically deep, winding gorges known as *quebradas.*

The river soon reaches the *yungas,* humid lowlands of the eastern piedmont. The La Paz River forms one of the major tributaries of the north-flowing Beni, which in turn is one of the major feeders of the great Amazonian tributary the Madeira. Following this river system into northeast Bolivia, one leaves behind the predominantly Incan inhabitants of the Altiplano and La Paz, as well as the primarily mestizo and European populations of the lower valleys and basins of the eastern cordillera, encountering the aboriginal dwellers of the rain forest of upper Amazonia.

See also Beni

LENA

Source: West Baikal Range, in southern Siberia
Length: 2,648 miles (4,261 kilometers)
Tributaries: Kirenga, Vitim, Olekma, Botoma, Aldan, Vilyuy
Outlet: Laptev Sea

The longest and easternmost of the great Siberian rivers rises west of Lake Baikal on Russia's southern rimland. It flows northeastward across the southern portion of the Central Siberian Plateau before making a large bend to the north, then northwest near Yakutsk. The river crosses the Arctic Circle (66°30'N) and, flowing northward, empties into an arm of the Arctic Ocean through an enormous delta.

The Lena's circuitous path to the sea begins in the faulted mountains on the western edge of Lake Baikal. The upper course of the river—approximately a third of its length—follows a narrow, steep-sided valley that has been carved from the old rocks of the Precambrian Shield surrounding Lake Baikal. The Lena (its name means "big river" in the Yakut dialect) passes out of this rugged landscape of deep gorges beyond the junction with the Vitim, a major right-bank tributary that also heads up on the Shield. As the river approaches the mouth of the Olekma River, it forms a broad, deep channel, and the wide valley is flanked by gentle, heavily wooded slopes.

Beyond the Olekma junction the river is again hemmed in by rocky crags. With the joining of the Aldan below the city of Yakutsk, the river's channel divides, separating into several branches interspersed with numerous islands and marshes. The channel here is as much as 9 miles (15 kilometers) wide. After crossing the Arctic Circle, the river follows for more than 400 miles (650 kilometers) the flat, inhospitable tundra, subject to permanently frozen subsoil beneath a shallow active layer that thaws only during the brief three to four months of summer.

Though one of the great rivers of the world, the Lena, like other Arctic rivers, has essentially no flow

Permafrost on the banks of the Lena River showing ice wedges (Jesse Walker)

during the winter. Spring arrives in late May. After the breakup of the river ice, surging floods inundate the broad lower valley and delta, aggravated by the frozen subsoil (permafrost) and consequent poor drainage. Huge blocks of ice and tree trunks rush downstream, contributing to bankside erosion and the collapse of deltaic materials. Discharge in June, the month of maximum flow, is sixty times that of April, when flow is reduced to a trickle. Like other long Arctic rivers, the Lena transports to its outlet the characteristic products of its temperate source region, particularly the sediments and warm water.

The Lena's delta, the largest Arctic delta and the third largest delta in the world, comprises a broad fan of sediments building outward into the open sea. Though its form is sometimes described as the classic triangle (after the fourth letter of the Greek alphabet), it more nearly resembles an irregular quadrilateral, and in this respect it is similar to Canada's huge Mackenzie delta. The apex of the delta begins some 47 miles (75 kilometers) from the sea, and it is believed that the delta was originally of the estuarine type, where the outlet was once an indented bay, but the large amount of sediments deposited at the mouth have built the delta outward. Large outlying islands have been incorporated into the growing delta, best exemplified by Erge-Muora-Sisse, with an area of 2,702 square miles (6,997 square kilometers). The delta has many of the characteristic forms and processes of Arctic deltas: numerous lakes and ponds, distributary channels, sandbars, frost-wedging, pingos (conical mounds cored by ice), erosion accentuated by breakup flooding, and a fragile tundra ecosystem.

More isolated than the other great Siberian rivers, the Lena nevertheless has extensive timber, fishing, and mineral resources that have long been exploited. The taiga, or coniferous forest, of Siberia not only provides rich timberland but is also the habitat of valuable fur-bearing animals, including the silver fox, ermine, sable, and marten. As trapping of these animals in the wild has decreased in importance, fur farming, the production of pelts from animals in captivity, has increased. The upper courses of the Lena and the Vitim have extensive gold deposits of the placer type found in the old Shield rocks around Lake Baikal. Curiously, these were long exploited by a company with mainly British capital until 1935, when the Soviets took over the company (with compensation). There are also important gold mining operations in the Aldan district. Although Russia was once responsible for about 50 percent of world gold production, that figure has dropped today to less than 10 percent.

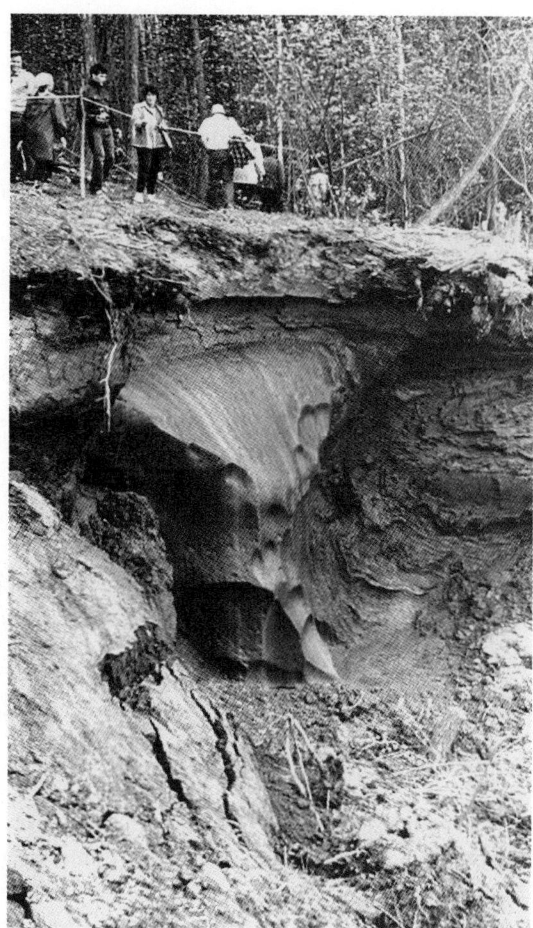

Ice wedges on the banks of the Lena River (Jesse Walker)

The major non-Russian population of the valley are the Yakuts, a Turkic-speaking people with Mongolian influence. Resembling the native peoples of Alaska, the Yakuts have control of an autonomous government within the Russian

Federation. Though supposedly independent, about 50 percent of the region's population is Russian. Situated at the great bend of the Lena in the valley's one district (the Lena-Aldan-Vilyuy Lowland) suitable for agriculture because of its somewhat milder climate, Yakutsk is a major river port and the capital of Yakutia.

See also Ob', Yenisey
Further Reading: Bobrick, Benson, *East of the Sun: The Epic Conquest and Tragic History of Siberia,* New York: Poseidon Press, 1992; Korotayev, V. N., "Geomorphology of River Deltas in the Arctic Coast of Siberia," *Polar Geography and Geology* 10, no. 2 (1986): 139–147; Taylor, Jeffrey, "White Nights in Siberia," *Atlantic Monthly,* December 2000, pp. 36–40.

LIFFEY

Source: Wicklow Mountains, in southeastern Ireland
Length: c. 50 miles (80 kilometers)
Tributaries: Kings, Dodder
Outlet: Dublin Bay, Irish Sea

A river with a short but circuitous course flows past the port and capital city of Dublin before emptying into the Irish Sea. The life-giving Liffey was the setting for most of the writing of the Irish novelist James Joyce.

The source of the Liffey River (Irish Gaelic: An Life) lies in the Wicklow Mountains south of Dublin. The river rises in a peaty depression between the granitic peaks of Kippure and Tonduff. The much-loved Irish river, named after a legendary Celtic woman, lies at about 1,800 feet (549 meters) above sea level at its source and is only about 20 miles (32 kilometers) south of the capital city; with its winding path, the Liffey travels about 50 miles (80 kilometers) to the sea. The river flows west past Manor Kilbride to the artificial Blessington Lakes, a reservoir used for generating hydropower and as a source of drinking water for Dublin. Then the river gradually turns to the north and east, across the fertile open plain of the Liffey valley, where some of the most desirable rural properties of the Irish elite, often in Protestant hands, are located. At Leixlip (from a Norse word meaning "salmon leap"), the river flows east, passing under several stone bridges through the old trading city of Dublin. The river finally empties into Dublin Bay, a protected arm of the Irish Sea that forms an excellent site for a city. After the Viking conquest in the ninth century, Dublin, meaning "black pool," was a Norse town, but the settlement dates back even earlier; on a map of the known world by Ptolemy, the second-century A.D. geographer, a camp is indicated on the north bank of the Liffey, near its mouth.

One of Ireland's most celebrated writers, James Joyce, often used scenes of the Liffey in his fiction. In the *Dubliners* story "An Encounter," the river is an important psychological boundary for two boys "miching" from classes at their parochial school. Upon reaching the docks, the sensitive boy who is the narrator gazes at passers-by, hoping to see a green-eyed Norwegian sailor, perhaps an allusion to the millennial-old conquest of the Irish by the Norse. The Liffey represents a social boundary in *A Portrait of the Artist as a Young Man,* and the young Stephen Dedalus is well aware of the significance of the family's move north of the Liffey to a less genteel residence. Joyce's *Ulysses* relates the peregrinations and thoughts of the young aesthete Stephen Dedalus, the same central character as in *A Portrait,* and the middle-aged advertisement salesman Leopold Bloom on a single day (June 16, 1904) in Dublin, along with the satisfied musings of Molly Bloom, Leopold's wife. The Liffey winds in and out of a complex plot. In the Wandering Rocks episode (chapter 10), for example, the river marks the narrative pace as it carries the torn fragments of the Alexander J. Dowie throwaway from O'Connell Bridge to Dublin Bay.

Joyce's last work, *Finnegans Wake,* is his most difficult. It is not written in English so much as an Indo-European amalgam of linguistic roots and neologisms. The Liffey flows circuitously through the entire novel from the opening passage "riverrun, part Eve and Adam's" to the last lines of Part IV, where Anna Livia Plurabelle, the mature female presence, compares her life to the Liffey's voyage from its source to the open sea. The river is the topographic embodiment of Anna Livia Plurabelle, as her middle name suggests. One whole chapter of *Finnegans Wake* (I.8) contains the disguised names of more than 300 world rivers over which Anna Livia Plurabelle exerts a gentle hegemony. The Anna Livia Plurabelle passage begins with two Irish washerwomen washing their clothes on opposite banks of the Liffey near its source. The last line of *Finnegans Wake* is an incomplete sentence that is completed by the first line of the novel, so that Joyce's final artistic statement is an endlessly recirculated river of words.

See also Boyne, Shannon
Further Reading: de Courcy, John W., *The Liffey in Dublin,* Dublin: Gill and Macmillan, 1996: Healy, Elizabeth, Christopher Moriarty, and Gerard O'Flaherty, *The Book of the Liffey from Source to the Sea,* Dublin: Wolfhound Press, 1988.

LIMPOPO

Source: Northern part of Republic of South Africa
Length: 1,100 miles (1,770 kilometers)
Tributaries: Marico, Shashi, Olifants
Outlet: Indian Ocean

Though rising only 300 miles (483 kilometers) from the Indian Ocean, the Limpopo makes a large, semicircular arc across the northern part of the Republic of South Africa; passes along the border with Botswana (formerly the Bechuanaland Protectorate) and Zimbabwe (formerly Rhodesia); then crosses southeastern Mozambique before emptying into the sea more than a thousand miles from its source.

Also known as the Crocodile River, especially in its upper course, the Limpopo rises west of Johannesburg on the northern side of the Witwatersrand (or, more simply, the Rand), the great gold-bearing reef of the Transvaal. Its source lies near Krugersdorp on the northern side of the Rand. The river flows northward across the veld (Dutch for "field"), the undulating plateau of South Africa and Zimbabwe. Crossing parallel quartzite ridges, the river has cut narrow *poorts,* or gaps, through the resistant rocks. The best known of these is Hartebeespoort, where a dam has been erected to provide irrigation water for the surrounding agricultural district, which produces wheat, tobacco, vegetables, and flowers. The veld has a semiarid climate, so supplemental water is often necessary for intensive agriculture and stock raising.

Crossing other quartzite ridges, the river eventually enters upon sandy country before being joined on its left bank by the Marico River. The northeastward-flowing river forms the boundary between South Africa and Botswana. Here it sheds the name Crocodile (Krokodil) and assumes the name Limpopo. Along this stretch it is joined by several intermittent streams from the south, one of which, the Nylstroom, was believed by Boer pioneers to be the source of the Nile. The river turns to the east at the junction of the Shashi, the primary tributary entering from Zimbabwe. It now forms the political boundary between South Africa and Zimbabwe. As the river enters Mozambique (formerly Portuguese East Africa), it crosses a type of semiarid veldt whose vegetation is open woodland; the characteristic tree here is the baobab, whose massive trunk raises it above the other trees.

The river falls quite steeply off the veld onto the plains of Mozambique (sometimes called low veld). As the river turns to the southeast, the grass-and-acacia savanna of the low plateau gives way to a more humid savanna, with occasional tracts of tropical rain forest. About 130 miles (209 kilometers) from its outlet, the river is joined by its largest tributary, the Olifants, whose source lies near Pretoria not far from the source of the Limpopo. The river is navigable only below this confluence. The river empties into the Indian Ocean 80 miles (129 kilometers) up the coast from the large seaport of Maputo (formerly Lourenco Marques), the capital of Mozambique.

The lowest stretch of the river is hot and humid. Reclamation of the overflow lands and construction of dams and weirs have led to the intensive cultivation of these alluvial lands for subtropical crops such as sugar cane. The crocodiles that gave their name to the river have been replaced by people. Here in southern Mozambique the colonial legacy of the Portuguese lies heavy on the land, particularly the development of ports at the expense of the hinterlands. As a result of the reclamation efforts in the lower valley, a high population density exists in a hazardous, flood-prone environment.

The port city of Xai-Xai at the mouth of the river has the same latitude as Miami, Florida, and the coastal region is just as susceptible to western-tracking hurricanes (known as cyclones in the Indian Ocean). With seasons reversed, however, in the Southern Hemisphere, the greatest danger is in the early months of the year, when sea surface temperatures rise during the Southern Hemisphere's late summer. The torrential flooding of February 2000 brought devastation to the lower Limpopo, inundating more than 1,000,000 acres (404,700 hectares) and resulting in the deaths of tens of thousands.

Further Reading: Mogg, E. H., "The Oliphants River Irrigation Scheme," *Africa* 18 (July 1948): 199–204.

LOIRE

Source: Vivarais Mountains, in southeastern France
Length: c. 630 miles (1,014 kilometers)
Tributaries: Allier, Cher, Indre, Vienne, Maine
Outlet: Bay of Biscay

The valley of the longest and most variable river of France forms historic Château Country. The Loire rises along the steep eastern edge of the Massif Central, a geologically diverse plateau region that has been described as "the water tower of France" because rivers flow from here in all directions of the compass. The source of the Loire is in the inner hills of the Vivarais, the highest elevations of the Cévennes. The traditional headstream begins at the foot of Gerbier de Jonc, a 4,500-foot (1,372-meter) volcanic cone known as the Reed-Stack. The source region includes many eroded volcanic landforms, most spectacularly at the Loire-skirted town of Le Puy, built on a volcanic dike in the midst of free-standing needle rocks formed as resistant volcanic necks, one of which supports seemingly in midair the eleventh-century chapel of St. Michel d'Aiguille.

The upper course of the Loire is not a natural route of travel, so the region has remained secluded. Flowing generally northward, parallel to the plateau's eastern edge, the river alternates between deep gorges, through which the river flows very rapidly, and open basins, which offer enough level land to have attracted human occupation. The first basin is that of Le Puy, floored by alluvial gravels as well as lava flows, after which the river enters the winding gorge of Peyredeyre. Then the Loire descends to the basin of Forez, which has been entrenched by a series of terraces on either side of the river. Again leaving through a gorge, the river flows through the basin of the Roannais. The road from Lyons to Moulins crosses the Loire at Roanne, the west-bank town that gives its name to the region. The Rhône Lateral Canal runs from Roanne to Briare, and other canals link the river with the Rhône and Seine Rivers. Here the Loire becomes part of the trading complex of central France, though the river has not yet broken clear of the highlands and entered the plains. Crossing the undulating plateau of Bourbonnais, the river gradually converges toward the Allier, with which it finally unites near Nevers. Some 40 miles (64 kilometers) farther north, the much enlarged Loire leaves the Massif Central and begins its course across the plains. It then begins to make a large northwestern bend in the direction of Orléans.

Here begins the historic Val de Loire, in which the graceful, slow-moving river flows with wide dignity for approximately 220 miles (354 kilometers) from Orléans to Angers. This is the Loire beloved of every Frenchman (and Frenchwoman) who learned as a child about the glorious history of the storied waterway of Château Country.

The river flows in a trench some 3 to 6 miles (4.8 to 9.6 kilometers) wide, along whose sides rise a series of well-defined terraces to the low plateau. The flow of the Loire is quite variable, like that of most Mediterranean streams. In the drier months of the summer numerous islets and sandbars appear, and the river has a braided form. In winter the branches of the river merge, and water fills the entire broad bottom of the valley, contained between the protective embankments of the levees set far back from the summer course. Much

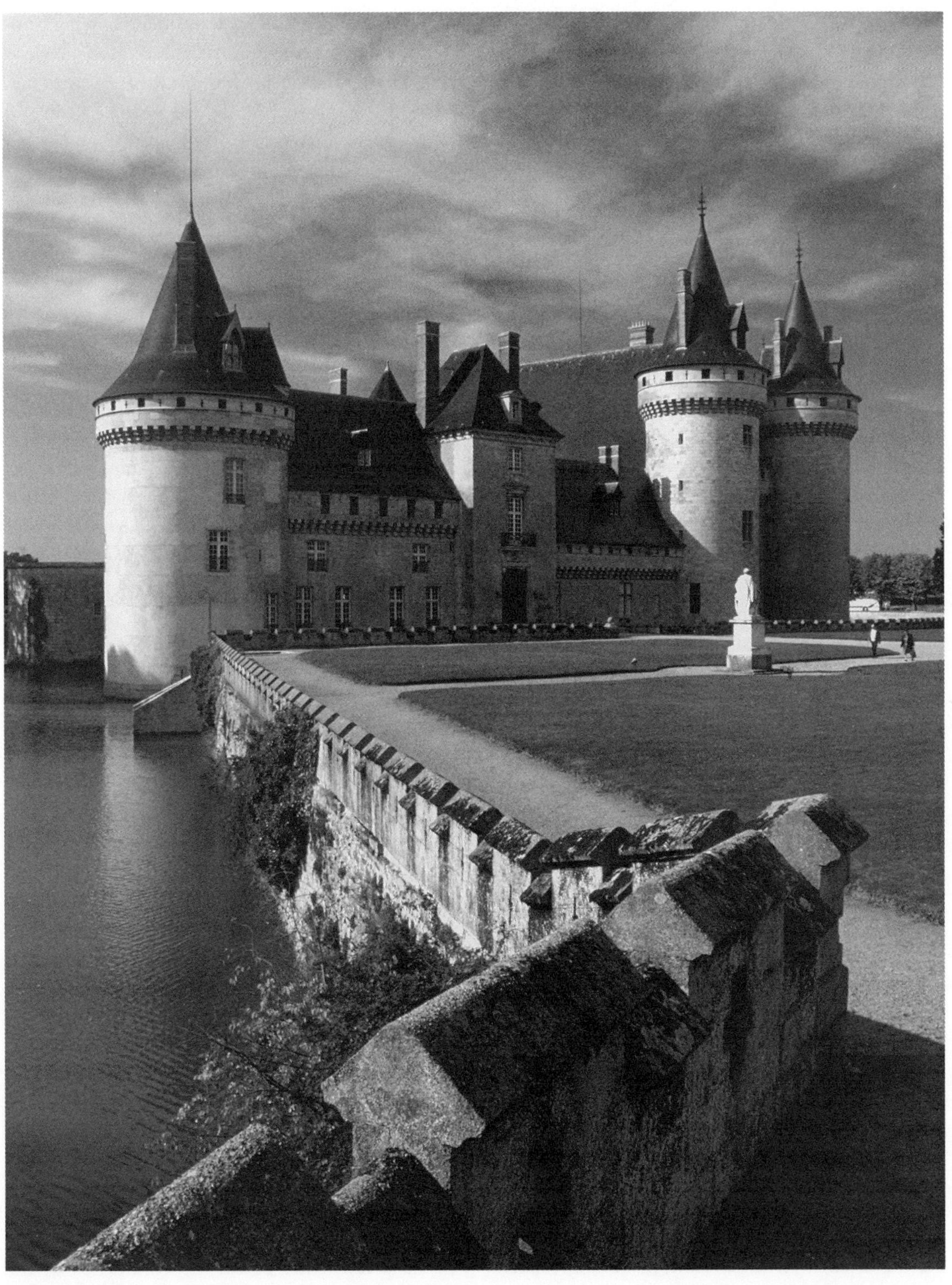

Imposing Château de Sully, with its battlements, courtyards, and moats, at Sully-sur-Loire, near Orléans, France (Adam Woolfitt/CORBIS)

drainage and reclamation have been undertaken. A regular pattern of agricultural land use characterizes the valley, with intensive market gardening of fruits and vegetables along a strip near the river and the towns; cereal cultivation on terraces farther removed; and forest patches, parks, and broom-covered heath on the uplands. Vineyards are of course to be expected in France, and some famous vintages originate here.

The cathedral town of Orléans owes its existence to a river-island that provided a suitable crossing point. The town serves as a market center for the fertile agricultural districts surrounding it—cereal-growing Beauce to the north (really a part of the Paris Basin) and Berry to the south. The city once was an important link in a multimodal transport system: Parisians outward-bound on the Atlantic would take a coach or carriage to Orléans, where they would then be carried on Loire boats to the port of Nantes.

Farther downstream is Tours, the venerable capital of the historic region, or *pays,* of Touraine (as Orléans is of Orleanais). The older part of this city lies on the southern bank of the river between the Loire and its tributary the Cher. The town carries the main road from Paris to Bordeaux across its grand bridge. Forty miles (64 kilometers) downriver is the Anjou town of Saumur, the center of a noteworthy wine industry. Vineyards occupy the slopes of the Loire valley and its tributary valleys. The *pays* of Anjou specializes in white wines, and sparkling wines of the Champagne type are made at Saumur.

The châteaux attract most of the attention. These ornate Renaissance residences were often built on prominent bluffs or spurs overlooking the river. The sites were initially defensible positions—that is, castles—but over time, and with the addition of much ornament, a castle becomes a home, and a château is born. The first château encountered coming down the river is the massive, moated fortress of Sully. It was here in 1429 that the most famous French heroine, Joan of Arc, prevailed upon the dauphin to be crowned king of France at Rheims. The châteaux of the fifteenth and sixteenth centuries in the Loire valley were no different from other ornate residences being built elsewhere at the time, but they were more concentrated in the river valley and its numerous tributaries. The early French kings did not like to live in Paris, which they considered spirit-haunted, so they retired to the Loire, which was located deep in their domains and whose forested uplands dividing the valley allowed the French nobility to indulge its favorite pastime: hunting. The nobles gladly followed the court to Amboise or Blois. Francis I (1494–1547) built perhaps the most elaborate château, that of Chambord, with its ornate skyline of domes and pinnacles. Francis I made his court a center of Renaissance culture and learning, inviting great Italian artists such as Leonardo da Vinci and Cellini to reside there. The middle Loire suffered as a result of religious wars between the Protestants and Catholics. The cloth-making towns in the valley were hurt when the Bourbon kings no longer kept their court on the Loire after Henry IV won Paris. The revocation of the tolerant Edict of Nantes (1685) undermined the prosperity of Tours and Saumur when its Protestant population of weavers left. Louis XIV left Chambord to the tenancy of various pensioners of the crown and moved the court to Versailles. The French Revolution finally emptied the châteaux.

The river was already sanding up when the railroads arrived, converting a once busy river to an idle stream for pleasure craft, since the railroad carried the trade of Nantes. It was not until the revival of romanticism in the nineteenth century that restoration projects brought these large residences back to life. We cannot say good-bye to the châteaux without mentioning the fairy-tale château of Ussé, startling white against a backdrop of dark trees. This château, built in the fifteenth century between the Indre and the Loire about 6 miles (9.6 kilometers) west of Tours, was the setting for the story of Sleeping Beauty, by the seventeenth-century French writer Charles Perrault.

The Loire enters its lowest section at Les Ponts-de-Cé a few miles above the confluence of the right-bank tributary the Maine, which itself has collected the waters of the Mayenne and the Loir (the latter stream having the same name as the river, but without the feminine "e"). Here the river flows across the schists and slates of the Armorican Massif, extending to the south from Brittany. Even as the river approaches the sea, it does not broaden but is contained within a narrow, gorgelike valley because of the effect of the resistant Armorican crystallines. The port of Nantes, 30 miles (48 kilometers) from the sea, has been built on a narrow ridge of granite known as the Sillon de Bretagne, which approaches the north bank of the river. The port's greatest period of prosperity occurred with the founding of the French colonies overseas, as an important triangular trade in sugar, rum, and slaves grew up from here. The abolition of the slave trade was a severe blow, as it was to Bristol. The later development of the port is associated with the tapping of the hinterland of Brittany. A canal links the lower Loire to Brittany and its major port, Brest. Below Nantes constant dredging and diking are required to maintain navigability. Many of the marshes have been carved up by dikes into "pans," where salt is recovered by evaporation, a traditional industry in decline for some time with the pans going to weeds. Before the river finally reaches the sea another granite headland approaches and forms the site of St. Nazaire, the outport of Nantes. Although the estuarine marshes between Nantes and St. Nazaire have been partly reclaimed, many of the wetlands and their teeming wildlife remain. The village of Coueron is situated in the midst of these marshes between the two once-great but now stagnant port cities. The naturalist and painter John James Audubon grew up and once roamed at leisure as a boy in these marshes. Audubon left France in 1806 to make his name in the New World, most famously with his majestic book *Birds of America.* Today the 750-acre (304-hectare) marsh around Coueron, now named after Audubon, is in danger of being turned into a dump site for dredged spoil from the Loire ship channel. The cause of local residents who have attempted to protect and preserve the Audubon Marsh has been championed by France's Bird Protection League as well as—appropriately enough—the National Audubon Society of the United States.

See also Dordogne, Garonne

Further Reading: Cospérec, Annie, *The Châteaux of the Loire,* Paris: Hermé, 1997.

M

MACKENZIE

Source: Great Slave Lake, Northwest Territories, Canada
Length: 1,120 miles (1,802 kilometers)
Tributaries: Liard, Ramparts, Great Bear, Arctic Red, Peel
Outlet: Beaufort Sea, an arm of the Arctic Ocean

Traveling more than a thousand miles from the point of outflow of Great Slave Lake to the Arctic, the Mackenzie is a substantial river by any standard. Yet the distance from its ultimate headwater—the Finlay River in British Columbia—is a total of 2,635 miles (4,241 kilometers), making it the second-longest river system on the North American continent. Thus the Mackenzie River is but the final segment of a drainageway exceeded in length in North America only by the Mississippi-Missouri-Yellowstone system.

Much of the region south of Great Slave Lake drains north into the Arctic Ocean via the Mackenzie. The Slave River links Lake Athabasca and its affluent, the Athabasca River, to the northern lake, and is joined by its own tributary, the Peace-Finlay River. Only the trunk stream north of Great Slave Lake bears the name Mackenzie. A major river-and-lake freight transport route links Alberta to the far north. A number of trading posts (bearing the obsolete appellation "forts") are scattered through the valley and its tributaries, especially at the junction of tributaries with the main stream (for example, Fort Simpson at the Liard confluence), or at constriction points of the water route (such as Fort Providence, near the outlet of Great Slave Lake). The river is navigable between Great Slave Lake and the Arctic for about four months of the year. The route along the Slave River has a serious obstacle in the 16-mile (26-kilometer) stretch of rapids between Fort Fitzgerald and Fort Smith, around which all cargoes are carried by truck. The lower course of the Athabasca River has shallow water and shifting channels. The lakes present some difficulties in that the breakup of ice on these broad surfaces does not occur until mid- or late June, a month later than on the river.

Named after the explorer Sir Alexander Mackenzie, who followed the river's main course to the Arctic in 1789, the river flows generally northwest in a broad valley that is forested as far north as the delta. Sandy terraces stand back from the river, merging inland with the spruce-fir coniferous forest. Following a path between the Rocky Mountains and the Canadian Shield, the river is wide and encounters only a few low hills, the one exception being the 5-mile (8-kilometer) constriction known as the Ramparts, where the river picks up velocity as it runs in a narrow channel under 200-foot (61-meter) cliffs.

The head of the delta is reached at the appropriately named Point Separation, whence the river branches into a maze of interconnected channels scattered with numerous lakes and ponds. The Mackenzie delta is the second largest Arctic delta after the Lena. Layer upon layer of sediment has been built up to form a rough triangle, which is more than 100 miles (161 kilometers) long and about 50 miles (80 kilometers) wide. The main town of Inuvik is located near the head of the delta, while a trading post can be found on the West Channel. As in all deltas, the salinity gradient is an important regulator of vegetation. The southern part of the delta receives more freshwater from the river and is tree-covered, whereas the northern part, more affected by tides and storm surges, is treeless. The Mackenzie delta is not only distinguished by its size but also by the large number of lakes (it has been estimated that 25 percent of its area is occupied by lakes), with numerous small ponds predominating in the north, while fewer, larger lakes are common in the south.

Conspicuous features that stand out from the flat tundra are the conical pingos. These mounds, which can reach 150 feet (46 meters) in height, are caused by a lens-shaped mass of ice freezing beneath the surface of the tundra and heaving the soil up into a domelike hill. When the ice melts, the soil slides off the hill to form characteristic water-centered polygons. Pingos seem to be more common in North America's Arctic than in Russia, and it has been estimated that there are 1,400 pingos in the Mackenzie delta. Other common Arctic processes and forms are the effects of permafrost, heightened erosion during spring breakup of the river, and ice-wedging.

The region was the domain of fur traders until the 1930s, when oil was discovered. The principal oil production site was upriver at Norman Wells until the 1970s, when major petroleum discoveries were made in the delta. By 1994, no fewer than forty-eight significant oil and gas fields had been established. Unlike Alaska's North Slope, the pipeline project that was to bring petroleum to the south, in this case to Alberta, was canceled in 1977 after a federal royal commission concluded that, though feasible, the project had too many legal, political, and environmental problems. Environmental impacts on the fragile tundra ecosystem are many, but especially damaging would have been the effects on the tens of thousands of migratory waterfowl—ducks, geese, swans—that converge on this watery wilderness each summer to mate, breed, and depart before the arrival of winter.

Further Reading: Roberts, Leslie, *The Mackenzie*, New York: Rinehart and Company, 1949 (Rivers of America Series); Walker, H. Jesse, "Arctic Deltas," *Journal of Coastal Research* 14 (1998): 718–738.

MADEIRA

Source: Confluence of **Beni** and Mamoré Rivers, in western Brazil
Length: c. 2,100 miles (3,380 kilometers)
Tributaries: Aripuanã, Canuma
Outlet: **Amazon** River

One of the great southern tributaries of the Amazon begins at the junction of the Mamoré and Beni Rivers in northern Bolivia, along the border with Brazil. The Beni, the primary headstream, cuts across the sandstone foothills of the eastern slopes of the Andes before reaching the lowland *selvas*, or tropical rain forests. Forming the border between Bolivia and Brazil for the first 60 miles (97 kilometers) of its course, the Madeira then turns northeast to cross the sparsely inhabited Brazilian territory of Guaporé. The river passes Pôrto Velho, the head of navigation for shallow-draft ocean vessels, where a series of rapids and falls are encountered. The Madeira-Mamoré Railroad begins here, a 227-mile (365-kilometer) section around the unnavigable river reaching as far as Guajará Mirim (meaning "small pebble") on the Mamoré River. Built as an outlet for rubber during the boom of the early twentieth century, the link was never extended far enough: northeast Bolivia was left unserved, as the rail connection failed to reach navigable water on the lower Beni at Riberalta.

Sugar cane and cotton have replaced rubber and cochineal as salable commodities from these distant portions of the Amazon basin. Distance and inaccessibility continue to trouble the area, however. As the Madeira winds across Rondônia and Amazonas states in northwest Brazil, it picks up several significant tributaries from the southeast, but navigation on these is also restricted by formidable falls. On an affluent of the Aripuanã, Theodore Roosevelt almost lost his life during an exploring expedition. This river is now known as the Rio Roosevelt (it had formerly been called the Duvida, or Doubt, because of its unknown course), a name sometimes applied also to the lower course of the Aripuanã. Carrying almost as much water as the Amazon during the wet season, the Madeira empties into the great equatorial trunk stream 90 miles (145 kilometers) east of Manaus. A minor branch joins the Amazon from the north, just downstream. At this confluence the distributaries of the Madeira are responsible for the formation of a large marshy island known as Ilha Tupinambaranas.

Although the Madeira is the largest tributary of the Amazon, its significance is eclipsed, in terms of human occupancy, by the fact of its unnavigability and its isolation from the main centers of Brazilian population. In this respect, the river is not alone but shares the fortune and fate of the other large Amazonian tributaries.

See also Amazon

Further Reading: Roosevelt, Theodore, *Through the Brazilian Wilderness,* London: Murray, 1914.

MAEANDER

See Menderes

MAGDALENA

Source: Cordillera Central, southwestern Colombia
Length: c. 1,000 miles (1,600 kilometers)
Tributaries: César, Cauca
Outlet: Caribbean Sea

The northern end of the Andes Mountains fray out into parallel cordilleras and wide longitudinal depressions. The Magdalena occupies a structural depression approximately 50 miles (80 kilometers) wide between the Cordillera Central, where it rises, and the Cordillera Oriental, the easternmost of the north-south trending mountain ranges.

The primary concentration of Colombia's population is in the highlands of the central and eastern cordilleras. The Magdalena valley has been only sparsely populated until recently, except for the port cities at its outlet. The main line of access between the coast and the highlands, however, has been the Magdalena River. It has been the chief commercial artery since colonial times and has served as a political unifier of a diverse people who occupy rugged terrain. Goods coming upriver are collected at river ports, from where connecting routes fan out east and west across the cordilleras.

The Magdalena is actually not a very satisfactory navigation route. The mouth has numerous sandbars, which have caused port functions, and even ports themselves, to shift location. Above Calamar the channel shifts frequently and is prone to flooding when the main stream receives the seasonal peak of inundation from its mountain tributaries. Nevertheless, stern-wheel river steamers once made their way on a regular schedule as far as the Honda rapids, the head of navigation for deep-draft vessels located 615 miles (990 kilometers) upstream. Smaller boats can reach as far as Neiva, beyond which navigation is impeded. Honda was at one time one of the most important commercial towns in interior South America. A road was built westward over the Quindío Pass to the Cauca valley crossing at Cali, and links were made to join the river port to the eastern mountain basins of Cundinamarca, where the capital city Bogotá is located. The construction of a railroad (begun in 1880, completed in 1909) from the capital to Girardot, upstream from the Honda falls, as well as the construction of a railroad in 1884 below the falls that tapped the traffic of the lower river and provided transport around the falls, undermined the importance of Honda as a commercial center without diminishing the significance of the Magdalena valley.

With a diverse population scattered in mountain basins and isolated valleys, Colombia has always been in need of something to overcome the friction of distance. It is not a mere coincidence that the country adopted the first regular airline service in the Western Hemisphere, a German line that started in 1920, flying along the Magdalena between Barranquilla and Girardot.

The mouth of the river has been a focus of colonization and intense rivalry for its control since the initial Spanish entry. Once the river emerges from the structural valley between the Cordillera Oriental and the Cordillera Central, it enters a broad alluvial plain. A maze of swamps, oxbow lakes, and rivers is formed by the conjunction of four streams: the Magdalena, the Cauca, the San Jorge, and the César. Much of the land east of the river is taken up by vast shallow lakes and reed-filled swamps with fluctuating outlines (*ciéngas*). Discharging into the tideless Caribbean, the Magdalena has built a large, protruding delta in the shallow waters of the sea. The breadth of the delta is suggested by the spread of the three major port cities. Founded in 1533, Cartagena, lying to the west of the main outlet, was once the preeminent port and stronghold along this strategically important stretch of the Spanish Main. Its site is a natural side channel connected to the main river known as El Dique. Cartagena's channel silted up in the early nineteenth century, and the port lost its pre-eminence (somewhat regained with railroads). On the eastern side of the delta lies the old port of Santa Marta. Shallow-draft boats once passed between the main river and the port through the *ciéngas*. When Cartagena's connection to the Magdalena was disrupted, Santa Marta enjoyed for a while its status as the dominant port, but with the arrival of steamboats neither of the older, colonial ports could be reached by the larger vessels. In this way Barranquilla, more centrally located at the outer edge of the delta, established itself as the most important port city. Barranquilla quickly rose to prominence in the mid-nineteenth century when steamboats began to navigate the river as far as the Honda falls. Sandbars continue to plague navigation, but massive dredging and the construction of short-line railroads to piers projecting out into the shallow waters of the Caribbean have allowed Barranquilla to maintain its preeminent position at the mouth of the river.

Sugar cane and cotton are grown in the lower valley, while coffee, cacao, tobacco, and coca (the source of cocaine) proliferate on slopes in the upper valley and its tributaries, especially in the valley of Magdalena's major tributary, the Cauca. The Cauca valley occupies the northern portion of the structural depression lying between Cordillera Central and Cordillera Occidental. The population is concentrated between Popayan in the south, where the river emerges from the Cordillera Central, and Cartaga, where the river enters its gorges. The city of Medellín is built along a valley east of the Cauca valley but relatively isolated from it. The reputation of the dynamic and culturally distinctive inhabitants of Antioquia has unfortunately been associated with the cocaine trade. Medellín lies along a small stream, the Río Porce, which drains eastward, eventually joining the Cauca-Magdalena system.

Although Colombia, unlike its OPEC neighbor Venezuela, is not well known for petroleum development, a large oil field near the river port of Barrancabermeja was brought under production as early as the 1920s. The primary role the river plays in the life of the country remains that of a commercial artery and a political unifier.

Further Reading: Griffin, E. C., "The Changing Role of the Río Magdalena in Colombia's Economic Growth," *Geographical Survey* 3 (1974): 14–24; Márquez, Gabriel García, *Love in the Time of Cholera,* New York: Knopf, 1988 (orig. pub. in Spanish, 1985); Nichols, Theodore E., "The Rise of Barranquilla," *Hispanic American Historical Review* 34 (May 1954): 158–174.

MAHAWELI GANGA

Source: Hatton Plateau, in Sri Lanka
Length: 208 miles (335 kilometers)
Tributaries: Amban Ganga
Outlet: Koddiyar Bay, Indian Ocean

Separated from peninsular India by the narrow and shallow Palk Strait, the pear-shaped island of Sri Lanka (formerly Ceylon) occupies an area slightly larger than that of Scotland in a range of latitude from 6 degrees north to 10 degrees north. Despite its more nearly equatorial location, the island shares with its larger neighbor a tendency to semiaridity. The dense, rural population (the country has more people than Australia) depends heavily on the efficient utilization of scarce water resources.

The Mahaweli Ganga (*ganga* meaning "river") rises in the crystalline highlands of interior Sri Lanka, a low mountainous range comparable geologically to India's great massif. The air is redolent of tropical spices, and the cool hill station of Nuwara Eliya (pronounced "Nuralia") is nearby. Flowing north across the Hatton and Kandy Plateaus—subdivisions of the interior highlands—the river passes tea and rubber plantations for which the island is famous. The river is lined by Sinhalese villages surrounded by orchards and gardens and terraced rice fields. The stream curves east past Peradeniya, famous for its botanical gardens, and the old capital Kandy, the center of Sinhalese culture. Built entirely around an artificial lake, Kandy has as its chief attraction a temple containing what is said to be a tooth of the Buddha. Kandy was the capital of the independent kings of Ceylon, and even when the coastal lowlands were occupied successively by the Portuguese, Dutch, and the British, the interior region retained a degree of political control. Not until 1815 did the British finally subdue the island and convert it into a crown colony (Sri Lanka attained its independence in 1948).

The longest river in Sri Lanka, the Mahaweli Ganga, flows north and east, away from the island's primary population concentrations. Exiting the highlands, the river drains a semiarid zone where irrigation is necessary for successful farming. The irregular hill lands of Bintenne have sufficient rainfall—about 75 inches (190 centimeters) per year—but until 1947 were malaria infested and difficult to irrigate, even with modern techniques. The river is linked to ancient irrigation works in the basin of its left-bank tributary, the Amban Ganga. In the late 1970s several multipurpose development projects were undertaken along the river, creating a series of reservoirs that provided 500 megawatts of hydropower and irrigated 500 square miles (1,295 square kilometers) of new land. The longest river in Sri Lanka empties into an arm of the Indian Ocean 7 miles (11.3 kilometers) south of Trincomalee, site of a splendid harbor that once sheltered ships of the British Royal Navy that oversaw the Indian Ocean.

Rice, coconuts, and tea are the main crops of the valley, with the proportion of tea higher in the hill lands and coconuts more abundant along the maritime strip. Irrigation from tanks (artificial ponds made by damming the river) was the traditional method of paddy cultivation under the British, but today reservoirs permit a larger amount of water to be used more efficiently. In addition to rice, agriculture in the delta also focuses on coconuts and tobacco. The delta is small as a result of the small size of the river and the high-energy coastal environment of the Indian Ocean, which sweeps away to sea any sediments deposited.

MARITSA

Source: Rila Mountains, in western Bulgaria
Length: c. 300 miles (483 kilometers)
Tributaries: Tundzha, Ergene
Outlet: Aegean Sea

The upper course of the Maritsa (Greek: Évros; Turkish: Meriç) flows eastward in southern Bulgaria in the broad lowland of an ancient lake basin lying between the Rhodope Mountains to the south and Stara Planina (Balkan Mountains) to the north. The Plovdiv Basin, named after its largest city, has fertile soils and produces a variety of irrigated crops, including rice, fruit, and tobacco. The towns along the upper Maritsa—Pazardzhik, Plovdiv (Greek: Philippopolis), and Dimitrovgrad—are marketing and processing centers for their agricultural hinterlands, and also produce textiles and metal goods.

Known to the ancient world as the Hebrus, the river has long been a focus of colonization and conflict. The Macedonian king Philip II conquered Plovdiv and made it the capital of Thrace, the ancient region bordered roughly by the north Aegean, the Sea of Marmara, the Black Sea, and Macedonia. Possessing both valuable cultivated land and a key strategic location, the sprawling region of Thrace has passed back and forth between contending powers from the time of the Romans to the present, when the territory is divided among three countries.

The river turns to the south at Edirne (Adranople) at the junction of the major left-bank tributary, the Tundzha, and forms the border between Greece and Turkey. With the course of the river so obstructed by rocks and sandbars, the Turkish town of Edirne is the head of navigation for small boats. The marshy, flood-prone valley below the confluence of the Tundzha impedes communications and is therefore a good natural frontier.

With the incorporation of northern Thrace into independent Bulgaria in 1878, the political meaning of "Thrace" was confined to southern Thrace, which was then in Turkish hands. The terms "Eastern Thrace" and "Western Thrace" referred to the territories on either side of the Maritsa, which passed back and forth between Greece and Turkey (sometimes even going to Bulgaria). By a complicated series of events, including two Balkan wars, World War I, and two different treaties after World War I, the Maritsa, along much of its lower course, eventually became the boundary between Greece and Turkey (there is a short stretch where it separates Greece and Bulgaria). As a result of modern population movements, the ethnic components of the region now roughly correspond to national divisions.

Below the confluence of the left-bank tributary, the Ergene, the river begins to widen and branch into two main channels. The last 20 miles (32 kilometers) of the river form a delta crossed by numerous dikes and paths with access to land growing cotton and maize. A wetland some 7 miles (11.3 kilometers) wide stretches across this deltaic plain. A refuge has been established to protect about 250 species of birds that must compete for their aquatic prey with the local fishermen. The Maritsa finally empties into the northeastern Aegean near Enez, Turkey, which lies to one side of the delta.

MARNE

Source: Langres Plateau, in northeastern France
Length: 325 miles (523 kilometers)
Tributaries: Rognon, Saulx, Somme-Soude, Petit-Morin, Ourcq, Grand-Morin
Outlet: **Seine**, just above Paris

The major river of northern France, the Seine, forms a large drainage network, with numerous tributaries focused on the country's capital. Geologically speaking, the Paris Basin consists of a sedimentary bowl into which a series of layers have been poured, resulting in a rock structure resembling a nested set of teacups. Outwardly tilted hills (scarps, or cuestas) represent the upended, resistant strata. These elevated *côtes,* including the one east of Épernay on the Marne, have served historically as good natural lines of defense.

The Marne River rises on the edge of this sedimentary basin, tracing a northwesterly path across the upland known as the Plateau of Langres, after the dominating fortress perched above the river near its headwaters. The Marne has eroded its way headward more than the upper course of the Seine, which reaches only the dry oolitic limestone. Draining a region that doesn't have its precipitation swallowed by porous limestone, the upper Marne thus has a larger discharge than does the nearby Seine. As the Marne crosses the chalky soil of the Champagne, much of the precipitation is absorbed. As a result, the river becomes large only below Brie.

The Marne makes several large meanders before joining the Seine at Charenton, just upstream from Paris. It is navigable from Saint-Dizier to its junction with the Seine. Lateral canals parallel the river as far as Épernay. Additional canals link the river system with the Aisne to the north, the Sâone to the south, and the Rhine to the east. Coal, building materials, pit props (supporting timbers), and agricultural products stream along these connecting routes, making the Marne an important commercial waterway. The valley of the Marne has extremely good agricultural and pasture land. The low hills of Champagne, which rise above the river, are renowned for their vineyards and the sparkling wines they produce.

The river's Latin name, Matrona, meaning "Good Lady" or "protecting goddess," proved true in the crucial first month of World War I on the Western Front. The Great War began in August 1914 with an initial advance by the German army that brought it within striking distance of the garrison of Paris. In early September the Allied forces began an offensive that drove the Germans toward the east, on the far side of the river for which this major battle was named. Vigorous fighting took place along the banks of the Marne and its lower tributaries, especially the Ourcq, the Grand-Morin, and the Petit-Morin. The extensive wetlands of the Marshes of the St. Gond, near the headwaters of the Petit-Morin, were the scene of fighting between Germany's Third Army under General von Hausen and the French Ninth Army led by General Foch. The banks of the Marne and its affluents were steep, the valleys presented precipitous slopes, sometimes resembling ravines. Though not as difficult a terrain as the Ardennes and the Vosges, traditional natural frontiers of French territory to the east, the Marne—its channel and banks—served as natural bulwarks of Paris almost as important as the fortress-protected high points such as Verdun and Langres.

The rivers of the Marne system were not wide enough to provide easy defense. Soldiers learned that it was easier to defend the far bank of the river than the near bank. If the near bank had to be defended, better to make a line of defense away from the river's edge. With the successful Allied drive to the Marne, the Germans fell back by mid-September to positions that gave them possession of only a limited area in northeastern France. The Allies swiftly followed, hoping to conduct open warfare, but discovered that the enemy had sought defense in the construction of well-fortified entrenchments. Thus ensued the horrible trench warfare that characterized World War I.

See also Seine

MEDWAY

Source: The Weald, in southeastern England
Length: 70 miles (113 kilometers)
Tributaries: Eden, Beult, Len
Outlet: **Thames** estuary

The rivers of southeastern England in the old counties of Surrey, Sussex, and Kent are not among the most sublime or picturesque, but many count them beautiful in a peaceful, civilizing way. The Medway rises on the northern slopes of the Weald, a formerly forested region between the North and South Downs. The Weald (German: *Wald,* "forest") was once noted for its iron industry. The Medway's headstreams begin on the margins of Surrey and West Sussex. The river flows generally north into Kent. It is the most important Kentish stream by virtue of its length, the quiet beauty of its inland stretches, and the historic anchorage at its lower end.

The river trenches a gentle valley—narrow but with steep slopes—as it cuts across the sandstones, clays, and chalk (limestone) of the Weald. Clearly defined gaps in the resistant sandstone and chalk strata contrast with the broader vales where softer clays are more easily eroded. Passing the first important Kentish town on its route, Tonbridge, the river enters the Vale of Kent in crossing the claylands. The river picks up several subsequent tributaries, particularly the Eden from the west and the Beult from the east. It appears likely that the upper Medway once continued northward as a headstream of the present Darent but was captured by the headward erosion of an east-flowing stream that now forms the Eden and the middle Medway.

After its confluence with the Eden, the river follows a generally easterly course. It passes through a sandstone escarpment in a distinct gap near Yalding before reaching the prosperous vale around Maidstone. In the dozen or so miles between Tonbridge and Maidstone, the Medway achieves the characteristically prosperous Kentish landscape of hop fields, orchards, fine country seats, and upstanding villages. Below Maidstone the river makes its passage through the high chalk ridge of the North Downs. The sides of the hills are scarred by several large quarries.

The tidal river broadens and begins to look less peaceful as industrial works become visible. At the head of the Medway estuary lie the nearly contiguous towns of Rochester, Chatham, and Gillingham. Compact Rochester with its cathedral is redolent of Dickens, while straggling Chatham was once an important naval base with dockyards, but those are now closed. The estuary widens into an expanse of open water with numerous islands. At low tide appears a maze of mud flats and tidal creeks. Narrowing briefly between Sheerness and the Isle of Grain, the river finally joins the great expanse of the Thames estuary.

At the close of the second Anglo-Dutch War (1664–1667), the English navy suffered a humiliating defeat on the Medway anchorage. Though the English generally had the better of the Dutch on foreign waters during this conflict occasioned by commercial rivalry in the East and West Indies, the Dutch fleet at times sailed unimpeded into the Thames estuary and nearby English waters. In June of 1667 a Dutch fleet entered the Medway estuary and burned English warships as they lay off Chatham. The humiliation was not just because English ships were lost at home, but also because English seamen served as pilots for the attackers. It turns out that the seamen had not been paid by their government for a long time.

See also Thames

Further Reading: Bradley, A. G., *The Rivers and Streams of England,* London: Bracken Books, 1993 (orig. pub. 1909).

MEKONG

Source: Eastern Tibetan Plateau
Length: c. 2,600 miles (4,184 kilometers)
Tributaries: Yangbi, Nam Phong, Nam Ngum, Tonle Sap
Outlet: South China Sea, southern Vietnam

Draining almost the entire length of the Indochina Peninsula in a southeasterly direction, the Mekong is truly a giant, but one subject to dramatic swelling and shrinking in response to seasonal changes in precipitation.

The river rises as a mountain stream in the Tanggula Range of the Tibetan highlands at an elevation of more than 16,000 feet (5,000 meters). The headwaters region is so secluded that it was not until 1994 that the source was finally pinpointed in eastern Tibet. The upper river runs in deep, narrow gorges down a steep gradient with numerous falls, characteristic of mountain streams. The Chinese name for the river in this section is Lancang Jiang, which means "turbulent river." Like many other Asian rivers rising in distant mountains, there are several names for the waterway. The Tibetans refer to the upper course as Dza Chu, or "river of rocks," while only farther downstream does the river adopt the Thai name Mae Nam Kong, or "mother of the waters," which is the basis of the stream's contracted Western appellation. At its lower end it is called either Song Lon, meaning "great river," or Song Cuu Long, referring to Nine Dragons, or deltaic mouths, that join the river to the sea. There are in fact many more than nine channels in the delta, if we count all the major and minor distributaries, but nine is a propitious number and the dragon is a powerful symbol for the Vietnamese.

Although the densely populated lower course of the river may be more life-giving, with millions of people depending on its waters for irrigation of rice crops, the headwaters of this giant stream also have a claim to a kind of beneficence. The English writer James Hilton's Shangri-La, the fanciful but realistically portrayed retreat from the troubled world of civilization, may have lain along one of the Mekong's tributaries. An ancient trade route carrying tea, horses, and salt between Tibet and China crossed Dequin and Zhongdian counties beneath lofty, snow-clad peaks marking the descent of the Tibetan plateau to the Chinese lowland. An isolated Buddhist monastery looming up like a fortress from a temperate valley protected by surrounding mountains—the setting of Shangri-La—is matched by a number of gorges cut by headstreams of the Yangtze and the Mekong Rivers.

The river crosses the southwest province of Yunnan running almost parallel to and between the Salween and the upper Yangtze. It is a raging torrent here, confined by bare rock walls and rushing at great speeds. The river was undammed and unbridged in this section until very recently, carrying only foot traffic across old iron suspension bridges. Today China has constructed a massive suspension bridge at Jinghong to facilitate the passage of heavy transport across the river, connecting Yunnan with Myanmar, Laos, and Thailand. A series of dams have been either built or planned, beginning with the Manwan Dam in

1993, to generate electricity for industrial development around Kunming, the provincial capital, and to even out the annual flow of the river, the latter an advantage, according to the Chinese, for downstream countries, which have objected to the possibility of decreased discharge.

Exiting China, the river briefly forms the border between Myanmar and Laos, before, at the convergence of a minor tributary, the territories of Myanmar, Laos, and Thailand converge. Known for decades as the "Golden Triangle," this rugged region long associated with the cultivation and sale of opium actually refers to the junction of the Ruak and the Mekong, not to the point where the three countries meet.

Along the river's middle course where Myanmar, Laos, and Thailand converge, people on opposite banks today move freely across the river, especially during the dry season. But in the 1890s, when these boundaries were delineated, they represented important geographic limits of imperial control, especially for the French, who controlled the eastern parts of Indochina, and the British, who occupied southern Asia as far east as Myanmar. A French toehold was gained in Indochina following the capture of Saigon (Ho Chi Minh City) and the creation of Cochin China in South Vietnam (1861). In one of the epic expeditions during the age of heroic exploration, Doudart de Lagrée led intrepid French explorers up the Mekong in 1866–1868. The party learned of the numerous falls and rapids on the middle course of the river in Laos, particularly at Khone Falls, which made the river unnavigable and undermined French imperial dreams of forging a major trade artery along the Mekong. Many of these knickpoints have today been developed as dam sites, to generate power (for sale to Thailand) and for irrigation, despite the environmental impacts of the decreased sediments reaching the delta for land building and altered flows leading to reduced fish population, especially in Cambodia's Great Lake, which the local population depends heavily upon for its diet.

Mekong River, floating gardens (Jesse Walker)

In this section the river zigzags between mountains as it travels in a generally southeasterly course. At times steep-sided canyons emerge; elsewhere the valley broadens as the river crosses undulating plains. Much of the massive Mekong Project, a series of dams and impoundments for providing steady irrigation water and hydropower, focused on this stretch of the Mekong and its tributaries. Directed from Bangkok, the project got its start in the late 1950s—at least in the information-gathering phase—and in the following decade European and American engineers and hydraulic experts descended on the region at just about the time that the Vietnam War began to spill across the border, threatening projects and participants alike. Some of the American consultants and engineers had had experience working on some of the giant projects on the Colorado in the American Southwest. The key feature of the Mekong Project was to store the surplus precipitation of the monsoon season (June–October) and to release some of that water during the dry months, when the river is reduced to a trickle.

As befits such an important river, the Mekong satisfies not just the multiple uses envisaged by reclamation engineers—irrigation, hydropower, and navigation—but also the numerous everyday activities that focus on the river. People along the river regularly bathe along its banks, traditionally before midday and evening meals. Small boats ply its waters for fish, an important part of the diet. A gigantic catfish that lives only in the Mekong, the *pla bük,* is threatened by dams that prevent its migration upstream to breed. Water buffaloes that are used to cultivate rice fields descend to the banks at the end of the day to cool off, and river water is used for cleaning, drinking, and washing.

In the Mekong basin, nature has provided a model of flow regulation. At Phnom Penh, a major port and capital of Kampuchea (Cambodia), a branch of the river connects it to the large interior Great Lake (Tonle Sap). During the flood season the river flows to the north, along the Tonle Sap River to the lake of the same name. In the dry season the flow reverses, and the water returns to the Mekong. The river confluence site of the Cambodian capital traditionally includes "Four Arms." One is the mainstream of the Mekong, flowing down from Laos to the north. This mainstream splits in two flowing into southern Vietnam: the second and third arms. The fourth arm is the Tonle Sap. Along the margins of the fluctuating lake connected to the Mekong lies the most visited tourist attraction in southeast Asia: Angkor Wat. The impressive ruins of this former civilization testify to an economy that depended on controlling the water supply along the edge of the Great Lake. The Khmer civilization of Angkor built canals, dams, and artificial lakes, manipulating the monsoonal environment of southeast Asia in ways that anticipated the Mekong Project of the 1960s.

The vast delta begins when the south-flowing river enters southern portions of Vietnam (formerly South Vietnam). Ho Chi Minh City lies a short distance to the east. The city is connected to the delta by a canal that carries an endless procession of barges bearing rice and other foodstuffs. In the delta, an endless panorama of rice fields are bounded by bunds, or embankments, to hold in the water. The paddies make for a neat mosaic of fields on river islands and riverbanks alike. Thousands of miles of interconnecting waterways lace the delta; during the Vietnam War, they provided excellent defensive coverts for the Viet Cong army. Not even heavily armed American gunboats and strafing Cobra helicopters could root out the guerrillas from the numerous hiding places provided by the densely vegetated delta, the heart and soul, and material basis, of Viet Cong resistance. The major towns of the delta—Soc Trang, Long Xuyen, Can Tho—are located where the largest canals connect with the rivers. Traffic follows the numerous canals in a region that has no roads. The U.S. Army and Navy discovered that the enormous jungly interstices of these access routes provided hard-to-get-at retreats and strongholds. Despite the flat terrain, the delta is a spider's web of canals and channels of various sizes, and most of the area is away from the large brown branches of the Mekong. No bridge had been built across the mainstream channel in the lower river until 1994, but bridges are now either planned or already constructed at a number of sites. The first was the Friendship Bridge linking the Thai and Lao banks of the river near the Lao capital of Vientiane, and there are plans to construct a major bridge and throughway in the Mekong Delta at My Thuan.

Further Reading: Osborne, Milton, *The Mekong: Turbulent Past, Uncertain Future,* New York: Atlantic Monthly Press, 2000; White, Peter T., "The Mekong: River of Terror and Hope," *National Geographic,* December 1968, pp. 737–787.

MENDERES

Source: Anatolian Plateau, western Turkey
Length: c. 240 miles (390 kilometers)
Tributary: Banaz
Outlet: Aegean Sea

The classical Maeander, from which is derived the English word *meander,* meaning "a winding stream," has for its full present name Büyük Menderes, or "Great" Menderes. This is to distin-

True to its name, the Maeander River of antiquity (today's Menderes) makes a tight loop along its lower course in western Turkey. (Atlas Geographic)

guish it from the Kücuk, or "Little" Menderes, which also drains the Anatolian Plateau but is located farther north. The shorter, northern stream, known in ancient times as the Scamander, passes near its mouth the windy plains of Troy, the setting of Homer's *Iliad.*

The Maeander River of antiquity rises in southern Anatolia not far from the Turkish lake district. Following a generally westerly course, it is the longest of the Turkish rivers draining westward into the Aegean Sea. Its upper course sometimes trenches itself into the bare plateau surface. As the river approaches the sea, the valley opens up to become a typical Mediterranean landscape of fig trees, olive groves, and vineyards. The river forms a series of regular serpentine loops resembling the general pattern made by rivers crossing low, level valleys around the world. There are much larger meanders than the classical ones—in the lower Mississippi valley, or along the Amazon once it leaves the cordillera—but the name itself is an echo of ancient times. Near its mouth the Menderes passes the site of Miletus, which has long since been abandoned because of the silting of the river. Miletus was once a great seaport of Ionian Greece and was the birthplace of some of the first, pre-Socratic philosophers. Known for its fertile soils and abundant olive production, the Menderes valley finally reaches the sea south of the island of Samos.

The Greeks populated their natural world with gods and goddesses, spirits and nymphs. According to legend, Maeander, son of Cercaphus and Anaxibia, was fighting a war in Phrygia, a region in central Asia Minor best known as a source of slaves and as a center of the cult of Cybele. He vowed to the earth goddess Cybele—a Persian deity but one that influenced Greeks and Romans—that if he were victorious he would sacrifice the first people who congratulated him upon his return. Those unfortunates turned out to be his family—his son, his mother, and his sister. After sacrificing them, he hurled himself into the river that afterward bore his name. The river's twists and turns, it might be suggested, register the convolutions of the soldier's vow, or the windings of his conscience upon his tragic return.

MEUSE

Source: Langres Plateau, in northeastern France
Length: c. 560 miles (901 kilometers)
Tributaries: Chiers, Bar, Sormonne, Semois, **Sambre**
Outlet: North Sea

The Meuse rises in eastern France in the southern part of Lorraine. This traditional region forms a transition zone between the outer scarps of the Paris Basin and the high Vosges. Flowing generally northward, the Meuse has entrenched itself in limestone to form the Côtes de Meuse, with the main scarp beyond the right bank of the river. In this long section the river receives no tributaries except for a few tiny streams originating as springs on the side of the limestone valley. The river wanders across a mile-wide valley, with braided sections, cutoff meanders, and backswamps. The size of the valley suggests that the river once carried more water, and it is likely that active erosion by Seine headwaters to the west and the Moselle to the east captured some of its tributaries. The flow of the river is highly variable, with rapid runoff from the impermeable claylands of southern Lorraine; in summer the flow reduces to a trickle. The most important town in this section is Verdun, a key fortress site dating from Roman times that guards the crossing of the Meuse by the Metz-to-Paris road. During a six-month period in 1916, the French held off the Germans in the hills around Verdun. The name is remembered mostly for the gruesome death tolls of World War I and the horrors of trench warfare: more than half a million men died fighting at Verdun.

Farther north the river makes a series of large loops and receives tributaries on each bank, with towns typically forming at or near the confluence of the tributaries (for example, Mézières at the junction of the Sormonne from the west; Monthermé at the junction of the Semois from the east). Most of the towns along this segment of the river are small manufacturing towns and like Verdun have associations with the devastation of the world wars. The fortified town of Sedan, just downstream from the confluence of the Chiers, was the site of the humiliating defeat of Napoleon III by the Prussians in 1870. The end of the Second Empire and the relinquishment of Alsace and Lorraine to Germany followed. The Meuse was the most important water obstacle on the Western Front in World War I, and devastation was rained on its towns—from Saint-Mihiel to the Ardennes. Fighting resumed during World War II, and devastation revisited this key valley.

Continuing northward, the Meuse crosses the western Ardennes, entering Belgium below Givet. The river is contained in a rocky gorge some 300 to 500 feet (91 to 152 meters) below the plateau, with deeply incised meanders producing sharp loops and prominent spurs. The citadel of the chief town of Dinant overlooks the river from a high limestone perch.

At Namur the river abruptly changes direction, flowing eastward along the trend of its tributary, the Sambre, as it skirts the coal basin of southern Belgium. The valley is broad and open as far as the major industrial city of Liège, though with a distinct, steep edge on its northern side. It receives numerous tributaries draining from the Ardennes to the south, in contrast to the river's isolation in the Lorraine scarplands. Navigability of the Belgian Meuse has been improved with a series of locks and dams to maintain a sufficient depth for barges in this busy iron and steel region. Between Liège and Maasbracht (in the southern Netherlands), the broad valley has a distinct set of terraces, associated with changing sea levels in the Pleistocene.

Not far north of Liège the river approaches the Netherlands frontier (the Dutch name for the river is the Maas). It forms an international boundary for some distance, but makes a loop to the west around the Dutch city of Maastricht, so that the river is wholly Dutch for 8 miles (12.9 kilometers) before the boundary once more runs down the center of the channel to Maasbracht. The complicated status of the river has created serious international problems. Flowing between the heath-covered Kempenland on the west and the south Limburg coal field on the east, the river is impeded by gravel, sandbars, and islets, whose removal would require cooperation between the two countries. Belgium has refused to cooperate, since improved navigation would be to the advantage of Rotterdam and to the disadvantage of Antwerp. The upshot is that the Dutch built the lateral Juliana Canal along the right bank between Maastricht and Maasbracht, bypassing the unnavigable stretch in entirely Dutch territory, while Belgium responded by extending the Albert Canal from Liège to Antwerp.

Below Maasbracht the river, flowing entirely in Dutch territory, curves to the west and joins the great Scheldt-Maas-Rhine delta. One branch joins the Waal, a major distributary in the estuary. Another branch, the Bergsche Maas, was cut in the late nineteenth century to provide a direct outlet distinct from that of the Waal. It flows into the Hollandsch Diep, an inlet of the North Sea south of Dordrecht. The Oude Maas (Old Maas) is a branch of the Waal, while the Nieuwe Maas (New Maas) is a continuation of the Lek River. In this intricate system of Dutch waterways the major channels are separated by massive dikes but linked by canals and locks. The menace of extensive flooding of inter-riverine areas has been reduced by a system of dams and locks. Navigability has to be maintained because the Maas is a commercially important waterway, and Dutch barges have to ply the river all the way to the south Netherlands province of south Limburg, which is remote from the rest of the country and dependent on the exploitation of bulky natural resources.

See also Rhine, Sambre

Further Reading: Monkhouse, F. J., *A Regional Geography of Western Europe,* London: Longmans, rev. ed., 1960; "Treaties to Protect Maas and Scheldt Rivers Signed by Dutch, French and Belgian Officials (Remediating Troubled Waters: Legal, Political and Institutional Frameworks)," *Ekistics: The Problems and Science of Human Settlements* 62, nos. 370–372 (January–June 1995): 109.

MISSISSIPPI

Source: Lake Itasca, in northern Minnesota
Length: c. 2,350 miles (3,780 kilometers)
Tributaries: Minnesota, **Wisconsin**, **Illinois**, **Missouri**, **Ohio**, Arkansas, Yazoo
Outlet: Gulf of Mexico

The river is a strong brown God—sullen, untamed and intractable.
T. S. Eliot, *Four Quartets*

The principal river of the United States is exceeded in length only by its major western tributary, the Missouri, which stretches 2,565 miles (4,130 kilometers) from its headwaters in the Rocky Mountains to its outlet on the Mississippi just north of St. Louis. The combined length of the Mississippi-Missouri ranks as the third longest river system in the world, after the Nile and the Amazon. The Missouri's drainage basin is about three times the size of that of the upper Mississippi north of the merger with the Missouri. The Ohio is the chief eastern tributary, entering the Mississippi near Cairo (pronounced KAY-ro), Illinois. The Ohio's discharge exceeds that of both the Missouri and the upper Mississippi.

Since the nineteenth century the primary federal agency responsible for flood control and navigation on the river, the Army Corps of Engineers, has made the Cairo junction the division point in their definition of the upper and lower valley. North of Cairo the upper valley carries less water; is confined within a comparatively narrow floodplain bounded by conspicuous bluffs; and has numerous small rapids and falls between St. Louis and the head of navigation at the Falls of St. Anthony at Minneapolis (these have been converted by the Corps into a series of locks and dams). The lower river valley comprises a vast alluvial plain, in which opposing valley sidewalls take the form of low bluffs. The valley stretches from horizon to horizon,

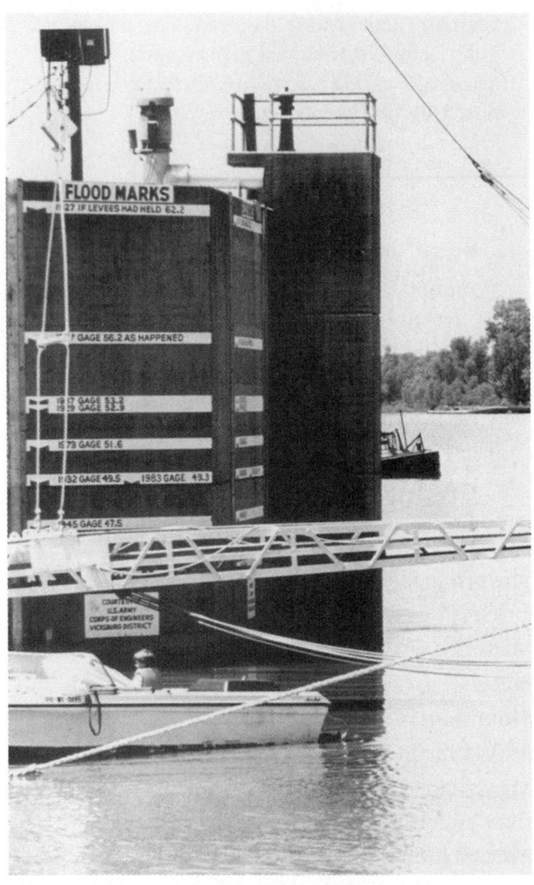

Mississippi River gauge at Vicksburg, Mississippi. Note the high level of the 1927 flood—"if levees had held." (Jesse Walker)

however, and cannot be taken in with a single view. This Mississippi "delta"—really an embayment of an ancient sea—is best seen from the air, with its broad floodplain and numerous meanders and oxbow lakes. The true head of the delta, defined as the Mississippi Embayment, lies about 30 miles (48 kilometers) north of the Ohio confluence at Cape Girardeau, Missouri.

The true geomorphic delta—an approximately triangular tract of land at a river's mouth—is found south of New Orleans in the Birdfoot delta of Plaquemines Parish, Louisiana. The primary distributary channels known here as "passes" include Southwest Pass, South Pass, and Pass à Loutre. Much of the coastal and interior lands of south Louisiana on either side of the Birdfoot (also known as Balize) delta has been built up by accumulation of sediments when the main channel discharged to the east or west of its current position. The two most important abandoned deltas are the Lafourche (pronounced la-FOOSH) delta, where the river debouched to the west of the presently active delta as recently as five hundred years ago; and the St. Bernard delta to the east, which has not received significant sedimentation for more than a thousand years and as a result is suffering from fragmentation of wetlands and land loss. The state of Louisiana is losing about 25 square miles (65 square kilometers) of land each year, much of that loss being a result of two causes: damage done by artificial canals and channels that cut across the marsh and encourage saltwater intrusion; and the loss of sediments resulting from the work of the Army Corps to prevent floodwaters (and sediments) from overtopping the levees.

The mandate of the Corps was initially focused more on navigation than flood control. The need to facilitate shipping and interstate commerce is a constitutionally specified federal responsibility. The elevation of earthen embankments (levees) to keep out floodwaters, however, would seem to be more of a local need, and so it was interpreted at a time when the federal government was smaller and its powers were more strictly defined. The Great Mississippi Flood of 1927 radically changed the federal role in regulating its greatest river. The levees-only theory—that by confining the river at high water between levees, the river's force would be concentrated and it would scour its channel—had been proven wrong. The idea of a self-scouring river, which had been criticized by the two most important engineers who dealt with the river in the early period, James Eads and Andrew Humphreys, had guided the actions of the Corps on the river: levees were raised to ever higher levels, and natural outlets (distributaries)—such as Cypress Creek, Arkansas, opposite and above Greenville, Mississippi; and Bayous Manchas and Plaquemine, south of Baton Rouge, Louisiana—were sealed off. The mistaken idea was that by sealing off the river, the velocity of the water would increase and bottom sediments would be removed, thus lower-

Eads' jetties at the mouth of the Mississippi in south Louisiana. The purpose of the jetties is to confine the flow of water and thereby to allow the river to scour and deepen its channel for purposes of navigation. (Jesse Walker)

ing the level of floods. Not only was this idea proven wrong by the 1927 flood, but, indeed, communities along the flood path made their own artificial crevasses or breaks to relieve the tension of the rising river. New Orleans dynamited a break in the levee at Caernarvon, just below the city, sacrificing properties in St. Bernard Parish. Curiously, Caernarvon turned out to be the site of an innovative project in the 1990s in which fresh water and sediments were allowed to pass through the levee at low-river stages to promote land building on a section of the coast that, as we have seen, is vulnerable to erosion. The Crescent City was in an especially vulnerable position in 1927 (it still is), since much of its downtown is below sea level. As it turned out, the artificial break was probably not necessary, because there were so many crevasses and inundations occurring upriver following the major crevasse at Mounds Landing, Mississippi (April 21, 1927), which put the whole Greenville-Yazoo delta under ten feet of water. From Missouri to the Gulf the river had been converted into an inland sea, with flood waters covering nearly a million acres (404,700 hectares) of land. Workers maintained twenty-four-hour watches on levees that they shored up with sandbags and makeshift retaining walls. Electric wires were strung out on the levee, and with the help of generators, workers (mostly blacks in the Deep South) kept up their arduous vigil at night. One learned to recognize the telltale signs of a weakening levee. The appearance of sand boils—cones of earth shaped like miniature volcanoes—discharging muddy water was a sign that something was about to give; they indicated that the levee was being eroded and would soon burst.

The aftermath of the Great Mississippi Flood of 1927 was that the Army Corps began to follow multiple goals in flood protection (flood control is only one of many activities on public waterways—navigation, recreation, and hydroelectric generation being others). Floodways are now used to divert high water into backwater channels and lakes. Among the most prominent of these are the Birds Point–New Madrid Floodway, which takes water off the main channel near Cairo and returns it at New Madrid; the Morganza Floodway above Baton Rouge, Louisiana, which directs floodwaters down the Atchafalaya; and the Bonnet Carré Spillway above New Orleans, which directs water to Lake Pontchartrain. Though levees are no longer relied upon exclusively, they are still the engineering backbone of the Corps's flood plan. Levees must be built to uniform standards, higher and wider now, and are reinforced by concrete revetments. An old idea of Eads, that cutting across the neck of horseshoe bends would move water faster and thus lower flood heights, has been put into practice along some sections of the river, particularly in "the Greenville bends."

The final piece of the Corps's plan to cope with floods has been the construction of the Old River Control Structure (ORCS) just above Morganza, Louisiana, where the Mississippi, the Red, and the Atchafalaya Rivers come close together. The ORCS, completed in 1962, is meant to divert as much as 30 percent of the flow of the Mississippi down the shorter Atchafalaya route to the Gulf of Mexico, a distance of 155 miles (249 kilometers) versus 325 miles (523 kilometers) via the current route past Baton Rouge and New Orleans. The other function of the ORCS (which was supplemented by an auxiliary structure because of problems during the 1973 flood) is to act as a giant floodgate in the event of a century flood (one that has a statistical probability of occurring once in a hundred years). The release of floodwaters down the overbank structure would cause the river to bypass the heavily populated cities of south Louisiana and flow in a torrent down the Atchafalaya Basin, thereby flooding Morgan City near its outlet. That small city, which was developed in the middle of the nineteenth century as an alternative port to New Orleans, would thereby be sacrificed, just as the properties of the inhabitants of St. Bernard Parish were in the flood of 1927. Despite such a prolonged effort pitting human willpower against the energies of the river, it is believed by many that the Mississippi will in the end take the shorter path to the sea.

See also Illinois, Missouri, Ohio

Further Reading: Barry, John M., *Rising Tide: The Great Mississippi Flood of 1927 and How It Changed America,* New York: Simon and Schuster, 1997; Carter, Hodding, *Lower Mississippi,* New York: Farrar and Rinehart, 1942 (Rivers of America Series); Havighurst, Walter, *Upper Mississippi,* New York: Farrar and Rinehart, 1937 (Rivers of America Series); Lee, Douglas, "The Land of the River," *National Geographic,* August 1983, pp. 226–252.

MISSOURI

Source: Rocky Mountains, southwest Montana
Length: 2,565 miles (4,130 kilometers)
Tributaries: Yellowstone, Little Missouri, Cheyenne, James, **Platte**, Kansas, Osage
Outlet: **Mississippi** River, 17 miles (27 kilometers) north of St. Louis

Rising high in the snow-covered peaks of the Beaverhead Mountains on the Montana-Idaho border, the mighty Missouri drains an enormous eight-state basin along an irregular course that takes it diagonally across the northern Great Plains before emptying into the Mississippi just north of St. Louis. The length of the combined Missouri-Mississippi system makes it the world's third-longest river, behind the Nile and the Amazon. Except for an accident of history that brought explorers and traders into contact with the upper Mississippi before they viewed the eastern end of the Missouri, it might have been designated the main stem of the greatest drainageway of North America.

Two key features of the upper Missouri are the Three Forks and Great Falls. It was already recognized by the explorers Lewis and Clark in the summer of 1805, during the course of their expedition up the Missouri, that the junction of three streams to form the Missouri in western Montana was an important gathering place and transit point. The Shoshone teenage girl Sacagawea, who had come along with her French-Canadian husband, Charbonneau, recognized it as the summer home of her people and the place where she had been recently captured by raiding Hidatsas, who lived among the Mandan villages near present-day Bismarck, North Dakota. She and her husband encountered the overwintering Lewis and Clark expedition there. A large bowl-shaped basin

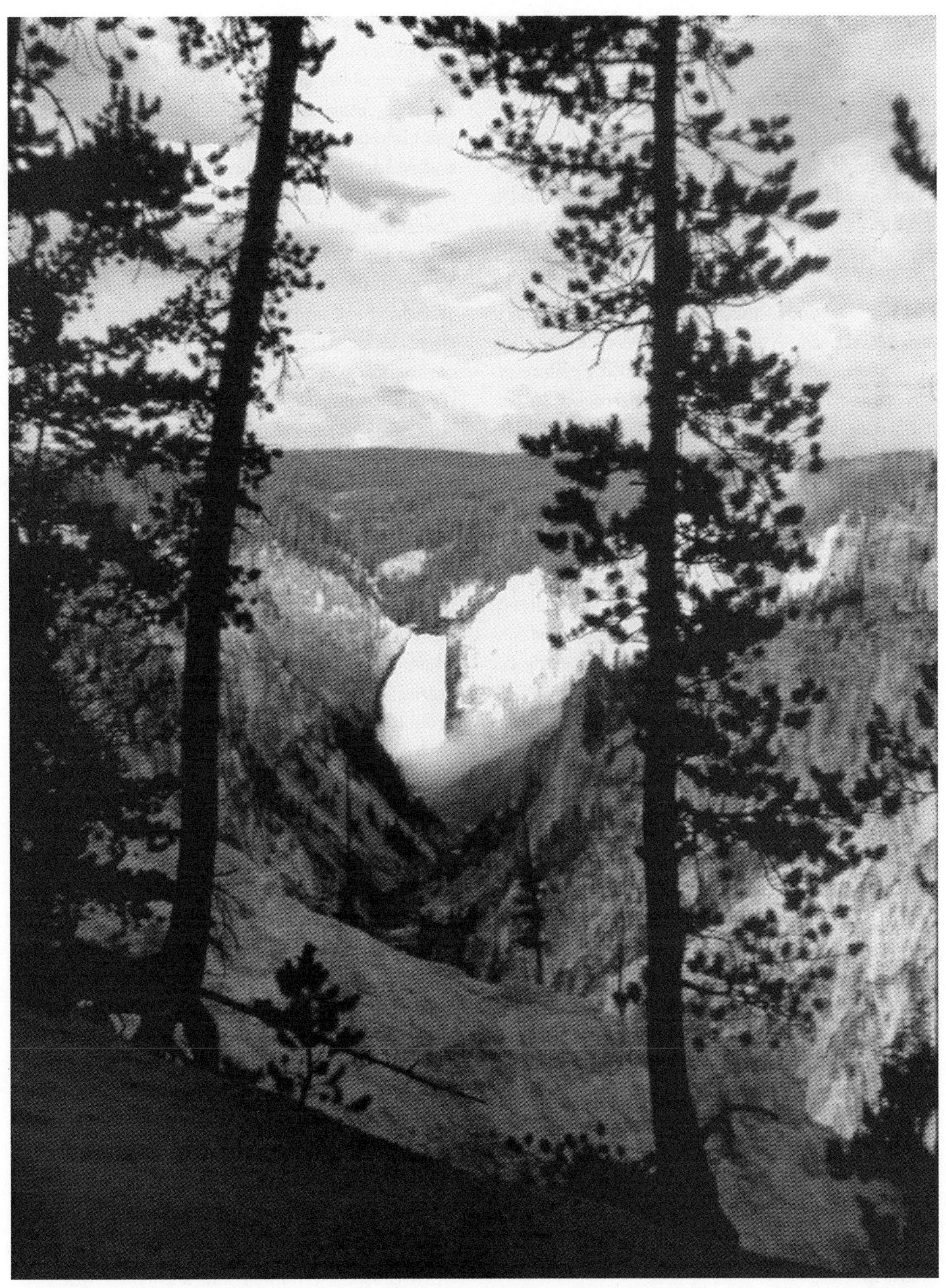

Lower Yellowstone Falls, knickpoint on the major Missouri River tributary (Jesse Walker)

contained the three interlinked valleys at Three Forks. Extensive meadows and grasslands were nearly surrounded by snow-girt mountains in a scene that yet today can be appreciated for its natural beauty. The headstreams of the Missouri were named by Captain Meriwether Lewis as the Jefferson, Madison, and Gallatin after, respectively, the third president of the United States, who had envisioned the great western exploration; his secretary of state; and his secretary of treasury. Lewis and Clark ascended the Jefferson and its tributary the Beaverhead, which is today considered the main-stem Missouri. Following another tributary stream, the Red Rock, the company of explorers crossed the Continental Divide at Lemhi Pass. This ascent of the Missouri, however, left the Corps of Discovery along an unnavigable section of the Salmon. Fortunately, a band of Shoshone Indians, Sacagawea's people, agreed to provide horses and a guide to take the men north along the Divide to the Bitterroot valley. From there a western tributary, Lolo Creek, gave access to the Lolo Trail, by which Lewis and Clark made their arduous crossing of the Bitterroot Mountains, bringing them down to the Clearwater-Snake-Columbia river system.

Lewis and Clark did not know it during the course of their westward journey, but trails existed that crossed the mountains and reached the Bitterroot valley downstream from the Three Forks region—routes that would have saved them hundreds of miles. They did make use of them, however, on their return trip. One of these trails reaches the river near Great Falls, where the Missouri plunges spectacularly over a series of five falls. This 12-mile (19-kilometer) stretch of falls and rapids presented a major obstacle for Lewis and Clark: they had to abandon their larger boats, which they called "pirogues" (large, flat-bottomed rowboats), and proceed with canoes, as well as making a difficult portage. Ever since then, Great Falls has been the head of navigation on the upper river. By 1859 steamboats plied the length of the river from St. Louis to Fort Benton, just below the falls.

Below Fort Benton the river enters a stretch that has been relatively undisturbed and has been set aside by the government as a Wild and Scenic River. The western section of this pristine part of the river is known as the White Cliffs, while to the east is the Missouri Breaks. Stretching for almost 160 miles (257 kilometers) from Fort Benton to the western end of Fort Peck Lake, the river is bounded by high, rugged bluffs composed of brown sandstones that beautifully capture the high, clear light of the plains. Entering the eastern section of the Breaks on their voyage upstream, Captain Lewis climbed a towering riverside bluff and saw for the first time the snow-covered mountains in the distance. His co-command, William Clark, thought he had seen the mountains the previous day. They were the first Americans to see the Rocky Mountains.

Among the many environmental problems along the upper river today is the loss of habitat for stream-side cottonwoods, a symbol of the riparian West. Although the main dams are farther downstream, there are numerous dams on tributary streams upstream that reduce the high spring flow necessary for scouring sandbars and for providing a place where seedlings can take root. Trampling of banks by grazing cattle and the development of riverfront property add to the degradation of the upper river.

After the Missouri's major tributary, the Yellowstone, joins the river from the south just inside North Dakota, the widening river makes a great bend, a gradual change in its course to the southeast and then to the south, as it crosses the plains and prairies of the Dakotas. Here the "Big Muddy," nicknamed for its heavy load of silt, enters a chain of reservoirs backed up by five major dams built since the 1940s (Garrison, Oahe, Big Bend, Fort Randall, and Gavins Point). Authorized by the U.S. Congress in 1944 as part of the Missouri River basin project (sometimes called the Pick-Sloan scheme, after Lewis Pick, an Army Corps of Engineers official, and Glenn Sloan, a Bureau of Reclamation engineer), the dams were built primarily to control flooding and provide irrigation water and secondarily to generate hydropower and ensure navigability. The high water in March and April caused by rainfall and snowmelt would be held back. Water would also be impounded during the second flood stage in June, when snow melts in the remote, western mountains. Summer water levels, when the flow is so low that boats can go aground, would be enhanced by releasing water from the lowest dam, at Gavins Point.

Since the dams have no locks, Sioux City, Iowa, below the lowest dam, is the head of navigation for deep-water barges. The 736-mile (1184-kilometer) segment of the river between St. Louis and Sioux City passes through rich corn and soybean country. Barges carry fertilizers and grain to and from Omaha, Kansas City, and lesser towns. Just as railroads killed the steamboats, they now outcompete the barges. Cargo traffic on the "Big Ditch," as the lower third of the river is sometimes called, is in decline, yet the maintenance of what is essentially an industrial canal remains a high priority for policy makers and planners trying to balance the multiple uses of the river.

Recreational use of the river, including power boating on the large reservoirs and paddling on smaller sections of the river, has become increasingly important, as have environmental issues. In the dry 1980s, the Army Corps released water downstream to salvage the barge channel. Lake Oahe in North Dakota got so dry that disgruntled recreationists protested, and the state of North Dakota initiated a flood of lawsuits. Environmentalists have clamored for water release that more nearly mimics the natural flow of the river: spring release to scour sandbars and provide spawning clues for fish, and low summer flow to expose sandbars for shorebirds. The latter would keep the reservoirs full for the boaters but require the suspension of downstream navigation. The environmental point of view is increasingly being incorporated into the plans of a new generation of Corps officials who attempt to balance the multiple uses of the river.

The greatest challenge faced by the Corps today concerns its historical mission of river channelization. The swollen, silt-choked river once flowed across a wide and twisting channel, passing over into numerous back channels, crossing chutes, making hairpin bends. Countless islands and sandbars interrupted the course of the river. As early as the 1880s the Army Corps began to construct wood and rock wingdykes to funnel water to the center of the channel, thereby deepening the river and increasing its speed. Soft, erosive banks were reinforced with rock revetments to prevent slumping. The creation of a deep, uniform, reliable channel for barge traffic along the lower river was the primary goal of the Corps. Wetlands and forests that once covered the riverbottoms were converted into agricultural land. Present plans call for leaving unrepaired levees open and letting nature reclaim some of the bottomlands, creating back channels and sandbars where endangered species such as the pallid sturgeon, the least tern, and the piping plover, among other more common species, can breed and feed.

For many, the traditional list of multiple uses of the river—flood control, navigation, irrigation, hydropower, and recreational boating—needs to be expanded, or perhaps tailored, to include the potential of the river for wildlife habitat, historic sites, and recreational use of the river by crafts not powered by the internal combustion engine. Some would like the chance to see the river, at least in places, as Lewis and Clark saw it, in the kind of craft they might have used. Not all users can be satisfied, of course, so priorities must be set. If the formula of "multiple use" degenerates into "too many uses," it is at the peril of all users and the river itself.

See also Platte

Further Reading: Ambrose, Stephen E., *Undaunted Courage: Meriwether Lewis, Thomas Jefferson, and the Opening of the American West,* New York: Touchstone, 1996; Hart, Henry C., *The Dark Missouri,* Madison: University of Wisconsin Press, 1957; Least Heat-Moon, William, *River-Horse: The Logbook of a Boat across America.* Boston: Houghton Mifflin, 1999; Vestal, Stanley, *Missouri,* New York: Farrar and Rinehart, 1945 (Rivers of America Series).

MOHAWK

Source: Central New York
Length: c. 140 miles (230 kilometers)
Tributary: Schoharie
Outlet: **Hudson**

The valley of the longest tributary of the Hudson provided for early migrants the only breach westward through the northern Appalachians. A histor-

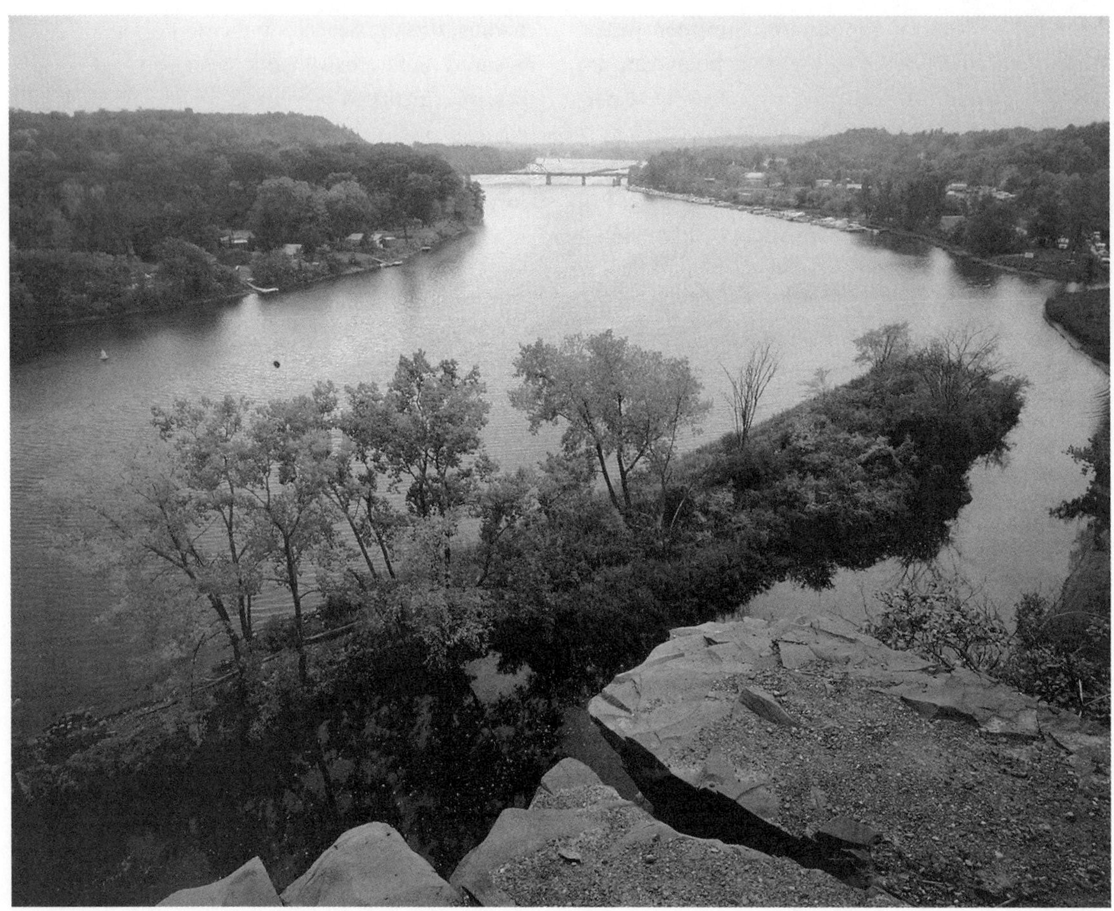

An island in the Mohawk River near Schenectady, New York (David Muench/CORBIS)

ical sequence of transport routes followed the course of the Mohawk valley, initiating local and regional change in population, town development, and technology. Named after its Native American inhabitants, the valley was the scene of many important battles and raids in the French and Indian War (1754–1763) and the American Revolution (1775–1783). The river is today canalized from Rome, New York, to its mouth as part of the New York State Barge Canal (formerly the Erie Canal), linking the Hudson River with the Great Lakes.

The Mohawk is formed by the junction of its east and west branches in central New York. It flows to the south and then to the southeast, past Utica, Schenectady, and a number of small manufacturing towns before entering the Hudson at Cohoes. Navigability of the river is generally good, but there are several small falls and rapids that were the object of improvement early in the nation's history. The widely used Schenectady boat was a freighter 50 feet (15.2 meters) long and capable of carrying 10 tons (9.07 tonnes) of produce if it could cope with shallows, snags, and seasonal changes in depth. By 1810 two sets of locks and dams had been installed: one around Little Falls, and the other across the old portage from the head of the river to Oneida Lake. The largest falls, Cohoes Falls, near the river's outlet, had not yet been circumvented.

The Mohawk Trail became the route of choice for thousands of settlers migrating westward from the Eastern Seaboard in the late colonial and early national periods. Often originating from older, settled New England states, migrants followed the

Indian Trail that wound along the ridgeline above the river. The Erie Canal, which has been described as the largest state-sponsored public project in American history, generally followed the route of the river (completed 1825). The project began when laborers started digging westward from Rome in 1817 (the large number of classical placenames suggests the importance Yankees and New Yorkers placed on education). Proceeding westward to Syracuse, Seneca, Palmyra, and Rochester, the canal gradually ascended thirty-four lock steps before reaching Buffalo at the eastern end of Lake Erie. The Oswego feeder canal linked the route to Lake Ontario. With freight costs reduced by 90 percent (and travel time cut by at least half), the rich commercial agricultural lands of the upper Midwest could now find their outlet along the Eastern Seaboard. Within fifteen years of the Erie Canal's opening, New York City, which had been the nation's fourth largest city, became preeminent, eclipsing Philadelphia.

The railroads outcompeted the canals, just as the canals had put the turnpikes out of business. One of the first railroads in the state was a portage route meant to complement river-based transport. The Mohawk & Hudson (1832) bypassed the tedious lockages around Cohoes that had been installed as part of the Erie Canal waterway. The New York Central Railroad, built in the 1840s, followed the path of the canal and the river, intersecting all the major towns along the route in a traffic-serving function so as to maximize receipts. The route of its competitor, the New York & Erie, lay farther to the south, following a straight line between New York and Buffalo to minimize construction costs. These two alternative strategies—revenue maximization versus cost minimization—are still very much in evidence today in building transportation systems, and they have a decidedly different geographical impact on service.

Just as the toll roads were superseded by the canal, and the canal by the railroad, so the railroad has been eclipsed by modern, paved roads: the New York State Thruway and Interstate 90 take most of the traffic across upstate New York, following the Mohawk valley in the eastern section. Though some cargo is moved by rail, the barge canal is today used mostly by leisure craft. The historical sweep from the Indian Trail to interstate highway has passed over the Mohawk during the course of three centuries like so many shadows from passing clouds. The people of upstate New York, as elsewhere in the nation, have derived untold rewards from the river that most take for granted. Cleanup efforts under the Clean Waters Program of 1965 have helped to remove industrial wastes and municipal raw sewage. A beautiful historic valley and a clean river are as appreciated today as economic benefits.

See also Hudson
Further Reading: Hislop, Codman, *The Mohawk,* New York: Rinehart, 1948 (Rivers of America Series); Swerdlow, Joel L., "Erie Canal: Living Link to Our Past," *National Geographic,* November 1990, pp. 38–65.

MORAVA

(In Czech Republic)
Source: Sudetes
Length: 240 miles (390 kilometers)
Tributaries: Becva, Dyje
Outlet: **Danube**

(In Yugoslav Federal Republic)
Source: Confluence of two branches northwest of Niš, in southern Serbia
Length: 134 miles (216 kilometers)
Tributary: Resava
Outlet: **Danube**

It is not surprising that two major rivers with this same name exist in eastern Europe, since the slavic root *morje* means "water." The central, restricted portion of the former Czechoslovakia comprised the historic region of Moravia. Incorporated today with Bohemia as the Czech Republic, this region embraces the fertile Morava valley, after which it is named. The Moravian Gate refers to the wide pass between the eastern end of the Sudetes and the western end of the Carpathians near the headwaters of the Oder and Vistula Rivers. The northernmost Morava drains southward into the Danube 8 miles (13 kilometers) west of Bratislava. It has been an important channel of communications between the North European Plain and the Danubian lands of eastern Europe since pre-Roman times, serving as a military line of contact as well as a trade artery between northern and southern Europe.

The southernmost Morava River in the Yugoslav Federal Republic is the main waterway of Serbia. Formed by the junction of a southern and western branch, this Yugoslav river flows in a northerly direction to its outlet on the Danube just downstream from Belgrade. Also known as the Velika Morava, it forms the wide, fertile, and densely populated valley of the Pomoravlje—the core area of Serbia. At its southern end the Morava approaches Skopje, the capital of Macedonia, providing a link to the south-draining Vardar, whose outlet is just west of Thessaloníki at the head of the Aegean Sea. The Morava-Vardar corridor thus provides an access route across the mountainous Balkans, joining the eastern Mediterranean to the lower Danube just as the northernmost Morava links the Danube to northern Europe.

See also Danube, Vardar
Further Reading: Magocsi, Paul Robert, *Historical Atlas of East Central Europe,* Seattle: University of Washington Press, 1993.

MOSELLE

Source: Vosges Mountains, in northeastern France
Length: 320 miles (515 kilometers)
Tributaries: Madon, Meurthe, Seille, Orne, Fentsch, **Saar**
Outlet: **Rhine**

The Moselle (German: Mosel) rises on the western slopes of the highly dissected crystalline massif of the High Vosges in eastern France. The highest granite peaks have been weathered and eroded to produce rounded humps that are known by the somewhat curious name *ballon* (or *bâlon*). The Moselle drains the slope of one of the highest of these, the Ballon d'Alsace, at an elevation of 4,101 feet (1,250 meters). It flows north-northwest along with its numerous headstreams across Lorraine. After crossing crystalline rocks, the river enters a sandstone country in which it is contained in a forested gorge. At Pont-Saint-Vincent, where the Madon joins from the left, the valley begins to cross limestone strata; this is important because the rocks contain one of the largest deposits of iron ore in Europe.

Farther downstream the river makes a sharp turn to the northeast for about 10 miles (16 kilometers) as far as Frouard. The abrupt change in course at Toul and the geological anomaly of the river's crossing and recrossing the limestone layers suggests river piracy in the past. The upper Moselle once followed a westerly path to join the Meuse, but the lower Moselle and its tributary, the Meurthe, which joins the main stream at Frouard, were more active (that is, possessed a steeper gradient and higher velocity of flow). They eroded headward until the "elbow of capture" near Toul diverted the upper river eastward, leaving a dry gap, the Val de l'Ane, utilized by the Marne-Rhine Canal. The town of Toul was for long a strategic fortress center commanding this important junction between the Moselle and Meuse valleys.

Below the Meurthe junction the river winds across a broad, flat-bottomed floor covered with alluvium and bounded on the west by the limestone escarpment of the Côtes de Moselle. Iron ore deposits of a rather low grade (the so-called *minette* deposits) are found at the surface on scarp faces and valley sides of the Moselle and its left-bank tributaries. An integrated iron-and-steel industry concentrates on the left bank near the foot of the limestone escarpment all the way from Metz to Thionville and along the lower valleys of the Orne and Fentsch.

Lorraine is the main iron-ore-producing area of France, and it is for this reason that the region was seized and annexed by the Prussians in 1871. The French-German borderland of the Saar furnishes complementary coal to Lorraine's iron ore. Just above the main metallurgical concentration in the valley is the old city of Metz, located at the confluence of the Seille. This town, the *chef-lieu* of the département of Moselle, is the only one in this part of Lorraine not directly concerned with the iron-and-steel industry; it had an earlier history as a fortress town since Gallo-Roman times and also functions as an agricultural service center for the

Moselle valley (Parisian food shops carry canned foods stamped "fabriqué en Metz").

Below Thionville the river turns to the northeast and approaches the international border where France, Germany, and Luxembourg converge. Almost all the drainage of the tiny duchy of Luxembourg focuses on the Moselle, by way of the Sûre.

As a German stream, the Mosel continues in a northeasterly direction for about 80 miles (129 kilometers). It picks up the important tributary of the Saar from the southeast. The river flows first through a broad open basin, where scenic Trier is situated, with its fine Roman ruins (some are surprised to learn that this is the birthplace of Karl Marx). Then the river crosses the middle Rhenish Highlands as far as its junction with the Rhine at Koblenz (a modification of the Roman name Confluentes, meaning "confluence"), with the Eifel plateau to the north and the Hunsrück to the south. In this section the Mosel forms a series of deeply incised meanders enclosing hilly spurs that impede navigation but promote lovely scenery. The steep north-facing slopes are covered with pinewoods, while the opposite sides of the valley are covered with vineyards that produce the vintage wines the region is best known for. Regularization of the lower river has resulted in the removal or alleviation of the problems of meandering channel, swift currents, variable depths, and gravel bars.

See also Rhine

MURRAY

Source: Australian Alps, in southeastern Australia
Length: 1,609 miles (2,589 kilometers)
Tributaries: Mitta Mitta, Ovens, Goulburn, Campaspe, Loddon, **Murrumbidgee**, **Darling**
Outlet: Indian Ocean

Occupation of the dry island continent of Australia has been largely along the periphery. All of Australia's large cities are ports, points of attachment between formerly separate colonies (now states) and the Mother Country. In only one significant exception did the British penetrate far into the interior: along the continent's greatest river system, the Murray-Darling. Traveling from Sydney on the southeast coast, early explorers crossed the southern end of the Great Dividing Range and intercepted the headwaters of the Murray. In 1830 Sir Charles Sturt made a fantastic journey by whaleboat down the Murrumbidgee to its confluence with the Murray, which he named after Sir George Murray, then British secretary of state for the colonies. Discovery of gold south of the Murray in the early 1850s set in motion a gold rush and subsequent agricultural colonization not unlike the nearly contemporaneous events in California.

The Murray rises in the Australian Alps, at the southern end of the Great Dividing Range, a major topographical feature in eastern Australia paralleling the coast; the Australian Alps have a geographical position and a geological structure similar to those of the Appalachian Mountains of North America. In its upper course the river tumbles over steep hills clothed with tall eucalyptus trees as it picks up numerous headstreams. It leaves the foothills at Albury, where it turns west, wandering across a wide plain. For much of its length the river forms the boundary between the states of New South Wales and Victoria. The broad, lagoonlike side channels of the meandering river are known by the colorful Australian term "billabongs." The word is enshrined in memory by Australia's most beloved song, in which a vagabond caught stealing a sheep commits suicide rather than get caught:

> Up jumped the swagman,
> Sprang into the billabong,
> "You'll never catch me alive,"
> said he.
> And his ghost may be heard as you
> pass by that billabong,
> "Who'll come a-waltzing Matilda
> With me?"

The once important upriver town of Echuca, located near the confluence of the Murray and Campaspe Rivers, was originally a cattle crossing. With the extension of the railroad from Melbourne

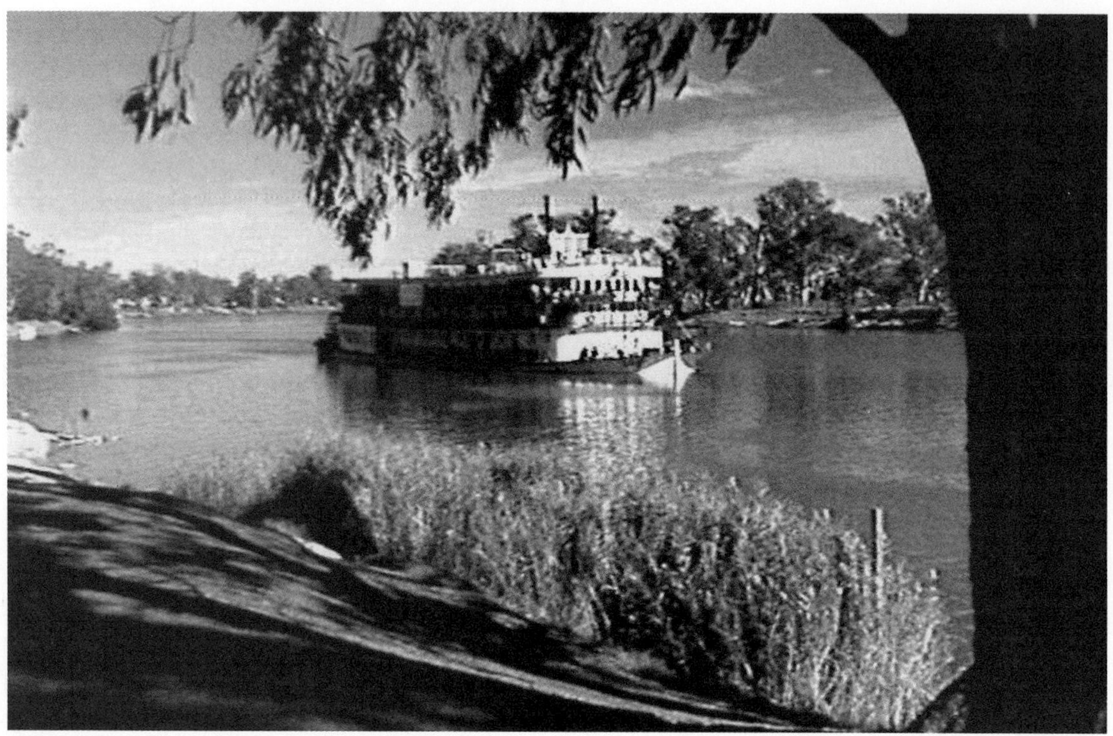

Once used for commercial traffic, the steamboats on the Murray River today carry leisure seekers. (Australian Tourist Commission)

in 1864, the town became a key transshipment point, where river steamers carrying wool from backcountry sheep stations were unloaded and cargoes destined for settlers—flour, tobacco, beer, sewing machines—were taken on board. As was generally the case when railroads intersected river routes, the boom was short-lived; as railroads extended their networks into the outback, river transportation was bypassed. Today the river is used primarily by pleasure craft, including restored paddlewheel steamboats and houseboats.

The river is joined by its major tributary and the longest river in Australia, the Darling, some 500 miles (800 kilometers) from the sea. The plain formed by the confluence of the Murray and Darling above their union is Australia's best agricultural land, known as the Riverina. The settlement around Mildura became a successful orchard and vineyard district in the late nineteenth century, bearing a similarity to California's Central Valley—including its dependence on irrigation.

The lower course of the river after its junction with the Darling crosses the dry mallee scrub of South Australia. Following a southerly course, the river is contained in a mile-wide gorge cut in marine sediments rich with fossils deposited when the lower end of the basin was an arm of the sea. The river empties into Lake Alexandrina, a shallow lake whose extensive shoals and high tidal ranges have impeded navigation and prevented the establishment of a major seaport at the outlet of this great hinterland. The river finally crosses the northern end of the Coorong, an 80-mile-long (128-kilometer-long) salt lagoon, before passing into Encounter Bay across a maze of shifting sandbars.

Environmental problems caused by the salinization of dry soils have increasingly threatened the Murray basin. As background, it must be borne in mind that more than 100 dams and weirs are in place along the river, some, like the Goulburn Weir, dating from the late nineteenth century. Without irrigation, the lands of the dry interior of Australia were worth about as much to Aussie settlers as arid Western lands were to American pioneers. Irrigation schemes expanded rapidly after the world wars to provide land and economic opportunity to returning soldiers. Best known of these is the famous Snowy River Scheme, by which the course of a stream that once flowed east to the Pacific Ocean has been reversed, its waters directed through tunnels in the mountains so that it now flows west to join the Murray system. The additional waters of the Snowy are used to generate hydroelectricity and to provide irrigation for the dry interior plains. Today more than 75 percent of Australia's irrigated land is in the basin. The elevation of the water table with irrigation brings salt to the surface. The problem is so bad that salt pans form on roadsides; the brick walls of old buildings turn white; and farms have to be abandoned. The problem is only partly the result of excessive irrigation, however: deforestation and unsuitable farming are also partly to blame. The towering eucalyptus, the river red gum that grows along the banks of the river and is almost a symbol of the valley, has been cut or its habitat has been destroyed by alteration of stream flow. Intensive cotton and rice cultivation are preferred to more appropriate crops such as olives and grapes, which require less water. The lower Murray in South Australia has become like the lower Colorado in Mexico—at times the river is reduced to a trickle. Excess withdrawal by upstream irrigators concentrates turbidity, salinity, and pollutants in the reduced volume of discharge.

See also Darling
Further Reading: Levathes, Louise E., "The Land Where the Murray Flows," *National Geographic,* August 1985, pp. 252–278; "The Salt that Won't Run to the Sea," *The Economist,* February 5, 2000, p. 38.

MURRUMBIDGEE

Source: Snowy Mountains, southeastern Australia
Length: c. 1,050 miles (1,690 kilometers)
Tributaries: Goodradigbee, Tumut, Lachlan
Outlet: **Murray**

The longest tributary of the Murray, Australia's principal river, is the Darling, but it drains from the dry north and its upper course includes frequently dry feeder streams. The Murrumbidgee, by contrast, begins in high alpine meadows of the Snowy Mountains at the southern end of the Great Dividing Range. Its head is located only a few miles from Canberra, and a traditional summer holiday for citizens of the Australian capital is to relax along the sandy banks of the tree-lined river. The Murrumbidgee (an Aboriginal word meaning "big waters") generally flows west in the southern part of New South Wales, paralleling the Murray for much of its course, but turns south to the junction with the larger stream after receiving its major affluent, the Lachlan. The river is navigable for small vessels for about 500 miles (800 kilometers) in the rainy season. West of Wagga Wagga the river crosses a broad alluvial plain with numerous meanders, oxbow lakes, and distributary channels. The colorful Australian term "billabong" refers to side channels of a river, and in the case of the Murrumbidgee some of these in high river stages can wander far enough away from the main river that they actually link with the Murray.

An important early exploration of the island continent focused on the Murrumbidgee. Six years after the initial discovery of the river in 1824 by Hamilton Hume and W. H. Hovell, a party under Sir Charles Sturt traveled the length of the river to determine if it flowed into the earlier-discovered Darling, or perhaps into the ocean at the southern rim of the continent. Crossing the mountains from the east, the explorers encountered green meadows near the river's source, but their initial delight turned to dismay when they began to cross a gloomy swamp vegetated with stunted gum trees. Horses and drays were abandoned in favor of a whaleboat that was roughly made on the spot from native eucalyptus. On January 13, 1830, the crude craft carried the party to a junction with a larger river, which was named the Murray, after the British secretary of state for the colonies. In their descent of the river to its mouth they discovered that treacherous shoals and sandbars near the outlet would prevent the establishment of a seaport there.

The river is today used extensively for irrigation. The basin receives water from the Snowy

Mountains Hydroelectric Scheme. The major reclamation project in the region is the Murrumbidgee Irrigation Area; there is a dam across the river at Burrinjuck, about 40 miles (64 kilometers) northwest of Canberra. The catchment of the large reservoir backed up behind the dam is largely the plateau north of Mount Kosciusko (the highest peak in mainland Australia), where average annual rainfall exceeds 60 inches (152.4 centimeters). In this project, dating from the 1920s, the water from the lake runs down the riverbed for 200 miles (322 kilometers) to Berembed, where a weir directs it to a main irrigation supply canal, which in turn branches into numerous channels reaching districts such as Mirrool and Griffith. The chief crops irrigated are fruits, rice, and vegetables. As with extensive irrigation in the Murray-Darling system generally, salinization of soils due to the elevation of the water table and evaporation has become a major environmental problem.

Further Reading: Clark, Manning, *History of Australia,* London: Chatto and Windus, 1993 (orig. pub. in six volumes, 1962–1987).

N

NARBADA

See Narmada

NARMADA

Source: Maikala Range, in central India
Length: 775 miles (1,247 kilometers)
Tributaries: None
Outlet: Gulf of Khambat

The Narmada (also Narbada) River rises in Madhya Pradesh state in central India and flows west between the Satpura and Vindhya ranges to its outlet on the Arabian Sea. Originating at almost the exact geographical center of India, the river is one of only a few in peninsular India that drains westward. Almost all other rivers in southern India, with the exception of the shorter nearby stream, the Tapti, rise in the Western Ghats not far from the Arabian Sea and flow eastward to the Bay of Bengal. A line of demarcation following the river, called either the Vindhya or Satpura, after its fringing hills, is a historic division between the Gangetic plain to the north and the ancient rocks of the Deccan Plateau to the south, where Aryan immigrants encountered trackless jungles and recalcitrant tribes. Important trade routes followed the valley connecting western ports to the Ganges region, and the river is mentioned by the Roman geographer Ptolemy (second century A.D.). Unlike the perennial rivers of the north, which are fed by snowmelt, the Narmada is subject to wide variations in level, as it is fed by monsoonal, summer precipitation.

The upper course of the river follows a circuitous route through deep gorges. The scenic Marble Rocks just downstream from the city of Jabalpur is a majestic limestone gorge hemmed in by walls as much as 100 feet (30 meters) high. The river then follows a rifted trench creating an alluvial plain. The river forms a broad estuary below Broach, an old trading port located on the north bank of the river, 30 miles (48 kilometers) from the mouth.

The river is generally regarded as second in sanctity only to Mother Ganga (the Ganges). It is believed by Hindus to have sprung from the body of the god Shiva. A traditional pilgrimage, the Pradakshina, requires the devout wayfarer to walk from the river's mouth to its source on one side of the river and then return on the other, a trip of roughly 1,600 miles (2,575 kilometers). Numerous pilgrimage sites and bathing ghats are found along the river. The gorge at Marble Rocks has a twelfth-century Hindu temple.

Contemporary economic development plans have come into conflict with traditional beliefs about the river and the need for environmental protection. Though the turbulent river is not navigable, except for a short distance along its lower end, and is unsuitable for irrigation in the valley, the Indian government in cooperation with the World Bank commenced a project in 1978 that would tap the river's water for agricultural districts in western Maharashtra and to benefit the parched southern Gujarat region. In the mid-1980s opposition focused on the fact that the reservoir to be backed up behind the planned dam would inundate 248 villages and 35,000 hectares (86,485 acres) of forested land upstream from the areas targeted for development. A nonviolent protest movement (a form of resistance almost invented by the Indians), combining the efforts of native and foreign environmentalists, brought the construction of the dam to a halt, and the project is presently under review.

See also Krishna
Further Reading: Kingsworth, Paul, "Small Things and Big Issues," *Utne Reader,* April 2001, pp. 46–51 (orig. pub. in the *Ecologist,* September 2000).

NEGRO

Source: Southeastern Colombia
Length: c. 1,400 miles (2,253 kilometers)
Tributaries: Branco
Outlet: **Amazon**, near Manaus

It is not surprising that so many rivers are named after the hue of light reflected by their waters: Red, Black, White, and Blue Rivers abound on almost every continent. South America has no fewer than six important rivers named after their dark appearance. Among these many Negro Rivers, perhaps the most important is the large tributary of the Amazon located in northwestern Brazil and eastern Colombia.

The river begins as the Río Guainía in southwestern Colombia. It flows northeasterly before turning to the south to form part of the boundary between Colombia and Venezuela. The river then flows southeasterly through Amazonas state, Brazil, to join the Amazon River 11 miles (17.7 kilometers) below Manaus, the major upriver town on the world's second longest river (ranking first in discharge and drainage area). The river is filled with islands and has numerous secondary channels. The blue-black waters of the Rio Negro join the light brown waters of the Solimões (the name for the Amazon in western Brazil) at the Encôntro das Aguas ("meeting of the waters"). The two rivers flow side by side for several miles before their waters merge. The name of the river stems from the tannin-rich mulch of the rain forest floor that discolors the Negro rather than its sediments, which are sometimes mistakenly referred to in explaining the name. The Negro is connected with the Orinoco basin via the Casiquiare waterway, a link first explored by the nineteenth-century naturalist and geographer Alexander von Humboldt.

The river was named by the Spanish explorer Francisco de Orellana, who first came upon it in 1541. By the middle of the seventeenth century, Jesuits had settled along its banks in the midst of numerous tribes: Manau, Aruák, and Tarumá Indians. After 1700 slaving along the river was common, and Indian populations were greatly diminished after contact with infectious European diseases. The age of the scientific explorer began when Alexander von Humboldt, Alfred Russel Wallace, Henry Walter Bates, and Richard Spruce arrived in the area. Wallace made the investigation of the biogeography of the river his personal quest, while his fellow adventurer Bates, an entomologist, followed up the main-stem Amazon. The discovery of the rich diversity of species in the rain forest by Wallace, here as well as in his later trip to the Malay archipelago, led him to a theory of organic evolution that he proposed independent of Charles Darwin.

See also Amazon, Casiquiare
Further Reading: Bates, Henry, *The Naturalist on the River Amazon,* New York: Dover, 1975 (orig. pub. 1863).

NIAGARA

Source: Lake Erie, near Buffalo, New York
Length: 34 miles (55 kilometers)
Tributaries: Buffalo, Cattaraugus, Tonawanda, Cezenovia, and Cayuga creeks
Outlet: Lake Ontario, near Fort Niagara, New York

Connecting the lowest of the two Great Lakes, the Niagara nicely illustrates the principle that a river doesn't have to be long to be important. At the risk of being overly clever, one is tempted to say that a river doesn't have to be a *river* to be impor-

Snow and ice patterns at the bottom of Niagara Falls at the end of winter (Jesse Walker)

tant: The Niagara is, strictly speaking, a strait: a length of water joining two larger bodies. But the river name has long been used to describe this waterway that, in passing between two large lakes, plunges over perhaps the most famous waterfall in the world.

From its beginning at the outlet of Lake Erie, the Niagara flows as a broad and serene stream. The difference in elevation between the two lakes is 99 meters (325 feet), and this drop must be accomplished in a short horizontal distance. The upper river is flat and fully navigable until, at about 20 miles (32 kilometers), a series of rapids above the falls appear. Then the river pours over two giant cataracts separated by rocky Goat Island. Approximately half the vertical drop between the lakes is attained by these plunges. The slightly higher American Falls, at 167 feet (51 meters), extends side-to-side for about 1,000 feet (323 meters) on the right-hand side of the river; the Canadian or Horseshoe Falls, lying on the left, is 158 feet (48 meters) high, with an impressive 2,600-foot (792-meter) crescent over which most of the water flows. The smaller, less-developed American Falls has an accumulation of rock debris (talus) at its base, which was partly cleared away by the U.S. Army Corps of Engineers in 1969 when it diverted the river to study the problem. The falls formed twelve thousand years ago at the end of the last Ice Age, when the Niagara encountered the resistant strata of Paleozoic dolomite (a magnesium-rich limestone). Forming the face of the falls, the resistant dolomite is undercut at the cascade's base because of the turbulence of falling waters, which hollows out the bottom rock layers. Overlying, unsupported rocks collapse, leading to headward erosion of the river as well as sloughed rock debris in the river. By such an erosional process Niagara Falls is retreating headward toward Lake Erie at the rate of about 1 kilometer (0.62 mile) per thousand years. Below the present falls is a narrow gorge extending 11 kilometers (6.8 miles) to Lewiston, where the Niagara escarpment emerges.

Niagara Falls–one of the best-known falls in the world but not the highest (Jesse Walker)

The flow of the Niagara is regulated today, with some of the river's water flowing over the falls and the rest diverted through underground tunnels, where, before returning to the lower river, the water passes through turbines that power a series of electrical generators. The responsibility for controlling the flow of the river is shared between the United States and Canada, with each country receiving an equal division of the water that doesn't go over the falls. The first large-scale hydroelectric plant in the world, the Adams Station, began generating alternating current here in 1895 (it was replaced between 1963 and 1965 by a plant capable of producing 2,100 megawatts). By 1896 electrical power from Niagara was used in running the streetcars of Buffalo. The cheap power provided by the falls has spawned a large number of industries on both sides of the river and at nearby locations: ceramics, abrasives, chemicals, steel, machinery, grain milling, paper, and many others. The Welland Ship Canal, located several miles west on the Ontario side, allows freighters to navigate between the lakes and is part of the Saint Lawrence Seaway.

The first widely read description of the falls was written by the Frenchman Louis Hennepin (in *Nouvelle Découverte,* 1697), who, exploring westward from Montreal, was led to the site by Seneca Indians. The French quickly realized the strategic value of the lakes, rivers, portages, and transfer points west of their Saint Lawrence settlements. Beginning in 1679 they established a series of forts near the outlet of the Niagara, at the site of what would eventually be Fort Niagara. A French *coureur de bois,* Louis Thomas de Joncaire, built a fur-trading post (1721) on the escarpment overlooking present Lewiston below the falls, and the British retaliated by establishing a post at Oswego to the east on the southern shore of Lake Ontario. The British captured Fort Niagara (1759) during the French and Indian War. By the treaty that settled the American Revolutionary War (Treaty of Paris, 1783), the middle of the Niagara River constituted the U.S.-Canadian border. Fort

Niagara went to the Americans, though it would not be until after another war with the British—the War of 1812, which included bloody battles fought along the Niagara—that the international frontier was stabilized and Fort Niagara remained in American hands.

The Niagara gorge—the narrows below the falls—was first spanned in 1848, but the wonder of the age was the construction of a double-roadway railroad and vehicular suspension bridge in 1855. Designed by John August Roebling (the father of Washington Roebling, who built the Brooklyn Bridge), the span attracted as many visitors as the falls at the time. Although the river's importance for concentrating industry and facilitating navigation cannot be gainsaid, for millions of people every year from around the world, the river is best known for its magnificent falls. Barrel jumpers, tightrope walkers, honeymooners, and ordinary tourists are all attracted to the falls. Many cascades in South America and Africa are higher, but Niagara receives more attention because it is accessible to the populated centers of the East Coast and to international visitors.

Further Reading: Braider, Donald, *The Niagara,* New York: Rinehart and Winston, 1972 (Rivers of America Series).

NIGER

Source: Fouta Djallon plateau, in southwestern Republic of Guinea
Length: c. 2,600 miles (4,184 kilometers)
Tributaries: Bani, **Benue**
Outlet: Gulf of Guinea

The course of the principal river of West Africa has two distinct segments following different directions, a peculiarity that helps us understand the long and colorful narrative of the Niger's discovery, exploration, navigation, and political history. The third longest river in Africa begins in the highlands of western Guinea, not far from the Sierra Leone border. Rising only a few hundred miles from the Atlantic Ocean, the Niger does not flow westward into the sea as do the other major West African rivers, such as the Sénégal and the Gambia. Instead, it traces a northeasterly path as far as the edge of the Sahara Desert where it turns east, then southeastward.

The key to the upper Niger lies at this bend of the river. It was here that trans-Saharan caravans carrying gold and slaves intersected the river. The fabled city of Timbuktu in Mali is found along the great bend of the river in a hollow among sandhills in the course of an old streambed, whose still-marshy bottom furnishes necessary water supplies. The town is not actually on the river but is located nearby and is served by the river town of Kabara. Rumored to have been built of gold, the actual city is a small mud-built town that has generally disappointed Western explorers and travelers. In the modern period the desert emporium was first reached in 1826 by the Scots explorer Gordon Laing via the northern Tripoli route. The first Westerner to see Timbuktu and return (Laing was murdered) was the relatively unheralded René Caillie, who, inspired by the French Geographical Society's two-thousand-franc prize for the first person to reach Timbuktu, journeyed from the west coast and reached the town in April 1828. His impression of the fabled city was no less disappointing than those of other travelers. He wandered through a dusty village and wondered how this collection of mud-built residences and mosques could have been considered the jewel of the Sudan. The disillusionment of early travelers was partly the result of exaggerated expectations based on the writings of the sixteenth-century author known as Leo the African, who enshrined many mistaken ideas about Africa and the Niger that would not finally be cleared up until the nineteenth century. Also important in travelers' reactions was the fact that the trading city had declined since its heyday in the late Middle Ages, when a succession of savanna empires—the Ghana, Mali, and Songhai—had controlled long stretches of the upper Niger and the gold trails crossing the river. After European traders and slavers reached the west coast, the longer and riskier trade routes across the Sahara were undercut.

About a third of the way along its course the Niger branches into a maze of channels, lakes, and low sandy islands. This inland delta stretches southwest from Timbuktu almost as far as the trading town of Segou. Inundated by floodwaters during the four months of the rainy season, this broad alluvial district retains enough water during the long dry season, which begins in October, for it to be a thriving oasis producing plentiful crops of rice, millet, and cotton. The French initiated irrigation projects here in the 1930s, including a large dam at Sansanding (1941) that opened up more than 100,000 acres (40,470 hectares) of farmland for intensive cultivation.

Beyond Timbuktu the river reaches its northernmost point at the Tosaye gorges, cutting a narrow bed through low, rust-colored cliffs. As if sensing that it has reached its northern limit, the river turns sharply south and reaches the city of Gao, like Timbuktu a trading link between desert and river peoples. Flowing in a generally southeasterly direction, the Niger passes out of Mali into the Republic of Niger, where its course forms part of the border with Benin, and then into Nigeria, the most populated country of Africa, which accounts for about one-third of the Niger's length. At the place along the Bussa rapids where the famous Scottish explorer Mungo Park died on his second expedition (1805), by either drowning or ambush, is the huge Kainji Dam, built in the 1960s, which impounds water as far back as the settlement of Yelwa in the Yauri emirate. At Lokoja in central Nigeria the river receives its largest tributary, the Benue, on the left bank, which drains a large catchment area extending to the east as far as Lake Chad. Flowing to the south with twice the discharge it had before the Benue junction, the river leaves behind the semiarid savanna and briefly crosses the zone of tropical rain forest before branching into the largest delta in Africa. This coastal region of mangrove swamps, lagoons, and numerous distributary channels is a dark, mist-enshrouded zone that was inhospitable to Europeans, who inevitably came down with the "agues" (malaria and yellow fever), but it was relatively densely settled by a large number of African tribes. Slave-trading centers in the delta were known as "counters," and they included such settlements as Bonny, Brass, and Calabar, small feudal states controlling the primary, more navigable outlets. With the end of the slave trade, these towns were converted in the late nineteenth century into palm oil depots. The oil used to make soap and to lubricate new metal machinery was collected in the interior and brought downriver by natives to ships waiting to load the valuable commodity. The term *Oil Rivers* applied to the lower Niger was not originally a reference to petroleum but to palm oil, although eventually both kinds of oil would be produced in this coastal region. Not until the late 1950s were substantial amounts of petroleum exported from Nigeria, but the country soon grew to depend upon petroleum production as its primary means of earning foreign exchange, and today the country is a member of OPEC. The low sulfur content of much of Nigeria's crude makes it especially desirable to a world concerned about pollution.

The two major segments of the long river—the upper course, which came under the influence of the French, and the British lower course—were once two separate rivers and hence the discrepancy in the direction of their flow. The upper Niger, which natives call the Joliba, originates in granite hills near the Atlantic, flows north past Timbuktu, and once emptied into the salt lake of Juf near the Taodenni salt mines. The lower Niger, called by natives the Quorra, rose in the presently desolate Sahara mountains of Ahaggar. With the drying up of the Sahara since the end of the Pleistocene (tropical and subtropical dry areas experienced "pluvials," or wet periods, during the Ice Age), the Quorra eroded its way headward until it eventually captured the other, northward-flowing river. The Niger bend—the seat of medieval empires and focus of a nineteenth-century French imperial thrust—thus represents the elbow of capture. It is as a result of the geological grafting of two amputated rivers that the circuitous course of the Niger can be explained.

The twisted path of this great river also helps us understand the colorful history of West African exploration. Numerous expeditions were sent out by the British between 1796 and 1830 to solve the mystery of the Niger's course. This more than two thousand-year-old puzzle had first been posed by the Greek historian Herodotus (fifth century B.C.), who speculated that a large branch of the Nile divided Africa just as the Danube divided Europe. It was not until the first century B.C. that a Berber king of Numidia (roughly modern Algeria) named Juba II, educated in Rome, referred to the river as the Niger, a name derived from the Taureg expression *n'ger-n-gereo,* meaning "river of rivers." The riddle of the Niger that exercised the imaginations of nineteenth-century gentlemen almost as much as that of the Nile included three separate problems: (1) the direction of the river's flow—whether to the east or west; (2) the related question of whether the Niger was a branch of the Nile; and (3) the location of the river's mouth. Notice that the geographical conundrum presented a problem opposite to that of the Nile: its source was known but not its mouth. The best known of the Scottish explorers, Mungo Park, reached the Niger from the west via the Gambia route in 1796 and showed conclusively that the current of the river flowed to the east. It was not until 1830, at the end of the heroic age of exploration of West Africa, when Richard and John Lander, navigating the deltaic swamps and channels of the lower Niger issuing into the Gulf of Guinea, established that the Niger does not flow into an interior drainage basin like Lake Chad or into the Nile. Upon his return to England, Richard Lander became the first recipient of the Royal Geographical Society's gold medal. It was a fitting tribute because the quest for knowledge about Africa's great rivers had begun with the 1788 formation of the Africa Association, which in 1831 merged with the more recently formed geographical society.

The stage was set for the commercial exploitation of the Niger Basin. The transformation of the Slave Coast into the Oil Rivers proceeded under the guise of high-minded idealism regarding the abolition of slavery, the ending of human sacrifice, and bringing material comforts to a backward people, but it was also very profitable. The region served as a source of raw materials and a market outlet for a European capitalist economy that was churning along as forcefully as the paddle-wheel steamers now navigating the lower third of the river. Nigeria was to exhibit all three primary forms of British colonial administration: Lagos, the coastal city west of the delta, became a colony; the coastal region of the Oil Rivers was administered as the Niger Coast Protectorate; and upriver districts in central and northern Nigeria came under the monopolistic control of the Royal Niger Company, a trading company. In the early years of the twentieth century all would be merged into a single colonial status until Nigerian independence was achieved in 1960.

The French moved from their position on the Sénégal River to establish a sphere of influence along the upper Niger. A series of international scuffles and treaty arrangements finally led to the delineation of British and French spheres of control (without the African people being asked where they wanted their political borders). An 1890 Anglo-French agreement drew an east-west line from Say on the Niger to Burruwa on Lake Chad, separating the two imperial powers. It was in such a way that the southernmost area became British Nigeria, the wealthiest and most populated region of the basin, and France occupied the drier upriver country. France obtained the lion's share of the territory, in Guinea, Mali, and Niger, but most of that land was savanna scrub at best, often just desert margin. When even greater imperialists than British prime minister Lord Salisbury challenged him with having given away too much, he replied that he had given "what agriculturalists would call 'light' land."

Always prone to marked seasonal variations in flow and occasional drying up, the upper Niger was truly desiccated in 1973 and 1974 when a severe drought struck West Africa. The world then learned the geographical meaning of the Sahel, the sub-Saharan border lands dependent upon livestock rearing and nomadism along a vulnerable ecological boundary. Hundreds of thousands of people, mainly children, died of thirst and hunger, and millions of refugees were on the move before the advancing desert. The social causes of the famine were as important as the natural ones. The former colonial administration, native feudal structures, and the dictates of the modern economy all encouraged the cultivation of export crops for foreign exchange at the expense of indigenous multiple and intercropping schemes that finely meshed arable and pastoral lands in an intricate system of local food production.

Ecological problems associated with overstocked pastures in the vicinity of wells and the elimination of grass cover and thickets exacerbated by rapid population growth led to a deterioration in the environment that was related to the unfolding human suffering. The Niger's flow has not completely recovered from the droughts that continued in an intermittent fashion throughout the 1970s and 1980s. With the various impoundments of the river, the water level of the Niger is substantially lower than it was in the period before the late 1960s.

See also Benue

Further Reading: de Gramont, Sanche, *The Strong Brown God: The Story of the Niger River,* Boston: Houghton Mifflin, 1976; Gerster, Georg, "River of Sorrow, River of Hope," *National Geographic,* August 1975, pp. 152–189; Jenness, Aylette, *Along the Niger River: An African Way of Life,* New York: Thomas Crowell, 1974.

NILE

Source: Junction of the **Blue Nile** and **White Nile** at Khartoum
Length: c. 4,160 miles (6,695 kilometers)
Tributary: **Atbara**
Outlet: Mediterranean Sea

If the length of its longest headstream (the White Nile) is counted, the Nile is the longest river in the world. Thousands of years before Christ, pharaonic Egyptians, who considered the river sacred, wondered about the source of the Nile and the cause of its annual life-giving inundations. In the fifth century B.C. the Greek historian Herodotus traveled upriver as far as the Aswan cataract, where he was blocked in his search for the river's upper course. He described Egypt as the "Gift of the Nile," referring to the soil-building capacity of the river, by which annual flooding deposits regular increments of silt, slowly building up the alluvial valley. The second-century A.D. Roman astronomer and geographer Ptolemy, who lived in Alexandria at the western end of the delta, speculated that the river that drains about 10 percent of Africa had as its headwaters a range of mountains he called the Mountains of the Moon—a range since identified as the Ruwenzori mountains on the border between Uganda and Congo (formerly Zaire). He wasn't too far off regarding one of the sources—that of the Albert Nile, which drains Lakes Albert, Edward, and George in western Uganda, but the longest feeder of the White Nile drains a large lake lying to the east: Lake Victoria. Several streams flowing into the southwestern end of this lake straddling the border of Uganda and Tanzania are today identified as the sources of the Nile. The solution to the puzzle of the Nile's source was not known until the late nineteenth century, when it was discovered that there are multiple sources. Some details of the Nile's hydrology remained unknown until the twentieth century.

The Nile proper begins at Khartoum at the confluence of the Blue Nile and the White Nile. Apart from the brief comments already made about the source of the Nile in the lake region of Uganda and adjoining countries, the reader is referred to separate entries in this book on the White Nile and the Blue Nile concerning the exploration and character of the Nile's two headstreams. A concise summary of the most important facts should set the stage. The longest headstream, the White Nile, drains north from its source region across the Sudd swamp, which prevented explorers from ascending the Nile almost as decisively as the cataracts farther downstream. At the key strategic city of Khartoum, Sudan's capital, the shorter Blue Nile joins from the east. Draining the Ethiopian highlands, the Blue Nile is far shorter than the White Nile, but it carries a greater and more variable volume of water, as well as large amounts of silt washed downstream in the summer rains. Precipitation falling in the highlands in the summer is the source of the floodwaters that reach Egypt in July and peak in September. The Blue Nile contributes almost 60 percent of the Nile's water throughout

A traditional Arab boat, or dhow, on the Nile River at Cairo (Jesse Walker)

the year. Even in ancient times the Egyptians had devised an ingenious method of measuring the level of the flood: at Aswan's Elephantine Island, markings on the stone constituted a "Nilometer" for recording the height of the river.

North of Khartoum the river flows in a broad *S*-shape for some 1,200 miles (1,930 kilometers) as far as the Egyptian border and the upper part of Lake Nasser. Two hundred miles (320 kilometers) north of the juncture of the White and the Blue Nile, the last major tributary, the Atbara, joins from the east, draining a region as far away as the Ethiopian highlands. From Khartoum to the Egyptian border at Wadi Halfa and on to Aswan, the river valley is narrow and entrenched, and there is little floodplain available for cultivation. The river is interrupted by six cataracts (actually, rapids), numbered in ascending order going up the river (because explorers encountered them that way). The first cataract is just above Aswan, making this town a key location where trade routes crossing the desert intersected the head of navigation on the river. From Aswan the river flows 550 miles (885 kilometers) north to Cairo in a broad floodplain as much as 20 miles (32 kilometers) in width. Irrigated by the river, this intensively cultivated strip supports a dense population, with the green, checked fields standing in sharp contrast to the tawny desert that looms nearby. The Nile valley and delta constitute only 3 percent of Egypt's area but are home to 96 percent of its people.

The traditional method of irrigating the fertile lands of the lower Nile has been to rely on the annual floods to provide *basin irrigation*—natural inundation of shallow basins in which a cool-season crop like wheat or barley was raised in the soaked, silt-enriched ground. Ancient irrigation devices still in use today—though increasingly rare—include the weight-pivoted *shaduf* and the ox- or buffalo-driven *saquia,* which transferred precious water to where it was needed most. Over the last 150 years the agricultural system has been converted to *perennial irrigation,* in which two or three crops are grown each year, including cotton, sugar cane, and peanuts. This is accomplished by a system of barrages, in both the valley and the delta, that channels water into feeder canals from whence it is applied to fields. The Aswan High Dam (completed in 1970) is a giant storage dam meant to hold back part of the autumn flood for later use. The water impounded behind the dam, Lake Nasser, is one of the largest manmade lakes in the world. The dam has the additional purpose of generating electricity for a highly populated Third World country. The dam has a capacity of 5,724 billion cubic feet (162 billion cubic meters) and is sufficient with existing dams to hold back the entire flood.

The Aswan High Dam has not just generated kilowatts: it has also stirred up controversy. First let's give the project its due: the dam has added approximately 1,800,000 acres (728,500 hectares) of irrigated land to Egypt's cultivable area and converted much risky basin irrigation to more dependable perennial irrigation. The electrification of villages and the jobs provided by industrial development have been a plus. The many problems with the dam, however, appeared almost as soon as it was built. Lake Nasser may be one of the largest artificial lakes in the world, but it is also one of the largest sediment traps. The enormous lake, which extends all the way from Aswan into northern Sudan (where it is called Lake Nubia), began filling with sediments almost as soon as it formed. The silt once deposited farther downstream in the valley to nourish and replenish the soil today accumulates behind the concrete barrier of the dam. Nutrients that used to be carried down the Nile and emptied into the Mediterranean Sea have been so reduced that the sardine fishery—once an important industry—has gone into decline. The incidence of the parasitical ailment schistosomiasis is on the rise because of the increased prevalence of stagnant water coincident with a larger area of irrigation; such an environment is a breeding ground for the flukes (trematodes) that carry the disease, which is spread by snails and contaminated water.

Groundwater levels are rising in the valley, and increased rates of evaporation and lack of flushing have led to salinization problems that remind one of the fate of so many overirrigated areas in the Mideast. The increased use of herbicides, pesticides, and chemical fertilizers by commercial farmers has led to the pollution of the Nile. Inasmuch as 90 percent of the natural flow of the Nile is used for irrigation or is lost in evaporation (much of it from Lake Nasser), the pollution is effectively concentrated in the remaining discharge. The water that reaches the Mediterranean carries a heavy load of pollution from irrigation drainage, municipal wastes, and industrial effluent. The High Dam may have protected Egypt against the biblical cycle of seven years of plenty followed by seven years of famine, with the water stored behind the dam serving the same function as Joseph's stored grain, but the ecological and environmental problems need to be counted a heavy price against the dam's benefits.

The delta north of Cairo closely resembles the classic triangular shape of the geographers. That is not surprising, since the Nile delta is the prototype of all others; it reminded the ancient Greeks of the fourth letter of their alphabet—delta—and ever since the characteristic landform at the mouth of major rivers has been so called. The Nile's waters reach the sea in a fan-shaped network of shallow channels that is approximately 100 miles (160 kilometers) long and up to 115 miles (185 kilometers) wide. Despite extensive swamps and lakes, the delta contains 60 percent of Egypt's cultivated land. Two primary distributaries bound the delta, the Damietta (Dumyat) on the east, and the Rosetta (Rashid) on the west (see Figure 3 on p. 179). Each channel, being approximately 150 miles (240 kilometers) long, carries the much reduced flow of the Nile after irrigation and evaporation.

Saltwater intrusion has become a large problem because of the High Dam and the consequently reduced volume of fresh water that passes through the delta. Coastal environments, including deltas, are fragile ecosystems. The dense population of lower Egypt and the rise of manufacturing have meant that large amounts of municipal and industrial waste have been deposited in the delta, especially on its eastern side. Lake Manzala, a 31-mile (50-kilometer) coastal lagoon located northeast of

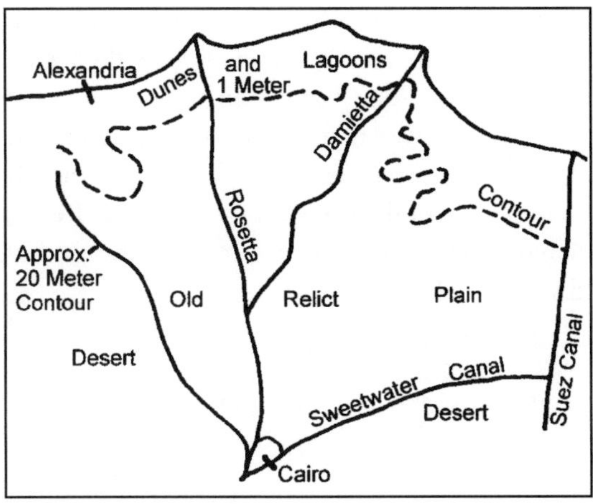

Figure 3. Nile Delta

Cairo near the Suez Canal and Port Said, contains untreated sewage and various contaminants that are (as of 2000) being studied by Monaco's Marine Environment Laboratory in conjunction with Egyptian scientists to determine the extent of the damage and whether such wetlands can be protected from future destruction.

See also Blue Nile, White Nile

Further Reading: Butzer, Karl W., *Early Hydraulic Civilizations in Egypt: A Study in Cultural Ecology*, Chicago: University of Chicago Press, 1976; Caputo, Robert, "Journey up the Nile," *National Geographic*, May 1985, pp. 576–633; Stanley, Daniel Jean, and Andrew G. Warne, "Nile Delta in Its Destructive Phase," *Journal of Coastal Research* 14 (1998): 794–825.

NORTH PLATTE

See Platte

NORTHERN DVINA

Source: Northern European Russia
Length: 465 miles (748 kilometers)
Tributaries: Vychegda, Vaga, Pinega
Outlet: White Sea

The Northern Dvina (Russian: Severnaya Dvina) is formed by the union of the Sukhona and Yug Rivers in the northern coniferous forest of European Russia. The river drains northwest and north across the low-lying Russian Plain, with approximately half its course draining marshes and swamps. The primary environment traversed by the river is the taiga, a vast evergreen forest composed primarily of fir, pine, and larch trees, a vegetation that is geographically associated with the harsh climate of Russia's north country. The Northern Dvina reaches the western section of the broadly embayed White Sea, an arm of the Barents Sea, just below Arkhangel'sk (Archangel). This wooden city of half a million people was founded in 1584 as a trading center linking the Arctic Ocean with the Russian settlements of the Volga basin such as Yaroslavl and Moscow. The city is located just below the river's confluence with the eastern tributary of the Pinega and above the extensive delta.

Russian pioneers had to be skillful navigators of the maze of interconnected rivers and lakes in the northern forest region. Early inhabitants soon learned where connecting routes required them to *volok*, or portage, their river boats, a term referring more to dragging or rolling than to carrying in the manner of American Indians and frontiersmen. The Russian term for portage is retained in many place-names, including the head of navigation on the Northern Dvina system at Vologda.

The important early trading city of Novgorod sent explorers and colonists as far as the Arctic coast by the end of the twelfth century. Settlers, who were known as Pomors ("dwellers by the sea"), reached the "Cold Sea," or White Sea, via the Severnaya Dvina estuary. With the arrival of traders who penetrated the Arctic Ocean and its various arms in pursuit of the Northeast Passage, the length of the trading links was extended but not fundamentally changed. Dutch, Flemish, and English contact with the Arctic coast led to the first sustained trading between western European powers and the incipient Russian Muscovite state. In 1555, Ivan IV (the Terrible) granted trade privileges to English merchants after Richard Chancellor reached the mouth of the Northern Dvina and traveled overland to Moscow. The Muscovite, or Russia, Company remained profitable but was soon eclipsed by another trading company that copied its idea of a joint-stock company with a government monopoly: the highly successful East India Company, chartered in 1600.

Arkhangel'sk was the chief Russian seaport until the establishment in 1703 of St. Petersburg at the mouth of the Neva River. The city went into a period of decline in the eighteenth and much of the nineteenth century, until at the end of the latter century a railroad was built to Moscow. Arkhangel'sk was an entry point for Allied aid in both World War I and II and was a focus of resistance against Bolshevik rule by the White Army in 1918–1920. After the furs of the taiga, timber has been the most valuable commodity of the region. The river has long been used to float and ship timber. The river is frozen from December until April and is navigable during the warmer months as far as its confluence with the Vychegda River, a major right-bank tributary draining the western flank of the Ural Mountains.

See also Western Dvina

Further Reading: Willan, T. S., *The Early History of the Russia Company, 1553–1603,* Manchester: Manchester University Press, 1956.

O

OB'

Source: Altai Mountains, in Central Asia
Length: c. 2,300 miles (3,701 kilometers)
Tributaries: Tom, Chulym, Ket, **Irtysh**, Kazym, Poluy
Outlet: Ob' Bay

With its chief tributary, the Irtysh, the Ob' (pronounced OB-ah) is the fourth-longest river in the world and almost as long as the Mississippi-Missouri system. From its source in the glaciated Altai Mountains near the Russian border with Mongolia, the river descends rapidly to the lowlands of western Siberia. This is a region of steppe and forested swamps stretching 1,250 miles (2,012 kilometers), all the way from the south Siberian city of Novosibirsk to the Kara Sea, an arm of the Arctic Ocean into which the Ob' empties via Ob' Bay (Russian: Obskaya Guba).

The river is formed on the northern flank of the Altai (an autonomous region within the Russian Federal Republic) by the junction of two fast-flowing mountain streams, the Biya and the Katun. Legend has it that when loggers discovered this union, they exclaimed "Oba!"—Russian for "both." From this point the river flows generally northward, getting wider and more sluggish as it crosses one of the largest extents of flatland in the world—the West Siberian Lowlands. The Ob' winds across this land of seemingly endless horizons, which is bounded by the Ural Mountains on the west and the Yenisey River on the east. The largest city in Siberia and the third largest in Russia, Novosibirsk, is located along the banks of the Ob' at a key site: the intersection of the Trans-Siberian Railway and the river. A large hydroelectric dam has been installed here, and the size of the reservoir backed up by the dam can be inferred from the name of the artificial lake—the Ob' Sea.

Below Novosibirsk the river traverses a northwesterly path across the swampy forests of the Tomsk and Narym regions, before being joined from the west by its principal tributary, the Irtysh. The broad, level plain of this section of the river—the middle Ob'—is subject to inundation each spring: the thaw in the upper course of the river occurs before melting and breakup frees the ice of the lower Ob'. The result is that floodwaters spread out widely across a wide plain in which lakes and ephemeral channels cover the low-lying area. Such springtime bottlenecking may explain why large Arctic rivers like the Ob' deliver relatively small amounts of sediment to the sea, the river's load being reduced by deposition during early season jamming.

Oil and gas development has expanded dramatically since the 1960s in northwest Siberia. The Ob' basin produces 78 percent of Russia's oil and 84 percent of its natural gas. Wells, pipelines, and ancillary petroleum-industry infrastructure are concentrated along the middle Ob' in the Tyumen, Surgut, and Samotlor regions. The principal activity in the oil fields has been to the south (or upstream) of the Ob'-Irtysh confluence, along both the trunk stream and its major feeder. Petroleum development has moved steadily northward, so that its impacts are now being felt in the far north.

The reorientation of the economy and transportation system caused by petroleum development has meant that the old Cossack city of Omsk, located on the Irtysh River where it is crossed by the Trans-Siberian Railway, has decreased in importance compared with the more northern city of Tobolsk, also on the Irtysh; the latter city sits in the midst of the Tyumen oil field. By a curiosity of the Russian winter and the spring flooding of the Ob', oil operations are best carried out in the winter, when the swamps and lakes are frozen. Workers can handle machinery and pipe more easily in this season than during the spring, when ice blocks the lower Ob' and a distended floodplain overflows with river water.

Much of the oil and gas development in Siberia takes place within the zone of permanently frozen subsoil, or permafrost. This is especially true of the newer districts being explored and developed to the north, including the Yamal-Nenets field (the Yamal Peninsula is the large block of land jutting out into the Kara Sea forming the western shore of the Ob' estuary) and the Khanty field at the Ob'-Irtysh confluence. The fragile Arctic ecosystem, with simplified food chains and low biological diversity, is in danger of severe environmental impact. Compounding the problem is the presence of native peoples—the Khanty and the Nenets—who depend on hunting and fishing for their subsistence. Caribou, seals and walruses, and whitefish are important parts of the diet of these indigenous, non-Indo-European people, a food supply threatened by oil and gas development. In June 1997, the presence of oil spills and blackened wetlands caused the Khanty peoples to deny their regional government permission to auction traditional lands for petroleum options in the Ob' confluence region.

Below the union with the Irtysh, the Ob' broadens considerably, so that in places the river is as much as 12 miles (19 kilometers) wide. A network of multiple channels and numerous low islands appears even before the delta is reached. The lower Ob' divides into two channels (the Great Ob' and the Small Ob'), which separate by as much as 200 miles (320 kilometers) before reuniting. The river crosses the Arctic Circle (66°30'N), turns briefly eastward, and finally discharges through a large delta into the head of Ob' Bay. This bay is more than 500 miles (800 kilometers) long, and is one of the longest narrow bays in the world. Like the outlet of the Yenisey River to the east, the Ob's delta is of the estuarine type. Because of the long, sinuous shape of the bay, the river discharges into a body of water that is almost landlocked. Like the Yenisey's, the Ob's delta is almost rectangular in shape because of its environmental setting as an in-filling bay. Oil and gas exploitation of the lower river and the delta has not been as intensive as along the middle Ob', but pollution of the river has reached levels where a once famous fishery has been damaged. Though the rivers of western Siberia do not deliver large amounts of sediment to the Arctic, they do contribute significant amounts of fresh water—87 percent of all fresh water entering the Kara Sea comes from the Ob' and Yenisey combined.

Even along the upper Ob' navigation is impeded by ice from October through April. The water route is nevertheless important and is used to transport lumber and grain. In the delta spring, the force of river water clears the river ahead of the bay, and in autumn the relatively warm river water delays freezing. As a result, the navigation season in the delta is nearly a month longer than in other Arctic places at similar latitudes.

Although the most proximate of the great Siberian rivers for Europeans, the Ob' did not gain notice in the West until fairly recently. Russian Pomors, or coastal dwellers of the White Sea, reached the lower Ob' in the later years of the sixteenth century. In the following century major advances in geographic exploration and discovery took place in Siberia as elsewhere in newly opened lands. The river is referred to in Milton's epic *Paradise Lost* (pub. 1667), but not in the works of Shakespeare. There is evidence that a Russian trading venture from the Ob' or Yenisey River sailed around the northern coast of Eurasia during this period, but such a northeast passage was not officially completed until the early twentieth century. By the time of Peter the Great (1672–1725) and the creation of a Russian navy, the entire Arctic coastline from the White Sea to the Bering Strait had been explored. Cossacks penetrated the upper and middle Ob' and established trading stations along the river and its tributaries at key confluences and crossings. The crossing of south Siberia by the Trans-Siberian Railway at the end of the nineteenth century and the discovery and exploitation of oil from the middle decades of the twentieth century have firmly placed western Siberia and the Ob' River in the geographical realm of terra cognita.

See also Lena, Yenisey

Further Reading: Jordan, Robert Paul, "Siberia's Empire Road, the River Ob," *National Geographic,* February 1976, pp. 145–181.

ODER

See Odra

ODRA

Source: Eastern Sudetes Mountains, in Czech Republic
Length: 562 miles (904 kilometers)
Tributaries: Nysa, Kaczawa, Bobr, Neisse, Warta
Outlet: Baltic Sea

This important waterway in east-central Europe rises in the northeastern, mountainous corner of the Czech Republic and flows north across the North European Plain before emptying into the Baltic. Along its lower course, the river—the second longest in Poland—constitutes the border between Poland and Germany and as such assumes a major significance in political geography.

The head of the Odra lies near Olomouc in the Czech Republic. The river initially follows a northeasterly path into Poland, then veers to the northwest. The principal city of the upper river is Wroclaw, whose picturesque site includes the baroque buildings of the university, a gothic town hall, and Ostrow Tumski, an island of architecturally interesting churches and cathedrals in the Odra's channel (one side of which has dried up, so it is not strictly speaking an island). The river and its tributaries crisscross the city, giving it the effect of being a miniature Venice.

The historic region of Silesia approximately corresponds to the upper Odra watershed. Long a borderland between German, Polish, and Czech peoples, Silesia possessed the two key raw materials necessary for steel making, coal and iron ore, and so attracted the early attention of industrialists. Settled since the Middle Ages by a mixed German/Polish population and ruled for much of the early modern period by the Austrian Hapsburgs, the upper Odra region was seized by Frederick the Great and annexed to Prussia in 1742. German migration and capitalization became especially important in the nineteenth century when the region's name became synonymous with coal mining and textiles.

The river is navigable as far as Racibórz, Poland, which is far upriver from Wroclv (the latter city was in fact the capital of Lower Silesia). Barges still carry iron, coal, and coke, suggesting the continued importance of steel making today. The river is linked to the west with Germany's Spree and Elbe Rivers, and to the east via the Warta to Poland's major river, the Wisla. Complementary economic regions are fostered by extensive canalization, especially in the river's middle and lower courses.

Industrialization of course has its costs, and pollution of the river and its tributaries by acid drainage from coal mines and industrial works has been detected. In the section of the river between the mounths of the Kaczawa and Warta Rivers, accumulation of toxic trace elements such as arsenic and cadmium from the mining and processing of copper and from lead-zinc mines has been detected in the riverbottom sediments (bed load), but the contamination of riverborne sediments (suspended load) has been less noticeable.

The lower river along the German border has been heavily modified since the time of Frederick the Great by canals, dikes, marsh drainage, and channelization. Pollution is less of a problem here than flooding. In the summer of 1997 devastating floods broke through dikes and inundated vast areas of populated lowland. The major seaport of Szczecin (formerly Stettin) near the mouth of the river did not suffer as much damage, because the large estuarine lagoon absorbed much of the floodwater, which then found its way into the Baltic, and also because the opening of the polders increased the cross section of the river and the effective runoff.

A key line of political demarcation follows the lower course of the Odra in the north, and the Odra's tributary, the Neisse, in the south. This Oder-Neisse Line, as it is sometimes called, forms the present political boundary between Poland and Germany. It was first proposed by Stalin at the Yalta Conference at the end of World War II. The Russian leader suggested the new boundary to compensate Poland for losing territory in the east to the Soviet Union: formerly German areas such as Silesia on the upper Odra and the Pomeranian coastlands near the river's mouth would henceforth be Polish. (Not all of Silesia became Polish territory, as parts of the Czech Republic and of Brandenburg, Germany, were also once included in the historic region.) At Yalta, Winston Churchill and Franklin Roosevelt, the leaders of the West, tentatively accepted the Oder-Neisse Line, today's boundary, and more definitely agreed to this delineation at the subsequent Potsdam Conference. Germans were forced to patriate west of the line after the war, in some cases to make room for Polish emigrants arriving from the east. With the division of Germany into an eastern and western state as a result of the dawning of the Cold War, Germany's opinion of such a boundary became problematic, especially that of the Federal Republic of Germany (West Germany). The government of West Germany finally accepted the Oder-Neisse Line in 1970, and with the 1990 reunification of Germany the 1945 border was reaffirmed.

OGOOUÉ

Source: Batéké Plateau, in People's Republic of Congo
Length: c. 560 miles (901 kilometers)
Tributaries: Leconí, Leyou, Sébé, Mvouna, Ahanga, Ngounié
Outlet: Gulf of Guinea

The Ogooué (also Ogowe) does not qualify as one of the great rivers of the world by virtue of length or general significance, but it is the principal drainageway of a country that once formed an important part of French Equatorial Africa. Though not the looked-for passage straight across central Africa, the river does link the west coast of equatorial Africa with the interior highlands.

The river rises on a plateau in the People's Republic of the Congo (Brazzaville, or French Congo). It flows northwestward across a densely forested upland, then veers southwest toward the Atlantic outlet, near Port-Gentil. In its upper course the river passes Franceville; farther downstream is the island town of Lambaréné, made famous by the mission hospital founded there by Albert Schweitzer. The latter town is situated at the head of year-round navigation, some 110 miles (175 kilometers) from the mouth. In high-water months the river is navigable for a short distance above Lambaréné. Beyond that are a series of rapids where the river descends from the interior highlands onto the coastal plain. This middle course of the river consists of stretches of quiet water alternating with sections of rapids where the river foams over outcrops of resistant granite. One of the most impressive whitewater portions of the river is the narrow, winding gorge known as the Gates of Okanda, named after a tribe that once inhabited the area.

The Ogooué Rapids today provide thrills for boating enthusiasts, but in the nineteenth century they were a major obstacle to Europeans trying to penetrate interior Africa. The initial foothold of the French along the Gabon coast was north of the Ogooué at the mouth of the Gabon River. Libreville was founded in the Gabon estuary in 1848 as a home for liberated slaves, as its name suggests (like Sierra Leone's Freetown). The broad mouth of the Ogooué with its several large islands was first discovered in 1857. Hoping to tap the lucrative trade in tropical products from equatorial regions, the French believed that the Ogooué offered a route straight across central Africa. They were to discover that the river does not extend very far into the interior before turning off to the south, and that the navigable portions are limited to the river's lower 150 miles (240 kilometers). Though the Ogooué Rapids impeded exploration, the traveler Pierre Savorgnan DeBrazza in 1880 followed the course of the river upstream and found that one of its headstreams rose close to a partially navigable tributary of the lower middle Congo, the Alima. He crossed the narrow drainage divide separating the Ogooué from the Congo Basin and proceeded to Stanley Pool, a lacustrine expansion of the Congo above the falls that is traditionally considered the lower end of the middle river. At about this same time, the left bank of the Congo was being staked out and claimed by the American newspaperman and explorer Henry Stanley (of "Dr. Livingstone, I presume" fame) on behalf of the Congo Association and the king of the Belgians. The indefatigable Stanley founded the town of Stanleyville (Kinshasa) on the strategic Pool. The intrepid DeBrazza in turn founded Brazzaville on the opposing shore of the Pool to lay claim for France to the right bank of equatorial Africa's greatest river. The Ogooué valley was thereby an indirect approach to the interior for the French. The second expedition of Mary Kingsley (1894) took this extraordinary Victorian lady clad in bonnet and petticoats up the Ogooué River as far as Ndjolé in search of zoological specimens and tribal lore.

Further Reading: Cousins, Norman, *Dr. Schweitzer of Lambaréné,* New York: Harper and Brothers, 1960.

OHIO

Source: Confluence of Allegheny and Monongahela Rivers at Pittsburgh, Pennsylvania
Length: 981 miles (1,579 kilometers)
Tributaries: Muskingum, Kanawa, Big Sandy, Scioto, Licking, Miami, Kentucky, Wabash, Cumberland, **Tennessee**
Outlet: **Mississippi** at Cairo, Illinois

The valley of the principal tributary of the Mississippi has been variously described as the crucible of participatory democracy in America, the testing ground of Corn Belt agriculture, and the gateway of the American Midwest. The river served as a primary transportation artery in the eighteenth and nineteenth centuries, linking east and west, north and south, in the prerailroad era.

The major east-to-west drainage encountered by westward-moving pioneers, the Ohio River early gained prominence for transporting passengers and cargo into the new Trans-Appalachian territories. Though not as long as the Missouri, the Ohio supplies more water to the Mississippi. The river has a number of advantages besides its direction. Most of its approximately one thousand miles is navigable except during a brief period in midwinter, when ice jams the channel above Louisville. The river is formed at the confluence of the north-draining Monongahela and the south-draining Allegheny Rivers in downtown Pittsburgh. Above the Forks of the Ohio, the headstream regions have navigation restrictions because of spring "freshes" or floods, low water in the fall months, and a longer ice-prone season, though the main-stem river is also subject to these kinds of problems, especially for the crude river craft of the early nineteenth century. The river once featured a diverse flotilla of boats—flatboats, keelboats, broadhorns, ferries, Kentucky boats, and New Orleans boats. The keelboat was a kind of express: it resembled a decked rowboat enlarged three or four times and fitted out with a narrow prow for greater navigability. With much pushing and pulling, poling and bushwhacking (grabbing ahold of overhanging branches), the boat could go both up and down the river, unlike the various flatboats, which were usually broken up and sold for scrap or just set adrift at their downriver destination.

The peak of the "flatboat era" on the Ohio and lower Mississippi was about 1820, by which time mechanized power in the form of steamboats had arrived on Western rivers. Two-way commerce on the Ohio-Mississippi system could be said to have begun when the *Aetna* carried 200 tons of freight and a few passengers from New Orleans to Louisville in sixty days in 1815, and made the return trip the following year in thirty days. A large number of shipbuilding centers sprang up along the Ohio River, most notably at Pittsburgh, which was sometimes even at this early date called the Birmingham of America. Construction of the new boats progressed rapidly in the second and third decades of the nineteenth century, interrupted only

The end of an era. Two steamboats, the Betsy Ann *of Pittsburgh (left) and the* Chris Greene *of Cincinnati (right) belch black smoke on the Ohio River in pursuit of the title "Queen of the River," circa 1915. The* Chris Greene *narrowly won the race. (Hirz/Archive Photos)*

by the Panic of 1819 and the short ensuing period of economic downturn. In 1826 fifty-six boats were built on the Ohio, whereas fifteen years earlier only one had been made.

The Falls of the Ohio at Louisville was a major navigation obstacle on the river. More accurately described as a series of rapids, the obstructed course consisted of a rock ledge that underlay the surface of the water at a shallow depth over a distance of 2.2 miles (3.6 kilometers). For more than half the year the 24-foot (7-meter) vertical drop at the Falls was a serious obstacle to transportation, and the city of Louisville was founded as a stopover place at this bottleneck (New Albany and Jeffersonville, Indiana, arose on the opposite bank of the river). A canal that opened in 1830 at Louisville bypassed the rapids with a three-stop lock that carried boats quietly around the tortuous channel. The canal was built and maintained by a private company, and for fifty years a toll was charged, until the federal government took it over. In the early twentieth century a grand plan to construct a series of locks and dams along almost the entire course of the river was eventually trimmed down, but upon its completion in 1929 there were fifty locks, at a time when the river was carrying 21,000,000 tons of shipping. After a slow start during the Great Depression, the project was vindicated at the time of World War II, when more and more industrial plants moved into the Ohio valley. A new lock and dam system with fewer but higher dams (boosting electricity production) has increased the 1929 tonnage figure many times over. The dams help maintain a 9-foot (2.7-meter) depth for shipping, carried on mostly by tug-pushed barges whose holds are filled with coal and oil.

Other obstacles on the Ohio, apart from the ever-present floating objects, snags, and "planters" (sunken logs), have been removed with modern improvements. Le Tart's Rapids, located 230 miles (370 kilometers) below Pittsburgh, were a stretch of rapidly moving water that was especially dangerous during periods of low water when navigated by rudderless flatboats. Farther downstream, near Shawneetown, Illinois, a limestone ledge known as the Great Chain was impassable by large boats in the lowest stage of water. This minor break in transportation was matched by a similar obstruction on the Mississippi below Cape Girardeau known as the Little Chain.

The major river city of Cincinnati benefited from its location near the mouth of fertile tributary valleys on both sides of the river—the Miami on the Ohio side, and the Licking on the Kentucky bank. Moreover, the river made a large bend to the south below the city, and many emigrants chose the city as the place from which to leave the river and travel overland to reach their preferred, northern destinations in Indiana and Illinois.

The demonstration effect of the Erie Canal (completed in 1825) encouraged the construction of a number of canals that cut across the low drainage divide separating the Ohio basin from the Great Lakes. Mostly completed in the 1820s and 1830s, these projects included the Ohio and Erie Canal, which linked the Ohio at Portsmouth to Cleveland on Lake Erie; the Miami and Erie Canal, linking Lake Erie at Toledo with the Ohio at Cincinnati; and the Wabash-Erie Canal, which provided a northern outlet for the fertile Wabash valley. Railroads with their greater speed and year-round service soon eclipsed the canals, just as the steamboats had the flatboats, and this "creative destruction," as one historian of entrepreneurial revolutions has described the change, was especially evident in the later-settled regions of southern Wisconsin and northern Illinois; there, a canal mania in the 1830s and 1840s gave way to a series of bankruptcies and uncompleted routes by the time of the Civil War. It has been shown that the orientation of Midwestern markets away from the southern outlet of New Orleans had already been substantially completed by the Ohio canals diverting produce to the Great Lakes and thenceforth to eastern cities before the railway network had been constructed linking Chicago and the East Coast centers of Boston, New York, Philadelphia, and Baltimore.

The Ohio River shares many of the water quality problems of the Mississippi and the Missouri. Population growth and industrial development have led to pollution problems from urban runoff, industrial discharge, and outflows from abandoned mines. The valley has imported the zebra mussel problem from the Great Lakes. An exotic species brought in by international shipping, the mussel has crossed into the watershed of the Ohio, where it is clogging pipes and disrupting the natural ecosystem, much as it has done in the Great Lakes.

See also Mississippi
Further Reading: Banta, R. E., *The Ohio,* New York: Rinehart and Company, 1949 (Rivers of America Series); Brown, Ralph H., *Historical Geography of the United States,* New York: Harcourt, Brace and World, 1948.

OKA

Source: Central European Russia, south of Moscow
Length: 925 miles (1,489 kilometers)
Tributaries: Nara, Moskva, Moksha, Klyazma
Outlet: **Volga**

The Oka (pronounced o-KUH) River drains a densely populated agricultural and industrial region south and east of Moscow. Flowing northward initially, the river makes a broad bend to the east that nearly matches the curved arm of the Volga, which surrounds Russia's capital on the northern side, though within a smaller compass. As the primary western tributary of Russia's most revered river, the Oka thus might be described as nestled within the embracing arms of Mother Volga, with Moscow resting between these two waterways like a protected child—which in a sense the city is, with its defensive position on a minor river, the Moskva, itself a tributary of the Oka.

The Oka rises on the Central Russian Plateau, an elevated tongue of land south of Moscow located between the Dnieper and Don lowlands. The river's course initially parallels the nearby Don, but flowing north instead of south. It follows a narrow, winding valley to Kaluga, where it veers sharply eastward across a broad alluvial lowland.

The Nara joins the river from the north and in the direction of Moscow. At the confluence is the strategic center of Serpukhov with its walled Kremlin and monasteries that have served as a frontier fortress facing south since the town was founded in 1328. Just downstream the new science city of Pushchino was established in 1962. Located on the right bank of the Oka River, 8 miles (13 kilometers) southeast of Serpukhov, the city is the home of the Russian Academy of Science's Biological Research Center. Sections of the Oka valley, including meadows, oxbows, and riverbanks, have been officially incorporated into the International Biosphere Reserve.

The river flows off to the east and passes another old fortified city lying along Moscow's southern rim: Kolomna is situated at the junction of the Moskva and Oka Rivers. First mentioned in 1177, the strategic importance of the town is suggested by the fact that it was sacked four times by the Tatars.

Farther along the middle course of the Oka lies Ryazan oblast (province) and the city of 500,000 of the same name. Located southeast of Moscow on the west bank of the Oka, Ryazan has a heritage similar to Moscow's. Founded in the eleventh century, burned by the Mongols in the twelfth century, the city was rebuilt and flourished; it is perhaps best known as the home of the pioneering physiologist Ivan Pavlov, famous for his stimulus-response experiments with drooling dogs. Extensive reed and grass marshlands with interspersed mixed forest (the Meshchera Lowland) lie to the north of the river, while to the south the gray-brown soils of the forest-steppe have long been under cultivation.

The path of the lower Oka turns to the northeast, joining the Volga at Nizhny Novgorod (formerly Gorki). This major industrial city at the eastern limit of Moscow's economic influence has been a key to the expansion of Russian power to the east ever since the late Middle Ages, when it was annexed (1392). The city was strategically important in the Russian conquest of the Volga through the sixteenth century. This trade center is famous for its annual fair, the Nizhegorodsky Yarmarka, which though discontinued in the Communist regime has been resumed and attended by international visitors since 1991.

See also Volga

OKAVANGO

Source: Highlands of central Angola
Length: 1,000 miles (1,609 kilometers)
Tributaries: Cuchi, Cuebe, Cuito
Outlet: Okavango Swamp, in northern Botswana

Rising as the Cuvango River in the moist tropical hills of Angola's Benguela Plateau, the Okavango (pronounced o-KAH-vahn-go), the third largest river of southern Africa, flows south and east *away* from the sea into an undrained interior depression. Forming part of the border between Angola and Namibia, the river crosses the Caprivi Strip—a good example of the political geographer's prorupt, or fingerlike, boundary—into the arid plains of northern Botswana. There the river spreads out into an array of distributary channels and disappears into the flat plains at the northern end of the Kalahari Desert as perhaps the world's most spectacular inland delta (it is certainly the world's largest oasis).

The northern part of the swamp is wet throughout the year. Hippopotamuses roll in the silty muck borne down by the river. The vegetation consists of papyrus beds, razor-sharp swamp grasses, and exposed roots. The swamp is the home of myriad animals, including leopards, cheetahs, Cape buffaloes, migrating zebras, numerous monkey species, and large herds of elephants. The native Bayei are able to navigate the maze of identical channels, but even they sometimes go into the swamp and never return, or at least fear such a happening as attested to by their legends and myths. The Afrikaners, of Dutch descent, refer to the Okavango as Riviersonderend, or "River without End." The southern portion of the inland delta is dry much of the year, filling with water only as the seasonal cycle progresses. At the southern edge of the swamp is a low ridge retaining water in most years, but during wet periods it overflows via the Boteti River to the arid Makgadikgadi Salt Pans to the southeast.

In the late 1990s there occurred a pronounced drying up of the delta. Villages in the Botswana town of Maun at the southeastern edge of the delta depend on the water for washing, for fish, and for roots and reeds that are used for building materials. Although part of the cause for increased aridity is the natural variation in precipitation and runoff, human-induced changes are increasingly blamed. The situation is likely to get worse in the future. The driest country in the world, Namibia, proposes to extend a network of pipelines and aqueducts from its capital, Windhoek, northeast to the Okavango River along the Namibia-Angola border. Water-management engineers and bureaucrats have arrived from Botswana to dredge its own canals and construct its own pipelines. A water war may be in the offing between Namibia and Botswana, two minor-league African countries to be sure, but ones occupying key subtropical locations and engaged in struggles that represent in microcosm global conflicts over scarce water resources.

Further Reading: De Villiers, Marq, *Water: The Fate of Our Most Precious Resource,* Boston: Houghton Mifflin, 2000; Eales, Kathy, Simon Forster, and Lusekelo Du Mhango, *Water Management in Africa and the Middle East,* ed. Egial Rached et al., Ottawa: IDRC, 1996.

OMO

Source: Ethiopian Highlands
Length: c. 500 miles (805 kilometers)
Tributaries: Gojeb, Gibe
Outlet: Lake Turkana

The East African Rift valley, cutting across Malawi, Tanzania, Kenya, and Ethiopia, provides scenes of some of the most isolated and desolate African landscapes. Tectonic forces along the boundary between lithospheric plates are evidenced in the thick layers of volcanic sediments that have built up along the shores of Lake Turkana (former Lake Rudolf) on the border between Kenya and Ethiopia. Though smaller than Lake Victoria and Lake Tanganyika, the lake may be considered one of East Africa's Great Lakes, occupying a depression in the foundered ground produced by rift activity along what geologists call a "spreading center."

From its source in the upland plateau of Ethiopia to its outlet in Lake Turkana, the Omo River is fairly short compared with the great rivers of the world. The upper course crosses the mountainous region west of the Ethiopian capital of Addis Ababa—it is one of the truly wild rivers of the world, not navigated by boat until 1973. The river plunges over foaming rapids hemmed in by nearly vertical cliffs. Tributary streams rush over the brink of valley sidewalls in magnificent waterfalls. This portion of the river is today a popular destination for whitewater rafters.

The remote African river eventually leaves the canyons as it broadens in its lower course. Flowing generally southward, the Omo crosses a district of rolling hills, passing hippopotamuses lounging in pools and crocodiles lurking on the banks. At Omo National Park the river meanders across a wide plain occupied by diverse wildlife, ranging from elands to warthogs to ostriches. Finally the river winds across a dry, brush-covered plain before pouring its rust-colored waters into the green expanse of Lake Turkana.

Along the river's lower course, north of the present lakeshore, has been found some of the oldest fossil evidence of the ancestors of human beings. Though the first discoveries were made by the French in 1901, the most significant finds were those of an international team of archaeologists operating between 1967 and 1975. Their discoveries included the jawbone of an individual of the genus *Australopithecus* dating from 2,500,000 years ago and the skeletal remains of a 100,000-year-old *Homo sapiens.* Crude, sharp-edged quartz tools were found associated with the latter remains. Some of these hominid fossils dated back to 3,000,000 years and considerably extended human evolution, as the earliest fossils previously discovered had been dated at 1,750,000 years. In the 1990s additional finds were made near the Omo delta as well as in the Afar depression, located to the northeast in central Ethiopia within the Rift valley.

Although the Turkana area today consists of semiarid savanna, during the Pleistocene epoch (between 2,000,000 and 10,000 years ago) the region experienced a wetter climatic regime: lake levels were higher, vegetation lusher, and biological resources greater. A more propitious physical environment than that which exists today, combined with the better chances for fossil preservation (and exposure) in the sedimentary beds and volcanic ash of the river valley, led to some of the most important clues to the ancestry of modern humans, not just here but also elsewhere in Africa's Rift valley.

Further Reading: Leakey, Richard, and Roger Lewin, *People of the Lake: Mankind and Its Beginnings,* Garden City, NY: Anchor Press, 1978.

ORANGE

Source: Maluti Mountains, in northern Lesotho
Length: c. 1,300 miles (2,090 kilometers)
Tributaries: Senqunyane, Makhaleng, Kraai, Caledon, **Vaal**
Outlet: Atlantic Ocean

The Orange is one of the major drainages of the African continent, along with the Nile, Niger, Congo, and Zambezi. It drains the South African highveld south of the Witwatersrand (or just Rand), the entire country of Lesotho, and parts of Botswana and Namibia. It features prominently in the history of white settlement of South Africa. Farmers of Dutch descent (Boers) left the Cape Colony between 1835 and 1843 to escape British domination. Migrating beyond the Orange River, the Afrikaner farmers, or Boers, who made this trek (*Voortrekkers*) settled in isolated communities that formed the nucleus of Natal, Transvaal, and the Orange Free State.

Like the Nile, the Orange rises in a well-watered upland region, then traverses a water-deficient area lacking any significant tributaries. The course is generally westward from the Great Escarpment of the Drakensberg to the sea, but the river makes a series of alternating southwesterly and northwesterly loops, especially in its middle course. Though the river rises within a few hundred miles of the Indian Ocean, it crosses the breadth of the southern African landmass before emptying into the Atlantic at Alexander Bay.

The river begins in the northern section of Lesotho, a former British protectorate (Basutoland) that is now a sovereign country albeit completely contained within the boundaries of the Republic of South Africa. The ridges of the Malutis—the source region—are actually spurs of the Drakensberg that separate the headstreams of the Orange. The migrating *Voortrekkers* in passing north of the Vaal drove the native Basutos from their best agricultural land and forced them to occupy the rougher terrain in the upper Orange basin, which is more suitable for grazing. The river cuts down from the escarpment in a series of deep valleys and gorges with numerous waterfalls and rapids.

Two hundred miles (322 kilometers) from its source, the Orange leaves Lesotho, and at a height of 4,400 feet (1,341 meters) above sea level becomes the boundary between Cape Province and the Orange Free State (today, Free State). Journeying across the fertile plateau of the highveld, the river continues to form this political border for the next 300 miles (483 kilometers). The valley is comparatively broad, except in places where its width contracts from many miles to a narrow gorge because of the outcropping of resistant rocks. Major fighting occurred in this section of the river in the first year of the South African (or Boer) War (1899–1902), especially in the vicinity of Colesberg; it ended when the British advanced beyond the Orange and captured Bloemfontein, capital of the Orange Free State. The most important tributary in this section is the Caledon, which rises near the source of the Orange but takes a more direct, southwesterly course to its confluence below the town of Aliwal North. From Norvals

Pont the river swings to the northwest until it reaches the confluence of its largest tributary, the Vaal. From this point it adopts the southwesterly course of the Vaal as far as Prieska, then reverts to its northwesterly course until reaching Upington.

Thenceforth the river flows generally westward along the edge of the Kalahari and Namib Deserts until reaching its mouth near some of the richest alluvial diamond beds in the world. From the confluence of the Vaal to the sea—more than 600 miles (966 kilometers)—the river receives no perennial tributaries. In the dry season the channel disappears, and in many years the river does not reach the sea. Much of the precipitation that falls, even over the more humid central districts of the Orange, does not reach the main river, but collects in shallow lakes known locally as "vleis" and "pans"; these undergo evaporation and percolation, with the result that a salt-encrusted surface is exposed during the dry winter months. Grasslands extend about as far west as Aliwal North, and drought-resistant shrubs predominate beyond that point. Douglas, near the Vaal confluence, receives an average of 13 inches (33 centimeters) of precipitation, while Upington's rainfall is 8 inches (20 centimeters).

West of Upington, red sand dunes stretch down to the north bank of the river. A braided section of the river ends abruptly at Aughrabies Falls, a spectacular cascade that is higher than the more famous Victoria Falls on the Zambezi. Just downstream the river becomes the political boundary between South Africa and Namibia (formerly South-West Africa), which status the waterway retains as far as its mouth.

The low and irregular flow of the river; the presence of falls and rapids; the heavy load of silt in the channel contributing to shoaling; and a river-mouth sandbar explain the lack of a river-based civilization or even a large city along the river. Though the river is heavily used today for irrigation, the obstacles to navigation contributed to a delay in tapping the river's potential. Beginning in 1963 the first steps were taken in the construction of a larger storage dam in a gorge above Norvals Pont. Today's Orange River Scheme includes a number of dams along the middle as well as the lower river (the largest being the Hendrik Verwderd Dam, completed in 1972). Tunnels have been built through the Great Escarpment to bring water southward to the Fish and Sunday Rivers in eastern Cape Province, as well as to provide water supplies for the city of Port Elizabeth.

Although it is commonly believed that the reddish color of the silty water gives the river its name, the watercourse was actually named in honor of the Prince of Orange by Colonel R. J. Gordon, commander of the Dutch garrison of Cape Town when he discovered the river in 1777.

See also Vaal

Further Reading: Moolman, J. H., "The Orange River," *Geographical Review* 36 (1946): 635–74.

ORINOCO

Source: Guiana Highlands, in southern Venezuela
Length: 1,281 miles (2,061 kilometers)
Tributaries: Guaviare, Vichada, Meta, Apure, Caura, Caroní
Outlet: Atlantic Ocean

One of South America's major waterways rises on the slopes of the Sierra Parima in extreme southeastern Venezuela on the border with Brazil. The river flows in a wide arc—to the northwest, then to the east—through tropical rain forests and savannas (llanos), forming part of the Venezuela-Colombia border, and enters the sea across a wide delta just south of the island of Trinidad.

The Orinoco has the third largest volume of flow of the world's rivers, and together with the Amazon accounts for 25 percent of the freshwater discharged to the oceans. Though possessing the third largest drainage basin in South America, the river's entire course had not been traced by travelers or explorers until comparatively recently. Columbus is believed to have first sighted the river (1498) when he sailed along the coast opposite the mouth during the course of his third voyage. Renaissance adventurers doubling as dubious scholars (one accompanied Raleigh on an expedition) sought the origin of the river in a lake reputed to be the burial place of the sacrificial gilt man, El

Dorado. Not until the epic journey of Alexander von Humboldt in 1800 did anyone actually explore the upper river, and even the reports of the celebrated naturalist and geographer about the region's native people, the Yanomami, whom he described as dangerous and bellicose, were based on few encounters; they contributed to the mistaken impression that the Yanomami were hostile by nature. The 1968 study *Yanomamö: The Fierce People* by the American anthropologist Napoleon Chagnon contributed to this undeserved reputation (the author later removed the subtitle). It was only in the early 1950s that a French-Venezuelan expedition pinpointed the river's source, near Mt. Delgado Chalbaud in the Guiana Highlands. Portions of the Yanomami lands have been set aside as an international biosphere reserve for the preservation of the rain forest ecosystem and the homelands of the native population. Gold-mining *garimpeiros,* or independent miners, pay no attention to international policy, however; they assault the ecological basis of the indigenes' material existence just as much as scholars in the past undermined their image.

At the western edge of the Yanomami lands near Esmeralda, the river branches, with one arm, the Casiquiare, flowing south in a natural canal joining the Rio Negro, a tributary of the Amazon. This unusual—virtually unique—link between two major watersheds is subject to wide variations in flow, as is the Orinoco, so that at times the Casiquiare receives as much as 20 percent of the Orinoco's discharge. The main branch of the river continues northwest to the town of San Fernando de Atabapo, where it receives the Guaviare River. Thenceforth flowing north along the border between Venezuela and Colombia, the river passes over the Maipures and Atures rapids, which divide the Orinoco for purposes of navigation into the upper and lower river (oceangoing vessels can reach only as far as Ciudad Bolívar). The river then receives on the left first the Meta River, then the Apure River, the latter its major left-bank tributary.

Turning northeast the river traverses the llanos, or plains, of central Venezuela, a vast alluvial plain encompassing nearly one-third of the national territory. The Venezuelan llanos turns into an inland sea in the rainy season months of May to November. The region is home to a diverse assemblage of wildlife, ranging from the oversized capybara, the world's largest rodent—said to resemble a cross between a guinea pig and a hippopotamus—to the deadly, coiled constrictor snake, the anaconda, to the alligator's cousin, the caiman. A delightful assortment of bird species includes Orinoco geese, crested bobwhite, yellow-headed parrots, and crested caracaras, to name just a few. It is perhaps something of a tall tale, but nonetheless has been reported, that during Venezuela's colonial period a Spaniard killed a capybara in the Lenten season and, as the colonists were starving, declared that since the pig-sized rodent spent most of its life in water it could be considered a fish and be eaten.

Crossing wide stretches of cattle ranches and wildlife pools, the Orinoco divides the mineral-rich central district of Venezuela. Vast petroleum deposits are found north of the river, while the hard-rock riches of the Guiana (Guayana) Shield lie to the south. Beneath flat-topped *tepuis* in the foothills of the highlands are gold deposits estimated to be 11 percent of the world's supply. The river's southern bank also has large deposits of iron ore, diamonds, and bauxite, the last the primary raw material in aluminum-making, the principal industry in Ciudad Guayana, the planned industrial city (est. 1961) located just upriver from the delta. The Caroní River passes through downtown Ciudad Guayana en route to its nearby confluence with the Orinoco, and the lower course of this tributary contains a string of hydroelectric plants providing energy for the industries of the largest city in the valley today.

To the north of the river is the Orinoco Belt, a large deposit of heavy crude oil and bitumen estimated at 270 billion barrels. Though requiring extra cost to transport and refine, these reserves are one of the largest accumulations of hydrocarbons in the world and are considered crucial for the future economic development of Venezuela, the only OPEC member in the Americas.

On a hillside along the south bank of the river

stands the key entrepôt of the past: Ciudad Bolívar. The site of this old colonial city is the Angostura Narrows, which also gives the town its former name, where the river's width is reduced sufficiently so that it is spanned by a suspension bridge, the only bridge crossing the thirteen-hundred-mile (2,100-kilometer) length of the river (there is no dam along the main-stem river).

About 50 miles (80 kilometers) northeast of Ciudad Guayana is the apex of the branching delta. The river splits into a number of distributaries (*caños*), the principal one being the Rio Grande, which empties into the Atlantic Ocean at Boca Grande. The remaining flow is primarily through the northern distributaries of the Caños Mánamo and Macareo, which also originate near the head of the delta at Barrancas. The primary outlet of this enormous river with two thousand tributaries has been confined to the south of the delta for the last few thousand years, but frequent channel jumpings from old channels to newer ones during floods has produced the northern delta plain. Two types of streams have been distinguished in the delta: *brown-water streams* directly connected to upland rivers and carrying suspended sediments, and *black-water streams* draining delta swamps carrying water rich in humic acids. Indigenous Warao use the delta's numerous creeks and channels to fish, swim, play, and build their stilt houses on. In their native tongue, the Orinoco's name means "a place to paddle," and though the river is still navigated in dugouts, they are often motorized today and are used by men seeking employment on large oil rigs along the coast.

The hundreds of miles of mangrove swamps and the maze of tidal inlets provide a better outlet for contraband than the closely watched drug routes and airfields of Colombia, where much of the illegal drug production takes place. The delta of the Orinoco has become a major gateway for cocaine en route to the Caribbean and the United States. The only delta town of any size, Tecupita, is located at the drier western end of the distributary fan. It has been accurately described as tumbledown, but one might add drug-infested. The movement of cocaine downriver has become the region's latest myth of riches, the most recent El Dorado.

See also Casiquiare
Further Reading: de Civrieux, Marc, *Watunna: An Orinoco Creation Cycle,* ed. and trans. David Guss, Austin: University of Texas Press, 1997 (orig. pub. in Spanish, 1970); Webster, Donovan, "The Orinoco: Into the Heart of Venezuela," *National Geographic,* April 1998, pp. 2–31.

ORONTES

Source: Bekáa valley, in north Lebanon
Length: c. 250 miles (402 kilometers)
Tributaries: Afrine
Outlet: Mediterranean Sea

Although it is not a particularly long river, the Orontes (Arabic: Nahr Al Nasi; Turkish: Asi Nehri) derives significance from its situation near the crossroads of the Mideast, where cultural influences of Hellenistic and Roman, Jewish and Arab worlds intermingled.

The river rises in the broad Bekáa valley of Lebanon and flows northward. It is said that its Arabic name—*Asi,* meaning "rebel"—refers to the fact that the river flows away from Mecca. The Orontes River does not alone drain the Bekáa, as the southern part of the trenched depression is occupied by the south-draining Litani River. Springs west of Baalbek (ancient Greek name: Heliopolis) have been identified as the headwaters of the Orontes, near the cave retreat of St. Maron, the founder of Maronite Christianity, the Uniate church using the Syriac liturgy. The great Roman temple of Jupiter lies in magnificent ruins in Baalbek, providing an excellent background for the music and ballet festival held there annually. The earliest rite associated with this ancient town was probably worship of the sun, but Baal is often identified with the sensual, naturalistic god of the Philistines.

The river follows a generally northerly course between the Lebanon Mountains (to the west) and the Anti-Lebanon Mountains (to the east), continuing on this path once it reaches Syria. Shortly after crossing the political border, the Orontes broadens into an artificial lake at Homs (anciently Emesa), one of the storied cities along the middle course of the river. Located 85 miles (137 kilometers) north of Damascus, Homs is today a large sugar and oil-refining center. Lying nearby on the Orontes is the ancient city of Kadesh, where Rameses II fought the Hittites (c. 1300 B.C.) in a great battle that ended in a truce. Devoted to sun worship under Roman rule, Homs was the scene of the defeat of Queen Zenobia of Palmyra in 272 by Emperor Aurelian.

The other famous town of antiquity along the middle Orontes is Hamah, or biblical Hamath, noted for its oversized water-lifting wheels, used for irrigation. Hamah was one of the traditional northern boundaries of Israel specified in the Bible.

The river eventually crosses into southern Turkey, where flowing westward it traverses a fertile strip of coastal plain. Cutting deeply into the plain, the Orontes passes Antakya (anciently Antioch) before debouching into the Mediterranean at Samandaq, 40 miles (64 kilometers) north of Latakia. Archaeologists have discovered sequences of cultural occupation near the mouth of the river at Antakya. In ancient times, the city, founded by the Macedonian general Seleucus I Nicator in 300 B.C., was the commercial rival of Alexandria. Not actually located at the mouth of the river, Antioch (to the Romans, Antiochia) is situated away from the sea and served by the port of Seleucia, also established by Seleucus I (the port was later damaged by an earthquake and left to deteriorate). The Roman general Pompey conquered Antioch in 64 B.C., and the city subsequently became a mission center for early Christianity. St. Paul sailed with Barnabus from the seaport of Antalya en route to Antioch on his first missionary journey. One of the largest and richest cities of the Mediterranean world until the collapse of the Roman imperium was the first place outside Palestine where Christianity took hold.

The Orontes is unnavigable along most of its course, but it is used extensively for irrigation, especially in the middle section of the river in Syria. The marshy Ghab depression below Hamah in western Syria has been drained and the land reclaimed for farming. In addition to irrigation there are several dams providing hydroelectric power.

OTTAWA

Source: Laurentian Highlands, in southwestern Quebec
Length: c. 700 miles (1,130 kilometers)
Tributaries: Mattawa, Coulonge, Madawaska, Gatineau, du Lièvre, South Nation
Outlet: **Saint Lawrence**

Best known today for its opportunities for whitewater enthusiasts and as the site of Canada's capital, the Ottawa River (French: Rivière des Outaouais) was for centuries the primary route into the western interior from the well-settled lower St. Lawrence valley.

The river rises in western Quebec in a chain of lakes resting on the ancient plateau of the Laurentian Highlands, or Canadian Shield. It first flows westward as far as Lake Timiskaming, then to the southeast, forming part of the Quebec-Ontario border. South of Lake Timiskaming the river is broad and forceful, its course alternating between expansions into marshy lakes and constrictions into turbulent rapids. Along its middle course above Ottawa, the river passes through a series of outreaches: Allumette, Chats, and Deschênes. At Ottawa the major tributary—the Gatineau—joins from the left on the other side of the river. On the near side, Ottawa is bisected by the Rideau Canal (completed 1832) joining the Ottawa River to Kingston on Lake Ontario. The attractive neo-Gothic parliament buildings of the capital city stand high on a hill near the confluence of the Ottawa River and the Rideau Canal. The Rideau (pronounced ri-DOUGH) Canal, with forty-seven locks, has attracted settlement along its 124-mile (199-kilometer) path. Bytown, as Ottawa was originally called (having been named after Colonel By), dates from the second decade of the nineteenth century. At that time a plan was drawn up to settle what was then an inhospitable section of the valley, vegetated with cypress swamps, by veterans of the War of 1812–1814 who had been given Crown

Colony land grants in exchange for their military service. It was not until the 1830s and 1840s, with the construction of the Rideau Canal, that the city grew rapidly in population and became the center of the lumber trade in the Ottawa valley. The rapid growth during this period bears comparison with nearly contemporaneous events in upstate New York upon completion of the Erie Canal (1825), except that Canada didn't have the vast American Midwest to tap as a market. The first few miles of the Rideau Canal wind through downtown Ottawa, and the tree-lined route is a pleasingly integrated natural design for the town center.

Across the river from Ottawa is present-day Hull, founded in 1806 by Philemon Wright, who was the first to send a raft of squared timber down the Ottawa to the Saint Lawrence. The Napoleonic Wars depleted the traditional British sources of timber in Scandinavia, and Canadian exports took up the slack. The logs were squared so that they could be more efficiently stacked in the hold of ships transporting the cargo back to Britain.

The river is navigable for large vessels as far as Ottawa. Farming occurs in the valley below Pembroke, benefiting from the fertile clays deposited by the Ottawa on its way to the sea. The valley itself was gouged out by Pleistocene glaciers, and, with the melting of the icesheets approximately 10,000 years ago, it was the Ottawa that drained the Great Lakes until the land was elevated enough to form a new channel along the Saint Lawrence. The lower valley represents an intrusion of fertile land into the barren Canadian Shield. Many of the river's southern tributaries—for example, the Rideau and South Nation—drain gentle land, in contrast to the rough country crossed by swift-flowing and wild northern tributaries. At St-André-Est the river expands to form Lac-des-Deux-Montagnes ("Lake of the Two Mountains"), from which it enters the St. Lawrence by a number of channels.

The French explorer Samuel de Champlain may not have been the first European to discover the river—its outlet had certainly been seen before—but his expedition in 1613 carried him along the route of what was to become the primary avenue for carrying furs for the next 200 years. Champlain traveled up the Ottawa, then followed the Mattawa, a western tributary, until he reached French River, which drains west into Georgian Bay and Lake Huron. The section of the route linking the Ottawa to Georgian Bay is called the Lake Nipissing route, after the large glacial lake lying on the divide between the Mattawa and French Rivers. The Ottawa–Lake Nipissing canoeway required eighteen portages, and, what with the need to unload and carry cargo and canoe (full portage) or cargo alone (half-portage) at rapids, the river route was a severe test even for the hardy voyageurs. Just as the fur trade gave way to the lumber industry by the mid-nineteenth century, so farming and second-growth harvesting of timber for paper and pulp processing came into prominence by the end of the nineteenth century. Most of the valley's stands of pine had been decimated by 1910. Fertile ground was reclaimed for agriculture, but vast tracts of stumps and debris proved excellent kindling for fires. The establishment of Algonquin Provincial Park (1893) saved some of the wilderness from the ax, and scientific forestry studied the effects of logging, disease, and fire, with an eye to fostering sustainable forestry. Although the lumber industry is still important in Canada's economy, it must be remembered that Ottawa, chosen as capital of the United Provinces in 1857, today depends for its prosperity on the federal government, not the resources of the valley or its riverine connections.

Water quality problems bedevil the river that runs past the national capital almost as much as they do on Washington's Potomac. High counts of coliform bacteria, traces of toxic elements, and excessive sediments settling out in channels are perennial environmental problems here as elsewhere where there are sizable concentrations of people and industry. Pulp and paper mills along the river are a source of sulfur. A recent and more troubling threat to the river comes from the proposal that a cavern located near the river at Deep River, Ontario, be used as a disposal site for radioactive wastes. Upstream from Ottawa, about 25 miles (40 kilometers) northwest of Pembroke, the proposed dump site for a million metric tons of radium and radioactive waste is a giant underground cave less than half a kilometer from the river. A long-standing political pledge dating from a 1984 election promise by Brian Mulroney commits the government to moving toxic materials from the watershed of Lake Ontario, where it was generated (at Port Huron, Ontario), to the watershed of the Saint Lawrence at Deep River. In 1995 a task force recommended that the Canadian minister of natural resources proceed with the disposal of the nuclear wastes at Deep River. Government technical reports indicate that within a hundred years arsenic, uranium, and radium will leak into the nearby Ottawa River, and environmentalists and concerned citizens are resisting the move by publicizing the harmful effects of such an action.

See also Saint Lawrence

Further Reading: Lafrenière, Normand, *The Ottawa River Canal System,* Ottawa: National Historic Parks and Sites Branch, Parks Canada, Environment Canada. Hull, Quebec, Canada: Canadian Govt. Pub. Centre, Supply and Services Canada, 1984; MacLennan, Hugh, *Rivers of Canada,* Toronto: Macmillan of Canada, 1974.

OXUS

See Amu Darya

P

PARAGUAY

Source: Mato Grosso Plateau, in southwestern Brazil
Length: c. 1,300 miles (2,090 kilometers)
Tributaries: Cuiabá, Apá, Ypané, Pilcomayo, Bermejo
Outlet: **Paraná**

The southern portion of the South American continent has for its major drainage a series of interconnected rivers that begin with the letter *P:* The Río de la Plata (or River Plate) is the major waterway at the lower end of the basin and is sometimes identified with the whole network. The La Plata, on whose southern bank stands the Argentine megacity of Buenos Aires, is continued upstream by the Paraná, a major drainage of Argentina and southern Brazil, which in turn is fed by the Paraguay, the primary river of the landlocked country of the same name and an important waterway in interior Brazil.

The long and sluggish Río Paraguay (Portuguese: Rio Paraguai) begins near the Brazilian town of Diamantino in Mato Grosso state in western Brazil (not to be confused with the diamond-mining center of Diamantina in Minas Gerais in eastern Brazil). The river rises amid numerous *serra,* or highlands, from which issue several of the headwaters of north-flowing tributaries of the Amazon. After gathering the waters from a number of tributaries, the river flows south toward the border with Paraguay, traversing the broad interior basin of swampland known as the Pantanal, a scene with beautiful and diverse wildlife not unlike the Venezuelan llanos along the middle course of the Orinoco. The river pursues an uncertain course with multiple channels across the Pantanal wetlands, which each summer flood as far as the eye can see. In the dry winter season the waters of the floodplain shrink, and the inundated immensity is reduced to myriad lakes, patches of swamps, and the braided channel of the Paraguay.

The Apá tributary entering from the east marks the boundary with Paraguay and also the transition to the better-drained hill country. In this section less extensive riverside swamps and seasonal lakes can be found east of the river. The river crosses the country from north to south and approximately bisects the landlocked nation. To the east the river pushes up against the harder rocks of the Brazilian *planalto,* or plateau (that portion in Paraguay), while to the west a dry plain is formed by the deposition of heavy loads of sediments sluiced out of the Andes. This vast region west of the Paraguay known as the Chaco, mainly in the country of Paraguay but also in Argentina and Bolivia, constitutes a territory of ill-defined river courses, dry scrubland vegetation, and only a sparse population of Guaraní Indians (who also compose the majority of the population in more thickly settled eastern Paraguay). Though not blessed with rich natural resources, the Chaco has been the scene of recurrent warfare, most recently in the Chaco War of 1932–1935.

The major city along the river is Asunción, the capital of Paraguay, situated at the confluence of the right-bank tributary, the Pilcomayo. With a population of half a million, this largely Indian city lies at the head of navigation for steamers plying upstream from Buenos Aires, though smaller craft can reach as far as Conceptión, Paraguay's second largest city. Below Asunción and the junction of the Pilcomayo, the river flows southwestward to the Paraná confluence, forming part of the Paraguay-Argentina border.

The forbidding nature of the terrain crossed by the river—savanna, swamps, and scrubland—in combination with the region's isolation has led to little attempt to colonize or develop this interior country. For more than four centuries the Spanish confined their activities to the establishment of military posts and religious missions. The chief contact between Paraguay's capital and the outside world has been the railway or, more recently, the airlines.

In 1995, with the establishment in the Southern Cone of the four-nation Mercosur trade zone (comprising Brazil, Argentina, Uruguay, and Paraguay), a waterway based on natural routes, but deepening and improving them, was envisaged that would link interior portions of the Paraguay with the coast. The proposed route of the so-called Hidrovia project links Caceres in western Brazil with Nueva Palmira in Uruguay and would essentially expand the navigability of the Paraguay-Paraná system. Critics of the plan have argued that the environmental effects of dredging, diking, and channel straightening would devastate the species-rich Pantanal swamplands, and that these costs should be taken into account in assessing the economic benefits of improving access to the landlocked countries of Paraguay and Bolivia. At a time when similar large navigation projects are being scrutinized more closely in the more developed parts of the world (for example, the proposed new additions to the upper Mississippi-Missouri navigation channel), it might be asked why such proposals in poorer countries should automatically be allowed to override environment considerations for the sake of the exaggerated benefit of increased barge traffic.

See also Paraná, Plata
Further Reading: For an assessment of the Hidrovia project, see the Web site: http://www.american.edu/projects/mandala/TED/HIDROVIA.HTM

PARANÁ

Source: Junction of **Paranaíba** and Rio Grande, in south-central Brazil
Length: c. 2,000 miles (3,200 kilometers)
Tributaries: Tietê, Verde, Paranápanema, Iguaçu, **Paraguay**, Salado, Carcarañá, Gualeguay
Outlet: **Plata**

Constituting a major river in southern Brazil and northern Argentina, the Paraná is a key avenue of communications in South America, and it is the exception to the rule that the continent's rivers flow away from rather than toward settlement zones. In conjunction with its principal tributary, the Paraguay, and the baylike estuary of its Río de la Plata ("River Plate") mouth, it is a vital accessway to the southern continent's broad hinterlands.

The Paraná (from Tupi-Guarani, meaning "like the sea") is formed by the confluence of two westward-flowing headstreams in the Brazilian Highlands. The more northern of these, the Paranaíba, demarks the northwestern border of Minas Gerais state with Goiás. The southern headstream, the Rio Grande, also forms a political border: the division between São Paulo state and Minas Gerais. The upper river, known as the Alto Paraná, continues this function of political delineation. Flowing to the southwest, it marks a political division, first between São Paulo state and Mato Grosso do Sul state, then between the latter state and Paraná state.

Following a course that turns slowly to the south, the river cuts across the diabase rocks of the Paraná tableland, furnishing some of the best coffeelands in the world. Diabase being volcanic in origin, the rocks are especially resistant to erosion. Deep gorges and spectacular falls characterize the valleys trenched out by the upper Paraná and its numerous tributaries. The impressive Iguaçu Falls, consisting of more than twenty cataracts averaging 200 feet (61 meters) in height, is located on a left-bank tributary, the Iguaçu, near its junction with the Paraná. Because so many people visit this easily accessible scenic attraction, it might be considered the "Niagara Falls" of South America (it is much higher than North America's famous falls, though

Magnificent cascades of Iguaçu Falls on the Brazil-Argentina border near the junction of the Iguaçu and Paraná Rivers (Jack Fields/CORBIS)

not the highest in South America). Iguaçu is only one of a series of cataracts along the river and its tributaries. The Urubu-Pungá Falls, just above the influx of the Tietê River, forms a spectacular sequence of cataracts. Farther downstream are the Guaíra Falls, which are the result of the river's crossing the resistant Serra de Maracaju. This falls comprises eighteen cataracts, the highest dropping about 100 feet (31 meters). Near the falls a Jesuit mission was founded at Ciudad Real in the eighteenth century. The Jesuits, early settlers of Brazil's backlands, have generally received good marks for their treatment of the indigenous population, in contrast to the depredations of the slave traders who replaced them and turned Ciudad Real into a ghost town.

Between the Guaíra Falls and the junction of the Iguaçu River, the Paraná divides Brazil from Paraguay. Below the falls the river turns to the southwest to form the border between the Corrientes Province of Paraguay and the Misiones territory of Argentina. Below Posadas (Argentina) and Encarnación (Paraguay), the river turns westward and is split by several large islands and a long stretch of falling water known as the Apipé Rapids, the river's traditional head of navigation. Just above Corrientes the Paraná receives its major tributary, the Paraguay, and the broad, navigable river flows southward to join the northern lowlands of Argentina.

After the river's junction with the Paraguay, its western banks encompass the Argentine portion of the dry Chaco region, shared with the landlocked countries of Paraguay and Bolivia. The banks are low to the west and are subject to regular overflow in times of flood. To the east lies the Mesopotamian region between the Paraná and the Uruguay River, the latter paralleling the Paraná for a considerable distance before joining it in the delta to form the River Plate. The northern limit of the Argentine

Pampa is marked by the complex delta of the Paraná, which begins below the city of Paraná. The rich agricultural region of the delta, whose chief crop is maté (from which "green tea" is made), includes a number of distributary mouths, of which the navigable northern channel, the Paraná Guazu (Great Paraná), is the largest. The principal southern distributary is the Paraná de las Palmas, also navigable, which is longer and deeper than the northern debouchure. The delta is long but comparatively narrow.

Oceangoing vessels can reach Rosario and Santa Fe, Argentina, via a dredged channel. Neither is far from the apex of the delta. Smaller craft can ascend to Corrientes and up the Paraguay as far as Asunción, the Paraguayan capital. The mainstream river is navigable for only a short stretch above the Paraguay junction, as far as the Apipé Rapids. Along the lower river islands, sandbars, shifting channels, and variable flow pose significant obstacles to navigation, while the upper course is virtually unnavigable except along brief stretches. Sailing vessels carrying passengers and freight once navigated the Plata estuary and the lower Paraná, but they soon lost out to steamers that could ride the strong current of the river and travel more swiftly upriver.

Most of the major knickpoints (falls and rapids) along the upper river have been developed for hydroelectric power. The impoundments formed behind the dams have almost converted the river into a string of lakes. This is not surprising if one considers that Brazil had a population of 170 million (as of 2000) and scant petroleum resources but many rivers falling from elevated escarpments. Ninety percent of Brazil's electricity is generated from hydroelectric plants. The proposed Porto Primavera project would inundate a large area and destroy the riverbank ecosystem with its diverse plant and animal communities. Animal species including jaguars, anteaters, tapirs, howler monkeys, and wetland deer (cervo do pantanal, the largest deer in South America) would be lost. Most of the electricity from this project would be used in the highly urbanized and industrialized São Paulo state, but 80 percent of the area of the reservoir would be in Mato Grosso do Sul state. The dam would flood an area seven times larger than Itaipu, which is the largest hydroelectric plant in the world. A recent proposal to construct a dam farther downstream, in Argentina, has met with resistance from environmentalists both at home and abroad. The Paraná Medio project, whose primary purpose is to produce hydroelectric power, would create the second-largest reservoir in the world, flooding an area seven times larger than Itaipu's yet generating only one-fourth of the electricity.

Chemical spills are always a threat along a river with a sizable number of people. In July 2000, some 1,000,000 gallons (3,800,000 liters) of crude oil leaked from a burst pipe at a refinery of Brazil's state-owned Petrobras company and ended up in the Iguaçu River. Although the leak was well above the falls and the confluence with the Paraná, downstream farmland and communities were at risk. Brazilian cleanup crews assisted by international experts used floating barriers and diversion canals to halt the movement of the oil slick 25 miles (40 kilometers) below the refinery.

See also Paraguay, Plata

Further Reading: Bonetto, A. A., and I. R. Wais, "Powerful Paraná: Environmental Health of South America's Second Largest River," *Geographical Magazine* 62, no. 3 (March 1990): S1–S3; Kohlhepp, Gerd, *Itaipú: Basic Geopolitical and Energy Situation: Socio-Economic and Ecological Consequences of the Itaipú Dam and Reservoir on the Rio Paraná,* Braunschweig: Friedrick Vieweg and Son, 1987.

PARANAÍBA

Source: South-central Brazil in western Minas Gerais state
Length: c. 500 miles (800 kilometers)
Tributaries: São Marcos, Araguari, Corumbá, Meia Ponte, Tijuco
Outlet: Merges with Rio Grande to form **Paraná**

The Paranaíba is the northernmost of the two headstreams of the Paraná, the second-largest river in South America. It forms a major drainage in Brazil's interior state of Minas Gerais (Portuguese: "general mines"). The river was colonized as much from the northeast as from the coast, due to the penetration of Minas by the headwaters of the São Francisco, which approach the sources of the Paranaíba. Diamonds and gold were found elsewhere in Minas, but diamond washings were the focus for settlers in the valley of the Paranaíba and its tributaries.

The river rises on the western slopes of the Serra da Mata da Corda (Portuguese *serra* corresponding to the Spanish *sierra:* "mountain range"). It flows to the west and southwest, collecting a number of sizable tributaries. Joining the river from the right are rivers draining the southern part of Goiás from as far away as Brasília, the national capital. The southern portion of the drainage includes fertile farming and ranching country. Most of the native savanna vegetation has long been converted to pasturage and arable land. The river forms the border between Minas Gerais and Goiás states and briefly separates Minas from Mato Grosso do Sul state. Turning southwest, the river joins the Rio Grande to form the Paraná.

Several hydroelectric dams have been constructed along the middle course of the river, such as the one at Itumbiara, backing up the river to form large lakes whose recreational potential has been increasingly valued. Since the late 1970s the basin has been used for government-backed irrigation projects, focusing on cattle raising and cultivation of sugarcane, rice, corn (maize), bananas, cotton, and *feijão* (beans).

See also Paraná
Further Reading: Goodland, Robert J. A., *Itumbiara Hydroelectric Project: Environmental Impact Reconnaissance,* Millbrook, NY: Cary Arboretum of the New York Botanical Garden, 1972.

PEACE

Source: Junction of Finlay and Parsnip, in north-central British Columbia, Canada
Length: 945 miles (1,521 kilometers)
Tributaries: Smoky
Outlet: Slave River at Lake Athabasca

Flowing out of the Stikine Mountains of northern British Columbia, the Finlay—one of the Peace's headstreams—follows a southeasterly course until its junction with the Parsnip. The resulting Peace River flows east across the flank of the Rocky Mountains into Alberta as far as the town of Peace River, an important transport and distribution center for Canada's Far North. Located just below the mouth of the Smoky River, this settlement occupies the former site of Fort Fork, where Sir Alexander Mackenzie wintered in 1792–1793. Though the American fur trader Peter Pond may have visited the river earlier, the Canadian explorer Mackenzie is credited with its first exploration. The river turns north as far as Fort Vermilion, where it begins to follow an east-northeasterly course to the Slave River just north of Lake Athabasca.

The river and its tributaries and headstreams were important entranceways into the beaver-rich Rocky Mountain region. The British established a series of forts along the watercourses to secure and provision the fur trade. The name of the river derives from Peace Point, along its lower reaches, where Cree and Beaver Indians amicably settled a dispute about riverside lands. The middle course of the river has especially suitable soils and climate for farming. This grain-growing district is the northernmost commercial agricultural region in Canada. With only a short growing season the region received a flush of late pioneer settlement because of high commodity prices. The completion of the railroad from Edmonton during World War I and the subsequent building of the provincial highway during World War II, the latter with access to the Alaska Highway, opened up the more westerly parts of the valley in Alberta and adjacent parts of British Columbia. Beyond the farming areas are the gray soils of the forests, which provide the materials for a well-developed forest products industry. Large reserves of natural gas are tapped in the valley, and coal, oil, salt, and gypsum resources are also worked here. Rocky Mountain canyons are excellent sites for hydroelectric development. Near Hudson Hope, British Columbia, is the W. A. C. Bennett Dam, opened in 1967, which impounds Williston Lake. The dam's power plant, the sixth largest in Canada, provides electricity for Vancouver.

See also Mackenzie
Further Reading: Irvine, Thelma, *Where the River Ran: The Story of the Peace,* Victoria, B.C.: Touchwood Editions, 2000.

PENOBSCOT

Source: Convergence of West and East Branch, in north-central Maine
Length: 350 miles (563 kilometers)
Tributaries: North Branch, South Branch, Piscataquis, Passadumkeag, Mattawamkeag, East Branch, West Branch
Outlet: Penobscot Bay

Encompassing about one-fourth of the total area of Maine, the Penobscot River drainage basin extends from the Atlantic Ocean to the remote north woods. The river, the longest in Maine, rises on the Quebec frontier northwest of Moosehead Lake along the North and South Branches. To the east the Mattawamkeag tributary drains water from within a few miles of the international boundary with New Brunswick.

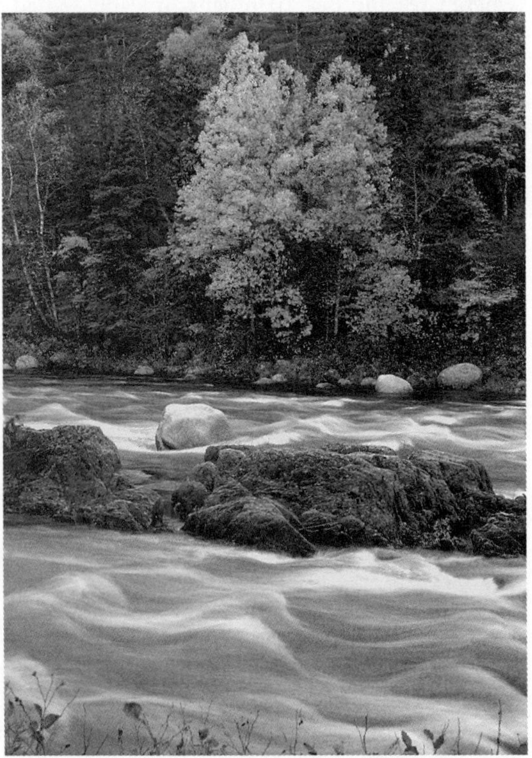

Grindstone Falls on the Penobscot River (David Muench/CORBIS)

The wilderness stream twists frequently in its upper course, receiving the influx of hundreds of smaller brooks and interconnected ponds. (One wonders who took the time to count them, but it has been determined that there are 1,604 rivers, streams, and brooks that flow into the Penobscot.) Major tributaries are large rivers in their own right, but the Penobscot proper is considered to begin at the convergence of the West and East Branch, at Medway. Mount Katahdin, the highest point engulfed by the East and West Branch and the highest point in the state, can be seen from miles away and is a landmark for travelers. This eminent peak, which anchors the Appalachian chain on the north, was held in reverence and fear by the native tribes of the region.

The creation tales of the Penobscot Indians linked human life with the beautiful, ramifying river system. By necessity the natives were knowledgeable about and well adapted to the river and its resources. Thousands of years of experience and countless results of trial-and-error went into the careful meshing of their cultural life with the environment. The harvesting of the fall-run eels is a good example of the natives' environmental savvy. After maturing in northern ponds, eels run south to the sea to reach their spawning grounds (the reverse of the reproductive path of the salmon). The Penobscot Indians ground to a powder jack-in-the-pulpit root, and by vigorously mixing this powder into the river's waters rendered the eels unconscious so they could be easily caught, brought to the surface, and smoked or salted for future eating. The root was available for only a short time, and the fish collected at obstacles on the river only at certain seasons, testifying to the Indians' remarkable powers of observation and deduction.

The place-names of the Penobscot country are a valuable source of information about the aboriginal use of the land. Kenduskeag means "eel weir place," and it was applied to the confluence of a tributary. Many names are in effect geographic features as viewed from the perspective of a canoer.

Mattawamkeag, for instance, means "at the mouth a gravel bar." Natural barriers to fish migration—both for eel going downstream and salmon coming up—were favorite fishing spots and village sites. European town sites, as at Bangor and Old Town, mimicked the Indian choices.

The French explorer Samuel de Champlain, the founder of Quebec City and discoverer of the Great Lakes, sailed up the course of the Penobscot in 1604. An early captive of the Maine Indians, the eleven-year-old John Gyles, who was seized in a French-led raid on Pemaquid, was taken up the Penobscot by canoe and held for eight years in captivity. He reported feelings amounting to religious awe that his Indian masters displayed toward the granite massif of Mt. Katahdin. Wolfe's capture of Quebec in 1759 marked the end of the long war between the surviving tribes of the interior and English settlers on the coast. As European colonists penetrated northward along the banks of the Penobscot, economic gain was sought and sometimes gained, but at the cost of wreaking ecological havoc. The principal attraction was cheap land and large stands of white pine and spruce. Harvesting timberlands and converting the forest to cutover, unattractive as the result might be, was financially rewarding. It was justified by the phrase "letting daylight into the swamp."

Power sites were plentiful along the river for grist- and sawmills. By the 1840s a large lumbering industry flourished along the Penobscot, with Bangor, at the head of navigation, as the boom town (literally, for a boom was a holding area where logs coming downstream could be retained until they needed to be cut into serviceable lumber). In the year 1832 Bangor shipped 37 million board feet of lumber. Between Bangor and Old Town—only a dozen or so miles away—nearly two hundred saw mills sprang up. During Maine's golden age of lumbering more efficient tools of the trade were created, including peaveys and driving boots, which would be used on later timber frontiers such as northern Wisconsin in the late nineteenth century.

The colorful adventures of river driving made for romantic stories, but it was dangerous work. The risk of accidental maiming or even death was always at hand, whether by being knocked down by an overhanging branch (a "widow-maker"), "sluiced" on an icy slope that gave way, or crushed by rolling logs. There are many unmarked graves along the Penobscot's banks, final resting place for the restless river drivers. The legends and lore of the river pigs would grow into the tall tales of Paul Bunyan and his fanciful friends—animal and otherwise—on the northern Great Lakes frontier.

In September 1846, Henry David Thoreau, author of *Walden,* made one of several trips to the Maine woods, canoeing extensively in the wilderness of the Penobscot. He questioned the utilitarian values of his commercial society: "Think how stood the white pine on the shore of Chescuncook, its branches soughing in the four winds, and every individual needle trembling in sunlight,—think how it stands with it now—sold perchance to the New England Friction Match Company!" A somewhat hypocritical comment this was, since the family business that employed and paid the young naturalist, thereby allowing him to pursue his solitude, was a pencil factory.

Pollution of the river was detected early and reacted to decisively by conscientious New Englanders. Sawmills and, later, pulpwood and paper mills have been the primary contributors to befouling the environment. Fish, notably salmon, have been harmed. In the 1860s commercial fishermen took 15,000 salmon from the river. Because of industrial pollution and the construction of power dams, only 1,500 were taken in 1920. Things got even worse: only 40 fish were taken in 1947, and commercial fishing ceased. It was soon realized that dumping of the lime used in paper-making was responsible for depopulating fish in rivers and streams. In the 1890s the Army Corps of Engineers had to dredge sawdust and slabs from below Bangor, as refuse from hundreds of sawmills blocked this inland port's channel. Textile mills, tanneries, dye houses, and municipal sewage (the last-named being the result of recent urban growth) all have contributed to the river's pollution. By 1960 the Penobscot River carried a pollution load equivalent to a population of 3.3 million people, although there were only about 150,000 permanent residents in the valley. Since the 1960s, public concerns about the environment have been translated into effective action to clean up the river. Moose can be seen wading the river's West Branch; salmon ascend the river, at least as far as the dams; and canoes again ply the quiet waters of the ponds, rivers, and brooks of the North Country.

See also Kennebec

PLATA

Source: Junction of **Paraná** and Uruguay, in southeastern South America
Length: c. 170 miles (270 kilometers)
Tributary: Riachuelo
Outlet: Atlantic Ocean

The broad estuary between Argentina and Uruguay is the focus of the continent's second-largest river system. Only approximately 20 miles (30 kilometers) wide at its head, the Río de la Plata widens to around 120 miles (190 kilometers) at its mouth on the Atlantic Ocean. The funnel-shaped indentation of the coastline is sometimes referred to by its English name, the River Plate. Considering that the waterway is the key riverine access into the interior, it is curious that the Plata is not a river at all, but a vast tidal estuary or gulf of the sea. So large a volume of fresh water enters at its head that the low salinity conditions of a river prevail at its western, narrow end.

The name of the river, literally Spanish for "River of Silver," is not based on its color, which, because of the high sediment load is decidedly not silverish, nor is it the result of any precious metal obtained in the valley. It has been suggested that the name may derive from the mines of distant Potosí, Bolivia, where, during colonial times, these rich sources of silver found their outlet down the Plata river system at a time when the viceroyalty of Río de la Plata embraced present Argentina, Uruguay, Paraguay, and Bolivia. The most likely explanation is that the river was given its name because of the many silver ornaments worn by local people at the time it was visited by early explorers and settlers.

The principal cities and capitals of Argentina and Uruguay—Buenos Aires and Montevideo, respectively—are located along its shores. Though extensive sandbanks and shoals reduce navigability, a constantly dredged channel permits movement along the Plata and through the merged Paraná-Uruguay delta. The two large cities that lie on opposite banks of the wide Plata are major ports for oceangoing vessels. Montevideo was named by Magellan, who, sailing up the river in 1520, noted high banks set amid generally flat terrain to the north and reputedly said, "*Mont-vide-eu*" ("A mount I saw"). The northern shores of the Plata in present Uruguay originally were colonized by Portuguese from Brazil, but Spain later took over this territory. Buenos Aires was initially a failed settlement, since the Spanish abandoned the town in the face of Indian attacks shortly after it was established in 1536. Resettled in 1580, the city has become a riverine hub for an extensive river network that comprises South America's most important navigable waterway.

The delta at the western end of the Plata is advancing at a rate of 230 feet (70 meters) per year. Dredging of selected Paraná distributaries needs to be undertaken continually, so that a sufficient depth—today about 65 feet (20 meters)—is maintained for the increasingly large ships that ply international waters. Artificial channels are maintained with deep-water ports near the apex of the delta, at Rosario and Santa Fe.

The proposed Hidrovia project, put in motion after the formation of the four-nation Mercosur trade region in the Southern Cone (1995), would link the Uruguayan port of Nueva Palmira on the Plata to Caceres in western Brazil on the Paraguay. Supporters of the giant project say it would be a major economic boon to the region by expanding the navigability of the Plata-Paraná-Paraguay system, while its opponents argue that the massive diking and dredging required, especially along the upper river (that is, the Paraguay) would cause the loss of wetlands and wildlife habitat. The likelihood of flooding on the lower river would actually be increased because of the reduction of the storage capacity of wetlands, which absorb floodwaters.

Straightening and shortening rivers to make artificial channels increases the speed of a ship's passage but also increases the velocity of the water, aggravating flood problems and increasing erosion.

See also Paraguay, Paraná

PLATTE

Source: Junction of North and South Platte, in west-central Nebraska
Length: c. 310 miles (499 kilometers)
Tributary: Loup
Outlet: **Missouri**

The Platte is one of the major right-bank tributaries of the Missouri, the longest river in North America. Since rivers literally form a branching network or system, it is best not to treat individual rivers in isolation. The branches of the Platte—both longer than the mainstream river—are best considered as part of the Platte system. Adding the distance traversed by its longest headstream, the North Platte, which is 680 miles (1,090 kilometers) long, the Platte system stretches approximately 1,000 miles (1,600 kilometers). Extending from the inner parks of the Colorado Rockies eastward to the Missouri River, the Platte, along with its two substantial branches, drains a large segment of the central Great Plains. Each headstream features prominently in the history of the American West.

The South Platte, which is 430 miles (690 kilometers) long, rises high in the Rocky Mountains, where tiny streams gather in a wet meadow near Fairplay in central Colorado. Tumbling through narrow canyons and changing direction frequently, the river eventually spreads out across the broad plains of eastern Colorado and western Nebraska. At the confluence of Cherry Creek is the original site—actually two sites—of Denver, Colorado, close to where alluvial gold was washed from a streambed in 1859, leading to a second Gold Rush in 1859 ("Pikes Peak or Bust"). The flatlands of the lower river had long been a hunting ground for Plains Indians who followed the buffalo. European impact began before the gold rush and the subsequent wave of settlement. Thousands of immigrants passed just northward along the Oregon Trail in the 1840s and 1850s. In northeastern Colorado, the South Platte flows through fertile irrigated farm- and ranchland, passing by or near Greeley, Fort Morgan, and Sterling. The cities of Boulder and Fort Collins are situated along left-bank tributaries near the mountains (Boulder Creek and Cache la Poudre River, respectively). Today the South Platte is used primarily for irrigation, with municipal demands and hydroelectric power secondary.

The northern branch of the Platte also rises in the Colorado Rockies. Its source is in North Park, Colorado, only a few hundred miles north of the head of the river's southern branch. The North Platte flows northward into Wyoming, then veers eastward across the plains of central Nebraska, merging with the South Platte at the town of North Platte, Nebraska, to form the Platte proper.

The valley of the North Platte formed a key section of the Oregon Trail. Crossing much of Nebraska in the broad valley of the Platte, western immigrants followed the northern branch of the river upstream, then traveled along one of its tributaries, the Sweetwater, which took them through South Pass, the best broad route across the northern Rocky Mountains. South Pass is situated at the southern end of the Wind River Range in southwestern Wyoming. The pass is more of an open corridor than a narrow defile, and travelers were surprised to find that they were already in the pass once they began to ascend the Sweetwater. For twenty-five years, from 1841 to 1866, the North Platte valley was covered with wagon trains rumbling along either side of the river. Both the Pony Express and the telegraph followed the North Platte route. At the site of a fur-trading post on the North Platte was established Fort Laramie in 1849, to protect travelers on the Overland Trail. Farmers and ranchers early settled the fertile lowlands in the valley. Already by 1889 farmers were irrigating with North Platte water. In 1910 the Pathfinder Reservoir was completed southwest of Casper, Wyoming. Since the 1930s a series of dams have been constructed on the North Platte for hydroelectric power and irrigation. These include the

George W. Kingsley Dam, near Ogallala, Nebraska; the Kendrick Project, which impounds water behind several dams south of Casper; and the Grayrocks Dam near Wheatland, Wyoming, on the Laramie River, a North Platte tributary (the last-named dam forms a reservoir that cools a coal-fired power plant). The lakes created by these dams are recreational draws, and they are especially popular for motor- and sailboating. The damming of so much of the North Platte's water has led to restricted downstream flow in Nebraska, which has a legal claim to most of the river's discharge. Conservationists point to reduced habitat along a major flyway for migratory birds.

Below the junction of the North and South Platte, the river is broad and shallow, traversing a wide alluvial valley. The aptly named Platte (meaning "flat") was used by French fur traders who skimmed its shallow waters in animal-skinned bullboats. Indians had earlier named the stream Nibraskier, a term carrying much the same meaning. The Platte was disparaged by early visitors who described it as a "mile-wide, inch-deep" river. However, its valley towns, such as Gothenburg, Lexington, Grand Island, Columbus, and Fremont, testify to the prosperity of some of the first places settled in Nebraska. On the roughly 70-mile (112-kilometer) stretch of the river between Lexington and Grand Island in central Nebraska is a flyway for thousands of migratory ducks and geese, including such large species as sandhill and whooping cranes, which feed, rest, and breed in the myriad islands and necks of land formed by the braided river.

Automobile drivers today crossing Nebraska on Interstate 80 may grow weary of the levelness and monotony of the Platte River valley, just as travelers in the last century surely did, but it must be remembered that one is following a historic route—the Oregon Trail, the Pony Express, and the Union Pacific Railroad all came this way—and that the lower courses of rivers generally produce broad, flat plains, to which fact the Platte is no exception.

See also Missouri

Further Reading: Ambrose, Stephen E., *Nothing Like It in the World: The Men Who Built the Transcontinental Railroad, 1863–1869,* New York: Simon and Schuster, 2000; Michener, James, *Centennial,* New York: Random House, 1974.

PO

Source: Cottian Alps of Piedmont, in northwest Italy
Length: 405 miles (650 kilometers)
Tributaries: Dora Riparia, Dorea Baltea, Tanaro, Ticino, **Adda**, Oglio, Mincio
Outlet: Adriatic Sea

Known to Italians as Padiana or the Valle Padana, the Po forms a broad drainage basin between the Alps and the Apennines. Its plain represents the largest extent of good agricultural land in Italy. The river flows through or forms a boundary of the provinces of Piedmont, Lombardy, Emilia-Romagna, and Veneto. The valley contains many historic towns that have been the prize of conquerors since Roman times. Napoleon I described the Po, with some exaggeration, as "the most fertile plain in the world," and made its conquest the object of his first military campaign (1796).

The Po Plain is not uniformly flat or lacking in variety as is sometimes represented. Two well-marked zones can be distinguished. The upper plain consists of a series of glacial terraces and morainic arcs on the north side of the valley flanking the Alps. Low moraines act as natural dams to left-bank tributary streams, impounding water in several large lakes (for example, Garda and Como) as well as numerous smaller ones. The terraces consist mostly of coarse gravel, the source of the debris being the nearby mountains. Below a line of *fontanili,* or springs, that provide irrigation for the meadows of Piedmont and Lombardy and help to maintain the flow of streams in low-water periods is the lower plain of finer sediments washed down from the mountains, recent alluvium, the Emilian plain (to the south of the river), and the deltaic zone. A series of alluvial fans emanating from the mountains and its left-bank tributaries have pushed the Po toward the foot of the Apennines.

Originating as a mountain stream on the flank of Monte Viso, the river accomplishes most of its

Marshy mouth of the Po River (Jesse Walker)

vertical drop by the time it reaches Piacenza. The Po then meanders widely across a marshy plain. Heavily diked, the lower Po approaches its delta in an elevated channel above the surrounding plain, which is constantly threatened with submersion. The wide delta south of Venice ends along a distinctive coastline where fluvial debris has been built up by the counterclockwise drift of Adriatic currents in lateral spits (*lidi*), with backing lagoons and penetrating gaps (*porti*), features best known in historic Venice, though this city has for a site a number of offshore islands north of the present Po outlet. The Po is navigable for small craft for much of its length, but seasonal variation in flow impedes the use of the river by large ships (also, the marshy mouth does not have a good site for a port city). High water comes in two periods—a spate in May from melting Alpine shows, and a major flood in November from the abundant fall precipitation characteristic of the Mediterranean region.

The modern delta stands out as a widely protruding coastline in the northern Adriatic. Though somewhat irregular in shape, it is of the cuspate type. More important than its deviation from some presumed ideal form are the major shifts in the river's channel and its many outlets in historical times. The ancient delta, dating from the middle of the first millennium B.C., stretches all the way from the Venice Lagoon to Ravenna. Some 800 miles (1,300 kilometers) in length, this former coastline is suggested by an old dune ridge extending from Chioggia to Ravenna. During Roman times, the primary outlet was well to the south, near present-day Comachio, as well as inland from its present location. A series of cuspate mouths and a complex shifting delta were already evident in ancient times, as described by the Latin writers.

Deforestation of the Po basin by the Celts and Romans caused siltation and progradation of the coast, leading to a situation in which former coastal sites lay far to the interior, as in the case of the Roman coastal city of Ravenna, which is today well inland of its former position. In the middle of the twelfth century, a major event, the so-called "breach of Ficarolo," caused the Po's main outlets to shift northward, approaching the Venice Lagoon. In 1604–1607 Venetians feared that discharged sediments might close the mouth of the lagoon, so they diverted the river to the southeast through a canal, the Porto Viro, thereafter called the Taglio di Po. The Po mouth subsequently began to accrete more rapidly and began to assume its present form. Human intervention increased in the eighteenth and nineteenth centuries when the delta extended itself an average of about 70 hectares (173 acres) per year, probably as a result of increased sedimentation caused by extensive deforestation and intensified upland tillage. The embankment of distributaries led to an increase of sediment yield to the river mouths. Old branches of the Po, such as the Volano and Primaro, which had opened up, respectively, during Roman times and in the early Middle Ages, became disconnected from the active network of the river.

Land reclamation, especially conversion of brackish marshes to agricultural and aquacultural plots, tourist development of the old delta around Ravenna, and exploitation of maritime natural gas deposits have all contributed to coastal erosion or the drastic alteration of the physical and natural environment. The present Po delta reached its maximum extent sometime in the middle of the twentieth century, and since then a reduced sediment load has resulted from reforestation, the decrease of tillage on slopes, the construction of dams, and sand extraction from riverbeds, all of which developments have been marked since World War II.

The floodplain of the Po and its slightly uplifted terraces are excellent for growing maize, rice, mulberries, and sugar beets, as well as cultivating specialty crops found in polycultural fields scattered throughout the valley. Though little used for navigation, the Po, its tributaries, and fontanili are particularly well suited for irrigation and have been so used since ancient times. The landscape of the North Italian Plain has been so altered by canals and diking that it has been said that the valley "is not the mother but the daughter of its inhabitants."

A prosperous agriculture has contributed to the rise of commercial trade and, more recently, manufacturing. The Po valley today contains the major concentration of Italy's industrial cities. The river flows by or near Turin, Pavia, Piacenza, Cremona, and Ferrara. The second city of Italy, Milan, is not located on the river (few of the large modern cities are), but as the Latinate name suggests (from *Mediolanium,* or "middle of the plain"), it stands away from the river in a central portion of the valley. A northern tier of cities lies away from the river, either on elevated terraces or at the foot of the Alps along corridor routes guarding the treacherous Alps (for example, Mantua, Verona, Padua), while to the south the main line of cities is along the foothills of the Apennines, where the mountains reach the plains (Reggio nell'Emilia, Modena, and Bologna).

The Latin name *Padus* was applied to one of the most important agricultural districts incorporated into Roman rule. Systematically colonized in the second century B.C., cis-Alpine Gaul, as the region south of the Alps was known, included the early Roman towns of Piacenza and Cremona, which were uncharacteristically located on the banks of the flood-prone river. Both guarded strategic bridge-crossing sites where the long, straight Roman roads intersected the Po. The Roman towns of Turin (in the west) and Verona (in the east) stood astride key routes that gave access to the Alps. By the fourth century A.D., Milan had become almost as important as Rome itself, and the work of the church father St. Ambrose, who was this city's bishop from 374 to 379, helped make it the religious center of northern Italy and the capital of the western Roman Empire after Rome collapsed. Renaissance princes tapped the trade across the Alps by controlling key Alpine pass routes while simultaneously developing a prosperous agriculture on lands that had been intensively cultivated since ancient times. Lombard bankers taught financial science to the rest of Europe. Large-scale commercial cultivation of rice and maize began only in the nineteenth century, when the region received reforming impulses not only in agriculture but also in political affairs from the likes of

Conte di Cavour (1810–1861). This Piedmont statesman and premier of the leading Italian state, Sardinia, extended lateral canals that are still known by his name and at the same time engineered the unification of the Italian states in 1861.

See also Arno, Tiber
Further Reading: Cencini, Carlo, "Physical Processes and Human Activities in the Evolution of the Po Delta, Italy," *Journal of Coastal Research* 14 (1998): 774–793; Robertson, C. J., "Agricultural Regions of the North Italian Plain," *Geographical Review* 28 (1938): 573–596.

POTOMAC

Source: Junction of North and South Branch, southeast of Cumberland, Maryland
Length: 285 miles (459 kilometers)
Tributaries: Wills Creek, **Shenandoah**, Monocacy, Rock Creek, Anacostia
Outlet: Chesapeake Bay

The passage of the Patowmac [sic] through the Blue Ridge is, perhaps, one of the most stupendous scenes in nature. You stand on a very high point of land. On your right comes up the Shenandoah, having ranged along the foot of the mountain an hundred miles to seek a vent. On your left approaches the Patowmac [sic], in quest of a passage also. In the moment of their junction, they rush together against the mountain, and rend it asunder, and pass off to the sea.
Thomas Jefferson, *Notes on Virginia*

This great river of American history is one of the most impressive rivers flowing eastward from the Appalachians to the Atlantic. The upper course may be considered to include its two headstreams, North and South Branch, both originating in West Virginia. This portion of the valley, along with the Shenandoah, the Potomac's principal tributary, which joins it in midcourse, has a widely ramifying drainage network in the form of a trellis. This characteristic pattern is a response to the regular folds of the Ridge and Valley Province of the Appalachians, which deflects minor drainageways parallel to the corrugated lay of the land but allows major drainages like the Potomac to cut across resistant sandstone ridges to reach the sea. Even relatively large rivers like the Shenandoah are forced to flow parallel to the coast, forming a broad valley hemmed in by its elongated, flanking ridges, until, after its junction with the Potomac at Harpers Ferry, the swollen waters of the two rivers pass through the mountains and emerge onto the piedmont.

The North and South Branch meet southeast of Cumberland, Maryland, to form the Potomac proper. After passing through the Harpers Ferry water gap, the river flows southeast, forming the boundary between Virginia and the District of Columbia. The Fall Line is reached just above Washington at Great Falls, where the river literally falls over a series of ledges as it passes from the crystalline piedmont onto the lower sedimentary coastal plain. The Potomac estuary—the broad meeting ground between fresh and salt water—begins at this point and runs almost 100 miles (160 kilometers) to the Chesapeake Bay. Along the tidal reach of the river on the Virginia side below Washington are the Mt. Vernon estate of the nation's first president and the site of the U.S. Military Corps base, Quantico.

When Europeans first arrived in the early 1600s, several Algonquian tribes lived in palisaded villages along the banks of the Potomac and its tributaries. The Piscataway tribe or confederacy claimed territory northward from the river almost all the way to the present city of Baltimore and east to the Chesapeake Bay. The native populations depended heavily on the river for subsistence. Besides using seines and set lines, they trapped fish by constructing a V-shaped rock structure that forced the fish into a narrow chute from which they could be scooped, speared, or netted. The arrival of Maryland settlers in 1634 led to a brief period of amicable relations, followed by a long period of land encroachment, disease, and warfare.

By a curious but long-standing legal ruling, the state of Maryland claims rights to the Potomac extending across the river to the low-water mark on the Virginia shore. Maryland thus controls the use of the river's water. Fast-growing communities in northern Virginia have recently (2000) challenged a ruling agreed upon first in 1785 at a meeting of the two states' representatives at George Washington's Potomac residence. Ruled on by the

Confluence of the Potomac River (left) and the Shenandoah River (right) at Harpers Ferry, West Virginia (Laura Penn)

Supreme Court three times—in 1894, 1910, and 1958—the status quo has come into question by Virginia's request to build a 725-foot (221-meter) water intake pipe above Washington.

Away from the rivers and the plantations ("Every planter had a river at his door" was a common saying in Colonial times), inland areas were slow to settle. Many early migrants followed the Monocacy River south from Pennsylvania, and as a result the northern portions of Maryland were some of the first places occupied away from the tidewater. Marylanders sometimes confused the Monocacy, rising in Pennsylvania and flowing southeast across Maryland, with the Potomac, and mistakenly believed that Maryland's western boundary was much farther east than it was. The inevitable contention between Pennsylvania and Maryland proprietors and settlers over the border between the two colonies led to the running of the famous Mason and Dixon Line in 1767, which has been described as the most professional survey in British North America.

In the late eighteenth century a perceptive traveler, Uria Brown, observed an abundance of coal just west of Cumberland in western Maryland. He noted that although the well-watered land in tributary valleys was thin and worn out, the hills contained "black gold." When coal was ten cents per bushel in Cumberland but ten times that rate in the nation's capital, local inhabitants began shipping fuel and farm produce to Georgetown, just west of Washington, D.C., during periods of high water on the Potomac. In exchange, boats brought back such commodities as plaster, herring, shad, and manufactured items. By 1820 large shipments of coal from Allegany County, Maryland, were reaching the major Eastern seaports. The construction of an inland transportation system along the Potomac to facilitate this trade—the Chesapeake and Ohio Canal—was promoted in the nation's capital, a ten-square-mile area straddling the Potomac selected by George Washington with congressional mandate and approval. A canal would provide a cheap route to the interior, lessen the expense of fuel, and bring flour, wheat, oats, and whiskey into the city at reduced prices. After much debate the canal project was launched on July 4, 1828, the same day that Baltimore began its own western transport enterprise: the Baltimore & Ohio Railroad. The canal project was plagued by labor unrest, financial difficulties, and a cholera epidemic. By 1842 all hopes of reaching the Ohio had been abandoned, and not until 1850—after twenty-two years of construction—was the C & O Canal opened as far as Cumberland, the strategic site on the North Branch of the Potomac at the junction of a major northern tributary that provided access to the Ohio country. The road west of Cumberland had been pioneered by General Braddock in 1758 during the French and Indian War, when he built a wilderness road from Fort Cumberland to Fort Duquesne (Pittsburgh). Unfortunately for the canal, the B & O Railroad had reached Cumberland in 1842, and it quickly pushed on to Pittsburgh. The C & O Canal continued to operate until the early twentieth century, but the faster, more reliable railroad made the waterway an increasingly obsolete means of transportation. It eventually attained historical status first as a National Monument (1961) and then as a National Historical Park (1971). Stretching 184 miles from Georgetown to Cumberland, this scenic waterway, which once counted seventy-four lift locks, can today be visited at selected locations, where towpaths, locks, and small gatekeepers' houses are open to the public. The nearly level towpaths once trod by mules are used now by bikers, hikers, and joggers who choose to get away from the snarl of Washington's traffic to appreciate the scenery of the Potomac valley and relax amid the pleasures of a bygone day.

The rivers crossing the Piedmont are not particularly long, but the valleys are often narrow, steep-sided, and prone to flooding. Stripping of the western forests for coal mining has led to increased runoff and decreased infiltration to the soil. Flooding of the Potomac occurs about once every ten years, with a devastating flood about every thirty years. A major flood in 1924 caused a breaching of the C & O Canal that led to its ceasing operations. Most Potomac floods occur in spring after heavy rainfall, but the most destructive floods happen when snowmelt and frozen ground preventing infiltration act together, as in the largest recorded flood, in January 1936. It has been pointed out that flooding has some beneficial environmental effects: flood-adapted habitats such as floodplain forests and scourbars increase biotic diversity and provide habitat for wildlife.

The Potomac River watershed is part of a larger hydrologic unit: the Chesapeake Bay. Discharge from the river eventually reaches the bay. Organic matter, nutrients, toxic chemicals—all find their way into the river and bay. Excessive contamination and eutrophication can cause algal blooms, affect fish populations, and destroy the fringing submerged aquatic vegetation (SAV) that researchers regard as crucial in preserving the treasured bay ecosystem. There are some success stories here. The District of Columbia's sewage used to be released directly into the Potomac. Since 1938 the Blue Plains Wastewater Treatment Plant has processed the liquid wastes of the growing population of the metro area. Today the largest water treatment plant in the world, Blue Plains produces farm fertilizer and returns an effluent to the river that actually improves the quality of the Potomac.

See also James, Shenandoah
Further Reading: Gutheim, Frederick, *The Potomac*, New York: Rinehart and Company, 1949 (Rivers of America Series); Stanton, Richard L., *Potomac Journey*, Washington, DC: Smithsonian Institution Press, 1993.

PRIPET

Source: Northwest Ukraine
Length: 473 miles (761 kilometers)
Tributaries: Stokhid, Yaselda, Styr, Tsna, Goryn, Sluch', Ubort', Ptsich
Outlet: Kiev Reservoir of the **Dnieper**

The Pripet, or Pripyat', River rises northwest of Kovel in northwest Ukraine, near the border with

Poland and the source of the Bug (Western) River. It flows northeast, crossing into Belarus, then generally east through this former Soviet state, before emptying into an impoundment of the Dnieper above Kiev.

The Pripet Marshes comprise the most extensive swamp in Europe. They consist of a broad alluvial lowland 140 miles (225 kilometers) wide and 300 miles (485 kilometers) long, stretching between Brest (to the west), Mogilev (to the northeast), and Kiev (to the southeast). Sometimes called the Pinsk Marshes after the town at the river's head of navigation, the wetlands are located in the extreme west of the former Soviet Union, where Poland, Belarus, and Ukraine meet. The basin is largely coextensive with the Polesye (Russian: "forest land"). This lowland occupies a broad, flat trough between the Volyno-Podolsk upland to the south and the Belarussian Ridge to the north. Numerous streams drain into this depression from the surrounding highlands to join the Pripet. The front of the icesheet in the last glaciation lay just to the north, and glacial meltwaters deposited large quantities of sand along the ice margin, choking and complicating the drainage. The swamp consists mostly of marshes of reeds, bulrushes, carex, and grasses. Occasional patches of sphagnum peat bog interrupt the herbaceous vegetation. Trees occupy the drier flanks of the Pripet, with willows, alder, and aspen being fairly common. Dry sites are thickly forested, with pines on sandy soils, and oaks, hornbeams, and other deciduous trees on heavier soils.

The river is navigable for about two-thirds of its length and carries mostly lumber. To the west the Pripet is connected by canals with the Bug—and thereby forms part of the Vistula-Dnieper system—and to the north via the Oginsky Canal with the Neman River.

Across the marshes and forests of the Pripet, the maze of waterways—rivers, lakes, canals, marshes—form a dense network that has traditionally discouraged both concentrated settlement and military incursion. This low-point barrier has become a cultural and political borderland between Poles oriented westward to the Vistula and Russians directed more toward the Dnieper; between Belarussians to the north and Ukrainians to the south. Military commanders generally avoid barriers—whether high or low—but sometimes are attracted to them for reasons of surprise or for other tactical considerations. Just as the hilly Ardennes on the border between Belgium and France was the scene of several battles during the two world wars, so the Pripet Marshes were the site of a battle in World War I, though the rapid-deploying Germans bypassed them in 1941. The largest nuclear disaster in history occurred in 1986 at Chernobyl, at the mouth of the Pripet on the Kiev Reservoir, 50 miles (81 kilometers) north of the capital of Ukraine. This disastrous accident—a meltdown—and the bungling of the follow-up, not least in the way the story was communicated abroad, must be considered a contributory factor to the collapse of the Soviet Union a few years later.

See also Dnieper

PRIPYAT'

See Pripet

R

RAVI

Source: Himalayan Mountains, in Jammu and Kashmir state, northern India
Length: 475 miles (764 kilometers)
Tributaries: Ujh, Degh
Outlet: **Chenab**

The historic Punjab (Persian: "five rivers") of the northwestern portion of the subcontinent of India comprises a broad alluvial plain of coalescing river valleys tributary to the Indus (see Figure 1 on p. 24). In addition to the Indus, the two main rivers are the Chenab to the northwest and the Sutlej to the southeast, with the Jhelum and Ravi tributaries of the Chenab. Below the junction of the Chenab and the Sutlej, the river is sometimes called the Panjnad ("five rivers").

Divided since the Partition of 1947 between Muslim Pakistan and Hindu (and Sikh) India, the Punjab is a fertile agricultural plain and the chief producer of wheat on the subcontinent. Although migration, amalgamation, and the passage of time have reduced some of the problems of this borderland, and there is no active fighting here today (2001) as there has been in nearby Kashmir, religious, ethnic, and historical animosities lie just beneath the surface of the region's parched soils. The partition line, an international border, follows part of the course of the Ravi and the Sutlej, allotting Lahore, Rawalpindi, and Multan to Pakistan and the remainder of the region to India.

The Punjab was formerly a province of British India, with Lahore as its capital (it summer capital was Simla). Alexander the Great reached and ruled the lands along the middle Indus. It became a cultural center for the late flowering Muslim power of the Mogul Empire in the sixteenth and seventeenth centuries, whose stunning architectural monuments are still very much in evidence at Lahore (for example, the Pearl Mosque and Shalamar Gardens). Annexed by the Sikhs under Ranjit Singh in 1767, the city, which stands near the left bank of the Ravi River, was conquered by British troops in 1846 and placed under British sovereignty in 1849. Lahore today is an important trade, communications, and manufacturing center.

In the early twentieth century the archaeological site of Harappa was discovered in the Pakistani Punjab on an old bed of the Ravi River. Along with the prehistoric city of Mohenjo-Dara located farther south, these finds provided evidence of an ancient civilization of brick cities, monumental buildings, and curious seals inscribed with a language that has yet to be deciphered. Even though there isn't much evidence, it's fun to speculate about a possible link between the lost civilizations of the Indus valley and the earliest Mesopotamian cities, such as Sumer.

Lahore is located in the Bari Doab, the alluvial tract of land between the Beas and the Ravi Rivers. In addition to wheat, the region produces cotton, oilseed, gram, and sugar cane. An extensive system of irrigation canals and feeder lines crisscrosses the large agricultural district. Overflow irrigation dating from time immemorial was replaced by the British with a well-engineered hydraulic distribution system that did for water transport and use in this dry and somewhat isolated province what the Great Northwest Railroad did for movement of people and goods on the subcontinent.

See also Beas, Chenab, Jhelum, Sutlej
Further Reading: Alter, Stephen, *Amritsar to Lahore: A Journey across the India-Pakistan Border,* Philadelphia: University of Pennsylvania Press, 2000.

RED (CHINA)

Source: Yünnan Province, in southern China
Length: 730 miles (1,175 kilometers)
Tributaries: Clear (Song Lo), Black (Song Da)
Outlet: Gulf of Tonkin

The Red River of southeast Asia is the key region of northern Vietnam, as the Mekong is of southern Vietnam, though the former river doesn't flow through as many countries in reaching its densely populated delta and the sea. Known as the Yuan in China where it rises, the Red takes the name Song Hong in Vietnam (formerly Song Coi). The French, who annexed Tonkin (northern Vietnam) as a protectorate in 1883, called this great artery of the north Fleuve Rouge, or Red River. The name derives from the large amount of iron-rich silt carried by the river. Flowing southeast across mountainous Yünnan Province and into northern Vietnam, the river runs through deep, narrow gorges before reaching the coastal plain, where it receives its major tributaries northwest of Hanoi. Downstream the river enters a giant delta that empties into the sea through many mouths.

As elsewhere in southeast Asia, there is a marked contrast between the isolated and sparsely populated mountains and the densely populated alluvial valley and delta (compare the Mekong, Chao Phraya, and Irrawaddy). The cultural and historical heartland of northern Vietnam—and its breadbasket—lies in the fertile delta of the Red, near whose apex stands the ancient capital of Hanoi. The delta contains fifteen million people (2000) and has one of the highest population densities in the world. It began to form 4,000 years ago when silt started to accumulate at the mouths of the Red and Thai Binh Rivers. It was here, at the junction of these two rivers, that the Viet people—as the French colonial name Indochina suggests, a mix of Chinese and indigenous peoples—began to settle. The delta embraces an area approximately 75 miles (121 kilometers) long, with the identical dimension in width. A variety of subtropical crops are grown in this economic center of northern Vietnam, but rice is the mainstay of the agricultural economy and the staple of the diet. The chief port, Hai Phong, is on the delta's northern branch.

The delta is a mostly artificial landscape today, with its patchwork of rice paddies intersected by dikes and canals. A dense forest once covered the region. In the eleventh century King Ly went elephant hunting near what is now Hanoi's West Lake. As late as the Tran Dynasty (1226–1400), black tigers still roamed the capital. Linguistic traces of former times survive in place-names containing the words *lam* and *rung* (meaning "forest"), as in Gia Lam district or Rung village. During periods of fallow in the annual rice-growing cycle, villagers have been free to pursue crafts ranging from the making of conical "non" hats to the production of traditional lacquerware (Bat Trang, a village near Hanoi, remains one of the best known of these ceramic-producing villages).

Rapid population growth in one of the fastest-growing economies in southeast Asia and intensification of agricultural production in response to free-market policies have led to increased environmental threats to the delta. Deforestation of the hills surrounding the delta has resulted in increased erosion, which in turn has caused increased sedimentation downstream. Levees dating from the eighteenth century prevent new materials (alluvium) from reaching portions of the delta that are sinking because of tectonic activity. The coastal areas, meanwhile, are aggrading—that is, growing outward—but in irregular, unpredictable, and unstable ways. The entire region is within the monsoon belt of south and southeast Asia, with heavy precipitation and flooding during the June–October wet season aggravated by the potential for Pacific typhoons. Government dikes, canals, pumps, headworks, and so on are badly in need of upgrading to avoid imminent disaster and to more efficiently distribute water to meet the growing needs of the population.

Further Reading: Lê, Phan Huy, Nguy-ên Quang Ngoc, Nguy-ên Dinh Lê, *The Country Life in the Red River Delta,* Hanoi: The Gioi Publishers, 1997.

RED (OF THE NORTH)

Source: Confluence of Otter Tail and Bois de Sioux, in southeast North Dakota
Length: 533 miles (858 kilometers)
Tributaries: Sheyenne, Red Lake, Goose, Pembina, **Assiniboine**
Outlet: Lake Winnipeg, Manitoba

The northern of the two Red Rivers of North America winds through the midsection of the flat-as-a-pancake basin forming the boundary between North Dakota and Minnesota continued northward into Canada. The Red River valley occupies an extensive former lakebed. At its greatest extent during the last ice advance, Lake Agassiz covered much of south-central Canada as well as the U.S. portion of the Red River valley. The lake formed during a warming period at the end of the Pleistocene epoch, when snowmelt was blocked in its northern path by ice and consequently accumulated as an ice-marginal lake. As the glacier receded, a broad river began to drain the central part of the former lakebed. Through time the river decreased in size, leaving behind siltlike layers of sediments on top of the original glacial till. The result was a fertile agricultural soil, though one prone to ponding and stickiness. Farmers call the district's soil "Red River Gumbo," referring to the claylike consistency of the soil's texture. Eventually the Red River became quite small in its southern portion, and its northern course was subject to wide meandering and low flow.

One of the two headstreams, the Bois de Sioux, begins in Lake Traverse on the Minnesota–South Dakota border. After joining with the Otter Tail at Breckenridge, Minnesota, and Wahpeton, North Dakota, the north-flowing river passes Fargo and Grand Forks, North Dakota. It crosses the Canada-U.S. border between Pembina, North Dakota, and Emerson, Manitoba, increasing in size as it receives the influx of the left-bank tributary, the Pembina River. The primary tributary, however, is the Assiniboine, which joins the Red from the west at Winnipeg, the large cosmopolitan city of Canada's prairie provinces and the capital of Manitoba. Since the time of the fur trade the confluence site known as the Forks has been the key location along the river. Winding through downtown Winnipeg, the river flows northward via the Nelson River into Hudson Bay.

French voyageurs and métis half-breeds navigated the Red River and its tributaries with Indian-style craft—large birchbark canoes and smaller timber dugouts. By the mid-eighteenth century French and English fur traders had established forts at key locales: the junction of the Red and Assiniboine at present-day Winnipeg and the junction of the Red and Pembina at the present international frontier. The first permanent white settlement dates from 1811–1812, when a group of Scottish immigrants known as Selkirkers, so called because they were under the sponsorship of Lord Selkirk, arrived intent on agricultural colonization. It was not until 1820 when a group of Selkirkers were brought by Mackinaw boat along with a cargo of seed from southeastern Wisconsin up the Mississippi, Minnesota, and Red Rivers that the first non-Indian conveyance appeared on the river. The district had a highly diverse population composition at the time, with Scottish traders, Assiniboine buffalo hunters, métis *coureurs de bois,* and a thin band of agricultural settlers aligned on long lots extending back from the river and its tributaries. In 1822 the Hudson's Bay Company, under whose administration the Canadian portion of the valley fell, built a trading post, Fort Garry, at the site of present Winnipeg. The bustling community that grew up at the Forks—plus flood problems—caused the orderly company officials to move the post downriver to lower Fort Garry (now a historical site), but that ploy didn't work, as the confluence site was destined to become a major city. The growth of Winnipeg fostered a demand for farm produce, which encouraged further settlement of a linear kind along the level and treeless river valley. Game was abundant in the prairies, along the strip of timber lining the river, and in the mixed forest nearby, so farmers could supplement their diet as well as vary their daily activities by hunting. Even today raccoons, foxes, beavers, and even occasionally a bear or moose is sighted within Winnipeg's city limits.

From 1830 to about 1870 little use was made of the Red River for navigation. Then a commercial link was forged between a burgeoning St. Paul, Minnesota, and the Red River valley. The means of transportation joining these two communities evolved rapidly. Creaking oxcarts soon gave way to paddle-wheel steamboats, though the latter were hampered in navigation by the shifting, shallow channel of the Red (the perennial trouble spot was midway between Fargo and Grand Forks, at Goose Rapids). Eventually the dynamic entrepreneur James J. Hill initiated the construction of the St. Paul and Pacific Railroad (Hill had earlier monopolized steam service on the river). Fargo-Moorhead, Grand Forks, and Winnipeg, whose heyday was in the 1870s, grew rapidly during this period. Huge bonanza wheat farms were carved from prairie sod, and they set the pattern for agribusiness-style farming in the nearly contemporaneous agricultural development of California's Central Valley.

The Red River valley has long been perceived as flood-prone. Its low banks, a glacial legacy, are easily overtopped, and the sticky soils of its broad floodplain—really a lakebed—are rapidly saturated. Heavy snowmelt combines with frozen ground in the spring to produce the severest floods. When the northern course of the river is still frozen—a seasonal condition mimicking what occurred year-round during the ice age—a backing up of the river occurs, and the worst floods are produced. A devastating flood on the lower river in 1950 drove 100,000 people from their homes, inundated 15,000 farm buildings and businesses, and caused Winnipeg to build a wide, shallow floodway around the city to divert future flood waters. The disastrous flood of 1993 spared Winnipeg but reaped havoc on cities upriver.

It has been pointed out that the 1993 flood was small in comparison with historical flooding (in the 1820s Selkirker settlers fled to Birds Hill, northeast of Winnipeg, to escape flooding). The conversion of grasslands and natural creeks into fields and drainage channels aggravates high-water problems. This creates a pulse effect, with heavy rains in the spring going directly into the river. The proposed Assiniboine Diversion, meant to draw water from the Red's major tributary for municipal, industrial, and agricultural use, may exacerbate water quality problems. The concentration of effluent in a reduced volume increases the effects of pollution. Until about 1970 the Red River's water quality was of little concern to Manitobans. They used the riverbank and the river itself as a dumping ground. Although sewage is now treated (it wasn't formerly) before its release into the river, heavy rainfall often overloads the city's sewage system, and the result is that raw sewage from toilets and industrial sources goes directly into the Red.

The multimillion-dollar redevelopment of the Forks—today a tourist, retail, office space, and park complex—has led to renewed interest and concern for preserving the river's water quality and protecting the riverfront. The city has tried to turn its face toward the river, reversing a long trend in U.S. and Canadian cities of sealing off the river from the downtown, making it almost impossible for pedestrians to reach the waterway that once gave birth to the city. With the success of the Forks project, canoes are once again seen navigating the Red in downtown Winnipeg, but today's vessels are less likely to be made of birchbark than of synthetic materials such as kevlar.

Further Reading: MacDonald, Jake, "The Red River Valley: Manitoba's Storied Waterway Is Rich in History and Biodiversity," *Canadian Geographic* 114, no. 1 (January–February 1994): 42–52.

RED (OF THE SOUTH)

Source: Confluence of Prairie Dog Town Fork and North Fork, in northwest Texas
Length: 1,290 miles (2,076 kilometers)
Tributaries: Wichita, Washita, Kiamichi, Black
Outlet: **Atchafalaya**

The upper and lower courses of the storied Red River of Texas, Oklahoma, and Louisiana are a study in contrast. At its source in the Panhandle of Texas, small but highly erosive streams carve out picturesque canyons south of Amarillo. Exiting the canyonlands and the Panhandle, the river's major headstream, the Prairie Dog Town Fork, flows southeasterly along the Texas-Oklahoma border, merging with the North Fork north of Vernon, Texas. The Red River proper begins at this confluence, curiously near the 100-degree longitude mark that has been proposed as the western limit of a humid climate. The broad, shallow, silt-laden river takes on the characteristics of a humid regime as it flows southeast, first along the Texas-Oklahoma border, then between Texas and Arkansas. At least from Lake Texoma just north of Denison, Texas, one of the largest impoundments of water in the United States, the river no longer flows through arid country (as the lake's name implies, it occupies the Texas-Oklahoma boundary). The river crosses briefly into southwest Arkansas, leaving the state at Fulton, then entering Louisiana. Here the Red adopts the characteristics of a sluggish Southern stream. Swamps, bayous, oxbows, and islands are scattered across its broad floodplain. Although the river is joined to the Mississippi in central Louisiana by a short, regulated linking waterway—Old River—the bulk of the flow enters the Atchafalaya, a 170-mile-long (270-kilometer-long) distributary of the Mississippi that empties southward into the Gulf of Mexico.

The Red River's course is no less differentiated in matters of culture, history, settlement, and economy. The rough-and-tumble history of the Red River valley of Texas and Oklahoma shares its story with that of the Wild West. It is a bleak and beautiful country, as the author of this book can attest from having crossed the region many times en route from humid Louisiana and east Texas across the Texas Panhandle and Raton Pass into southern Colorado. The Red River was a natural highway into the southern Great Plains in Texas and Oklahoma. Early explorers looking for the river's source exaggerated its length. In 1806 Lieutenant Zebulon Pike headed westward into Spanish territory in search of the Red's headwaters and mistook the upper course of the Rio Grande for the Red. Another early explorer, Stephen H. Long of the Topographical Engineers, believed he was floating down the Red only to discover it was the Canadian. Not until 1852 did Colonel Randolph B. Marcy discover that the Red has two main branches that come together near the 100th meridian. And only in 1896 did the U.S. Supreme Court accept the Prairie Dog Town Fork as the main stream, since it carries more water than the North Fork; the court switched the Texas-Oklahoma boundary from the latter to the former. Atlas maps today routinely show the source of the Red's feeders with dashed lines, suggesting intermittent and changing courses.

The colorful history of the region—with its explorers, Indian wars, and Civil War battles—results in the term "Red River country" taking on a diffuse quality. To enhance regional importance, geographical accuracy is sometimes sacrificed. The author came across an otherwise authoritative reference work that listed the Canadian, Grand, and Cimarron Rivers as tributaries of the Red, when they actually flow into the Arkansas. The outlet of the Red is commonly reported to be the Mississippi River, when in fact the Mississippi has no large natural tributaries in the state of Louisiana.

The river's course was initially a no-man's-land between French Louisiana and Spanish Texas. The French established their first permanent settlement in present-day Louisiana not along the bayous in the southern part of the state or at New Orleans, but in north Louisiana at Natchitoches (1714), on a short, right-bank tributary of the Red, at the meeting of the outer edge of the floodplain and the wooded ridge of the Nacogdoches Wold.

Improvement of navigation along the lower Red was the order of the day in the mid-nineteenth century. Not only was the river sluggish, but trees and brush accumulated in the river above Campti—roughly halfway between Alexandria and Shreveport—forming what was then known as the Great Raft. Steamboatman and entrepreneur Henry Shreve, who has been credited with designing the first true steamboat, used a battering-ram vessel of his own design to do battle with the Raft. Shreve's name was adopted by the river town of Shreveport in northwest Louisiana, which benefited from Shreve's improvements in river navigability just as it still does from the Army Corps's work to maintain a dredged channel at least as far as the city. The immediate effect of Shreve's efforts was not only to produce a cotton plantation economy along the lower Red but also to make the valley the scene of several Civil War engagements. Union and Confederate forces came to something of a draw here. After the war attention shifted upriver to Indian conflicts and cattle trails crossing the river. In what might be described as the last stand of the Indians on the southern plains, the Red River Indian War (1874–1875) pitted tribes of Comanches, Cheyenne, and Arapahos against the U.S. Army. The Indians were defeated, the buffalo banished, and the land was made ready for white settlers and the railroad. During the brief interlude of the cattlemen's open range, several famous trails crossed the Red in north Texas, including the Chisholm Trail, which crossed north of Henrietta, Texas, and the Western Trail, which crossed the river at Doan's Store, north of Vernon, Texas.

No part of the Red River valley is especially robust economically at the present time. Alexandria, in central Louisiana, has not benefited as much as the two ends of the state—the Baton Rouge–New Orleans southeastern corner and the Shreveport–Bossier City metro area in the northwest. The Texas-Oklahoma stretch has fallen far behind the staggering overgrowth of the Dallas–Ft. Worth metroplex. Recreational outlets for a weary Dallas population can be found nearer at hand than Lake Texoma. Depressed oil, agricultural, and property prices in the 1980s led to a disproportionate number of banks closing their doors in the Red River region of northeast Texas. "Little Dixie," the Oklahoma portion of the valley just across the river, which is best known for its predilection for football, country music, and fundamentalist religion, has suffered even more. Although hunting has provided some economic opportunities—more than recreational boating, anyway—hopes for Lake Texoma have snagged on the water's salinity, a problem for future irrigation plans. An ambitious scheme, the Red River Chloride Control Project, aims to desalinate ten salt springs that discharge into the upper river in Texas and Oklahoma. The plan is to use the purer water for irrigation and for industrial or municipal use. Water projects are no longer approved as a matter of course, however, and judging by the difficulty of acquiring congressional approval for the final steps in improving the navigability of the lower Red River, Texas and Oklahoma have a much harder sell than in the past, when those states had representatives like Sam Rayburn (Texas) and Carl Albert (Oklahoma) holding the key Speaker of the House positions.

See also Atchafalaya

Further Reading: "America's Rivers: Is Big Red to Work for Its Living?" *Economist* 313, no. 7630 (November 25, 1989): 29–30.

RHINE

Source: Swiss Alps
Length: c. 820 miles (1,320 kilometers)
Tributaries: **Aare**, Ill, Neckar, Main, **Moselle**, **Ruhr**, Lippe
Outlet: North Sea

The principal waterway of a highly industrialized section of Europe passes through or adjoins Switzerland, Liechtenstein, Austria, France, Germany, and the Netherlands. Linking the diverse peoples and landscapes of *Mitteleurope,* the river crosses the disparate terrain of the Central Uplands. Other major rivers of western Europe, including the Seine, Rhône, Saône, Ems, and Elbe, are linked to it by canals. Valued since Roman times for its strategic location, the river has been a source of friction and international rivalry as well as an avenue of trade and migration.

The celebrated Rhine (German: Rhein) begins its course as a tumultuous mountain stream draining snowfields and glaciers in eastern Switzerland. Its two headstreams, the Vorderrhein and the Hinterrhein, unite to form the Rhine proper at the town of Reichenau. The word *rein,* meaning "pure"

Thyssen steel works at Mülheim, Germany, near the junction of the Rhine and Ruhr Rivers. The Rhine is visible in the background (1955). (Erich Lessing)

or "clear," doesn't fit the clouded, turbulent torrents of the headstreams as they sweep down from the Swiss Alps, though the mountainous section of the river is comparatively free of manmade pollution. Flowing northward past the orchards and meadowlands of Liechtenstein and Austria, the river widens into Lake Constance on the border between Switzerland and Germany, which moderates its pace somewhat. Vast accumulations of silt and sediment settle out in the lake, so that when the river emerges at the opposite end it truly is *rein*—pure and clean. Reverting to its Alpine character, the river plunges over the picturesque Rheinfall near Schaffhausen, Switzerland. Only 75 feet (23 meters) high—small by comparison with the great waterfalls of the world—the falls is quite broad and is famous for its multiple, thundering cascades. After receiving several Alpine tributaries, most notably the Aare, the Rhine reaches Basel, Switzerland, the traditional head of navigation, after having traveled some 230 miles (370 kilometers) and descended nearly 7,000 feet (2,100 meters) from its mountain source.

At Basel the river turns northward and enters the Rhine Graben, a wide, flat-floored geological depression (technically, a parallel fault) that lies between the Vosges Mountains in eastern France and the Black Forest (Schwarzwald) of southwestern Germany. Strasbourg, France, is the focal point for merging water routes from the Paris Basin that intersect the Graben. Navigation in this section is by lateral canal through France as far as Strasbourg, then farther downstream along the river whose channel has been improved for the large barge traffic that plies the waterway. Some of this section of the river serves as the international boundary between France and Germany. Beyond the border with France, two major tributaries, the Neckar and the Main, enter from the east, stabilizing the river's flow: the Alpine sources receive maximum meltwater and flood stage in early summer, while the lower basin tributaries tend to have their greatest flow in winter. The city of Worms on the west bank not only played a key role in the story of Martin Luther's rebellion against the Roman Catholic Church but in addition is the setting for the epic poem, the *Nibelungenlied*, about treachery and treasure buried in the Rhine that inspired Richard Wagner's famous *Ring* cycle of musical dramas.

The most romantic stretch of the river, however, is the narrow, winding gorge of the middle river between Bingen and Bonn. Slicing through resistant slate formations, the Rhine for some 90 miles (145 kilometers) passes along terraced hill slopes graced with flourishing vineyards beneath castellated cliffs where medieval warlords once levied tolls on river traffic passing beneath. It was not until 1868 that the Rhine was declared a free waterway by the Mannheim Convention. The "heroic Rhine" of the gorges is perhaps best known in literature for the rock face of the Lorelei, which inspired the famous lyric *Die Lorelei* by the German poet Heinrich Heine; it tells the tale of a beautiful Siren sitting atop the rock, singing a seductive song to lure sailors to their death in the treacherous currents swirling below. Farther downstream are the Siebengebirge, or "Seven Mountains," said to be dropped from the shovels of giants as they excavated the streambed. On one of these, the Drachenfels, or "Dragon's Rock," Wagner's hero Siegfried slew his mythical dragon.

Below Bonn the river widens and begins to cross the coastal plain. Passing Cologne in an embayed section of the plain, it flows by Düsseldorf and the Ruhr conurbation, focused on coal mining and steel manufacturing. The river is not so *rein* as it crosses the densely populated North Rhine–Westphalia state, and the channel is heavily polluted from industrial wastes.

The changing river takes on its last alteration when it enters the Netherlands and becomes a delta. Branching into two major channels, the Lek and the Waal, the delta comprises a lowland that has been extensively diked and ditched since medieval times. Merging with the Maas (Meuse), draining Belgium and northeastern France, the delta with its many old channels and artificial canals exemplifies the conversion of a natural landscape into a cultural landscape. Canals connect river-mouth distributaries to nearby cities. The Rhine's principal seaport is Rotterdam, which, along with nearby Europort, ranks among the world's major deep-water seaports.

The Rhine-Meuse delta, of Holocene age, comprises three physical environments: fluvial areas characterized by broad meandering rivers and relatively small flood basins; back-barrier coastal plain, subject more to fluvial influences or tidal influences, depending on the location; and barrier beach and coastal dune area. Sea level changes associated with deglaciation since the Pleistocene era have been fundamental factors in the complex, shifting pattern of channels and lowland forms.

Humans have been present in the Rhine-Meuse delta for at least 200,000 years and have significantly altered the environment. In Neolithic times (6400 to 3650 B.P.), forests were first cleared and cultivation on levees and on higher Pleistocene sand began. The Old Rhine was the northern border of the Roman Empire (c. 50 B.C.– A.D. 400). The Romans founded many villages in the delta and dug canals to locally influence the course of rivers. Human influence increased greatly in the Middle Ages, especially after about 1000. The damming of the Old Rhine in 1122 reduced the number of Rhine branches to three: the lower Rhine-Lek, the Waal, and the IJssel, which today carry, respectively, 2/9, 6/9, and 1/9 of the river's discharge. As the river mouth of the Old Rhine and the ebb-tide delta were eroded, sand became available to transport to the coast, stimulating the formation of the so-called Younger Dunes up to 131 feet (40 meters) high in western Netherlands. The embanking of the rivers opened the possibility of draining the peat bogs in the western part of the deltaic plain, which has led to the creation of the famous Dutch agricultural polderlands. Elsewhere in the delta, in the southwest, a new "man-made" landscape was formed by closing some estuaries, shortening the coastline, and allowing only the Westerschelde, the Scheldt outlet and entrance to the port of Antwerp, to remain open. The closing of the Haringvliet tidal inlet forced discharge to flow through the Rotterdam Waterway to ensure sufficient water depth for shipping and additionally to counteract saltwater intrusion. The closing off of outlets had the unintended consequence of degrading ebb-tide deltas of former estuaries by wave action, producing a new pattern of sandy ridges parallel to the coast. Space is so precious in the Netherlands that virtually every inch of the embanked floodplain is in demand for agriculture, industrial activity, recreation, and, today, nature conservancy.

Industrial pollution is almost inevitable with the high level of economic development and heavy barge traffic along the Rhine. After years of improvement in water quality since the 1960s, however, a series of incidents in the 1980s showed how much more needed to be done. A chemical spill in 1986—the so-called Sandoz accident—resulted from putting out a fire at a warehouse in Basel, releasing massive amounts of pesticide and mercury into the river. Nearly 30 tons of toxic wastes entered the river, killing 500,000 fish and causing the closing of water systems in Germany, France, and the Netherlands. In 1988 high levels of polychlorinated biphenyls (PCBs) were found in the necrotic tissue of the last river otter in the Netherlands. In that same year, 70 percent of the seals in the Wadden Sea died of a virus as a result of the weakening of immune systems caused by pollution.

The principal causes of environmental degradation of Europe's most stressed river are channel alterations for flood control and shipping—a human impact about a century in duration—and the discharge of pollution from agricultural, industrial, and municipal sources (it is estimated that 10 percent of the world's chemical industry is concentrated in the Rhine basin). Seven of forty-seven indigenous fish species cannot be found anymore. Dredging of bottom sediments often stirs up heavy metals and other pollutants, so navigation policies tend to conflict with other priorities such as ecological protection and habitat restoration.

Since the Rhine is shared by six countries, the problem of environmental cleanup is compounded by the need for international cooperation. Old mandates for cooperation in matters of navigation need to be supplemented by agreements about environmental protection, which is nominally the purpose of the International Commission for the Protection of the Rhine (ICPR) and more recently the Rhine Action Plan. National directives often pit one ministry against another, or one country against another. It is in the obvious interest of the European Union representative who sits as a separate participant on the ICPR to foster national cooperation in the cleanup of the major river of western Europe.

See also Moselle, Ruhr

Further Reading: Berendsen, H. J. A., "Birds-Eye View of the Rhine-Meuse Delta," *Journal of Coastal Research* 14 (1998): 740–752; Carbiener, R., and M. Tremoliere, "The Rhine Rift Valley Groundwater-River Interactions: Evolution of Their Susceptibility to Pollution," *Regulated Rivers: Research & Management* 5 (1990): 375–389; Fredrich, G., and V. Muller, "Rhine," pp. 265–315 in B. A. Witton, ed., *Ecology of European Rivers,* Oxford: Blackwell, 1984; Gray, Malcolm, "Death in Europe's Grandest River," *Maclean's,* November 24, 1986, pp. 48–49.

RHÔNE

Source: Rhône Glacier in Swiss Alps
Length: 505 miles (813 kilometers)
Tributaries: Arve, Ain, **Saône**, Isère, Drôme, Ardèche, Durance, Gard
Outlet: Gulf of Lions

Along with its principal tributary, the Saône, the Rhône forms an elongated north-south corridor in southeastern France running between the Massif Central to the west and the Alpine mountains to the east. Despite the inadequacy of the Rhône for navigation, with its numerous gorges, the valley has carried the major transport routes connecting the western Mediterranean littoral of southern France to the Paris Basin since Roman times.

It rises as glacial meltwaters high in the Rhône Glacier at an elevation of 5,740 feet (1,750 meters).

Issuing from a lofty ice cavern just below the Furka Pass in upper Valais, Switzerland, the river flows west through a gradually widening, flat-bottomed valley separating the Bernese Alps to the north from the Pennine or Valais Alps to the south. After making several turns and passing some small towns, the river enters Lake Geneva at its eastern tip near Montreux. Leaving the western end of the lake at Geneva, the river follows a twisting course across the Jura Mountains of eastern France. The long, parallel folds of the Jura deflect the river southward; it breaks through in places at narrow gorges, or *cluses*.

At Lyons the river turns to the south and flows to the Gulf of Lions in the Mediterranean Sea. The third-largest city of France, Lyons (ancient Lugdunum), was built by the Romans on a prominent hilltop on the right bank of the Saône, just above its confluence with the Rhône. The city thus occupied a strategic position approximately halfway along the Rhône-Saône passageway. It has become a vital road and rail center and, despite navigation problems of the lower Rhône, a major river port. After much destruction during the French Revolution in reprisal for its support of the royal cause, the city expanded in the nineteenth century to the hilly interfluve of La Croix-Rousse and then east of the Rhône.

Below Lyons the middle river consists of an alternation between narrow gorges and open basins. The latter often constitute distinctive *pays*, with towns such as Vienne, Valence, and

Vincent Van Gogh's "Starry Night on the Rhône" painted at Arles, France, in September 1888. The more famous, visionary "Starry Night" was composed at Saint-Rémy nine months later. (Réunion des Musées Nationaux/Art Resource, NY)

Montélimar serving the fertile agricultural lowlands opened up by tributaries joining the main stream. Orchards, vineyards, and mulberry groves cover the natural terraces of the Rhône valley here. As one passes southward, with the red-tiled villages surrounded by an opulent rural landscape with orchards and vineyards—green in winter, blossoming magnificently in spring, dry and dusty in summer—it dawns on one that a different, Mediterranean region has been reached: Provence. Most of the cities are located away from the flood-prone valley bottom on terraces or rounded knolls in the valley, or at strategic crossing-points where outcrops of hard rock narrow the valley.

The lower Rhône presents much the same prospect as it passes between Donzère and the apex of the delta at Arles. The plains of Pierrelatte, Orange, and Avignon are crossed, each separated by a narrow defile. Avignon, where the popes sojourned in the Middle Ages, and the scene of a famous bridge across the Rhône ("Sur le Pont d'Avignon"), has for its original site (cathedral and papal palace) a limestone outcrop that overlooks the divided channels of the Rhône enclosing the Ile de Barthelasse.

The Rhône reaches the sea in a two-armed delta, with the major channel lying to the east (Grand Rhône) and the smaller branch to the west (Petit Rhône). Between them lie the wetlands of the Camargue—part lagoon, part grassland—representing the current delta. A broader deltaic region, however, encompasses about twice as large an area, including lands beyond the approximately 25-mile-wide (40-kilometer-wide) present delta. The entire region has been so modified by human activity for so long that it is difficult to discern where the natural channel has been at different historical periods in the midst of old and abandoned channels and so-called economic mouths—backwaters and lagoons, with little current, which have been dredged as routes linking the marshlands to the river and the sea.

The delta and its inhabitants were mentioned by the ancient writers Herodotus and Strabo. Crusades were launched from small ports at the seaward edge of the delta (the major port of Marseilles is located to the east, well away from the shifting channels of the flood-prone Rhône). The region boasts a plenitude of interesting geographical terms of a descriptive kind: *craus,* gravel terraces sometimes referred to as "dry-delta," even though they are the result of the lower channel of the Durance formerly taking a more southerly course; *etangs,* brackish lagoons, the largest of which is the interior Etang de Vaccarès; *marais,* fringing marshes; *graus,* shallow channels connecting the marsh to the sea (for example, that for the Grand Rhône is the Grau de Pégoulier, for the Petit Rhône the Grau d'Orgon; and *montilles,* sweeping sand spits backed by coastal dunes. Extensive engineering works and training walls along the Grand Rhône have caused an increasing amount of discharge and sediment to take the southeastern route, so that this part of the delta is gradually accreting.

Near the head of the delta, Arles is situated on the left bank of the Grand Rhône at its lowest bridging point. The Romans connected Arles to the sea by a canal, and it was the most prosperous ancient city after Rome during the early Roman Empire. The surrounding region was an important granary for the Roman world. The drier northern part of the Camargue is still a productive agricultural region yielding grain, olives, and wine. The countryside around Arles is perhaps best known today for the vivid, sun-drenched paintings produced by Vincent Van Gogh during the fifteen months that he spent here (February 1888–May 1889) at the peak of his creative powers.

The Rhône is the hardest-working waterway in France. With a flow exceeding that of any other French river, a series of hydroelectric dams have been installed along its course. Additionally, the Rhône provides cooling water for several nuclear power plants, a form of energy that fossil fuel–poor France is heavily dependent upon. Many improvements in the navigation of the Rhône have been carried out through the years. Below Lyons, standard-size barges carry bulk merchandise to and from Mediterranean ports. Above Lyons the Saône is navigable as far as Chalon-sur-Saône, where the

Rhône-Rhine Canal follows the Doubs River through the low Belfort Gap to Basel, Switzerland. Other canals link the Rhône to the port of Marseilles (through Arles) and to the Canal du Midi (via the port of Sète). The irregular flow of the Rhône, especially that issuing from right-bank tributaries draining the Massif Central, has led to the creation of a multiple-use planning agency, the Compagnie Nationale du Rhône (est. 1934), to harness the river for electrical power as well as to prevent flooding and to provide irrigation along the lower course of the river.

See also Saône

Further Reading: "In a Brilliant Light: Van Gogh in Arles," Metropolitan Museum of Art video, 1984; Russell, Richard Joel, "Geomorphology of the Rhône Delta," *Annals of the Association of American Geographers* 32 (1942): 149–254.

RHUMEL

Source: Northern Algeria
Length: 145 miles (233 kilometers)
Tributaries: None
Outlet: Mediterranean Sea

The arid portions of the earth's surface are naturally underrepresented in a treatment of rivers. Nevertheless, watercourses can play a major role in sculpting desert landscapes and often significantly influence the cultural and historical milieu of such areas. That is the case with the Rhumel gorge and the natural setting of the Algerian city of Constantine.

The intermittent stream of the Oued Rhumel rises on a high plateau in northeastern Algeria and flows to the northeast past Constantine. There it turns to the northwest and then the north, entering the Mediterranean as the Oued el Kebir. On the east and north of the ancient city of Constantine is the precipitous chasm of the Rhumel gorge. The city, which is built on a high limestone bluff known as the Rock of Constantine, lies more than 800 feet (244 meters) above the valley floor. The fortress site is nearly surrounded by bluffs and cliffs, with only a narrow, ramplike neck of land on the southwest connecting the Rock of Constantine with the adjoining hills.

Cut off from the surrounding area, the defensive potential of this natural fortress was realized as early as the third century B.C., when the principal city of the ancient kingdom of Numidia occupied the location. Conquered by the Romans, the city was destroyed in a civil war in A.D. 311. Constantine the Great then rebuilt the city, which was renamed in his honor. Taken over by the Arabs and French in turn, the city was briefly occupied by American troops in November 1942.

The city of nearly half a million is no longer so isolated. Several bridges now span the wadi, one occupying the same position as a Roman bridge. Below the gorge a series of waterfalls have been harnessed to provide hydroelectric power. In the nineteenth century, the French built the seaport of Philippeville (present Skikda) well to the east of the river's outlet, so there was no question of the commercial development and settlement of the lower valley. The Rhumel's primary role has been to provide a moatlike, defensive site for Algeria's largest interior city.

See also Ziz

RIO GRANDE

Source: San Juan Mountains, in southwestern Colorado
Length: 1,885 miles (3,034 kilometers)
Tributaries: San Juan, Alamosa, Chama, Jemez, San Jose, Conchos, Pecos, Salado
Outlet: Gulf of Mexico

The river that citizens of the United States refer to as the Rio Grande, and that Mexicans call Río Bravo del Norte, is the fifth longest waterway in North America. Long a cultural and political borderland, the "Big River" today figures as an important corridor of industrial development, migration, and natural resource conflict.

The Rio Grande rises on the Continental Divide in the San Juan Mountains of southwest Colorado. The river begins by collecting melting snowfields and mountain rushes in tumbling streams that drain steep, forested slopes. On the left bank of the upper course of the river in Colorado is the broad tributary valley of the San Juan. The tallest sand

Rio Grande in Big Bend National Park (Jesse Walker)

dunes in North America have grown on the eastern, or lee, side of the large alluvial flat of the San Juan valley. Sand has accumulated up to 700 feet (213 meters) over thousands of years as a result of the erosion of the volcanic San Juan Mountains to the west. The sand being too heavy for the prevailing southwesterly winds to carry over the high mountain passes in the Sangre de Cristo range to the east, it is deposited at the base of the foothills, as spectacularly seen at Great Sand Dunes National Park.

In its upper course the Rio Grande flows to the east, then south into New Mexico. As the river crosses the central part of New Mexico, it enters a canyon 70 miles (113 kilometers) long and up to 800 feet (244 meters) deep. It passes Taos, Albuquerque, and Las Cruces on its way to Texas. The piñons, junipers, and sagebrush of the semi-arid environment of the river's middle course gradually give way to a desert zone of cactus, mesquite, and other drought-adapted plants. Rich in history and folklore, the great river forms the Texas–New Mexico border approximately 20 miles (32 kilometers) above El Paso, Texas. It trends generally southeasterly to the Gulf of Mexico along the U.S.-Mexico border. The river forms a large loop in the Big Bend region of west Texas, contributing to the distinctive shape of the Texas outline as well as forming a magnificent national park on the U.S. side of the border—Big Bend—which combines in a single large area three major environmental types: forested mountains (Chisos Mountains); desert (Chihuahua lowlands); and riparian zone (Rio Grande floodplain). The river has carved three spectacular, sheer-walled canyons in the park.

The phenomena of paired cities, not unusual along political boundaries, is especially pronounced along the Rio Grande, where cultural and economic differences on opposite sides of the river are striking. Among the border pairs are El Paso, Texas, and Juárez, Mexico; Eagle Pass, Texas, and

Piedras Negras, Mexico; Laredo, Texas, and Nuevo Laredo, Mexico; and Brownsville, Texas, and Matamoros, Mexico.

Although one of the longest rivers in North America, the Rio Grande is too shallow for commercial navigation. Brownsville is reached by a ship canal that parallels the river. A number of dams on the river—Elephant Butte and Caballo in New Mexico, Amistad and Falcon in Texas—are used for irrigation, flood control, and regulation of the river flow. The citrus fruit and vegetable-growing agricultural area near the mouth of the river referred to as the Rio Grande Valley is an irrigated district developed principally in the 1920s. A long-standing agreement between the United States and Mexico (1945) calls for sharing the river's water in future projects, but the disparity in economic clout and political power between the two nations inevitably has meant that Mexico's interests have been short-changed. Like many of the world's great rivers running through arid regions, by the time the Rio Grande reaches the sea it is often dry. Shifting channels have led to border disputes, some lasting for more than a century. A 114-year controversy over the location of the border of El Paso was settled in 1968 when the Rio Grande was diverted into a concrete channel. The shallowness of the river plus the length of the international border between two countries with such large differences in living standards contribute to the problem of illegal crossing by Latin American immigrants.

The Spanish captain Alonso Alvarrez de Pineda in 1519 explored the Gulf Coast and first sighted the river's mouth, calling the Rio Grande the "River of Palms" after the trees that lined the shore, which were as tall as a ship's masts. When the ill-fated Narvaez expedition washed up in the region, the fantastic survivor-cum-explorer Cabeza de Vaca was rescued in 1536 near where the Conchos River empties into the Rio Grande. Although de Vaca's tales of golden cities—which inspired Coronado's famous exploration of the Southwest—have been generally discredited by historians, he may have seen the numerous pueblos that were thriving on the basis of irrigated agriculture on the river's banks, north of present-day Las Cruces, New Mexico. In 1540 Coronado explored the Rio Grande and its main tributary, the Pecos River of Texas, and examined the pueblos, though without discovering any large, exploitable source of gold. The establishment of Santa Fe in the upper valley, and El Paso farther downriver, in the seventeenth century was primarily the work of the episcopal and missionary extension of New Spain toward the north. The rise of French interest along the lower Mississippi and the Gulf Coast after LaSalle's 1682 expedition down the Mississippi from the Great Lakes reactivated Spanish settlement along the upper Rio Grande; Santa Fe was rebuilt, Albuquerque established, El Paso resupplied, and numerous new missions erected. In the early 1800s the American explorer Zebulon Pike was captured by the Spanish along the upper Rio Grande, and he was taken to Santa Fe before being released along the border of Louisiana Territory.

The river featured as an important divide and focus of rivalry in both the creation of an independent Texas (1835) and the Mexican War (1846). Less well known is the prominence of the river in the Civil War. The Rio Grande was important to the Confederacy because it marked the border of the only neutral country that touched the newly formed rebel nation. Mexico served as a market for Texas cotton and could provide supplies to the South. The subjection of Mexico to French occupation during the Civil War complicated matters, but the lower Rio Grande valley had a sizable amount of trade: wagon teams laden with cotton bales coming from San Antonio, ships of many nations putting in at Matamoros. Union invaders put an end to this activity when they seized the lower reaches of the river, and Lincoln tied up a British ship over an international legal issue. Thereafter cotton shipments from Texas had to be rerouted through Eagle Pass, and from there hauled to Bagdad, a boom town some 30 miles (48 kilometers) above the mouth. Foreign ships waited beyond the sandbars for lighters to bring them bales of cotton. At the end of the war, General Philip

Sherman brought 40,000 troops to the Rio Grande to ensure that the French puppet regime left Mexico. In the late nineteenth and early twentieth centuries the U.S. Army was kept busy along the border subduing recalcitrant Indians (Apaches and Comanches), raiding bandits, and monitoring restless Mexican politicos.

Today, life along the Rio Grande border is better for most, but not for all. Banks and department stores line the U.S. side of the border, while industrial plants known as *maquiladoras* ("sister," or branch, plants) cluster on the Mexican side to take advantage of the low wages and weak environmental laws of the poorer country. Recent rapid immigration and urban growth along the border have resulted in water-scarcity problems—perennial in this dry, subtropical location. Since 1906 the United States has been obliged to deliver 60,000 acre-feet (7,380 hectare-meters) of water from the upper Rio Grande to Mexico each year, much of it used to irrigate the Mexicali valley. It is becoming increasingly difficult to develop water-delivery systems and wastewater treatment plants while maintaining a clean, safe environment. With the signing of the North American Free Trade Agreement (NAFTA) in 1993, the two countries are required to promote economic development by the free movement of labor, goods, and services across and along the border. To traditional natural resource institutions such as the International Boundary and Water Commission, which has had authority over both water allocation and sanitation since 1944, has been added the transboundary environmental agency, the Border Environment Cooperation Commission, which is responsible for certifying environmental infrastructure projects.

Further Reading: Horgan, Paul, *Great River: The Rio Grande,* New York: Rinehart and Company, 1954 (Rivers of America Series); Maxwell, Ross A., *The Big Bend of the Rio Grande: A Guide to the Rocks, Landscape, Geologic History, and Settlers of the Area of Big Bend National Park,* Bureau of Economic Geology, University of Texas at Austin, Guidebook 7, 1968.

RUBICON

Source: Apennine Mountains, near San Marino
Length: Short stream
Tributaries: None
Outlet: Adriatic Sea

A three-legged stool is more stable than the political triumvirate that took control of ancient Rome in the middle of the first century B.C. The three-way alliance begun in 60 B.C. among Pompey the Great, Crassus, and Julius Caesar—the so-called First Triumvirate—was an attempt to balance the opposing forces of popular and patrician rule, civilian and military government. Gaius Julius Caesar (100? –44 B.C.) was appointed governor of the Roman province of Gaul in 58 B.C. This province included places south of the Alps that had already been conquered and incorporated into the Roman imperium (cis-Alpine Gaul), as well as the region north of the Alps inhabited by recalcitrant Celts (trans-Alpine Gaul), an area approximating present-day France. Although he had previously distinguished himself as governor of Spain, Caesar earned his military laurels in the conquest of northern Gaul (58–49 B.C.). His *Commentaries on the Gallic Wars,* containing descriptions of the events of the campaign and the people of the region, is considered a model of clear and concise Latin prose.

Meanwhile the other two legs of the political stool—Pompey and Crassus—naturally reacted to Caesar's swelling pride and reputation. After Crassus died during the Syrian campaign in 53 B.C., Pompey was made sole consul. He moved to exclude Caesar from power, goading the Senate into calling upon Caesar to resign his command and disband his army.

Refusing to do so, Caesar in 49 B.C. crossed the Rubicon (Latin: *Rubico*), a small stream on the eastern coast of northern Italy near Ariminum (modern Rimini). The stream rises in the Apennine Mountains near the miniature state of San Marino, flowing eastward to its outlet on the Adriatic Sea. During this period of the Roman Republic the Rubicon River formed part of the political border between cis-Alpine Gaul, under

"The die was cast" in 49 B.C. when Julius Caesar crossed the Rubicon River, a small stream in northern Italy, against the Senate's orders, as shown here in an illuminated manuscript page. (Jean Fouquet, circa 1415/1420–1481, Louvre, France (Giraudon/Art Resource, NY)

Caesar's rule, and Italy proper, controlled by Pompey and the Roman Senate. Caesar's crossing the Rubicon directly contradicted the wishes of the Senate and amounted to an act of rebellion. The public safety of the Roman people had been placed in the hands of Pompey. He had more troops at his command, but they were dispersed throughout the provinces. Pompey fled southward to Brundisium, and from there to Greece. He was eventually assassinated in Egypt, and Caesar became dictator of the Roman Republic by 48 B.C. when he was elected consul. The republic did not allow its leader to become a king (Rex), but Caesar expanded and multiplied his powers, thereby laying the foundation of thc Roman Empire.

"Crossing the Rubicon" is a phrase that has come to mean the taking of a decisive step that commits oneself to a hazardous enterprise. Curiously, the words do not appear in Shakespeare's play *Julius Caesar,* perhaps because the events surrounding the death of Caesar rather than his rise to power make up the story of this popular play. The phrase crops up frequently in the Age of Dryden, the words taking on the connotation of both a decisive action and an important boundary. Charlotte Bronte in *Jane Eyre* employs the words feelingly: "A Pause—in which I began to steady the palsy of my nerves, and to feel that the rubicon was passed" (1847). By the late Victorian period the term had been seriously inflated, at least in its meaning as a boundary. In Boscawen's *Bible & Monuments* (1896), we find these words: "The

Deluge formed the rubicon between the mythic period and the heroic and polyarchal age." Without worrying about the meaning of "polyarchal," it might be said that the small river in northern Italy has come a long way, from being a tiny stream actually crossed by Julius Caesar en route to his seizure of power to being the limit of the antediluvian period.

Further Reading: Meier, Christian, *Caesar,* New York: Basic Books, 1982.

RUHR

Source: Western Germany, just north of Winterberg
Length: 145 miles (233 kilometers)
Tributaries: Lenne, Möhne
Outlet: **Rhine**

A short, right-bank tributary of the lower Rhine is one of the principal manufacturing areas of Europe and was once the largest concentration of heavy industry in the world. The Ruhr, whose name derives from the Celtic word for "red brook," after the red sandstone in the drainage basin, rises in the hilly uplands of west-central Germany and generally flows westward, though in a highly tortuous route, to its junction with the Rhine not far south of the border with the Netherlands.

The river passes by or near the primary industrial cities of Dortmund, Essen, Mülheim, and Duisburg. On the north bank of the river at its confluence with the Rhine is the coal port and industrial site of Ruhrort, at the head of the Rhine-Herne Canal. Though the Ruhr region proper encompasses only the area between the Lippe River (north) and the Ruhr River (south), a broader concentration is also identified so as to include the industrial zone farther south in a belt east and west of Düsseldorf.

High-quality coking coals necessary for modern steel production are found at the surface just north of the Ruhr River, along a fringe of hills known as the Haarstrang, or "Hair String." Farther north near the Lippe River, where the modern mines are located, extensive coal measures lay at some depth, but with modern hydraulic equipment to keep the mine shafts drained, these deposits proved to be commercially exploitable. Large-scale coal mining and steel making in the region are associated with the late-nineteenth-century rise of Germany to economic prominence. Such internationally famous firms as Krupp, Thyssen, and Stinnes first began integrating mines, blast furnaces, and mills and organized fellow producers and the government to discriminate favorably on matters of transportation rates and prices. (This form of organization—a trust or monopoly—was given the German term *Kartell,* from which derives the English word *cartel.*) The famous Krupp works at Essen epitomized the size of the operations, their diversity, and organizational principles. Krupp was an industrial giant producing coal, coke, coal tar, pig iron, steel, and armaments, all closely controlled by the cartels and the national government.

Local reserves of iron ore were not sufficient for steel making on such a scale, so the Ruhr depended on complementary economic regions such as Lorraine (controlled by Germany after 1871) to provide ore and in turn be provided Ruhr coke. A dense network of canals, railroads, and highways traverse the region. The Ruhr carries bulky cargoes of coal, chemicals, and iron and steel as far as the head of navigation at Witten. The Rhine-Herne Canal links the valley to the Rhine and the Dutch coast, while the Dortmund-Ems makes a connection to the north-flowing Ems and the north German ports. The right-bank tributary, the Möhne, provides a reservoir at Günne that constitutes a major water and power supply of the Ruhr.

The primary heavy industrial base of German armament manufacturing in both World War I and World War II, the Ruhr was the focus of contention between the wars and a major target of Allied bombing in World War II. Because of disputes about German payment of World War I reparations, French and Belgian forces occupied the Ruhr between 1923 and 1925. Allied air attacks nearly leveled the industrial Ruhr in March–April 1945. The region was considered so vital in the postwar period that its control was in the hands of international authorities until 1954, when it was returned to the Federal Republic of Germany (West Germany). Although coal mining and steel production in the Ruhr suffered severe setbacks in the 1980s, the region has recovered today (2001), so that it still produces the bulk of German iron and steel, machinery, chemicals, and textiles. Today, the majority of its working population is employed in the service sector and lives in the large cities of the Ruhr megalopolis, away from the coal fields and the old steel works.

See also Rhine

Further Reading: Harris, Chauncy D., "The Ruhr Coal-Mining District," *Geographical Review* 36 (1946): 194–221.

S

SAAR

Source: Western slope of Vosges Mountains, in northeastern France
Length: c. 150 miles (241 kilometers)
Tributaries: Blies, Sultz, Rosselle, Bisten, Prims, Nied
Outlet: **Moselle**

The coal deposits of Saar (French: Sarre) and the iron ore of nearby Lorraine are brought together in important complementary economic regions.

The river rises in two headstreams near Le Donon, the summit of the Vosges Mountains in northeastern France near the border with Germany. It flows northward through the French *départements* of Moselle and Bas-Rhin. The river crosses Lorraine, passing Sarrebourg and Sarreguemines. It then enters the Saar (today's German state of Saarland) and, following a northwesterly course, soon passes the leading industrial city of the coal basin and an important road and railroad junction, Saarbrücken. Winding through low, wooded hills, the river flows past Saarlouis, originally a fortress site founded by Louis XIV of France (1680) and designed by the famous military architect Vauban; past Merzig; and finally past German Saarburg before reaching the Moselle (German: Mosel) just upstream from Trier.

The Saar region is highly industrialized, with a large iron and steel industry based on a vast coal field. Though the Saar coal measures are not as extensive as those of the Ruhr, the Warndt deposits in the south furnish coking coals necessary in the production of steel. French Lorraine provides iron ore to complement the Saar's coal reserves. Linked by canal, superhighway, electric rail, and airport to the Rhine-Main area, the Saar also manufactures machinery, motors, ceramics, processed foods, and textiles.

Long divided politically between France and Germany, Alsace-Lorraine experienced rapid industrial development after 1871, when the region passed to Germany at the end of the Franco-Prussian War. By 1913 the Saar coal mines had an annual output of 17 million tons (15.5 tonnes), some of which was contributed by annexed Lorraine. Between 1920 and 1935 the Saar territory was placed under the administration of the League of Nations and granted to France. After a League-sponsored plebiscite in 1935 the region was restored to Germany as Saarland. In 1940, during World War II, Hitler again unified the complementary regions when he annexed French Lorraine and combined it with Saarland to form what he called Westmark. Heavy fighting along the Saar River occurred at the end of World War II in December 1944. The region's economic resources and its key geopolitical status as a borderland made it so important in the postwar period that Saarland was not fully integrated into the Federal Republic of Germany (West Germany) until 1957.

See also Moselle

SACRAMENTO

Source: Near Mount Shasta, in northern California
Length: c. 380 miles (612 kilometers)
Tributaries: Pit, McCloud, Feather, Cache, American, Putah
Outlet: Merges with **San Joaquin** in delta that feeds into Suisun Bay, an eastern arm of San Francisco Bay

The 14,162-foot (4,317-meter) peak of perpetually snow-capped Mount Shasta stands like a sentinel guarding the northern end of California's Central Valley. The headwaters of the river that constitutes the northern section of this great valley issue from a small lake on Mount Eddy in the Klamath Mountains near Shasta's giant volcanic cone. The longest river in California begins as a wild mountain stream that is delightful to experienced boaters. Within 40 miles (64 kilometers) of the source, near Redding, the Shasta and Keswick dams block the river's flow and that of its tributaries, the McCloud and the Pit, to form the enormous reservoir of Lake Shasta. This body of water, along with the snowfields of the mountains that feed it, is a valuable source of water not only for the irrigation of Central Valley farms but also as drinking water for the state's rapidly growing coastal population.

The river follows a generally southerly course between the Coastal Ranges to the west and the Cascade Range, with its southern extension, the Sierra Nevada, to the east. The drainage basin includes all or parts of five terrain regions: the Sacramento valley, the Sierra Nevada, the Coast Ranges, the Cascade Range, and the Modoc Plateau—the last being an upland terrain unit bridging the Cascade and Sierra Ranges. The relatively humid climate of northern California ensures that the river and its tributaries are a major source of water for the populous but parched southern part of the state. The eastern tributaries and subtributaries of the Sacramento—the Feather, Yuba, and American Rivers—and the feeders of the Shasta reservoir receive their peak flow from winter rains and spring snowmelt. The

Yuba River, subtributary of the Sacramento, showing evidence of hydraulic gold mining (Jesse Walker)

Covered bridge on the western slope of Sierra Nevada in gold rush country, Bridgeport, Nevada County, California (Jesse Walker)

stored water is then released during the normally dry summer months.

Passing by or near Red Bluff, Chico, and Colusa, the river reaches the largest city of the valley and the state capital, Sacramento. From there the river flows to the southwest for approximately 40 miles (64 kilometers) to join the north-flowing San Joaquin, the two jointly forming an estuary that runs westward a short distance to Suisun Bay, connected westward via Carquinez Strait to San Pablo and San Francisco Bay. Not only does the fresh water of the Sacramento ultimately pass under the famous Golden Gate Bridge, exiting the bay and reaching the Pacific, but some of this water also mixes with brackish water in the estuarine zone to ensure a proper environment for aquatic species and birds in the bay area. Without this fresh water, or with less of it, saltwater intrusion—a major problem in deltas—would alter or destroy the natural environment at the river's mouth.

Land use in the Sacramento valley is dominated by agriculture. Rice is one of the principal crops, and it grows well on the relatively impermeable soils of the floodplain and in basin areas. This cash crop depends heavily on irrigation water from the Sacramento River. Orchard crops, principally walnut, almond, prune, and peach, tend to be near the river channel or on alluvial fans to benefit from well-drained soils. On slopes farther away from the river, and dominating land use in the upper basin, forest, rangeland, and mining are more important.

The valley was the scene of the Gold Rush of 1849, when placer, or alluvial, mining of the Sacramento's eastern tributaries (along the western foothills of the Sierra Nevada) initiated the rapid growth of northern California. Although the Central Valley had been occupied by the Spanish since 1769, it was not until 1808 that Ensign Gabriel Moraga led a small group of soldiers from Mission San Jose to the northern part of the valley, giving the name Sacramento, meaning "Holy Sacrament," to the lower reaches of the Feather River, a tributary of the Sacramento. Soon the name was adopted by the primary river. In the early decades of the nineteenth century, Hudson's Bay trappers ventured southward from their Canadian base. A brigade commanded by Alexander McLeod explored and gave names to the streams of the region, though the name Buenaventura, or "Big River," which appeared on several maps of the 1830s, was not widely used.

The first permanent European settler was the Swiss immigrant John Sutter, who established Fort Sutter (within present Sacramento) near where the American River empties into the Sacramento. Encompassing a range of enterprises, the somewhat incorrectly named "Fort" was a service center for agriculture and the fur trade, and a point of entry for overland immigration. A lumber mill was set up by Sutter on the South Fork of the American River to provide for immigrant needs, and it was here that gold was discovered by an American frontiersman, James Marshall, in January 1848. During the ensuing rush, mining claims spread from the Mariposa River in the south to Mt. Shasta in the north, with the relatively narrow foothills zone where ore was most concentrated deemed the Mother Lode. Even while the most accessible ore deposits were played out, bonanza wheat farms encompassing thousands of acres spread across the Central Valley. The holdings of Dr. Hugh J. Glenn in the Sacramento valley, for instance, extended for 20 miles (32 kilometers) along the west bank of the river and totaled 55,000 acres (22,258 hectares). California wheat passed through the Golden Gate en route to world markets. Sacramento grew rapidly as the western terminus of the Central Pacific Railroad, the western unit of the first transcontinental railroad, built between 1863 and 1869. All of the four elite business leaders in early California who dominated railroads and finance (the so-called "Big Four" of Leland Stanford, Charles Crocker, Mark Hopkins, and Collis Huntington) resided in Sacramento.

The Sacramento Deep Water Channel parallels or follows the lower course of the river, from Cache Slough to West Sacramento, giving the capital city the status of an inland port. Through time the agricultural economy of the valley has diversified, and the delta region, where the Sacramento joins with the San Joaquin, is notable as an intensive fruit, nut, and vegetable region, with asparagus an especially important crop.

Authorized first by the state in 1933, the Central Valley Project has been the primary hydraulic agency by which, via dams, reservoirs, and canals, surplus water from northern California reaches the thirsty San Joaquin valley as far south as Bakersfield. At the same time, provisions have been made for transmission of electrical power and for flood protection.

Numerous problems with the quality of ground and surface water in the Sacramento valley have arisen. Elevated concentrations of trace metals, especially from abandoned mines, have been detected. Several mines near Lake Shasta are particularly offensive. High pesticide use in the valley by agriculturalists threatens both surface water and groundwater. Overflows from irrigation, storm runoff, and percolation are the primary means by which nitrates and other nutrients threaten the river. The highly permeable soils of the natural levees and alluvial fans facilitate the infiltration of nitrates into the groundwater. Rapid urban growth brings with it environmental problems associated with compacted surfaces, decreased permeability, and increased runoff of volatile organic compounds. Fish and other aquatic species, including the chinook salmon, are affected by the dams that restrict upstream migration. And in addition to the effects of acidic mine discharge and agricultural chemicals, overfishing and the introduction of nonnative species have also harmed aquatic life.

See also San Joaquin

Further Reading: Dana, Julian, *The Sacramento,* New York: Farrar and Rinehart, 1939 (Rivers of America Series).; for treatment of water-quality issues, see the Web site: http://water.wr.usgs.gov/sacval.html

SAINT LAWRENCE

Source: Northeast side of Lake Ontario
Length: 744 miles (1,197 kilometers)
Tributaries: Richelieu, Saint Francis, **Ottawa**, Saint Maurice, Chaudière, Saguenay
Outlet: Gulf of Saint Lawrence

Although not the longest river in Canada, the Saint Lawrence (French: Saint-Laurent) is the most important in terms of settlement, commerce, and history. It occupies a broad trough separating the Canadian Shield (Laurentian Highlands) to the northwest from Appalachian-era highlands to the southeast. Nowhere else in North America does an eastward-flowing river penetrate so far into the interior. It is the chief outlet of the Great Lakes, the largest bodies of fresh water in the world. Although the river measures slightly less than 750 miles (1,207 kilometers) from the eastern end of Lake Ontario to its mouth on the Gulf of Saint Lawrence north of Cape Gaspé, its length extends to 2,300 miles (3,701 kilometers) if one counts the distance from the westward end of Lake Superior. The ultimate source is sometimes considered to be the Saint Louis River, which flows past Duluth, Minnesota, adding another 150 miles (240 kilometers), but this claim is subjective and far-fetched, based as it is on the apparent assumption that rivers cannot begin in lakes.

The upper Saint Lawrence forms part of the boundary between Ontario and New York state. It includes the scenic Thousand Islands, now the

Political leaders of the United States and Canada at the groundbreaking of the Saint Lawrence Hydroelectric Power Project, Cornwall, Ontario, Canada, August 1954 (Bettmann/CORBIS)

western section of the Saint Lawrence Seaway. Below this stretches Lake Saint Francis, which serves for a short distance as the boundary between Ontario and Quebec (French: Québec) before flowing entirely within the French Canadian province. At Montreal (French: Montréal) the river expands to create Lake Saint Louis. Montreal, the largest French-speaking city in Canada, was founded in 1642 at the foot of Mount Royal, after which the city is named, on a large island in the river at the traditional head of navigation; nearby, an important left-bank tributary, the Ottawa, joins the Saint Lawrence. During the early French colonial period, light boats navigated the Ottawa to its headwaters and thus permitted a more direct access to the beaver-rich country of the upper Great Lakes than the westward-penetrating Saint Lawrence. Montreal soon became the primary fur-trading entrepôt, its urban dominance reinforced by commercial water links forged during the canal-and-steamboat era in the early nineteenth century and later by the arrival of the railroads.

Just upstream from Montreal are the Lachine Rapids, a major impediment to navigation. The somewhat satiric name of this obstacle derives from the time when the French explorer La Salle thought that by going up the Saint Lawrence and down the Mississippi he would reach the Pacific Ocean and gain access to the long-sought luxury trade with the Orient. The remarkably persistent belief in a mythical Northwest Passage circumventing or threading the northern latitudes of the North American continent was made fun of by down-to-earth Canadians; they called the obstacle the *Lachine* Rapids, that is, "the China" rapids to poke fun at illustrious La Salle's pretensions.

Below Sorel the river expands to form the large Lake Saint Peter (French: Lac Saint-Pierre). Some 200 miles (322 kilometers) east of Montreal, where the river approached from its mouth begins to narrow, lies the earliest French settlement and still the heart of French Canada, Quebec City. For years after the explorer Jacques Cartier coaxed his ships into the broad estuarine mouth of the Saint Lawrence (1535), giving the river and the gulf the name of the Roman Catholic martyr on whose feast day the discovery had been made, French fishermen had been dropping anchor at the river's mouth and landing to dry their fish. Associated with the shift in European interest from exploitation and exploration to colonization and settlement, Samuel de Champlain in 1608 established a town at the Quebec narrows, which were the head of navigation for oceangoing vessels at the time. He envisioned a permanent colony of farmers producing enough that they would be able to overcome their dependence on the annual spring convoy from France. Champlain meanwhile explored farther west, discovering the Great Lakes by 1615, and quickly established French hegemony as far as the upper Mississippi headwaters. The strategic significance of the Quebec gateway to the St. Lawrence should not be overlooked. Even though the French eventually lost their New World empire to the British (1763), Quebec continued to be known as the Gibraltar of North America. The old city lay on a low bluff 300 feet (91 meters) above the river. It was considered unassailable from the river but open to attack from the land. General Wolfe's victory on the Plains of Abraham above Quebec City led to the French defeat during the French and Indian War, or Seven Years War (1754–1763). The English victory and takeover of Canada can be related to their successfully playing the Iroquois tribes of upstate New York against the French allies and fur-trading middlemen, the Algonquin and Huron Indians of the Saint Lawrence–Great Lakes corridor.

The broad, fertile lowlands of the lower Saint Lawrence, extending from Montreal to Quebec City, represent the cultural hearth of French Canada. A distinctive land survey and disposal system was practiced here, still evident in the cadastral, or property map, and visible from the air. The crown granted large parcels of land, or seigneuries, which were surveyed in characteristic long lots extending back from the Saint Lawrence and its tributaries to maximize river frontage and ensure that properties had a mix of land types: from well-drained levees to game-rich swamp backlands. Large owners subdivided their tracts into smaller units suitable for occupation by *habi-*

tants, as farmers of modest means called themselves in French Canada. Since the land was surveyed using the antiquated measure of the arpent (1 arpent = 192 feet), the long-lot system came to be known as the arpent system. As in other places in North America where this land survey was practiced (for example, southern Louisiana), distinctive pie-shaped properties arose clinging to the meandering river, as well as associated features; these included semidispersed linear settlement ("straggling village") and a focus around the parish church, both contrasting with the dispersed settlement of stereotypical Anglo settlers.

The second Treaty of Paris (1783), signed at the end of the American Revolution, proved just as decisive in the decline of French-speaking Canada as the first treaty, which had granted sovereignty to the British. In 1792 the British divided Canada into two provinces: Upper Canada (Ontario), for the loyal Americans; and Lower Canada (Quebec), mainly for the French, who continued to resent that their leaders twenty years earlier had, as they put it, traded snow for sugar (France retained control of the Caribbean sugar islands of Martinique and Guadaloupe). Loyalist and commercial-minded colonists from Pennsylvania and upstate New York migrated to the fertile peninsular region lying between Lake Ontario, Lake Erie, and Lake Huron, especially the sedimentary soils of the southern part of the area. A series of cities located in the rich limestone country between Windsor, Ontario, and Toronto were well on their way by the middle of the nineteenth century to becoming prosperous agricultural and industrial counterparts of the American upper Midwest.

Although artificial channelization of the Saint Lawrence between Kingston, Ontario, and the Lachine Rapids began in the nineteenth century (between 1821 and 1845, eight canals were built to compete with the Erie Canal), the construction of a deep-water channel became a reality only with the completion of the Saint Lawrence Seaway in 1959; this ensured access of commercial vessels to a continuous channel with a minimum depth of 14 feet (4.3 meters). The project, undertaken jointly by the United States and Canada, involves a series of locks, canals, and dredged channels above Montreal that allow oceangoing vessels to reach Great Lakes ports. The Saint Lawrence and Great Lakes are thereby transformed into a fourth coastline for Canada and the United States. Commodity flows consist primarily of upstream shipments of iron ore from Quebec and Labrador to ports on the Great Lakes, and downstream cargoes of wheat, corn, barley, and soybeans.

With a large volume of flow and a relatively steep descent, the Saint Lawrence is well suited to the production of electricity. The Saint Lawrence Power Project was built in the 1950s concurrently with the Seaway, at the International Rapids downstream from the Thousand Islands. It includes the Iroquois Dam (at Iroquois, Ontario); the Long Sault Dam,near Massena, New York (both used to control the river's flow); and the Robert Moses–Robert H. Saunders Power Dam, built between Cornwall, Ontario, and Barnhart Island, New York, with a generating capacity of 1,600,000 kilowatts. The electrical capacity of the power dam is shared equally by the two countries.

The Seaway handles large quantities of cargo during the open months of May through November, but it is closed by ice for the rest of the year. Proposals to keep the waterway open year-round have been criticized by environmentalists who argue that winter ship traffic would have damaging effects on fishery resources and habitat, and by certain utilities that oppose winter navigation because they fear it would disrupt the usual pattern of flow they have maintained using artificially anchored ice booms that can be opened to allow "lakers" through, releasing regular flow to nearby hydroelectric plants.

See also Ottawa

Further Reading: Beston, Henry, *The St. Lawrence,* New York: Farrar and Rinehart, 1942 (Rivers of America Series); Creighton, Donald G., *Empire of the St. Lawrence,* Boston: Houghton Mifflin, 1958; Ellis, William S., "Canada's Highway to the Sea," *National Geographic,* May 1980, pp. 586–623; Harris, R. Cole, *The Seigneurial System in Early Canada: A Geographical Study,* Madison: University of Wisconsin Press, 1966.

SALT

Source: Convergence of Black and White, on Fort Apache Indian Reservation in eastern Arizona
Length: c. 200 (322 kilometers)
Tributaries: Big Bonito Creek, Diamond Creek, Carrizo Creek, Cibecue Creek, Canyon Creek, Cherry Creek, Tonto Creek, Verde River
Outlet: **Gila** River

A map of hot and dry regions is scattered with Salt or Salado Rivers, as a result of the high rate of evaporation and saline accumulation in tropical and subtropical locations. Of the many hundreds of Salt Rivers in the world, the one in central Arizona is perhaps the best known, as it is the locale of the oldest multipurpose reclamation project in the United States within the fastest-growing urban areas in the country.

The headwaters of the Salt River lie in the White Mountains of eastern Arizona at an elevation of 11,400 feet (3,476 meters). Springs and seeps along the Mogollon Rim and in the mountains are caused by the geological barriers presented by volcanic rocks to groundwater, which is discharged as small but perennial streams. Volcanic rocks are exposed in the east-central highlands of Arizona, where water is forced to the surface through joints and fractures; where these lithological breaks intersect the surface, springs appear.

There are some two dozen perennial streams of more than a few miles' length in the Salt River watershed. Many are little more than washes, but the Black and White Rivers, fed in the headwaters by countless seeps, together form the Salt proper, approximately 40 miles (64 kilometers) northeast of Globe, Arizona. With the Black, the river constitutes the boundary between the Fort Apache Indian Reservation (north) and the San Carlos Indian Reservation (south). It flows generally westward to the Gila River in Maricopa County, 15 miles (24 kilometers) southwest of Phoenix.

The upper river in eastern Arizona is a favorite of river runners attracted by a fast-running stream with rapids. A day trip to the Salt River Canyon begins by heading out of Phoenix via U.S. 60. Soon the traveler comes into sight of the Superstition Mountains, where the legendary Lost Dutchman's Gold Mine is believed to be. The prospector Jacob Waltz is said to have discovered a mother lode of gold somewhere in the desert hills, but he died without telling anyone its whereabouts. Pass by volcanic Weaver's Needle and enter into Arizona's saguaro country. After going through Superior (site of the "World's Smallest Museum") and Globe, an old copper mining town, turn left onto U.S. 60/ Arizona 77 and follow the twisting canyon road. The erosional work of the Salt River acting together with wind and freezing water is evident in the geological splendors of the canyon, as well as in the sculpting of the valley itself.

The lower course of the river is often referred to as the "Salt River Valley." The channel is usually dry in Phoenix because of upstream dams. The water is utilized for irrigation and waterpower through a system of dams forming a 60-mile (97-kilometer) chain of lakes: Roosevelt Lake (dam of the same name); Apache Lake (Horse Mesa Dam); Canyon Lake (Mormon Flat Dam); and Saguaro Lake (Stewart Mountain Dam). Water from the Salt River is impounded by the Phoenix metro area for municipal, industrial, and agricultural use. Roosevelt Lake, named after Theodore Roosevelt, is the key feature of an intricate hydraulic system known as the Salt River Project. The reservoir is by far the largest, with a storage capacity of 1,336,700 acre-feet (164,414 hectare-meters), compared with the second-largest reservoir, Apache Lake, with 245,100 acre-feet (30,147 hectare-meters). Roosevelt Dam was the first major structure constructed by the infant Bureau of Reclamation in the early twentieth century. Completed in 1911 and subsequently modified in the 1990s, the dam has been the focus of a recent controversy over the issue of whether to enlarge the dam to create a larger potential reservoir to provide flood protection for Phoenix. The paradox of flood problems in a desert environment is explained by urban growth: construction and development compacts and paves the surface, decreasing the permeability of the soil and increasing overland flood. With little vegetation to slow the movement of water, the rare but intense storms of the desert are converted into major inundations in a highly artificial urban environment. An enlarged area for a reservoir would endanger several species of the southwestern willow flycatcher and threaten critical habitats and green areas. Debates are often sharply polarized exchanges between harshly depicted adversaries: water power gluttons versus tree-hugging environmentalists (though there are precious few trees to hug here). Additional elements of the Salt River Project include Granite Reef Dam, 4 miles (6.4 kilometers) downstream from the confluence of the Salt and its major tributary, the Verde, which diverts water to canals to irrigate the Phoenix area; and Bartlett Horseshoe Dam on the Verde River, used primarily for flood protection. Below Granite Reef Dam the river forms the southern boundary of the Salt River Indian Reservation, then successively flows past Mesa, Tempe, and Scottsdale, and through the city of Phoenix south of downtown.

Native Americans had an extensive system of irrigated farming in the lower valley. In the nineteenth century Mormons used some of the old canals, including those at Mesa. The native inhabitants include the Pima-Maricopa tribes, who now have a federally mandated community 15 miles (24 kilometers) northeast of Phoenix, adjacent to Scottsdale, Tempe, and Mesa. The Pima are descendants of the Hohokam, the ancestral dwellers who created the elaborate system of irrigation canals. The Maricopa, by contrast, originally lived along the lower Gila and Colorado Rivers and migrated into the region in the early nineteenth century. The emblem of the Pima-Maricopa Community is the Man in Maze, which is an apt symbol for a people caught in the web of burgeoning urban growth. When the traveler reaches the center of the maze—one's dreams and goals—he or she is met by the Sun God, who greets and blesses the sojourner en route to the next world.

The Salt River Project was the first large irrigation project undertaken under the federal Reclamation Act of 1902. Construction started on Roosevelt Dam in 1903 in a canyon east of Phoenix. The dam, completed in 1911, impounds enough water to irrigate fields for two years even if no rain falls. The project is considered one of the most economically successful reclamation efforts in North America. The rich agricultural district is a major producer of citrus fruits, lettuce, melons, and other crops. What was once an attractive winter resort and retirement destination is today one of the fastest-growing metropolitan areas in the United States.

Explosive urban growth of course has its consequences, not least in environmental impact. The deleterious effects of an increased size of Roosevelt Lake on habitat has already been mentioned. Turbidity problems exist along many stretches of the Salt and its tributaries. High sediment load is caused primarily by poor range management (overgrazing), mining, and sand and gravel operations. High levels of fecal coliform bacteria and ammonia have been reported for Carrizo Creek and White River. Several creeks and washes in mining country exceed allowable levels of metals and have acid leaching (low pH). The broad issue of uncontrolled urban growth cannot be addressed here except in passing. City dwellers are attracted to beautiful natural environments (and the desert, though desolate, *is* beautiful); many are tired of being caught in the snarl of congested traffic and in modern hurry-and-worry lifestyles. Urban sprawl has of late become an important political issue, and not just in Phoenix.

Further Reading: For the water-and-power perspective, see the Bureau of Reclamation Web site: http://dataweb.usbr.gov/html/saltriver.html

SALWEEN

Source: Tanglha Range, in eastern Tibet
Length: c. 1,750 miles (2,816 kilometers)
Tributaries: Yunzali, Kyaukhyat
Outlet: Gulf of Martaban

One of the wildest and most picturesque rivers in the world begins in the eastern Tibet Autonomous Region of western China, then flows southward through Yunnan Province. The Salween has cut deep, narrow gorges along its upper course parallel to the upper Mekong, Chang Jiang (Yangtze), and Irrawaddy. The geological character of the headwaters of four of the great rivers of Asia consists of folded mountains trenched by mighty rivers into deep valleys five million years ago when a northward-moving lithospheric plate carrying India encountered the southern end of the Eurasian plate, buckling up not only the Himalayas but also the Tibetan plateau (see Figure 4).

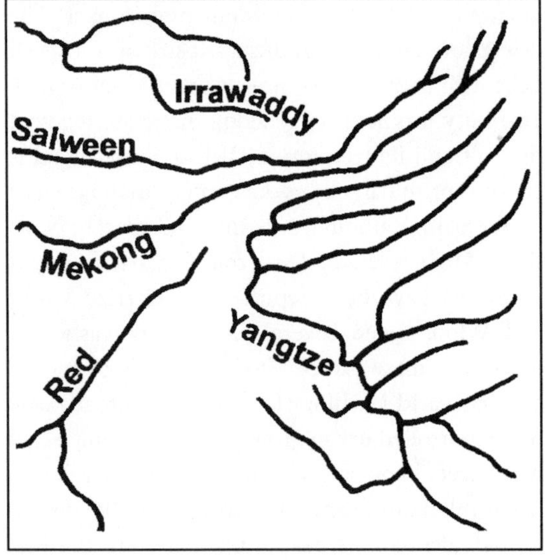

Figure 4. River knot in Southeast Asia

Unlike the other three rivers, the Salween (Mandarin Chinese: Nu Jiang; Tibetan: Chiama Ngu Chu) is navigable for only a short distance above its mouth and has therefore not served as a transportation corridor or focus of settlement. Flowing through gorges for most of its length, the Salween has been a major obstacle to east-west movement. It is crossed by the Burma Road and several road ferries in western China. The variation in the river's depth between wet and dry seasons renders the river useless except for floating logs downstream. Small launches and native boats, however, navigate along local stretches.

The river flows out of China into Myanmar (formerly Burma), cutting through the Shan plateau and the Karenni Hills. Called the Thanlwin River in Myanmar, it forms for a short section part of the border between Myanmar and Thailand. Flowing generally southward, the river empties into an arm of the Andaman Sea, the latter being the part of the Bay of Bengal east of the arc of the Andaman Islands, near Moulmein. This port is also a road hub and terminus of a railroad leading south to Ye. Many noted pagodas and caves are found in the town and on surrounding ridges. Formerly a ship-building center of considerable importance, Moulmein was the chief town of British Burma from 1827 to 1852. Today it is known primarily as an exporter of teak and rice. Rubber plantations are common to the south of the city. The river enters the sea at Moulmein by two mouths, north and south of Balugyin Island in the Gulf of Martaban. The southern mouth is the more important, being the route by which ocean-going ships approach Moulmein.

The upper course of the river is narrow, constricted, and forbidding. A chaos of boulders and shingle in the valley bottom during the dry season is converted during summer snowmelt into a torrent 50 to 90 feet (15 to 27 meters) above its low season flow, raging against the flanks of the steep, tree-clad valley sides. Submerged rocks, points jutting partially across the stream, and rock ledges forming rapids create perilous conditions on the river. Settlement is sparse except at ferry villages, which are sometimes built 1,000 feet (305 meters) above the banks.

The international conservation group Nature Conservancy is working with the Chinese government to balance economic development and environmental protection in the headwaters of four of Asia's great rivers. A series of national parks and wilderness areas, it is hoped, will be reserved as part of the Yunnan Great Rivers Project, a multi-million-dollar venture focusing on a spectacular swath of 16,500,000 acres (6,700,000 hectares) in northwest Yunnan. The region encompasses the upper courses of the Yangtze, Mekong, Irrawaddy, and Salween. Logging, along with its environmental impacts of siltation and aggravated flooding, will be replaced by more sustainable and environmentally friendly economic activities, such as ecotourism and adventure travel if the reserve is established. Endangered species in the Four Rivers region include the snow leopard, the red panda, and the snub-nosed monkey. A deputy director of the project, the Harvard-trained attorney and environmentalist Ed Norton, gave up his five-bedroom house in Columbia, Maryland, and moved with his wife, Ann McBride, who also gave up a high-profile job as president of the citizens action group Common Cause, to work to achieve a balance between economic development and respect for the land in this remote region. Although Norton is well aware of the criticisms of the project as wildly ambitious and unrealistic, he maintains his idealism and a respect for the Chinese people: "It's their country, these decisions are theirs to make. There is still plenty of time to do things right in Northwest Yunnan."

SAMBRE

Source: Aisne department, in northeast France
Length: 120 miles (193 kilometers)
Tributaries: Helpe Mineure, Helpe Majeure, Samme, Orneau
Outlet: **Meuse**

Along the northern edge of the Ardennes, an uplifted block in northeastern France and southern Belgium, runs the structural basin of the west-to-east Sambre-Meuse valley. An industrial crescent based on this southern coal field, or *Basin Sud,* contains the larger share of Belgium's industrial population. The coal measures extend across the frontier into the French *départements* of Nord and Pas de Calais.

The upper course of the river in northeastern France is paralleled by the Oise-Sambre Canal, which links it to the Paris Basin to the south, the Oise being a tributary of the Seine. Flowing northeasterly across France's Nord department, the river passes Maubeuge before crossing into Belgium. The river successively passes by or near a series of towns identified with this old coal district: Mons, Charleroi, and Namur, to mention just the largest. All have become large industrial cities making steel and steel products as well as consumer goods, depending less and less over time on the extraction of coal or coal products. Mons is situated on the western part of the coal furrow but is not on the Sambre, which enters the coal district just above Charleroi. The Charleroi-Brussels Canal takes off from this central location along Belgium's portion of the river and connects northward with the capital. Situated at the confluence of the east-flowing Sambre and the north-flowing Meuse, Namur is the strategic gateway to the Ardennes. It has been a fortress town for centuries and has suffered many sieges, including the battles of 1914 when the Germans finally captured this key location after destroying its outer rings of defense. The coal fields and industrial region continue eastward along the structural trough as far as Liège on the Meuse River, the major industrial city of the district.

The southern Belgian coal field developed rapidly in the nineteenth century on the basis of pre-existing charcoal-making, using the raw materials of the Ardennes, the discovery of accessible coals that outcropped along the sides of the Sambre-Meuse valley, and new techniques of coke- and steel-making. The coal deposits might have been accessible, but they were thin, sometimes buried deep beneath the surface, and contorted and fractured, defying easy exploitation. The Liège coal fields are some of the oldest to be worked in continental Europe, as vertical shafts were cut well before the Industrial Revolution to provide coal for smiths and metal-workers of Liège. Horizontal adits could be easily driven along the margins of deeply cut valleys to facilitate drainage. Mining led to metallurgical industries, and soon large integrated steel companies combined coke ovens, blast furnaces, and steel mills on a large scale, though never as large as on the nearby Ruhr, partly because its coal field was less extensive and less varied than those of the premier German heavy industrial region. The Sambre valley is today something of a Black District—an old industrial region whose buildings are darkened by coal soot and whose population is subject to high rates of unemployment. The mines of the Sambre-et-Meuse employ fewer than 1,000 workers, and the region is undergoing a difficult process of economic reconversion.

The numerous bridges, small towns, industrial buildings—and above all, the river itself—were critical elements in the fiercely fought Battle of the

Sambre (British: Battle of Mons) at the outbreak of World War I. On August 21, 1914, outliers of the advancing German army crossed undefended bridges on the Sambre between Charleroi and Namur. On the morning of August 22, elements of the French 5th Army tried to retake two large meander loops of the Sambre held by Germans, but were repelled with heavy losses. The French infantry was described as advancing gallantly across Belgian beet fields with colors unfurled and bugles sounding before being mowed down by German machine guns. On the French army's left in the vicinity of Mons, the British Expeditionary Force (BEF) more successfully defended another water obstacle on August 23—the Mons-Condé Canal. In the heart of mining country, the canal, spoil heaps, cottages, and buildings served as excellent defensive coverts and spying positions for the professional, all-regular BEF, which had been schooled in a dozen colonial wars. With losses on both sides numbering in the thousands, the BEF was ordered the following day to retreat along with Allied forces to defensive positions around the fortress of Paris, behind key waterways that ring the French heartland.

Further Reading: Keegan, John, *The First World War,* New York: Knopf, 1999.

SAN JOAQUIN

Source: Sierra Nevada, in northeast Madera County, eastern California
Length: c. 320 miles (515 kilometers)
Tributaries: Mokelumne, Tuolumne, Merced, Fresno
Outlet: Merges with **Sacramento** to form delta emptying into Suisun Bay, an eastern arm of San Francisco Bay

An alluvium-filled structural trough lying between the Coast Ranges and the Sierra Nevada extends for more than 400 miles (644 kilometers) from Redding, in northern California, to the east-west trending Tehachapi Mountains linking the southern end of the Sierra and Coast Ranges in south-central California. The southern two-thirds of the great Central Valley is drained by the San Joaquin, the northern third by the Sacramento River. The latter is smaller, better watered, and composed of an Anglo population. The cotton fields, orange groves, vineyards, and oil wells that are characteristic of the San Joaquin are not found in the north. Wider and more intensively developed than the Sacramento valley, the San Joaquin includes six substantial cities, from Stockton in the north to Bakersfield in the south. The southernmost part of the San Joaquin is actually drained by other streams: the Kings, the Kaweah, and the Tule drain into Tulare Lake Basin, which is prevented from entering the San Joaquin system by the fan of the Kings River. Despite the apparent flatness of the valley, there is a pronounced asymmetry to its profile, with the alluvial fan of the Sierra streams shifting the low axis of the valley to the west.

From its headwaters in the Sierra the San Joaquin flows southwest, then northwest through Mammoth Pool Reservoir and Millerton Lake Reservoir (Friant Dam) into the Central Valley. Passing Fresno—a central location in the valley—the river flows to the north and northwest past Merced, Modesto, and Stockton before joining the Sacramento River in the delta east of San Francisco Bay.

Large cattle ranches were the dominant land use in the valley during the Spanish and Mexican periods of its history. Exportable hides and tallow were exchanged for the staples and manufactured goods needed by rancheros. With American conquest and the discovery of gold in the Sierra foothills east of Sacramento at midcentury, the northern end of the valley became the focus of agricultural colonization, especially the navigable waterways of the delta and the bay. Stockton grew up rapidly on the route to the southern mines. A major drought in "cow country" in 1862 and the completion of the Central Pacific, whose western terminus was Sacramento, led in 1869 to the arrival of thousands of settlers. The first railroad in California was actually not the Central Pacific but the San Joaquin Railroad, serving the commercial needs of the north-south valley. The latter line soon amalgamated into the western unit of the first transcontinental rail link (the Central Pacific's name was changed to the Southern

Intensive irrigation of the San Joaquin Valley via the California Aqueduct makes the Central Valley a fruit and vegetable capital. (Jesse Walker)

Pacific). The connection to Los Angeles via the Tehachapi Pass was completed in 1876, opening up the southern part of the valley to outside markets, just as the Stockton–San Francisco outlet opened up the north.

Ranchos were carved up into bonanza wheat farms, and by the 1870s California became the second wheat state in the nation. The process of mechanization of agriculture that has been such a prominent feature in American history was well advanced during the nineteenth century on the large-scale farms of the valley, but it must be remembered that the motive power at the time for the reapers, mowers, and the like was provided by horses. Specialized grain farming soon evolved into what one thinks of as characteristic California-style agriculture: intensively cultivated specialty fruit and vegetable crops. California is the top agricultural state in the nation, and the San Joaquin is the primary agricultural region of the Golden State. Fresno, Kern, and Tulare regularly are the first, second, and third agricultural counties in the United States. The diversity of crops is bewildering and almost as great as the ethnic diversity of the Central Valley's population. Some crops, such as almonds and alfalfa, are found almost everywhere. But specialty crops abound: olives are grown at Lindsay, cherries at Linden, asparagus on the delta, Tokay grapes at Lodi, sweet potatoes at Atwater. Cotton, a dry crop but one that does better with irrigation, is confined to the southern two-thirds of the valley, with the northernmost gins in Merced County.

Environmental issues focus both on water quantity and quality. The Central Valley Project, dating from the 1930s, is the linchpin of a water allocation scheme that redistributes water from the humid Sacramento valley to the thirsty lands of the semiarid San Joaquin. In the most populous state of the nation (2000 population: thirty-four million), and one of the fastest growing, irrigation water for agriculture consumes about 80 percent of

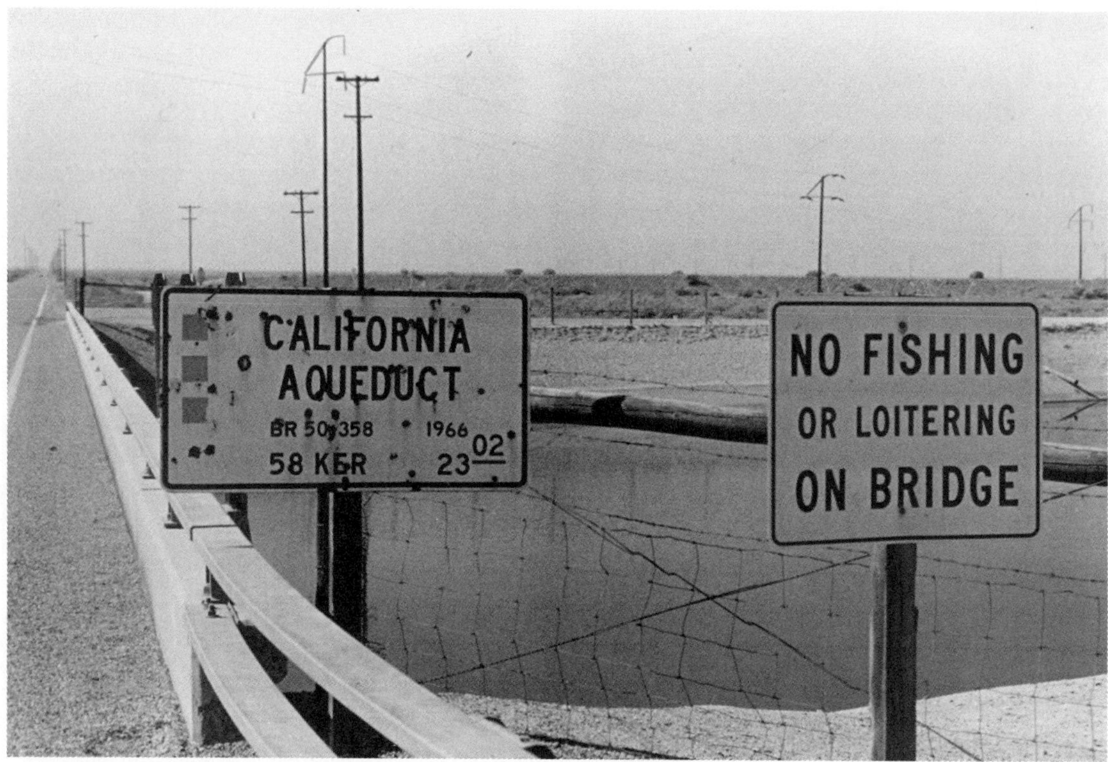

California Aqueduct (Jesse Walker)

the water pumped from California's rivers. Aqueducts take off from the Sacramento–San Joaquin delta and carry water to the south. Politically connected land owners have long had access to subsidized, low-cost water because of the public nature of the projects (there is also a California State Water Project). With demand exceeding supply, free marketeers urge California to create private markets for water with communities outsourcing the management of their water needs to private firms such as American States Water and California Water Service.

The pumping of fossil groundwater, increasingly necessary to make up for deficits, depletes nonrenewable (actually, slowly renewable) water resources and leads to salinization and land slumping. Attempts at water storage, whether underground or above, though well-intentioned in some cases (and even favored by critical analysts of resource use in the water-short West, such as Marc Reisner, author of *Cadillac Desert)*, struggle with the problem of limited supplies facing exploding demands. One of the most widely reported pollution problems was the befouling of the waters of the Kesterson Wildlife Reserve near Los Banos on the west side of the San Joaquin valley. Migratory wildfowl in this preserve, which adjoins the large Westlands Water District, were discovered to be deformed and dying. Two-headed, three-legged, or just plain dead birds have been found along the slough that drains wastewater from the agricultural Central Valley. Excessive fertilization, depletion of underground aquifers, and the deleterious effects of overirrigation of dry soils have led to unanticipated impacts on habitat. A perched water table caused by the presence of impermeable, subsurface clay has resulted in the ponding of irrigation water, whose toxic chemicals (for example, selenium) bioaccumulated in the morbid and necrotic tissues of wildlife. Decreased freshwater reaching the delta leads to saltwater intrusion and loss of habitat. In environmentally conscious California, problems focused on one of the state's major waterways and source of irrigation and drinking water will surely increase in the future.

See also Sacramento
Further Reading: Parsons, James J., "A Geographer Looks at the San Joaquin Valley," *Geographical Review* 76 (1986): 371–389.

SAN JUAN

Source: Southeast corner of Lake Nicaragua
Length: c. 110 miles (177 kilometers)
Tributaries: Frio, San Carlos, Chirripó
Outlet: Caribbean Sea

The waist of the Central American isthmus in southern Nicaragua consists of a diagonal rift occupied in the northwest by the largest freshwater lake between Bolivia and Michigan, and to the southeast by the Río San Juan, connecting the lake to the Caribbean Sea. A short and low divide, the Rivas Isthmus, joins Lake Nicaragua to the Pacific across a rich, fertile volcanic plain whose primary entrepôt is Grenada. The depression is not only situated between two oceans but between two countries, since part of the lower course of the Río San Juan forms the boundary between Nicaragua and Costa Rica.

The lake, river, and sea connections have encouraged actual and imagined transportation routes and trans-isthmian passages. In 1522 the Spanish explorer Gil González Dávila inferred from the fresh water of Lake Nicaragua that it drained to the sea, and he named the stream the *Desaguadero* (today's San Juan), the Spanish term for "outlet." The following year Grenada was founded at the northern end of the lake, and it quickly became a focus of trade and trans-shipment across the region. At the other end of the lake, where the San Juan begins, lies the lake-mouth town of San Carlos. From here the river winds across tropical rain forest, freshwater wetlands, and brackish delta until it reaches the Caribbean near the port of San Juan del Norte.

The Spanish established ports at both ends of the trans-isthmian route, but rivalry with the British and skirmishes with pirates (the two groups abetting one another), plus the hostility of the Miskito Indians, made this passage less useful than the Panamanian route, which eventually carried a canal. With the discovery of gold in the foothills of California's Sierra Nevada in 1848 and the subsequent rush of migration to the west coast, the San Juan–Lake Nicaragua route across the isthmus could potentially save several months over the journey around Cape Horn, but the passage up the river by native craft was dangerous and unhealthy. In 1849 the railroad and shipping magnate Cornelius Vanderbilt opened a shipping route across Nicaragua providing transit between the oceans. The uncomfortable passageway combined shallow-draft dugout canoes (*bongos*), which permitted navigation of the numerous rapids of the San Juan, with lake steamers and horseback. A young San Francisco newspaper man, Samuel Clemens (Mark Twain), took the Nicaraguan route in traveling back East to regale city slickers with his Western tales and yarns.

In the 1980s the border region—long a corridor for exchange of plants, animals, cultures, and peoples—once again received pulses of activity, but this time from warring nations. The socialist Sandinistas' revolution in Nicaragua (1979) and the subsequent Contra guerrilla campaigns led to rivalry in the San Juan river valley. Cross-border attacks, the posting of base camps in enemy territory, and the use of the river to transport supplies and as a staging area all became prominent features in the war between the Nicaraguan Sandinistas and Costa Rican supporters of ARDE (Democratic Revolutionary Alliance). Among the effects of the 1980s war was the increased agricultural colonization of the Costa Rican side of the San Juan and the decreased population of the formerly well settled Nicaraguan side. Because of the sparsity of settlement in the north, Costa Rica had built roads and encouraged colonization of its northern lowlands even before the wars. In the 1980s Nicaragua was fighting wars on two fronts (the larger Contra movement was Honduras-based), so people were relocated from the farming and ranching frontiers of the south. As a result of the war the felling of the tropical rain forest decreased north of the border but increased to the south.

In the 1990s the use of the river for drug and contraband trafficking and continued ecological destruction led to the creation of a binational agency to protect the largest extent of tropical rain forest north of the Amazon. Formally agreed to in 1991 by the presidents of Nicaragua and Costa Rica and the natural resource ministers of those two countries, SIAPAZ (International System of Protected Areas for Peace) seeks to join existing and new parks, reserves, and wildlife refuges in order to preserve the natural environment and the cultural heritage of the San Juan basin.

Further Reading: Girot, Pascal O., and Bernard Q. Nietschmann, "The Río San Juan," *National Geographic Research & Exploration* 8, no. 1 (1992): 52–63.

SÃO FRANCISCO

Source: Serra da Canastra, in southwestern Minas Gerais state, Brazil
Length: c. 1,800 miles (2,900 kilometers)
Tributaries: Velhas, Jequitaí, Paracatu, Urucia, Verde Grande, Corrente, Grande, Pajeú, Moxotó, Ipanema
Outlet: Atlantic Ocean

The tropical giant Brazil encompasses about half the area of South America, and touches every country of the continent except Chile and Ecuador. Its numerous rivers rise in many cases near the escarpment overlooking the sea but flow to the west and north, away from the major coastal concentrations of population. The rivers of the relatively densely settled southeastern plateau drain to the interior, emptying into the Paraná, which by a circuitous route eventually debouches into the Plata past Buenos Aires. The great tributaries of the lower Amazon, the Tocantins and the Xingu, rise in the south (the Tocantins heads up near the federal capital of Brasília) but flow northward and away from the older settlements.

The Rio São Francisco is something of an exception to this pattern and thereby gains its historical significance. The river, the largest flowing entirely within Brazil, originates near the sea and then flow for thousands of miles parallel to the coast. However, its lower course crosses an old settlement region in northeastern Brazil, and the river thus links the *Nordeste* to the southeastern interior. The river rises in southeastern Brazil on the slopes of the Serra da Canastra in southwestern Minas Gerais state (the Portuguese *Serra* = Spanish *Sierra,* meaning "mountain range"). The river traverses the crystalline uplands of the Brazil plateau, passing occasionally an outlier of cemented tabular sandstone. It flows northeastward, then to the southeast across the semiarid *sertão,* or backland, of interior Brazil. In its headwaters it collects a network of tributaries draining half of Minas in a zone of mountains and forests. Along its middle course the river valley narrows as it passes across the Campo Gerais. Downstream from Joazeiro along its lower course the river becomes poor in tributaries, and most of these are intermittent, shown as dashed lines on atlas maps. The river becomes a corridor as it crosses the semidesert of the *caatinga,* a distinctive vegetation consisting of scrub forest. The caatinga—from a Tupi Indian word meaning "white forest"—appears pale and lifeless, but it is well adapted to drought, with its waxy leaves and stems and its defensive thorns.

After making its great bend, the river breaks through the granite escarpment of the coast range, plunging over a series of waterfalls at Paulo Afonso Falls with a total height of approximately 275 feet (85 meters), nearly twice as high as Niagara. From here the river flows to the southeast for about 190 miles (305 kilometers) along the border between the two northeastern states of Alagoas and Bahía to its mouth northeast of Aracaju, the capital of Sergipe state. It is believed that the ancient river probably entered the sea near Cape São Roque, northeast of the great bend, as suggested by the near right-angle bend the river makes near Cabrobó, indicative of river piracy.

The middle course of the São Francisco is navigable for 850 miles (1,368 kilometers), but the lower course is interrupted at three points: (1) the rapids of Pirapóra, (2) near the border of Bahía state, and (3) at the break in the escarpment at Paulo Afonso Falls. Traffic is carried around this last point by a railroad line.

Subject to periodic drought, the interior *sertão*

is traversed by the river most identified with Brazilian national feelings. The backlander is hardy and independent, somewhat nomadic, certainly restless, and attracted by pastoral pursuits. The Rio São Francisco featured prominently in what has been described as Brazil's greatest book, *Os Sertões* (*Rebellion in the Backlands*), by Euclides da Cunha, published in 1902. The story concerns a short-lived rebellion fostered by a religious leader in primitive desert and mountain backwoods communities at the end of the nineteenth century, a rebellion ending in destruction and the death of every man, woman, and child who resisted the military impositions of the new republic (the young author was also to meet a tragic and violent end). In da Cunha's depiction of the resistance of the backland natives at the siege of Canudos in 1896–1897, he managed not only to defend the culture of the people of the sertão against seaboard civilization but also turned what might have been a journalistic account of a military campaign into an epic treatise on geography, geology, climatology, local plants, animals, and the customs and manners of the *vaqueiro.*

With the decline of the sugar plantations of the northeast in the eighteenth century, the São Francisco served as a funnel of migration into the newly opening mining districts of Minas Gerais, which also attracted colonization from the southeastern coastal districts. During this period of frontier settlement along the São Francisco, the *bandeirante,* the Jesuit, and the *vaqueiro* met and mingled, producing a characteristic backlander sensibility. The São Francisco gained its reputation as the great highway of Brazilian civilization, a unifier of the Portuguese-speaking people, and a major conduit of migration.

Brazilians are enthusiastic about the damming of the rivers that cross the country's highland plateau and the creation of large reservoirs for hydroelectric power generation and irrigation of the parched lands of the sertão. One can't blame them for this, especially in the dry backlands where periodic droughts—such as the severe drought of 1877–1879—have devastated communities almost like biblical acts of destruction. The São Francisco valley is today the object of a large-scale river development and control scheme. There is a large dam and impoundment on the upper river upstream from the confluence of the Velhas, and a series of dams and reservoirs are in place along the lower river to furnish water for a fruit and vegetable agricultural region that stands in marked contrast to both traditional pastoralism and the sugar and cotton plantations of a bygone era. The falls of the Paulo Afonso have been harnessed to generate power to improve the economic conditions of a drought-ridden and sparsely settled region.

Further Reading: da Cunha, Euclides, *Rebellion in the Backlands* (*Os Sertões*), Chicago: University of Chicago Press, 1944 (orig. pub. 1902).

SAÔNE

Source: Vosges Mountains, in east-central France, near Épinal
Length: 268 miles (431 kilometers)
Tributaries: Ognon, Doubs
Outlet: **Rhône**, at Lyon

The valley of the Saône, continued south of Lyon as the Rhône, forms a distinctive, elongated depression sometimes called "le Fosse Saône-Rhône." This corridor, running generally north-south between the Massif Central and the Alpine forelands, has long been a line of communications between western Mediterranean shorelands and northwest Europe. As a transport route and traditional gateway, the structural depression has been described as *un vestibule de Nord pour le Midi, du Midi pour le Nord* ("an entranceway of the North for Midi, of Midi for the North").

Although the Saône possesses the unity of features sought by regional geographers, the valley exhibits considerable diversity of traditional *pays* and landscapes. The river begins by collecting a group of headstreams from the southwestern sandstone flanks of the Vosges. Following an exceptionally serpentine course, it receives a number of affluents from the Vosges, notably the left-bank tributary of the Ognon. The major tributary from the Jura is the Doubs, which joins the Saône some 20 miles (32 kilometers) above Chalon-sur-Saône.

Draining from the east, the Doubs has carved a gap between the Vosges and Jura, which forms the traditional means of access between the Rhône-Saône and the German Rhineland past the fortified town of Belfort. The strategic Burgundy Gateway (or Belfort Gap) has been a key control point, from prehistoric times—when a Celtic population from southwestern Germany crossed into France—to the late nineteenth century, when valiant French holders of Belfort endured a lengthy siege during the Franco-Prussian War (1870–1871). The historic region of Burgundy (French Bourgogne) was at different times a kingdom, a duchy, and a county, and is today administered by several French *départements*. Its traditional core has been the Saône River above Lyon because of the fertility of the agriculture in this region.

Between Chalon and Mâcon lie the rich agricultural lands that once helped the rulers of medieval Burgundy become such potent players in western Europe. East of the Saône is the Bresse district, known for its cattle and poultry. Most celebrated in this area of intensive agriculture are the vineyards cultivated on terraces along the sides of hills (*côtes*) west of the Saône. The vines are situated on the south-facing slopes of lowlands flanking the Val de Saône to the northwest. Among the famous vintage wines of Burgundy can be counted the Mâconnais (west of Mâcon), including the renowned Pouilly-Fuissé and Solutré vineyards, and those of Chalon at Givry and Mercurey.

Across the northern end of Burgundy lies the low Langres plateau and an easy crossing by road, rail, or canal to the Paris Basin. The river is connected by canal to the Moselle, Marne, Yonne, and Loire Rivers. Because of its regular and even flow, the Saône receives a substantial amount of commercial traffic, including barges carrying tourists through a region that was arguably once second in economic and political power among French regions only to the fertile, sedimentary plains around the French capital.

See also Rhône
Further Reading: Davenport, William, "Living the Good Life in Burgundy," *National Geographic*, June 1978, pp. 794–817.

SASKATCHEWAN

Source: Confluence of North and South Branches, near Prince Albert in central Saskatchewan
Length: c. 340 miles (550 kilometers)
Tributaries: Carrot (see text for tributaries of branches)
Outlet: Lake Winnipeg

If one considers the Saskatchewan only as the river downstream from the junction of its two branches, it is relatively short and drains only the eastern part of Canada's prairie provinces. The full length of the Bow–South Saskatchewan–Saskatchewan river system, however, stretches from the eastern slopes of the Rocky Mountains to Lake Winnipeg. This enlarged Saskatchewan drainage basin is approximately 1,200 miles (1,930 kilometers) long and represents the primary waterway of the prairie sections of Alberta, Saskatchewan, and Manitoba.

Both branches of the Saskatchewan originate in the sharply uplifted fault-block mountains of the Canadian Rockies in Alberta. The North Saskatchewan River is approximately 760 miles (1,220 kilometers) in length. It rises in the Columbia ice field at the foot of Mt. Saskatchewan in southwestern Alberta. The river flows generally east past Edmonton into Saskatchewan Province and then to Prince Albert, where it joins the South Saskatchewan. Its major tributaries are the Clearwater, Brazeau, Vermilion, and Battle Rivers. The South Saskatchewan, approximately 550 miles (890 kilometers) in length, is formed in southern Alberta by the junction of the Bow and Oldman Rivers. It flows to the east past Medicine Hat, then northeast into Saskatchewan Province, where it receives on its left bank the Red Deer River; then it flows past Saskatoon to Prince Albert. Farther west on the Red Deer, in south-central Alberta, is the city of the same name, approximately halfway between Edmonton on the North Saskatchewan and Calgary on the Bow.

Between the Saskatchewan and the Churchill drainage immediately to the north lies a belt of mixed forest (evergreen conifers and deciduous hardwoods) with much marketable timber. A section of this forest is reserved as the Prince Albert National Park. The river flows eastward past

Nipawin into Manitoba. In this easternmost of the prairie provinces the river enters an extensive lowland of lakes, marshes, and interconnected drainageways, whose irregular and disrupted pattern provides evidence of the effects of Pleistocene glaciation. The river flows through The Pas and then out into Cedar Lake. This relatively large glacial lake is connected by a narrow strait at Grand Rapids to the even larger Lake Winnipeg, at whose southern end is the traditional gateway to the Canadian plains, the cosmopolitan city of Winnipeg. Such an overview of the drainage of the Saskatchewan and the identification of its major settlements show that nearly all of the major cities of the Canadian prairie—Calgary, Edmonton, Red Deer, Saskatoon, and Winnipeg—are located along the river, its affluents, or outlet (the exception is Regina, the capital of Saskatchewan Province).

Early French and British explorers and fur traders penetrated the Canadian prairies along the two branches of the Saskatchewan. Though the river and its headstreams have no navigational value today, in the eighteenth century they were widely used as routes to conduct the fur trade. The British set up posts along the region's waterways, initially administering the territory through the Hudson's Bay Company, then turning over its governance to Canada. It must be remembered that Canada was late in forming compared with the United States (the confederation of four eastern provinces did not occur until 1867), and that Saskatchewan did not become a province until 1905.

The influential Palliser Expedition (1857–1860) made primary use of the north and south branches of the river in exploring the resources of the plains and searching for passes in the western cordillera. Perhaps the most influential finding of the expedition, as publicized in a parliamentary blue book, was that the southern part of the plains along the South Saskatchewan and its tributaries, the Bow and the Red Deer, was barren of trees and therefore less suitable for agriculture than the mixed parklands of aspen groves and prairie meadows growing along the North Saskatchewan in a wide and fertile belt. The arrival of the transcontinental Canadian Pacific Railroad (1882) brought many settlers from the east and later from Europe. Winnipeg became the funnel of the plains, located at its eastern edge, while Calgary and Edmonton increasingly became the gateways for routes crossing the Rockies.

In the years between World War II and the late 1960s, Canada, like its southern neighbor, exhibited a penchant for large water-and-power projects. The South Saskatchewan River scheme may be smaller than California's Central Valley Project, the Columbia Basin Project, or the nearby damming of the Missouri River, but it is similar in conception and purpose. The Gardiner and Qu'Appelle valley dams south of Saskatoon (completed 1967) impound the waters of Lake Diefenbaker for irrigation and hydropower generation. The Grand Rapids Dam at the mouth of the Saskatchewan River also has a power installation. The cost of irrigation has increased, and with low prices for primary agricultural products, large governmental projects in the West now attract the same kind of criticism they receive in the United States.

Further Reading: Campbell, Marjorie W., *The Saskatchewan,* New York: Rinehart and Company, 1950 (Rivers of America Series)

SAVANNAH

Source: Confluence of Tugaloo and Seneca
Length: 314 miles (505 kilometers)
Tributaries: Broad, Brier Creek (for tributaries of the Tugaloo and Seneca, see text)
Outlet: Atlantic Ocean

Along with the Tugaloo, the Savannah forms the political border between the southeastern states of Georgia and South Carolina. Because the river presents similar economic activities and social life on opposing banks, the region is not a culturally divided borderland after the European fashion so much as a straightforward political boundary, with the river anchoring certain of the valley's activities and sites.

The Savannah is one of the major streams draining the Appalachians eastward. The watershed includes portions of North Carolina as well as Georgia and South Carolina. The river proper

The Statue of "The Waving Girl" on the Savannah River waterfront (Jesse Walker)

begins at Hartwell Reservoir, where the Seneca and Tugaloo meet. Above this point the major headstreams include the Keowee River and Twelve Mile Creek (for the Seneca) and Tallulah and Chattooga Rivers (for the Tugaloo). Dams above Augusta and the Fall Line, the boundary between the elevated Piedmont and the low-lying Coastal Plain, include Clark Hill Dam (completed 1954) and Hartwell Dam (1961). In the humid East such multipurpose dams and accompanying reservoirs are designed primarily for flood control, power generation, navigation, and recreation (in the dry West, irrigation is usually the priority).

Georgia came into existence as a downcoast extension of the South Carolina Low Country around Charleston. Rice was intensively cultivated there on slave-worked plantations reclaimed from the wetland margins of tidal rivers. Georgia in the early Colonial period was defined as the region southward from the Savannah River to the Altamaha River. Settlement clung to the river-mouth site of Savannah, which quickly became a plantation region rivaling Charleston. Not until Georgia enters the history books with the arrival of James Oglethorpe (1733) and its adoption of the modified name of the British monarch George II does settlement make its way up the Savannah River into the interior.

Major interior cities in the southeastern states often lie along the Fall Line, and this site characteristic is especially notable in towns established during the Colonial period. Augusta, Georgia, is located at the head of navigation on the Savannah River, where the river literally falls from the crystalline Piedmont onto the sedimentaries to the south and east. An important industrial city, Augusta has harnessed the energy of the falling river to drive its mills, whether grist and lumber mills in the early period or textile mills more recently. The city serves as a trade center for a broad band of counties in Georgia and South Carolina known as the Central Savannah River Area. Embedded in the resistant metamorphic rocks of the Piedmont are Carolina slates, which erode more easily to form broad basins conveniently used as reservoir sites above Augusta. The assemblage of nuclear fuel reactors—the Savannah River Plant (now Site)—is located 25 miles (40 kilometers) southeast of Augusta, adjacent to the river south of Aiken, South Carolina.

Environmental concerns about the Savannah River focus on the effects of the Piedmont dams, potential contamination caused by the nuclear fuel plants, and any further damage to the coastal marsh as a result of renewed dredging of the Savannah port. Water-quality problems include pollution from specific, identifiable industrial sources, as well as nonpoint sources such as forestry, agriculture, and urban development.

Nutrients washed into the river lead to low dissolved oxygen levels, resulting in harm to fisheries. Sediments cloud the water and obtrude biological systems. The dams above the Fall Line trap sediments and release cold water in large discharges, damaging fish and sometimes leading to large kills. The estuary of the coastal zone is particularly vulnerable to alterations in discharge and sediment caused by these dams.

The Savannah River Site (SRS) represents an approximately 325-square-mile (842-square-kilometer) area along the Savannah River on the upper coastal plain. Commissioned by the Atomic Energy Commission in 1950 to produce weapons-grade plutonium and tritium for national defense, the site comprises five reactors where materials are irradiated with neutrons, as well as supporting chemical separation plants, a water extraction plant, and waste management facilities. Production of weapons materials ended in the late 1980s, when the five production reactors were shut down; the plant today is primarily involved in waste processing and environmental restoration. Westinghouse replaced Du Pont as the principal contractor in the late 1980s, and the name was changed from the Savannah River Plant to the SCS. At that time the area was deemed a Superfund site, joining a list of the most dangerously polluted locations in the United States. Nuclear plants require large amounts of cooling water for their operation, and that is the primary reason to locate near rivers. Leaking or discharge of radioactive materials from the Savannah plants is a constant threat, though less so now that the reactors have been shut down. Also of concern is the long-term potential of raising the localized temperature of surface and groundwater (thermal pollution).

The Army Corps of Engineers—inveterate dam builders and harbor dredgers—have proposed deepening the channel to the port of Savannah, located near the mouth of the river. The Savannah National Wildlife Refuge and several coastal fisheries would be negatively affected by such a move. Deepening the channel would increase saltwater intrusion, causing seawater to advance farther upstream, with a damaging effect on the refuge's freshwater marshes—an essential habitat for many species. Increased salinity threatens to wipe out the shortnose sturgeon and the striped bass. Charleston, South Carolina, is engaged in major harbor expansions, as is Jacksonville, Florida, and it is wondered whether all these harbors need to accommodate the newest megaships. The engineering costs for Savannah would be high, since the port does not have a natural deep-water harbor so much as a shallow, dredged river mouth.

Further Reading: Stokes, Thomas L., *The Savannah,* New York: Rinehart, 1951 (Rivers of America Series).

SCHELDT

Source: Aisne department, in northern France
Length: c. 270 miles (435 kilometers)
Tributaries: Scarpe, Leie, Dender, Rupel
Outlet: North Sea, via Wester Schelde estuary

The various rivers composing the Scheldt (Dutch and Flemish: *Schelde;* French: *Escaut*) drainage system flow more or less parallel across the Flanders Plain and central Belgium. The greater part of the course of the Scheldt, including its tributaries and subtributaries, trend southwest to northeast, approximately paralleling the North Sea coast. The upper Scheldt and the Leie (French: Lys), the latter the most northern and the most important affluent, cross French Flanders into Belgium following a northerly path that is almost at right angles to the west-to-east course of the middle Scheldt.

The old industrial town of Ghent (Flemish: *Gent;* French *Gand*) lies at the confluence of the Leie and the Scheldt. The rivers meet in the southeast of the city, which is crossed by many minor rivers and canals. With hundreds of bridges, and the built-up area of the city lying on twenty-three islands, the town resembles nothing so much as a northern Venice.

The river heads eastward to Antwerp, a major port and the largest city of Belgium, lying on the east bank of the river just beyond its confluence with the Rupel. The river turns sharply to the north past the city, which is situated at the river's most easterly elbow. The Scheldt flows 58 miles (93 kilometers) to its outlet on the Wester Schelde, with its delta forming the western part of the great Rhine-Meuse-Scheldt delta, stretching from Flanders to the Danish Straits. More than half of the estuary downstream from Antwerp lies in Dutch territory: thus arises the long, difficult story of "the Scheldt question." For many years the Dutch tried to cripple the trade of Antwerp by denying maritime access to the port. The lower Scheldt was therefore closed from 1648 to 1792. Not until 1863 was the Dutch right to levy tolls on the traffic of the lower river bought out by Belgium and other interested countries. This rivalry was a modern instance of a long-standing struggle for control of Flanders and the Scheldt basin by West European powers not confined to the nations of the Low Countries. Just as Antwerp surpassed Bruges, located on the silting river Zwin, so Amsterdam surmounted Antwerp in its financial and market innovations as well as the broader trade it tapped—most notably after 1595, when the first Dutch fleet reached the Indies and attached the Moluccas and adjoining islands to their overseas empire (today's Indonesia). The Wester Schelde is today dredged to allow deep-water access in its western part, known as the Honte, to the docks and quays of Antwerp.

Inland waterway traffic up and down the Scheldt connects via canals to major drainages in northern France and Belgium. The Albert Canal links Antwerp to the Sambre-Meuse coal furrow and industrial concentration of southern Belgium at its eastern end. The chalk ridge of Artois is traversed by the Saint-Quentin Canal, joining the Scheldt at Cambrai, France, to the Seine system via the Oise Lateral Canal. The Mons-Condé Canal joins the western end of the southern Belgium–northeastern France industrial region to the French Scheldt at Condé. In France the river and its tributaries are served by an intensive network of transverse canals interlinking each other and the primary tributaries of the Lys and the Scarpe; thus barges can move to the southeast from Calais and Dunkirk as far as the Scheldt, following a line parallel to, but a short distance inland from, the Belgian frontier. Thereby they serve the Lille industrial district (on the Deûle Canal joining the Scarpe and Lys) and the numerous agricultural *pays* and industrial zones of northeastern France.

See also Meuse, Rhine
Further Reading: "Treaties to Protect Maas and Scheldt River Signed by Dutch, French and Belgian officials (Remediating Troubled Waters: Legal, Political and Institutional Frameworks)," *Ekistics: The Problems and Science of Human Settlements* 62, no. 370–372 (January–June 1995): 109.

SEINE

Source: Langres Plateau, Côte d'Or department, in northern Burgundy
Length: c. 480 miles (772 kilometers)
Tributaries: Aube, Yonne, Loing, **Marne**, Oise, Eure
Outlet: English Channel

Although not one of the great rivers of the world by virtue of its length, France's Seine, like England's Thames, attains significance as the primary commercial artery and the cultural and political center of a nation.

The Seine's headwaters lie on a limestone plateau joining the ancient masses of the Vosges and the Morvan in the northern part of southeastern France. The source is at the northern end of the Saône basin, not too far from the headwaters of some of its primary affluents, including the Marne and the Aube. The river rises as a spring bubbling to the surface in a grove of fir northwest of Dijon; the spot is identified for tourists by a statue of the goddess Sequana. According to myth, the river was formed by the tears of a nymph pursued by a lecherous satyr into this grove on the Plateau of Langres. Still searched for by lovers and day-trippers in quest of its romantic and inspirational associations, the source is technically in Paris, since the site was purchased in the nineteenth century by the Paris Commune and made a part of the city.

The Seine trickles from its source across forest and meadowlands. In hot summers it is no more than a string of small puddles. In extremely dry periods the bed of the river can be dry as far downstream as Châtillon. The permeable lime-

Eighteenth-century engraving of Paris as viewed from the Pont Royal. Many of the palaces and large residences (hôtels) on or near the Seine River have been converted into museums. (Giraudon/Art Resource, NY)

stone of the upper valley swallows up the river's flow in places, and the springs breaking out in the deeply cut valley floor represent the sources of the river as much as any particular spring identified for tourists.

The river flows generally to the northwest through Champagne, past Troyes, where Joan of Arc girded the reluctant French king Charles VII to attack the English. Upon receiving one its few left-bank tributaries, the Yonne, it enters the Paris Basin, the heartland of the French nation. The capital city stands in the center of a bowl-shaped basin of sedimentary rocks, which by differential erosion form a concentric pattern of rings consisting of resistant eastward-facing scarps (*côtes*) and more easily worn valleys or plains. The Champagne region, producing a distinctive grape used to produce the famous sparkling wine, actually comprises several subunits of the low-lying plains to the east of Paris (*champagne* in French means "field," from which comes the sports term "champion," originally referring to an outstanding field performance, as in track and field).

The historic Île-de-France, domain of the Capetian monarchy, represents the fertile, innermost agricultural ring in the sedimentary basin. Paris is not located so much at the bottom of a bowl as in a low point of the drainage pattern. The Marne, the longest tributary, joins the river just above Paris, and the Oise just below. The river bisects the capital: hence the right- or left-bank designations of its landmarks and districts. The banks of the river in Paris are concreted and lined with wharves and quays (and today high-speed roadways).

A large island in the river, the Île de la Cité is the site of the sublime medieval edifice of Notre Dame Cathedral as well as the city's judicial and administrative center. It was here that Julius Caesar defeated a fierce Celtic population that had been using the island as a fishing place. Caesar conquered this village because he needed the river-ford site to control the lower Seine. The Roman town established on the Île de la Cité, known as Letetia Parisiorum, soon spread to the left bank, which grew under subsequent rulers. The left bank became the haunt of students, teachers, and universities in the Middle Ages, especially the Latin Quarter, the oldest part of Paris except for the river island site. The larger area of the right bank, by contrast, became the center of business activity and amusements. The story of the "City of Light," so called for the brilliant illumination of its broad avenues and numerous monuments, as well as for its intellectual leadership, cannot of course be told here, but it might be noted that one cannot think of the city apart from the river that serves it. Significantly, the coat of arms of the city of Paris is that of the Seine boatman's guild.

The Seine has not just brought civilizing influences to this former Gallic fishing village. It carries a large amount of cargo, especially from ships going to and fro between the seaports of Le Havre and Rouen and the French capital. The river is navigable for river tugs below Bur-sur-Seine and for ocean shipping as far as Rouen. A system of canals links the Seine with the Scheldt, Meuse, Rhine, Rhône, and Loire Rivers. It should be noted that many of these are shallow and were designed in former times, and so are more often used today to transport tourists than cargoes of coke or steel. The lower Seine is known for its broad meanders, some of which have been cut across for purposes of saving time for the barges that ply these waters. A number of towns lie along the lower Seine in a stretch of river described by Napoleon I as the "main street of a single city." The Seine is the most navigable of French rivers because of its low gradient, the permeability of the region's soils (thus reducing runoff), and the staggered flood stages of its principal affluents. Though Paris is located some 110 miles (177 kilometers) from its outlet on the English Channel (the French prefer the name La Manche), the river distance is actually about twice that length on account of meandering.

The Seine below Paris forms a series of wide meanders incised 300 feet (91 meters) or more below the surface of the chalk plateau. As the river meanders, bordering meadows alternate sides of the river, broaden, and become seamed with drainage channels as the estuary is reached. The river widens considerably below the port of Rouen, though it is still embanked by prominent bounding walls. The broad estuary opens to the west between Le Havre and Trouville, where it is nearly 9 miles (14 kilometers) across. The old seaport of Rouen, where Joan of Arc was burned at the stake and her ashes (and unconsumed heart, according to legend) were thrown into the nearby river, is situated along the right bank of a large meander on a terrace above the river, and therefore immune from all but the most exceptional flooding. Some 80 miles (129 kilometers) from the sea, Rouen takes in less trade than Le Havre, which developed as an outport of the older inland city and benefited from the silting of the river below Rouen. Le Havre, the second-largest port of France, has as a site the northern shore of the Seine estuary to the southeast of Cap de la Hève. Until the sixteenth century the area was an arm of coastal marshes from which its docks were excavated. The young United States shipped much of its agricultural products—cotton, sugar, and tobacco—to Le Havre for distribution to the rest of Europe. Pummeled by both German and Allied military raids and bombings during World War II, the port of Le Havre was rebuilt, with its manmade harbor constructed of dikes and breakwaters extending into the estuary of the river.

See also Marne
Further Reading: McCarry, Charles, "The Civilizing Seine," *National Geographic,* April 1982, pp. 478–511.

SÉNÉGAL

Source: Confluence of Bafing and Bakoy, in southwestern Mali
Length: c. 1,000 miles (1,609 kilometers)
Tributaries: Falémé
Outlet: Atlantic Ocean

The two headstreams of one of the largest rivers in West Africa come together in the southwestern corner of the jigsaw-puzzle-shaped country of Mali. Both streams rise in the Fouta Djallon plateau, an important watershed and political divide in northern Guinea. From the confluence the river flows generally northward, then to the west to its Atlantic outlet near the old colonial port of St. Louis. The Sénégal forms the political boundary between the country of the same name and Mauritania, while its chief tributary, the Falémé, forms the Sénégal-Mali border.

Reached by the Portuguese explorer Bartholomew Diaz in 1445, the sandy mouth of the river did not attract permanent settlement until the mid-seventeenth century, when the French founded Saint-Louis, the first French settlement in West Africa and the tropical port nearest to Europe. Shifting sandbanks and a wide variation in water level between wet and dry seasons limited the use of the river for navigation. French interest in exploring the entire length of the valley and attaching interior lands to French West Africa was retarded until the mid-nineteenth century, at which time Gallic enthusiasm for new territories was spurred on by British competition as much as the need for tropical exports to the mother country. Many of the Muslim remnants of the once vast Songhai Empire proved difficult to conquer, especially on the Fouta Djallon plateau. Even with these successes, it was only late in the nineteenth century that the French colonial office showed an interest in the inclusion of the region into what emerged in 1904 as the Federation of French West Africa, which comprised four coastal settlements—Senegal, French Guinea (today's Guinea), the Ivory Coast (Côte d'Ivoire), and Dahomey (Benin)—and four hinterland districts: Mauritania, French Sudan (Chad), Upper Volta (Burkina Faso), and Niger.

The river is navigable during the rainy season as far as Kayes, Mali. This strategically located town became important because of its link to the upper and middle Niger River valley—the core area of French imperial interest in interior West Africa. Below some low falls the river's gradient is very gentle, and during floods the river spreads out widely across the lower river and broad delta. Distributary channels (*marigots*) are a feature of the Sénégal. The lower river regularly fills or receives water from Lakes Guiers and Rkiz.

Rice, cotton, and groundnuts (peanuts) are grown widely in the valley. Groundnuts are well adapted to light, sandy soils and do not require irrigation, a significant factor in the semiarid belt of the Sahel traversed by the river. Heavier textured soils are more suitable for cotton, a competing cash crop, while rice functions primarily to feed the local population.

St. Louis has long since been superseded by the better-situated port at Senegal's capital city of Dakar. Below St. Louis the river flows in a broad channel for 20 miles (32 kilometers) behind a sand spit called Lange de Barbarie before emptying into the sea. The location of the old port was mostly the choice of French general Faidherbe in 1854, who sought to make the Sénégal the line of advance into the interior for imperial strategic reasons. He needed the site for a headquarters.

See also Gambia

SEVERN

Source: Cambrian Mountains, in central Wales
Length: c. 200 miles (322 kilometers)
Tributaries: Vyrnwy, Stour, Teme, Avon, Wye
Outlet: Bristol Channel

A beloved river draining eastern Wales and western England rises on the eastern slope of the Plynlimon plateau of the Cambrian Mountains. Generations of British schoolchildren have learned that the sources of the Wye (Welsh: *Gwy*) and Severn (Welsh: *Hafren*) lie less than a mile apart, but since the rivers flow in opposite directions they do not meet until reaching the Severn estuary.

The Severn flows to the northeast and east to Shrewsbury. The river in this highland region noted for its trout winds across broad vales within sight of small wooded hills that stand back from the valley. The upper river enters the flat-floored trench of the Vale of Powis, deepened by the action of glaciers, which contains a sizable agricultural population and several small towns, the largest being Welshpool. On leaving this valley, the Severn receives its major mountain tributary, the Vyrnwy. The river makes a large horseshoe bend around the old market town of Shrewsbury, almost reversing its course and subsequently flowing southwestward as a result of a combination of river piracy and glacial action. The easterly course of the upper Severn below the Vyrnwy confluence was once continued to the north by the Trent. The ancestral Dee extended itself southward, capturing not only the river that now forms its upper mountainous course but also the Severn. During the Ice Ages a moraine dam was thrown across the north-flowing river and dammed up its waters, which collected in the Shropshire basin until, having cut an overspill outlet at Ironbridge Gorge, the river escaped south and thereby completed the nearly continuous semicircular course of the present-day Severn.

A long north-south section of the valley extends from Shrewsbury to Tewkesbury, the latter at the junction from the left of the "Shakespeare," or Upper Avon. The Upper Avon drains a broad area eastward to Warwickshire (the Lower Avon empties into the Bristol Channel at Avonmouth). The right-bank tributary of the Teme, which joins the Severn farther upstream at Worcester, drains a large area of the Welsh border. These two affluents with large drainage basins contribute to making the Severn the largest river in southwestern Britain. It is an important transportation route and is connected by canal to the Trent, Mersey, Thames, and other rivers.

At Tewkesbury the river turns southwest toward its estuary. This alignment follows the northeast-southwest trend between the Cotswold escarpment and outliers of the Welsh highlands. Gloucester is the largest city in the lower valley and is situated at the lowest convenient bridging point of the Severn. The river meanders so much below Gloucester that a canal has been constructed to enable seagoing vessels to reach the city directly from the estuary. Because of the funnel shape of the estuary, rising tides force a wall of water, the famous Severn Bore, up the shallow, narrow lower basin, making necessary enclosed dock basins at Avonmouth and Chepstow. A railroad tunnel was opened as early as 1886 under the estuary to provide a more direct link from London to south Wales and avoid the roundabout route through Gloucester. The Severn Road Bridge, one of the world's longest suspension bridges at 3,240 feet (988 meters), also crosses the estuary. Entering from the west is the Wye affluent, which drains the border region west of Hereford. William Wordsworth's well-known pastoral poem "Lines Written a Few Miles above Tintern Abbey" was inspired by the Romantic poet's revisit to the Wye valley early in his career.

See also Trent

Further Reading: Bradley, A. G., *The Rivers and Streams of England,* London: Bracken Books, 1993 (orig. pub. 1909); Rowbotham, Fred, *The Severn Bore,* Newton Abbot: David and Charles, 1970.

SHANNON

Source: Cuilcagh Mountains, County Cavan, Republic of Ireland
Length: c. 240 miles (390 kilometers)
Tributaries: Black, Suck
Outlet: Atlantic Ocean

The Shannon (Gaelic: *An tSionainn*) is not only the longest river in Ireland, it is also the longest in the British Isles. The terrain of Ireland has been compared to a saucer with a central depression and upturned edges. The Shannon rises in the uplands of northwest County Cavan—on the edge of the saucer—not far from Sligo Bay. It flows to the south and west along a course that drains the western portion of the Central Plain (the saucer's depression). A series of lakes, or loughs, represent expansions of the river's channel.

For about half its length the Shannon forms the boundary between the western province of Connaught and the eastern province of Leinster. The river valley includes a diversity of land types and uses, including farmland, pasture, and peat bogs. Ireland's major river flows mostly over a slightly undulating surface of Paleozoic limestone on which has been plastered glacial drift of variable thickness. The river traverses black peat bogs, with *Calluna* dominant, elsewhere passing contrasting winding ridges of glacial materials that stand out as bright-green dry sites. The limey waters of the lakes and adjoining marshes are colonized by calcium-adapted plants and animals. In the marshes *Juncus subnodulosus* and *Cladium* are the dominant vegetation, rather than peat. The ubiquitous peat of former days is rarely used today to heat homes, but at Shannonbridge, a small market town at the mouth of the Suck River, a power station utilizes milled peat as fuel. The river and lakes abound in salmon and trout, and the fishery is still important.

Within a few miles of its source the river enters

Lough Allen, an elongated lake basin between the Bralieve Mountains and the Slieve Anierin–Benbrack range of hills. In the eighteenth and early nineteenth centuries the river was canalized and, with the aid of short canals, was made navigable for light vessels to Lough Allen. In the years 1846–1859 a canal was dug below Lough Allen to link the Shannon to the Erne. The town of Carrick-on-Shannon is 9 miles (14 kilometers) below Lough Allen, where a string of small lakes occupies a portion of the floodplain. Along the lowlands and around the lake shores are found the meadows, or "callows," prone to regular inundation that were the traditional homes of Irish smallholders and tenants who have long since left. The Shannon pursues a wayward course toward Loughs Ree and Derg. The river is joined from the east by the Royal Canal, linking Dublin with the Shannon through Mullingar. Farther downstream the Grand Canal also provides access to eastern Ireland. Exiting island-studded Lake Derg, replete with seabirds, the river attains a sufficient increase in gradient to make possible the establishment of the Shannon hydroelectric scheme below Killaloe. The seaport of Limerick, the valley's major city, is located at the head of a 60-mile-long (97-kilometer-long) estuary. The tidal river turns west at this point en route to the distant Shannon mouth. Formerly the first landfall for North Atlantic air routes, Shannon Airport (Gaelic: *Aerfort na Sirnanne*) lies about three-fourths of the way up the estuary due west of Limerick. It is today an international airport and a prosperous duty-free industrial zone.

See also Boyne, Liffey

SHARI

See Chari

SHATT AL ARAB

Source: Confluence of the **Tigris** and **Euphrates**, in southeastern Iraq
Length: 120 miles (193 kilometers)
Tributary: Karun
Outlet: Persian Gulf

The waters of the Tigris and Euphrates gave life to the ancient civilizations of Mesopotamia, literally the land between the rivers. Some five thousand years ago these two great rivers of southwestern Asia flowed separately into the Persian Gulf (which Arabs prefer to call the Arabian Gulf). Because of siltation at the head of the gulf, the rivers now meet at Al Qurnah, just above Basra, Iraq, and flow together in a generally southeasterly direction as the Shatt al Arab.

Withdrawal of water upstream for dams and irrigation and the inevitable loss of water caused by high evaporation in a desert environment have resulted in the flow of the Tigris and Euphrates being much reduced. But below their confluence, discharge is augmented by the Karun, a major tributary, entering in a long and winding course from Iran, where its source lies in the Zagros Mountains. Because the Shatt al Arab is influenced by the tides on the gulf, water levels are deep enough to allow oceangoing vessels access to the port of Basra, which is 60 miles (95 kilometers) inland.

The lower course of the conjoined rivers is actually the main course of a complex delta consisting of numerous marshes, channels, lakes, and islands. Some of the distributaries have been dammed to regulate the river's flow, yet extensive marshlands and large lakes, most notably Hor al Hammar, still remain.

The myriad lakes and marshes provide a refuge for a way of life dating back to antiquity. The "Marsh Arabs" (their name for themselves is *Ma 'dan*) depend on the river and its resources in their capacities as buffalo herders, rice cultivators, mat weavers, and fishermen. In the region above Basra they harvest date palm and other crops, but *qasab,* or giant reeds, are the mainstay of their economy. Growing up to 20 feet (6 meters) high, these reeds are cut, chopped, then used to provide food for the people and their livestock, as well as fuel and materials for weaving mats and constructing reed houses. The material is also used to build the indispensable reed boats with which the Marsh Arabs navigate the maze of waterways.

The political complications of the Shatt al Arab, whose lower course forms part of the boundary between Iraq and Iran, have nothing really to do with shifting channels or even water-resource conflicts. Rather, problems arise from the need to agree to a boundary in what had been, until the mid-nineteenth century, a broad zone of transition between two different cultures and traditions. Petroleum development in the twentieth century only aggravated a boundary dispute that the British had tried to resolve in the previous century.

As background it must be remembered that the British East India Company established an agency (called a "factory") in Basra as early as 1639. British attempts to extend lines of access by river steamboats up the Shatt al Arab and up the Tigris to Baghdad were frustrated by the lack of a clear line of demarcation between Ottoman Turkey's territory and that of Persia (today's Iran). Under strong prodding from the British and the Russians, the Treaty of Erzerum (1847) was accepted by the two countries that lay astride the critical waterway. By terms of the agreement, Ottoman Turkey (including Syria and Iraq) and Persia (Iran) both enjoyed free and unrestricted use of the Shatt al Arab. For much of the length of the river Ottoman Turkish sovereignty extended to the east bank of the river, while Persian control began at that point. Because of the location of a number of islands at the head of the gulf, Persia also gained sovereignty of Abadan Island, which is today a major Iranian oil terminal and shipping point. Since the Iranian city of Khorramshahr lay at the mouth of the left-bank tributary of the Karun, it was granted to Persia. However, 10 miles (16 kilometers) above Khorramshahr both banks of the Shatt al Arab became Turkish territory by the 1847 agreement, as well as the entire course of the Tigris. Numerous conflicts have been fought, at least partially, over this nineteenth-century border, most notably the Iran-Iraq War of 1980–1988, yet the Erzerum line remains substantially in effect today.

One of the problems of the old agreement line was that it was drawn without consideration of the distribution of people's languages or religions. The population on both sides of the Shatt al Arab are generally Arabs (like the Iraqis), but Shiite Muslims (like the Iranians). Persia gained access to the waterways at the head of the gulf but complained that most of the territory of the Shatt al Arab was in Iraqi hands. The Iraqis in turn felt that their Arab kinsmen on the eastern side of the river, in what they called Arabistan (Iranian Khuzistan), were cut off from their rightful country. It is significant that one of the first acts of the Iran-Iraq War in 1980 was the Iraqi invasion of Khuzistan.

The British discovery of oil in southwest Iran in 1908 and in Iraq in 1923 accentuated the poorly drawn boundary. Both the search for oil and its subsequent development and transportation required river transportation on the Shatt al Arab. Almost inevitably, the nascent country of Iraq (founded 1932) and the modern country of Iran would dispute old settlement lines that had been forced upon them almost a hundred years before. In 1937 Iraq and Iran accepted the *thalweg,* or line of greatest depth of water, near the port of Abadan. This port, opened in 1912, is today, with its refineries, one of the largest oil-processing and -loading facilities in the world. Except for specifying more carefully the situation of Khorramshahr and Abadan, the 1937 treaty left the river boundary where it had been placed by the treaty of Erzerum.

The political instability of the post–World War II period contributed to the problems of the riverine border. The rise and fall of the Shah of Iran and the accession to power in Iraq of the socialist Baathist party led by Saddam Hussein were not conducive to making amicable agreements about the river. There was a need to dredge a deep-water channel for the new tankers, but because of political enmity, both countries resorted to building larger and larger oil facilities *away* from the Shatt al Arab. Iran constructed new terminals on Khor Musa, an inlet of the Gulf that lay to the east of the Shatt al Arab, and later on Kharg Island, a small island in the northwestern gulf. Iraq dredged a new port south of Basra at al-Faw for exporting crude oil, and then built a new terminal at Khor Al-Amaya on an artificial island west of the river mouth connected by submarine pipeline to the mainland.

Although conflicts over scarce water resources have not been important in the geopolitical tensions and conflicts just discussed, the increased withdrawal for irrigation on the Tigris and Euphrates may increase the salinity of the Shatt al Arab and not only undermine the marsh habitat by that most common problem of modern deltas—salt water intrusion—but also potentially increase conflicts over reduced flow of sweet water (fresh water) in civilization-nourishing Mesopotamia and the adjacent region of the Shatt al Arab.

See also Euphrates, Tigres
Further Reading: Melamid, Alexander, "The Shatt Al Arab Boundary Dispute," *Middle East Journal* 22, no. 3 (summer 1968): 351–357.

SHENANDOAH

Source: In Augusta County, Virginia, near Steeles Tavern
Length: c. 150 miles (241 kilometers)
Tributaries: North River, Middle River, South River, North Fork, South Fork
Outlet: **Potomac**, at Harpers Ferry, West Virginia

Oh, Shenandoah, it's far I wander,
Away, you rolling river!
Oh, Shenandoah, it's far I wander,
Away, we're bound to go,
'Cross the wide Missouri!
—Anonymous song

Upstream from the town of Front Royal, Virginia, rise two parallel branches or forks separated by the forested slopes of the Massanutten Mountains. The South Fork is the larger, but the main road since Colonial times (today's Interstate 81) follows the North Fork past Harrisonburg. Below the confluence of the two forks, the Shenandoah is only 55 miles (89 kilometers) long, and even counting its major headstream (the South Fork), the length increases by only a factor of three, so this river of Virginia and West Virginia, rich in history and legend, is not long by the standards of the great rivers of the world.

The main stream of the river that inspired a beloved American folk song of the same name flows northeasterly in a broad, limestone-floored depression between the Blue Ridge and the folded mountains of the Allegheny Mountains. The surrounding slopes rise thousands of feet above the valley and offer spectacular overlooks of fertile agricultural land traversed by a widely meandering river, especially as viewed from Skyline Drive in Shenandoah National Park to the east. Technically, the Shenandoah valley is only the watershed of the Shenandoah River, extending as far south as Steeles Tavern, Virginia, site of the farm and shop of the Virginia-born reaper manufacturer Cyrus McCormick. Since a similar landscape continues to the southwest through Lexington and Roanoke, a more encompassing description of the valley is sometimes used.

Tributaries draining from the northwest are long and tortuous, while tributaries from the southeast tend to be short and direct. It is presumed that this asymmetry is a result of river piracy: a series of streams that flowed northwest to southeast have been captured by the main branch of the Shenandoah, which eroded more easily along the weaker limestone belt. The breaks in the Blue Ridge on the eastern side of the Shenandoah valley, as at Snickers, Ashby, and Manassas Gaps, are interpreted as evidence of the former courses of southeasterly flowing streams. The river is shallow and interrupted by rapids, so it has no commercial value for navigation. The vertical drop of the river has been harnessed at several locations for the production of hydroelectric power. The conspicuous meanders of the river above Front Royal have been incised into the broad floor of the valley, so that the river is more often than not hidden from sight.

The land beyond the Blue Ridge represented one of the first and most promising American frontiers. As in many later trans-Appalachian regions, fertile soils were tapped in the production of the most important cash crop, wheat. Forming part of the Great Valley of the Appalachians, extending all the way from Pennsylvania to Tennessee, the Shenandoah was a key link in the interior migration route originating in southeastern Pennsylvania; it followed the Great Valley to the south and west through Maryland and Virginia into the upland Southern states of Kentucky and Tennessee. Many early valley settlers were German,

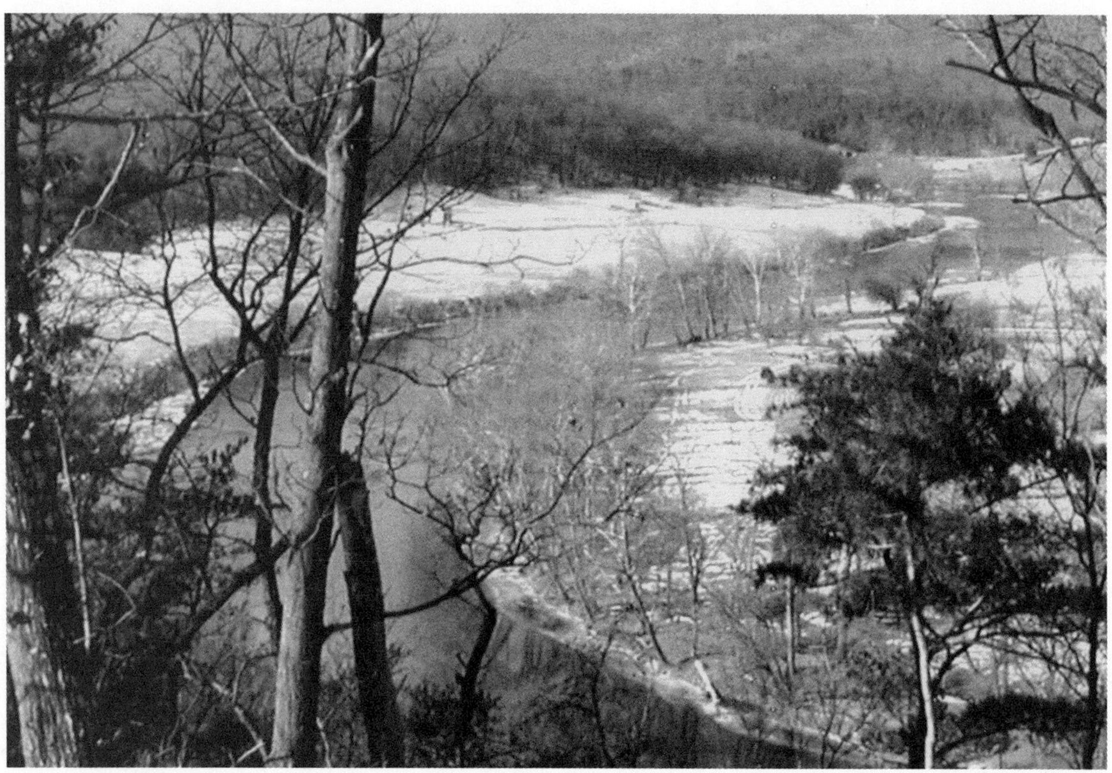

Three Bends overlook, Shenandoah State Park, Virginia (Laura Penn)

English, or Scotch-Irish, coming from or through Pennsylvania. Although stereotypical associations between national groups and agricultural practices have been refined by modern scholarship (Germans don't *always* make the best farmers and end up on the best land), it cannot be doubted that immigrant groups, especially continental Europeans, contributed importantly to the prosperity and success of this newly settled region. Land acquisitions by eastern Virginians of English background in the lower (northern) valley, however, must be emphasized.

By 1750 Winchester had established itself as the primary service center of the lower valley, while Staunton assumed that role in the upper valley; the road south to Roanoke had yet to be cleared. Livestock, tobacco, wheat, hemp, and local manufacturing were important economic elements on the eve of the American Revolution. The nation's first president had close associations with the Shenandoah valley, especially the counties of Winchester and Frederick. When Lord Fairfax received a royal grant of 5,000,000 acres (2,023,472 hectares) of land in the valley, a callow youth of sixteen from a good eastern Virginia family—George Washington—helped survey the estate. During the French and Indian War, Colonel Washington was posted for three years at Winchester, which was Virginia's frontier garrison. At Washington's urging, three of his younger brothers settled in the valley (he, of course, inherited the Mount Vernon estate on the Potomac after the death of his half-brother).

During the Civil War the valley was the scene of numerous battles, as Confederate and Union armies successively occupied the region. Stonewall Jackson made control of the valley, a valuable storehouse for the Confederacy, the object of his "valley campaign" of 1862. Lee retreated through here after defeats at Antietam (1862) and

Gettysburg (1863). Following up on Union victories late in the war, General Philip Sheridan laid waste to the valley (1864–1865) in a manner reminiscent of Sherman's better-known depredations in Georgia and the Carolinas.

In contrast to the heavily urbanized Eastern Seaboard nearby, the Shenandoah valley is still a lovely, rural region, and its clear rivers and peaceful vistas lift the heart of harried city dwellers temporarily away from their homes and workplaces. Eighteenth-century Colonial farmhouses and church spires dot the valley. Though clean rivers and attractive scenery lure the visitor or tourist as they beckoned to the early settler, environmental problems threaten the river's health. In the 1970s, workers at the Du Pont nylon factory in Waynesboro (on the South Fork) discovered pools of mercury that had been dumped during manufacturing processes decades before and that had been leached into the streambed, making fish dangerous to eat in quantity. It was then discovered that Avtex Fibers, a subsequently closed rayon factory, had released carcinogenic polychlorinated biphenyls (PCBs), making fish unfit for any consumption. The rich agricultural fields of the valley—with grain, beef and dairy cattle, orchards, and poultry houses—contribute to silt and nutrients that threaten to cloud and overenrich the river's waters, leading to eutrophication, oxygen depletion, and algal blooms. Though hardly the Rhine or even the Potomac in its level of pollution, constant monitoring and enforcement of environmental laws are in order in this classic American region.

See also Potomac

Further Reading: Davis, Julia, *The Shenandoah,* New York: Farrar and Rinehart, 1945 (Rivers of America Series); Mitchell, Robert D., "The Shenandoah Valley Frontier," *Annals of the Association of American Geographers* 62 (1972): 461–486.

SHIJIANG

See Xi He

SNAKE

Source: Yellowstone National Park, in northwestern Wyoming
Length: 1,038 miles (1,670 kilometers)
Tributaries: Gros Ventre, Henry's Fork, Bruneau, Owyhee, Boise, Payette, Imnaha, Salmon, Grand Ronde, Clearwater, Palouse
Outlet: **Columbia**, near Pasco, Washington, flooded by McNary Dam

I walk upstream from the confluence and then wade far into the Snake River. Beyond a shallow sandbar, I lie back and let the water pour over me, and then I float with my face in the evening sun and let the river take me away. The current carries me over sand and stone toward the eddy where the Columbia picks up this water of Yellowstone, of the Tetons, and of the enriching cottonwood forests. The Columbia picks up the cool spring flows of the Fort Hall Bottoms and the rampage of undiverted gorge below Milner. An unpiped Thousand Springs wells beneath me. Sturgeon-filled for hundreds of miles, the middle river washes up around me; I am pushed also by the powerful forces of Hells Canyon—an undammed canyon of 200 miles from Weiser to Lewiston. Here I am buoyed by the incomparable Salmon and Clearwater with chinook and sockeye and coho so plentiful that a civilization was based on them. Here, too, is the lower river where salmon and steelhead swam in hordes resembling a solid mass and where grizzly bears and eagles gorged themselves until they could eat no more. I swim on and join the Columbia. I swim on.

Tim Palmer, *The Snake River: Window to the West,* 1991

Draining the mountain heartland of Idaho, the Snake has no parallel among American rivers. With twenty-five dams, numerous diversions, and hydroelectric plants, the river is a "working river," as irrigators and Idaho Power Company officials are prone to describe the river that is the largest tributary of the Columbia. Yet, unlike the Columbia, whose only free-flowing section in the United States ironically is across the Hanford Nuclear Reservation, the Snake runs free for about half its length, looping across southern Idaho before turning west to join the mighty Columbia in southeastern Washington. It traverses biotically diverse cottonwood bottomlands, closes in at dramatic "narrows," plunges over a horseshoe cascade that is higher than Niagara (at Shoshone Falls), and cuts a slot in the surrounding lava plateau that is deeper than the Grand Canyon of the Colorado (at Hells Canyon).

The Snake begins on a height of land in the southern part of the nation's oldest national park, Yellowstone. Pinpointing the precise source of a major river is an exercise in futility. One can't identify the single spring, gorge, or slope from which the Snake emanates. Nevertheless, the river rises along the Continental Divide, not far from the headwaters of the Yellowstone, which, flowing to the north and east, joins the Missouri-Mississippi system, whereas the Snake empties to the south and west into the Columbia.

The river threads its way across Jackson Hole, meandering widely in front of the spectacular, much-photographed peaks of the Grand Tetons that loom to the west of the river. The Snake winds around these geologically young and seismically active fault-block mountains. Crossing into Idaho, it arcs to the northwest, then southwest. Exiting the mountains, the river crosses all of southern Idaho in a generally southwesterly direction, forming the rich agricultural district of the Snake River Plain. The looping, or wraparound, course of the Snake differs from that of other western rivers, including the Yellowstone, Colorado, and Rio Grande. The numerous turns of the Snake's path—not the tight meanders, but the major alterations in the trend of the river—are the result of the many types of faulting and volcanism in the headwaters region. Since the Teton Range is active seismically, even a geologically minor event could send the upper river over the low divide separating the Snake's upper basin, down the fly-fisherman's paradise that is Henry's Fork.

No river in America has such diverse tributaries. The Salmon, or "River of No Return," is a right-bank affluent draining the largest wilderness area in the United States outside Alaska. Joining the river from the left are the Bruneau and Owyhee Rivers, which flow through forbidding desert high country. In southern Idaho the Snake traverses a highly permeable lava plain that includes water-guzzling tubes, tunnels, and cinder cones. As a result, surface waters do not reach the Snake from the north bank, and the flanking Sawtooth Range and Lost River Mountains of south-central Idaho lack surface drainage features. Instead, an enormous underground aquifer gurgles and cascades in the form of the beautiful "Thousand Springs" from the sheer rock cliffs of the canyon.

The river has had many names, and its current one is a mistake. Fish, especially the salmon and the steelhead, are central to the culture of the native peoples of the region: the Shoshone and Bannock tribes. A Shoshone Indian probably once identified the river in sign language: a curving motion of the hand moving outward from the chest, probably signifying a swimming fish, or "people of the fish." But the sign was misread as a snake.

Lewis and Clark crossed Lolo Pass at the northern end of the drainage basin along the Lochsa headwaters. Making trail across the Bitterroot Mountains, the most arduous leg of their epochal expedition, the explorers followed the Clearwater River downstream to the Snake (the Lochsa along with the Selway forms the Middle Fork of the Clearwater). The confluence of the Snake and its principal tributary, the Clearwater, is at today's appropriately named twin cities of Lewiston, Idaho, and Clarkston, Washington, which represent the largest urban concentration along the river. The exploring party first named the Snake "Lewis's River," after calling it the Southeast Fork of the Columbia. Though a few men from the Corps of Discovery ventured up Hells Canyon a short distance, Lewis and Clark never gained a true conception of the Snake's course and extent.

One of the distinctive features of the Snake River is the way it has become segmented and sealed off along its 1,000-mile-plus course connecting the northern Rockies to the Pacific Northwest. Different agencies, organizations, even levels of government make decisions about the different segments of the river. Twenty-five dams have backed up flatwater bulges that cover about half of the river's length. For purposes of the federal Bureau of Reclamation, the river terminates at one of the largest dams, Milner Dam above Twin Falls. Irrigation lines from that point draw remaining upstream water to such an extent that there is zero flow below the dam. Any flow farther downstream must come from groundwater seepage or affluents. Above Milner Dam, the Snake has been extensively dammed, impounded, and canalized to deliver irrigation water not only to potato producers but also to grain and livestock farmers and ranchers who contribute more agricultural value than do Idaho's more celebrated spud growers. The middle river below Milner is the province of more recent hydroelectric projects of the Idaho Power Company. When these dams were developed, during the Eisenhower years, the federal government preferred local and private initiative over the earlier national control provided by the New Deal's Bonneville Power Administration along the Columbia. Dam building in Hells Canyon has so far been successfully resisted, as, for example, at the Nez Percé Crossing site at the mouth of the Salmon and at the alternative High Mountain Sheep Dam site farther upstream. The Army Corps of Engineers has, however, built a number of dams along the river below Hells Canyon, creating back-to-back impoundments for purposes of inland navigation and hydroelectric power.

The Snake is no more manipulated than the Tennessee, which also has twenty-five dams along its course, but the Snake stands out by virtue of its remaining free-flowing miles and the possibility that some unneeded dams might be breached for the sake of the migration of anadromous fish and the re-establishment of healthy riparian habitats. Bald eagles gather in the wetlands of the Snake floodplains, but they depend on healthy fringing cottonwoods for shelter, nesting, and food. Rare trumpeter swans congregate in the upstream section of the valley, but the drawdown of the river's flow caused by irrigation threatens this largest bird in North America, which requires slow-moving, unfrozen waters in which to eat tubers and the stems of aquatic plants. As sediments gather behind and fill up aging dams, "hungry water" downstream erodes beaches, islands, and the regular pattern of shallow riffles and deep pools so vital to healthy fish populations.

Two major environmental concepts have been advanced by those seeking to balance the need for environmental protection with economic development, especially as applied to the nation's rivers and streams. One is the idea of *instream flow,* the notion that there is an overriding public right to maintain a minimum stream flow below dams in order to prevent irreparable damage to fish and wildlife and the degradation of the floodplain. Maintaining minimum streamflow is considered by many to be one of the most critical issues along the Snake River from Jackson Hole to the Columbia. Other Western rivers face similar problems—the United States now guarantees a minimum flow of Colorado waters at the Mexican border—but the rich diversity of wildlife and habitat along the Snake puts the river in a special class.

The other significant public policy tool is actually an old and revered notion, but one given a new twist since the 1960s. The issue that gave rise to the environmental application of the *public trust doctrine* arose over disputes about where to build a dam in the Hells Canyon section of the Snake River. Appealed to the U.S. Supreme Court, the historic case's decision has been hailed as a judicial landmark. Justice William O. Douglas, an avid outdoorsman and conservationist, wrote that the Federal Power Commission, the permitting agency, had a duty not just to decide *where* to build a dam but *whether* to build one. The spectacular Hells Canyon extends for approximately 125 miles (201 kilometers) along the Idaho-Oregon state line, with a vertical drop of 7,900 feet (2,410 meters) at the He Devil Mountain—deeper than the Grand Canyon, which is 5,500 feet (1,680 meters) from rim to floor, and second in North America only to the canyon of the Kings River in the Sierra Nevada, which has a vertical drop of 8,240 feet (2,510 meters). Justice Douglas felt that interests other than just the calculation of kilowatt-hours and acre-feet needed to be considered: "The test is whether the project will be in the public interest. And that determination can be made only after an exploration of all issues . . . including future power demand and supply, alternate sources of power, the public interest in preserving reaches of wild rivers and wilderness areas, the preservation of anadromous fish for commercial and recreational purposes and the protection of wildlife."

With the support of Idaho's senator Frank Church and Senator Bob Packwood of Oregon, legislation was introduced to protect Hells Canyon, and in 1975 a wilderness area of 213,993 acres (86,602 hectares) was established within a broader National Recreation Area. Wild river designation was granted to the 31.5 miles (50.7 kilometers) of the Snake from Hells Canyon Dam to Pittsburgh Landing, and scenic river status was given to the 36 miles (58 kilometers) from Pittsburgh to the Washington border. A momentous decision had been made: at least along a portion of the Snake, a river should not be just a "working river"—but a "living river."

Conflict over the Snake obviously did not end with this decision. As recently as the 2000 presidential election, controversy swirled over problems with the four lower dams on the Snake constructed by the Army Corps of Engineers in the 1960s and 1970s for purposes of barge navigation and hydroelectric power. Located below Hells Canyon, these four dams—Lower Granite, Little Goose, Lower Monumental, and Ice Harbor, proceeding downstream—have been the target of environmentalists who have a special animus against the Army Corps (an agency that is considered to consist of two types of people, who are really one and the same: dam builders and damn builders). Salmon and other anadromous fish blocked by the dam are trucked around the obstacle, but, like more traditional fish ladders, this procedure increases mortality and tips the balance of survival in favor of hatchery-raised stock rather than wild fish, to the detriment of the genetic population. The political ground has shifted in the environmentally conscious Pacific Northwest. Today the Army Corps has to calculate the costs and benefits of breaching dams. Critics point to the Corps's biased data and calculations, exaggerating the benefits of the dams for farming (reduced barge costs) and downplaying the recreational use of the river and the value of a healthy fishery and floodplain. With the breaching of Maine's Edwards Dam on the Kennebec in the summer of 1999, under the eye of the superintending secretary of the interior, Bruce Babbitt, many began asking questions that were unthinkable only a few years before: Can the rivers of the West be undammed? Can the Snake River dams, at least on the lower river, be broken, and the fish and the river be let run free?

See also Columbia

Further Reading: Palmer, Tim, *The Snake River: Window to the West,* Washington, DC: Island Press, 1991.

SOMME

Source: Near Saint-Quentin, in northern France
Length: c. 150 miles (241 kilometers)
Tributary: Avre
Outlet: English Channel

The marshy valley of the Somme has been the locale of peaceable, even civilizing activities—say, the intensive cultivation of horticultural plots outside Amiens, the river's major city—but it has also been the site of a battlefield that is synonymous with the atrocity of modern warfare.

The river rises near Fontsomme (literally, fountain of the Somme) in the Department of the Aisne but soon enters and then traverses the whole of the department to which it gives its name. Flowing generally northwesterly, it passes by Saint-Quentin, Saint-Simon, Péronne, Amiens, and Abbeville before emptying via a broad estuary into the English Channel (French: La Manche). The river flows through a gradually widening flat-bottomed marshy valley that lies between the hills of Artois to the northeast and the plain of Picardy to the south. In terms of drainage, the river abuts the Oise-Seine system to the south and the Scheldt to the northeast, to both of which river systems the Somme has linking canals.

The name of the river comes from the Celtic word *Samara,* meaning "tranquil." With only a slight drop in elevation along its course, the river does not have a large erosive force. As a result, the valley bottom is choked with silt, and the course of the river is obstructed by numerous marshes, some of which were laid out long ago in fishponds that today constitute part of the river's channel. From

British artillery transporting a gun in the Somme Valley during World War I, October 1916 (Tropical Press Agency/Archive Photos)

Saint-Simon on, a lateral canal runs alongside the river, generally at the left margin of the floodplain, but the silting up of the estuary restricts traffic to local produce. This comparatively short river has never been as important for navigation or extraregional transportation as the great nearby river systems to which it is joined by canals. Abbeville was once an important medieval port at the head of the tidal estuary, but because of silting it now lies well inland.

Most of the major cities of the valley were founded as fortress sites, including Abbeville, Péronne, and Amiens. A textile center and market for the fertile surrounding agricultural plain, Amiens lies at the convergence of a number of side valleys, most of which today carry road and rail routes. The citadel of Amiens stands on a bluff overlooking the right bank of the river and the densely canalized floodplain (Amiens is known as the Venice of France). The city's defensive advantages, however, derive less from its high point location than its extensive, impeding marshes that nearly surround the town. The need to cross the river between the citadel to the north and the old hill city to the south gave significance to the old Roman station. Below the town an expansive marshy floodplain reinforced by a group of affluents joining the valley and the ponding up of tidal waters made the river difficult to cross and a good natural barrier. On the outskirts of Amiens are found the famous market gardens known as *hortillonages,* conjured as if by a sleight of magical industry from the peat bogs. The canals interlacing this intensively cultivated area not only serve the purpose of irrigation but also permit communication: owners visit their gardens in punts.

The nineteenth-century French writer Jules Verne adopted Amiens as his home in later life, mostly because his wife's family was from there, but also because of its civilizing traditions and its distinctive dialect (Verne's family was of Breton stock). In this ancient capital of Picardy the imaginative writer, who is best known for his ability to spin out a tale with state-of-the-art or slightly-in-advance-of-fact science, wrote many of his greatest tales. The prolific Verne worked in the shadow of France's largest cathedral, not far from embankments carrying trains on a regular schedule to and from Paris, where he had earned his fame. He wrote many of his most famous novels, including *Around the World in Eighty Days,* at Amiens, or at the seaside retreat of Le Crotoy at the mouth of the Somme.

The magnificent Gothic cathedral at Amiens was, unlike the Château de Péronne, only slightly damaged during the devastation of World War I. The Battle of the Somme (1916) was the worst nightmare of trench warfare. After a sustained pounding by artillery, the British commanders launched an assault on July 1 of well-defended and well-emplaced German positions in which trenches were sometimes dug 30 feet (9.1 meters) deep. Allied soldiers, both British and French, advanced across a no-man's-land, with uncut wire facing them, after artillery had prematurely pulled cover without accomplishing its intended effects. Rising from their trenches and assuming positions at defensive parapets, the German soldiers, who well knew that their own lives were at stake, mowed down wave upon wave of advancing Allied soldiers. Some died instantly, some few escaped, while others crawled into shell holes, wrapping their waterproof sheets around them, taking out their Bibles, and dying in that way.

Although the French lost heavily (as did the Germans), for the British it was a holocaust: the country's casualty figure for four months of warfare was 419,654. It was the largest loss of life in British military history. By the time the Allied offensive was officially brought to a halt on November 19, the gain was an insignificant seven miles ahead of the front line of July 1. The cemeteries that mark the Somme battlefield not only memorialize the young men who died in the bloody wilderness of no-man's-land but also symbolize a key retrenchment of British vitality—a loss that many would view in retrospect as leading to the eventual collapse of the British empire.

The French landscape only slowly recovered, if at all. Much rebuilding and remaking had to be done. An authoritative geography written between the two world wars evoked poignantly the shattering changes in the Somme region:

> Its [the Somme's] mangled villages and churned-up subsoil will, in some places, never be brought back to use and habitation. Vast craters and crude, infertile exposures of chalk have taken the place of the fertile loamy fields.... The War of 1914–18 has made a crude break with the past, and there is a certain incongruity in the aspect of the reconstructed settlements, as of a peasant girl when she exchanges her native costume for the garb of the town.

Further Reading: Macdonald, Lyn, *Somme,* New York: Atheneum, 1989; Ormsby, Hilda, *France: A Regional and Economic Geography,* London: Methuen, 1950 (orig. pub. 1931).

SONGHUA JIANG

Source: Changbai Mountains,
in northeastern China
Length: c. 1,150 miles (1,851 kilometers)
Tributaries: Erdaobai, Nen
Outlet: **Amur**

The Songhua Jiang (sung-HWAH JYAHNG), the northernmost river system in China, is also the largest river in China's northeastern region of Manchuria. Also known as the Sungari, it flows generally northward through Jilin and Heilongjiang Provinces until reaching the Amur River along the border with Russia. Its name means "Heavenly River" in Manchurian.

The river rises in a series of parallel mountain ranges trending northeast-southwest in southeastern Manchuria near the border with North Korea. The Changbai Shen consist of volcanic, snow-covered peaks representing the headwaters of many of northeastern China's border rivers. Tianchi Lake ("the lake of heaven") forms the source of the Songhua Jiang, as well as the Yalu and Tumen Rivers. Changbai Waterfalls is a famous scenic spot on the northern slope of the mountain range, plunging 223 feet (68 meters) into Erdaobai River, which flows into the Songhua.

The drainage basin includes the largest coal deposits in Manchuria. The valley is one of the major agricultural regions of China, often referred to as the Manchurian Plain. The industrial city of Durbin is on the river at the head of navigation for steamships. Songhua Lake, an artificial lake, lies approximately 16 miles (26 kilometers) southeast of the city of Jilin. This popular recreational area has fish hatcheries and is used for irrigating surrounding farmland. In 1959 vast oil reserves were found in the Songhuajiang-Liaohe Basin, and the Daqing oil field went into operation the next year.

See also Amur

SOUTH PLATTE

See Platte

STIKINE

Source: Stikine Mountains, in northwest British Columbia
Length: 335 miles (539 kilometers)
Tributaries: Klappan, Tuya, Iskut
Outlet: Pacific Ocean

Most of the rivers draining the rugged northern portion of the Rocky Mountains in British Columbia and southeastern Alaska have short courses and include major sections that are longitudinal, not transverse, as they follow the southeast-northwest trend of the mountains. During the late-nineteenth-century Klondike Gold Rush, the Stikine River, the largest river crossing the Coast Mountains, provided one of the preferred routes for migrants seeking to reach the interior of Canada from the Inner Passage of coastal Alaska.

The Stikine (meaning "Great River" in Tlingit) rises in the mountains of the same name in northwest British Columbia. In addition to the Stikine, these mountains are the source of the Skeena and Finlay Rivers. The Stikine flows in an arc to the west and southwest, crossing southeastern Alaska and emptying into the Pacific Ocean north of Wrangell Island. Before crossing the Coast Ranges and the Alaska Panhandle, the Stikine traverses a 68-mile (109-kilometer) stretch known as the Grand Canyon of the Stikine. The deep, narrow valley of the middle Stikine is a favorite of river adventurers who navigate the section in canoes, kayaks, and rafts. The Iskut River and many other glacial streams distribute water and rock materials to the broad, silt-laden river flowing through forested ranges. The peaks of the flanking mountains rise to 10,000 feet (3,048 meters) and are permanently capped with snow.

Only about 130 miles (210 kilometers) of the river are navigable. Apart from a few trappers' cabins, the only settlements along the Stikine are Wrangell, Alaska, about 10 miles (16 kilometers) south of the river mouth; and Glenora and Telegraph Creek, British Columbia, at the head of low and high water navigation, respectively.

The Klondike District refers to the auriferous region on the border between Yukon Territory and Alaska, near the confluence of a small tributary, the Klondike, with the Yukon River. During the 1897–1898 rush to the gold-mining district, the Stikine was one of the preferred routes for prospectors. Though not as well known as the Skagway and Dyea entranceway from the navigable Inner Passage of southern Alaska, the Wrangell route also provided a means of reaching the gold fields from the coast. As many as twenty riverboats waited at the mouth of the Stikine to carry the Argonauts to Glenora, where they camped before heading overland to the headwaters of the north-flowing Yukon. Upstream at Telegraph Creek was a Hudson's Bay Company post and a link to the all-Canadian route from Edmonton. The routes that represented alternatives to the Dyea and Skagway crossings of Chilkoot Pass and White Pass, respectively, which passed Lake Lindeman, were the Copper River Trail and the Teslin Trail, which followed the Stikine River and Teslin Lake.

The Stikine River provides almost unsurpassed recreational opportunities, from the glacial valleys of its upper course to the delta flats north of Wrangell. The 16-mile-wide (26-kilometer-wide) delta is one of the largest coastal marshes in the Pacific

Northwest. It is a haven for 120 species of migratory birds in the spring and fall, including tundra (whistling) swans, Canada geese, snow geese, sandhill cranes, mergansers, waterfowl, and more than 150,000 shorebirds. In April, when bald eagles gather along the lower river to feast on the "hooligan" run (eulachon, a fish in the smelt family), the number of birds represents the second-largest concentration of bald eagles in the world. The numbers of shorebirds such as plovers, sandpipers, dunlins, and snipe, dependent on the grassy mudflat habitat, generally peak in the first week of May.

Further Reading: Bronson, William, *The Last Grand Adventure,* New York: McGraw-Hill, 1977; Pool, Rollo, "Stikine and Iskut Rivers in Transition," *Alaska* 48 (July 1982): 17–19.

SUSQUEHANNA

Source: Otsego Lake, New York
Length: 444 miles (715 kilometers)
Tributaries: Chenango, Chemung, Lackawanna, West Branch, Juniata
Outlet: Chesapeake Bay at Havre de Grace, Maryland

The largest river draining the Appalachians to the east served as a bridge between different sections of the emerging nation and subsequently became a key coal- and steel-producing region for an industrializing America.

Rising in Otsego Lake in central New York, the Susquehanna flows alternately to the southeast and the southwest through east-central Pennsylvania before emptying into the Chesapeake Bay. The river has numerous tributaries, most of them draining the Appalachian Plateau from the west. In its upper reaches, called the North Branch, the river is joined at Binghamton, New York, by the Chenango, and a little farther south, across the border in Pennsylvania, by the Chemung. The Susquehanna then meanders across Pennsylvania's appropriately named Endless Mountains, from which automobile drivers have many spectacular views of the twisting river from overlooks. The river begins to straighten out as it crosses the Wyoming valley and the anthracite coal region of northeastern Pennsylvania, passing by the steel centers of Wilkes-Barre and Scranton, the latter located on the Lackawanna, a left-bank tributary. At Sunbury the river is joined by its main tributary, the West Branch, which has zigzagged eastward from its source in the Alleghenies for 238 miles (383 kilometers). Just above Harrisburg the last major tributary, the Juniata, joins the river, again draining from the west. From there to the river's mouth the Susquehanna is a large, wide river with an average width of about 1 mile (1.6 kilometers). The Chesapeake Bay is the drowned river mouth of the Susquehanna. The lower reaches of the former Susquehanna and its previous outlet were inundated some 10,000 years ago with the melting of the last Pleistocene icesheet and rising sea levels. Ships bound for Baltimore on the western shore of the Chesapeake Bay trace out the ancient river's route as they follow the ship channel.

The Susquehanna is large enough in central Pennsylvania near Harrisburg to erode a "water gap" at right angles to the sandstone ridges of the Appalachian Ridge and Valley. Its tributaries, however, follow the trend of the folded sedimentary rocks, paralleling the ridges before joining the Susquehanna, which is the only river that cuts across the ridges and reaches the sea. A map view of the Susquehanna and its tributaries in this portion of the watershed shows a classic trellis drainage pattern. Farther west along the West Branch, a dendritic or branching pattern reflects the less elevated but irregular Appalachian Plateau. The road map of Pennsylvania follows this geological trend: Roads in the west are more likely to wind about, while in the east they follow the straight lines of the linear valleys and make sharp turns, just as the rivers do.

This long and crooked river was one of the most important corridors in the early settlement and development of colonial British America, linking the grain- and livestock-producing Middle Colonies of New York and Pennsylvania to the tobacco-producing Chesapeake. The river not only provided a transportation route—the valley, anyway, since the shallow, swift-flowing river impeded navigation—it also opened up a broad, fertile, agricultural region, one of the American

Conowingo Dam on the lower Susquehanna, Maryland (Laura Penn)

cultural hearths, in fact: southeastern Pennsylvania. Much has been written and said about this storied region, with its innovative agriculture based on livestock and careful husbandry, and its influential material culture that included flintlock rifles, large forebay barns, and Conestoga wagons (from Conestoga Township, just outside of Lancaster, Pennsylvania), the covered wagons that carried pioneers across successive frontiers. The population of Native American tribes in the area, such as the Susquehannocks, was low, and the Iroquois from New York overwhelmed them, traveling down the Susquehanna River from their homelands in the Finger Lake region. Europeans in turn displaced their Iroquoian antagonists, who made the unfortunate mistake of forging an alliance with the British during the Revolutionary War.

The natural setting of the Wyoming valley attracted native tribes as it did later Europeans. Twenty-five miles (40 kilometers) long and 3 to 4 miles (5 to 6.4 kilometers) wide, its lush meadowlands and open forests carpeted with grasses and wildflowers were especially attractive to early European colonists, even though today, after a century and a half of smoke and industrial blight, the visitor may have a hard time visualizing the pristine environment. The alliance of the Iroquois with the British doomed the Iroquois. Many veterans of the war returned to settle lands they had seen during periods of fighting. Among the settlers was William Cooper, who founded Cooperstown near the river's source at Otsego Lake. Cooperstown is the site of the Baseball Hall of Fame and the nearby Farmer's Museum. The son of the founder, James Fenimore Cooper, wrote a celebrated saga of the early American frontier, *Leatherstocking Tales,* based upon his experience of growing up along the upper Susquehanna in upstate New York.

An entire volume could be devoted to the canal and railroad era of nineteenth-century America in Pennsylvania. The Keystone State was the preeminent transportation state. A system of canals was built during the 1820–1850 period connecting the waterways of the Susquehanna and Delaware systems in order to reduce the time and cost of transportation. It might be noted that Pennsylvania even combined these two modes of transportation by means of an innovative portage railroad. The Main Line Canal from Harrisburg ran via the Juniata River and then cut across the Allegheny Front with a single locomotive on a narrow-gauge track carrying boats up and over the steep divide.

Flooding continues to be a problem for the largest river of the Eastern Seaboard. A humid climate combines with a dense pattern of urbanization to create high flood potential. Major floods devastate the region every few decades, with the latest disaster occurring in 1972, when Hurricane Agnes's torrential rains flooded the basin, even inundating the governor's mansion at Harrisburg.

In recent decades, environmental problems have been acute. Acid drainage from coal rock wastes that are sometimes heaped as high as 500 feet (152 meters) pollutes streams and kills fish. Vacant mine shafts slump or fill up with chemical wastes, in some instances catching fire. Denuded slopes in logged and mined areas contribute to the siltation of streams. Logging has been practiced everywhere in the basin for a hundred years. The scale of commercial lumbering a hundred years ago is suggested by the fact that in the late nineteenth century, 300 million board feet of timber were held in a boom of logs on the West Branch of the Susquehanna at Williamsport, Pennsylvania. Acidic drainage from abandoned coal mines is the primary source of pollution of the Susquehanna and its tributaries. Telltale signs of this degradation are the orange-colored waters and smeared banks produced by a large concentration of iron hydroxides in the sulfate-rich mine wastes. This kind of pollution prevails in both the bituminous coal fields of the basin of the Western Branch, where mining is still active, and the now-abandoned anthracite region of northeastern Pennsylvania. (Curiously, the anthracite era came to a sudden halt in January 1959 when the Knox Coal Company dug too close to the riverbottom near Wilkes-Barre, and the Susquehanna broke through the ceiling of the mine, flooding the entire subterranean Wyoming Valley and preventing the operators from reopening the mines.)

Historical problems of untreated discharge of lime and bleaches from tanneries and organic materials from slaughterhouses and dairies have given way to inadequately treated municipal wastes and the danger of toxic and even radioactive discharge. Nonpoint sources of pollution that have proved especially intractable of solution include surplus agricultural nutrients from fertilization, especially in the lower Susquehanna valley. Excessive siltation has traditionally been caused by rock materials washed into the river from mine washings. Heavy river siltation gave rise to the so-called Hard-Coal Navy, a fleet of steamboats and barges that used to ply the river as far north as Sunbury, vacuuming up coal particles and silt from the riverbottom to sell to utilities and industries as fuel. Although not all the thousands of miles of

Three bridges across the lower Susquehanna, in Maryland, looking south from Conowingo Dam (Laura Penn)

rivers and streams in the basin are "fishable and swimmable" as prescribed by the 1972 Clean Water Act, biological oxygen demand, a key factor in fish vitality, has been decreased along many stretches and is closely monitored. Clean stream laws in Pennsylvania date from the 1960s and were promoted by a strong coalition of sportsmen, scientists, and conservationists who were at the forefront in the Keystone state's fight for cleanup of the Susquehanna against strong vested interests, especially mine owners.

A large population and a river with a gentle gradient have led to the harnessing of the natural forces of the river for hydroelectric power. The lower Susquehanna has most of the power plants—including the Three-Mile Island nuclear plant, a serious accident at which in 1979 virtually put a stop to new construction of nuclear power plants for a generation. The giant Conowingo plant in Maryland, near the river's mouth, is the largest nonfederal power station in the nation. Unfortunately, the dams on the lower river have prevented the spawning of anadromous fish such as American shad, which need to migrate upstream to fresh water to breed. Agricultural runoff, which is rich in nitrogen, finds its way into the Chesapeake Bay, whose biological productivity has been sharply diminished. The oyster catch now is perhaps 1 percent of its historic highs (the Baltimore sage, H. L. Mencken, once described the Chesapeake as an "immense protein factory"). The state of Pennsylvania has finally started to reverse a 150-year trend of cutting off the spawning runs: fish are today lifted by ladders at hydroelectric dams. Gone however are the days when single hauls of a net near the river's mouth took days to empty.

The Susquehanna is the largest source of fresh water for the Chesapeake Bay. An estuarine environment like the bay's is a transitional zone where fresh and salt water mix. The ecology and biological productivity of the bay depends crucially on the amount and timing of fresh water releases. Low flows on the Susquehanna, especially in late summer or during droughts, cause salt water to stretch farther up the bay, threatening salt-intolerant submerged grasses along the bay's shores—grasses that are considered critical in filtering and reducing agricultural runoff. The city of Baltimore itself contributes to the problem by diverting the flow of the Susquehanna for the use of the city and adjoining counties when its own reservoirs are inadequate. The multistate Susquehanna River Basin Commission has blocked Baltimore's river diversions on occasion (such as in June 1998), when it found the water use to be in conflict with overriding public and environmental concerns.

Further Reading: Burmeister, Walter F., *The Susquehanna and Its Tributaries,* Oakton, VA: Appalachian Books, 1975; Carmer, Carl, *The Susquehanna,* New York: Rinehart, 1955 (Rivers of America Series); Stranahan, Susan Q., *Susquehanna, River of Dreams,* Baltimore: Johns Hopkins University Press, 1993.

SUTLEJ

Source: Kailas Range, in southwestern Tibet
Length: c. 900 miles (1,448 kilometers)
Tributaries: Gar Zangbo, **Beas**
Outlet: Merges with **Chenab** to form the combined Panjnad, which empties into the **Indus**

The broad alluvial plain of the Punjab in northwest India and eastern Pakistan is drained by an intricate network of waterways sloping westward from the Himalayas in the direction of the great river of south Asia that gave India its name. The largest of the five rivers of the Punjab (Persian: "five rivers") is the Sutlej, which along with its principal tributary, the Beas, traverses the southern extent of this important borderland (see Figure 1 on p. 24).

The Sutlej originates in Rakas Lake on the southern slope of Mount Kailas at about 15,000 feet (4,572 meters). Because of the reverence felt by both Hindus and Buddhists for natural features such as rivers and mountains, it is not uncommon for a swami- or pilgrim-cum-geographer to be seen circumnavigating an isolated peak and perhaps discovering a hitherto overlooked headstream. At its head the Sutlej flows northwesterly in a narrow structural trough between the Kailas Range and the Kamet–Nanda Devi section of the Himalayas. The river traverses an arid belt developed on glacial detritus, into which the Sutlej, swollen by snowmelt and glaciers, has cut a 3,000-foot (914-meter) canyon. At the Shipki Pass the river turns to the southwest and cuts a deep gorge in the Zaskar Range. Dropping rapidly in elevation, the river bulges into impoundments behind the Bhakra and Nangal dams, which function as storage reservoirs. The river then flows southeasterly for some distance along the fertile Jaswan Dun, a valley consisting of coarse sediments nestled between the outer Himalayan folds and the Siwalik Hills. Turning to the southwest again, the river emerges onto the plains at Rupar.

Like the other rivers of the Punjab, the Sutlej has long been used to irrigate the floodplains and lower terraces of this enormous coalition of overlapping valleys. Modern canal irrigation began in 1859 with the construction of the headworks at Madhopur on the Ravi feeder canals (though the 300-year-old Mogul canals were partly remodeled). The headworks at Rupar feed the Sirhind Canal and the fingers of distributary channels that reach the desert margins of the semiarid plain to the south and east. Soon after the Beas joins from the northeast are the headworks of the long Rajasthan Canal, extending irrigation lines far to the southwest into the desert. Along the Indian-Pakistan border a series of ramifying canals serve both sides of the political fence. Inside Pakistan the Sutlej receives the Chenab, which has already taken the waters of the Jhelum and the Ravi. The 40-mile (64-kilometer) stretch between the Chenab-Sutlej confluence and the junction with the Indus River is known as the Panjnad, also meaning "five rivers."

Although the land in the divided region of the Punjab is no longer disputed between India and Pakistan, as Kashmir is, access to headwater remains a source of contention. The upper courses of the rivers of the Punjab as well as of the Indus, however, lie in Indian-controlled territory. India thereby commands the waters flowing down from the Himalayas. It controls the Bhakra-Nangal project, the Rajasthan Canal, and even the Dipalpur Canal serving Pakistan, since its headworks lie on the Indian side of the 1947 partition line. An international treaty signed in 1960 guarantees that India will deliver water to the lower Sutlej from the northern rivers, to ensure that the lower river will not suffer from aridity.

See also Beas, Chenab, Jhelum, Ravi

SWAN

Source: Rises as the Avon in hills near Corrigin, in Western Australia
Length: 240 miles (386 kilometers)
Tributaries: Helena, Canning
Outlet: Indian Ocean

Two generations after the first convicts arrived to colonize southeastern Australia in 1788, the English frigate *Challenger* cruised along the coast of western Australia and eased into the Swan River estuary. The ship's captain, Charles Fremantle, took formal possession in May 1829 of 1,000,000 square miles (2,590,000 square kilometers) of territory on behalf of James Stirling, the new colony's lieutenant-governor and the British crown. In contrast to the earlier colonization at Sydney Harbor, the Swan River Settlement, at it came to be called, didn't depend initially on the servile labor of transported convicts.

Western Australia, the western third of the continent, was the last to receive English settlers. Except for coastal patches, the land was mostly arid or semiarid, its vegetation consisting of forbidding saltbush and spinifex, and the isolated coast was far off the shipping routes. Captain Fremantle entered the mouth of the river and named the enormous wastes he was taking possession of "Western Australia," the first time the term "Australia" had been officially used. The name derives from the ancient Greek belief in the need for a southern hemisphere counterweight—*terra australis,* or "southern lands"—to balance the Northern Hemisphere's landmasses.

With a small number of colonists—and without asking the permission of the Aborigines—the Swan River colonization scheme of 1829 was launched. The port city of Fremantle was established at the mouth of the river, while just upstream, beyond the reach of the new steamships,

Drought-adapted vegetation on a hill slope above the Swan River in western Australia (Australian Tourist Commission)

was the capital city of Perth. It was noted that black swans glided on the river, and this symbol of antipodean inversion gave the name to the river. (Lieutenant-Governor Stirling, who first recommended the Swan River settlement, had wanted to name it Hesperia because it faced the westering sun.) Curiously, the eastern boundary of the colony was the meridian line of 129°E, which corresponded to the famous Tordesillas Line, drawn in the late fifteenth-century as a division of the world into Spanish and Portuguese spheres.

The fertility of the soils and the bounty of the harvests proved to be a mirage. The colony regularly depended on shipments of wheat and flour from the not-so-nearby British settlements of Cape Town and Hobart. Token amounts of a few hundred bales of wool were sent yearly to England. By 1850, after two decades of settlement, Western Australia counted only 5,886 people, of which the governor, Charles Fitzgerald, said two-thirds would gladly quit the colony tomorrow.

At just about that time, Britain stopped "transporting" convicts to eastern Australia and began sending them west. The first convict ship arrived off Fremantle in June 1850, carrying almost as many guards as felons. The symbol of the convict-colonization efforts in Western Australia was the long, low barracks known as the "Establishment," which overlooked the sea at the river's mouth. This building housed prisoners who worked in chain gangs around Fremantle, while other groups of convicts were housed at Perth and worked on roads and public buildings in and around the capital. The last convict ship disgorged its human cargo—sundry criminals and political dissidents, the last-named group including many Irish Fenians—in January 1868. The 1871 census reported approximately 25,000 people in Western Australia, while the colonies of New South Wales and Victoria, where the convict system of servile labor had been abolished earlier, numbered 500,000 and 730,000, respectively. The last colony's population growth was set off by a gold rush at midcentury sustained by subsequent land development.

Gold mining would arrive in the western districts in the late nineteenth century. A series of strikes beginning in 1883 culminated in the discovery of the richest field of all, the Coolgardie, in 1892. A coining facility was soon established as an adjunct of the British Royal Mint. The Perth Mint today is a major producer of bullion coinage for Australia. Kangaroos, kookaburras, and koalas may not be as common in Western Australia as elsewhere in the Land Down Under, but their images stream from Perth in the form of minted gold, silver, and platinum collector coins.

Further Reading: Hughes, Robert, *The Fatal Shore,* New York: Alfred A. Knopf, 1987.

SYR DARYA

Source: Tien Shan Mountains
Length: c. 1,380 miles (2,200 kilometers)
Tributaries: Naryn, Kara Darya
Outlet: Northern end of Aral Sea

One of the major rivers in Central Asia played an important role in the Great Game of imperial strategy and intrigue played between Russia and Britain in the nineteenth century.

The Syr Darya (anciently Jaxartes) is formed by the junction of two streams, the Naryn and the Kara Darya, which rise far to the east in the Tien Shan Mountains. At the junction of the two headstreams lies the fertile Fergana valley, historical crossroads between Chinese Turkestan (Sinkiang) and Russian Turkestan, the latter now the independent Muslim republics carved out of former Soviet Central Asia. Overrun by Arabs in the eighth century, the Mongol leader Genghis Khan in the thirteenth century, Tamerlane the Great in the fourteenth century, and the Uzbeks in the sixteenth century, the Fergana basin was eventually taken by the Russians in 1875–1876. This key region in the upper course of the Syr Darya was divided between the Uzbek and Kyrgiz socialist republics during the era of the Soviet Union.

Alexander the Great in his conquest of Persia reached the river in approximately 329 B.C. and established the city of Khodzent (formerly Leninabad) on the left bank of the river about 90 miles (145 kilometers) south of Tashkent, near where the river exits the hills onto the arid plains. Among the more than thirty cities named Alexandria, the conqueror honored this city as Alexandria Eschate—the Farthermost. Contact between the Han Chinese and the West first took place in the Fergana region in the second century B.C.

The lower course of the river crosses sandy desert wastes interrupted only by occasional oasis towns. Forming the northern border of the Kyzyl Kum Desert (Red Desert), the Syr Darya empties into the northern end of the Aral Sea. In the nineteenth century the three powerful khanates of Bokhara, Khiva, and Kokand (Quqon) occupied the desert wastes and oases of Central Asia and blocked the southern expansion of Russia. The legendary cities of Samarkand and Tashkent were political dependencies of conniving Muslim potentates who controlled these lands. The region's leaders were as wary of Persian incursions as they were of the Russians, and they were known as much for their long knives as their long beards. Extension of the czar's domain to the south of the Black Sea into the lands of the decaying Ottoman Empire was effectively checked by the British, who worried about foreign control of the key straits linking the Black Sea to the Mediterranean—the Bosporus and the Dardanelles. After the humiliating defeat of Russia in the Crimean War (1853–1856), Russia turned its gaze toward Siberia and Muslim Central Asia.

Already by midcentury the Russians had established a garrison at Orenburg on the lower Ural River, just above its mouth on the Caspian Sea. They had begun to reconnoiter the vast sandy deserts east of the Caspian and had assembled two small steamers on the Aral Sea from sections brought overland. By 1853 a fortress that could be resupplied by steamer was established 250 miles (402 kilometers) upstream on the Syr Darya at Ak-Mechet. A disruption of Russia's traditional supply of cotton caused by the American Civil War (1861–1865) provided an additional reason for expansion, for Uzbek cotton was a valuable prize. The construction of the Trans-Caspian Railway across the Kara Kum Desert (Black Desert) in the 1880s linked the cities of Bokhara, Samarkand, and Tashkent—only recently taken by the Russians—to the West.

The British in India meanwhile stirred at this new posturing of the Russian bear. Now troops and supplies could be brought to within hundreds of miles of their borders, rather than thousands. The snow-covered passes surrounding the borderlands of mountain-begirt India were now being watched closely with telescopes, as the Great Game of imperial rivalry reached a high pitch. Exciting adventures and intrigues, on both the British and Russian sides, resulted from the need to achieve one-upmanship by stealing a march on the enemy. The British treated any incursion into the lands surrounding India as an attempt to gain access to the road to India, while the Russians feared that the British would launch a takeover of their new domain in Muslim Asia from such a flanking position. The Great Game officially ended with the signing of the Anglo-Russian Convention of 1907, but numerous elements of the struggle took on new life with the accession of the Bolsheviks in 1917, especially during the Cold War period following 1945.

The lower course of the Syr Darya is practically unfit for navigation because of its shallowness. The river is used for irrigating cotton and for hydroelectric power. So much water has been withdrawn for irrigation from the Syr Darya and its twin river, the Amu Darya, that the Aral Sea is being rapidly depleted. From 1974 to 1986, almost no water reached the Aral Sea from the Syr Darya. It has been estimated that the volume of the Aral Sea as of 1998 was only 30 percent of its pre-1960 level. The sea (more properly called a lake) has been so reduced in size that boats lie high and dry many miles from the current shoreline. The sea has even split into sections, and the Syr Darya now flows into the Small Aral Sea, which since 1988 has been separated from the Large Aral Sea.

See also Amu Darya

Further Reading: Hopkirk, Peter, *The Great Game: The Struggle for Empire in Central Asia,* New York; Kodansha International, 1994; Meyer, Karl E., and Shareen Blair Brysac, *Tournament of Shadows: The Great Game and the Race for Empire in Central Asia,* Washington, DC: Counterpoint, 1999.

T

TAGUS

Source: Sierra de Albarracín, in east-central Spain
Length: 585 miles (940 kilometers)
Tributaries: Alagón, Jarama
Outlet: Atlantic Ocean

One of the major rivers of southwestern Europe, the Tagus (Spanish: Tajo; Portuguese: Tejo) drains the central portion of the Iberian Peninsula westward past Lisbon, Portugal, into the Atlantic. Only the lower course of the river is navigable, since steep gorges broken by waterfalls are found along both the upper and lower-middle river. The Tagus, the longest river of the Iberian Peninsula, is navigable for approximately 80 miles (130 kilometers) upstream. The broad estuary that provides the setting for Portugal's capital and its major city is one of Europe's finest harbors. Ponte 25 de Abril, one of the longest suspension bridges in Europe, spans the estuary.

The Tagus rises in the mountains of eastern Spain about 80 miles (130 kilometers) east of Madrid. It flows northwestward through rugged sierra, past Teruel, then north across the Meseta, or tableland, of central Spain. The river passes the historic city of Toledo, the seat of the Catholic primate of Spain and the major center of medieval culture in Iberia, which is located 40 miles (64 kilometers) south-southwest of the modern city of Madrid (where Philip II moved his capital in 1560). The river's central course around Toledo is dammed to irrigate the valley's fertile farmland and to generate hydroelectric power. The river flows west to form a section of the Spain-Portugal border 25 miles (40 kilometers) in length. Entering Portugal, it veers to the southwest past Santarém, on the right bank of the Tagus, 43 miles (69 kilometers) northeast of Lisbon. The river begins to expand into a lagoon below there, but it again narrows to a navigable channel as it approaches the capital city. To heavy industries such as steel making, ship building, and refineries, which concentrated in the Tagus estuary during the post–World War II economic boom, have been recently added elements of a modern service economy, including modern tourism, which unfortunately converts natural coastal strips and estuarine bays into high-rise buildings.

By virtue of Portugal's fronting on the Atlantic and having its major rivers, the Douro and the Tagus, linking the coast to the interior, the country is united as a geographical entity. Independent since the twelfth century, the country represents in effect an oceanic strip of arid Spain and became, in the sixteenth century, a powerful maritime power during the Age of Discovery. The Tagus divides Portugal into two distinct regions. North of the river the land is mostly mountainous; to the south, undulating lowlands. The north is wetter, experiences less extreme variation in temperature, and cultivates maize, rye, and the vine. The south is drier, hotter in the summer (crops require irrigation), and cultivates wheat, oats, and the cork oak. With the dissolution of its colonial legacy in the mid-1970s, Portugal is now a minor player in Europe, not to

Mouth of the Tagus River, Lisbon, Portugal with a statue of Prince Henry the Navigator (Jesse Walker)

speak of the world. Its greatest effect remains the legacy of populating and culturally unifying half of South America, in the form of the country of Brazil.

See also Douro
Further Reading: Walker, D. S., *The Mediterranean Lands,* New York: Wiley, 1960.

TARIM

Source: Karakorum Range, in extreme northern India
Length: 1,300 miles (2,092 kilometers)
Tributary: Hotan
Outlet: Lop Nur, a salt lake

The principal drainage of the Xinjiang Uygur (Sinkiang Uighur) Autonomous Region in northwest China rises in the mountainous borderlands straddling Pakistan, India, and China. Its upper course is known as the Yarkant (Yeh-er-ch'ing). The river proper begins at the junction of the Kashi and the Yarkant Rivers at the western end of the Taklimakan Desert. The river flows northward, is joined by the Hotan River, then flows generally eastward across the northern rim of this giant arid depression that is approximately 800 miles (1,287 kilometers) long and 400 miles (644 kilometers) wide. Surrounded by the lofty Tianshan, Kunlun, and Pamir Mountains, this internally drained region is given its name by the river: the Tarim Basin. The river empties into a district of ephemeral lakes and marshes known as the Lop Nur (Lob Nor). In common with interior sinks in continental interiors at these latitudes (compare the Salt Lake of Utah), the base of the river forms salt lakes and flats. Because of the shifting channels of the lower course of the river, the Lop Nur posed difficulties for navigation.

The Tarim Basin is the largest sedimentary basin in China. Most of the rivers and streams, with the exception of the Tarim, are dry for much of the year. The basin is one of the driest places on earth. With less than 0.79 inch (20 millimeters) of precipitation per year, it is the driest region on the Eurasian landmass. Occupying the center of the depression, the Taklimakan Desert is classified as dune-type desert, whose shifting dunes measure up to 984 feet (300 meters) in height (by contrast, the dunes in the Great Sand Dunes National Park in southern Colorado, the tallest in North America, are only about 700 feet (213 meters). Meltwaters from the permanently snow-capped peaks encircling the basin permit irrigated agriculture, and most of the native population (Muslim Uighurs) live in irrigated oases that hug the surrounding mountains.

The historical significance of the Tarim Basin derives less from its geological character or climatic peculiarity than from its location. The Tarim constituted the most hazardous portion of the long and arduous Silk Road connecting Europe and

China, intermittently bringing great wealth to the celestial empire, from the period of the Han Dynasty (206 B.C.–A.D. 220) to the Qing (1644–1911). The key strategic point along this route lay at the 43-mile-wide (70-kilometer-wide) gap at the eastern edge of the Tarim Basin. This relatively narrow opening in the mountains permitted a road to cross at the Jade Gate Pass (Jiayuguan).

Most of the great caravans of the Silk Road skirted either the northern or southern end of the basin. The southern route, believed to be the first, followed the northern foothills of the Altun and Kunlun Mountains and passed just south of the salt lake of Lop Nur. After this route was abandoned because of the drying up of the vital oases that provided water, food, and shelter for passing caravans, a later route, known to Chinese historians as the Central Route, came into play along the southern edge of the Tianshan. For some distance this route followed the north bank of the Tarim River. The routes converged at the western end of the basin at the historic market center of Kashgar (Kashi). The northern route of the Silk Road, perhaps most important in recent times, lies outside the basin, passing north of the Tianshan and connecting the cities of Hami, Urumchi, and Yining. It must be kept in mind when assessing the importance of the Silk Road that it was not just the source of fabulous wealth from the silk and tea trade but also a conduit for new ideas and religions entering China. Settled by Islamic peoples from Central Asia, the Tarim Basin was referred to by Westerners as "Eastern Turkestan" or "Chinese Turkestan," and those names, suggesting the link to other Turkic populations of inner Asia, persisted—at least until the founding of "New China" (Communist China) in 1949. The term *Sinkiang* (*Xinjiang*), meaning "New Region," is of relatively recent date, stemming from the permanent acquisition of this border region in 1884 by conquering Qing armies.

Since the late 1970s the production of Tarim crude oil has increased, particularly on the southwestern periphery of the region. China's nuclear testing is carried out at the eastern edge of the basin near Lop Nur. As the petroleum industry expands, the number of ethnic Chinese increases, but a majority of the population remains Uighur. Recent political unrest is the result of rising Islamic fundamentalism in the wake of the breakup of the Soviet Union. Former Sinkiang and the Tarim Basin remain important for strategic and political reasons, as well as for their vast mineral reserves.

Further Reading: Whitfield, Susan, *Life along the Silk Road,* Berkeley: University of California Press, 1999.

TAY

Source: On Ben Lui in the Grampians
Length: 118 miles (190 kilometers)
Tributaries: Lyon, Tummel, Isla, **Earn**
Outlet: Firth of Tay, North Sea

A classic example of a glaciated river valley is that of the longest river in Scotland, the Tay. Draining the heart of the Grampian Highlands, the headstreams of the Tay, the Lochay and the Dochart, flow through steep-sided, glacier-gouged troughs strewn with morainic rubble. At the village of Killin the headstreams converge to form Loch Tay, a ribbon of water impounded by an Ice Age dam. This lake occupies a glacial-scoured rock basin more than 500 feet (152 meters) deep. At the exit of the loch, the Tay meanders across a wide plain, receiving the waters of the Lyon, whose source lies in remote glens and corries to the west. After the small town of Aberfeldy the valley closes in and the river flows through a wooded defile before opening up again onto an open, flat-bottomed valley at Grandtully.

It is then only a short distance downstream before the principal tributary, the Tummel, joins the river from the west, where it rises on the barren Moor of Rannoch. Along the course of the Tummel are various lochs, natural and artificial, that have been integrated into a hydroelectric scheme, but the Scots have been careful to build fish ladders to allow spawning salmon to go upstream—as at the tourist stop of Pitlochry. Nearby is the Pass of Killiecrankie, where road and rail routes (as well as the Garry River, a tributary of the Tummel) manage to squeeze through a deep, narrow gorge.

After the junction of the Tummel, the river valley again narrows, and at the old cathedral town of Dunkeld the river occupies a narrow trench, part of which is known as the Pass of Birnam. On the right bank of the river is Birnam Wood, which provides the basis for the prophetic passage in Shakespeare's Scottish tragedy: "Macbeth shall never vanquish'd be until/ Great Birnam wood to high Dunsinane hill/Shall come against him." Unfortunately for the regicide and his wife, such a conjunction of events does come to pass by the use of the stratagem of carrying vegetation as camouflage, and thus the drama comes to its sad conclusion.

The river opens onto the broad, fertile lowlands of Strathmore. After receiving the meandering Isla, the Tay flows swiftly to Perth, a cathedral town, route center, and head of navigation for small boats. The tidal river flows through a breach in the Sidlaw Hills, receives the last of its tributaries, and gradually opens onto the 20-mile-long (32-kilometer-long) Firth of Tay with its many sandbanks.

A tragedy many Scots consider second only to Shakespeare's took place in the Tayside region in the late nineteenth century. A railroad bridge completed in 1877 across the Firth collapsed on a stormy December night in 1879 while a passenger train was steaming across it. Ninety lives were lost, and though a new bridge was soon built to provide access to Dundee, local people for some decades feared to cross it by train.

See also Earn

TENNESSEE

Source: Junction of Holston and French Broad Rivers, near Knoxville, Tennessee
Length: c. 650 miles (1,046 kilometers)
Tributaries: Hiwassee, Little Tennessee, Clinch, Flint, Elk, Duck, Big Sandy, Clark
Outlet: **Ohio**, at Paducah, Kentucky

The Tennessee is distinctive as an American river because of its circuitous course and the numerous obstacles it once posed to pioneers and developers, until in the 1930s the Tennessee Valley Authority (TVA) converted it into a chain of lakes. The southwesterly-flowing Tennessee was the first major river encountered by Southern frontiersmen crossing the Appalachians. To the chagrin of the pioneer, the river does not continue to flow south. Nor is the course of the upper river any less confusing. The upper end drains a vast section of Appalachian highlands and valleys, where it is difficult to distinguish tributaries from the river's main channel; watercourses from all points of the compass contribute their output to the river there, which was known to the Indians as just the Big River. The Holston, its longest branch, rises in southwest Virginia and drains young sedimentary rocks and alluvial deposits of the folded Appalachians. It is 916 miles (1,474 kilometers) from the Tennessee's mouth at Paducah, Kentucky, to the farthest reach of the Holston. Yet the Tennessee River is considered several hundred miles shorter because of the conventional acceptance of the confluence of the Holston and French Broad Rivers, just upstream from Knoxville, Tennessee, as the river's origin.

Historically, the name Tennessee was applied to the river's headstreams and its tributaries. The north-flowing affluent, the Little Tennessee, was often referred to as *the* Tennessee in the early period. An 1890 federal statute declared that the Tennessee should be considered the river below the key junction near Knoxville. The old Cherokee town of "Tanase" or "Tenese" on the Little Tennessee gave its name to the Little Tennessee, the Big Tennessee, and the sixteenth state of the Union. The name Tennessee, applied to the river's branches or tributaries, persisted throughout pioneer times, and readers of letters and old documents must be careful to avoid confusion.

If the Holston is the primary drainage of the northern end of the upper basin, the French Broad, the Little Tennessee, and the Hiwassee are the primary affluents on the southern bank of the upper river. These three left-bank tributaries (the French Broad is, strictly speaking, a branch) cut across the older crystalline rocks of the Blue Ridge. They rise on the lofty flanks of the Smoky Mountains, occupying the border of east Tennessee, western North Carolina, and north Georgia.

The *U*-shaped course of the Tennessee—by which it crosses and recrosses the state that bears its name and thereby encloses on all sides but the north the region known as Middle Tennessee—is one of the most distinctive features of the river. The Tennessee has three distinct segments that have meaning for both geologists and historians of settlement: (1) the southwest-trending upper river from Knoxville to the vertex of the parabolic curve in northern Alabama; (2) the Great Bend of the river in northern Alabama, which includes the flex point (actually a curve that includes three minor bends as well as the treacherous Muscle Shoals above Florence, Alabama); and (3) the river's quiet lower course, where it is diverted northward across the western portions of Tennessee and Kentucky into the Ohio River.

The middle segment of the river—the Great Bend—presented major navigation obstacles for boatmen trying to reach east Tennessee. It was also an insuperable obstacle for those who wanted to bring flatboats and keelboats downriver to New Orleans; even if one could navigate the river, it ran in the wrong direction. The Tennessee gained a reputation in the early period as a contrary river—and it was its tumbling, twisting midsection that was the source of the problem. As a result of these difficulties, the river was always more an obstacle to be crossed than a path to be followed.

The earliest European occupants of the valley gave vivid names to the constricted course of the middle river below Chattanooga, which presented obstacles almost as great as those of Muscle Shoals farther downstream: the Suck, the Boiling Pot, the Skillet, the Frying Pan. This approximately 30-mile-long (48-kilometer-long) stretch was collectively known as "the Narrows." There is no truth to the notion that the Indian word *Tennessee* meant "great bend" or "bends" (we do not know the Indian meaning), though settlers who thought so can be forgiven for identifying the river's most salient aspect with its linguistic meaning.

After making a number of twists and turns, the river approaches the center of the Great Bend, where it turns southward. Then, near Guntersville, Alabama, it turns northwest once again in the direction of its most formidable barrier, the boiling whitewater passage of Muscle Shoals, so called because it was the site of traditional shellfish gathering, mussels being scooped from the shallow waters. This navigational knot of the middle Tennessee is located near the Alabama tri-cities of Florence, Sheffield, and Tuscumbia.

The Tennessee valley was the domicile and hunting grounds of native Cherokee. Along with their neighbors, the Creek and the Chickasaw, they occupied alluvial lands, built stockades, and established strategic villages at key points along the river, especially at confluences. The Cherokee came out losers in both the French and Indian War (1754–1763) and the American Revolution (1775–1783). In the former conflict, the Cherokee as a group sided with the French, but to protect the independent Overhill Cherokees the British built their westernmost redoubt near the mouth of the Little Tennessee. This is the notorious Fort Loudoun, named after the British commander-in-chief, a site that in 1761 was captured by warring Cherokee who then allowed their captives to go only to ambush and kill them on their way to South Carolina. Again at the end of the American Revolution, in 1783, the Indians were on the wrong side, and it was a foregone conclusion that their western lands must be vacated for veterans who had been paid in bounty warrants to be taken out in the public domain of trans-Appalachia. Even before the end of the Revolutionary War, settlers crossed into east Tennessee, followed the river downstream, and crossed the short distance to the paralleling Cumberland, which they followed to French Lick—presently Nashville.

During the Civil War the Tennessee provided a direct line of access for Northern troops into the upper South. From the time federal gunboats appeared off Paducah in September 1861 until Sherman's march to Atlanta (May–September 1864), the control of the Tennessee River was a major strategic focus for the armies of both the Union and Confederacy. Some of the key battles in the West were fought along the banks of the river and its tributaries: Shiloh, fought to a bloody draw near Pittsburg Landing (south of Savannah,

Tennessee), allowing the lower Tennessee to come under Union control; Chickamauga, an important Confederate victory fought on the side of Lookout Mountains opposite Chattanooga, amid wooded hills and a cove formed by the west branch of Chickamauga Creek, a Tennessee tributary; and the ensuing battle of Chattanooga, fought for control of the strategic heights of Lookout Mountain and Missionary Ridge overlooking the river and the city. Chattanooga was a key location not because of the river, but because it was the rail link between Nashville and Atlanta. Incorporated only in 1841, Chattanooga was a railroad town, as was Atlanta, the latter founded only a few years earlier (as the town of Terminus). The fateful importance of the "Battle above the Clouds" concerned control of the southern route into Georgia. Once Grant lifted the siege of Chattanooga on November 23–25, 1863, the way was open to Atlanta (May–September 1864) and the notorious March to the Sea (beginning November 16, 1864). The war in the West was virtually over, and when Grant swung northward through the Carolinas to close in on Lee's army from the south, the bloody days of the Civil War were almost over.

A sustained attack on the river was subsequently mounted by the Army Corps of Engineers. Between 1875 and 1900 the army engineers built canals and aqueducts, deepened channels, and made tentative plans to untie the navigational knot at Muscle Shoals. The first power proposal directed to the island-studded stretch of reefs, bars, and rapids was introduced in Congress in 1898 by Joseph Wheeler, a former Confederate cavalryman. From then until 1933 no session of Congress was without a bill to develop Muscle Shoals. Mobilizing for World War I, legislation was passed authorizing a nitrate plant that required a hydroelectric power plant, but the war ended before the project was completed. Senator George Norris of Nebraska was a tireless advocate of a combined flood control–power project along the middle Tennessee. It was during the famous Hundred Days of F. D. R.'s first New Deal administration that the TVA legislation was passed (May 1933). An overriding purpose of TVA, besides bringing jobs and electricity to a depressed region, was the integrated planning and development of an entire watershed. Soils, forests, agriculture, and industry were to be managed together according to an overall plan for the basin.

With twenty-five dams on the river today (nine of them major dams), the Tennessee is an example of a highly engineered waterway: the middle Tennessee has been converted into a chain of lakes. The river symbolizes for many environmentalists an excessively controlled system, less a managed river than a manacled river. The Army Corps, though, is nothing if not busy. To overcome the problem of the circuitous course of the Tennessee, a canal linking the southern arc of the middle Tennessee to the south-flowing Tombigbee, a branch of the Mobile River, permits easier access to the Gulf Coast. Built between 1972 and 1984 at a cost of $2 billion (the same price as the TVA), the Tennessee-Tombigbee Waterway—or the Tenn-Tom—was justified primarily on the basis of the economic benefits of improved barge traffic. At a time when the recreational, aesthetic, and ecological values of rivers have come to the forefront of public consciousness, it is questioned why considerations of megawatt-hours of power, acre-feet of reservoir space, and tons of cargo should be given precedence. The recent removal (fall 1999) of the unfinished Columbia Dam, a TVA project on the tributary Duck River, suggests that the era of the dam builders may be over. Demolition and removal of unnecessary dams has become an important political issue, as was seen in the presidential election of 2000.

See also Ohio

Further Reading: Davidson, Donald, *The Tennessee,* New York: Holt, Rinehart and Winston, 1946 (Rivers of America Series), rev. ed. University of Tennessee Press, 1978.

THAMES

Source: Cotswold Hills
Length: c. 210 miles (338 kilometers)
Tributaries: Windrush, Cherwell, Thame, Kennet, Wey, Mole, Lea, Roding, **Medway**
Outlet: The North Sea, at the Nore

St. Paul's Cathedral, London, and heavy boat traffic on the Thames River, George Chambers (Fine Art Photographic Library, London/Art Resource, NY)

> *Old Queensberry was entertaining at his villa in Richmond, which had a magnificent view of the Thames River. Guest after guest admired the panorama until the duke burst out, "What is there to make so much of in the Thames? I am quite tired of it. Flow, flow, flow, always the same."*
> Anecdote about William Douglas,
> Forth Duke of Queensberry

Draining a sizable portion of England's southern lowlands, the east-flowing Thames is not long compared with the great rivers of the world. From its source in the hills west of Oxford to the funnel-shaped estuary below London, the river justifies its original Celtic name (Tamese), meaning "Tranquil River." Once a major commercial artery, the Thames above London is no longer an important transportation route, and it is valued for its scenic beauty (except by the occasional jaded aristocrat), for angling, and for boating (the annual Henley regatta is rowed on the river).

Although a certain amount of doubt exists about the river's precise source, which is almost always the case for major rivers, the Thames is usually considered to begin with the merging of its four headstreams—the Isis (or Thames), Churn, Coln, and Leach—which converge on the university town of Oxford. In its upper course around and above Oxford—the town was originally a fording site—the river is often referred to as the Isis. The four headstreams rise near one another on the eastern slope of the Cotswolds in Gloucestershire, not far from Cheltenham. The upper valley of the Thames encompasses a broad basin, in which the river frequently twists and turns as it traverses the clay soils of the alluvial plain. The valley narrows at Goring Gap, which divides the Chiltern Hills from the North Downs. The lower end of the valley forms a second large alluvial basin, across which the river also meanders.

The river is navigable by barges to Lechlade, below which are a series of locks. The upper portion of the river, however, is used today primarily by fishermen and pleasure boaters. Downstream from London, just past Gravesend, the channel expands to a wide estuary. Whereas at London Bridge the width of the river is about 870 feet (265 meters), at Gravesend pier it is 2,400 feet (732 meters); only 3 miles (5 kilometers) farther downstream, below Gravesend, the river swells to a width of 3,870 feet (1,180 meters). The river is tidal above London as far as Teddington (a fact captured by the name). There is a difference of 23 feet (7 meters) between high and low tides, and navigators have to pay careful attention to this regular, diurnal variation in flow in entering and leaving the port of London. The part of the stream near London Bridge is known as the Pool, which stretches downstream as far as Blackwall.

The London docks represent artificial pools of enclosed waters just off the main channel, linking the waterway to the country's roads and rails—its circulation system—like so many intestinal villi lining an organism's alimentary tract linking it to the vascular system. The development of the docks was spurred by the need to overcome the congestion of the Thames banks, where hundreds of vessels pulled up alongside densely packed wharves, as is evident in old prints of the town and the river. Vessels today are moved along the river for 35 miles (56 kilometers) between Tower Bridge and Tilbury Docks. The upper docks are tidal, but the lower docks (for example, Tilbury) admit oceangoing vessels at any stage of the river. Once redolent of the exotic spices and foodstuffs of the Orient, today many of the docks are either closed or have changed their function. (Tilbury Docks closed in 1981 and has been redeveloped into an area of light industry.) The trend in new dock construction is for larger basins located farther downstream. Not only are the new docks not subject to the high tidal range of the river, but, in addition, they are served by good road connections that allow roll-on, roll-off trans-shipment service for the large container ships, which no longer require extensive warehouses.

The long and noble history of England has taken place largely along the willow-shaded banks of the Thames. The Roman city of Londinium (London) was located at the lowest bridging point of the river, just above the broad estuary. Only one bridge crossed the river until the eighteenth century—London Bridge—but today twenty-seven bridges span the tideway. The original London Bridge has indeed fallen down—or, at least, has been taken down—and transported to Lake Havasu, Arizona, where it has been reconstructed; a new London Bridge has been put up across the Thames.

During the Middle Ages the valley was prosperous, with a number of towns and religious houses strung out along the river. Beginning in the eighteenth century, with the expansion of the British Empire (especially the addition of the Indian subcontinent after Robert Clive's victory at Plassey in 1757), mercantile trade increasingly funneled into the Thames estuary. The historic wharves and docks from London Bridge to Blackwall received and trans-shipped a new and increasing bounty that underpinned the British imperium. The West India, East India, and Millwall Docks were enclosed in a wide meander just below the city. New docks were opened in the late nineteenth and early twentieth centuries to accommodate additional expansions of trade: the Victoria and Albert Docks (opened in 1885 and 1880), known collectively as the Royal Docks; the King George V Docks (added in 1921); and the already mentioned Tilbury Docks (opened in 1886). With places like Gravesend being virtually annexed to the city, and the new docks functioning as outports, it can no longer be said, in the words of the poet John Masefield, that London is a "great street paved with water, filled with shipping."

Two recent developments related to flood control and environmental protection might be noted. Unlike the flooding of most rivers, the lower Thames has the problem of high water coming *up* the river, the most feared condition being a destructive surge caused by a combination of a winter storm and high tide. Against such an eventuality, the Thames Barrier, the largest moving flood barrier in the world, was completed in 1983. With eight massive piers that allow shipping to pass unhindered, the giant retractable gate revolves upward to a vertical position only when needed. In mind of the Thames Barrier across the lower river and the numerous weirs that regulate the level of the upper course, it would be accurate to say that the Thames, like most major rivers in the world today, does not flow freely to the sea.

Although the river above London is not industrialized, the Greater London conurbation is the major industrial concentration of Great Britain. The cumulative effect of untold wastes discharged into the river by the country's primary port has led to significant pollution problems. Major cleanup efforts did not get going until the 1960s. The level of toxicity reached such a level by 1970 that not only had almost all the fish life been killed but the pollution was eating away at boat hulls. As fish species began to return to the lower river, the government offered a prize of twenty-five pounds sterling to the first angler to catch a salmon in the river—an event that hadn't occurred for 150 years. In 1985 a salmon was hooked, a 6 pound, 12 ounce trophy. Credit for revitalizing the river was given to a native Yorkshireman, who had worked in various capacities for river and environmental agencies since serving in the Royal Navy during World War II. In 1989 Hugh Fish was knighted for his efforts to clean up England's major river.

Further Reading: Dury, George H., *The British Isles: A Systematic and Regional Geography,* 5th ed., London: Heinemann, 1973.

TIBER

Source: Etruscan Apennines, in central Italy
Length: 251 miles (404 kilometers)
Tributaries: Paglia, Nera, Aniene
Outlet: Tyrrhenian Sea

After the Po and the Arno, the Tiber River is the third-longest river in Italy, but it is almost certainly the most famous, since along its banks stands the Eternal City of Rome. The Tiber is one of the most celebrated rivers of Europe. It has gone by many names: the ancient Romans referred to it variously as the Tiberis, the Amnis Tiberinus, and the Thyber, the first-named being the usually attributed Latin name (the Italian name is Tevere). According to legend the river was originally called Albula, but the name was changed to Tiber after Tiberinus, the King of Alba, was drowned in its swift current. The Latins granted river-god status to Tiberinus. The river's sacred character is attested to by the famous passage of Virgil's *Aeneid* (Book VIII), in which Tiberinus, the river god of the Tiber, appears to sleeping Aeneas and soothes him by describing the future city of Rome that will arise on the Tiber's banks, as well as promising to guide the oared boats of the refugee from the Trojan War upstream against his enemies. The ancient Romans believed that the river was under the patronage of the divine personification of the river. A festival was held every May 14, during which a bundle of rushes shaped to resemble a human form—the *argii*—was tossed into the Tiber to appease the divine nature. Although the central coast of Italy was not as attractive to colonists as the south, an ancient town of Tibur existed not far from Rome on the river Anio. Its founders were emigrants from Greece. Much of the historical background for the founding of Rome as set forth in Virgil's classic must be taken with a grain of salt, for the poet was attempting to produce a creative synthesis of myth, legend, and historical understanding meant to inspire and prolong the Augustan Age.

The actual river emerges from springs in the Apennines near Arretium. The source is not far from that of the Arno, and the two river systems are joined by the Paglia River and the Chiana Canal. Picturesquely meandering in its upper course, the river flows generally southward across Tuscany, Umbria, and northern Latium, until it turns to the southwest through Rome to empty into the Tyrrhenian Sea by two mouths. The upper Tiber and its chief tributaries, the Nera and the Aniene Rivers, have been harnessed to produce electricity.

The river is noted for its flooding, the heavy load of silt it carries, and navigational difficulties. After rains, the Tiber was wont to overflow the lower areas of Rome (today, the river is embanked). The Roman demand for timber for its navy's ships and for construction in the capital city led to the denudation of Apennine slopes, which made the soils less permeable, thereby increasing soil erosion and overland flow (as opposed to base flow). Most attempts to prevent flooding in Rome were unsuccessful, even by Augustus. Because the silt turned the river's waters a muddy yellow color, the river was known as *flavus Tiberis,* or yellow Tiber. Silt accumulation at the river's mouth has been so great that the ancient coastal city of Ostia, once Rome's port, now lies 4 miles (6 kilometers) from the sea. Siltation made it increasingly difficult to maintain the port. Claudius sought the radical solution of making an artificial outlet. The Tiber delta today has two channels: the Fiumara, which enters the sea near the ancient site of Ostia; and the Fiumicino, an artificial waterway used by ships. Though smaller craft can travel upriver as far as the junction of the Nera, frequent dredging of the lower course is necessary to permit navigation as far as Rome.

The growth of Rome had less to do with its site than its relative location. The marshy site of the city comprised a set of low hills (the celebrated Seven Hills) and intersecting valleys. Unlike other Greek and Italian towns located on a defensible high point, or acropolis (for example, Athens), Rome lacked a citadel. It did derive a measure of security from its interior location, for the city is some 15 miles (24 kilometers) from the river's mouth. Rome was a natural center of trade and communication along Italy's most navigable river at the approximate midsection of the peninsula. Timber and stone were brought downstream from the Apennines to build the largest city in the ancient world, a city whose estimated population of one million would not be exceeded until London attained that number in the first decade of the nineteenth century. Seagoing vessels of light draft brought grain and other commodities upstream from the coast. The city of Rome is at a river island that is the lowest point that supported bridge abutments. But what was more important than such physical considerations, the Roman region of Latium was at a central location. It became the natural focus of an extensive road system fanning outward from the imperial center.

See also Arno, Po

Further Reading: Cary, Max, *The Geographic Background of Greek and Roman History,* Oxford: Clarendon Press, 1949; Eberlein, Harold Donaldson, Geoffrey J. Marks, and Frank A. Wallis, *Down the Tiber and Up to Rome,* Philadelphia: J. B. Lippincott, 1930.

TIGRIS

Source: Taurus Mountains, in eastern Turkey
Length: c. 1,150 miles (1,850 kilometers)
Tributaries: Great and Little Zab, Diyala
Outlet: Merges with the **Euphrates** to form the **Shatt al Arab**, in southern Iraq

After flowing through a corner of southeastern Turkey and almost the entire length of Iraq, the Tigris forms in its lower course one-half of the famous riverine pair that encloses the rich alluvial land of Mesopotamia. The river rises in two branches in Turkey, far from the major concentrations of the Turkish population in the west. One branch originates south of Lake Hazar, the other southwest of Lake Van. The headstreams meet at Til, and the river winds in a southeasterly direction, forming part of the boundary between Turkey and Syria, before passing into Iraq. The Tigris unites with the Euphrates River at Al-Qurnah, below which the Shatt al Arab, the waterway forming part of the Iran-Iraq border, empties into the head of the Persian (Arabian) Gulf. Five thousand years ago, when the ancient civilizations of Sumeria, Babylonia, and Assyria had followed one another in rapid succession in controlling the valuable but flood-prone "land between the rivers" (Greek: *mesopotamia*), the Tigris and the Euphrates flowed separately into the gulf. Large accumulations of sediment since then have built the land outward from approximately Basra, and the 120-mile-long (193-kilometer-long) Shatt al Arab, the joint drainage of the Tigris and Euphrates, now traverses this deltaic plain.

The Mesopotamian interfluve of southern Iraq (in India it would be called a doab) is now in part known as al-Jazirah. The city of Baghdad lies on the Tigris, but it is a late, Islamic addition. The ruins of the ancient cities of Nineveh (opposite Al Mawsil), Seleucia, and Ctesiphon all stand on the banks of the Tigris. (The well-restored ruined city of Babylon is on the Euphrates.) The bed of the Tigris south of Baghdad lies several meters higher than that of the Euphrates. This made it possible in ancient times for Tigris water to enter irrigation canals and pass into the lower Euphrates. The floods of the Tigris are sudden and unpredictable, unlike those of the lower Nile. The need for a strong centralized authority stemmed in part from the requirement to control the river and to assign and enforce land rights. The instability of the political regimes in ancient times, which was evident in their regular rise and fall, was partly a consequence of the government's failure to predict and manipulate the river successfully, given the then-current state of technology.

Ancestors of the Abrahamic peoples—Jews, Christians, and Muslims—originated here, but the founder of the monotheistic traditions migrated westward across the Fertile Crescent (the wide extent of arable land arcing from the Tigris-Euphrates valleys to the Mediterranean) to the less promising but more predictable (and less well settled) lands west of the Jordan River. Babylonia was not just a place of fleshpots where stern Jewish patriarchs in exile prophesied the end of the world. The twin river valleys were a prototype of hydraulic civilizations, in both their advantages and disadvantages. The Tigris and Euphrates were two of the four rivers flowing out of Eden in Genesis (the location of the other two is not known).

The Tigris is navigable by small boats and rafts for much of its length. Some river steamers can ascend the waterway as far as Baghdad. The problem for British ships in the nineteenth century was not that they couldn't travel up the river, but that in negotiating the lower river, particularly the Shatt al Arab, they had to pass along the uncertain boundary between the (declining) Ottoman Empire and the domain of the Persian Shah. Modern nations in the region date from the post–World War I period (the name "Mesopotamia" for Iraq went out of favor only at that time).

In response to the need to protect its people from the Tigris's devastating floods, Iraq built the Samara Dam and put in place the Wadi Ath Tharthar Scheme, Iraq's largest flood-control project, which additionally irrigates an increased acreage of farmland. Turkey has planned a new, large-scale Southeast Anatolia Project (at a cost of $32 billion), aimed at generating electricity and providing irrigation water. Iraq feels threatened by the possibility of reduced flow downstream in its country. An additional impact of the new Turkish dam would be the inundation of archaeological sites and ruins. The Zeynel Bey tomb, an onion-domed temple in the medieval town of Hasankeyf, is the only example of Central Asian architecture in the region. Located on the banks of the Tigris, it would be submerged by an artificial reservoir if the new dam were built. Since a Kurdish minority is concentrated in southeastern Turkey, critics have charged that the removal of a contentious ethnic group is one of the purposes of this megaproject. The projected Ilisu Dam on the Tigris would be the second-largest Turkish dam after the Ataturk Dam on the Euphrates.

The importance of the river as a transportation artery has declined with improved road and rail service. The river still functions as an important political boundary (Iran-Iraq War of 1980–1988). As a source of scarce water resources that need to be divided between rivals, the river will shape the economic future of the region.

See also Euphrates, Shatt al Arab
Further Reading: Roaf, Michael, *Cultural Atlas of Mesopotamia and the Ancient Near East,* New York: Facts on File, 1990.

TRENT

Source: Staffordshire, in west-central England
Length: c. 170 miles (274 kilometers)
Tributaries: Tame, Dove, Derwent, Soar
Outlet: Merges with the Ouse to form the **Humber** estuary

England's third-ranking stream after the Thames and the Severn drains central England eastward to the Humber. It rises on Biddulph Moor and flows generally northeastward across the Midlands, the agricultural and industrial heart of England. The valley is underlain by sedimentary rocks, with widespread glacial deposits. Arable and pasture land predominate, especially on the dry, fertile terraces, but there are scattered patches of wetlands and woodlands in the valley.

The largest city on the upper river is Stoke-on-Trent, 38 miles (61 kilometers) north of Birmingham. This is the center of the Staffordshire pottery-making industry, but coal mining and the iron industry also concentrate here. An intricate network of canals links the river to the Severn, Mersey, Thames, and a host of other, minor waterways. During the prerailroad era (c. 1800), this web of waterways with accompanying aqueducts, tunnels, and side cuts (lateral canals) gave this central region of England maximum accessibility to raw materials, foodstuffs, and markets. Stoke-on-Trent and the surrounding, formerly separate Five Towns constitute the Potteries, an industrial district specializing in the production of china and earthenware. The Five Towns were the setting of Arnold Bennett's finely drawn *Clayhanger* trilogy of novels about small-town life in Edwardian England.

Farther downstream the Trent passes through the central English county of Nottinghamshire. The river has historically been an important boundary as well as an obstacle between northern and southern England. A diagonal line running southwest-northeast across Britain—the Severn-Trent Line—has often been considered to divide England into two regions on the basis of both physical and social geography. To the northwest are the Celtic uplands, while to the southeast are the lowlands, occupied by the Anglo-Saxons (and Romans). On opposite sides of the river stood at different times the Danes and Saxons, parliamentarians and royalists, labor and Tory voters. During the conflicts of the Middle Ages the Trent was deemed of enough strategic significance that fortified castles were built at Nottingham and Newark. The county was important because of its central position and the physical obstacle of the river. Because of the public's overwhelming consciousness of the associations of the Robin Hood legend with this region, it should be noted that the ancient royal forest of Sherwood extended from Nottingham to the vicinity of Worksop: it was some 25 miles (40 kilometers) in length and perhaps one-third that dimension in width.

The lower valley in Lincolnshire was once subject to regular inundation, but such natural cycles have been restricted by the regulation of the river's level. The tidal river reaches as far as Gainsborough, the head of navigation for merchant ships at the beginning of the nineteenth century. Barges moved farther up the river as far as Nottingham and were able to navigate between different river systems using the well-developed network of interconnected internal waterways. A high tidal bore known locally as the *agar* pushes a violent wave of water up the estuary and the lower reaches of the river (the word is believed to be a corrupt pronunciation of the word *eager*).

A note for the many golf lovers. The innovative golf course designer Robert Trent Jones was born in 1906 in Ince, England, on the Trent River, from which his middle name was taken. He immigrated to the United States in 1911 and became the first person to train himself as a golf course architect, designing or modifying many famous golf courses.

See also Humber

TWEED

Source: Southern Uplands of Scotland
Length: 97 miles (156 kilometers)
Tributaries: Ettrick, Teviot, Till, Whiteadder
Outlet: North Sea, at Berwick, England

The Tweed is one of the world's most famous (small) rivers, primarily among salmon fishermen, but it is also a celebrated border region. Since 1157 the Tweed has formed part of the English-Scottish border. For centuries prior it had been—and since that time has continued to be—a battleground across which two different peoples raided and fought.

The Tweed rises in the west of the Southern Uplands in southern Scotland. The valley forms a depression lying between the hard-rock Lammermuirs to the north and the volcanic Cheviots to the south. The river begins by trending to the northeast, following the guiding direction of

Scottish faults and folds. It then turns to the northeast at Hawick, the largest town on the middle Tweed, which lies at the head of Teviotdale. A river cliff overlooking a small tributary nearby, the Jed, is famous to earth scientists as the site where the Scottish geologist Hutton identified "gaps," or unconformities, in the rock strata, an important clue in the interpretation of geological history. Most of the region's towns (for example, Selkirk, Melrose) are sheltered in the valley of the middle Tweed. The river's waters were used in the early period to run looms for making the distinctive Tweed fabric woven from Cheviot sheep. The broad mainstream of the Tweed traverses glacial deposits, while the tributaries have cut narrow gorges in the shaly bedrock. Turning to the northeast, the river forms the Anglo-Scottish boundary for 17 miles (27 kilometers) before crossing into northeast England and emptying into the North Sea at Berwick.

The Tweed is not in itself a formidable natural barrier. Historical accounts referring to the "crossing of the Tweed" often seem to be using a figure of speech rather than literally describing the inevitable need to cross this stream in passing to and from Scotland. The only English city on the Tweed is also the most important. The walled fortress of Berwick-on-Tweed lies on the north bank of the river near the river's outlet. The Tweed boundary was important during the Scandinavian incursions, beginning in the ninth century; in the Scottish War of Independence, during the late thirteenth and early fourteenth centuries; and during the English Civil War, in the eighteenth century. In the struggle between King Charles I and the parliament, the Scottish earl Montrose led his forces across the Tweed on the open east side of the Borders in August 1640. He swept around the fortified English site of Berwick and repulsed the English army at Newburn on the Tyne. He soon occupied Newcastle, and thereby controlled London's vital coal supply. The Scottish victories were crucial in swinging the momentous struggle between king and commons against the monarchy, and the beheading of the king and the inauguration of the republican commonwealth were important events that followed.

Further Reading: For additional information about the Tweed valley and its towns, see the Web site: http://www.curriculumvisions.com/river/worldRivers

V

VAAL

Source: Mpumalanga Province, in northeastern Republic of South Africa
Length: c. 750 miles (1,210 kilometers)
Tributaries: Wilge, Sand, Vet, Riet, Modder
Outlet: **Orange**

It is perhaps not surprising that on the semiarid plateau lands of South Africa, rivers assumed importance as sources for irrigation and as political boundaries but not as avenues of transportation. The two Boer states that came into existence in the nineteenth century as a result of the *Voortrekkers*, or pioneers, venturing out from the Cape onto the forbidding veldt (open grazing land) were named after rivers: Orange Free State (today's Orange Province); and the Transvaal, the land beyond the Vaal (divided today between Mpumalanga in the east and Northern Province). These two rivers are actually part of one system, for the Vaal is the major tributary of the Orange. Both drain generally westward across the veldt, away from the towering Drakensbergs that overlook the southeastern coast. After the Vaal's confluence with the Orange, the latter turns away from the high, cool plateaus and traverses the hot, dry Karoo on the edge of the Kalahari Desert before emptying into the sea.

The valleys of the Vaal and the upper Orange are cool and temperate, at least compared with the subtropical climates of the lowlands. The high veldt, corresponding to elevations between 4,000 and 6,000 feet above sea level (1,219 and 1,829 meters), includes most of the basin of the Vaal and the upper Orange. The lower portion of the Vaal receives enough precipitation to be classified as semiarid, with a climate similar to that of the American Great Plains, while the eastern or upper valley has a moderate maritime climate, like that of northwest Europe but with a dry winter.

The Vaal rises in Mpumalanga Province in north-central Republic of South Africa near the railroad junction point of Breyton, about 120 miles (193 kilometers) east of Johannesburg. Its course is approximately west-southwest to join the Orange near Douglas. For most of this distance it forms the boundary between the former Orange Free State and the Transvaal, once independent Boer states. The river has not cut a deep valley into the upland surface, for in most places the bed of the river lies only a few tens of feet below the surface. The difference in elevation between the headwaters, at approximately 6,000 feet (1,829 meters), and the Orange confluence, at 3,500 feet (1,067 meters), approximately defines the vertical limits of the topographical high veldt

For most of the year the river is shallow and includes many "drifts," or fords that were used as easy crossing places. In the summer months heavy rains in the catchment area cause the river to swell and raise its level to as much as 30 feet (9 meters) above its winter level. (*Vaal* has no relation to the English words *vale* or *valley,* but instead signifies "muddy," hardly a very specific meaning for an

African river—or any river.) The river has no right-bank tributaries of any significance, since the land is more arid to the north and the drainage basin of the northward- and eastward-flowing Limpopo lies nearby. On the other hand, there are a number of important left-bank affluents, draining different sections of the Orange Free State to the north.

The entire length of the Vaal has been developed, and further water supplies for the republic must be found elsewhere. The waters of the Vaal and its tributaries are used for irrigation, chiefly of alfalfa and other fodder crops, while the unirrigated lands along the banks are used for raising cattle and sheep and cultivating maize. With the gold mines of the Witwatersrand (or simply, the Rand) lying only 35 miles (56 kilometers) north of the middle stretch of the Vaal, the river has long been used to serve the mining industry and the large towns of the gold belt. Discovery of coal and gold deposits south of the river only accentuated the intensive utilization of the river's waters. In southwestern Transvaal, there are alluvial "diggings" of diamonds along the lower course of the river, although the largest diamond mines in this region are in basaltic pipes—as, for example, at Kimberley, in northern Cape Province. The Vaal Dam, 24 miles (39 kilometers) above Vereeniging, is the largest storage dam on the river, but there are several others, including the Vaal-Harts Dam within Cape Province, used for irrigation of the Harts valley. The river has never been used for transportation, but recreational use of the artificial lakes strung out along its course has increased lately.

See also Orange

VARDAR

Source: Sar Planina, in northwest Macedonia
Length: c. 240 miles (390 kilometers)
Tributaries: Bregalnica, Crna Reka, Treska
Outlet: Gulf of Salonica

The north-flowing Morava and the south-flowing Vardar form a furrow crossing the mountainous Balkan Peninsula that has historically been an important route between eastern Mediterranean lands and the lower Danube valley of central and eastern Europe. In a region of inhospitable mountain ranges and dry karstic terrain (terrain formed by limestone solution), the two valleys, which approach one another in northern Macedonia, provide scarce, fertile farmland and exhibit a relatively dense pattern of settlement.

The Vardar (Greek: Axios) rises north of the Macedonian capital of Skopje. The course twists through the mountainous borderlands between Kosovo and Macedonia, both parts of the former Yugoslavia (although only Macedonia has attained independence), before passing Skopje. This old city—once a Roman center, later the capital of medieval Serbia—stands on the banks of the Vardar in a large basin with a Mediterranean-style climate (dry summers and temperate winters). The surrounding peaks are more than 6,500 feet (1,981 meters) high, but the valley is fertile and productive. An earthquake devastated the city in 1963, but it has been largely rebuilt today.

The ancient kingdom of Macedonia, whose most famous son was Alexander the Great, was anchored at the head of the Aegean Sea in the Vardar valley. The Macedonians were less sea-minded than the Greeks, and they appropriately demonstrated a genius for the continental organization of a vast land empire. The second-largest city of Greece, Thessaloniki (Salonika)—a major port and industrial center—lies 15 miles (24 kilometers) east of the river's mouth at Cape Vardaris.

The structural depression of the Vardar-Morava has been crossed and recrossed by invaders and conquerors since time immemorial. The corridor has been a meeting place not just between north and south but also between east and west. The river route was used in the Middle Ages by marauding Crusaders as well as by southward-expanding Serbs.

Downstream from Skopje the Vardar flows through a series of narrow gorges on its way to Greece. The lower course of the river flows 50 miles (80 kilometers) through Greece before emptying into the Gulf of Salonika, an arm of the Aegean. The Greek portion of the river traverses a marshy lowland that was once prone to flooding and malaria. Flood control and reclamation were initiated in 1925, and these plains today are intensively cultivated for rice production.

The entrance of the river into northeastern Greece is a key strategic location, traditionally called the "iron gates," not to be confused with the Iron Gate, a gorge on the lower Danube, also an important military control point in southeastern Europe. During World War II, the Germans used the Vardar valley to invade Greece.

The Macedonian culture is not easy to pigeonhole, but the language is considered to be in the Slavic family. The designation of a broader Macedonian region comprising the area peopled by ethnic Macedonians includes the borderlands between Greece, Bulgaria, and the former Yugoslavia. The present Republic of Macedonia consists of only a part of this traditional homeland, as people in northeastern Greece (in the Central Macedonia department) and in bordering Bulgaria are quick to point out. The entire length of the Vardar valley in Macedonia and Greece continues to be an important spatial anchor for a people who can trace their history back to the centuries before Christ when Alexander ruled much of the known world.

See also Morava
Further Reading: Kaplan, Robert D., *Balkan Ghosts: A Journey through History,* New York: St. Martin's, 1993.

VISTULA

Source: West Beskid range of the Carpathians, in southern Poland
Length: 665 miles (1,070 kilometers)
Tributaries: Dunajec, San, Narew, **Western Bug**, Brda
Outlet: Gulf of Gdansk on the Baltic Sea

One of the major rivers of eastern Europe rises in southwestern Poland on the flanks of the Carpathian Mountains. Poland's longest river flows generally northward toward the Baltic, but not without making some wide turns.

The Vistula (Polish: Wisla) originates in the traditional region of Galicia in southern Poland. The headwaters of the river approach nearby the upper course of the Oder (Polish Odra), which occupies the traditional region of Silesia. Both these historic regions occupy natural and political borderlands, where the western Carpathians, the Moravian Gate, and the North European Plain converge, and Germany, Poland, and the former Czechoslovakia have contended for political dominance here.

The major town on the upper river is Kraków, where a new, planned German section of the city was built during the late Middle Ages as an extension of the original Slav settlement attached to the fortified enclosure of the Wawel. The capital of Poland, however, lies in the central part of the country. Warsaw occupies both banks of the river at an important east-west crossing point, where the river could be easily forded. Such geographical advantages of course attracted the attention of military forces. The fate of Poland—partitioned three times in the late eighteenth century and wiped off the map of Europe in the nineteenth—is epitomized by the tragic history of Warsaw. Succeeding Kraków as the Polish capital in 1609, the city was destroyed by Charles Gustavus of Sweden in 1656 and by the Russians in 1794; it was conquered by Napoleon, who made it a Grand Duchy, and then it came under the domination of the Russian monarchy until World War I. It is estimated that German bombing in September 1939 destroyed 75 percent of the city. World War II began with the September 1, 1939, German crossing of the portentous Polish Corridor—a thin strip of Polish territory along the lower Vistula that permitted Polish access to the independent Baltic port of Danzig (today's Gdansk).

Like most of the rivers draining the North European Plain, the Vistula flows obliquely from southeast to northwest, at least in its middle and lower course. Unlike the rivers of Germany and the Low Countries, its navigability has never been assured, and it did not carry as large or as diverse cargoes as the Rhine, the Elbe, or even the Oder. Subject to freezing in the winter, the river also was more prone to low and undependable flow during drier summers. Unlike many of the western rivers, it had no coal and iron ore to sustain shipping. It did carry grain and timber, however, and the Baltic trade in these commodities was important as an early linkage between the economies of western and eastern Europe. Today canals link the Vistula to the Oder, Dnepr, Neman, and Pregel Rivers.

The last-named river—perhaps least familiar to the reader—raises the subject of the deltaic portion of the river. The estuary comprises two main distributaries: the Nogat River, which passes Malbork to the Vistula Lagoon (to the east); and the Martwa Wista (or "dead Vistula"), which flows past Gdansk (to the west). The Vistula Lagoon (Polish: Zalew Wislany) is an arm of the Baltic separated from the Gulf of Gdansk by a narrow spit approximately 60 miles (97 kilometers) in length. The Nogat and Pregel Rivers flow into this lagoon, which is shared between Poland and a tiny Russian outlier, whose main town is Kaliningrad, sheltered behind the Vistula Spit at the eastern end of the inlet.

See also Bug, Western
Further Reading: Hartshorne, Richard, "The Polish Corridor," *Journal of Geography* 36 (1937): 161–176.

VOLGA

Source: Valday Hills, northwest of Moscow
Length: c. 2,300 miles (3,700 kilometers)
Tributaries: **Oka**, Sura, Vetluga, Kama, Samara
Outlet: Caspian Sea

Russia's Volga, the longest navigable waterway in the largest country in the world, and the longest river of Europe, rises in a small lake among the Valday Hills about halfway between Moscow and the Baltic Sea. The name of the source of this river is something of a misnomer: the Valday are not so much hills as lakes, marshes, and low morainic ridges resembling the glaciated lake district of northern Minnesota and Wisconsin. Although this low plateau is sparsely populated today (partly as the result of World War II destruction), it once commanded key control points in a riverine communication system formed by the convergence of the watersheds of some of Russia's greatest western rivers: the Volga, Dnieper, and Western Dvina. After the Mongol invasion (1237–1240) overthrew Kievan Russia, population movement and political control shifted to the protected forest interior southeast of the Valday—at Yaroslavl, Suzdal, Vladimir, and, later, Moscow.

From the Valday plateau the Volga flows north to a point above Moscow, where it turns southeast in a large bend. The river passes Gor'kiy (Nizhney Novgorod), picking up its major western tributary, the Oka. Then the magnificent Volga flows south until it reaches the important town of Kazan, where it is joined by the Kama, the major eastern tributary that rises 1,262 miles (2,031 kilometers) to the northeast in the Ural Mountains. At Kazan the river enters the enormous Kuibyshev reservoir covering 2,500 square miles (6,500 square kilometers), an area larger than the state of Delaware. The river continues to flow southward as far as Volgograd (formerly Stalingrad). Below Volgograd the lower course of the river crosses marshlands and parched deserts and semideserts before it enters the landlocked Caspian Sea.

The heavily industrialized river corridor of the middle and lower Volga from Gor'kiy to its Caspian outlet is known by the Russians as the Povolzhye, or land along the Volga. Including the important left-bank tributary, the Kama, the Povolzhye was primarily an oil- and gas-producing region until the 1930s, when Josef Stalin sought a more protected eastern location for steel-making and metal industries beyond the reach of invading German armies. In the post–World War II period, the Povolzhye became the key new industrial zone of the rapidly expanding Soviet Union, and though the landscape resembles chemical corridors elsewhere around the world, such as the northern gulf coast of Texas and Louisiana, the Volga region is increasingly diversified and does not rely solely on the petrochemical industry.

Extending from the cool forests of the north to the steppes and semideserts of the Caspian lowlands, the Volga is revered by all Russians, and it has earned the appellation "Mother Volga," by which it is referred to in popular Russian folk stories. The river sweeps around Moscow before it veers to the south, seeming to embrace the capital city in the crook of its northern arm like a loving mother. The Volga valley had already been claimed for the Russians by Ivan IV ("the Terrible") in the sixteenth

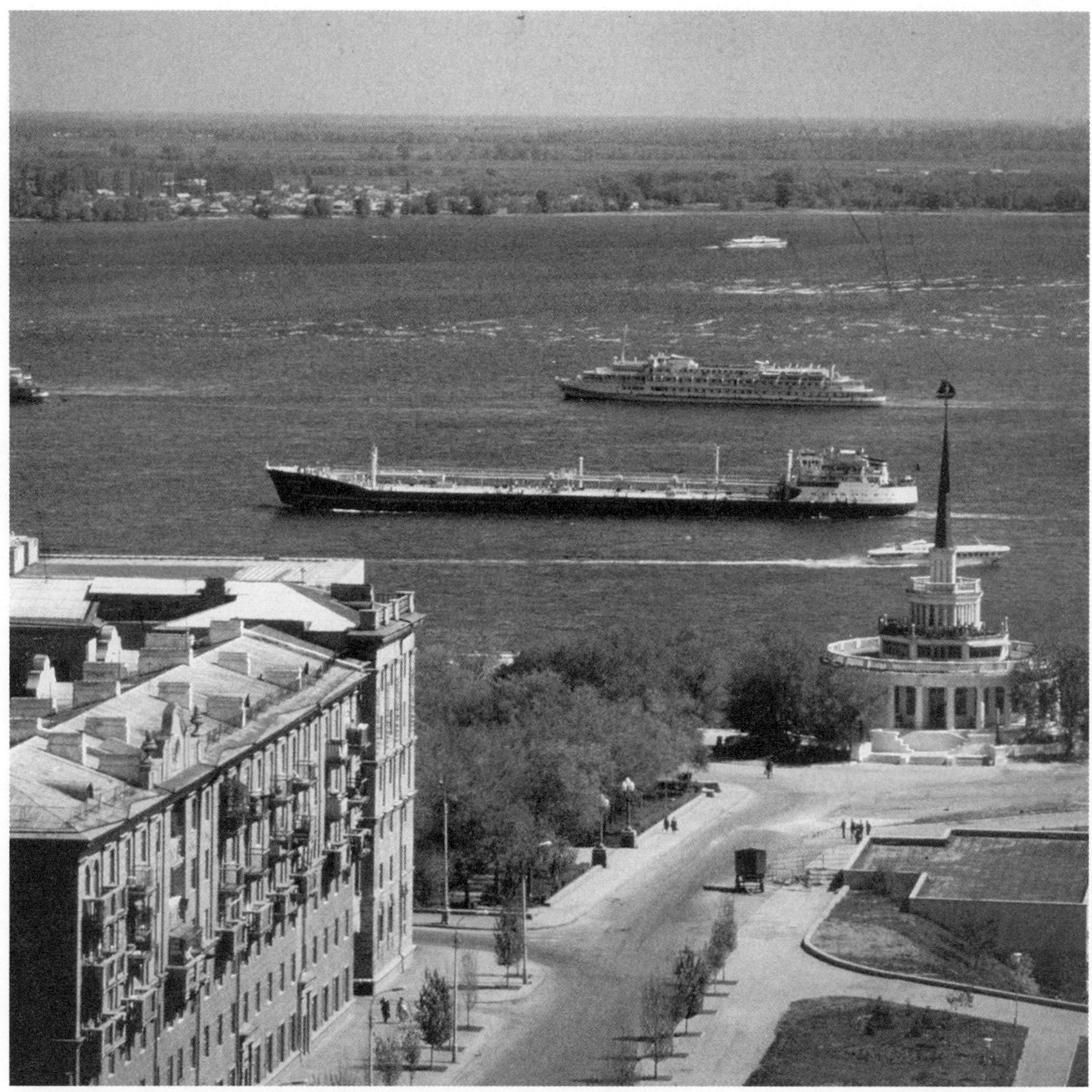

View of the Volga River from Volgograd (formerly Stalingrad) showing river traffic (Novosti)

century. Although the industrial Volga lies well to the east of the core concentration of the Russian population, the river has been an important corridor for trade and migration, and its accessibility was crucial in Russia's plans for eastern expansion. As early as the eighteenth century a portion of a navigable route between the Volga and the Baltic was constructed, joining rivers and lakes in what was then known as the Mariinsk Waterway. Periodically expanded and improved, the transportation artery was completed in 1964 and reopened as the Volga-Baltic Waterway. Combining navigable rivers, canals, and reservoirs, this aquatic highway joins the Rybinsk Reservoir on the Volga to the Neva River at St. Petersburg (formerly Leningrad). The Volga-Don Canal, completed in 1957, joins the lower course of the Volga at a point just south of Volgograd to the eastern tip of Tsimlyansk Reservoir on the Don. Extending 63 miles (101 kilometers), this artificial waterway effectively links the Caspian and Black Seas. Once prone to dangerous flooding in May and June because of melting snow, the Volga has been converted to a chain of reservoirs connected by navigable stretches of river, thereby providing flood protection as well as generating hydroelectric power.

On a contemporary map one can scarcely discern where the Volga begins in the midst of the maze of artificial lakes west of Moscow. Much of the river is still navigable, an important fact since Russia's bulk freight—fuel, timber, agricultural products—moves by the slow but reliable mode of river transportation. Two out of every three tons of freight shipped by water in the Soviet Union were once carried on the far-flung Volga system. Rail and air transport are more important in a relative sense today, but cheap water transportation continues to be suitable for heavier cargoes. The nearly landlocked position of Russia, with few outlets to warm waters, has historically meant that its large western rivers had to be kept open and accessible to the warm water ports on the Black and Baltic Seas. Today, the Volga is linked via canal to the Baltic Sea, Black Sea, Sea of Azov (an arm of the Black Sea), White Sea, Don River, and Moscow. One might picture the mighty Volga and its tributaries as an enormous heart with a circulating system encompassing much of European Russia.

See also Oka

Further Reading: Chamberlain, Lesley, *Volga, Volga: A Voyage down the Great River,* London: Picador, 1995; de Villiers, Marq, *Down the Volga: A Journey through Mother Russia in a Time of Troubles,* New York: Viking Penguin, 1992; Hooson, David J. M., "The Middle Volga: An Emerging Focal Region in the Soviet Union," *Geographical Journal* 126 (June 1960): 180–190.

WEI

Source: Southeastern Gansu Province, in northern China
Length: c. 450 miles (724 kilometers)
Tributaries: Jing, Lo
Outlet: **Huang He**

The Wei (WAI) River rises on a plateau in north-central China north of the Qinling Mountains. The small but important area drained by the river represents an extension of the fertile, loess-derived soils associated with the great bend of the Huang He, or Yellow River. The river begins in Gansu Province, flowing southeast and then east across populated Shaanxi Province before joining the Yellow River where the great river makes its bend from south to east (at Huayin). The main tributary of the Wei is the Jing, at whose confluence is modern Xi'an, formerly known as Chang'an, the ancient capital of China. The Wei valley has long been the major east-west route into Central Asia, bypassing the circuitous course of the Yellow.

The broad alluvial valley was the site of some of the earliest centers of Chinese culture, most notably during the Zhou dynasty that ruled for much of the first millennium B.C. Though not the first culture to develop floodplain agriculture and metallurgy (the earlier Shang dynasty did that) or the first to unify the Chinese people (the brutal, succeeding Qin did that), the Zhou encompassed the classical age of Confucius, Lao-Tze, and Mencius, from which all later Chinese learning and thought derives, as well as making progress in the use of iron for ox-drawn plows. It could be said that the cultural hearth of Chinese civilization lies along the banks of the Wei and Yellow River valleys. Without the fertile soils formed from silt blown eastward from the interior deserts, the Chinese civilization—the oldest continuous civilization in the world today—could not have risen, grown, and thrived.

The early Neolithic culture known as the Yangshao arose in the valleys of the Wei and Yellow. Zhou people migrated down the Jing River and formed the state of Zhou in the Wei valley. They overthrew the Shang dynasty (1750–1040 B.C.) and established the Zhou dynasty (1100–256 B.C.), which lasted longer than any other in Chinese history. Between about 1000 B.C. and A.D. 1000, the Chinese capital alternated between Chang'an in the Wei valley and Luoyang in Henan Province to the east. In the Wei Valley the brutal ruler of the Qin state defeated his rivals and later unified the Qin dynasty (221–206 B.C.), calling himself the Qin Shi Huangdi, the First Emperor. The Wei was the site of the first major irrigation system in China, constructed in the third century B.C., abandoned after the ninth century, and reconstructed and repaired in the twentieth century. The Wei valley today is the agricultural and population center of Shaanxi. Major cities, besides Xi'an, include Xianyang, Baoji, and Tianshui. More than half the land in the valley is intensively cultivated with cotton, wheat, millet, and fruits.

See also Huang He

Further Reading: Perkins, Dorothy, *Encyclopedia of China: The Essential Reference to China, Its History and Culture,* New York: Checkmark Books, 1999.

WESER

Source: Hannoversch-Münden, in north-central Germany
Length: 273 miles (439 kilometers)
Tributaries: Aller, Hunte
Outlet: North Sea

The north-flowing Weser cuts across the Mittelgebirge, or Central Uplands, of Germany before passing across the northern plains en route to its estuarine outlet on the North Sea. With its southwestern branch, it provides a traditional route from the vicinity of Frankfurt am Main to the lowlands of the north and the port of Bremen.

The river begins at the junction of the Fulda and Werra Rivers in the midst of the low hills and plateaus of central Germany. The southwest branch of the river—the Fulda—was an important traditional gateway to the south, and the valley has been dignified as the Fulda Gap. A Benedictine abbey established in A.D. 744 at Fulda was the basis of a pre-eminent cultural center, which also benefited from the valley's being a transportation corridor. Farther north in the Fulda valley near the junction of the two branches of the Weser is the old town of Kassel, once the residence of the elector of the German state of Hesse-Cassel (German: Hessen-Kassel), as well as the home in the early 1800s of the pioneering philologists and folklorists Jacob and Wilhelm Grimm.

The Weser flows northward past Minden (Münden) onto the level lands of the North German Plain. At Minden the river passes through a hilly plateau in the Porta Westphalia, another traditional gateway. Farther downstream the river traverses the Lüneburger Heath, a sandy, sterile outwash plain stretching southward from Hamburg between the Elbe and the Ems.

Like other streams draining the North European Plain, the Weser turns to the northwest and crosses the lowlands obliquely. This disruption of the drainage pattern is the result of morainic obstacles placed in the path of the river by the melting of Pleistocene icesheets. This lateral, east-west deflection of the lower courses of the Elbe, Weser, Ems, and Rhine facilitates the linking of these waterways via canals (best known of which is the Mittelland Canal). After crossing sandy heathlands, the river passes the port of Bremen. The estuary stretches downstream as far as the seaport of Bremerhaven. From south to north there is a regular succession of belts of land: sandy heath, followed by extensive fenlike marshlands, then the tidal flats along the coast and the estuary, and finally an interrupted chain of sand dunes across the North Sea that includes the East Frisian Islands. The mouth of the Weser faces the tiny North Sea island of Helgoland, as does the mouth of the Elbe not far to the east. This island was able to cover the German navy in the ports of the lower sections of these rivers; therefore Helgoland became a pawn in the military rivalry between Great Britain and Germany in the late nineteenth and early twentieth centuries. All of the rivers emptying into the North Sea are polluted, as a result of a dense population and a high concentration of industry. Although the Weser isn't as bad as the notoriously dirty Rhine, that is mostly because it is a shorter stream with fewer industrial cities in its valley.

See also Elbe, Rhine

WEST

See Xi He

WESTERN DVINA

Source: Valdai Hills, in northwest Russia
Length: 635 miles (1,022 kilometers)
Tributaries: Aiviekste, Ogre
Outlet: Gulf of Riga of the Baltic Sea

The multiple names of this comparatively short, smooth-flowing stream—German: Düna; Lettish: Daugava; and Russian: Zapadnaya Dvina—suggest its character as a borderland. The river is called the

Western Dvina to distinguish it from the Northern Dvina, the primary affluent of the White Sea, lying far to the east.

The river's headwaters are in the Valdai Hills, a region of low glaciated ridges about halfway between Moscow and the Baltic. Nearby are the sources of the Dnieper and Volga river systems. The terrain of the headwaters more nearly resembles a plateau of irregular drainage than a true highland. With its many lakes and marshes, it bears comparison with the glaciated landscapes of northern Minnesota and Wisconsin.

From its source, the Dvina flows to the south and then generally the west en route to its outlet on the Gulf of Riga, an arm of the Baltic. Along its course the river crosses a small section of western Russia, northern Belarus, and most of the small Baltic country of Latvia. It is the principal drainage of this Baltic nation, and the capital city of Riga lies near its mouth. Latvia is the only Baltic country whose capital is at a maritime rather than an interior location.

The basin of the Western Dvina was added to the territory of an expanding Russia during the eighteenth century at the expense of Sweden and Poland-Lithuania. The part of the watershed north and east of Riga and the lower course of the river itself came under Russian rule as a result of the northern wars of Peter the Great (reigned 1689–1725). The Treaty of Nystad in 1721 granted to Russia control of Karelia, Estonia, and Livonia (Latvia plus parts of Estonia). The southern expansion of Catherine the Great (reigned 1762–1796) led to the addition of lands on the left bank of the middle and lower river almost as far south as the Black Sea following the last two partitions of Poland (1793, 1795).

The river was once a key waterway linking the Baltic and Black Seas. Only a low divide separates its headwaters from those of the south-flowing Dnieper. Water transportation on rivers and seas remained the primary mode of moving goods until the transport innovations of the nineteenth century—especially in Russia, which was slow in building a road and rail system to serve its vast land area. Whereas the Dvina was used in medieval times as a route for the exchange of exotic northern furs for Byzantine silver in the markets of Constantinople, today the river is used primarily for floating timber. The Dvina has some rapids and shallows in its lower course, as well as a series of hydroelectric dams and reservoirs near Riga. The waterway therefore illustrates the unusual case of a river that is more navigable in its upper course than in its lower. The river is connected by canals to the Dnieper, Neman, Berezina, and Volga river systems.

See also Northern Dvina

WHITE NILE

Source: Luvironza, in Burundi, central Africa
Length: 600 miles (970 kilometers) or
c. 2,300 miles (3,700 kilometers)
Tributaries: Victoria Nile, Albert Nile, Bahr Al-Zeraf, Bahr Al-Gabal, Bahr Al-Ghazal, Sobat
Outlet: Merges with **Blue Nile** at Khartoum, Sudan, to form **Nile** proper

The name White Nile (Arabic: al-Bahr al-Abyad) is applied on maps to only a limited section of the river: in northern Sudan, extending upstream from Khartoum to the junction of the Bahr Al-Gabal and the Bahr Al-Ghazal at Lake No. In a wider sense, the Nile's longest headstream embraces the headwaters of Lake Victoria (Victoria Nyanza), whose most remote feeder, the Luvironza River, has been identified as the source of the world's longest river. This latter stream flows into the Ruvuvu River, which in turn merges with the Kagera, one of the principal streams draining the western side of Lake Victoria. So conceived, the White Nile has already flowed more than 2,000 miles (3,200 kilometers) and half the length of the Nile by the time it passes Khartoum, the capital of Sudan, located at the strategic intersection of the White and Blue Nile.

Although a remote mountain spring in Burundi has been marked with a small pyramid bearing the inscription *Caput Nili*—"Source of the Nile"—it is perhaps best to speak of *sources* of the Nile when considering the mountainous headwaters region. In the beautiful yet treacherous lake district of central Africa where the Nile has its origins, the drainage is composed of a series of

White Nile riverside scene (Caroline Penn/CORBIS)

large freshwater bodies—Lakes Victoria, Albert, and Kyoga are only the largest—each of which is fed by numerous affluents.

The historic search for the source of the Nile dates from the time of the Greek historian Herodotus, who in about 460 B.C. reached as far as the first cataract (actually, rapids) before turning back. The English explorer John Hanning Speke reached Lake Victoria from the east coast in 1858, and four years later in a subsequent expedition with Augustus Grant he discovered the river that issued from the north end of the lake (Victoria Nile). Thus began a fervid search for the most distant source of the great river by a remarkable series of explorers—Richard Burton, David Livingstone, and Henry Morton Stanley—all of whom tried to trace more southerly sources than Lake Victoria (Livingstone mistakenly identified the Nile's source—Ptolemy's Mountains of the Moon—as draining into Lake Tanganyika). In the end, Speke was right, although he died tragically and mysteriously on the very day he was to defend his position against Burton at a public meeting. Lake Victoria and its affluents provide the most remote source of the world's longest river. In addition to "discovering" the medical missionary and explorer Dr. Livingstone, Stanley, a newspaperman and later a writer of travel books, descended the Lualaba to show that it was a tributary of the Congo and not, as Livingstone had believed, an influx of the upper Nile system.

The discovery, exploration, and conquest of the Nile were a principal achievements of Victorian England. Its adventurers appropriately gave names to the lakes, rivers, and falls reflecting their leaders, their monarch, and her family. Although it was not until 1937 that a German explorer, Dr. Burkhart Waldecker, traced the southernmost spring of the Nile in Burundi, by the conclusion of the nineteenth century the entire length of the valley had been explored and solidly placed within the British sphere of influence (Sudan became a condominium administered jointly by Egypt and Great Britain in 1899, Uganda a British protectorate in 1894).

A major obstacle to early expeditions on the White Nile was presented by the marshlands of Bahr Al-Ghazal and Bahr Al-Gabal known as the Sudd. Located in southern Sudan, this extensive wetland encompasses a lowland where the White Nile spreads out over 60,000 square kilometers (23,166 square miles). The region is covered by water lilies, papyrus rushes, and other aquatic plants (the ubiquitous exotic invader, the water hyacinth, has now made its appearance). Each year the Nile brings down more vegetation and chokes the Sudd marshes (sometimes mistakenly called swamps) with more material. Debris breaks away and forms islands. Matting of vegetation can produce enough "land" that elephants can walk on it. Though today the marshes are channelized and partially converted into an irrigation canal, rather like the Everglades of southern Florida, the drifting reeds and ooze posed almost insuperable difficulties for early explorers, including the Englishman Samuel Baker, who first encountered the malarial wetlands.

Farther upstream beyond the Sudd, after passing the strategic location of Gondokoro, where the English early established a stronghold, cataracts and rapids make ascent of the river practically impossible. The major falls in order of ascent are Fula Rapids (formerly Fola Falls), near where the Albert Nile merges into the Bahr Al-Gabal; Murchison Falls on the lower Victoria Nile; and, near Jinja and the outlet of Lake Victoria, Ripon Falls, which today is inundated by the storage reservoir of a hydroelectric plant.

Although the White Nile loses much water by evaporation, especially in the Sudd morass, and contributes only half as much water to the lower Nile as the Blue Nile draining the Ethiopian highlands, its flow is more regular than that of the highly variable Blue Nile. In terms of hydrology, it might be stated that the White Nile provides the *baseflow* while the Blue adds *peakflow* to the world's greatest river. Thus it is the Blue Nile that was responsible for the regular September flooding in Egypt of the lower valley and delta, now checked by the Aswan High Dam.

See also Blue Nile, Nile

Further Reading: Moorehead, Alan, *The White Nile*, New York: Harper and Brothers, 1960.

WILLAMETTE

Source: Cascade Range, in western Oregon
Length: 240 miles (386 kilometers)
Tributaries: McKenzie, Calapooya, Clackamas
Outlet: **Columbia**

The Willamette (pronounced wuh-LAM-et) valley lies on the western side of Oregon, but it is central to the history of the state and indeed the whole Pacific Northwest. The river drains a broad, north-south trending depression between the subdued Coast Ranges and the towering Cascades. The river meanders widely across a floodplain whose main floor lies slightly to the west of center, and the channel, carrying a heavy load of sediments with little gradient, is braided. The floodplain includes characteristic features of a mature valley: sloughs, abandoned channels, and oxbow lakes. Foothills slope up to the Cascades to the east, the Coast Range to the west, and the Calapooya Mountains to the south. The valley stretches from the river's mouth just north of Portland, Oregon's largest city, to Eugene, the state's second largest city, at its southern end. The main-stem river begins 4 miles (6.4 kilometers) southeast of Eugene at the confluence of the Middle and Coast forks. The longer of the two, the Middle Fork, rises approximately 75 miles (120 kilometers) away in southeast Linn county and flows to the northwest through a series of reservoirs before reaching the junction of the two rivers. The north-flowing Coast Fork flows through a reservoir en route to the junction of the Willamette's headstreams, some 55 miles (89 kilometers) away near Eugene. As the Willamette winds through its sloping alluvial plain, the relief is interrupted by small basaltic ridges and rolling hills. Above Oregon City, which is 15 miles (24 kilometers) south of Portland, a range of basaltic hills forces the river into a narrow gorge that ends at Willamette Falls in a picturesque but small vertical drop.

The fertile soils and mild climate of the valley have long attracted human occupation. *Willamette* is a native Indian word, but not one applied by the indigenous people to the river (its meaning has been lost). The Kalappuyan Indians, the predomi-

Willamette riverfront scene at Portland, Oregon (John Elk)

nant group upstream from the falls, depended on the spring run of the chinook salmon as a food source. A member of George Vancouver's expedition in search of the elusive Northwest Passage was the first European to view the Willamette River. In the fall of 1792 the commander of the British expedition dispatched Lieutenant William Broughton up "the river of the West" (the Columbia). In late October, Broughton sighted the mouth of a large left-bank tributary of the Columbia and named it the River Mannings, after another member of the Vancouver expedition. Lewis and Clark were little interested in the Willamette's mouth as they passed down the Columbia in their haste to reach the Pacific (1805). On their return trip, however, they paddled up the stream's mouth for a short distance and gave it the name of an Indian people who inhabited an island just below the entrance—another name that didn't stick. Only with the publication of Lt. Charles Wilkes's *U.S. Exploring Expedition* (1845) did the present name become attached to the river, and with the government's imprimatur even the spelling has not changed since then.

Agents of the Hudson's Bay Company established the first town at Oregon City at the key location of the falls, which was not only the head of navigation but also an important source of power for saw- and gristmills. The American tide of immigration was inexorable. In 1844 alone, 800 people followed the Oregon Trail to its terminus at Oregon City. The head start of Oregon City as an urban center was soon dissipated, as new cities sprang up along the river. Portland soon replaced Oregon City as the largest city in Oregon Territory because of its strategic location near the mouth of the river. The valley was rapidly settled after 1846. Following the midcentury Gold Rush in California, and the later rush in eastern Oregon-Idaho, the Willamette valley became the primary source of food on the West Coast.

Salem was founded in 1840 and had the definite

advantage of being a central location in the valley. Unfortunately, about half of its population wandered off to California with the discovery of gold. A new era of growth was inaugurated in the midvalley by the arrival of the railroad in 1871. Upriver towns such as Corvallis and Eugene initially prospered as markets for products of their hinterlands: Corvallis serving a dairy- and fruit-producing area, Eugene a center for wheat, lumber, and mineral products. These towns sustained their growth in the twentieth century by being the homes of the state's two principal universities.

Environmental modifications of a major kind began in the nineteenth century. From 1850 to 1853 the federal government spent thirty thousand dollars clearing rocks from a stretch of the lower river to improve navigation for steamboats. It was hoped that oceangoing steamers would be able to travel as far as the falls. Even though that aim was never achieved, navigation for river boats on the lower river was improved, and steamers began to ply the river's upper waters for a number of years—but only at high water. The completion of locks at Oregon City in 1873 allowing circumvention of the falls made the river continuously navigable. The arrival of the railroad ended the romantic era of steamboat travel, because wherever rail lines intersected the river, cargoes were redirected to the faster, more reliable trains.

In the twentieth century the lead agency of the federal government for rivers, the Army Corps of Engineers, emphasized flood control more than navigation. The valley is particularly vulnerable to flooding, with disastrous floods occurring about every twenty to thirty years (1861, 1881, 1890, 1927, 1964). The clayey soils of the floodplain are prone to inundation because they impede drainage. Following the passage of legislation in 1936, the Army Corps constructed a series of storage reservoirs along the Willamette and its tributaries to control runoff. One of the subsidiary effects of controlling flooding was making the floodplain more suitable for agricultural, commercial, and industrial development.

By the 1950s the Willamette valley was, despite its image as a land newly reclaimed from the wilderness, suffering the effects of high population density and increased levels of pollution. Among the sources of its water-quality problems were raw sewage, waste from pulp and paper mills, and untreated industrial effluents. The oxygen of the river's waters was low, and fish populations were in decline. Even toxic trace metals were appearing in the river. Oregon responded rapidly to clean up and protect the largest river flowing entirely within its boundary. By the 1970s water quality had already improved markedly, and fish populations had returned to the river. To coordinate a sensible plan that would balance the need for land use with the need for environmental protection, Oregon implemented its innovative Greenway program in 1973. An environmental corridor stretches south from Portland for some 150 miles (241 kilometers), in which natural, historical, scenic, and recreational values are recognized and protected. Land use in this corridor is strictly regulated. A buffer strip of vegetation has been established or allowed to remain in place along the river to slow down runoff from adjacent lands. Construction visible from the river and alteration of the riverbanks are not allowed, or at least are kept to a minimum. The Willamette River has been transformed over the years from a raw wilderness, to a commercial and industrial artery, to a protected and enhanced environmental corridor. The continuing success of Oregon's Greenway program suggests that a society and a culture can evolve in its relationship to the land.

See also Columbia

Further Reading: Bowen, M. A., *The Willamette Valley: Migration and Settlement on the Oregon Frontier,* Seattle: University of Washington Press, 1979; Web site for the protection of the main-stem Willamette River (Willamette Riverkeeper): http://www.willamette-riverkeeper.org/

WISCONSIN

Source: Lac Vieux Desert
Length: c. 430 miles (690 kilometers)
Tributaries: Rib, Eau Claire, Big Eau Pleine, Plover, Lemonweir, Baraboo, Kickapoo
Outlet: **Mississippi**

One of the marvels of early Wisconsin was the Round River, a river that flowed into itself, and thus sped around and around in a never-ending circuit. Paul Bunyan discovered it, and the Bunyan saga tells how he floated many a log down its restless waters.

No one has suspected Paul of speaking in parables, yet in this instance he did. . . .

The current is the stream of energy which flows out of the soil into plants, thence into animals, thence back into the soil in a never-ending circuit of life.
Aldo Leopold, *Round River*

The largest northern tributary of the Mississippi rises in the lake district of northeastern Wisconsin on the border with Michigan. The river flows generally southward before making a large bend near the place where only a short distance separates it from the Fox River, an important link in the historic Fox-Wisconsin waterway. From that point, the broad waters of the many-islanded river flow west past the important early fur-trading entrepôt of Prairie du Chien, near the river's outlet.

The Fox-Wisconsin waterway was featured in the earliest history of Wisconsin. In 1673 Père Jacques Marquette and Louis Jolliet pioneered the easiest portage from the Great Lakes to the Mississippi River. Guided by friendly Miami Indians, Jolliet, whose primary interests were in the fur trade, and Father Marquette, a Jesuit priest who had lived among the Huron Indians, traveled up the Fox from Green Bay in two birchbark canoes and soon were shown across the mile and a half distance separating the watersheds of the two rivers. At the site of present-day Portage (early Fort Winnebago), the team of explorers with their small crew of five encountered a wide, sandy river that Marquette reported as having numerous shoals and small islands covered with vines. The Indians told the explorers that the southwest-flowing stream was called "Meskousing," which was transformed by French orthography into "Ouisconsin," which the British then turned into "Wisconsin." The eastern end of the broad lower river where the two river systems approach closest to each other furnished the site of Portage, Wisconsin. Located 34 miles (55 kilometers) north of the state capital of Madison, Portage became an important trans-shipment point for fur trading during the French regime (the spot was originally called Carrying Place), and later was a strategic center and fort site when British, American, and Indian forces met and collided along the lower Wisconsin. At the other end of the lower river, near its junction with the Mississippi, there grew up the earliest white settlement in the valley, Prairie du Chien, not named after prairie dogs but taking its name from a local Indian chieftain, Chien. It was here, on the plain skirting the confluence of the Wisconsin and Mississippi Rivers, that a regular fur exchange arose during the French period. The various Indian tribes arrived here in late May, bringing their furs to trade before scattering for the winter. It was at the dawn of the American period when a man who has been described as Wisconsin's first millionaire, Hercules Dousman, arrived at Prairie du Chien in 1826 as an agent for Astor's American Fur Company. Dousman's span at the historic town embraced the final defeat and removal of the native tribes, in the series of events following the Winnebago Uprising (1827) and the Black Hawk War (1832), as well as the arrival of agricultural settlers in the valley. The elegant residence of this headstrong entrepreneur was built on the site of an abandoned fort. Villa Louis is today a major tourist draw for those who want to glimpse early Wisconsin life.

The headwaters region encompasses myriad lakes, ponds, and small feeder streams, so that it is difficult to pinpoint the river's source. The political border of Michigan and Wisconsin almost equally divides the shallow but relatively large source of Lac Vieux Desert. On an island in the lake was located an old Indian potato-planting ground, which in corrupted French came out "vieux desert," better translated as "old planting-ground" than "old desert." The river flows from the southwest end of this lake and proceeds across a dense, mixed forest—once valuable timberland—comprising pine, hemlock, tamarack, and cedar, with birch, maple, poplar, and linden interspersed. It meanders widely and begins to bend to the south. The early lumbermen said that the upper river twisted and turned so much that it was "like the intestines of a hog."

The extensive windings of the upper Wisconsin probably gave rise to the legend of the Round River. This story came from the pen of Douglas E. Malloch at a comparatively late date, but it was soon attached to the larger Paul Bunyan saga of the Northwoods. As the tale goes, a huge pile of timber, one hundred million board feet, was once removed from a single "forty" (40 acres) and driven downriver in search of a sawmill town. After two weeks of navigating the river, Paul and his men came upon the camp from which they had started, which they could identify by the way the logs had been stacked. It was then they realized that the river they were on was round:

> And though we'd driven for many a mile
> We'd drove in a circle all the while!
> And that's the truth as I'm alive,
> About the great Round River drive.

The numerous rapids and falls of the upper Wisconsin were more of a problem to the early loggers than the meanders. A partial list of obstacles feared by early loggers would include Big Bull Falls (Wausau); the Jenny Bull Falls (Merrill); Little Bull Falls (Mosinee); Wisconsin Rapids; and Whitney's Rapids (below Nekoosa). The 150 miles (241 kilometers) from Rhinelander to Nekoosa (first called Pointe Bar) presented the largest drop in elevation and the greatest number of navigation problems. Numerous hydroelectric dams came to occupy these sites, and even during the heyday of the logging era, at the end of the nineteenth century, early dams were major obstacles for raftsmen. Large rafts consisting of a number of smaller cribs had to be broken up before these obstacles could be passed. Slides in dams needed to be installed to allow passage of the logs. Navigation of the large dams, such as the Kilbourn Dam at the lower end of the Dells constriction, was dreaded by raftsmen in the early days. If the raft were not steered properly below the chute, there was the danger of *saddlebagging*, or running the raft against a rock or obstruction and doubling it up, requiring large amounts of labor to unjam it. The pioneer logging industry—with its timber cruisers, lumberjacks, dam builders, and mill owners—was considered so important (it was Wisconsin's first industry) that early dams were rarely built all the way across the river, thereby allowing passage of the rafts. When it came time to create a series of reservoirs to regulate the river's flow in the twentieth century, planners carefully studied the various dams and impoundments that had been put in place by early loggers to float and guide logs, especially on the upper river's tributaries.

The lower river below Portage is a study in contrast to the upper river. Though interrupted by a power dam near the twin villages of Sauk City and Prairie du Sac, the river runs broad and free to its junction with the Mississippi. It slides past the German-settled Sauk City and Yankee Prairie du Sac, settlements parceling out between them the fertile Sauk Prairie Indian lands. The river passes the large Badger Ordnance Plant near Baraboo, built at double pace during the early years of World War II and the site of an abortive bombing attempt during antiwar protests in the 1960s. The river soon passes Spring Green on its right bank, and on the opposite bank, on the low brow of a hill, the residence and school of the iconoclastic architect Frank Lloyd Wright, who was born nearby. As the Wisconsin approaches the greater river, the unusual situation is presented of a valley narrowing downstream rather than broadening. Imposing bluffs rise on both sides of the river. The volume of water carried by the river is not decreasing, however, only the width of the floodplain. The explanation of this conundrum lies in the geological structure of the region. The Wisconsin River in this section traverses resistant layers of dolomite (calcium-magnesium carbonate) and as a result has carved out a narrower valley than, say, in the central parts of the valley, where soft sandstones are encountered. Whereas the river at Wisconsin Dells has shaped the bedrock into fantastic shapes including standing rocks and witches' bowls, the mouth of the Wisconsin, no less spectacular, features towering bluffs, most notably at Wisconsin's Wyalusing State Park, where the confluence can be grandly viewed.

Further Reading: Derleth, August, *The Wisconsin: River of a Thousand Isles,* New York: Farrar and Rinehart, 1942 (Rivers of America Series); Martin, Lawrence, *The Physical Geography of Wisconsin,* Madison: University of Wisconsin Press, 3d ed., 1965 (orig. pub. 1916).

WISŁA

See Vistula

X

XI HE

Source: Eastern Yunnan Province, in southwest China
Length: c. 1,250 miles (2,012 kilometers)
Tributaries: Zuo Chiang, Liu Chiang, Gui, Bei, Dong
Outlet: South China Sea

The upper and lower courses of the Xi He (SHEE-huh), the longest river in southern China, are a study in contrast. The river rises on Maxiong Mountain in eastern Yunnan Province. It goes by many names and includes many headstreams, the principal one being the Hongshui. The Xi's main stream is formed at the meeting point of the Hongshui and You Rivers at Guiping in Guangxi Province. Farther downriver, below Wuzhou, the river is called the West River (*Xi* meaning "west").

Li River karst landscape in Guangxi, China (Jesse Walker)

Chinese junk at mouth of Pearl River (Jesse Walker)

The generally easterly-flowing stream traverses mountainous Guangxi within narrow, confined valleys. There are numerous scenic and historical spots in the Xi (sometimes spelled Si) basin in Guangxi Province, including the Lingyang Gorge, forming the passageway between the upper reaches of the West River and Guangzhou (Canton). Towns are few, with the most important, Wuzhou, lying at the junction of the navigable tributary Gui. This was once the collecting center for the cinnamon, mace, and cabinet woods for which Guangxi is famous. A tributary of the Gui, the Li River, offers some of the most spectacular karst mountain peaks in this region, and the area around Guilin has been praised and painted since ancient times. Limestone peaks rise from the fertile plain of the river, reflected on clear days in the smooth surface of the water. The Chinese compare the 51.5-mile (82.9-kilometer) stretch of the Li River between Guilin and Yangshu to a landscape painting on a scroll. The Ling Canal, connecting the Li and the lower Xi, was originally built as a transportation route and line of invasion between central and southern China.

Although the province to the east that the Xi flows into is also mountainous, the large triangular delta of the lower river is set in the midst of the Guangdong highlands, each of its three sides measuring about 100 miles (160 kilometers). The Pearl River (Zhujiang) delta is formed in southern Guangdong by the convergence of three major rivers: the West (Xi), the North (Bei), and the East (Dong). The Pearl is the name given to both the geomorphic delta and the lower course of the Xi after the convergence (Chinese names are nothing if not confusing to the Westerner). The delta—a maze of canals and channels—drains about half the area of Guangdong Province.

Geographers classify the climatic type of southeastern China as Humid Subtropical. The rivers that make up the Pearl River delta receive heavy precipitation and are subject to extreme seasonal fluctuations because of monsoonal reversal of atmospheric flow. Even though its basin is half as

Heavily laden boat in Pearl River Delta (Jesse Walker)

large as the Yellow's, the Pearl River system discharges six and a half times as much water to the sea as the great river of north China.

The numerous streams and canals occupying the delta flow between paddies, wet fields where rice is cultivated (properly speaking, *paddy* refers to the rice, not to the field). In the twelve-month growing season of southern Guangdong Province, three rice crops can be grown a year. The Pearl River delta is one of the most important economic areas in China. Besides rice, the rich alluvial soils furnish sugarcane, tropical fruits, tobacco, and oil-bearing plants. Other major economic activities include fish farming and the raising of silkworm cocoons.

Guangzhou (Canton), the capital of Guangdong Province, is just downstream from the convergence of the three rivers. On the north bank of the Pearl, it has long been one of the major cities of south China and a major port. Until the opening of the coastal ports, Guangzhou was the port of entry for the whole of China. The road to the interior lay up the North River (Bei) to the Plumtree Pass (Meiling), a low notch communicating with rivers draining in the direction of central China; farther to the west, a pass (Lesser Meiling) leads to Hengyang in Hunan Province. The island port cities of Hong Kong and Macao are situated south of Guangzhou, with the former British colony located just east of the mouth of the Zhujiang and the former Portuguese colony to the west.

Further Reading: Lin, George C. S., "Evolving Spatial Form of Urban-Rural Interaction in the Pearl River Delta, China," *Professional Geographer* 53 (2001): 56–70.

Y

YALU

Source: Changbai Mountain Range, in northeastern China
Length: 490 miles (789 kilometers)
Tributaries: Hun, Changjin, Tongno
Outlet: Bay of Korea of the Yellow Sea

On the southern slopes of the Changbai, or "Eternal White," Mountains, rise the most important rivers of northeastern China: the Sungari (Songhuajiang), the Tumen, and the Yalu. All issue from Tianchi Lake ("lake of heaven"), a volcanically formed lake that is the deepest in China. The headwaters of these rivers are dear to the Chinese not just because of the traditional Chinese reverence for nature but also because the mountains are the primary source of timber for the country, and provide the "three treasures" of Manchuria: the medicinal herb ginseng; the sika deer, whose antlers are also used for medicine; and the sable, whose valuable fur is prized.

The Yalu (Korean: Amnok) flows in a generally southwesterly direction along the border between China and North Korea. Draining Liaoning and Jilin Provinces in northeastern China (Manchuria), the river forms with the Tumen River the boundary that has been the scene of important battles during the last hundred years or so. The river empties into an arm of the Yellow Sea just south of Dandong, China. This port city just upstream from the outlet remains ice free year-round and accommodates large ships. On the Korean side of the border near the mouth is Sinuiju. Bridges across the Yalu link Dandong with Sinuiju, as they do the other twin cities separated by the frontier: Ji'an, China, with Manpu, North Korea; and Shanghekou, China, with Supung, North Korea. The river is navigable for large ships only along its lowest course, but barges and small craft ply the river's waters along most of its length. The Yalu is used principally for floating timber downstream to sawmills. It is also an important source of hydroelectric power for industrial Manchuria. The Supung Dam above Sinuiju, which supplies power to both North Korea and China, is one of the largest dams in Asia.

The longest river in Korea has featured prominently in modern warfare. In a major battle of the Sino-Japanese War (1894–1895) a rising Japanese power defeated a Chinese naval squadron around Haiyang Island off the mouth of the river. By the terms of the negotiated peace, Japan received Korea and Formosa (Taiwan), the first step in a territorial aggrandizement that would continue until the end of World War II. Ten years after the fracas with the Chinese, Japan again went to war, this time with Russia. In February 1904 Japan launched a surprise attack on the Russian naval base at Port Arthur, located at the tip of the Liaodong Peninsula covering the Yalu mouth to the east, thus precipitating the Russo-Japanese War (1904–1905). In the first land battle of the war, the Russians were defeated by the Japanese near the Yalu River on May 1, 1904. A Japanese victory in this war resulted in new acquisitions to the growing east Asian empire and access to the coal deposits of Manchuria. Most recently, the Yalu River was important in the Korean War (1950–1953). On October 25, 1950, Chinese People's Liberation Army troops crossed the Yalu River and succeeded in defeating some United Nations' troops, including some Americans. In the next year the U.N. charged China with being the aggressor. Yet China perceived a threat to its valuable industrialized northeastern region and was responding to a request by communist North Korea for help as U.N. forces advanced northward in their country. General Douglas MacArthur was relieved of his command by President Truman when the popular general voiced his opinion that the Western forces should cross the Yalu and punish the Chinese in their own territory.

Further Reading: Alexander, Bevin, *Korea: The First War We Lost,* New York: Hippocrene Books, rev. ed., 2000 (first pub. 1986).

YAMUNA

Source: Himalaya Mountains
Length: c. 850 miles (1,370 kilometers)
Tributaries: **Chambal**, Sind, Betwa, Ken
Outlet: **Ganges**

This major tributary of the Ganges enters India's holiest river from the right bank, yet its source lies in the Himalayas. For most of its length the river parallels the Ganges, and the fertile interfluve between these two rivers (the Doab) constitutes a densely settled region of great strategic and political significance.

The Yamuna (formerly spelled Jumna) rises at an elevation of nearly 11,000 feet (3,353 meters) in the western part of the Himalayas. It runs to the southwest, cutting deeply into the mountains, forming the boundary between Uttar Pradesh and Himachal Pradesh. The river trenches a gorge through the coarse, easily erodible Siwalik Hills, a Himalayan outlier. Reaching the Indo-Gangetic plain—the great alluvial lowland stretching across northern India—the Yamuna, like other rivers draining from the mountains to the north, has built up an alluvial fan of coarsely textured materials about 100 miles (161 kilometers) wide, into which it has incised a narrow floodplain. An irrigation barrage at Tajewala raises the water levels and provides for the Western and Eastern Yamuna Canals. Paralleling the banks on both sides of the river, these canals ramify to form an intricate network of canals and branches. A channel of the western canal taking water to Hisar, which is chronically struck by famine, was built in the fourteenth century and repaired by the Mogul emperor Akbar in 1568. Under British administration in the nineteenth century the canal system was extended, with many branches and channels added. In the twentieth century the digging of modern wells has tapped underground aquifers and allowed the pumping of water away from fixed lines of irrigation. Precipitation declines steadily to the west, and wheat, a winter crop (or *rabi*), becomes increasingly more important than the monsoonal summer crop (*kharif*) of rice as one goes in that direction.

The long fillet of land between the Yamuna and the Ganges has a preeminent position as *the* Doab. Elsewhere a doab requires specification of the enclosing rivers, but if unstated it is assumed that the reference is to the Yamuna-Ganges interfluve. The region is anchored by Delhi to the west and Agra to the east. Delhi—both the old capital and new—is situated at a key location that has been vital since prehistory. The city lies on the west bank of the upper Yamuna almost on the drainage divide between the Indus and Ganges basins. The city has easy access to the two great fertile plains of the Punjab and the Ganges at a point where the Thar Desert approaches somewhat closely the Himalayan chain. Invaders of India were compelled to pass near Delhi if they were to reach the densely settled and prosperous Gangetic plain. Delhi was, moreover, at the head of navigation so that boats could go all the way from Delhi to Calcutta.

Near the eastern end of the Doab's axis, the city of Agra, the Mogul capital, stands on the right bank of the Yamuna. Boasting numerous examples of Mogul architecture at its fullest flower, the city is best known for the magnificent, white-marbled Taj Mahal, built approximately 1631–1645 to commemorate a much-loved empress, a classic structure of geometric design that has become a symbol of India even though its creator was a Muslim. Agra has a strategic location, commanding the routes to the south into Malwa and the Deccan. With access to the Malwa passage the Doab was the core of the pre-Mogul Delhi sultanate.

The Ganges and the Yamuna are both holy rivers, and the confluence point, at Allahabad, is especially sacred. The place is a pilgrimage site, or *prayag,* where believers purify themselves by bathing. Below Akbar's great fort, on dry sandbanks in the angle of the rivers, pilgrims gather in large numbers at the annual Magh Mela fair. Every twelfth year the Kumbh Mela attracts even larger numbers of people, sometimes exceeding a million. The separate waters of the two rivers can be distinguished below the confluence for some distance: the Ganges brown, the Yamuna clear and blue.

See also Chambal, Ganges
Further Reading: Moynihan, Elizabeth B., ed., *The Moonlight Garden: New Discoveries at the Taj Mahal,* Seattle: University of Washington Press and the Arthur M. Sackler Gallery, Smithsonian Institution, November 2000.

YANGTZE

Source: Tibetan highlands, in southwest Qinghai Province, western China
Length: c. 3,450 miles (5,550 kilometers)
Tributaries: Yalong, Min, Jailing, Wu, Han, Xian
Outlet: East China Sea

The fourth longest river in the world and the longest in Asia rises in the Tibetan highlands of western China and flows 3,450 miles (5,550 kilometers) before emptying into the East China Sea. The river is known for most of its length as Chiang Jiang ("Long River"), or just Jiang ("the river"). With more than 700 tributaries, Long River bisects China's agricultural and industrial heartland, at once uniting and dividing the country. The river is a major commercial artery in central China and the primary rice-growing area in the world's most populous country.

The upper course of the Yangtze flows first to the southeast, then the northeast, across the Yunnan Plateau and the Red Basin of Sichuan (*Sichuan* means "four rivers" in Chinese, referring to four major tributaries of the Yangtze). Above Yibin, the river is known as the Jinsha Jiang, or the River of Golden Sand. The left-bank tributary of the Min joins the river at Yibin, emptying its clear water into the reddish, silty water of the main stream. Since the Min is more navigable and has been more important for trade than the Yangtze above this point, the Chinese used to consider the Min, flowing past the Sichuanese capital of Chengdu, as the mother river. The confluence of the two rivers is marked by an old eight-story pagoda. Not until the end of the Ming dynasty in the 1640s did the Chinese realize that the Jinsha, lost farther west in mountains and navigable upstream only for another 60 miles (96 kilometers), was the longer and thus the primary river.

Thousands of miles farther west the great river begins its journey to the sea. The precise location of its source has been a matter of considerable doubt until recently. Above the town and bridge of Yushu the river adopts the name Tongtian He, the River to Heaven. In turn, two feeders of this stream are candidates for the true *fons et origo* of the legendary river: the Tuotuo, draining from the west; and the Dam Qu, flowing from the south. In 1976 the China Geographical Research Institute dispatched an expedition to determine the actual source of the river: the team explored the small glacial lake of Qemo Ho at the head of the Tuotuo, which lay beneath a picturesque glacier at the base of 21,723-foot (6,621-meter) Gelandandong Mountain. A later expedition in 1985 led by a Hong Kong Chinese found that the Dam Qu head stream was a little longer and had a larger discharge. This expedition, sponsored by the National Geographic Society (United States), identified a far less scenic site as the source: a small pool at the base of a subdued hill known to the local Tibetans as Jari. If that is the true source, a partial recompense for its lack of scenic beauty can be gained by noting that on the far side of Jari Hill rises another tiny stream, the head of the Mekong (though this is disputed, too).

The river stretches across the vastness of China

Three Gorges Dam under construction on the Yangtze River, November 1999 (Andrew Warne)

and its western territory, making giant swinging loops rather like the arches of a dragon's back. The generally southerly course of the river's upper section—the Jinsha Jiang—is diverted sharply to the northeast at Shigu by upturned limestone mountains. According to Chinese tradition, more than 4,000 years ago Emperor Yü, the founder of the Hsiq dynasty, raised Cloud Mountain in front of the river at Shigu, causing the great bend and preventing the river from flowing out of Chinese territory into present-day Vietnam and the Gulf of Tonkin.

The section of the river between Yibin—where the Min enters, and the traditional head of navigation for junks and smaller vessels—and Ichang is best known for the treacherous but beautiful Three Gorges, towering pinnacles that constrict and deepen the river, turning it into a boiling mass of whirlpools and dangerous rapids. A massive hydroelectric dam with eight times the power-generating capacity of the Nile's Aswan Dam is being built across a narrow part of the valley at Sandouping, just above Yichang, despite mounting international concern over both its environmental and engineering problems (not to mention the fact that millions of people will have to be moved). The Three Gorges Dam was first conceived by the redoubtable Chairman Mao, who boosted his image by swimming the Yangtze on a number of occasions. The construction of the giant dam could be considered the fulfillment of imperial ambition and communist propaganda to control and subdue the inequalities of nature in the name of the collectivized state. (Even the U.S. Army Corps of Engineers, which had acted as adviser, withdrew from the project because of criticisms.) Although river steamers once warped through this stretch on tautly wound cables, the traditional head of navigation for steamers was at Yichang.

The river emerges from the gorges to meander across a broad lake basin that is considered the rice bowl of China. Here in the central province of

Hubei (Hubeh) the river passes the town of Shasi and the tri-city cluster of Wuhan: Hankow, Wuchang, and Hanyang. The head of navigation for oceangoing vessels is at the industrial city of Hankow. During the heavy monsoonal precipitation of the summer, overflow lakes such as Dongting and Poyang absorb some of the overflow of the Yangtze. During the winter months these lakes are almost dry. As a result of sedimentation, the lakes have become shallower and less effective in regulating the river's flow.

Most of the five hundred million people who live along the banks of the river occupy the lower, near-sea-level section of the river. The river forms an important though approximate boundary—the wheat-rice line—dividing China into geographic regions based on subsistence diet. At Namjing the Jiang is crossed by a large modern bridge, the lowest on the river, first opened in 1968. This section of the river once had dolphins disporting in its waters—they were revered as Yangtze goddesses—before pollution and overhunting reduced their numbers almost to nil. Just below Zhenjiang (Chinkiang) the Grand Canal, the longest manmade waterway in the world, built mostly during the Sui and Tang dynasties in the seventh century, joins the river, linking it to north China and the Huang He (Yellow River).

The Long River finally enters its deltaic plain, with its mouth consisting of two main arms separated by a tongue of land known as Chongming Dao. The giant city of Shanghai lies just south of the mouth, joined to the river by its tributary, the Whangpo. Not until the removal of the obstruction of the Woosung Bar, at the mouth of the Whangpo, did Shanghai emerge in the early twentieth century as a major trading city, allowing ships to move along the estuary of the Yangtze, up the Whangpo, and pull alongside the wharves on Shanghai's Bund, or waterfront road. The 50-mile-wide (80-kilometer-wide) estuary of the river ends—or begins, depending on one's perspective (for ship pilots it is where the river meets the ocean)—at Zhong Sha or Middle Sand Light, a barnacle-crusted floating platform with a bell and a flashing lamp to guide mariners at the busy entrance to China's greatest river.

Further Reading: Hersey, John, *A Single Pebble*, New York: Alfred A. Knopf, 1956; Winchester, Simon, *The River at the Center of the World: A Journey up the Yangtze, and Back in Chinese Time*, New York: Henry Holt, 1996.

YELLOW

See Huang He

YENISEY

Source: Tuva Republic, in Central Asia
Length: c. 2,500 miles (4,023 kilometers)
Tributaries: **Angara**, Stony Tunguska, Lower Tunguska
Outlet: Kara Sea

One of the great Arctic rivers, the Yenisey forms the western boundary of the Central Siberian Plateau (the geologists' Angaraland). This plateau represents folded hill lands, not unlike the Appalachian Plateau in the eastern United States. The eastern limit of this plateau is marked by another of Russia's great Siberian rivers: the Lena. The Yenisey, with its major tributary, the Angara, flows steadily and strong as it drains northward from the world's largest lake by volume (Lake Baikal). In a country of great rivers, the Yenisey exceeds the flow not only of any of the other rivers in Siberia but also of any Russian river, including the Volga, Europe's longest river.

The river is formed at Kyzyl, in Tuva Republic, by the junction of the Bolshoi ("greater") and the Maly ("lesser") Yenisey. The headstreams rise in the lofty East Sayan Mountains, stretching eastward to Lake Baikal along the Russian-Mongolian border. The upper course of the river and its branches are turbulent and offer excellent opportunities for hydroelectric power development, which Russians have taken advantage of starting in the mid–twentieth century. The large Irkutsk Dam and the larger Bratsk Dam were constructed primarily for generating electricity (for pulp and paper mills and aluminum manufacturing). Where the river squeezed into a gorge, the Krasnoyarsk Dam was begun in 1955. The first two 500,000-kilowatt generators were installed by 1967, and a total of twelve such generators were planned, with a total capacity of 6 million kilowatts.

The wider middle Yenisey is navigable. The old town of Yeniseisk lies on the river below the Angara confluence. It is a major river port, saw-milling center, and fur-collecting entrepôt. Established in 1619 as one of a series of *ostrogs,* combined forts and trading posts, which Russia used to settle and control Siberia, the city has declined with the construction of the Trans-Siberian Railroad, which crosses the river farther south at the growing city of Krasnoyarsk.

The Yenisey enters the Kara Sea, an arm of the Arctic, by a long narrow bay and gulf of the same name. Unlike the Lena's delta to the east, which protrudes into the sea, the Yenisey's is at the head of a sinuous, island-filled estuary. Because of the restricted environmental setting, sediments fill in the embayment, forming a floodplain in which former deltaic islands can be distinguished only on air photos, and the main discharge shifts to the largest remaining channels.

Spring breakup and flooding are especially important events here, as elsewhere in the Arctic. Along the upper Yenisey, ice thaws earlier than farther north, and the river begins to flow even as it is blocked by ice in its lower reaches, with the result that water backs up and inundates the broad expanses of the river's lower valley. Because of the position of the delta at the end of a gulf, ice is cleared from the river earlier and freeze-up occurs later.

Negative human impacts on Arctic environments have been increasingly observed. In the lower Yenisey, just east of the delta, nickel- and copper-mining operations at Norilsk have polluted the Yenisey—its tributaries and delta—in one well-publicized case. Located south of the delta, Igark has become the region's chief lumber-loading port. Logs floated down the river have broken loose from booms and rafts and have washed up on the riverbanks, becoming stranded on sandbars and in channels of the delta to such an extent that their recovery is now an economic activity. The effects of vehicular activity on the fragile tundra ecosystem, deforestation, and global warming are just a few of today's environmental concerns about Arctic rivers like the Yenisey.

See also Angara, Lena, Ob'
Further Reading: Tropkin, Alexander, "Down the Yensei: The Main Route of Siberia," *Soviet Life,* June 1983, pp. 29–36; Walker, H. Jesse, "Arctic Deltas," *Journal of Coastal Research* 14 (1998): 718–738.

YUKON

Source: Coastal Range of northwest British Columbia
Length: c. 2,000 miles (3,220 kilometers)
Tributaries: Teslin, Pelly, White, Stewart, Klondike, Porcupine, Tanana, Koyukuk
Outlet: Norton Sound, in the Bering Sea

One of the last unspoiled great rivers, the Yukon has figured prominently in the history, exploration, and development of the forty-ninth state. A portion of the middle river in central Alaska—the Yukon Flats—constitutes a wildlife refuge and summer home to 1.5 million waterfowl.

The third-longest river in North America (after the Mississippi-Missouri and Mackenzie systems), the Yukon rises in extreme northwestern British Columbia, Canada, near the border with the Yukon Territory. The source lies on the eastern side of the Coastal Range, not far from the border of the panhandle of southeastern Alaska. The headwaters are less than 50 miles (80 kilometers) from the sea, yet the river flows in a large arc for some 2,000 miles (3,220 kilometers) before emptying into its mouth on the Bering Sea. One of a series of glacial lakes, Atlin Lake, is identified as the source. Investigators have even pinpointed the most distant feeder of the lake as the ultimate source: a trickle of silty water issuing from an ice cave high above, in Llewellyn Glacier.

The upper river (which used to be called the Lewes) flows to the northwest across Yukon Territory. It passes the first, and last, city along its course at Whitehorse, which is located at the head of navigation during the short shipping season. Picking up right-bank tributaries—the Teslin, Pelly, and Stewart—the river's discharge is augmented, especially in the spring and summer

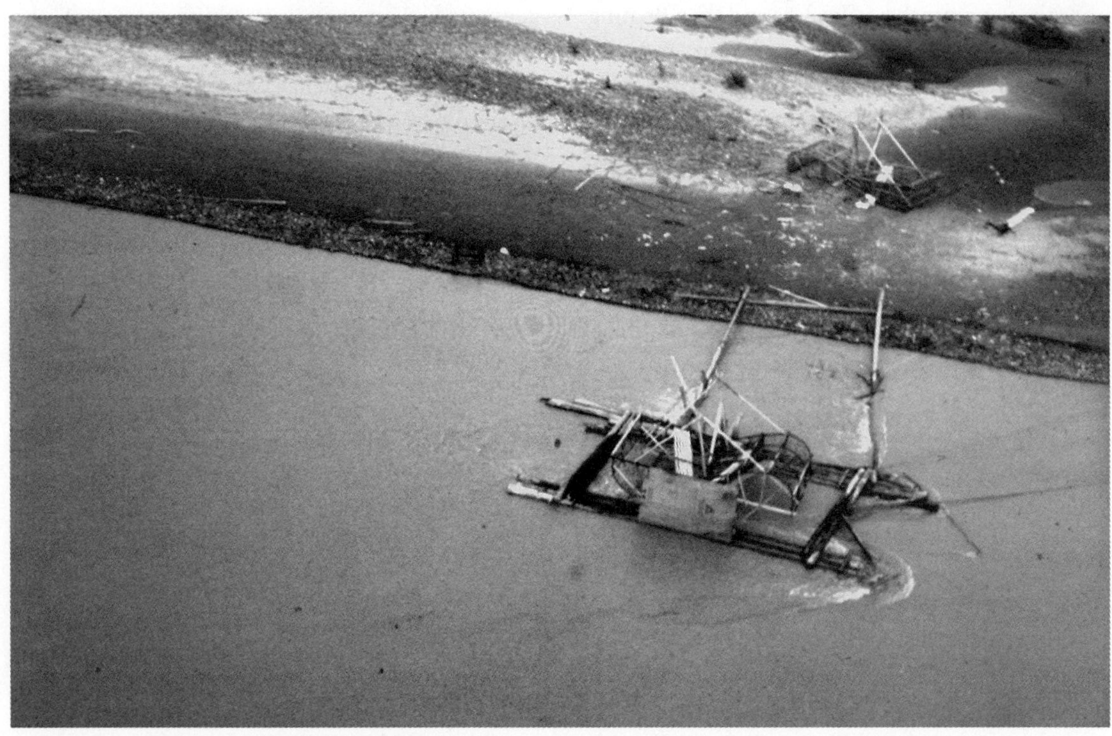

Fish wheel on the Yukon River (Jesse Walker)

months, when snow and ice melt in the upper basin. The major burden carried by the river is silt, fine rock material ground by the glacier. Along most of the river's course the water is opaque, and one can see only a few inches beneath the surface (making for difficult navigation) on account of the milky white color of the silty water. Long before the fall freeze, reduced flow has converted many stretches of the river into a braided stream. The river breaks up into a multitude of channels that weave in and out of hundreds of islands and sandbars that clog the riverbed. The Yukon is joined by Pelly River at Fort Selkirk. At this strategic location a Hudson's Bay Company agent, Robert Campbell, built a secure fur-trading post in 1848. Being subject to Indian attack, the fort was abandoned in 1852.

Near the border with Alaska the river passes Dawson, where it receives one of its smaller but most famous tributaries, the Klondike. It was along one of the Klondike's feeder streams, Bonanza Creek, that gold was discovered in 1896, triggering the Klondike Gold Rush (1897–1898). The Yukon was the major entryway to the Klondike gold fields. One could either cross the steep passes from the Alaskan coast (for example, Chilkoot, Chilkat, or White pass) and follow the headwaters of the Yukon downstream to Dawson; or one could take the more obvious but difficult route up the river from its mouth via steamboat, facing a notoriously treacherous river that was prone to early freeze-up.

Entering the United States, the Yukon continues to the northwest until it reaches its northernmost point, just within the Arctic Circle (66°30'N) at Fort Yukon. Then the great river turns to the southwest across the desolate wilderness of central Alaska. At the northern point of the arc, where the Yukon turns to the southwest and the Porcupine River comes in from the northeast, the Hudson's Bay Company under Alexander Hunter Murray built the fur-trading post at Fort Yukon that still exists today as a settlement. Murray had reached the site by crossing the short distance separating a western affluent of Canada's Mackenzie River from the Porcupine's headwaters and then floating downstream to the junction with the Yukon. At the time, the Hudson's Bay Company and the two men who built the forts were unaware that Fort Selkirk and Fort Yukon were on the same river.

Much of the middle river across central Alaska is incised in the Yukon Plateau, a central upland of comparatively low relief between the Brooks Range to the north and the Alaska Range, including Mount McKinley (Denali) to the south. At places the hills surrounding the plains approach the riverbanks; elsewhere the valley and the channel widen to a horizonless expanse of meandering and braided channels, myriads of islands, and extensive marshes. Such is the character of the Yukon Flats, a federal wildlife refuge occupying the northern arc of the river's course in northeastern Alaska stretching between Circle and Stevens Village. The vast aquatic maze of Yukon Flats—easy to get lost in—comprises 6,500,000 acres (2,600,000 hectares) and 40,000 lakes.

Although some small dams exist in the Yukon's headwaters, the main river flows freely to the sea. But not without a challenge. After attaining statehood in 1959, Alaska was expected to achieve a modern economy, so the U.S. Army Corps of Engineers proposed an enormous hydroelectric project, with a dam to be built at Rampart Canyon that would have flooded Yukon Flats and created an impoundment larger than Lake Erie. Five million kilowatts of electricity would have been generated. Fortunately, nothing came of the scheme, and with the passage of the Alaska Land Act (1980) by President Carter, Alaska's wild lands received new and expanded protection.

Only a scattering of villages lie along the lower river, many of them only accessible by river craft or airplane. Isolated native settlements of Athabascan Indians wait patiently for the spring breakup, which occurs near the beginning of May and is an event of both geomorphic and cultural significance. The heaving of the ice ("keep anything of value well back from the riverbanks" is common advice) and the slow but relentless movement of ice and water lead to a sense of relief and renewal. The river once more can travel to the west, then abruptly north, before reaching its delta in Norton Sound, an inlet of the Bering Sea. As with the Mississippi's Birdfoot delta south of New Orleans, the apex of Yukon's giant triangle is called Head of Passes. The river subdivides here into a maze of distributaries that all reach the salt sea as imperceptibly as gushes of ice water trickle from countless glacial caverns, far away at the source.

Further Reading: Mathews, Richard, *The Yukon,* New York: Holt, Rinehart and Winston, 1968 (Rivers of America Series); McPhee, John, *Coming into the Country,* New York: Farrar, Straus and Giroux, 1977; Parfit, Michael, "The Untamed Yukon," *National Geographic,* July 1998, pp. 100–127; Hildebrand, John, *Reading the River: A Voyage down the Yukon,* New York: Houghton Mifflin, 1988.

Z

ZAMBEZI

Source: Northwestern Zambia, in south-central Africa
Length: c. 1,700 miles (2,736 kilometers)
Tributaries: Kabombo, Lungwebungu, Luanginga, Chobe, Shangani, Kafue, Luangwa, Shire
Outlet: Mozambique Channel of the Indian Ocean

The Zambezi (Portuguese: Zambeze) was first explored by the medical missionary David Livingstone, who hoped the river would be "God's Highway" into the interior—an avenue of commerce and enlightenment. But a century and a half later the river flows through an impoverished region trying to come to terms with the aftermath of colonialism and civil war.

The fourth longest river in Africa rises in a corner of northwestern Zambia pushed up between Angola and the Democratic Republic of Congo (Zaire). The headwaters lie in a region of tropical rain forest that might be called the watershed of Africa, for there is only a short distance separating the springs that are the ultimate sources of the west-flowing Congo and the east-flowing (eventually) Zambezi.

The great river of southern Africa traces a path to the south and east in a giant loop resembling the letter *S* on its side. Along its route to the sea the Zambezi passes through or forms the borders of six countries. For some 500 miles (800 kilometers) it constitutes the entire boundary between the two former British colonies of Zambia (Northern Rhodesia) and Zimbabwe (Southern Rhodesia, or later just Rhodesia).

Somewhat perversely, the river begins by heading to the north and west into Angola for a couple of hundred miles before returning to western Zambia. The headstreams and tributaries of the upper river are fed by extensive wetlands in eastern Angola and northern Botswana. In southwestern Zambia the south-flowing river crosses the Barotse Plain, a marshland that absorbs excess rainwater during the wet season and releases water during dry months. Near the harbor of Mongu—several miles away from the river—is situated a mound of high ground in the marshes known as Lealui, the island capital of the paramount chief of the Barotse tribes. During the rainy season a ceremonial procession accompanies the royal barge up a canal to the Litunga's dry-site palace. Below the Barotse Plain the now southeast-flowing river passes on its right the Caprivi Strip—a tongue of Namibia separating Angola from Botswana. Within a short stretch the river becomes the border with Namibia, Botswana, and Zimbabwe.

Along the Zambia-Zimbabwe border above Victoria Falls the river is lined by sultry shores of reeds backed by thorn trees. It resembles the poet T. S. Eliot's description of a great river as "a strong brown god—sullen, untamed, and intractable." Imperceptibly the Zambezi widens, and yet remains placid, before plunging spectacularly over the precipice of the falls, recognized as one of the most impressive cascades in the world. Livingstone had heard about *Mosi-oa-tunya,* or "the smoke that

Spectacular Victoria Falls on the Zambezi River between Zambia and Zimbabwe was named by the medical missionary and explorer Dr. Livingstone after his sovereign Queen Victoria. (Richard Bickel/CORBIS)

thunders," before observing it for himself in 1855. After camping upstream, he landed his canoe on a small island above the precipice, which is cut like a slot into the basaltic plateau. The profusion of wild vegetation on the banks and islands, the plume of vapor mingling with the clouds, and the booming sound of the falls all combined to affect his senses profoundly. The falling water seems to have drawn him back to his past. The immense wall of whiteness reminded him of snow, something he hadn't seen for years. Pious, courageous, and ruthless by turn, the Scotsman once said he never saw anything more beautiful in Africa. Back home in Britain, he wrote that the falls offered "scenes so lovely [they] must have been gazed upon by angels in their flight." An American businessman's one-line cable home showed a different response: "Have seen Victoria–sell Niagara."

Beyond the falls the river zigzags through a narrow gorge that has been incised into Central Africa's basalt plateau. Emerging from this 400-foot-deep (122-meter-deep) canyon, the Zambezi traverses a thorny bush country with few affluents. Some 80 miles (129 kilometers) downstream from Victoria Falls the river changes as if by magic (actually, by engineering) into Kariba Lake, three times the size of Lake Geneva and one of the largest artificial reservoirs in the world. This was once the homeland of 50,000 Batonga tribesmen, but they were removed to make way for the dam and impoundment. The native population didn't object because their snake-headed, fish-tailed god Nyami-nyami stayed in the floodplain and looked after his people. It is said that one shouldn't fish near a Batonga man, because he'll pull in one fish after another and you'll catch nothing.

Flowing eastward the river passes into Mozambique at Zumbo. After forming the Zambia-Zimbabwe border for some 500 miles (800 kilometers), the river has another 500 miles to go on its course across the territory of this former Portuguese colony. The valley widens but is not without obstacles. The treacherous waters of the Cabora Bassa gorge wrecked Livingstone's plans for a navigable highway of commerce and enlightenment that would reach far into the African interior. A huge dam has been built in the gorge, backing water all the way to Zumbo. Beyond the Quebrabasa Rapids, the last major navigation obstacle on the river, the Zambezi turns southeast past Tete, the head of steamboat navigation.

The lower river flows across a broad plain en route to its junction with the sea 130 miles (209 kilometers) north of Beira, Mozambique. The chief tributary in this section of the river is the south-flowing Shire, which drains Lake Malawi (Lake Nyasa). Chinde is a small port in the center of the delta that is used for navigation. At the mouth of the delta's northern branch is located Mozambique's main fishing port, Quelimane. It was here in 1497 that the Portuguese explorer Vasco da Gama touched briefly on his voyage to India, thus initiating contact between Europe and the Zambezi. The Arabs had already been using the river for centuries as a trading artery. The Portuguese arrived in the sixteenth century seeking to develop commerce in ivory, gold, and slaves. Livingstone became the first white man to cross the African continent from coast to coast when he reached Quelimane, which he described as a low, pestilential place suffering from the slave trade. In the modern period, the effects of long years of Portuguese rule, a socialist-led independence (1975) movement, and ensuing civil war have not been kind to the country that occupies the lower end of the Zambezi.

Further Reading: Wollaston, Nicholas, "The Zambezi," pp. 130–141 in *Great Rivers of the World,* ed. Alexander Frater, Boston: Little, Brown and Company, 1984.

ZANGBO

See Brahmaputra

ZHUJIANG

See Xi He

ZIZ

Source: Southeast Morocco
Length: 175 miles (282 kilometers)
Tributaries: None
Outlet: Sahara Desert

Deserts receive scant attention in a book about the world's major rivers. Dry regions have characteristic intermittent streams, known in the Mideast and north Africa as *wadis,* which can attain local and even regional significance. Such is the case with Oued (Wadi) Ziz, which traverses the Atlas Mountains of north Africa. Though only an intermittent stream, the watercourse has notched the high mountains with a series of limestone gorges that have been used since ancient times as passageways.

The Ziz rises on the southern slope of the Jbel Ayachi (High Atlas) in southeast Morocco. It flows southward past Errich and Errachidia through the Tafilalt oasis. Much reduced in flow, the wadi is joined by the Oued Ghéris to form the Oued ad-Daoura, which soon disappears into Saharan sands within the territory of Algeria. There is some potential for irrigation, and the Hassan Addakhil north of Errachidia has been in service since 1971.

The Ziz gorges are caused by the upper course of the Oued Ziz eroding the elevated mountains. The watercourse provides one of the few routes across the Atlas Mountains, a range named after the defeated Titan of classical mythology who was forced to carry the world on his shoulders. The Roman general Paulinus followed the wadi in the first century A.D. when he crossed the High Atlas. The pass route has been for centuries part of a traditional caravan route linking the oases and market towns of the northern Sahara to the Mediterranean littoral. Towering limestone walls cleft by narrow crevices offer rugged beauty, and today this comparatively isolated place is often visited by tourists. Occasionally the valley widens enough to form a fertile valley where palm groves flourish. The sparkling blue-green waters of the Ziz contrast sharply with the reddish-brown color of the lofty limestone peaks. During snowmelt and the rare but intense rainstorms, the waters of the Ziz become a raging torrent, sweeping fallen debris from the bed of the river. Rock materials are carried farther downstream as abrasive tools that are capable of cutting deeper into the rock and enlarging the canyon. Located on the edge of the Sahara in a corner of southeastern Morocco, the Ziz today is an exotic stop on the itinerary of travelers who want to visit secluded villages, desert oases, and abandoned forts.

See also Rhumel

GLOSSARY OF RIVER TERMS

Affluent A stream or river flowing into a larger stream or river (also tributary).

Aggradation When the sediment load of a stream exceeds the stream's capacity, sediment accumulates in the channel. This process of aggradation increases the slope of the bed. *See also* Graded Stream

Alluvial Fan A cone-shaped body of alluvium deposited at abrupt changes in slope, typically where a canyon in a mountainous environment opens onto a plain. First used to describe the broad fans of sediment radiating from the Himalayas, these surfaces consisting of coarsely textured sediments often coalesce to form a Bahada, or a Piedmont alluvial plain. The alluvial fan is most associated with dry environments, because the alternate drying up and flooding of mountain streams favor its formation.

Alluvial Terraces Level areas appearing like topographic stair steps above a floodplain. Terraces are former floodplains that have been cut into when the river has surplus energy, usually as a result of a steepening of the river's slope or gradient. Since rivers are symmetrical (that is, rivers have two banks and two levees), terraces are usually paired, though older terraces are often eroded and difficult to detect. The process of cutting down into a floodplain and creating a new valley bottom can be repeated, resulting in a series of terraces, with the oldest terrace lying at the highest level and farthest away from the current floodplain.

Alluvium Sediments consisting primarily of sand, silt, and clay transported by running water and deposited on a floodplain, delta, or streambed.

Antecedent River A river that has cut down through younger land that has risen in its path, and has maintained its path. An example is the Columbia River's course through the Cascades.

Arpent An antiquated unit of measurement equal to 192 feet. This unit was the basis of a riverine survey method used by the French in their colonies of North America. Known as the long lot or arpent system, narrow lots fronted the river and extended back from it, maximizing accessibility to the river. Property boundaries along the Mississippi River and other major streams in south Louisiana, as well as along the lower Saint Lawrence, still conform to the original arpent system. A pattern of pie-shaped wedges along the winding river is especially evident from the air.

Arroyo A term used in North and South America to describe a normally dry streambed that becomes a stream only during comparatively rare periods of rainfall. Then the stream may become a torrent, and flash flooding becomes a serious problem.

Backswamp *See* Floodplain

Bahada *See* Alluvial Fan

Batture The short slope between the levee crest and the river (lower Mississippi). Pronounced BATCH-er, this frequently flooded bankside has sandy soils and is vegetated by hardy trees, such as cottonwood and willow, that are adapted to alternate periods of drought and flooding.

Bayou A French borrowing of an Indian term meaning a small stream, most commonly used in south Louisiana (for example, Bayou Lafourche); homelands of the Cajuns, originally from Acadia or French Nova Scotia.

Billabong In Australia, the cutoff loop of a river, approaching the size of a large lagoon; a cutoff meander.

Blind Valley In a karst landscape (formed by limestone dissolution), a valley that ends suddenly when its stream disappears underground.

Bolson A term applied in the arid or semiarid region of the American Southwest and Mexico to an area of interior drainage. The flat-floored, alluvium-filled depression becomes a shallow, muddy lake during rare rainstorms; at other times it is a dry alkali flat. Sloping down from the flanks of the surrounding mountains are a number of alluvial fans. The term is from the Spanish for "large purse."

Bourne An intermittent stream in England. The linguistic root is similar to that of a Scottish *burn,* or small stream, but the term is usually applied to seasonally dry watercourses in the chalk regions of southern England.

Brae In Scotland, a hill slope or bank overlooking a valley.

Braided Channel A channel that separates into a maze of interconnected channels. A stream's channel typically separates, rejoins, and divides again when it is loaded with excess sediments (for example, as a result of a landslide upstream), or when the stream's transportation ability is curtailed (for example, a sluggish coastal plain river).

Broad An English term referring to a wide stretch of a river or adjoining lands in the estuary of a river, particularly in East Anglia.

Burn A small stream or brook in northern England, Scotland, and northern Ireland. Formerly also applied to a spring or seep.

Canyon A relatively narrow gorge of large size, bounded by steep slopes. From Spanish *cañon,* this feature is often formed by a river's cutting through soft rocks in arid regions. Although nearly vertical rock walls are sometimes present, it is more common for an irregularity of slope to be caused by the differential erosion of rock types. Where a smaller ravine joins the main river, a side-canyon can form.

Carse In Scotland, the low alluvial land bordering a river near its mouth, as in the Carse of Gowrie.

Cascade A small waterfall, or a series of falls resembling steps.

Cataract A large waterfall or a series of falls; or, as on the Nile, a rapids.

Channel The deepest portion of a river (sea, lake), or the three-dimensional shape of the contained flow of a river. In a technical analysis, the term *thalweg* refers to the deeper, navigable part of a stream, while the cross-sectional area of flow reveals variations in channel geometry: roughness versus smoothness, depth, width.

Chute A narrow channel between a towhead and the nearest shore; also a "shortcut" across a meander bend. More generally a chute is any narrowing of a channel through which water velocity increases. In this way, water confined by protruding rocks in waterfalls or rapids produces chutes.

Combe In southern England, a short valley or hollow in the side of a hill, especially in the chalk downlands (also coombe).

Consequent River A river flowing down the dip or primary slope of the land. Its flow is thus a necessary consequence of that slope (see Figure 5).

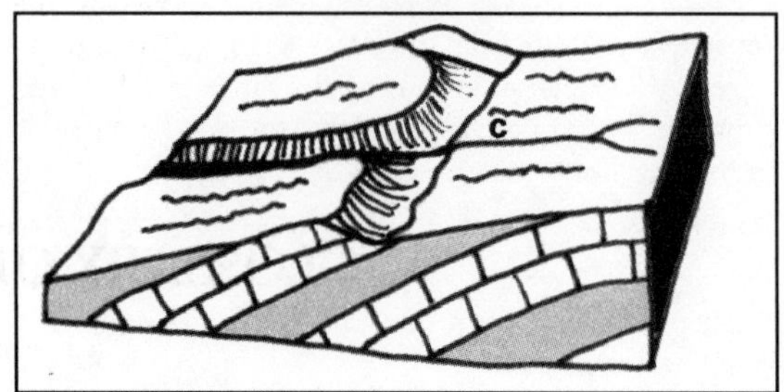

Figure 5, consequent river (c).

Coulee From French *coulée,* the past tense of the verb "to flow," a dry ravine or gulch in the western United States that is dry in the summer but flows during snowmelt or in a heavy rain. A related meaning refers to a consolidated lava flow. In the portion of the Driftless Area of southwestern Wisconsin north of the Wisconsin River, a coulee is a short stream draining a narrow, steep-sided valley that ends in an abrupt headwall.

Crevasse A breach in the bank of a river, especially in the elevated natural or artificial levee (an embankment) of the lower Mississippi. Such a break usually occurs during flood stage and can lead to a new set of distributary channels.

Cutbank Outer or concave bend of a meandering stream. *See also* Meander

Dale A wide, open valley, especially in southern Scotland and northern England; similar to the Scandinavian *dal.*

Dead-Head A water-soaked log lying at the bottom of a stream or lake, or more dangerously a partially submerged log.

Degradation Applied to a river, this refers to the process of the deepening of a valley. If a river's discharge exceeds what is needed to transport the sediment load, the river will cut down into its valley. *See also* Graded Stream

Delta An approximately triangular-shaped tract of land at the mouth of major rivers. Named after the resemblance of the Nile River north of Cairo, Egypt, to the fourth letter of the Greek alphabet, this alluvial landform is formed when sediment is deposited at a river's outlet because of the reduction in velocity and load-carrying capacity as the river empties into the sea. As materials are deposited, new branches form, and the delta extends itself outward in the shape of a fan or triangle. The sides of the triangle are represented by the two outermost branches and the sea. Formation of a major delta has an additional requirement: the body of water into which the river flows must not have large currents or tides, for that would sweep the sediments out to sea, preventing the creation of a landform. As inventors of geometry, the Greeks saw perfect forms everywhere, but most deltas deviate from the classic triangle. The seaward edge of the delta may consist of arcs (arcuate delta); may protrude outwardly (cuspate delta); or may be indented in the coastline (estuarine delta).

Dingle A small, narrow, well-wooded valley.

Discharge The rate of stream flow; the volume of water passing any point in a unit of time (measured in cubic meters per second).

Distributary A branch or outlet that diverts water from a main river, usually in the delta, carrying water to the sea or a lake; an effluent.

Doab Chiefly in India, the alluvial tract of land between adjacent rivers (for example, Ganges and Yamuna).

Donga In South Africa, a steep-sided ravine or dry watercourse, similar to a wadi or nullah.

Drainage Basin The area drained by a river and its tributaries (also watershed, catchment area). The network of tributaries gathers all the water and sediment to the main river, which then empties into the sea or a lake. The boundary of the basin is defined by the line—usually a ridge—beyond which water flows in the opposite direction. The primary characteristics that determine runoff and sediment load are relief, soils, vegetation, climate, rock type, and land use. The drainage basin has proved to be one of the most useful units for landscape analysis, for both physical geographers and planners.

Drainage Pattern The geometric arrangement of streams in a region. The pattern made on a map by streams is a result of climate, slope, rock resistance, and geological structure. The most common drainage patterns are dendritic or branching, trellis, parallel, radial, annular or ringlike, and disrupted (see Figure 6).

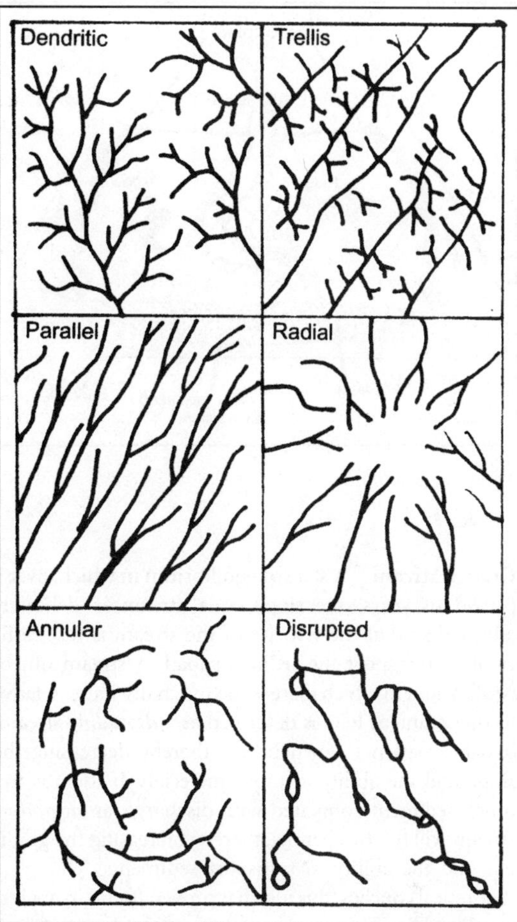

Figure 6, drainage pattern.

Effluent The outlet of a river, the channel by which its waters reach the sea (also distributary). At the mouth of the Mississippi River such channels are known as passes (for example, Southwest Pass).

Elbow of Capture *See* River Piracy

Estuary The lowest course of a river where tidal effects are felt and fresh and salt water mix. Some of the world's greatest seaports are located on the estuaries of the Hudson, Thames, Elbe, and Plata, just to cite a few.

Exotic Stream A river rising in a humid environment that crosses an arid region. Discharge decreases downstream in exotic rivers like the Nile and the Colorado.

Floodplain That portion of a river valley inundated during flooding. The plain adjacent to a river or stream receives sediments when the river overtops its banks during a flood. The comparatively elevated embankment of the levee along the river is produced by the deposition of the more coarsely textured sediments of sand and silt. Away from the river the back swamp receives fine, less permeable clays. Floodplains often comprise wide belts within which rivers meander, producing such characteristic alluvial features as cutbanks, point bars, oxbow lakes, and yazoo tributaries (see Figure 7).

Fluvial Stream-related process, from Latin fluvius.

Geomorphology The branch of physical geography treating landforms. Geomorphologists investigate the arrangement of landforms on the earth's surface and the relationship between physical processes and specific forms and features. Those specializing in river-related processes are known as fluvial geomorphologists.

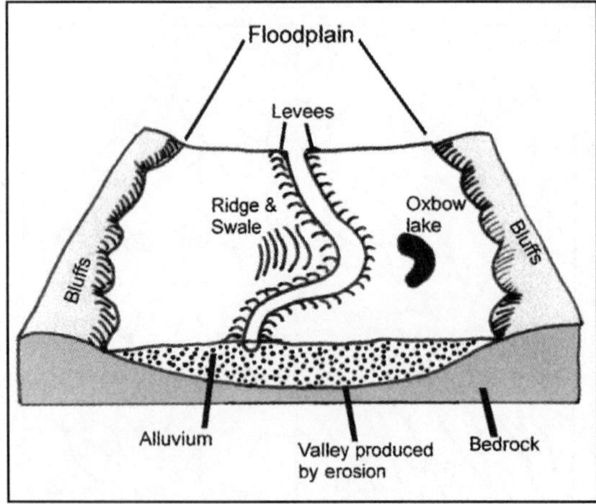

Figure 7, floodplain.

Graded Stream A state of equilibrium in which, over a period of years, the slope of a stream is delicately adjusted so that the velocity of the stream is just sufficient to transport the sediment load. A stream out of equilibrium in which there is too much discharge relative to the sediment load is described as a *degrading* stream; it will experience downcutting, thereby decreasing the slope and the ability to move materials. If there is too much sediment compared with discharge, an *aggrading* stream will fill the channel, thereby increasing the gradient and the ability to transport sediments. Though a theoretical concept, this idea has proven useful in analyzing the relationships among volume and velocity of flow, sediment load, slope, and channel characteristics.

Gradient The degree of inclination or slope of a river; its rate of decline in elevation. *See also* Longitudinal Profile

Headward Erosion The extension of a stream valley by erosion at its head or upland end (see Figure 8).

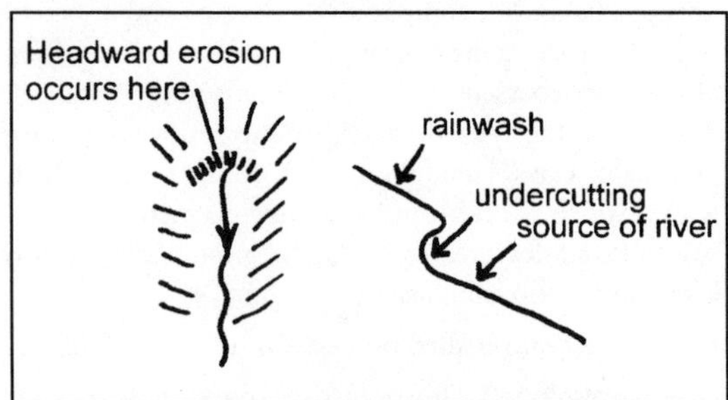

Figure 8, headward erosion.

Hydrologic Cycle The continuous motion of water and vapor from the land to the sea and back again. Its various segments include evaporation, precipitation, groundwater, and surface water, the last including stream flow. The idea is as old as Aristotle, or even the Old Testament's Ecclesiastes, but its elaboration in the seventeenth and eighteenth centuries was an important step forward in earth science.

Interfluve The tract of land, usually elevated, between adjacent river valleys.

Knickpoint An irregularity in the usually smooth profile of a river, resulting in rapids or falls.

Levee The natural bank of a river formed during flooding. The levee receives the largest proportion of coarsely textured sediments (sand) during flooding and is thus built up as the highest portion of the lowland. A levee is continually being raised by floods, and a levee and the river's channel can be elevated above the level of the surrounding country, as in the lower Mississippi, the Po in northern Italy, and the Huang He in northern China. Artificial levees shore up and elevate the natural embankment to protect against flooding and to keep the river in its channel.

Load, River Materials carried along by a river. This includes: (1) the suspended load, fine-grained particles held up by their light weight and the random upward motions of water; (2) the bed load, larger and heavier materials that move along the bottom of the river by bouncing (saltation) or by being dragged (traction); and (3) the dissolved load, materials carried in chemical solution such as minerals, soluble salts, and pollutants.

Longitudinal Profile The profile of a stream drawn along its length from its source to its mouth. An idealized cross section of the longitudinal profile (also known as long profile) shows a steeper slope upstream and a gentler slope downstream, with more irregularities or knickpoints along the stream's upper course.

Meander A bend in a river's course. The natural tendency for a stream to follow a winding course is accentuated by the river itself (see Figure 9), which wears away the outer or concave bank of the curve (cutbank) and deposits sediments on the inner or convex bank (point bar). The name derives from the river Menderes (ancient Maeander) in Asia Minor (present-day Turkey), whose lower course twists notably. Ultimately a river may form a large enough meander, a nearly circular loop, that during subsequent flooding the narrow strip of land, or neck, may be eroded. The result is that this part of the river's course will become almost straight, and the former channel will survive as an oxbow lake. An entrenched meander is produced when a river incises itself into resistant bedrock and becomes trapped—that is, unable to erode the rocky neck separating adjacent loops. A classic example is the goosenecks of the San Juan River, a tributary of the Colorado.

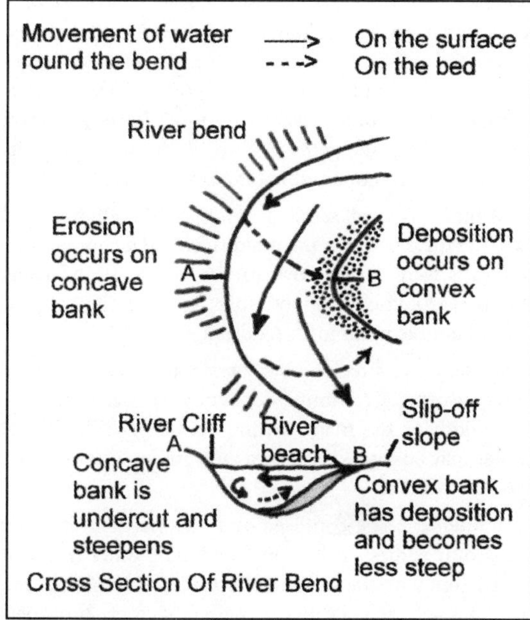

Figure 9, meander.

Nullah In India, a dry watercourse that becomes a stream only after a heavy rainfall.

Obsequent River A tributary to a subsequent river, flowing in the direction opposite that of the initial dip of the slope (see Figure 10).

Figure 10, obsequent river (o).

Outwash Plain A broad alluvial plain formed by streams originating on a melting glacier. Consisting of stratified deposits, many are sandy, infertile wastelands best left in unimproved pasture or woodland. The Lüneburger Heath south of Hamburg, Germany, is a good example of this landform.

Oxbow Lake A cutoff meander, hence a former channel of a river. This type of lake is formed, after a river makes an exaggerated loop, when the base of the loop is eroded during high water. The river then takes the shorter path across the eroded neck—called a chute—leaving behind a shallow crescentic body of water whose name derives from its curved shape, resembling the horn of an ox. A good example of this lake type can be observed at False River in Pointe Coupee Parish, Louisiana, the parish name itself suggesting the historical cutoff of a wide meander of the Mississippi above Baton Rouge in 1722.

Point Bar The inner or convex bend of a meandering stream. *See also* Meander

Raft A jam in a river formed by accumulated debris—brush, limbs, and logs—impeding navigation. The most common rafts in the nineteenth century occurred where tributaries dumped excessive sediments into a major stream, building up alluvium across the channel.

Reach A straight stretch of river channel between meanders.

Ridge-and-Swale A series of low ridges and intervening depressions along the inside bend (point) of a meandering stream.

River Bar A ridgelike accumulation of alluvium along the channel or at the mouth of a river. As a result of channel shifting or during low water, the bar appears, constituting a navigational obstruction.

River Pig Lumberjack lingo for one who drives logs down a river (also river rat, river jack).

River Piracy The action of a river in enlarging its drainage basin by capturing the headstreams of a second river. Also known as river capture, the process is carried out by the more powerful river, which erodes its valley more vigorously than does its weaker neighbor. When the weaker river's headstreams are cut off and diverted into those of the stronger, it is said to have been beheaded. The bend at which the capture takes place is known as the elbow of capture.

Stream A body of flowing water confined within a channel. The term "stream" is all-encompassing, referring to all sizes of watercourses, from the smallest rill to the greatest river.

Stream Order The numeric expression of a stream's hierarchical position in a stream network. The number assigned to a stream is in direct proportion to its size: a first-order stream lacks any tributaries and is smallest in size; a second-order stream receives at least two first-order streams and is next larger in size; a third-order stream receives at least two second-order streams, and so on (note that the addition of a first-order stream to a second-order stream does not form a third-order stream). By such an accounting, the Amazon is a twelfth-order river and the Mississippi is a tenth-order (see Figure 11).

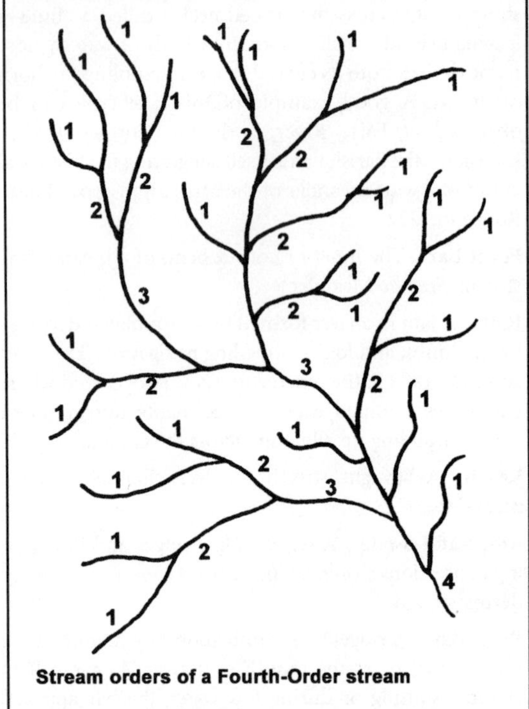

Figure 11, stream order.

Subsequent River A tributary to a consequent river, following a line approximately perpendicular to the general slope of the land (see Figure 12).

Figure 12, subsequent river (s).

Subtributary A tributary of a tributary. *See also* Stream Order

Superimposed Stream When a stream maintains a winding course through mountains and doesn't follow the trend of the local geological structures and rock types, it is sometimes inferred that the stream was superimposed on a new surface and eroded its way downward into the underlying rocks.

Thalweg The deepest, most navigable channel of a river, often used in defining water boundaries between states and political units (from the German for "valley way"). A line joining the lowest point of the channel from the source of the river to its mouth forms a concave curve marking the general slope of the river along its course. *See also* Longitudinal Profile

Towhead A small sandbar or an island with grass and willows on it between the main river and a chute. When log rafts were driven downstream by rough-and-ready lumberjacks known as river pigs, a raft striking a bar would double up to form saddlebags.

Tributary A smaller river or stream flowing into a larger waterway. A tributary does not necessarily increase the width of the main stream, because the additional water may be carried off by an increased velocity of flow. *See also* Affluent

Turbulence The confused and chaotic flow of water caused by eddies. Turbulence in running water is caused by friction with the sides and bottom of the channel and by channel irregularities (roughness, rock protuberances). Turbulent flow contrasts with laminar or layered flow, which occurs when stream lines are distinct and remain unchanged through time. Turbulent flow is most common in rivers and streams, while laminar flow characterizes the movement of groundwater. A stream's erosive force is as much a result of turbulence as volume and velocity of flow.

Underfit Stream A stream that appears too small for the valley in which it flows. Among the possible explanations are past glaciation, climatic change, and river piracy.

Valley A river valley is a long, narrow depression in the earth's surface carved out from the surface rocks by the channelized flow of water. In the upper course of a stream, a valley is usually narrow and steep-sided, while farther downstream a valley is broad and terminates in low bluffs or none at all when the river reaches the deltaic plain. A valley carved out by a glacier is a *U*-shaped trough, while the normal cross section of a nonglaciated stream is *V*-shaped. The two essential parts of a valley are the valley bottom, consisting of alluvium deposited in a floodplain, and the valley side walls or bluffs, although the proportion of these components varies along the river's course.

Wadi A normally dry watercourse in the desert that contains water only after a heavy rainfall. The term is usually in reference to the Sahara and the deserts of the Mideast.

Water Gap A deep gorge across a mountain ridge in which a stream flows, especially a narrow defile or ravine cut through resistant rocks by an antecedent stream (for example, the Delaware Water Gap).

Weir A dam placed across a river or canal to divert water, as for a millrace, or to measure the flow.

Wind Gap A shallow notch in the upper part of a mountain ridge, usually at a higher level than a water gap. The term can also be applied to a former water gap whose pass is no longer occupied by a stream.

Yazoo Tributary A tributary of a river paralleling the course of the main stream in the floodplain. Named after the Yazoo River in west-central Mississippi, such a tributary is blocked from joining the main stream by the levees and the elevation of the stream channel.

BIBLIOGRAPHY

General and Reference Works

Baird, David M., and Dane Lanken. "Wandering Rivers: Why They Twist and Turn Is One of Nature's Secrets." *Canadian Geographic* 113 (July–August 1993): 58–65.

Bangs, Richard, and Christian Kallen. *Rivergods: Exploring the World's Great Wild Rivers.* San Francisco: Yolla Bolly Book (Sierra Club Books), 1985.

Brittain, Robert. *Rivers, Man and Myths: From Fish Spears to Water Mills.* Garden City, NY: Doubleday, 1958.

Brown, Ralph H. *Historical Geography of the United States.* New York: Harcourt, Brace and World, 1948.

Canby, Courtlandt. *The Encyclopedia of Historic Places.* 2 vols. New York: Facts on File, 1984.

The Columbia Encyclopedia. 6th ed. New York: Columbia University Press, 2000.

The Columbia Gazetteer of the World. New York: Columbia University Press, 1998.

Cronin, John, and Robert F. Kennedy, Jr. *The Riverkeepers: Two Activists Fight to Reclaim Our Environment as a Basic Human Right.* New York: Touchstone, 1999.

Czaya, Eberhard. *Rivers of the World.* New York: Van Nostrand Reinhold, 1981.

Eblen, Ruth A., and William R. Eblen. *The Encyclopedia of the Environment.* Boston: Houghton Mifflin, 1994.

Espenshade, Edward B., Jr., ed. *Goode's World Atlas.* 19th ed. Chicago: Rand McNally, 1995.

Gresswell, R. Kay, and Anthony Huxley, eds. *Standard Encyclopedia of the World's Rivers and Lakes.* New York: G. P. Putnam's Sons, 1965.

Huber, Thomas P., Robert P. Larkin, and Gary L. Peters. *Dictionary of Concepts in Physical Geography.* New York: Greenwood Press, 1988.

Ingpen, Robert, and Philip Wilkinson. *Encyclopedia of Mysterious Places: The Life and Legends of Ancient Sites around the World.* Bergenfield, NJ: Viking Studio Books, 1990.

Kazman, Raphael G. *Modern Hydrology.* New York: Harper and Row, 1965.

Leopold, Aldo. *Round River: From the Journals of Aldo Leopold.* Edited by Luna B. Leopold. New York: Oxford University Press, 1953.

Leopold, Luna B. *The View of the River.* Cambridge: Harvard University Press, 1994.

_______. *Water, Rivers and Creeks.* Sausalito, CA: University Science Books, 1997.

Leopold, Luna B., and W. B. Langbein. "River Meanders." *Scientific American,* June 1966, pp. 60–70.

Leopold, Luna B., and Thomas Maddock, Jr. "The Hydraulic Geometry of Stream Channels and Some Physiographic Implications." *Geological Survey Professional Paper* 252. Washington, DC: G.P.O., 1953.

Lopez, Barry. *Crossing Open Ground.* New York: Vintage, 1989.

Maclean, Norman. *A River Runs through It.* Chicago: University of Chicago Press, 1976.

McPhee, John. *Encounters with the Archdruid.* New York: Farrar, Straus and Giroux, 1971.

Merriam-Webster's Geographical Dictionary. 3d ed. Springfield, MA: Merriam-Webster, 1997.

Michael, Pamela, ed. *The Gift of Rivers: True Stories of Life on the Water.* San Francisco: Travelers' Tales, 2000.

Milich, Lenard, and Robert G. Varady. "Managing Transboundary Resources: Lessons from River-Basin

Accords." *Environment* 40 (October 1998): 10–15; 35–41.

Morisawa, Marie. *Rivers.* London: Longman, 1982.

Murray, John A. *The River Reader.* New York: Lyons Press, 1998 (Nature Conservancy Book).

National Geographic Society. *Great Rivers of the World,* 1984.

Ondaatje, Christopher. *Journey to the Source of the Nile.* Toronto: HarperCollins, 1998.

Pringle, Laurence. *Rivers and Lakes.* Planet Earth Series. Alexandria, VA: Time-Life Books, 1985.

Reader's Digest. *Natural Wonders of the World.* Pleasantville, NY: Reader's Digest Association, 1980. Based on *Dictionnaire Illustre des Merveilles du Monde,* published in France, 1978, 1977. Selection du Reader's Digest, S.A.

Schama, Simon. *Landscape and Memory.* New York: Alfred A. Knopf, 1995.

Shirley, Martha Lou, and James A. Ragsdale. *Deltas in Their Geologic Framework.* 2 vols. Houston, TX: Houston Geological Society, 1966.

Sinclair, Bryan T. "Merging Streams: The Importance of the River in the Slaves' Religious World." *Journal of Religious Thought* 53 (Fall 1997): 1.

Stamp, L. Dudley, ed. *A Glossary of Geographical Terms.* New York: John Wiley, 1961.

Torrance, Robert M., ed. *Encompassing Nature: A Sourcebook.* Washington, DC: Counterpoint, 1998.

Tuan, Yi-Fu. *The Hydrologic Cycle and the Wisdom of God: A Theme in Geoteleology.* Toronto: University of Toronto Press, Department of Geography Research Publication no. 1, 1968.

Wilson, Edward O. *The Diversity of Life.* New York: Norton, 1992.

Studies of Individual Rivers and Regions

Abbey, Edward. *Desert Solitaire.* New York: McGraw-Hill, 1968.

_______. *Down the River.* New York: E. P. Dutton, 1982.

Alexander, Bevin. *Korea: The First War We Lost.* Rev. ed. New York: Hippocrene Books, 2000 (orig. pub. 1986).

Alexander, Caroline. *One Dry Season: In the Footsteps of Mary Kingsley.* New York: Knopf, 1990.

Alter, Stephen. *Amritsar to Lahore: A Journey across the India-Pakistan Border.* Philadelphia: University of Pennsylvania Press, 2000.

Ambrose, Stephen E. *Undaunted Courage: Meriwether Lewis, Thomas Jefferson, and the Opening of the American West.* New York: Simon and Schuster, 1996.

_______. *Nothing Like It in the World: The Men Who Built the Transcontinental Railroad, 1863–1869.* New York: Simon and Schuster, 2000.

Amery, Hussein A. "The Litani River of Lebanon." *Geographical Review* 83, no. 3 (July 1993): 229–237.

Ash, Jean. "Damming the Yangtze." *Forum for Applied Research and Public Policy* 13, no. 3 (Fall 1998): 76–83.

Asprey, Robert B. *The Rise of Napoleon Bonaparte.* New York: Basic Books, 2000.

Atkinson, Thomas Witlam. *Travels in the Regions of the Upper and Lower Amoor and the Russian Acquisitions on the Confines of India and China.* New York: Harper and Brothers, 1860.

Banks, Francis Richard. *Your Guide to the Bernese Alps.* London: A. Redman, 1965.

Banta, R. E. *The Ohio.* New York: Rinehart, 1949 (Rivers of America Series).

Barry, John M. *Rising Tide: The Great Mississippi Flood of 1927 and How It Changed America.* New York: Simon and Schuster, 1997.

Bates, Henry Walter. *The Naturalist on the River Amazon.* New York: Dover, 1975 (orig. pub. 1863).

Beattie, Malcolm Hamilton. *On the Houghly.* London: P. Allan, 1935.

Beek, Steve Van. *The Chao Phya: River in Transition.* Oxford: Oxford University Press, 1995.

Berendsen, H. J. A. "Birds-Eye View of the Rhine-Meuse Delta." *Journal of Coastal Research* 14 (1998): 740–752.

Beston, Henry. *The St. Lawrence.* New York: Farrar and Rinehart, 1942 (Rivers of America Series).

Bobrick, Benson. *East of the Sun: The Epic Conquest and Tragic History of Siberia.* New York: Poseidon Press, 1992.

Bonetto, A. A., and I. R. Wais. "Powerful Paraná: Environmental Health of South America's Second Largest River." *Geographical Magazine* 62, no. 3 (March 1990): S1–S3.

Bourne, Russell. *Rivers of America: Birthplaces of Culture, Commerce, and Community.* Golden, CO: Fulcrum Publishing, 1998.

Bowen, M. A. *The Willamette Valley: Migration and Settlement on the Oregon Frontier.* Seattle: University of Washington Press, 1979.

Boyle, Robert H. *The Hudson River: A Natural and Unnatural History.* New York: W. W. Norton, 1979.

Bradley, A. G. *The Rivers and Streams of England.* London: Bracken Books, 1993 (orig. pub. 1909).

Braider, Donald. *The Niagara.* New York: Holt, Rinehart and Winston, 1972 (Rivers of America Series).

Breton, Jean-Francois. "Manhattan in the Hadramaut." *Aramco World Magazine* 37, no. 3 (May–June, 1986): 24–27.

Bronson, William. *The Last Grand Adventure.* New York: McGraw-Hill, 1977.

Bullard, Oral. *Crisis on the Columbia.* Portland, OR: Touchstone Press, 1968.

Burmeister, Walter F. *The Susquehanna and Its Tributaries.* Oakton, VA: Appalachian Books, 1975.

Butzer, Karl W. *Early Hydraulic Civilization in Egypt: A Study in Cultural Ecology.* Chicago: University of Chicago Press, 1976.

Campbell, Marjorie W. *The Saskatchewan.* New York: Rinehart, 1950 (Rivers of America Series).

Caputo, Robert. "Journey up the Nile." *National Geographic,* May 1985, pp. 576–633.

Carbenier, R., and M. Tremoliere. "The Rhine Rift Valley Groundwater-River Interactions: Evolution of Their Susceptibility to Pollution." *Regulated Rivers: Research & Management* 5 (1990): 375–389.

Carmer, Carl. *The Hudson.* New York: Farrar and Rinehart, 1939 (Rivers of America Series).

_______. *Songs of the Rivers of America.* New York: Farrar and Rinehart, 1942 (Rivers of America Series).

_______. *The Susquehanna.* New York: Rinehart, 1955 (Rivers of America Series).

Carter, Hodding. *Lower Mississippi.* New York: Farrar and Rinehart, 1942 (Rivers of America Series).

Cary, Max. *The Geographic Background of Greek and Roman History.* Oxford: Clarendon Press, 1949.

Cencini, Carlo. "Physical Processes and Human Activities in the Evolution of the Po Delta." *Journal of Coastal Research* 14 (1998): 774–793.

Chagnon, Napoleon A. *Yanomamö, the Fierce People.* New York: Holt, Rinehart and Winston, 1968.

Chamberlain, Lesley. *Volga, Volga: A Voyage down the Great River.* London: Picador, 1995.

Clark, Christopher. "Household Economy, Market Exchange and the Rise of Capitalism in the Connecticut Valley, 1800–1860." *Journal of Social History* 13 (1979): 169–189.

Clark, Manning. *History of Australia.* Abridged by Michael Cathcart. London: Chatto and Windus, 1993 (orig. pub. in 6 volumes between 1962 and 1987).

Clark, Robert. *River of the West: Stories from the Columbia.* New York: HarperCollins, 1995.

Coffin, Robert P. Tristram. *Kennebec.* New York: Farrar and Rinehart, 1937 (Rivers of America Series).

Connelly, Owen. *Blundering to Glory: Napoleon's Military Campaigns.* Wilmington, DE: Scholarly Resources, 1987.

Corle, Edwin. *The Gila.* New York: Rinehart, 1951 (Rivers of America Series).

Cospérec, Annie. *The Châteaux of the Loire.* Paris: Hermé, 1997.

Cousins, Norman. *Dr. Schweitzer of Lambaréné.* New York: Harper and Brothers, 1960.

Creighton, Donald G. *Empire of the St. Lawrence.* Boston: Houghton Mifflin, 1958.

Da Cunha, Euclides. *Rebellion in the Backlands (Os Sertões).* Translated by Samuel Putnam. Chicago: University of Chicago Press, 1944 (orig. pub. 1902).

Dana, Julian. *The Sacramento.* New York: Farrar and Rinehart, 1939 (Rivers of America Series).

Davenport, William. "Living the Good Life in Burgundy." *National Geographic,* June 1978, pp. 794–817.

Davidson, Donald. *The Tennessee.* New York: Holt, Rinehart and Winston, 1946 (Rivers of America Series) (rev. ed., University of Tennessee Press, 1978).

Davis, Julia. *The Shenandoah.* New York: Farrar and Rinehart, 1945 (Rivers of America Series).

Davis, Wade. *One River: Explorations and Discoveries in the Amazon Rain Forest.* New York: Simon and Schuster, 1996.

De Civrieux, Marc. *Watunna: An Orinoco Creation Cycle.* Edited and translated by David Guss. Austin: University of Texas Press, 1997 (orig. pub. in Spanish, 1970).

De Courcy, John W. *The Liffey in Dublin.* Dublin: Gill and Macmillan, 1996.

De Gramont, Sanche. *The Strong Brown God: The Story of the Niger River.* Boston: Houghton Mifflin, 1976.

De Villiers, Marq. *Down the Volga: A Journey through Mother Russia in a Time of Troubles.* New York: Viking Penguin, 1992.

_______. *Water: The Fate of Our Most Precious Resource.* Boston: Houghton Mifflin, 2000.

Derleth, August. *The Wisconsin: River of a Thousand Isles.* New York: Farrar and Rinehart, 1942 (Rivers of America Series).

Dury, George H. *The British Isles: A Systematic and Regional Geography.* 5th ed. London: Heinemann, 1973.

Eales, Kathy, Simon Forster, and Lusekelo Du Mhango. *Water Management in Africa and the Middle East.* Edited by Egial Rached et al. Ottawa: IDRC, 1996.

Earle, Carville. "Environment, Disease, and Mortality in Early Virginia." *Journal of Historical Geography* 5 (1979): 365–390.

Eberlein, Harold Donaldson, Geoffrey J. Marks, and Frank A. Wallis. *Down the Tiber and Up to Rome.* Philadelphia: J. B. Lippincott, 1930.

Edwards, Mike. "An Eye for an Eye: Pakistan's Wild Frontier." *National Geographic,* January 1977, pp. 111–139.

———. "The Danube: River of Many Nations, Many Names." *National Geographic,* October 1977, pp. 454–485.

Ellis, William S. "Canada's Highway to the Sea." *National Geographic,* May 1980, pp. 586–623.

Fairley, Jean. *The Lion River: The Indus.* New York: John Day, 1975.

Fernea, Elizabeth Warnock. *A View of the Nile: The Story of an American Family in Egypt.* Garden City, NY: Doubleday, 1970.

Ferrero, Guglielmo. *The Gamble: Bonaparte in Italy, 1796–1797.* London: G. Bell, 1961.

Fitzgerald, Carol. *The Rivers of America: A Descriptive Bibliography.* Edited by Jean Fitzgerald. New Castle, DE: Oak Knoll Press, 2001.

Forbath, Peter. *The River Congo: The Discovery, Exploration and Exploitation of the World's Most Dramatic River.* New York: Harper and Row, 1977.

Fradkin, Philip L. *A River No More: The Colorado River and the West.* Rev. ed. Berkeley: University of California Press, 1996 (orig. pub. 1981).

Frater, Alexander, ed. *Great Rivers of the World.* Boston: Little, Brown, 1984.

Fredrich, G., and V. Muller. "Rhine," pp. 265–315 in B. A. Witton, ed., *Ecology of European Rivers.* Oxford: Blackwell, 1984.

Gayton, Don. "The Cartography of Catastrophe: Harlan Bretz and the Great Spokane Flood." *Mercator's World* 4, no. 3 (May–June 1999): 54–61.

Gerster, Georg. "River of Sorrow, River of Hope." *National Geographic,* August 1975, pp. 152–189.

Girot, Pascal O., and Bernard Q. Nietschmann. "The Río San Juan." *National Geographic Research & Exploration* 8, no. 1 (1992): 52–63.

Goell, Theresa. "Throne above the Euphrates." *National Geographic,* March 1961, pp. 390–405.

Goodland, Robert J. A. *Itumbiara Hydroelectric Project: Environmental Impact Reconnaissance.* Millbrook, NY: Cary Arboretum of the New York Botanical Garden, 1972.

Graves, Robert. *The Greek Myths.* 2 vols. Baltimore: Penguin Books, 1955.

Gray, James. *The Illinois.* New York: Farrar and Rinehart, 1940 (Rivers of America Series).

Gray, Malcolm. "Death in Europe's Grandest River." *Maclean's,* November 24, 1986, pp. 48–49.

Great Rivers of Europe. Introduction by Alan Bullock. London: Weidenfeld and Nicolson, 1966.

Greener, Leslie. *High Dam over Nubia.* New York: Viking Press, 1962.

Griffin, E. C. "The Changing Role of the Río Magdalena in Colombia's Economic Growth." *Geographical Survey* 3 (1974): 14–24.

Grove, A. T., ed. *The Niger and Its Neighbors: Environmental History and Hydrobiology, Human Use and Health Hazards of the Major West African Rivers.* Rotterdam: A. A. Balkema, 1985.

Gulick, Bill. *Snake River Country.* Caldwell, ID: Caxton Printers, 1971.

Gutheim, Frederick. *The Potomac.* New York: Rinehart, 1949 (Rivers of America Series).

Hall, B. C., and C. T. Wood. *Big Muddy: Down the Mississippi through America's Heartland.* New York: Dutton, 1992.

Hard, Walter. *The Connecticut River.* New York: Rinehart, 1947 (Rivers of America Series).

Harden, Blaine. *A River Lost: The Life and Death of the Columbia.* New York: W. W. Norton, 1996.

Harris, Chauncy D. "The Ruhr Coal-Mining District." *Geographical Review* 36 (1946): 194–221.

Harris, R. Cole. *The Seigneurial System in Early Canada: A Geographical Study.* Madison: University of Wisconsin Press, 1966.

_______. *The Resettlement of British Columbia: Essays on Colonialism and Geographical Change.* Vancouver: University of British Columbia Press, 1997.

Hart, Henry C. *The Dark Missouri.* Madison: University of Wisconsin Press, 1957.

Hartshorne, Richard. "The Polish Corridor." *Journal of Geography* 36 (1937): 161–176.

Havighurst, Walter. *Upper Mississippi.* New York: Farrar and Rinehart, 1937 (Rivers of America Series).

Healy, Elizabeth, Christopher Moriarty, and Gerard O'Flaherty. *The Book of the Liffey from Source to the Sea.* Dublin: Wolfhound Press, 1988.

Hendrie, William F. *Discovering the River Forth.* Edinburgh: J. Donald Publishers, 1996.

Hersey, John. *A Single Pebble.* New York: Alfred A. Knopf, 1956.

Hildebrand, John. *Reading the River: A Voyage down the Yukon.* New York: Houghton Mifflin, 1988.

Hislop, Codman. *The Mohawk.* New York: Rinehart, 1948 (Rivers of America Series).

Hochschild, Adam. *King Leopold's Ghost: A Story of Greed, Terror, and Heroism in Colonial Africa.* Boston: Houghton Mifflin, 1998.

Holbrook, Stewart. *The Columbia.* New York: Rinehart, 1956 (Rivers of America Series).

Hooson, David J. M. "The Middle Volga: An Emerging Focal Region in the Soviet Union." *Geographical Journal* 126 (June 1960): 180–190.

Hopkirk, Peter. *The Great Game: The Struggle for Empire in Central Asia.* New York: Kodansha International, 1994.

Horgan, Paul. *Great River: The Rio Grande.* New York: Rinehart, 1954 (Rivers of America Series).

Howat, John K. *The Hudson River and Its Painters.* New York: Viking Press, 1972.

Hughes, Robert. *The Fatal Shore.* New York: Alfred A. Knopf, 1987.

Humboldt, Alexander von. *Personal Narrative of Travels to the Equinoctial Regions of America, during the Years 1799–1804 by Alexander von Humboldt and Aimé Bonpland.* Vol. II, ch. 23, 1852. Translated and edited by Thomasina Ross. London: Bohn Scientific Library.

Hunt, Charles B. *Natural Regions of the United States and Canada.* San Francisco: W. H. Freeman, 1974.

Hutchison, Bruce. *The Fraser.* Toronto: Clarke Irwin, 1950 (Rivers of America Series).

Huxley, Elspeth. *Their Shining Eldorado: A Journey through Australia.* New York: William Morrow, 1967.

Hyland, Paul. *The Black Heart: A Voyage into Central Africa.* New York: Henry Holt, 1988.

Irvine, Thelma. *Where the River Ran: The Story of the Peace.* Victoria, BC: Touchwood Editions, 2000.

Jenness, Aylette. *Along the Niger River: An African Way of Life.* New York: Thomas Crowell, 1974.

Jordan, Robert Paul. "Siberia's Empire Road, the River Ob." *National Geographic,* February 1976, pp. 145–181.

Kaplan, Marion. "Iberia's Vintage River." *National Geographic,* October 1984, pp. 460–489.

Kaplan, Robert D. *Balkan Ghosts: A Journey through History.* New York: St. Martin's, 1993.

Keegan, John. *The First World War.* New York: Knopf, 1999.

Kelley, Pat. *River of Lost Dreams: Navigation on the Rio Grande.* Lincoln: University of Nebraska Press, 1986.

Kemper, Steve. "Madidi: Will Bolivia Drown Its New National Park?" *National Geographic,* March 2000, pp. 2–23.

Kingsworth, Paul. "Small Things and Big Issues." *Utne Reader,* April 2001, pp. 46–51 (orig. pub. in *The Ecologist,* September 2000).

Kohlhepp, Gerd. *Itaipú: Basic Geopolitical and Energy Situation—Socio-Economic and Ecological Consequences of the Itaipú Dam and Reservoir on the Rio Parana.* Braunschweig: Friedrick Vieweg and Son, 1987.

Korotayev, V. N. "Geomorphology of River Deltas in the Arctic Coast of Siberia." *Polar Geography and Geology* 10, no. 2 (1986): 139–147.

Lafrenière, Normand. *The Ottawa River Canal System.* Ottawa: National Historic Parks and Sites Branch, Parks Canada, Environment Canada. Hull, Quebec, Canada: Canadian Govt. Pub. Centre, Supply and Services Canada, 1984.

Lê, Phan Huy, Nguy-ên Quang Ngoc, Nguy-ên Dinh Lê. *The Country Life in the Red River Delta.* Hanoi: The Gioi Publishers, 1997.

Leakey, Richard, and Roger Lewin. *People of the Lake: Mankind and Its Beginnings.* Garden City, NY: Anchor Press, 1978.

Least Heat-Moon, William. *River-Horse: The Logbook of a Boat across America.* Boston: Houghton Mifflin, 1999.

Lee, Douglas. "The Land of the River." *National Geographic,* August 1983, pp. 226–252.

Lee, Katie. *All My Rivers Are Gone: A Journey of Discovery through Glen Canyon.* Boulder, CO: Johnson Books, 1998.

Levathes, Louis E. "The Land Where the Murray Flows." *National Geographic,* August 1985, pp. 252–278.

Lin, George C. S. "Evolving Spatial Form of Urban-Rural Interaction in the Pearl River Delta, China." *Professional Geographer* 53 (2001): 56–70.

Lopez, Barry. *Crossing Open Ground.* New York: Vintage, 1989.

Lowi, Miriam R. *The Politics of Water: The Jordan River and the Riparian States.* Montreal: McGill Studies in International Development, no. 35, 1984.

Lunt, W. E. *History of England.* 4th ed. New York: Harper and Row, 1957.

MacDonald, Jake. "The Red River Valley: Manitoba's Storied Waterway Is Rich in History and Biodiversity." *Canadian Geographic* 114, no. 1 (January–February 1994): 42–52.

Macdonald, Lyn. *Somme.* New York: Atheneum, 1989.

MacLennan, Hugh. *Rivers of Canada.* Toronto: Macmillan of Canada, 1974.

Magocsi, Paul Robert. *Historical Atlas of East Central Europe.* Seattle: University of Washington Press, 1993.

Magris, Claudio. *Danube: A Sentimental Journey from the Source to the Black Sea.* Translated by Patrick Creagh. London: Harvill Press, 1999 (orig. pub. 1986).

Malcolm, Andrew H. *Mississippi Currents: Journeys through Time and a Valley.* New York: William Morrow, 1996.

Margolis, Mac. *The Last New World: The Conquest of the Amazon Frontier.* New York: Norton, 1992.

Márquez, Gabriel García. *Love in the Time of Cholera.* New York: Knopf, 1988 (orig. pub. in Spanish, 1985).

Martin, Lawrence. *The Physical Geography of Wisconsin.* 3d ed. Madison: University of Wisconsin Press, 1965 (orig. pub. 1916).

Masters, Roger D. *Fortune Is a River: Leonardo Da Vinci and Niccolo Machiavelli's Magnificent Dream to Change the Course of Florentine History.* New York: Free Press, 1998.

Mathews, Richard. *The Yukon.* New York: Holt, Rinehart and Winston, 1968 (Rivers of America Series).

Mattes, Merrill J. *The Great Platte River Road: The Covered Wagon Mainline via Fort Kearny to Fort Laramie.* Lincoln: University of Nebraska Press, 1969.

Maxwell, Ross A. *The Big Bend of the Rio Grande: A Guide to the Rocks, Landscape, Geologic History, and Settlers of the Area of Big Bend National Park.* Bureau of Economic Geology, University of Texas at Austin, Guidebook 7, 1968.

McCarry, Charles. "The Civilizing Seine." *National Geographic,* April 1982, pp. 478–511.

McCullough, David. *The Johnstown Flood.* New York: Simon and Schuster, 1968.

McCully, Patrick. *Silenced Rivers: The Ecology and Politics of Large Dams.* London: Zed Books, 1996.

McNamee, Gregory. *Gila: The Life and Death of an American River.* Albuquerque: University of New Mexico Press, 1998.

McPhee, John. *Coming into the Country.* New York: Farrar, Straus and Giroux, 1977.

_______. *The Control of Nature.* New York: Farrar, Straus and Giroux, 1989.

_______. "Farewell to the Nineteenth Century: The Breaching of Edwards Dam." *New Yorker,* September 27, 1999, pp. 44–53.

Meier, Christian. *Caesar.* Translated by David McLintock. New York: Basic Books, 1982.

Meinig, D. W. *The Great Columbia Plain: A Historical Geography, 1805–1910.* Seattle: University of Washington Press, 1968.

Melamid, Alexander. "The Shatt Al Arab Boundary Dispute." *Middle East Journal* 22, no. 3 (Summer 1968): 351–357.

Meyer, Karl E., and Shareen Blair Brysac. *Tournament of Shadows: The Great Game and the Race for Empire in Central Asia.* Washington, DC: Counterpoint, 1999.

Michener, James. *Centennial.* New York: Random House, 1974.

Millward, Roy. *Scandinavian Lands.* London: Macmillan, 1964.

Mitchell, Robert D. "The Shenandoah Valley Frontier." *Annals of the Association of American Geographers* 62 (1972): 461–486.

Mogg, E. H. "The Oliphants River Irrigation Scheme." *Africa* 18 (July 1948): 199–204.

Monkhouse, F. J. *A Regional Geography of Western Europe.* Rev. ed. London: Longmans, 1960.

Moolman, J. H. "The Orange River." *Geographical Review* 36 (1946).

Moorehead, Alan. *The White Nile.* New York: Harper and Brothers, 1960.

_______. *The Blue Nile.* New York: Harper and Row, 1962.

Morgan, Dale L. *The Humboldt.* New York: Farrar and Rinehart, 1943 (Rivers of America Series).

Moynihan, Elizabeth B., ed. *The Moonlight Garden: New Discoveries at the Taj Mahal.* Seattle: University of Washington Press and the Arthur M. Sackler Gallery, Smithsonian Institution, November 2000.

Murray, Stanley Norman. *The Valley Comes of Age: A History of Agriculture in the Valley of the Red River of the North, 1812–1920.* Fargo: North Dakota Institute for Regional Studies, 1967.

National Research Council. *Upstream: Salmon and Society in the Pacific Northwest.* Washington, DC: National Academy Press, 1996.

Newby, Eric. *Slowly down the Ganges: An Enthralling and Hilarious Voyage down India's Sacred River.* New York: Viking Penguin, 1966.

Nicholl, Charles. *The Creature in the Map: A Journey to El Dorado.* New York: William Morrow, 1995.

Nichols, Theodore E. "The Rise of Barranquilla." *Hispanic American Historical Review* 34 (May 1954): 158–174.

Niemeyer, Lucian, and Julia Davis. *Shenandoah: Daughter of the Stars.* Baton Rouge: Louisiana State University Press, 1994.

Niles, Blair. *The James.* New York: Farrar and Rinehart, 1939 (Rivers of America Series).

Norton, Boyd. *Rivers of the Rockies.* Chicago: Rand McNally, 1975.

Ohlsson, Leif, ed. *Hydropolitics: Conflicts over Water as a Development Constraint.* London: Zed Books, 1995.

Ondaatze, Christopher. *Journey to the Source of the Nile.* Toronto: HarperCollins, 1998.

Ormsby, Hilda. *France: A Regional and Economic Geography.* 2d ed. London: Methuen, 1950.

Osborne, Milton. *The Mekong: Turbulent Past, Uncertain Future.* New York: Atlantic Monthly Press, 2000.

Palmer, Tim. *The Snake River: Window to the West.* Washington, DC: Island Press, 1991.

_______. *The Wild and Scenic Rivers of America.* Washington, DC: Island Press, 1993.

_______. *America by Rivers.* Washington, DC: Island Press, 1996.

Parfit, Michael. "The Untamed Yukon." *National Geographic,* July 1998, pp. 100–127.

Parsons, James J. "A Geographer Looks at the San Joaquin Valley." *Geographical Review* 76 (1986): 371–389.

Perkins, Dorothy. *Encyclopedia of China: The Essential Reference to China, Its History and Culture.* New York: Checkmark Books, 1999.

Pisani, Donald J. *To Reclaim a Divided West: Water, Law, and Public Policy, 1848–1902.* Albuquerque: University of New Mexico Press, 1992.

Pitlick, John. "A Regional Perspective of the Hydrology of the 1993 Mississippi River Basin Floods." *Annals of the Association of American Geographers* 87 (March 1997): 135–151.

Pool, Rollo. "Stikine and Iskut Rivers in Transition." *Alaska* 48 (July 1982): 17–19.

Powell, John Wesley. *The Exploration of the Colorado River and Its Canyons.* New York: Dover, 1961 (orig. pub. 1874).

Putnam, John J. "The Ganges, River of Faith." *National Geographic,* October 1971, pp. 445–483.

Raban, Jonathan. *Old Glory: A Voyage down the Mississippi.* New York: Simon and Schuster, 1981.

Reed, John. *The Hudson River Valley.* New York: Bonanza Books, 1960.

Reid, Anna. *Borderland: A Journey through the History of Ukraine.* Boulder, CO: Westview Press, 1997.

Reisner, Marc P. *Cadillac Desert: The American West and Its Disappearing Water.* New York: Viking, 1986.

Ren, Mei-e, and H. Jesse Walker. "Environmental Consequences of Human Activity on the Yellow River and Its Delta, China." *Physical Geography* 19 (1998): 421–432.

Roaf, Michael. *Cultural Atlas of Mesopotamia and the Ancient Near East.* New York: Facts on File, 1990.

Roberts, Leslie. *The Mackenzie.* New York: Rinehart and Company, 1949 (Rivers of America Series).

Robertson, C. J. "Agricultural Regions of the North Italian Plain." *Geographical Review* 28 (1938): 573–596.

Robertson, Robert A., and Rabel J. Burdge. "The Interface between Commercial and Industrial Development and Recreational Use in an Urban River Corridor: Illinois & Michigan Canal National Heritage Corridor." *Journal of Leisure Research* 25, no. 1 (1993): 53–69.

Roosevelt, Theodore. *Through the Brazilian Wilderness.* London: Murray, 1914.

Roux, Georges. *Ancient Iraq.* London: Allen and Unwin, 1964 (Penguin, 3d ed., 1992).

Rowbotham, Fred. *The Severn Bore.* Newton Abbot: David and Charles, 1970.

Rudloe, Jack, and Anne Rudloe. "Trouble in Bayou Country: Louisiana's Atchafalaya." *National Geographic,* September 1979, pp. 377–397.

Russell, Richard Joel. "Geomorphology of the Rhône Delta." *Annals of the Association of American Geographers* 32 (1942): 149–254.

_______. "Alluvial Morphology of Anatolian Rivers." *Annals of the Association of American Geographers* 32 (1954): 149–154.

Sanchez-Arcilla, Agustin, Jose A. Jimenez, and Herminia I. Valdemoro. "The Ebro Delta: Morphodynamics and Vulnerability." *Journal of Coastal Research* 14, no. 3 (1998): 754–772.

Sastri, K. A. Nilakanta. *A History of South India, from Prehistoric Times to the Fall of Vijayanagar.* Oxford: Oxford University Press, 1958.

Scargill, Ian. *The Dordogne Region of France.* London: David and Charles, 1974.

Shoumatoff, Alex. *The Rivers Amazon.* San Francisco: Sierra Club Books, 1978.

Spurr, Daniel. *River of Forgotten Days: A Journey down the Mississippi in Search of La Salle.* New York: Henry Holt, 1998.

Stamp, L. Dudley. "The Irrawaddy River." *Geographical Journal* 95 (1940): 329–356.

Stanley, Daniel Jean, and Andrew G. Warne. "Nile Delta in Its Destructive Phase." *Journal of Coastal Research* 14 (1998): 794–825.

Stanton, Richard L. *Potomac Journey.* Washington, DC: Smithsonian Institution Press, 1993.

Stegner, Wallace. *Beyond the Hundredth Meridian: John Wesley Powell and the Second Opening of the West.* Boston: Houghton Mifflin, 1954.

Stokes, Thomas L. *The Savannah.* New York: Rinehart, 1951 (Rivers of America Series).

Stranahan, Susan Q. *Susquehanna: River of Dreams.* Baltimore: Johns Hopkins University Press, 1993.

Stutz, Bruce. *Natural Lives, Modern Times: People and Places of the Delaware River.* New York: Crown Publishers, 1992.

Sundborg, Åke. "The River Klarälven: A Study of Fluvial Processes." *Geografiska Annaler* 38 (1956): 127–316.

Sunset Books. *Rivers of the West.* Menlo Park, CA: Lane, 1974.

Swerdlow, Joel L. "Erie Canal: Living Link to Our Past." *National Geographic,* November 1990, pp. 38–65.

Taylor, Griffith. "Trento to the Reschen Pass: A Cultural Traverse of the Adige Corridor." *Geographical Review* 30 (1940): 215–237.

Taylor, Jeffrey. "White Nights in Siberia." *Atlantic Monthly,* December 2000, pp. 36–40.

Thomas, Bill. *American Rivers: A Natural History.* New York: W. W. Norton, 1978.

Thubron, Colin. *The Hills of Adonis: A Quest in Lebanon.* Boston: Little, Brown, 1968.

Tropkin, Alexander. "Down the Yensei: The Main Route of Siberia." *Soviet Life,* June 1983, pp. 29–36.

Van Beek, Steve. *The Chao Phya: River in Transition.* Oxford: Oxford University Press, 1995.

Van Dyk, Jere. "Long Journey of the Brahmaputra." *National Geographic,* November 1988, pp. 672–711.

Van Slyke, Lyman P. *Yangtze: Nature, History, and the River.* Reading, MA: Addison-Wesley, 1988.

Vestal, Stanley. *Missouri.* New York: Farrar and Rinehart, 1945 (Rivers of America Series).

Vincent, Mary, and R. A. Stradling. *Cultural Atlas of Spain and Portugal.* New York: Facts on File, 1994.

Walker, D. S. *The Mediterranean Lands.* New York: Wiley, 1960.

Walker, H. Jesse. "Arctic Deltas." *Journal of Coastal Research* 14 (1998): 718–738.

Walker, H. Jesse, and Warren E. Grabau. "World Deltas and Their Evolution." *Acta Geographica Sinica* 54 (1999): 30–41.

Walker, Jesse, Lennart Arnborg, and Johan Peippo. "Riverbank Erosion in the Colville Delta, Alaska." *Geografiska Annaler* 69A (1987): 711–720.

Waters, Frank. *The Colorado.* New York: Rinehart, 1946 (Rivers of America Series).

Watkins, T. H. *Mark Twain's America: A Pictorial History of America's Greatest River.* Palo Alto, CA: American West, 1974.

Watson, Francis. *India: A Concise History.* London: Thames and Hudson, 1974.

Webber, John W. "Down Mexico's Río Balsas." *National Geographic,* August 1946, pp. 253–272.

Webster, Donavan. "The Orinoco: Into the Heart of Venezuela." *National Geographic,* April 1998, pp. 2–31.

Wheeler, Sir Mortimer. *Civilizations of the Indus Valley and Beyond.* London: Thames and Hudson, 1966.

White, Peter T. "The Mekong: River of Terror and Hope." *National Geographic,* December 1968, pp. 737–787.

Whitfield, Susan. *Life along the Silk Road.* Berkeley: University of California Press, 1999.

Willan, T. S. *The Early History of the Russia Company, 1553–1603.* Manchester: Manchester University Press, 1956.

Wilder, Henry E. *The Delaware.* New York: Farrar and Rinehart, 1940 (Rivers of America Series).

Wilkinson, Henry Robert, George De Boer, and Adrienne Thunder. *A Cartographic Analysis of the Changing Bed of the Humber, A Report to the Humber Estuary Research Committee.* Hull: Department of Geography, University of Hull, 1973.

Wilson, Roy R. "An Integrated River Management Model: The Connecticut River Management Program." *Journal of Environmental Management* 41, no. 4 (1994): 337–348.

Winchester, Simon. *The River at the Center of the World: A Journey up the Yangtze, and Back in Chinese Time.* New York: Henry Holt, 1996.

________. "Black Dragon River: On the Edge of Empires." *National Geographic,* February 2000, pp. 2–33.

Winternitz, Helen. *East along the Equator: A Journey up the Congo and into Zaire.* New York: Atlantic Monthly Press, 1987.

Wood, Michael. *In the Footsteps of Alexander the Great: A Journey from Greece to Asia.* Berkeley: University of California Press, 1997 (companion volume to BBC television series).

Woodlief, Ann. *In River Time: The Way of the James.* Chapel Hill: Algonquin Books of Chapel Hill, 1985.

Worster, Donald. *Rivers of Empire: Water, Aridity, and the Growth of the American West.* New York: Pantheon, 1985.

Wyatt, David K. *Thailand: A Short History.* New Haven: Yale University Press, 1982.

Zich, Arthur. "China's Three Gorges: Before the Flood." *National Geographic,* September 1997, pp. 2–33.

Zwinger, Ann H. *Run, River, Run.* Tucson: University of Arizona Press, 1984.

________. *Downcanyon: A Naturalist Explores the Colorado River through Grand Canyon.* Tucson: University of Arizona Press, 1995.

INDEX

Page numbers in **boldface** refer to main encyclopedia entries.

ABOUT THE AUTHOR

James Penn received a Ph.D. in geography at the University of Wisconsin (1983). He has taught geography at the University of Maryland–Baltimore County, the University of Delaware, Louisiana State University, and Southeastern Louisiana University. He is the author of *Encyclopedia of Geographical Features in World History*.